INTRODUCTION TO THE OLD TESTAMENT

INTRODUCTION TO THE OLD TESTAMENT

GEORG FOHRER
Emeritus Professor at the University of Erlangen-Nürnberg

Translated by
David Green

First published in the U.S.A. in 1968
by the Abingdon Press

First published in Great Britain in 1970
Second impression with corrections, 1974
First published in paperback in 1976
Seventh impression 1986
S.P.C.K.
Holy Trinity Church
Marylebone Road
London NW1 4DU

Printed in Great Britain
Hollen Street Press Ltd., Slough

This volume is a translation of Ernst Sellin's *Einleitung in das Alte Testament,* tenth edition, completely revised and rewritten by Georg Fohrer and published in 1965 by Quelle & Meyer, Heidelberg.

Scripture quotations unless otherwise noted are from the Revised Standard Version of the Bible, copyrighted 1946, 1952, and 1957 by the Divison of Christian Education, National Council of Churches, and are used by permission.

ISBN 0 281 02961 X

FOREWORD TO THE TENTH EDITION

In the year 1910, when the first edition of this *Introduction to the Old Testament* appeared, the author, Ernst Sellin, explained in his foreword why he had written a short, concise textbook and what he conceived its advantages to be. The work remained a short textbook through the seven editions that appeared during Sellin's lifetime and through the two following editions, which Leonhard Rost revised. Its content, however, underwent significant alterations, both at the hands of Sellin, whose openness to change produced a succession of varying theses, and also in the revisions made by Rost, whose last edition "preserves only in scattered passages a text deriving from the seventh edition, the last prepared by Sellin." Rost once again intended basic changes for his tenth edition. In order to devote his undivided attention to other plans, however, he suggested that I prepare the new edition. In addition to my gratitude for the confidence in me demonstrated by him and the publisher in turning this job over to me, I also owe an explanation in detail for the far-reaching changes made in the present book with respect to previous editions. I hope that the presentation itself will, for the most part, provide its own explanation. It may suffice to emphasize at this point that the greatly increased scope and different organization of the whole work—to mention only the most striking changes—were unavoidable if it was to do justice to the present state of Old Testament studies and make a contribution to scholarship above and beyond mere elementary instruction. There was, nevertheless, much that had to be presented briefly—perhaps too briefly for many readers—or merely alluded to if the book was not to attain twice the size of the present volume.

The discussion is limited to the canonical books of the Old Testament. The noncanonical writings are not included, except for a mention of their titles at the appropriate place. Leonhard Rost intends to treat them in a separate supplementary volume.

I am grateful first of all to Frau Hildegard Hiersemann, who with indefatigable perseverance wrote the manuscript from my dictation. I am also grateful to Dr. Gunther Wanke, my assistant, and Hans Werner Hoffmann, stud. theol., for reading the manuscript, preparing the lists of introductions, commentaries, and abbreviations, making the indexes, assisting in the proofreading, and many other kinds of help.

I am grateful to the translator, Mr. David Green, for the care he has taken to bring out my meaning and for the patience with which he has done a work which was not easy. My thanks go likewise to the publishers for making this book available in the English edition as a contribution to the further study and teaching of the Old Testament.

Erlangen, May 1965 GEORG FOHRER

TRANSLATOR'S PREFACE

The present translation incorporates several minor corrections of the original furnished by the author. In addition, I should like to thank Prof. Fohrer for reading the entire manuscript of the translation and pointing out inaccuracies. His help has been invaluable.

A few words on terminology may be helpful to the reader. There are as yet no agreed translations of the German terms used in form criticism. Where there is some consensus, I have followed current English usage even where it does not completely reflect the meaning of the German word. In particular, *Gattung* has been translated as "literary form," even though the form in question may not be "literary" in the general sense of the English word. The term is not intended to imply of itself that the forms are either written or oral. The names for many of the forms are more conventional than descriptive; the best way to gain an accurate notion of the form is to refer to the examples cited.

Heilsprophet has been translated as "optimistic prophet"; the literal translation "prophet of salvation" is too strong a rendering, and awkward to use in English. The reader should bear in mind, however, that the "optimism" referred to is based on a conviction of God's favor.

Finally, biblical passages are cited according to the Hebrew verse numbering. The English numbering, when different, is noted afterward.

CONTENTS

Bibliographic Information 17

1. Introductions to the OT. 2. Commentaries. 3. Periodicals and Series. 4. Note on Bibliographies.

INTRODUCTION: ISRAELITE LITERATURE, THE CANON OF THE OLD TESTAMENT, AND INTRODUCTORY STUDIES

§1 The Purpose, History, and Methods of Introduction 23

1. The OT and introductory studies. 2. Beginnings. 3. The growth of historical-critical scholarship. 4. New methods. 5. The task of introduction.

§2 Presuppositions of Israelite Literature 32

1. Historical and geographical presuppositions. 2. Cultural presuppositions. 3. Literary presuppositions. 4. The significance of Yahwism.

§3 Oral Tradition and Literature 36

1. The problem. 2. Oral and written tradition. 3. Oral and written tradition in Israel.

§4 Prose 41

1. Present form 2. Linguistic peculiarities. 3. Stylistic peculiarities.

§5 Poetry 43

1. The use of poetry. 2. Long verse. 3. Short verse. 4. Meter and rhythm. 5. Poetic devices.

§6 Israelite Literature and the Old Testament 49

1. The OT as the remains of Israelite literature. 2. The problems of literary history.

Part One

The Formation of the Historical and Legal Books

CHAPTER ONE: GENERAL

§7 Law, Instruction, Narrative, and Report in the Ancient Near East and in Israel 51

1. Survey. 2. Law in the ancient Near East. 3. Instruction in the ancient Near East. 4. Narrative in the ancient Near East. 5. Report in the ancient Near East. 6. Letters in the ancient Near East. 7. Israel.

§8 The Directive Literary Types and Their Traditions 63

1. The formulas and sayings of everyday life. 2. Rules of conduct in apodictic form. 3. Legal maxims and decisions. 4. Rhetorical forms in legal proceedings. 5. Treaties and contracts.

§9 The Requesting and Wishing Literary Types and Their Traditions 74

1. Request and wish. 2. Formulas of salutation. 3. Blessings and curses. 4. Oaths.

§10 The Proclaiming and Instructing Literary Types and Their Traditions 77
1. Oracles. 2. Judgment by ordeal. 3. Torah. 4. Cultic regulations and priestly professional lore. 5. Approval, rejection, rebuke.

§11 The Communicating Literary Types and Their Traditions 80
1. Conversation. 2. Formal speeches. 3. Preaching. 4. Prayers. 5. Letters. 6. Epistles.

§12 The Narrative Literary Types and Their Traditions 85
1. Their common relationship. 2. Myth. 3. Fairy tale. 4. Novella. 5. Anecdote. 6. Saga and legend. 7. Historical and theological significance.

§13 The Reportorial Literary Types and Their Traditions 95
1. Lists. 2. Annals and chronicles. 3. Historical narrative and historiography. 4. Biography. 5. Dream-narrative.

§14 Other Literary Types and Influence on Other Books 99
1. Other literary types. 2. Influence on other books.

§15 Compilation and Transmission 100
1. Legal codes. 2. Narrative and historical sections. 3. Later historical and legal books.

CHAPTER TWO: THE PENTATEUCH

§16 Terminology and Content 103
1. Terminology. 2. Content.

§17 History of Pentateuchal Studies 106
1. Tradition. 2. Attempts to solve the problem. 3. New approaches.

§18 Methods, Results, and Problems 113
1. Results of previous studies. 2. The addition method. 3. The supplement method. 4. The composition method. 5. Motives and forces.

§19 The Growth of the Historical Traditions 120
1. The patriarchs. 2. Moses. 3. Other narratives of territorial occupation. 4. The development of the groundworks. 5. The two groundworks.

§20 The Origin of the Dependent Legal Collections and Codes 132
1. Survey. 2. The Covenant Code. 3. The Holiness Code. 4. Other collections of laws.

§21 The Growth of the Source Strata 143
1. Further redaction of the groundworks. 2. Inclusion of legal collections and codes. 3. The nature and character of the source strata.

§22 The Source Stratum J 146
1. Terminology and content. 2. Extant tradition and the contribution of J. 3. Characteristic content. 4. Theology. 5. Origin.

§23 The Source Stratum E 152
1. Terminology and content. 2. Other views and variations. 3. Extant tradition and the contribution of E. 4. Characteristic content and theology. 5. Origin.

§24 The Problem of a Third Early Source Stratum (J^1, L, N) 159
1. The assumption of a third stratum. 2. Terminology and content. 3. Extant

tradition and the contribution of N. 4. Characteristic content and theology. 5. Origin.

§25 The Source Stratum D 165
1. Terminology, scope, structure, and style. 2. Connection with Josiah's reformation. 3. Scope and content of Proto-Deuteronomy. 4. Growth of the Proto-Deuteronomic law code. 5. The development from the original lawbook to the present book of Deuteronomy. 6. Deuteronomy within the Pentateuch. 7. Theology.

§26 The Source Stratum P 178
1. Terminology and content. 2. Extant tradition and the contribution of P. 3. The problem of literary unity. 4. Characteristic content. 5. Theology. 6. Origin.

§27 Passages Not Belonging to the Source Strata 186
1. Genesis 14. 2. Exod. 15:1-19. 3. Exod. 19:3b-8. 4. Deuteronomy 32.

§28 The Growth of the Pentateuch 190

Transition

§29 The Assumption of Larger Works 192
1. Hypotheses. 2. Criticism. 3. The development of the historical books.

CHAPTER THREE: JOSHUA THROUGH KINGS
(The Former Prophets)

§30 The Book of Joshua and Judg. 1:1–2:5 196
1. Terminology, content, source strata. 2. N. 3. G[s]. 4. J and E. 5. Deuteronomistic redaction. 6. P. 7. Separation from the Pentateuch.

§31 The Book of Judges 205
1. Terminology and content. 2. The "Judges." 3. The traditions concerning the hero figures. 4. The pre-Deuteronomistic book of Judges. 5. The Deuteronomistic book of Judges. 6. Later additions. 7. Retrospect. 8. Historical reliability and theological characteristics.

§32 The Books of Samuel 215
1. Terminology and content. 2. Continuous sources or independent fragments? 3. The basic stratum. 4. The formation of the basic stratum and its supplements. 5. The supplementary stratum. 6. The Deuteronomistic redaction. 7. Conclusion. 8. Historical reliability and theological characteristics.

§33 The Books of Kings 227
1. Terminology and content. 2. The formation of the books. 3. The framework. 4. The historical sources. 5. The narrative complexes. 6. The Deuteronomistic books of Kings. 7. Later additions. 8. Historical reliability and theological purpose.

CHAPTER FOUR: THE CHRONICLER'S HISTORY

§34 The Chronicler's Work (I–II Chronicles, Ezra, Nehemiah) 238
1. Unity, transposition, division. 2. Terminology. 3. Content and purpose. 4. Origin.

§35 The Formation and Nature of the Chronicler's Work 240
1. Sources for the preexilic period. 2. Sources for the postexilic period. 3. Expan-

sions and later additions. 4. Use of sources. 5. The Chronicler's special material. 6. Historical reliability. 7. Theological character.

CHAPTER FIVE: OTHER BOOKS

§36 The Book of Ruth 249
1. Terminology and content. 2. Literary type and historical background. 3. Connection with David. 4. Interpretation. 5. Origin.

§37 The Book of Esther 252
1. Terminology and content. 2. Literary type. 3. Origin of the narrative material and historical background. 4. Origin. 5. Supplement and later additions. 6. Value.

Part Two

The Formation of the Poetic Books

CHAPTER ONE: GENERAL

§38 Lyric Poetry in the Ancient Near East and in Israel 256
1. Mesopotamia. 2. Egypt. 3. Elsewhere in the ancient Near East. 4. Israelite poetry.

§39 The Literary Types of the Psalms and Their Traditions 260
1. Distinguishing the literary types. 2. Hymnic songs. 3. Lament. 4. Thanksgiving. 5. Royal songs. 6. Other forms. 7. Psalms in other books of the OT.

§40 The Song Types of Everyday Life and Their Traditions 272
1. Work song, harvest song, vintage song, watchman's song. 2. Drinking song. 3. Taunt song. 4. Love song and epithalamium. 5. War song and victory song. 6. Dirge. 7. Connection with historical events.

§41 The Characteristics of the Old Testament Literary Types 277
1. Adaptation of foreign material. 2 Adaptation of foreign forms. 3. Development within Israel.

§42 Compilation and Transmission 278
1. Compilation and transmission. 2. Later songs or songbooks.

CHAPTER TWO: THE SONGBOOKS

§43 The Psalter 280
1. Terminology and enumeration. 2. Significance of the superscriptions. 3. Authorship and age. 4. Survey of literary types, origin, and cultic association of the psalms. 5. Compilation and growth of the Psalter. 6. Theological ideas.

§44 Lamentations 295
1. Terminology. 2. Literary type and style. 3. Occasion and content. 4. Origin. 5. Authorship. 6. Significance.

§45 The Song of Solomon 299
1. Terminology. 2. History of interpretation. 3. Love songs and epithalamia. 4. Literary form. 5. Formal literature. 6. Origin. 7. Significance.

Part Three

The Formation of the Wisdom Books

CHAPTER ONE: GENERAL

§46 Wisdom in the Ancient Near East and in Israel 304
1. The concept. 2. Mesopotamia. 3. Egypt. 4. Elsewhere in the ancient Near East. 5. Israel. 6. Significance of wisdom.

§47 The Literary Types of Wisdom and Their Traditions 311
1. Mashal. 2. Proverb. 3. Riddle and numerical saying. 4. Aphorism. 5. Wisdom and didactic poetry. 6. Parable, fable, allegory. 7. Lists. 8. In other books of the OT.

§48 Compilation and Transmission 316
1. Compilation and transmission. 2. Formation of wisdom books. 3. Later wisdom books.

CHAPTER TWO: THE WISDOM BOOKS

§49 Proverbs 318
1. Terminology and structure. 2. Collection A. 3. Collection B. 4. Collection C. 5. Collection D. 6. Collection E. 7. Collection F. 8. Collection G. 9. "The Perfect Wife." 10. Redaction.

§50 The Book of Job 323
1. Structure. 2. The framework. 3. The poem. 4. Later additions. 5. The original book and its origin. 6. Relationship to tradition. 7. History of the material and motifs. 8. Form criticism. 9. The problem of the book.

§51 Ecclesiastes (Qoheleth) 334
1. Canonical status, terminology, authorship. 2. Development and structure. 3. The aphorisms. 4. Origin. 5. Form criticism. 6. The character of Qoheleth.

Part Four

The Formation of the Prophetical Books and the Apocalyptic Book

CHAPTER ONE: GENERAL

§52 Prophecy in the Ancient Near East and in Israel 342
1. The ancient Near East. 2. Ancient Israel. 3. The period of so-called literary prophecy. 4. Eschatological prophecy. 5. Apocalyptic.

§53 Prophetical Preaching: Its Literary Types and Their Traditions 347
1. The function of the prophets. 2. Development of the prophetic oracle. 3. Style of the prophetic oracle. 4. Literary types. 5. Relationship to tradition.

§54 Compilation and Transmission 358
1. The development of the tradition. 2. The development of the prophetical writings. 3. Structure of the collections and books. 4. Later prophetic-apocalyptic books.

CHAPTER TWO: THE PROPHETICAL BOOKS

(The Latter Prophets)

§55 Survey 363

§56 Isaiah I (Isaiah 1–39) 363

1. Isaiah. 2. Isaiah's ministry. 3. Sayings and reports. 4. Later passages. 5. Growth of the book. 6. Message.

§57 Isaiah II (Isaiah 40–55) 373

1. Deutero-Isaiah. 2. Place and date. 3. Literary forms. 4. Oracles concerning the Servant of Yahweh. 5. Composition and structure. 6. Message.

§58 Isaiah III (Isaiah 56–66) 384

1. Trito-Isaiah. 2. Authorship and origin. 3. The sayings or sections. 4. Thematic groups.

§59 Jeremiah 388

1. Jeremiah. 2. Jeremiah's activity. 3. Written transmission. 4. The Baruch document. 5. Later passages. 6. Growth of the book. 7. Message.

§60 Ezekiel 403

1. The data of the book. 2. The historical problems. 3. Ezekiel's activity. 4. The manner of Ezekiel's preaching. 5. Later passages. 6. Transmission of the sayings and reports. 7. Ezekiel's personality. 8. Ezekiel's message and its problems.

§61 Hosea 418

1. Hosea's personal situation. 2. Hosea's wife and children. 3. Sayings. 4. Transmission. 5. Message.

§62 Joel 425

1. Joel. 2. Interpretation of chapters 1–2. 3. Unity of the book. 4. Date of Joel's activity. 5. Message.

§63 Amos 430

1. Amos and his profession. 2. Date of Amos' activity. 3. Sayings and reports; minor collections. 4. Later passages. 5. Growth of the book. 6. Message.

§64 Obadiah 438

1. The individual sayings. 2. Date. 3. Message.

§65 Jonah 440

1. Narrative. 2. Historicity and origin of the narrative material. 3. Literary type. 4. Date. 5. Thanksgiving psalm. 6. Purpose.

§66 Micah 443

1. Micah. 2. First collection. 3. Second collection. 4. Third collection. 5. Fourth section. 6. Structure of the book. 7. Message.

§67 Nahum 447

1. Nahum. 2. Date. 3. The hymn. 4. The sayings. 5. The book as a whole. 6. Message.

§68 Habakkuk 451

1. Habakkuk. 2. Transmission and individual problems. 3. The prophecy as a whole. 4. The central problem: the wicked man and the Chaldeans. 5. Date. 6. The character of Habakkuk.

§69 Zephaniah 456
1. Genealogy and date. 2. Sayings. 3. Redaction. 4. Message.

§70 Haggai 458
1. Haggai. 2. Sayings. 3. The book. 4. Message.

§71 Zechariah (Zechariah 1–8) 460
1. Zechariah and his date. 2. Sayings and reports. 3. Growth of the book. 4. Message.

§72 Zechariah 9–14 464
1. Major problems. 2. Deutero-Zechariah. 3. Trito-Zechariah. 4. Summary.

§73 Malachi 469
1. Malachi. 2. Sayings. 3. Date. 4. Message.

CHAPTER THREE: THE APOCALYPTIC BOOK

§74 Daniel 471
1. The claim of the book; Daniel. 2. Literary problems. 3. Narratives. 4. Reports. 5. Growth of the book. 6. Date. 7. The two languages. 8. Apocalypse.

Part Five

The Compilation and Transmission of the Old Testament

CHAPTER ONE: ORIGIN AND HISTORY OF THE CANON

§75 Terminology and Traditional Theory 480
1. The canon; deuterocanonical and noncanonical books. 2. Traditional theory.

§76 The Formation of the Hebrew Canon 483
1. Basis. 2. Prehistory. 3. The formation of the Hebrew canon. 4. Structure.

§77 Other Forms of the Canon 487
1. Samaritans. 2. Hellenistic Judaism. 3. Christianity.

CHAPTER TWO: TEXTUAL HISTORY OF THE OLD TESTAMENT

§78 The Masoretic Text 489
1. The text has a history. 2. Traditional theory. 3. Scroll and writing system. 4. Efforts to guarantee accurate transmission. 5. Basic form of the Masoretic text. 6. The work of the "scribes." 7. The Masoretes. 8. Development of the *textus receptus*. 9. Division of the text.

§79 Non-Masoretic Text Forms 502
1. Survey. 2. The Samaritan Pentateuch. 3. The Targums. 4. The Peshitta. 5. The Septuagint. 6. The translations dependent on the LXX. 7. The independent Greek translations. 8. The Vulgate. 9. Polyglots.

§80 Textual Corruption and Textual Criticism 513

BIBLIOGRAPHICAL SUPPLEMENT 517

INDEX 531
1. Index of passages. 2. Index of subjects.

BIBLIOGRAPHIC INFORMATION

1. Introductions to the Old Testament

(An author's name followed by * refers to these works.)

G. C. Aalders, *Oud-Testamentische Kanoniek,* 1952.

G. W. Anderson, *A Critical Introduction to the Old Testament,* 1959.

W. W. Graf Baudissin, *Einleitung in die Bücher des Alten Testaments,* 1901.

A. Bentzen, *Introduction to the Old Testament,* 1948-49; 5th ed., 1959.

J. A. Bewer, *The Literature of the Old Testament in its Historical Development,* 1922; 3rd ed. (rev. by E. G. H. Kraeling), 1962.

K. Budde, *Geschichte der althebräischen Literatur. Apokryphen und Pseudepigraphen von A. Bertholet,* 1906; 2nd ed., 1909.

J. Coppens, *Introduction à l'étude historique de l'Ancien Testament,* I, 1938; 3rd ed., 1942; II, 1950; III, 1944; 2nd ed., 1950.

C. H. Cornill, *Einleitung in das Alte Testament,* 1891; 7th ed., 1913 (English: *Introduction to the Canonical Books of the Old Testament,* 1907).

S. R. Driver, *Introduction to the Literature of the Old Testament,* 1891; 9th ed., 1913, reprinted 1961.

J. G. Eichhorn, *Einleitung ins Alte Testament,* 1780-83; 4th ed., 1823-24.

O. Eissfeldt, *Einleitung in das Alte Testament,* 1934; 3rd ed., 1964 (English: The Old Testament: an Introduction, 1965).

I. Engnell, *Gamla Testamentet: en traditionshistorisk inledning,* I, 1945.

H. Gunkel, *Die israelitische Literatur* ("Kultur der Gegenwart," ed. P. Hinneberg, Teil I, Abt. VII), 1906, pp. 51-102; 2nd ed., 1925, pp. 53-112.

J. Hempel, *Die althebräische Literatur und ihr hellenistisch-jüdisches Nachleben* ("Handbuch der Literaturwissenschaften," ed. O. Walzel), 1930-34.

H. Höpfl, *Introductionis in sacros utriusque Testamenti libros compendium,* 1921-22; II: *Introductio specialis in Vetus Testamentum,* 6th ed., 1963 (cur. S. Bovo).

A. Hudal, *Kurze Einleitung in die Heiligen Bücher des Alten Testaments,* 1920; 6th ed., 1948 (neubearbeitet von F. Sauer).

A. Kuenen, *Historisch-kritisch Onderzoek naar het onstaan en de verzameling van de boeken des Ouden Verbonds,* 1861-65; 2nd ed., 1885-93.

C. Kuhl, *Die Entstehung des Alten Testaments,* 1953; 2nd ed., 1960 (ed. G. Fohrer) (English: *The Old Testament, Its Origins and Composition,* 1961).

A. Lods, *Histoire de la littérature hébraïque et juive depuis les origines jusqu'à la ruine de l'état juif (135 aprés J.-C.),* 1950.

J. Meinhold, *Einführung in das Alte Testament,* 1919; 3rd ed., 1932.

G. F. Moore, *Literature of the Old Testament,* 1913; 2nd ed., 1948 (rev. by L. H. Brockington).

W. O. E. Oesterley and T. H. Robinson, *Introduction to the Books of the Old Testament,* 1934; 3rd ed., 1958.

R. H. Pfeiffer, *Introduction to the Old Testament,* 1941, reprinted 1957.

———. *The Books of the Old Testament,* 1957.

A. Robert and A. Feuillet, *Introduction à la Bible. Tome I: Introduction genérale, Ancien Testament* par P. Auvray *et al.,* 1957; 2nd ed. 1959.

H. H. Rowley, *The Growth of the Old Testament,* 1950.

S. Sandmel, *The Hebrew Scriptures. An Introduction to Their Literature and Religious Ideas,* 1963.

E. Sellin, *Einleitung in das Alte Testament,* 1910 (English: *Introduction to the Old Testament,* 1923).

E. Sellin and L. Rost, *Einleitung in das Alte Testament,* 9th ed., 1959.
W. R. Smith, *The Old Testament in the Jewish Church,* 1881; 2nd ed. 1892.
C. Steuernagel, *Lehrbuch der Einleitung in das Alte Testament. Mit einem Anhang über die Apokryphen und Pseudepigraphen,* 1912.
T. C. Vriezen, *Oud-israelietische Geschriften,* 1948.
———. *De Literatuur van Oud-Israel,* 1961.
A. Weiser, *Einleitung in das Alte Testament,* 1939; 5th ed., 1963 (English: *The Old Testament: Its Formation and Development,* 1961).
J. Wellhausen, *Die Composition des Hexateuchs und der historischen Bücher des Alten Testaments,* 1876-77; 3rd ed., 1899; 4th ed., 1963.
G. Wildeboer, *De letterkunde des Ouden Verbonds,* 1893; 3rd ed. 1903.
E. J. Young, *An Introduction to the Old Testament,* 1949 (1954).

2. Commentaries

a) Commentaries cited in the text:

ATD	Das Alte Testament Deutsch, Göttingen.
BK	Biblischer Kommentar, Neukirchen.
BOT	De Boeken van het Oude Testament, Roermond en Maaseik.
COT	Commentar op het Oude Testament, Kampen.
EH	Exegetisches Handbuch zum Alten Testament, Münster.
HAT	Handbuch zum Alten Testament, Tübingen.
HK	Handkommentar zum Alten Testament, Göttingen.
HS	Die Heilige Schrift des Alten Testaments, Bonn.
IB	The Interpreter's Bible, Nashville.
ICC	The International Critical Commentary, Edinburgh.
KAT	Kommentar zum Alten Testament, Leipzig.
KAT²	Kommentar zum Alten Testament, Gütersloh.
KeH	Kurzgefasstes exegetisches Handbuch zum Alten Testament, Leipzig.
KHC	Kurzer Hand-Commentar zum Alten Testament (Freiburg i. Br., Leipzig), Tübingen.
SAT	Die Schriften des Alten Testaments, Göttingen.
SZ	Kurzgefasster Kommentar zu den Heiligen Schriften Alten und Neuen Testamentes (ed. Strack-Zöckler), (Nördlingen) München.

b) Other commentaries and exegeses:

Anchor Bible, Garden City.
La Biblia, Montserrat.
Biblischer Kommentar über das Alte Testament (Keil-Delitzsch), Leipzig.
Die Botschaft des Alten Testaments, Stuttgart.
Commentaire de l'Ancien Testament, Neuchâtel.
Echter-Bibel. Die Heilige Schrift in deutscher Übersetzung, Würzburg.
Det Gamle Testamente, Oslo.
Harper's Annotated Bible, New York.
Die Heilige Schrift des Alten Testaments (E. Kautzsch), Tübingen.
Herders Bibelkommentar, Freiburg.
Korte Verklaring der Heilige Schrift, Kampen.
Peake's Commentary on the Bible, Edinburgh.
Dismo Święte Starego Testamentu, Posen.
La Sacra Bibbia, Turin.
La Sainte Bible (L. Pirot—A. Clamer), Paris.

La Sainte Bible traduite en français sous la direction de l'École Biblique de Jérusalem, Paris.
The Soncino Books of the Bible, Bornemouth.
Sources Bibliques, Paris.
Tekst en Uitleg, den Haag/Groningen.
Torch Bible Commentaries, London.
The Westminster Commentaries, London.
Zürcher Bibelkommentare, Zürich.

3. Periodicals and Series

A. Alt, Kleine Schriften .... A. Alt, Kleine Schriften zur Geschichte des Volkes Israel.
AASOR .... Annual of the American Schools of Oriental Research.
ABR .... Australian Biblical Review.
AcOr .... Acta Orientalia.
AfK .... Archiv für Kulturgeschichte.
AfO .... Archiv für Orientforschung.
AIPhHOS .... Annuaire de l'Institut de Philologie et d'Histoire Orientales et Slaves.
AJSL .... American Journal of Semitic Languages and Literatures.
ANET .... J. B. Pritchard (ed.), Ancient Near Eastern Texts Relating to the Old Testament, 2nd ed., 1955.
AnSt .... Anatolian Studies.
AOT .... H. Gressmann (ed.), Altorientalische Texte zum AT, 2nd ed., 1926.
ArOr .... Archiv Orientální.
ARM .... A. Parrot and G. Dossin (ed.), Archives Royales de Mari.
ARW .... Archiv für Religionswissenschaft.
ASTI .... Annual of the Swedish Theological Institute in Jerusalem.
AThR .... Anglican Theological Review.
BA .... The Biblical Archaeologist.
BASOR .... Bulletin of the American Schools of Oriental Research.
BEThL .... Bibliotheca Ephemeridum Theologicarum Lovaniensium.
BHET .... Bulletin d'Histoire et d'Exégèse de l'Ancien Testament.
Bibl .... Biblica.
BiOr .... Bibliotheca Orientalis.
BJRL .... Bulletin of the John Rylands Library.
BMB .... Bulletin du Musée de Beyrouth.
BS .... Bibliotheca Sacra.
BSOAS .... Bulletin of the School of Oriental and African Studies.
BWAT .... Beiträge zur Wissenschaft vom Alten (und Neuen) Testament.
BZ .... Biblische Zeitschrift.
BZAW .... Beihefte zur Zeitschrift für die Alttestamentliche Wissenschaft.
Canadian JTh .... Canadian Journal of Theology.
CBQ .... Catholic Biblical Quarterly.
ChQR .... Church Quarterly Review.
ColBG .... Collationes Brugenses et Gandavenses.
CRAI .... Comptes Rendus de l'Académie des Inscriptions et Belles-Lettres.
CuW .... Christentum und Wissenschaft.
CV .... Communio Viatorum.
DTT .... Dansk Teologisk Tidsskrift.

EstBibl	Estudios Bíblicos.
ET	The Expository Times.
EThL	Ephemerides Theologicae Lovanienses.
EThR	Études Théologiques et Religieuses.
EvTh	Evangelische Theologie.
FF	Forschungen und Fortschritte.
GThT	Gereformeerd Theologisch Tijdschrift.
HThR	Harvard Theological Review.
HTSt	Hervormde Teologiese Studies.
HUCA	Hebrew Union College Annual.
HZ	Historische Zeitschrift.
IEJ	Israel Exploration Journal.
Interpr	Interpretation.
Irish ThQ	Irish Theological Quarterly.
JAOS	Journal of the American Oriental Society.
JBL	Journal of Biblical Literature.
JBR	Journal of Bible and Religion.
JCSt	Journal of Cuneiform Studies.
JDTh	Jahrbücher für Deutsche Theologie.
JEA	Journal of Egyptian Archaeology.
JEOL	Jaarbericht van het Vooraziatisch-Egyptisch Gezelschap (Genootschap) Ex Oriente Lux.
JJS	Journal of Jewish Studies.
JNES	Journal of Near Eastern Studies.
JPOS	Journal of the Palestine Oriental Society.
JQR	Jewish Quarterly Review.
JR	Journal of Religion.
JRAS	Journal of the Royal Asiatic Society of Great Britain and Ireland.
JSOR	Journal of the Society of Oriental Research.
JSS	Journal of Semitic Studies.
JThSt	Journal of Theological Studies.
MAA	Mededeelingen der Koninklijke Akademie van Wetenschappen te Amsterdam.
MDAI	Mitteilungen des Deutschen Archäologischen Instituts, Abt. Kairo.
MGWJ	Monatsschrift für Geschichte und Wissenschaft des Judentums.
MIOF	Mitteilungen des Instituts für Orientforschung.
Münchner ThZ	Münchner Theologische Zeitschrift.
MV(Ä)G	Mitteilungen der Vorderasiatisch(-Ägyptisch)en Gesellschaft.
NC	La Nouvelle Clio.
NedThT	Nederlands Theologisch Tijdschrift.
NkZ	Neue Kirchliche Zeitschrift.
NRTh	Nouvelle Revue Théologique.
NThSt	Nieuw Theologisch Tijdschrift.
NTT	Norsk Teologisk Tidsskrift.
NZSTh	Neue Zeitschrift für Systematische Theologie.
OLZ	Orientalistische Literaturzeitung.
Or	Orientalia.
OrBiblLov	Orientalia et Biblica Lovaniensia.
OrChr	Oriens Christianus.
OTS	Oudtestamentische Studiën.
OuTWP	Die Ou Testamentiese Werkgemeenskap in Suid-Afrika.

PAAJR .... Proceedings of the American Academy for Jewish Research.
PBA .... Proceedings of the British Academy.
PEFQSt .... Palestine Oriental Fund, Quarterly Statement.
PEQ .... Palestine Exploration Quarterly.
PJ .... Preussische Jahrbücher.
PJB .... Palästinajahrbuch.
PRU .... Le Palais Royal d'Ugarit.
PSBA .... Proceedings of the Society of Biblical Archaeology.
RA .... Revue d'Assyriologie et d'Archéologie Orientale.
RB .... Revue Biblique.
RdQ .... Revue de Qumran.
REJ .... Revue des Études Juives.
RES .... Revue des Études Sémitiques.
RevBibl .... Revista Bíblica.
RGG .... Die Religion in Geschichte und Gegenwart.
RHA .... Revue Hittite et Asianique.
RHPhR .... Revue d'Histoire et de Philosophie Religieuses.
RHR .... Revue de l'Histoire des Religions.
RIDA .... Revue Internationale des Droits de l'Antiquité.
RivBibl .... Rivista Biblica.
RThPh .... Revue de Théologie et de Philosophie.
SEÅ .... Svensk Exegetisk Årsbok.
SJTh .... Scottish Journal of Theology.
StC .... Studia Catholica.
STKv .... Svensk Teologisk Kvartalskrift.
StTh .... Studia Theologica cura ordinum theologorum Scandinavicorum edita.
ThBl .... Theologische Blätter.
ThGl .... Theologie und Glaube.
ThLBL .... Theologisches Literaturblatt.
ThLZ .... Theologische Literaturzeitung.
ThQ .... Theologische Quartalschrift.
ThR .... Theologische Rundschau.
ThRev .... Theologische Revue.
ThSt .... Theological Studies.
ThStKr .... Theologische Studien und Kritiken.
ThT .... Theologisch Tijdschrift.
ThW .... Theologisches Wörterbuch zum Neuen Testament.
ThZ .... Theologische Zeitschrift.
Trierer ThZ .... Trierer Theologische Zeitschrift.
TTKi .... Tidsskrift for Teologi og Kirke.
VD .... Verbum Domini.
VT .... Vetus Testamentum.
VTSuppl .... Supplements to Vetus Testamentum
WdO .... Die Welt des Orients.
WuD .... Wort und Dienst, Jahrbuch der Theologischen Hochschule Bethel.
WZ .... Wissenschaftliche Zeitschrift.
WZKM .... Wiener Zeitschrift für die Kunde des Morgenlandes.
ZA .... Zeitschrift für Assyriologie.
ZÄS .... Zeitschrift für Ägyptische Sprache und Altertumskunde.
ZAW .... Zeitschrift für die Alttestamentliche Wissenschaft.
ZDMG .... Zeitschrift der Deutschen Morgenländischen Gesellschaft.

ZDPV	Zeitschrift des Deutschen Palästina-Vereins.
ZKTh	Zeitschrift für Katholische Theologie.
ZKWL	Zeitschrift für Kirchliche Wissenschaft und Kirchliches Leben.
ZLThK	Zeitschrift für die gesamte Lutherische Theologie und Kirche.
ZMR	Zeitschrift für Missionskunde und Religionswissenschaft.
ZNW	Zeitschrift für die Neutestamentliche Wissenschaft.
ZRGG	Zeitschrift für Religions- und Geistesgeschichte.
ZS	Zeitschrift für Semitistik und verwandte Gebiete.
ZSTh	Zeitschrift für Systematische Theologie.
ZThK	Zeitschrift für Theologie und Kirche.
ZWTh	Zeitschrift für Wissenschaftliche Theologie.

4. Note on Bibliographies

The bibliographies at the beginning of the individual paragraphs list first, whenever appropriate, the relevant commentaries, followed by general or survey literature. These are listed alphabetically according to author; different works by the same author are listed in order of publication. Special studies of particular problems or texts are cited in the footnotes. When an author's name followed by * is mentioned in the course of the presentation, it refers to the Introductions to the OT mentioned above; when not followed by *, it refers to the bibliography immediately preceding, including the commentaries, and only rarely to the notes cited in the immediate context.

It is impossible to give more than a representative selection from the scholarly literature, which has increased enormously in recent years. Those who seek additional bibliographical information on specific points have numerous resources at their disposal, particularly the bibliographies in the commentaries, the bibliographical articles in ThR, the "Zeitschriftenschau" and "Bücherschau" in ZAW, the "Elenchus bibliographicus" in Bibl (published separately starting in 1968), as well as the *Internationale Zeitschriftenschau für Bibelwissenschaft und Grenzgebiete.*

INTRODUCTION: ISRAELITE LITERATURE, THE CANON OF THE OLD TESTAMENT, AND INTRODUCTORY STUDIES

§1 The Purpose, History, and Methods of Introduction

L. Alonso Schökel, *Estudios de Poética Hebrea,* 1963; W. Baumgartner, "Alttestamentliche Einleitung und Literaturgeschichte," *ThR,* NF VIII (1936), 179-222; *idem,* "Eine alttestamentliche Forschungsgeschichte," *ibid.,* XXV (1959), 93-110; *idem,* "Zum 100. Geburtstag von Hermann Gunkel," *VTSuppl,* IX (1963), 1-18; A. Bentzen, "Skandinavische Literatur zum Alten Testament 1939–1948," *ThR NF,* XVII (1948/49), 273-328; K.-H. Bernhardt, *Die gattungsgeschichtliche Forschung am Alten Testament als exegetische Methode,* 1959; J. Bright, "Modern Study of Old Testament Literature," in *Essays Albright,* 1961, pp. 13-31; L. Diestel, *Geschichte des Alten Testaments in der Kirche,* 1869; O. Eissfeldt, "The Literature of Israel: Modern Criticism," in *Record and Revelation,* 1938, pp. 74-109; I. Engnell, "Methodological Aspects of Old Testament Study," *VTSuppl,* VII (1960), 13-30; G. Fohrer, "Tradition und Interpretation im Alten Testament," *ZAW,* LXXIII (1961), 1-30; D. N. Freedman, "On Method in Biblical Studies: The Old Testament," *Interpr,* XVII (1963), 308-18; C. H. Gordon, *New Horizons in Old Testament Literature,* 1960; H. Gunkel, "Die Grundprobleme der israelitischen Literaturgeschichte," in *Reden und Aufsätze,* 1913, pp. 29-38; H. F. Hahn, *The Old Testament in Modern Research,* 1954 (1956); G. Horning, *Die Anfänge der historisch-kritischen Theologie: Johann Salomo Semler's Schriftverständnis und seine Stellung zu Luther,* 1961; H. Hupfeld, *Über Begriff und Methode der sogenannten biblischen Einleitung* (1844), *ThStKr,* 1861, pp. 3 ff.; R. Kittel, "Die Zukunft der alttestamentlichen Wissenschaft," *ZAW,* XXXIX (1921), 84-99; K. Koch, *Was ist Formgeschichte?* 1964; E. G. Kraeling, *The Old Testament since the Reformation,* 1955; H.-J. Kraus, *Geschichte der historisch-kritischen Erforschung des Alten Testaments von der Reformation bis zur Gegenwart,* 1956; J. Lindblom, "Einige Grundfragen der alttestamentlichen Wissenschaft," in *Bertholet-Festschrift,* 1950, pp. 325-37; J. Muilenburg, "Modern Issues in Biblical Studies," *ET,* LXXI (1959/60), 229-33; L. Perlitt, *Vatke und Wellhausen,* 1965; H. H. Rowley, "Trends in Old Testament Study," in *The Old Testament and Modern Study,* 1951, pp. xv-xxxi; H. H. Schrey, "Die alttestamentliche Forschung der sogenannten Uppsala-Schule," *ThZ,* VII (1951), 321-41; S. Schulz, "Die römisch-katholische Exegese zwischen historisch-kritischer Methode und lehramtlichem Machtspruch," *EvTh,* XXII (1962), 141-56; St. Segert, "Zur Methode der alttestamentlichen Literarkritik," *ArOr,* XXIV (1956), 610-21; S. J. de Vries, "The Hexateuchal Criticism of Abraham Kuenen," *JBL,* LXXXII (1963), 31-57; G. E. Wright, "Archaeology and Old Testament Studies," *ibid.,* LXXVII (1958), 39-51; W. Zimmerli, "Die historisch-kritische Bibelwissenschaft und die Verkündigungsaufgabe der Kirche," *EvTh,* XXIII (1963), 17-31; cf. G. Fohrer in *ThR,* NF XXVIII (1962), 326-35.

1. *The OT and introductory studies.* The collection of books commonly called the Old Testament (OT) by Christian theology and the church goes back to the Judaism of the period before and after the birth of Christ, when, after going through a long series of preliminary stages, it was selected and assembled. Judaism in this period faced the problem of rejecting theologically dubious internal movements and carrying on a debate with the Christian church; to meet these religious needs, Judaism began to codify its foundations and its way of life. The resulting collection of books, however, became Holy Scripture not only for Judaism, but also for Christianity and Islam.

The term "OT" derives ultimately from biblical usage. The word "testament" comes from the Latin *testamentum*, which translates the Hebrew *bᵉrît* and the Greek *diathēkē*, "contract, agreement, treaty, covenant (also, in Greek, 'last will')." The term is connected with the concept of the covenant that Yahweh entered into with Israel through Moses. The new stamp that Old Testament prophecy puts upon this faith lies behind Jer. 31:31-34, which announces a new covenant that Yahweh will make with his people. In the NT, especially II Cor. 3:5-18, the word is interpreted as the announcement of a future that is fulfilled in Jesus Christ. Since in him the "new covenant" has been given, the term "old covenant" was applied to the period preceding him. Both terms were then extended to the sacred writings treating these covenants, the books of the old and new covenant (or testament). Thus the OT, the book of the old covenant, became Holy Scripture for Christianity. Originally, in fact, it alone was Christianity's Holy Scripture, because the NT came into being only gradually, and also because, notwithstanding all the critical distinctions that remain the task of OT theology, Jesus Christ himself accepted it as an undisputed authority (Matt. 5:17-19; Luke 10:25-28; 16:19-31).

Despite the reservations of Marcion and Harnack,[1] not to mention absolute rejection on the part of ignorant politicians and racists, the OT is still considered Holy Scripture by Christian theology and the church. For this reason it is necessary to understand it correctly both as a whole and in detail and to subject it to scholarly study. Alongside other approaches to study and understanding, this is the job of OT introduction. Its task is to examine and describe the growth of the Old Testament from its earliest beginnings to its conclusion. More precisely, within the framework of the ancient Near East that archaeology is recovering, it traces the formation and transmission of the writings constituting the OT from the growth of oral traditions through the written fixing of the individual texts and their arrangement in the form of books down to their coalescence in the OT canon and the final definition of the text.

2. *Beginnings.* Any document at all can be provided with an introduction, intended to render its understanding easier or even possible by introducing the reader to the vocabulary and grammar, the historical situation and institutions, the intellectual milieu and content of the text. A document must be provided with such an introduction if it is to be made accessible to readers belonging to a completely different period and environment and lacking such preliminary

[1] A. von Harnack, *Marcion*, 2nd ed., 1924.

data. The OT itself contains notes of this sort, especially in the headings and glosses introduced by later scribes or readers without regard for their correctness. These include the headings of most of the prophetic books and of the thirteen psalms that are derived from situations in the life of David, e.g., Pss. 18, 51, 52, 54, 56, 57, 59, and 60, as well as such isolated glosses as Ezek. 1:2, which is intended to explain the date in 1:1, and Zech. 1:7, which defines "the eleventh month" by giving its name.

Truly scientific introduction did not exist for many centuries after the writing of these glosses. At first the rabbis handed down their views on the authorship, date, and place of origin of the OT books; the ancient and medieval church borrowed these traditions and added to them. These and other details were discussed in the form of introductions to the books of the OT, like those written by Jerome, or in other works, like Augustine's *De doctrina christiana* and Junilius Africanus' *Instituta regularia divinae legis*. As far as we know, the term "introduction" was first used by Adrianus, a monk (d. *ca.* 440), in his work *eisagōgê eis tàs theías graphás, Introduction to the Divine Scriptures*. This was latinized as *isagoge* and *introductio* and translated into German as *Einleitung* by J. D. Michaelis in 1750. English borrowed the Latin term directly.

From the Middle Ages, two Jewish scholars deserve special mention: Rashi (d. 1105) and Ibn Ezra (d. 1167). The latter occasionally ventured critical comments, even though the doctrine of verbal inspiration forced him to do so allusively. On the basis of the phrase "beyond the Jordan" in Deut. 1:1, referring to the lands east of the Jordan, as well as Deut. 3:10-12; 27:1-8; 31:9, he concluded that Moses could not be the author of Deuteronomy: " 'Beyond the Jordan': When you understand the mystery of the twelve, and also 'And Moses wrote this law,' as well as 'The Canaanite was then in the land,' and 'On the mountain of God he shall reveal himself,' and finally 'Behold, his bedstead was a bedstead of iron,' then you will know the truth." But as for him who knows it—"Let him keep silent!" On the Christian side, those active as scholars included Isidore of Seville (d. *ca.* 636), who summarized all the available knowledge of his time in an encyclopedia, the *Prooemiorum liber*; and Nicolas of Lyra (d. *ca.* 1340), who knew Hebrew and therefore could transmit the works of the Jewish scholars and preserve contact with the original text.

Humanism and the Reformation created the conditions necessary for the formation of a real science of introduction. Humanism led to the rediscovery of Hebrew (J. Reuchlin) and the original text; the Reformation took this text as its basis in place of the Vulgate and promoted its philological study. At the same time, the traditions concerning authorship and date of the books of the OT were subjected to critical examination in the light of the text. Alongside Luther, with his remarks on the canonicity of the book of Esther and the late redaction of certain prophetic books, Karlstadt deserves special mention. In his work *De canonicis scripturis libellus* (1520), he recorded his stylistic observation that the narrative sections of the Pentateuch and Joshua did not differ stylistically and that the same hand had been at work in both. The author, he added (again on stylistic grounds), could not have been Ezra. But the first general introductions, by Sixtus Senensis (Catholic, 1566), Rivetus (Reformed, 1627), and Walther (Lutheran, 1636), did not advance beyond the traditional views and sought to accommodate the new critical discoveries to these views.

The decisive steps leading to scientific introduction were taken in the period of the Enlightenment and rationalism. In *Leviathan* III (1651), Thomas Hobbes insisted that the date of the OT books should be determined directly from the books themselves without recourse to tradition. In his *Tractatus theologico-politicus*, B. Spinoza gave to critical studies, which previously had been based on isolated contradictions and stylistic analysis, the methodological principle that the proper guidepost for the study of the OT is "natural reason, which is the common property of all men, not supernatural enlightenment or external authority." He also discussed the questions that were to be the subject matter of the introductory studies: the origin of the individual books and the history of the canon and of the text. Linguistic analysis of the text furnished a fourth impetus; for the Pentateuch—thanks to the inspiration of R. Simon—it had already led to the first source analysis by H. B. Witter (1711) and J. Astruc (1753). After J. S. Semler and his *Abhandlung von freier Untersuchung des Canon* (1771-75) and *Apparatus ad liberalem Veteris Testamenti interpretationem* (1773), demanding that the OT be studied according to the same principles that apply to other literature, free from dogma and tradition, and the new artistic and aesthetic appreciation of the OT on the part of J. G. Herder and R. Lowth, J. G. Eichhorn assembled all the previous observations and suggestions in his encyclopedic *Einleitung in das AT**; like Spinoza, he discussed the three questions of the origin of the individual books, the history of the canon, and the history of the text. He inaugurated introductory studies in the strict sense.

3. *The growth of historical-critical scholarship.* Subsequent history begins with the influence of the historical method and the history of religions. According to W. M. L. de Wette (1806-7; 1817), the books of the OT illustrate the development of its religious ideas, which in turn make it possible to date the books. De Wette's major contribution was the identification of Josiah's lawbook with Deuteronomy. Besides H. G. A. Ewald (1835 ff.; 1840-41; 1843 ff.), there remains to mention W. Vatke (1835), who, under the influence of Hegel, described the growth of the OT literature against the background of the history of the OT religion. Against this tendency, there was an attempt to revive the tradition of the synagogue and the ancient church on the part of E. W. Hengstenberg (1831 ff.) and K. F. Keil (1833). Keil, for example, strove to demonstrate the authenticity of the Pentateuch and the book of Daniel, or the unity of the book of Zechariah.

Historical-critical scholarship won the day, however. Despite the basic contributions of A. Kuenen* (1861 ff.) and K. H. Graf (1866), this school is associated with the name of J. Wellhausen* (1876 ff.), whose lead was followed by F. Bleek (1878), B. Stade (1881 ff.), W. Robertson Smith* (1881), C. H. Cornill* (1891), S. R. Driver* (1891), and, as it were definitively, C. Steuernagel* (1912). By equating Josiah's lawbook with Deuteronomy, de Wette had gained a fixed point of reference for chronology. Kuenen and Graf dated the Priestly stratum of the Pentateuch in the postexilic period, and Wellhausen created the great summary in which the sources, separated by literary analysis, yield a definite picture of Israelite history, within which the sources themselves are assigned to their proper periods. Since this picture simply could not be reconciled with the traditional views, Wellhausen was subjected to attacks that have lasted down to the present time, accusing him of Hegelianism and evolutionism if they do not indeed treat him as a kind of devil. As Perlitt most recently has shown, with all the clearness one could wish, these accusations are completely unjustified.

In fact, even Wellhausen's opponents have learned from him and made use of his approach to the problems and his methods, even when, like H. L. Strack (1883), E. K. A. Riehm (1889-90), E. König (1893), W. Graf Baudissin* (1901), and E. Sellin* (1910, 7th ed. 1935), they sought to present in their results a conservative synthesis with the views of the synagogue and the ancient church.

The purely analytic approach, however, created feelings of uneasiness that found expression in a pun: "Is the Pentateuch Mosaic or a mosaic?" Therefore such scholars as G. Wildeboer* (1893), E. Kautzsch (1897), K. Budde* (1906), J. Meinhold* (1919, 3rd ed. 1932) J. A. Bewer* (1922), and, belatedly, A. Lods* (1950) tried to achieve a synthetic description of how the OT was formed. The individual books were detached from their canonical sequence and discussed in a chronological framework. But before this program could be fully realized, another approach came to the fore, which produced several new methods of study.

4. *New methods*. The approach associated with the names of H. Gunkel and H. Gressmann was based on two types of study. On the one hand, it drew on the results of Near Eastern archaeology and general studies related to the Near East, fully recognizing the importance of these disciplines, an importance that has continued to increase down to the present day. On the other hand, it applied the methods of comparative literature to the OT. The literature of the OT was viewed within the framework of ancient Near Eastern literature as a whole, and the relationship between the two was examined. The first subject to attract interest was the history of rhetorical forms and literary types, together with the history of the material and motifs drawn upon. Both the present form and the prehistory of the OT texts became subjects of study.

a) The work of Gunkel, influenced by classical and Germanic philology, paved the way for the study of literary types. This approach is based on the assumption that in ancient times rhetorical forms and literary types were more fixed than they are today, following a certain structural pattern, exhibiting more or less well established motifs, and originating in a specific *Sitz im Leben*. The narrator or poet chose the type to follow as opportunity or occasion presented itself, but was then restricted to its pattern, so that the possibilities for individual variation were limited while conventional and typical elements exercised control. Starting from these considerations, Gunkel* wanted to replace previous "introductions" with a history of Israelite and Jewish literature, conceived as a history of the literary types current in Israel. This approach is especially attractive because it recognizes the possibility of reaching conclusions that go beyond the limits of what has been handed down in literary form, taking account of the actual singing and speaking, tracing the prehistory of the rhetorical forms back to the earliest periods, and explaining thereby the peculiarities of the OT texts. Hempel* produced a presentation along these lines.

In the meantime, the theory of literary types was further refined and developed into form criticism, which studies the development and transformation of the individual forms and formulas. This soon resulted in a tendency to ascribe primary or absolute authority to the form-critical method, not to go beyond it, and to exalt it as the sole or at least basic principle of interpretation. This tendency must be resolutely opposed. Form-critical study must be based on literary analysis and thought of as literary analysis developed further along one of several lines.

Occasional exaggerations and distortions concerning the study of literary types and form criticism need to be set right: 1. The method is applicable primarily to the original literary or rhetorical units. It is a dubious procedure, however, to apply this method to individual phrases (in which case the method threatens to degenerate into "formula criticism")[2] or to larger units or even entire books, whose structure does not usually depend on formal principles. 2. It is also dubious to overrate conventional and typical elements at the expense of personal and individual elements; to do so contradicts the personal structure of Yahwism and its resulting individual expression. This approach is based less on Israelite ideas and concepts than on the modern anti-psychological and anti-subjective influence of sociology and the natural sciences. 3. The attempt to find an institution or office in every case is a deception. The tacit assumption seems frequently to be that the rhetorical forms are firmly linked to a specific institution, that their structure reflects and brings to light a real (perhaps cultic) proceeding, that this proceeding can be localized and dated, and that the person using the form is therefore fulfilling an office in the institution and (cultic) proceeding. It is true that the concept of a *Sitz im Leben* refers to a specific occasion: the *Sitz im Leben* of a dirge is a death; but this is now suddenly transformed into an association with an institution, usually cultic or legal. It is not difficult to show that this view does not account for the actual situation. 4. It is not true to say that form and content of a literary unit always agree; to prove this point, it suffices to point out the prophets' use of the dirge as a threat or mock threat. This means that we must probably distinguish

[2] M. Noth, *Developing Lines of Theological Thought in Germany*, 1963.

between the rhetorical form and its function, between the original *Sitz im Leben* and the rhetorical setting.

b) Gunkel and Gressmann also took the lead in pioneering and promoting the study of themes and motifs. The discoveries of archaeology and Near Eastern studies exposed this approach, as they still do, in a special way to the danger of deriving the themes and motifs of the OT from its environment whenever possible and overlooking the uniqueness of Yahwism. OT studies actually succumbed to this danger in Pan-Babylonism and the Babel-Bible controversy. This approach nevertheless remains an indispensable tool for studying the origin and transformation of these themes and motifs in Israel's environment and in the OT itself. This, too, must be done on the basis provided by literary criticism and is itself a specific outgrowth of literary criticism.

Out of this approach has grown tradition history, which seeks to trace not only isolated motifs but also the streams of tradition consisting of clusters of motifs through the OT. As in the case of form criticism, however, we may note a tendency toward one-sidedness and exaggeration that exalts the study of traditions to the status of an absolute criterion, looking upon nearly all the utterances of the OT as deriving from a few traditions and tracing these traditions as they undergo transformation throughout the course of history. According to this school, there really is "nothing new under the sun" (Eccles. 1:9); what is unique about a statement is in the last analysis only the particular form assumed by a transformation.

Once again a few points should be set straight for the sake of the correct principles: 1. There seems to be frequent confusion between a multitude of motifs that appear together and a tradition. It is absolutely necessary to distinguish between a tradition and the separate motifs, which can of course be components of a tradition. The memory of Israel's deliverance from Egypt is a tradition; the elements of the later Zion theology, on the other hand, such as occur in the Korahite psalms, do not go back to a pre-Israelite cult tradition of Jerusalem, but are individual motifs that have been brought together.[3] Real caution is necessary to avoid confusing late theologoumena with streams of tradition. 2. Corresponding to the duality of form and function, there is a duality of tradition and interpretation; the latter can proceed variously and must not be subjected to the canons of an a priori uniformity. Interpretation can go so far as to transform a tradition into its opposite and clothe it in new forms. 3. In other cases, one must ask whether investigation into the origin of a theme, of scholarly interest in itself, is relevant to an understanding of how it is used in the text. Often the authors of a text were no longer aware of the former significance of a theme and simply read their own meaning into it; our goal is comprehension of this latter meaning. 4. Probably no part of the OT, least of all the prophets, can be viewed exclusively from the standpoint of its traditional content or the duality of tradition and interpretation. Almost always

[3] For a detailed discussion, see G. Wanke, *Die Zionstheologie der Korachiten in ihrem traditionsgeschichtlichen Zusammenhang*, 1966.

there is a more or less imposing mass of individual ideas and expressions, spontaneous or planned, that do not derive from the tradition. The prophets in particular were primarily charismatics, claiming to preach not a tradition but the living word of Yahweh that had been delivered to them.

c) In traditio-historical criticism we have a further method, which should not be considered an antithetical alternative to literary criticism (the view especially of I. Engnell*) nor accorded a superior position, but must rather be looked upon as a further step subsequent to literary analysis (e.g., M. Noth, W. Beyerlin, G. Fohrer). It deals with the prehistory of the books of the OT and examines the gradual accumulation of traditions from the preliterary stages until their final written form. The books for the most part are not "literature" in the sense that specific authors planned, formulated, and wrote them as a single connected process. Instead, the written copy usually marks the final element in the preservation of a specific subject matter in one stage, long or short, of its transmission, the stage in which it finally achieved its present form. Traditio-historical study not only inquires how the textual units achieved their final form but also seeks to trace the entire process by which the units came into being. Account must of course be taken of the diversity of the OT material; it must not be reduced to a uniform pattern. Obviously this kind of investigation often does not lead to a definite solution because the transmission of the material does not admit one.

d) Recently stylistic analysis has enjoyed a revival, unfortunately coupled with a certain tendency toward one-sidedness and exclusiveness instead of as a supplement to previous methods. L. Alonso Schökel, for example, employs the principles of the New Criticism from the literary realm to study sound patterns, verse structure, use of images, and composition. This approach, of course, runs the danger of falling into sterile aestheticism.

e) Many other approaches also enrich the picture and lead to new knowledge and insight. One might mention the results of archaeology and topography, of investigation of territorial history, and of the new light cast on historical circumstances in the ancient Near East. The texts discovered in the Judean Desert, especially in the Qumran caves, make many questions appear in a new light; they create problems, however, in at least equal number. The study of devotional forms traces the origin, development, and transformation of ideas and expressions of devotion. The cultic approach traces the cultic background of large portions of ancient Near Eastern and OT literature, the formation of the cult legends behind sanctuaries and festivals, together with the formation and transmission of traditions in the context of the cult in its widest sense. The redactio-historical approach, finally, devotes itself to the purposes of those who assembled and edited the larger complexes.

5. *The task of introduction.* The present multiplicity of scholarly approaches and methods of interpretation may seem confusing. This may in part be the reason why many are prepared to pledge themselves to a single method and let all the others go by the board. For this very reason the science of intro-

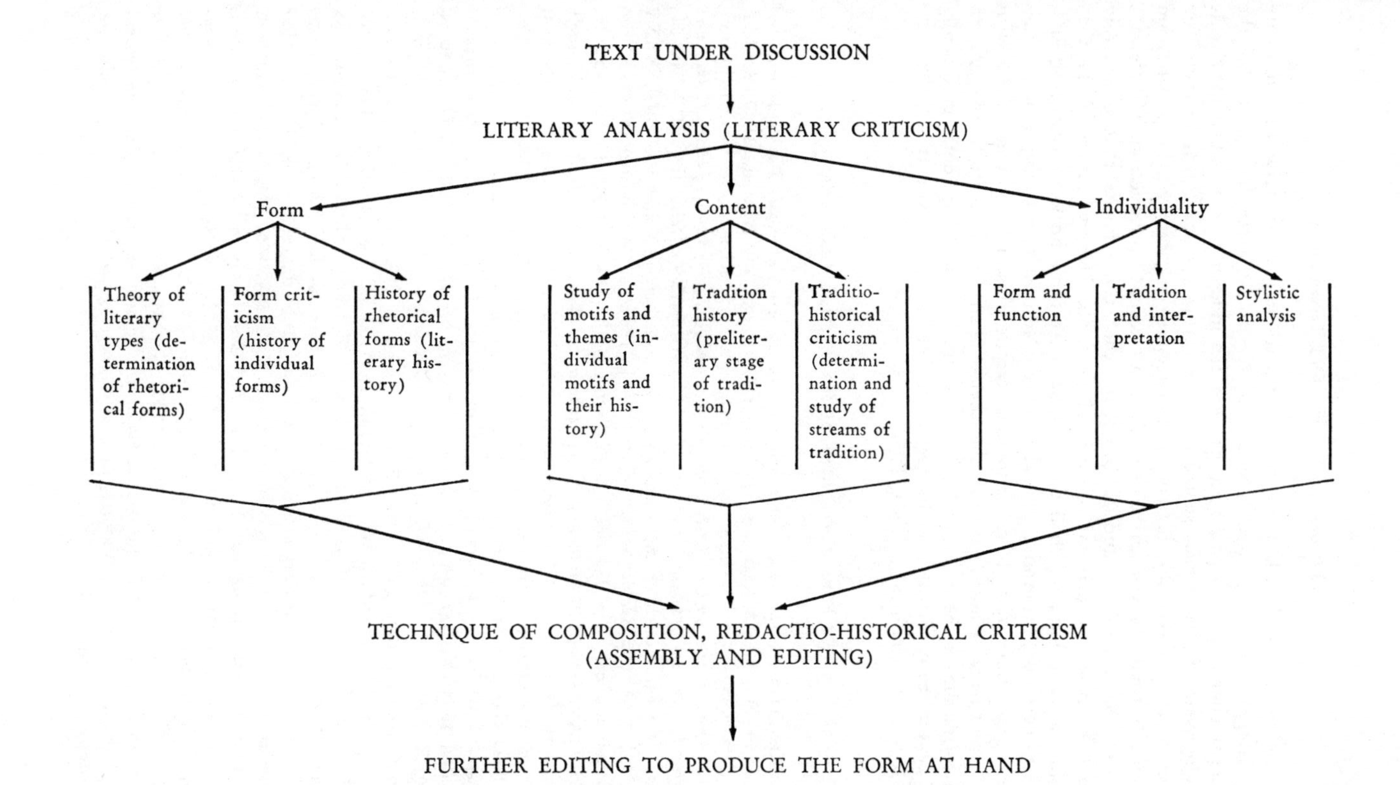
TEXT UNDER DISCUSSION
LITERARY ANALYSIS (LITERARY CRITICISM)
Form
Content
Individuality
Theory of literary types (determination of rhetorical forms)
Form criticism (history of individual forms)
History of rhetorical forms (literary history)
Study of motifs and themes (individual motifs and their history)
Tradition history (preliterary stage of tradition)
Traditio-historical criticism (determination and study of streams of tradition)
Form and function
Tradition and interpretation
Stylistic analysis
TECHNIQUE OF COMPOSITION, REDACTIO-HISTORICAL CRITICISM (ASSEMBLY AND EDITING)
FURTHER EDITING TO PRODUCE THE FORM AT HAND

duction has a special task in the present situation: it must strive to coordinate and integrate the divergent methods and tendencies after the fashion of the adjacent chart. Our purpose is to prevent the independent or mutually hostile development of the various schools and constitute the science of introduction as an organic whole. To this end, it is necessary to organize the presentation differently than has been the case in the more recent introductions (Eissfeldt*, Weiser*, Sellin-Rost*), and to bring together those books that objectively belong together independent of their place in the Hebrew canon of the OT. Within these groups, we shall discuss first what those books constituting each have in common, beginning with the ancient Near Eastern background, discussing the questions of form criticism and tradition history, and concluding with the growth and transmission of the texts. Then we shall study the growth and formation of the individual OT books within each group, both analytically and synthetically. Finally, the history of the canon and of the text will illustrate the further development of the OT.

§2 Presuppositions of Israelite Literature

J. Aistleitner, *Die mythologischen und kultischen Texte aus Ras Schamra*, 2nd ed., 1964; W. F. Albright, *Archaeology of Palestine*, 1949, 4th ed., 1960; A. Alt, *Die Landnahme der Israeliten in Palästina*, 1925 (= *Kleine Schriften*, I [1953], 89-125 [Eng. *Essays on Old Testament History and Religion*, 1966]); *idem*, *Völker und Staaten Syriens im frühen Altertum*, 1936 (= *Kleine Schriften*, III [1959], 20-48); *idem*, "Erwägungen über die Landnahme der Israeliten in Palästina," *PJB*, XXXV (1939), 8-63 (= *Kleine Schriften*, I [1953], 126-75); W. Baumgartner, "Ras Schamra und das Alte Testament," *ThR* NF, XIII (1941), 1-20, 85-102, 157-83; K.-H. Bernhardt, *Das Problem der altorientalischen Königsideologie*, 1961; I. Engnell, *Studies in Divine Kingship in the Ancient Near East*, 2nd ed., 1967; G. Fohrer, "Die wiederentdeckte kanaanäische Religion," *ThLZ*, LXXVIII (1953), 193-200; H. Frankfort, *Kingship and the Gods*, 1948; *idem*, *The Problem of Similarity in Ancient Near Eastern Religions*, 1951; J. de Fraine, *L'aspect religieux de la royauté israélite*, 1954; K. Galling, *Textbuch zur Geschichte Israels*, 1950; C. H. Gordon, *Ugaritic Literature*, 1949; *idem*, *Ugaritic Textbook*, 1965; *idem*, *Geschichtliche Grundlagen des Alten Testaments*, 2nd ed., 1961; J. Gray, *The Legacy of Canaan*, 1957; S. H. Hooke, ed., *Myth and Ritual*, 1933; *idem*, *The Labyrinth*, 1935; *idem*, *Myth, Ritual, and Kingship*, 1958; A. Jirku, *Die Ausgrabungen in Palästina und Syrien*, 1956; *idem*, *Kanaanäische Mythen und Epen aus Ras Schamra-Ugarit*, 1962; A. R. Johnson, *Sacral Kingship in Ancient Israel*, 2nd ed., 1967; C. R. North, "The Religious Aspect of Hebrew Kingship," *ZAW*, L (1932), 8-38; M. Noth, *Die Welt des Alten Testaments*, 4th ed., 1962 (Eng. *The Old Testament World*, 1966); *idem*, "Gott, König, Volk im Alten Testament," *ZThK*, XLVII (1950), 157-91 (= *Gesammelte Studien zum Alten Testament*, 1957, pp. 188-229); H. W. Robinson, *The History of Israel, Its Facts and Factors*, 1941; H. Schmökel *et al.*, *Kulturgeschichte des Alten Orient*, 1961; P. Thomsen, *Palästina und seine Kultur in fünf Jahrtausenden*, 3rd ed., 1931; G. E. Wright, *Biblical Archaeology*, new ed., 1962; see also the presentations of the history of Israel.

1. *Historical and geographical presuppositions.*[1] Because of the nature of the terrain, Palestine is not a unified, unbroken territory for settlement. Its division into broad strips running north to south—the coastal plain, the central mountain range, the Rift Valley, and Transjordan—crossed from east to west by plains, valleys, and sloping hills, favors sociological tensions between its various population groups, independent development of the separate regions depending on their proximity to trade routes, and political fragmentation into a multitude of autonomous political entities. At the same time, its valleys provide thoroughfares, making it the bridge between Africa and Asia, between Egypt, Mesopotamia, and Asia Minor. It was therefore continually drawn into the conflicts between the dominant powers of the Near East; during most of its history it has been subject to foreign rule. Geographic, ethnic, historical, and political diversity existed side by side. From the eighteenth to the sixteenth century B.C., the ruling class of the Hyksos divided the land into numerous city-states and rural estates; this system lasted through the following period of Egyptian domination and did not come to an end until the kingdom of David and Solomon. The juxtaposition of various ethnic groups, particularly —apart from the ruling class of Philistines—the Canaanites and the Israelites (most of the latter settled in the sparsely populated mountains), continued to affect Northern Israel through Solomon's division of the country into administrative districts, which followed the old boundaries. Both groups gradually coalesced; during this process, the influence of the Canaanites divided the Israelites ethnically, socially, and culturally. The decisive factor was the acceptance of permanent agriculture by the seminomadic Israelites, followed by their assimilation into urban life and economy.

All this must have made it difficult if not impossible for the Israelite people to preserve its own political, cultural, and intellectual life. It also must have made the formation of a specifically Israelite literature seem unlikely. That it nevertheless came into being and—apart from certain differences due to the separate development of the Northern and Southern Kingdoms after the breakup of the kingdom of David and Solomon—exhibits great uniformity runs counter to the geographical and historical presuppositions. Two factors account for it (apart, once more, from the gradual process of selection, which lasted for centuries): the sense of ethnic and national solidarity that had its groundwork laid in the period of the Judges, appeared in the time of Saul, and flourished in the Davidic and Solomonic kingdom; and the unifying force of Yahwism, which the band of Moses' followers brought to the Israelite tribes and groups in Palestine. This religion also had a decisive influence upon the growing sense of ethnic and national solidarity. The religious factor proved to be more powerful than the opposing forces.

2. *Cultural presuppositions.* When they settled in Palestine, the Israelites brought with them the elements of their nomadic culture, together with some Mesopotamian or Egyptian influences. At the same time, they entered the

[1] Following the description of Hempel*, which Weiser* also uses.

realm of an advanced Canaanite civilization, characterized by much more than a fertility cult based on sexual magic. The more excavations reveal of this civilization, the clearer becomes the immense heritage of form and content, both material and spiritual, that the Israelites borrowed. Its rejection by the Nazirites and Rechabites was a sterile and inappropriate reaction; had they succeeded it would have meant Israel's downfall. At the same time, the people were living in a land infiltrated by neighboring tribes, non-Israelite and non-Canaanite, particularly from the steppe country south of Judah. The whole region still showed the influence of the Hittite civilization of Asia Minor, following the collapse of the Hittite Empire about 1200, and even preserved traces of the Eastern Mediterranean civilization of the Aegean period, before the arrival of the Greeks, which had come through the Phoenician ports. There was also the lasting association with Egypt, to whose sphere of influence Palestine belonged culturally and often politically; it is hard to imagine the Israelite concept of wisdom apart from this influence. Finally, the eastern powers, from the Sumerians through the Babylonians and Assyrians down to the Persians, left traces in Palestine, which may be due to the early migrations of the seminomadic Israelites, the mediation of the Canaanites, or later direct contact. Foreign influences impinged upon Israel from all sides. It is therefore easy to see that Israel's literature must first be considered as one part of the entire literature of the ancient Near East. We may then ask whether it constitutes no more than that or also bears its own unique stamp.

This question is vital in view of the thesis represented by some English and Swedish scholars, who assert the cultural unity of the ancient Near East, especially in the cultic sphere, and speak of a cultic pattern shared by the whole Near East in which the divine king is the central figure. This pattern of necessity includes Israel, whose culture, religion, and cult are said to share its traits, as these scholars seek to show on the basis of Israel's literature. This approach reduces Israel's literature to a mere tiny sample of the religious and cultic literature of the ancient Near East. In his study of the book of Nahum, for instance, A. Haldar finds only four verses in which the cultic and mythical motifs of the pattern are not present (the status of two others remains vague in his presentation).

The positive contribution of this approach lies in its admonition to draw upon the whole range of ancient Near Eastern texts when determining the literary types of the OT. There is in fact a certain degree of agreement and uniformity among the civilizations of the ancient Near East. There are, however, several reasons for denying the existence of a unified cultic pattern: 1. As seen through our eyes, the civilization of the ancient Near East can appear as much a unity as modern European civilization will to later observers. But just as European civilization is in fact highly differentiated and at times even contradictory, so the individual civilizations of the ancient Near East also possessed their own peculiarities, differences, and contrasts. 2. The presupposition on which the thesis is based, namely, that the ancient Near East was a unified, monolithic block, is becoming more and more dubious. Even the Hittites do not fit into this picture completely. Above all, interpretation of the excavations at Ugarit shows that the Near East was open to the Eastern Mediterranean world. The same holds true for the relationship of the eastern regions to India. 3. There is no evidence for the existence of the entire pattern in a single civilization of the ancient Near East; each contains only a few traits, which must be brought together from all sources to yield the whole. 4. Parallels are discovered prematurely in the texts being compared. One must remember that identical words can have divergent meanings and overtones among various peoples and in various lands or civilizations. 5. The purported discovery of a wealth of overtones and undertones of the pattern, especially in late texts of the OT, presupposes that the average Israelite possessed a fantastic knowledge of the history of religions.

Even if the thesis of a cultic pattern is untenable, it remains astounding that, despite all the foreign influences, Israelite literature developed along its own individual and homogeneous lines. This fact must once more be considered due to Yahwism, which established itself so successfully that it could accommodate the Israelite tribal traditions and eliminate or assimilate Canaanite and alien material. Its creative power permeated religiously the heritage of Israel's own past and the Near Eastern environment.

3. *Literary presuppositions.* At the time the Israelites settled in Palestine, writing had long been familiar there and was taught in scribal schools. In official and diplomatic correspondence, Babylonian cuneiform was usually employed; even during the period of Egyptian ascendancy in Palestine, hieroglyphics could not displace cuneiform. Most important, however, about the middle of the second millennium a consonantal alphabet was developed in the Phoenician region, for which cuneiform signs were used at first, and later more specialized signs. The Hebrew alphabet, the archaic Hebrew script, and ultimately our own alphabet all derive from this, since the Greeks borrowed alphabetic writing from the Phoenicians during the ninth century B.C. and developed it further.

Considerable portions of Mesopotamian and Egyptian literature were likewise known in Palestine, not least because they furnished practice texts for the scribal schools. The most important categories are hymns, epics, myths, and wisdom teaching. There are numerous fragments, but no great continuous works. The present Pentateuch narrative can also be analyzed into its original stories and story cycles, which were gradually assembled on the basis of an all-encompassing idea. But the Joseph story and the court history of David, which came into being long after the settlement in Palestine, are carefully and systematically constructed.

Literarily, it turns out that the Israelites brought with them a very simple narrative technique and found a similar technique already in use in Palestine. Then, however, they assembled the individual stories or cycles in great general works dominated by specific ideas and created systematic presentations. We find nothing like this in the rest of Near Eastern literature. If we seek the reasons behind this startling development, we may formally trace its course from the Canaanite epic through the Israelite epic to the historical narrative. The decisive element, however, was Yahwism, which, for example, with its growth as a national religion involving the concept of Israel as a whole provided the ideas and connecting links by which the earlier narrators forged the materials of the Pentateuch into a unity. The faith that Yahweh determined the destiny of men and nations provided the chance—despite the literary presuppositions—for a unique literature. Similar observations hold true for the prophetic oracles, the psalms, and other rhetorical forms that differ considerably from the comparable phenomena of the ancient Near East.

4. *The significance of Yahwism.* Yahwism is again and again the decisive force that makes possible an autonomous Israelite literature despite the unfavorable presuppositions. This Israelite literature differs profoundly in its religious conceptions from the other literatures of the ancient Near East. Of course we are dealing here with a process that lasted for centuries, and it is a gross oversimplification to restrict this process to the premonarchic period. In this period we find only the roots, from which the tree gradually grew. The process is still going on in the period of the so-called writing prophets, when it grows constantly clearer that the driving forces of Yahwism are the idea of God's dominion and of personal relationship with God.

§3 Oral Tradition and Literature

H. Birkeland, *Zum hebräischen Traditionswesen,* 1938; R. C. Culley, "An Approach to the Problem of Oral Tradition," *VT,* XIII (1962), 113-25; O. Eissfeldt, "Zur Überlieferungsgeschichte der Prophetenbücher des Alten Testaments," *ThLZ,* LXXIII (1948), 529-34; I. Engnell, *Gamla Testamentet, en traditionshistorisk inledning,* I, 1945; *idem, "Profetia och tradition," SEÅ,* XII (1947), 110-39; B. Gerhardsson, *Memory and Manuscript,* 1961; *idem,* "Mündliche und schriftliche Tradition der Prophetenbücher," *ThZ,* XVII (1961), 216-20; A. H. J. Gunneweg, *Mündliche und schriftliche Tradition der vorexilischen Prophetenbücher als Problem der neueren Prophetenforschung,* 1959; J. Hempel, "The Literature of Israel: The Forms of Oral Tradition," in *Record and Revelation,* 1938, pp. 28-44; A. S. Herbert, "Literary Criticism and Oral Tradition," *London Quarterly and Holborn Review,* 1959, pp. 9-12; J. Laessøe, "Literary and Oral Tradition in Ancient Mesopotamia," in *Studia Orientalia Pedersen,* 1953, pp. 205-18; A. Lods, "Le rôle de la tradition orale dans la formation des récits de l'Ancien Testament," *RHR,* LXXXVIII (1923), 51-64; S. Mowinckel, "Opkomsten av profetlitteraturen," *NTT,* XLIII (1942), 65-111; *idem, Prophecy and Tradition,* 1946; E. Nielsen, *Oral Tradition,* 2nd ed., 1956; C. R. North, "The Place of Oral Tradition in the Growth of the Old Testament," *ET,* LXI (1949/50), 292-96; H. S. Nyberg, *Studien zum Hoseabuche,* 1935; J. van der Ploeg, "Le rôle de la tradition orale dans la transmission du texte de l'Ancien Testament," *RB,* LIV (1947), 5-41; H. Ringgren, "Oral and Written Transmission in the Old Testament," *StTh,* III (1950/51), 34-59; H. F. D. Sparks, "The Witness of the Prophets to Hebrew Tradition," *JThSt,* L (1949), 129-41; C. Stuhlmueller, "The Influence of Oral Tradition upon Exegesis and the Senses of Scripture," *CBQ,* XX (1958), 299-326; G. Widengren, *Literary and Psychological Aspects of the Hebrew Prophets,* 1948;

idem, "Oral Tradition and Written Literature among the Hebrews in the Light of Arabic Evidence, with Special Regard to Prose Narratives," *AcOr Kopenhagen*, XXIII (1959), 201-62; *idem*, "Tradition and Literature in Early Judaism and in the Early Church," *Numen*, X (1963), 42-83; cf. G. Fohrer in *ThR*, NF XIX (1951), 282-85; XX (1952), 199-203; XXVIII (1962), 33-35.

1. *The problem*. Up to now we have used the expression "Israelite literature." This raises the problem of how and when it came into being. Was it written down from the outset, as many have assumed rather ingenuously, or were there stages leading up to written literature? If the latter, when did this literature come into being, and how did the reduction to writing take place? In recent decades these questions have been the subject of lively discussion.

Nyberg has given the decisive impulse in this field. In his view, traditions were usually handed down orally in the Near East, rarely in writing. The written form of a literary work was preceded by a longer or shorter period of oral tradition, which remained the normal form in which the work was used and handed down even after it had been reduced to writing. This holds true for the OT, which until the Exile had a mostly oral prehistory in circles or centers that preserved and handed down the traditional material. In its written form, the OT is the creation of the postexilic Jewish community. It follows that critical study can recover only this postexilic written tradition for examination; textual and literary criticism becomes superfluous. Engnell has developed these hypotheses to their ultimate limit: not only were the OT narratives handed down for centuries exclusively by oral tradition, there were also complete oral "literatures," and oral tradition continued to be of primary importance even after the material was written down; without this oral tradition, the nascent literature of Israel would never have survived the Exile. These oral forms, fixed in writing, are the final material for investigation. Engnell and Birkeland have applied this high estimation of oral tradition to the prophetic books especially. Engnell finds there a liturgical type (intended from the very outset to be written down) and a divan type (collections of oracles and narratives, for the most part transmitted orally). Nielsen took up Nyberg's hypotheses and developed them in his own fashion.

Widengren has expressed a contrary view in his studies. He accords considerably less significance and reliability to oral tradition and assumes its presence only in exceptional cases. Even in the earliest period, he thinks the texts were written down at once and transmitted in writing.

Both views leave no place for literary criticism. According to the one view, such studies are no longer possible because investigation cannot penetrate beyond the tradition of the postexilic community; according to the other, they are unnecessary because from the very outset everything was written down and transmitted in the very form that we now have. Both views seem one-sided. Mowinckel therefore soon pioneered a middle course; he avoids exalting the present form of the tradition, emphasizing instead its historical development, in order to work back from the tradition to its historical basis. He seeks to distinguish between earlier and later strata of tradition and refers to the oral development from individual unit to collection, as well as to the fixed written text with canonical authority, which presupposes a fixed oral tradition. Since Mowinckel, many scholars, such as Gunneweg, Hempel, and Stuhlmueller, have assumed the existence side by side of both types of tradition, each scholar espousing a slightly different theory.

In discussing this question, two complexes of problems must be distinguished: references to oral and written tradition in the ancient Near East and the OT quite generally, and the application of the results to the various kinds of Israelite literature.

2. *Oral and written tradition.* How shall we resolve the problem of oral and written tradition? Primary evidence for the possibility of oral tradition is the observation that natives of the Near East have outstanding memories; they can even retain material of enormous scope and recall it years later. This observation, however, points up the accuracy of such tradition; it is not constantly subject to revision and alteration, as Nyberg and others assert. Between a narrative handed down orally and its later written form there are hardly likely to have been significant differences, unless of course a writer has altered the narrative for his own purposes. In addition, oral traditions were circulated by storytellers and singers, both in Israel and elsewhere in the Near East. There were, for example, singers of taunt songs (Num. 21:27); there were also men and women who performed laments and dirges and passed on their ability to others (Jer. 9:16 [Eng. 9:17]; Amos 5:16). The numerous stories in the Pentateuch witness to a long tradition of storytelling, a point already made by Gunkel with reference to Genesis. The prophetic oracles were for the most part intended to be proclaimed orally and only later were given fixed written form. The like holds true for the maxims of the wisdom teachers and for proverbs and legal dicta joined in series.

Such considerations support the existence of oral tradition. The duration and significance of this tradition, however, is limited by a further consideration: in the ancient Near East, and therefore in Israel, written tradition came into use very early. In Mesopotamia and Egypt, literary traditions go back into the dim past. The archaeological evidence is unambiguous. Much, of course, was learned by rote. This is true, however, even in our own day. In the ancient Near East, it held for memorization of texts by students and learning of prayers that one might want to know by heart in case of need. In the instances cited by Nielsen, we are not dealing with oral tradition itself, but with the appropriation of traditions already extant in writing, so that written tradition is in fact assumed. Failure to distinguish between oral transmission of traditions not yet committed to writing and appropriation of written texts for the purpose of oral recitation leads to erroneous conclusions.

In addition, the ancient archives and libraries point to an early date for written tradition.[1] Apart from the numerous local archives found in palaces,

[1] Cf. the details in H. Schmökel *et al.*, *Kulturgeschichte des Alten Orient*, 1961, pp. 204-5, 402-8, 471.

private dwellings, and temples in Mesopotamia and Asia Minor, in which the tablets, subdivided into sections and series, lay on wooden shelves or were preserved in jars or other containers, there were also libraries at a very early period. The tablets stored in them were made permanent, arranged according to definite principles, and listed in catalogs. Several such catalogs date from the second millennium; the earliest so far discovered—a neo-Sumerian hymn-catalog containing the incipits of forty-two hymns—dates from the Ur III period.[2] The Hittite archives and libraries, along with their catalogs, belong to the same millennium; excavations furnish a very good picture of their arrangement. Most of the religious texts from Ugarit, too, come from private collections dating from the second half of the second millennium. The earliest Assyrian library seems to have been planned by Tiglath-pileser I; the most famous is that of Ashurbanipal, dating from the seventh century, in which the old literature was to be collected as completely as possible. From these same centuries there is preserved a library of six hundred tablets from the house of a priest at Sultantepe, near Harran. This period of ancient Near Eastern history, the time of the late Israelite monarchy, can well be called an Age of Writing. This agrees with the frequent mention of writing, scrolls, and reading in the OT, as well as the immediate assumption that Moses received the Decalogue from Yahweh in written form. Judg. 8:14 assumes that even children knew how to read and write; there is evidence of preexilic literary works that were later lost (§§ 13, 42). No less important, we must mention the professional scribe, who took a special part in the writing down and preserving of the traditions.[3]

We must therefore reckon with the existence of written records and literature at a very early period. We must nevertheless express reservations about Widengren's assumption that everything was written down immediately and then handed down intact. The texts have suffered all kinds of interference and alteration, which cannot be disregarded. For the OT, comparison of the MT with the LXX shows that such textual distortions occurred at least until the third century B.C.

We must conclude that both types of transmission have existed since the beginning of writing: oral tradition in certain cases, continuing until a certain point in time at which the tradition was committed to writing; and also, even at a very early date, written tradition, which was, however, still subject to alteration.

3. *Oral and written tradition in Israel.* What relationship must we assume in Israel between oral tradition and the growth of literature? In some cases, a considerable period of oral tradition certainly preceded commitment to writing. This is true for a large portion of the stories in the earlier narrative books (Genesis–Judges), as well as for ancient poetry and proverbs. These were

[2] W. W. Hallo, "On the Antiquity of Sumerian Literature," *JAOS*, LXXXIII (1963), 167-76.

[3] Knowledge of the language of neighboring peoples, such as is shown by E. Ullendorff, "The Knowledge of Languages in the Old Testament," *BJRL*, XLIV (1961/62), 455-65, also supports a certain level of education.

at first passed on from place to place, from tribe to tribe, from generation to generation. This can explain the numerous variants of the same story in the sources of the Pentateuch, as well as the transference of the identical motif to various figures. In agreement with the literary presuppositions obtaining in Israel (§2.3), it is mostly individual units that were handed down by oral tradition; the sources of the Pentateuch undoubtedly had a fixed written form. Chronologically, oral tradition was most common in the pre-Palestinian period of Israel's history and in the early Palestinian period. Although we encounter it occasionally at a later date, as in the legends concerning Elijah and Elisha, which at first were transmitted orally, from the time of Solomon on, as culture advanced, the importance of oral tradition continuously decreased. The court history of David must be termed a literary work from the very outset.

Even in the earlier period, however, there must have been written as well as oral tradition; this would be the usual mode of transmission for legal texts, lists, and documents. Furthermore, it is not impossible that sizable narrative complexes or cycles had their own written form before they were subjected to further editing and incorporated into the present historical books. Many poetic idioms suggest that there may have been Israelite epics like the Ugaritic epics, dealing with figures of the distant past. If so, they were certainly written down, as they were at Ugarit.

From the later period, the most important material is the prophetic oracles. There is much to suggest that they were written down not long after they were proclaimed orally. When this did not take place, we possess no traditions of any sort, and do not even know the names of the many persons who functioned as prophets. When it did take place, a long period of oral tradition is out of the question. The prophetic schools mentioned as passing on these traditions never existed; they have merely been postulated on the basis of a corrupt gloss in Isa. 8:16.[4] The prophetic oracles are in fact part of the poetic material that the proponents of oral tradition think first achieved fixed written form. They also illustrate the personal idiosyncrasies of their authors; they have not been reduced to uniformity by a long process of transmission. Ezekiel had his oracles before him in writing, for he (and subsequent readers also) appended additions to some of his oracles. Jeremiah, too, dictated at least part of his oracles to Baruch. This particular event also provides an important reason for writing the oracles down: in this way the effect of the spoken word was preserved or even increased. This in turn demands that the writing be done without delay (§54.1).

All this means that we must think neither in terms of a long oral tradition, nor in terms of an exclusively written tradition, nor even in terms of parallel and simultaneous oral and written tradition of the same texts. Instead, the situation differs, depending on the specific rhetorical form or literary type. Some of them thrive especially in a soil of oral tradition and are particularly at home there. Other varieties seem to grow in the direction of a fixed

[4] Cf. G. Fohrer, "The Origin, Composition and Tradition of Isaiah I–XXXIX," *Annual of Leeds University Oriental Society*, III (1961/62), 29-32.

written form. In the case of large-scale or artistic works and in the case of prophetic oracles, there were additional circumstances favoring or promoting written transmission. As a result, the closer to the present we move, the more written tradition predominates.

§4 Prose

L. Alonso Schökel, *La formación del estilo: Libro del alumno*, 1961; *idem*, "Erzählkunst im Buche der Richter," *Bibl*, XLII (1961), 143-72; E. Auerbach, *Mimesis*, 1946 (Eng. *Mimesis*, 1953); M. Buber and F. Rosenzweig, *Die Schrift und ihre Verdeutschung*, 1936; J. Hempel, *Geschichten und Geschichte im Alten Testament bis zur persischen Zeit*, 1964, pp. 152-73; J. Muilenburg, "A Study in Hebrew Rhetoric: Repetition and Style," *VTSuppl*, I (1953), 97-111; A. Schulz, *Erzählkunst in den Samuel-Büchern*, 1923; M. Weiss, "Einiges über die Bauformen des Erzählens in der Bibel," *VT*, XIII (1963), 456-75.

1. *Present form*. In the present form of the text, the linguistic and stylistic peculiarities of prose are frequently the outcome of a long process of transmission and editing. The individual stages of this process have all left their traces, from the original formation of oral tradition—in such cases as it was in fact present at the beginning—to the final editing, and even later additions and glosses. Therefore the peculiarities of the original independent units are for the most part masked and hard to discover once these units have been incorporated into the great connected narratives, sources, or literary works. Even the peculiarities of these latter units have at best been studied and defined rudimentarily. Obviously the stylistic resources of the Elohistic or Priestly source of the Pentateuch, as well as of the Deuteronomistic school, differ from each other. A thorough study utilizing new methods, however, still remains to be carried out, as in the case of other books. Only after all the prose forms have been determined can inquiry be made into their common basic stylistic resources. In this field there is an enormous job to be done.

Identification of the stylistic resources of prose[1] must take account of the way in which the large-scale works have manipulated the earlier material, so that the two may be distinguished. Sometimes, as in the books of Kings, the statement that additional material can be found in the royal chronicles suggests that the present text to a great extent represents an extract from such sources, chosen according to the theological bias of the author. For the earlier period, the narrators were more closely bound by tradition and treated it more cautiously. The same is true for the redaction of the books from Genesis through Samuel, which repeatedly incorporated several traditions dealing with the same theme in the narrative in order to preserve them, accepting the resultant internal contradictions. As a result, it is possible to study Israelite prose even of an early period.

2. *Linguistic peculiarities*. Among the general marks of prose are certain

[1] Hempel* has provided an outline, which is largely followed in our presentation.

linguistic peculiarities. In agreement with the purposeful and impassioned side of Israelite nature, the language presses forward; progression from word to action and from one action to the next is reflected in numerous short sentences. They are linked together loosely by *and;* this technique may appear monotonous, but when the text is read aloud or recited, as it was intended to be, the effect is of active progress toward a sudden conclusion. The use of infinitives provides a certain variety: the infinitive absolute is used to express a series of actions and for commands; the infinitive construct does duty for subordinate clauses. Additional variety is provided by circumstantial clauses inserted without any conjunction (Num. 22:24) and appropriate imperatives (II Sam. 1:15).

The reality-centered and concrete side of Israelite nature corresponds to the lively, vivid, and impressive method of description, which loves to work with similes, sees psychological processes reflected in outward conduct, and depicts the individual scenes of an event like sections of a picture placed one beside the next. It thus succeeds in presenting the change of mood from violent anger to composure or from elation to black despair, which springs from the impassioned soul of the Israelite,[2] in all its sudden variability.

3. *Stylistic peculiarities.* One stylistic peculiarity is inversion, i.e., departure from the usual predicate–subject order used in verbal sentences.[3] It can serve to divide the narrative into sections and thereby direct attention to a particular turning point, as well as providing a mnemonic aid for oral utilization. When used merely for emphasis, it should be thought of more as a literary device. In narrative prose, the nominal sentence serves to describe a situation, mention important circumstances, or confirm certain consequences. It is properly connected with direct discourse, where it serves many functions.

Another stylistic resource is the repetition of important words or phrases in order to describe a situation (Gen. 22:6, 8) or emphasize the importance of an event (II Sam. 11:17, 21, 24). The repetition involved in a command and its execution (II Kings 13:15-16) or the repetition of entire scenes (Esther 5:3, 6; 7:2) serves the same purpose.

Another deliberate stylistic device is the withholding of information: explanatory details are omitted and then later revealed in order to indicate the strangeness and mystery surrounding an event (Gen. 20:4, 18) or the fulfillment of a prophetic oracle (Jer. 39:15-18; 45).

Finally we must mention the introduction of direct discourse into the narrative; it can enliven the action and urge it forward or bring a sense of repose and retardation. Indirectly, it can characterize the speaker, a technique skillfully employed by the author of Job. Such direct discourse involves monologue or duologue, even when the narrative implies the presence of several persons; only exceptionally do more than two of them take part in the conversation (I Kings 3:16-28).

[2] Cf. L. Köhler, *Der hebräische Mensch*, 1953 (Eng. *Hebrew Man*, 1956).

[3] Cf. W. Richter, *Traditionsgeschichtliche Untersuchungen zum Richterbuch*, 1963, pp. 354-61.

§5 Poetry

E. Balla, "Ezechiel 8,1-9; 11,24-25," in *Bultmann-Festschrift*, 1949, pp. 1-11; J. Begrich, "Zur hebräischen Metrik," *ThR*, NF IV (1932), 67-89; *idem*, "Der Satzstil im Fünfer," *ZS*, IX (1934), 169-209 (= *Gesammelte Studien zum Alten Testament*, 1964, pp. 132-67); G.-W. Bickell, *Carmina Veteris Testamenti metrice*, 1882; *idem*, *Dichtungen der Hebräer zum ersten Male nach den Versmassen des Urtextes übersetzt*, 1882-83; A. Bruno, *Rhythmische (und textkritische) Untersuchungen von Gen, Ex, Jos, Ri, I-II Sam, I-II Kön, Jes, Jer, Ez, Zwölf Propheten, Ps, Hi, Prov, Ruth, Cant, Qoh, Thr, Esth, Dan*, 1953-59; K. Budde, "Das hebräische Klagelied," *ZAW*, II (1882), 1-52, with supplements in III (1883), XI (1891), XII (1892), and *ZDPV*, VI (1883); A. Condamin, *Poèmes de la Bible. Avec une introduction sur la strophique hébraïque*, 1933; G. Fohrer, *Die Hauptprobleme des Buches Ezechiel*, 1952, pp. 60-66; *idem*, "Über den Kurzvers," *ZAW*, LXVI (1954), 199-236; D. N. Freedman, "Archaic Forms in Early Hebrew Poetry," *ZAW*, LXXII (1960), 101-107; I. Gábor, *Der hebräische Urrhythmus*, 1929; S. Gevirtz, *Patterns in the Early Poetry of Israel*, 1963; G. B. Gray, *The Forms of Hebrew Poetry*, 1915; G. Hölscher, "Elemente arabischer, syrischer und hebräischer Metrik," in BZAW, XXXIV (1920), 93-101; F. Horst, "Die Kennzeichen der hebräischen Poesie," *ThR*, NF XXI (1953), 97-121; E. König, *Hebräische Rhythmik*, 1914; C. F. Kraft, *The Strophic Structure of Hebrew Poetry as Illustrated in the First Book of the Psalter*, 1938; J. Ley, *Grundzüge des Rhythmus, des Vers- und Strophenbaues in der hebräischen Poesie*, 1875; *idem*, *Leitfaden der Metrik der hebräischen Poesie*, 1887; R. Lowth, *De sacra poësi Hebraeorum*, 1753, 2nd ed. 1763 (Eng. *Lectures on the Sacred Poetry of the Hebrews*, 1847); E. Z. Melamed, "Break-Up of Stereotype Phrases as an Artistic Device in Biblical Poetry," in *Scripta Hierosolymitana*, VIII (1961), 115-53; H. Möller, "Der Strophenbau der Psalmen," *ZAW*, L (1932), 240-56; J. A. Montgomery, "Stanza-Formation in Hebrew Poetry," *JBL*, LXIV (1945), 379-84; S. Mowinckel, "Zum Problem der hebräischen Metrik," in *Bertholet-Festschrift*, 1950, pp. 379-94; *idem*, "Metrischer Aufbau und Textkritik an Ps. 8 illustriert," in *Studia Orientalia Pedersen*, 1953, pp. 250-62; *idem*, "Der metrische Aufbau von Jes 62,1-12 und die neuen sog. 'Kurzverse'," *ZAW*, LXV (1953), 167-87; *idem*, "Zur hebräischen Metrik II," *StTh*, VII (1954), 54-85, 166; *idem*, "Die Metrik bei Jesus Sirach," *ibid.*, IX (1956), 97-123; *idem*, "Marginalien zur hebräischen Metrik," *ZAW*, LXVIII (1956), 97-123; J. Muilenburg, "A Study in Hebrew Rhetoric: Repetition and Style," *VTSuppl*, I (1953), 97-111; T. Piatti, "I carmi alfabetici della Bibbia chiave della metrica ebraica?" *Bibl*, XXXI (1950), 281-315, 427-58; L. Prijs, "Der Ursprung des Reimes im Neuhebräischen," *BZ*, NF VII (1963), 33-42; T. H. Robinson, "Some Principles of Hebrew Metrics," *ZAW*, LIV (1936), 28-43; *idem*, "Basic Principles of Hebrew Poetic Form," in *Bertholet-Festschrift*, 1950, pp. 438-50; *idem*, "Hebrew Poetic Form: The English Tradition," *VTSuppl*, I (1953), 128-49; J. W. Rothstein, *Grundzüge des hebräischen Rhythmus*, 1909; S. Segert, "Vorarbeiten zur hebräischen Metrik," *ArOr*, XXI (1953), 481-542; XXV (1957), 190-200; *idem*, "Problems of Hebrew Prosody," *VTSuppl*, VII (1960), 283-91; E. Sievers, *Metrische Studien*, I–III, 1901–1907; W. Staerk, "Ein Hauptproblem der hebräischen Metrik," in *Kittel-Festschrift*, 1913, pp. 193-203.

1. *The use of poetry.* Israel accompanied many of life's events with appropriate songs. The narrative books of the OT confirm this fact over and over

again and even preserve small remnants of the various types of song. The Song of Miriam (Exod. 15:20-21) and the Song of Deborah (Judges 5) furnish evidence that poetry was known and used even in the earliest period. Besides lyric poetry proper, in which the poetic form can help express particular moods and emotions, the proverbs, longer oracles, and poems of the prophets and wisdom teachers show metrical and rhythmic organization. This goes hand in hand with the importance of what is being said. Poetry is not merely an art form; it has functioned since the beginning as a mark of inspiration, of intercourse with the supernatural world. Poetic form therefore lends the spoken word such power and authority as is believed present, for example, in blessings and curses. It appears that a prophet claiming to preach in the name of Yahweh or a wisdom teacher claiming to be passing on an insight or maxim learned from God or previous generations could gain a hearing only if he gave his words metrical and rhythmic form.[1]

In its use of poetic forms, Israel followed the universal tradition of the ancient Near East. Texts exhibiting metrical or rhythmic structure have been discovered everywhere. They will be discussed in the following sections and in the paragraphs devoted to the poetic literary types in parts two through four of this book. In particular, as the Ugaritic texts show, we must think in terms of a well-defined poetic tradition in Syria and Palestine during the last two millennia B.C., so that Canaanite and Israelite poetry illuminate each other. This is all the more important because there is almost no native Israelite or Jewish tradition about the rules of poetry and its stylistic devices; some of the Qumran texts contain a very few hints.[2] These latter do appear to confirm the stylistic conjectures that scholars have derived from the texts of the OT. The metrical and rhythmic problems, however, remain unsolved and may be in fact insoluble. The question whether we may generally assume strophic structure in larger texts also remains unanswered. Despite all the difficulties surrounding metrical and rhythmic problems, most of which are bound up with the shift of the word accent from the initial to the final syllable and the consequent change in pronunciation, scholarship must not lose heart, but must look for new avenues of approach. The Ugaritic texts can assist these studies greatly.

The first task is to reexamine the principles that have guided stylistic analysis up to the present time, which have remained almost unchanged since their presentation by Lowth in 1753. They can be reduced to two general principles or rules: 1. Verses consist of two (alternatively, two or three)[3] members. 2. The structural principle is parallelism (*parallelismus membrorum*). This approach, however, is much too narrow and schematic to describe and explain all the observed facts. Quite apart from the solution of the metrical

[1] Cf. A. Guillaume, *Prophecy and Divination*, 1938.

[2] Eccles. 12:9*b* and Ecclus. 47:9 contain the verb *tqn*, "make straight," in the sense of "give metrical form"; Ecclus. 45:5 speaks of those who write songs "according to the rules." These passages, however, merely indicate the existence of rules of poetry. Whether 1QH i. 28-29, with the words "measuring line" and "measure," also refers to these rules is disputed.

[3] Mowinckel in particular recognizes only a rule of dualism applying to the members, and seeks to eliminate three-member verses wherever possible.

and rhythmic problems, we must instead take as our point of departure two principles more loosely formulated: 1. A verse can consist of one, two, or three members. A verse need not have more than one member, even though most extant verses do in fact have two or three. We may say at most that a verse potentially consists of two or three members. 2. The wording of the members is not absolutely determined by *parallelismus membrorum*. It is therefore more correct to speak of a repetitional and often parallelizing style.

Since there is no agreed common terminology, it should be noted that the following terms are equivalent:

member = half line = stich = colon

long verse = period = di- or tristich = bi- or tricolon.

In addition, the following must be distinguished: (1) stylistic organization, (2) meter or rhythm, (3) strophic structure, and (4) poetic devices.

2. *Long verse*. The first type of verse is long verse. Its stylistic organization differs distinctly from that of prose and constitutes an unmistakable external criterion: it consists of two or three members that together constitute a greater unit. Verses consist more commonly of two than of three members; the latter are found, for instance, throughout Psalm 45, in a section of text that may be a single strophe (Isa. 28:7-8), or in a single verse (Isa. 8:8*a*). A section sometimes concludes with an isolated member, e.g., Isa. 3:24; Hos. 4:14.

Ancient evidence confirms our knowledge of this organization at many points. It is common to all the poetry of the ancient Near East, as studies of Egyptian[4] and Ugaritic[5] texts have shown. On Akkadian clay tablets the division between members is shown by the writing system.[6] In an Aramaic funerary inscription of the fifth century B.C. from Egypt, a space separates the two members in the first line.[7] Hebrew manuscripts used this same procedure for the poetic books (Psalms, Job, Proverbs) and for isolated poetic passages in prose books, e.g., Exod. 15:1-18; Deut. 32:1-43. A fragmentary psalm scroll[8] and a fragment of Deut. 32[9] from the fourth cave at Qumran confirm that members were separated by a space in this fashion during the late pre-Christian period.

The mutual relationship between the members of a verse, which Ibn Ezra seems to have been among the first to recognize, is usually called *parallelismus membrorum*, following Lowth. We prefer to speak more generally of a repeti-

[4] A. Erman and H. Ranke, *Ägypten*, 1923, pp. 468-74; W. S. Golénischeff, "Parallélisme symétrique en ancien égyptien," in *Studies Presented to Griffith*, 1932, pp. 86-96; H. Grapow, "Stilistische Kunst," in *Handbuch der Orientalistik*, I.2 (1952), 21-29.

[5] W. F. Albright, "The Old Testament and Canaanite Language and Literature," *CBQ*, VII (1945), 5-31; C. H. Gordon, *Ugaritic Manual*, 1955, pp. 108-20; R. de Langhe, "La Bible et la littérature ugaritique," *OrBiblLov*, I (1957), 65-87; J. H. Patton, *Canaanite Parallels in the Book of Psalms*, 1944; G. D. Young, "Ugaritic Prosody," *JNES*, IX (1950), 124-33.

[6] B. Meissner, *Babylonien und Assyrien*, II (1925); *idem*, *Die babylonisch-assyrische Literatur*, 1928, pp. 25-27.

[7] G. Hölscher, *Syrische Verskunst*, 1932, pp.3-4.

[8] P. W. Skehan, *RB*, LXIII (1956), 59.

[9] W. H. Brownlee, *The Meaning of the Qumran Scrolls for the Bible*, 1964, p. 9.

tional and often parallelizing style. The style is truly parallelizing in the first two categories of so-called *parallelismus membrorum:* (1) "synonymous parallelism," in which the second member repeats the content of the first in different words, e.g., "But his delight is in the law of Yahweh, / and on his law he meditates day and night" (Ps. 1:2); (2) "antithetical parallelism," in which the second member illuminates the content of the first by means of a contrasting idea, e.g., "For Yahweh knows the way of the righteous, / but the way of the wicked will perish" (Ps. 1:6). There are also long verses whose members are not linked by any kind of parallelism and some consisting of three members, one of which is not parallel to the other two. The third category usually mentioned, "synthetic parallelism," is not parallelism at all, because the second member advances and supplements the thought of the first, e.g., "He is like a tree / planted by streams of water" (Ps. 1:3).

The single long verse constitutes the basic poetic and stylistic unit that can exist independently. In point of fact, we always find at least two long verses joined together, e.g., Gen. 9:6, to form larger units. These in turn can be formed into strophes made up of several long verses. Here we must distinguish between strophes as metrical and as stylistic entities. The former, which must always exhibit the same number of verses with the same meter, seem to have been very rare in Israelite poetry. The latter, which simply represent smaller units of a text, usually containing the same number of verses, seem to have been common. We find clear evidence of these strophes in the regular repetition of refrains, e.g., in Pss. 42–43; 46; 80; 107; and in the acrostic psalms with the same number of verses for each letter, e.g., Pss. 9–10; 119; Lam. 1–4. Arguing from these observations, we should also assume the presence of strophes in many cases where content supports their existence but external criteria are lacking.

3. *Short verse.* Contrary to the traditional restriction of poetry to long verse made up of two or three members, and despite the strictures of Mowinckel, we must assume the existence of another kind of verse: short verse, consisting of one member. Following Sievers, who never put his views in writing, Balla and Fohrer have studied this kind of verse. Similar observations have been made by Köhler[10] (who holds that the original form of Hebrew verse was a verse of four beats without further division), J. Schmidt[11] (who holds that proverb-verse of one member is the earlier form of wisdom aphorism), and Piatti (who holds that the original form of verse was the single member; single members were juxtaposed to form long verse).

The existence of this kind of verse is indicated by the following considerations: 1. In Arabic, besides prose and strictly regulated metrical poetry, there is a third form of composition, which Gray calls "unmetrical poetry." 2. In non-Israelite poetry of the ancient Near East we frequently encounter single-member verses in the context of long verses; in such cases we are dealing with composite sections, in which both kinds of verse are employed side by

[10] L. Glahn and L. Köhler, *Der Prophet der Heimkehr,* 1934, p. 251.

[11] J. Schmidt, *Studien zur Stilistik der alttestamentlichen Spruchliteratur,* 1936.

side.[12] A new study of ancient Near Eastern texts would probably yield sections consisting solely of short verses. 3. In the OT, similarly, we find several prophetic oracles written in long verse but concluding with a short verse as the crowning touch.[13] 4. The acrostic psalms 111 and 112 consist of short verses, each of which begins with one letter of the alphabet. 5. The poetic structure of Isaiah 62 is most striking. It contains fives strophes of five long verses each; the meter changes from one strophe to the next. Verse 10 contains five single members that together constitute a strophe of five short verses:

Isa. 62:1-3	5 long verses	3 + 3
62:4-5	5 long verses	3 + 2
62:6-7	5 long verses	2 + 2
62:8-9	5 long verses	3 + 2
62:10	5 short verses	3 (with one 2)
62:11-12	5 long verses	3 + 2

In contrast to the long verse, the short verse is not the basic poetic and stylistic unit; it is a dependent and auxiliary member of the serial strophe, which generally consists of an odd number of short verses (with a preference for five or seven) and contains a single idea or complex of ideas. Poetically and stylistically, it is a unit employed like the long verse. Its use in strophes is what distinguishes it from prose; a real prose text is never structured in this fashion. Several short-verse strophes are frequently linked to sections between which the continuity of thought is interrupted; these sections correspond to long-verse strophes.

Unlike long verses, short verses were clearly considered a type to be restricted to specific cases whenever possible.[14] The earliest examples are series of apodictic rules of conduct and series of legal dicta, e.g., the *ʿerwâ* series in Lev. 18:7-17*a* and the *ʾārûr* series in Deut. 27:15-26 as originally formulated. Then short verse came to be employed for "narrative poetry" (for which long verse is not suited): for the handing down of prophetic calls (Jer. 1:4-10), visions and auditions (Amos 7:1-3; Zech. 1:7–6:8), symbolic actions (Isa. 8:1-4) and events (Isa. 7:1-9; Amos 7:10-17), and later even for the messages proclaimed by the prophets, e.g., in the Elijah legends and the Baruch source of the book of Jeremiah. In addition, the later prophets, from Jeremiah and Ezekiel on, often put down their oracles in short verses or combined long and short verses in a single text (as in Isa. 62; also Jer. 14:2–15:2; Ezek. 17:1-21). Finally, we find short verses in late lyric poetry.[15] It is also possible that the priestly rituals, with their balanced structure, and lost epic-like historical works made use of short verses.

4. *Meter and rhythm.* Even more than stylistic structure and strophic

[12] G. Fohrer, "Über den Kurzvers," *ZAW*, LXVI (1954), 205-7.

[13] *Ibid.*, p. 210.

[14] Detailed examples *ibid.*, pp. 213-33.

[15] W. Rudolph, for example, who disputes their presence in the book of Jeremiah, assumes them in his commentary on the Song of Songs (1:2-4, 5-6, 7-8; 3:1-5; 4:9-11; 6:8, 9*a*; 7:7-11 [Eng. 7:6-10]).

organization, meter and rhythm determine the unique nature of poetry. That Israelite poetry possessed rhythmic motion follows from the fact that songs were sung to the accompaniment of music and choral dancing (Exod. 15:20-21; I Sam. 18:6-7). Since, however, there are no extant traditions about any details, the only possibility open is to analyze the text in such a way as to find a theory that satisfies the data as completely as possible. Refusal on theoretical grounds to construct such a theory is not a justifiable scholarly position, especially since metrical rules for Egyptian and Akkadian can be determined with some assurance.[16] On one of the Akkadian tablets mentioned in subsection two, the individual members of the verse are themselves divided, probably to mark the metrical feet. Of the four theories to be mentioned, the one described in paragraph (*d*) below seems to stand up best.

a) It is generally agreed that a quantitative metrical system counting long and short syllables in the fashion of Greek and Latin is a priori impossible for Hebrew. In *Antiq*. II. xvi. 4 § 346 and IV. viii. 44 § 303, Josephus mentions the use of hexameters in OT poetry; but he is merely seeking to explain the poetry to his Hellenistic readers.

b) For the earliest Israelite poetry, Segert assumes a metrical system in which the word as such constitutes the basic element, regardless of the number and nature of its syllables and the location of the stress. The question arises whether such a system can be ascertained with any assurance after a process of transmission that has lasted for centuries.

c) There is more support for the alternating system with feet consisting of two syllables, one stressed, the other unstressed. Bickell extended this system from Syriac to Hebrew poetry; Hölscher improved it by assuming that the accent always fell on the second syllable and allowing the possibility of feet consisting of one (accented) syllable, with the unaccented syllable included in the previous accented one (syncope). This system, however, runs counter to the character of the Hebrew language and Hebrew syntax; it necessitates textual emendations and suspiciously artificial pronunciation, as when a consonant with *šᵉwâ mobile* must be read as an accented syllable.[17]

d) The situation is different when we come to the accentual system developed by Ley, Budde, and Sievers, in which accented syllables alternate with one or more unaccented syllables. This system can be applied as well to ancient as to Masoretic Hebrew, so that it becomes unnecessary to follow Segert in assuming that Hebrew meter was first based on words, then changed to the accentual system, and finally to the alternating system. According to Ley, the verse is determined exclusively by the regular number of accented syllables, while the

[16] Besides Erman-Ranke (n. 4) and Grapow (n. 4), as well as Meissner (n. 6), see also G. Fecht, "Mitteilungen über Untersuchungen zur altägyptischen Metrik," in *Acts of the XXV International Congress of Orientalists* (Russian), I (1962), 161-66; F. M. T. de Liagre Böhl, "Bijbelse en Babylonische dichtkunst, een metrisch onderzoek," *JEOL*, XV (1957/58), 133-53; *idem*, "La métrique de l'épopée Babylonienne," in *Cahiers du Groupe F. Thureau-Dangin*, I (1960), 145-52.

[17] Fohrer, *op. cit.*, pp. 211-12.

number of unaccented syllables is irrelevant; according to Sievers, however, the unaccented syllables were also fixed in number, with two for every accented syllable. Both Ley's indifference and Sievers' regularity in the question of unaccented syllables are doubtful. Their number varied in any case. In exceptional instances one accented syllable could follow another directly; generally from one to three unaccented syllables would fall between them. This agrees with a Babylonian creation-hymn written with notation for singing, in which the accented syllables are usually separated by two, less frequently by one or three, unaccented syllables. If one does not fall into the trap of expecting strict regularity, the accentual system satisfies all the poetic texts of the OT.

5. *Poetic devices.* Poetic devices include rhyme (Exod. 29:35; Isa. 7:11; 31:9; Pss. 55:7 [Eng. 55:6]; 75:7-8 [Eng. 75:6-7]; *et al.*), key words (Gen. 32:21 [*pānîm*]; Isa. 42:15 [*'ôbîš*]), internal rhyme and alliteration (Jer. 4:30), vocalic and consonantal assonance,[18] anacrusis,[19] and antiphony.[20]

§6 Israelite Literature and the Old Testament

1. *The OT as the remains of Israelite literature.* The OT, whose formation will be discussed in the following paragraphs, comprises neither the whole of Israelite literature, which has so far been the subject of our study, nor a specific stratum of this literature. The OT is rather the extant remains of Israelite literature, whose development continues in Jewish literature, much more of which is preserved. It is a sacred collection of writings that represent fragmentary remains of a much more comprehensive literary whole. These writings themselves consist in large part of various literary units, frequently quite small, originating within a period of roughly a millennium and within a territory comprising several dialect regions. These units were variously revised and edited by speakers of Aramaic; their consonantal text did not assume definitive form until 100 B.C.–A.D. 100, and their pronunciation not until much later. These considerations mean frequently insurmountable difficulties for discovering how the individual writings came into being.

The numerous works of Jewish literature, especially the so-called Apocrypha and Pseudepigrapha of the OT and the recently discovered Qumran documents, give us an idea how many documents of the earlier period have perished, even if we assume scant literary activity. The OT itself mentions such works as the book of the Wars of Yahweh, the book of Jashar (or book of the Upright) (§42), the book of the Acts of Solomon, and the books of the Chronicles of the Kings of Judah and Israel (§13). These books have perished in the confusion of the centuries. If one recalls that the canon, too, exists in several forms, that it is impossible to determine its scope and limits by systematic principles and

[18] G. Boström, *Paronomasi i den äldre Hebreiska Maschalliteraturen*, 1928.
[19] T. H. Robinson, "Anacrusis in Hebrew Poetry," in BZAW, LXVI (1936), 37-40.
[20] I. Slotki, "Antiphony in Ancient Hebrew Poetry," *JQR*, XXVI (1935/36), 199-219.

define its nature with any precision,[1] then the canon turns out to be a more or less random variable without anything sacrosanct about it. The rest of our discussion will restrict itself to this canon, not for theoretical reasons, but for practical reasons: the OT is actually used as a canon of Holy Scriptures, and a line must be drawn somewhere between Israelite and Jewish literature.

2. *The problems of literary history.* The situation here outlined justifies our using the methods of literary history as we study the problems involved in the formation of the OT. In the case of poetry and the earlier prose, we must think of an oral tradition preceding written tradition (§3), and must therefore remember that the present written form is not original, but has a history behind it. We must seek the traces and remnants of what was once a much greater variety, which fell victim to later standardization. As far as possible we must determine both the pre-Yahwistic material and the rhetorical and literary forms of primitive origin, Israelite or foreign, so as to understand and appreciate how they were permeated and transformed by the creative forces of Yahwism.

Quite generally we must recall that Israelite literature, and therefore the books of the OT, were not written as autonomous works of art but to serve practical religious purposes. The emphasis can rest on nationalistic, cultic, or ethical elements. The crucial fact is that this literature is intimately linked with human existence, and attempts to make possible and guarantee a comprehensive regulation of life on the basis of the divine will. We see this reflected in various ways in the laws, narratives, poems, wisdom aphorisms, and prophetic oracles.

For this reason also it is almost impossible to distinguish between religious and secular rhetorical forms and literary types and to distribute them according to such a criterion. This is not even possible in the case of the common types of lyric poetry, all of which exhibit religious elements (§ 40). For life was not divided into secular and religious spheres, but in general constituted a unity under the sign of religion. This does not mean that there were religious texts exclusively; each text must be examined for religious content on its own merits. Even if it is impossible to distinguish between religious and secular literary types, it may still happen that a particular type included predominantly religious or secular compositions. As in many other questions, one is well advised not to generalize prematurely and not to proceed with bias.

[1] F. Hesse, "Das Alte Testament als Kanon," *NZSTh*, III (1961), 315-27.

PART ONE

The Formation of the Historical and Legal Books

CHAPTER ONE: GENERAL

§7 Law, Instruction, Narrative, and Report in the Ancient Near East and in Israel

A. Boissier, *Mantique babylonienne et mantique hittite*, 1935; S. G. F. Brandon, *Creation Legends of the Ancient Near East*, 1963; G. Cardascia, "Les droits cunéiformes," in *Histoire des institutions et des faits sociaux des origines à l'aube du moyen âge*, ed. Monier-Cardascia-Imbert, 1957, pp. 53-71; G. Contenau, *La magie chez les Assyriens et les Babyloniens*, 1947; R. C. Dentan, ed., *The Idea of History in the Ancient Near East*, 1955; H. Frankfort, H. A. Frankfort, J. A. Wilson, and T. Jacobsen, *The Intellectual Adventure of Ancient Man*, 1946; T. Gaster, *Thespis, Ritual, Myth and Drama in the Ancient Near East*, 1950; H. Gese, "Geschichtliches Denken im Alten Orient und im Alten Testament," *ZThK*, LV (1958), 127-45; H. Goedicke, "Untersuchungen zur altägyptischen Rechtsprechung," *MIOF*, VIII (1963), 333-67; H. W. Haussig, *Wörterbuch der Mythologie*, I. Abteilung: Die alten Kulturvölker, Teil I: Vorderer Orient, 1961-63; E. O. James, *Myth and Ritual in the Ancient Near East*, 1958; A. Jolles, *Einfache Formen*, 2nd ed., 1956; S. N. Kramer, *Sumerian Mythology*, 1944; *idem*, *History Begins at Sumer*, 1958; *idem*, *The Sumerians*, 1963; F. R. Kraus, ed., *Altbabylonische Briefe in Umschrift und Übersetzung*, I, 1964; S. Moscati, *Historical Art in the Ancient Near East*, 1963; A. L. Oppenheim, "Mesopotamian Mythology," *Or*, XVI (1947), 207-38; XVII (1948), 17-58; XIX (1950), 129-58; *idem*, *The Interpretation of Dreams in the Ancient Near East*, 1956; *Orientalisches Recht*, Handbuch der Orientalistik, I, Erg.-Bd. III, 1964 (E. Seidl, "Altägyptisches Recht"; V. Korošec, "Keilschriftrecht"); J. Pirenne, *Histoire des institutions et du droit privé de l'ancienne Égypte*, 1932-35; *idem*, "Lois et décrets royaux en Égypte sous l'Ancien Empire," *RIDA*, 3e série, IV (1957), 17-31; H. Schmökel, H. Otten, V. Maag, and T. Beran, *Kulturgeschichte des Alten Orient*, 1961; E. Seidl, *Einführung in die ägyptische Rechtsgeschichte bis zum Ende des Neuen Reiches*, 2nd ed., 1951; *idem*, *Ägyptische Rechtsgeschichte der Saiten- und Perserzeit*, 1956; B. Spuler, ed., *Handbuch der Orientalistik, I: Ägypten, 2. Abschnitt: Literatur*, 1952; W. Wolf, *Kulturgeschichte des alten Ägypten*, 1962.

1. *Survey*. The writings referred to as historical and legal books constitute a considerable part of the OT. In bulk and—according to the present classification—in number they form the largest group, including the Pentateuch, the following books of Joshua, Judges, Samuel, and Kings, together with the Chronicler's History (the books of Chronicles, Ezra, and Nehemiah) and the books of Ruth and Esther, which stand in isolation.

Just as the volume of the material is large, so is the number of rhetorical forms and literary types employed. Their roots go back in most cases to the more primitive traditions of the ancient Near East; the complex material derives in part from the milieu of the ancient Near East and pre-Yahwistic Israel, in part from the intellectual world that came into being in Palestine under the influence of Yahwism. Before describing the literary types, it is therefore necessary to discuss their occurrence in the ancient Near East, because this background shows clearly how closely the literary types used in Israel are interwoven with those used elsewhere in the ancient Near East and also how unmistakably different they are at many points. The multiplicity of forms means that we must restrict our discussion to the salient points; a thorough presentation would exceed the broadest limits.

In order to present the OT literary types as clearly as possible, they will be divided into six groups. Assignment of two or more types to the same group does not imply identical origin or purpose. The first group, the "regulating types," comprises those forms that refer to life and conduct as well as the whole realm of law; the second group, the "requesting types," comprises those forms and formulas, however various, that express a request or wish; the third group, the "proclaiming and instructing types," comprises those forms in which, on the basis of special authority, something is proclaimed, instruction is issued, or knowledge is transmitted. The fourth group, the "narrative" types, comprises those forms that depict events or situations whose historical nature is improbable or questionable, while the "reporting types" of the fifth group include those accounts or descriptions that at least in form claim faithfully to reproduce reality. The sixth group, the "communicating types," comprises the forms involving direct communication with other men or with God. For the sake of simplification and concentration, the following survey of the ancient Near East will deal primarily with law, instruction, narrative, and report.

2. *Law in the ancient Near East.* As one valuable result of the excavations carried out in the Near East, there is textual or other evidence for legal maxims and laws, law codes and strictly regulated legal procedure, private contracts and state treaties at an early period for each culture. In Mesopotamia several types of cuneiform law can be distinguished after Sumerian, Old Babylonian, Neo-Babylonian, and Assyrian forms begin to diverge.[1] For about a millennium, until the end of the period of Hammurabi, the "Old Law" [2] was in force. Its documents include economic texts from Shuruppak and Lagash (middle of the third millennium), the account of the "reform" of Urukagina (twenty-fourth century) [3] and the fragmentary Code of Ur-nammu (about 2000),[4]

[1] *AOT*, pp. 380-422; *ANET*, pp. 159-88.

[2] Following H. Schmökel, *Kulturgeschichte des Alten Orient*, 1961, which provides the basis for this survey.

[3] M. Lambert, "Les 'réformes' d'Urukagina," *RA*, L (1956), 169-84.

[4] J. Klima, "Zu den neuentdeckten Gesetzesfragmenten von Ur-Nammu," *ArOr*, XXI (1953), 442-47; S. N. Kramer and A. Falkenstein, "Ur-Nammu Law Code," *Or*, XXIII (1954), 40-51; E. Szlechter, "Le code d'Ur-Nammu," *RA*, XLIX (1955), 169-77.

then, after scattered additional Sumerian laws, the Neo-Sumerian legal documents of the Ur III period,[5] and some evidence bearing on the legal situation in the commercial colonies of Asia Minor, the numerous documents from the kingdom of Mari on the middle Euphrates[6] and additional documents from Elam, but especially for the first third of the second millenium the law codes of Lipit-Ishtar of Isin (*ca.* 1870),[7] the land of Eshnunna (eighteenth century),[8] and Hammurabi (*ca.* 1700).[9] "Middle Law" is known from the economic and legal documents from Nuzi and Arrapkha (middle of the second millennium), Kassite land grant documents (second half of the second millennium), and the so-called Middle Assyrian laws and harsh court and harem edicts (thirteenth-twelfth centuries).[10] The "New Law," from the first half of the first millennium, is known from chancellery documents of the Sargonides, cases settled according to Neo-Assyrian legal practice, and an enormous number of Neo-Babylonian and Late Babylonian contracts, official documents, sections of law codes, legal communications from the temple authorities, etc.[11] Basically all law—as in the OT—is considered a gift of the gods; the power to issue laws is of divine origin. This idea, at first associated with the god of the particular city, gradually becomes restricted first to a few specific gods and then to the sun-god Shamash. The king is the god's representative and deputy; he delegates jurisdiction to city princes and governors and, through them, to professional judges and jurors. Such power the Israelite king did not possess. Although we find interruptions or reverses such as Hammurabi's introduction of the *lex talionis,* the historical development of the law tends generally toward a refinement of legal thought, although the procedural rules and formularies remain much the same and do not undergo basic changes in the course of many centuries.

Two points deserve special stress. First, the international treaties, which occur in ever increasing number from the second millennium on, are constructed according to an internationally agreed upon norm: an oath must be taken by the

[5] M. Çiğ, H. Kizilyay, and A. Falkenstein, "Neue Rechts- und Gerichtsurkunden der Ur III-Zeit aus Lagaš," *ZA,* LIII (1959), 51-92; A. Falkenstein, *Die neusumerischen Gerichtsurkunden,* 1956.

[6] G. Boyer, "Textes juridiques," *ARM,* VIII (1958).

[7] A. Falkenstein and M. San Nicolò, "Das Gesetzbuch Lipit-Ištars von Isin," *Or,* XIX (1950), 103 ff.

[8] A. Goetze, *The Laws of Eshnunna,* 1956; J. C. Miles and O. R. Gurney, "The Laws of Eshnunna," *ArOr,* XVII (1949), 174-88; E. Szlechter, *Les lois d'Ešnunna,* 1954.

[9] M. David, "The Codex Hammurabi and Its Relation to the Provisions of Laws in Exodus," *OTS,* VII/VIII (1950), 149-78; W. Eilers, *Die Gesetze Chammurabis,* 1932; J. Köhler, P. Koschaker, F. E. Peiser, and A. Ungnad, *Hammurabis Gesetz,* 6 vols., 1904-23.

[10] E. Weidner, "Das Alter der mittelassyrischen Gesetzestexte," *AFO,* XII (1937), 46-54; *idem,* "Hof- und Haremserlasse assyrischer Könige," *ibid.,* XVII (1955/56), 257-93.

[11] G. R. Driver and J. C. Miles, *The Assyrian Laws,* 1935; *idem, The Babylonian Laws,* 1952-55; H. Petschow, *Neubabylonisches Pfandrecht,* 1956; *idem, Babylonische Rechtsurkunden aus dem 6. Jahrh. v. Chr.,* 1960; A. Ungnad and M. San Nicolò, *Neubabylonische Rechts- und Verwaltungsurkunden,* 1929-37.

gods of both partners to the treaty; sacrificial rites and symbolic actions must be performed when the treaty is concluded.[12] Second, legal practice seems to be based not on law codes, but on traditional common law, for which collections of various judgments probably were at the disposal of judges in the particular cities. The famous legal codes are clearly not intended to state the total body of law obtaining at a given time, but to lay the groundwork for legislative reforms in which new authoritative judgments of the king—put in the form of laws—change earlier decisions. This is important for an understanding of the legal books of the OT.

The legal texts from Egypt are considerably fewer. Frequently certain legal conceptions can be derived only by arguing backward from literary and religious texts. In particular, there is no trace of any law code, although the *Admonitions of an Egyptian Sage,* dating from the end of the third millennium, tells how at that time of revolution the lawbooks of the court were thrown upon the street. This probably refers to collections of judgments like those in Mesopotamia. Later, Bocchoris (eighth century) is said to have been an important lawgiver, Amasis (sixth century) is said to have reformed administrative law, and Darius I is said to have collected the Egyptian laws; no trace of them remains extant, however. Though the immediate basis of the law is, in practice, tradition, the law is at the same time royal, because, thanks to his divine descent, the king makes decisions in individual cases that can then be applied to future cases. Jurisdiction is delegated almost completely to subordinates; the king appears as judge only in special cases involving members of his own house. Court procedure can be ascertained in considerable detail. A noteworthy Egyptian peculiarity is the written accusation and the written reply to it. The legal documents, which are more abundant for the late period than for earlier periods, refer mostly to transactions involving property and cash values.

Hittite law,[13] which is written down in a collection of a mere two hundred paragraphs, is also thought to be of divine origin, with the sun-god (as in the late period in Mesopotamia) as its creator. The three versions, formulated in different periods, show legal development, especially in the reduced threat of capital punishment. Other documents witness to the multiplicity of local common law, so that the royal law collection should probably be considered similar to those in Mesopotamia, an attempt to standardize new judgments. Private documents and documents permitting us to reconstruct court procedure

[12] R. Borger, "Zu den Asarhaddon-Verträgen aus Nimrud," *ZA,* LIV (1961), 173-96; V. Korošec, "Quelques traités de l'époque néo-assyrienne," *Romanitas,* III (1961), 261-77; E. Weidner, "Der Staatsvertrag Aššurnirâris VI. von Assyrien mit Mati'ilu von Bît-Agusi," *AfO,* VIII (1932/33), 17-34; D. J. Wiseman, "The Vassal-Treaties of Esarhaddon," *Iraq,* XX (1958), 1-90.

[13] J. Friedrich, *Die hethitischen Gesetze,* 1959; R. Haase, "Zur Systematik der zweiten Tafel der hethitischen Gesetze," *RIDA,* VII (1960), 51-54; *idem,* "Zu den hethitischen Gesetzen," *ZA,* LIV (1961), 100-104; E. Neufeld, *The Hittite Laws,* 1951; K. K. Riemschneider, "Zu den Körperverletzungen im hethitischen Recht," *ArOr,* XXIX (1961), 177-82; V. Souček, "Einige Bemerkungen zum hethitischen Strafrecht," in *Orientalia Pragensia,* I (1960), 3-11.

are sparsely represented. It is noteworthy that in cases of murder, manslaughter, and bodily injury Hittite law does not apply the *lex talionis,* but rather seeks first to compensate the injured party. Last but not least, we come to the numerous international treaties of the Hittite kings, characteristic of the foreign diplomacy by which they gain the allegiance of smaller states as vassals and also political freedom of action.[14] Even disregarding treaties signed by other kings, Suppiluliumas alone concludes such treaties with Khuqqana and the people of Khayasha (in northeast Asia Minor), as well as with the kings of Kizzuwatna, Hurri, Nuhassi, Ugarit, Amurru, and Mitanni. These treaties follow a definite formal pattern that has recently been adduced to explain the "covenant" texts of the OT.

Treaties of the Canaanites[15] and Arameans[16] are also extant, but there are few documents to represent other aspects of Syro-Palestinian law. In its essential points it resembled Mesopotamian and Hittite law.[17] It was drawn upon in large measure for Israelite law in Palestine, so that it constitutes the historical link between Israelite law and the earlier law of other ancient Near Eastern civilizations.

3. *Instruction in the ancient Near East.* Throughout the ancient Near East oracles are obtained, blessings or curses are pronounced, instruction and advice in religious and cultic questions is given, and the cult is performed according to specific rituals and regulations. Practices forbidden in Israel as being contrary to Yahwism are found to a far greater extent than the OT would indicate: prognostication,[18] which reached its highest development in Mesopotamia, making use of astrology as well as omens from the animal and human worlds, hepatoscopy, and artificially produced omens (smoke, oil); calculations to determine auspicious and inauspicious days;[19] the whole broad realm of

[14] H. Freydank, "Eine hethitische Fassung des Vertrages zwischen dem Hethiterkönig Suppiluliuma und Aziru von Amurru," *MIOF,* VII (1960), 356-81; J. Friedrich, *Staatsverträge des Ḫatti-Reiches in hethitischer Sprache,* 2 vols., 1926-30; V. Korošec, *Hethitische Staatsverträge,* 1931; *idem,* "Les Hittites et leurs vassaux à la lumière des nouveaux textes d'Ugarit (PRU IV)," *RHA,* XVIII (1960), 65-79; H. Otten, "Ein althethitischer Vertrag mit Kizzuwatna," *JCSt,* V (1951), 129-32; I. Sugi, "Der Vertrag des Tudḫalijaš IV. mit IŠTAR-muwaš von Amurru," *Orient,* I (1960), 1-22; E. Weidner, *Politische Dokumente aus Kleinasien,* 1923.

[15] V. Korošec, "Quelques remarques juridiques sur deux traités internationaux d'Alalaḫ," in *Mélanges Lévy-Bruhl,* 1959, pp. 171-78; J. Nougayrol, "Les nouvelles tablettes accadiennes de Ras-Shamra," *CRAI,* 1953, pp. 40-51; *idem,* "Les archives internationales d'Ugarit," *CRAI,* 1954, pp. 30-41, 239-53; *idem, Textes accadiens et hourrites des archives est, ouest et centrales* (PRU III), 1955; *idem, Textes accadiens des archives sud* (PRU IV), 1956; S. Smith, *The Statue of Idri-mi,* 1949; D. J. Wiseman, *The Alalakh Tablets,* 1953.

[16] For the most recent edition and commentary, see H. Donner and W. Röllig, *Kanaanäische und aramäische Inschriften,* I (1962), 41-45; II (1964), 238-74, with bibliography.

[17] A. Alt, "Eine neue Provinz des Keilschriftrechtes," *WdO,* I (1947), 78-92 (= *Kleine Schriften,* III [1959], 141-57); G. Boyer, "La place des textes d'Ugarit dans l'histoire de l'ancien droit oriental," in PRU III (1955), 281-308.

[18] T. Bauer, "Eine Sammlung von Himmelsvorzeichen," *ZA,* XLIII (1936), 308-14; L. Dennefeld, *Babylonisch-assyrische Geburtsomina,* 1914.

[19] R. Labat, *Hémérologies et ménologies d'Assur,* 1939.

magic, especially exorcism,[20] for which we possess whole series of rituals from Babylonia, such as *The Evil Utukkē* (16 tablets) and *The Wicked Asakkē* (12 tablets) for protection against demons, and *Burning* (*Šurpu*, 9 tablets) and *Consuming* (*Maqlû*, 8 tablets) for protection against witches.

Apart from these aspects, the Mesopotamian cult was precisely regulated by cultic regulations that differ remarkably little from one of the numerous temples to the next.[21] The daily cult accompanies the daily life of the deity in the sanctuary like that of a king from his rising in the morning until his retiring at night. There are also rituals for the various sacrificial offerings, all kinds of prayer, penance, and purification rituals, and a multiplicity of festivals. On all occasions, liturgies corresponding to the cultic, magical, or sacramental actions were recited; myths were most commonly associated with the festivals.

In the Egyptian rituals[22] for those festivals on which the story of a god or gods was solemnly repeated, cult and myth clearly coalesce. They lead easily into mystery plays if ritual actions are referred to events recounted in the myth, as the relatively recent sources containing the rituals of the Osiris cult show.[23] As in Mesopotamia, we also find in Egypt cultic service performed daily for the deities and the other customary cultic actions;[24] mythological motifs are used to interpret the cultic action by analogy. The cultic procedure, not the narrative thread of the myth, is determinative; details of myths seem even to have been drawn from the cult. We must also mention the elaborate burial ritual, especially that of the king.

The Hittites, too, have a funerary ritual for the king,[25] which lasts two weeks.[26] There are also various magical rituals, intended for the most part to furnish protection or cultic purification, like the rituals found in the former royal archives, but also in part to harm or bewitch others. When new deities are borrowed, the corresponding rituals are introduced, as the example of Queen Puduhepa shows, who orders ritual texts from her Hurrian homeland to be copied. Recourse is also had to oracles, whether by means of hepatoscopy and augury or through female seers and priestly soothsayers, who do not cavil to use incantations in order to determine the will of the gods.

[20] A. Falkenstein, *Die Haupttypen der sumerischen Beschwörung*, 1931; G. Meier, *Die assyrische Beschwörungsserie Maqlû*, 1937; E. Reiner, *Šurpu*, 1958.

[21] *AOT*, pp. 295-330; *ANET*, pp. 331-45; S. Langdon, *Babylonian Liturgies*, 1913.

[22] For rituals, oracles, incantations, etc., see G. Roeder, *Die ägyptische Religion in Texten und Bildern*, III-IV (1960-61); A. M. Blackman, "Oracles in Ancient Egypt," *JEA*, XI (1925), 249-55; XII (1926), 176-85; H. W. Fairman, "The Kingship Rituals of Egypt," in S. H. Hooke, ed., *Myth, Ritual, and Kingship*, 1958, pp. 74-104; O. Kaiser, "Das Orakel als Mittel der Rechtsfindung im alten Ägypten," *ZRGG*, X (1958), 193-208; A. Moret, *Le rituel du culte divin journalier en Égypte*, 1902.

[23] E. Drioton, *Le texte dramatique d'Edfou*, 1948; H. Junker, *Die Stundenwachen in den Osirismysterien*, 1910; K. Sethe, *Dramatische Texte zu altägyptischen Mysterienspielen*, 1928.

[24] *Hieratische Papyrus aus den Kgl. Museen zu Berlin*, I (1901), discussed by A. Moret (see n. 22).

[25] H. G. Güterbock, "An Outline of the Hittite AN.TAH.SUM Festival," *JNES*, XIX (1960), 80-89; H. Otten, "Ritual bei Erneuerung von Kultsymbolen hethitischer Schutzgottheiten," in *J. Friedrich-Festschrift*, 1959, pp. 351-59.

[26] H. Otten, *Hethitische Totenrituale*, 1958.

It is obvious that the Canaanites were equally familiar with this sort of thing. Some of the texts found at Ugarit from the middle of the second millennium are probably priestly rituals and liturgies.[27] Even the much later Carthaginian festival sacrificial tariff bears witness to Canaanite-Phoenician cultic regulations.[28] Such forms and customs Israel borrowed in great measure from the Canaanite cult.[29]

4. *Narrative in the ancient Near East.* It has long been well known that myth and epic, which frequently assume the role played in Israel by saga and legend, are of immense significance in the ancient Near East. It has been said that myth always accompanies ritual, joining with it as a kind of "verbal ceremony" to produce a powerful event. This view, however, is exaggerated. Myth and ritual frequently go together, especially in the context of the religious festivals; but this is not always true as a general rule.[30] The myth of the Deluge, for example, was never recited as part of the cult. Other myths furnish religious propaganda for a particular sanctuary or a theological tenet,[31] or else political propaganda, like the Babylonian myth of the plague-god Erra.[32]

Within the complex of Mesopotamian myths and epics,[33] the Sumerian heritage of the third millennium is the most extensive, even though it has been subjected to revision by Semites. One can follow Kramer in classifying the myths into three general groups: myths dealing with the origin and structure of the cosmos, myths dealing with the underworld, and other myths; or one may follow Schmökel in distinguishing three major narrative cycles: one dealing with the deities Enki and Eridu, another with Enlil of Nippur, and a third with Inanna of Uruk. In fact most of the myths in which Enki and Enlil figure deal primarily with the creation and structure of the world, with all its component parts and institutions, while those that center on the goddess Inanna deal more with battle, revenge, and cunning, even telling how she hands over her partner Dumuzi-Tammuz, the "shepherd-god" and king of Uruk, to the powers of the underworld.[34] Among the other myths, one tells of the Deluge and its hero Ziusudra (later Atraḫasis or Utnapishtim).

[27] C. H. Gordon, *Ugaritic Manual*, 1955, pp. 124-67: nos. 1-3, 5, 9, 14, 17, 19, 22, 23, 41, 44, 47 and others; *idem*, *Ugaritic Literature*, 1949, pp. 107-15.

[28] *AOT*, pp. 449-50; cf. J.-G. Février, *Cahiers de Byrsa*, VIII (1958/59), 35-43.

[29] R. Dussaud, *Les origines Cananéennes du sacrifice Israélite*, 2nd ed., 1941; D. Kellermann, "'āšām in Ugarit?" *ZAW*, LXXVI (1964), 319-22; R. Schmid, *Das Bundesopfer in Israel*, 1964; R. de Vaux, *Les sacrifices de l'Ancien Testament*, 1964.

[30] R. de Langhe, "Myth, Ritual, and Kingship in the Ras Shamra Tablets," in S. H. Hooke, ed., *Myth, Ritual, and Kingship*, 1958, pp. 122-48; E. Otto, *Das Verhältnis von Rite und Mythus im Ägyptischen*, 1958; S. Schott, "Ritual und Mythe im altägyptischen Kult," *Studium Generale*, VIII (1955), 285-93.

[31] S. G. F. Brandon, "The Propaganda Factor in some Ancient Near Eastern Cosmogonies," in *Hooke Festschrift*, 1963, pp. 20-25.

[32] F. Gössmann, *Das Era-Epos*, 1956.

[33] *AOT*, pp. 108-240; *ANET*, pp. 37-119.

[34] A. Falkenstein, "Inannas Gang zur Unterwelt," *AfO*, XIV (1941/44), 113-38; T. Jacobsen and S. N. Kramer, "The Myth of Inanna and Bilulu," *JNES*, XII (1953), 160-88; S. N. Kramer, "Inanna's Descent to the Nether World," *JCSt*, V (1951), 1-17.

The Sumerian epics center on demigods and heroes, primarily Enmerkar,[35] Lugalbanda, and Gilgamesh (who is the subject of at least five Sumerian poems); the Akkadian Epic of Gilgamesh—the first poem in a Semitic language, an independent and much admired work—then made use of the Sumerian poems.[36] This latter work came into being in the Old Babylonian period and achieved its final form toward the end of the second millennium. It was familiar to the Hurrians, the Hittites, and even in Palestine (Megiddo),[37] while the best-preserved texts of other myths come from as far away as Egypt. The most important Semitic myth is the creation epic, called *Enuma Êliš* ("When above . . .") after its first two words.[38] There are also myths dealing with Adapa, Atraḫasis, Nergal and Ereshkigal, Etana, and many others.[39] A cycle of legends has grown up around the two Akkadian rulers Sargon and Naramsin.[40]

In the Egyptian texts[41] we find for the most part only isolated motifs taken from myths; these are embedded in rituals, hymns, and incantations. We may mention, for example, the dramatic Ramesseum Papyrus, the divine utterances in rituals found in the burial chambers of the pyramids dating from the end of the Old Kingdom, as well as other hymns and rituals. Coherent parts of myths are preserved in the *Monument of Memphite Theology*, the *Book of the Cow of Heaven*, a text from the ceiling of the false tomb of Seti I at Abydos, and in portions of a *Ritual to Defeat Seth*. Thematically, the myths seek on the one hand to fill out the present world and the beyond, and on the other to comprehend the origin, arrangement, and earliest history of the world. In addition, the myths of the Heliopolitan or Memphite theology show a propagandistic religious or political bias. In fact, it has been suggested that reference to immediate political events and circumstances is the basic organizing principle of most of the well-known Egyptian myths.[42] With the passage of time, whole complexes of myths grew up about the system of gods

[35] S. N. Kramer, *Enmerkar and the Lord of Aratta*, 1952.

[36] P. Garelli, ed., *Gilgameš et sa légende*, 1960; A. Heidel, *The Gilgamesh Epic and the Old Testament*, 2nd ed., 1954; F. M. T. de Liagre Böhl, "Das Problem ewigen Lebens im Zyklus und Epos des Gilgamesch," in *Opera minora*, 1953, pp. 234-62; A. Schott and W. von Soden, *Das Gilgamesch-Epos*, 1958.

[37] A. Goetze and S. Levy, "The New Megiddo Fragment of the Gilgamesh Epic," *'Atiqot*, II (1959), 121-28.

[38] R. Labat, *Le poème babylonien de la création*, 1935; S. Langdon, *The Babylonian Epic of Creation*, 1923.

[39] J. Laessøe, "The Atrachasis Epic," *BiOr*, XIII (1956), 90-102; W. G. Lambert, "New Light on the Babylonian Flood," *JSS*, V (1960), 113-23; F. M. T. de Liagre Böhl, "Die Mythe vom weisen Adapa," *WdO*, II (1959), 416-31.

[40] O. R. Gurney, "The Sultantepe Tables: The Cuthaean Legend of Naramsin," *AnSt*, V (1955), 93-103.

[41] *AOT*, pp. 1-8; *ANET*, pp. 3-36; A. Erman, *Die Literatur der Ägypter*, 1923; M. Pieper, *Das ägyptische Märchen*, 1935; G. Roeder, *Die ägyptische Religion in Texten und Bildern*, II (1960); S. Schott, *Mythe und Mythenbildung im Alten Ägypten*, 1945; *idem*, "Die älteren Göttermythen," in *Handbuch der Orientalistik*, I (1952), 67-75; J. Spiegel, "Göttergeschichten, Erzählungen, Märchen, Fabeln," *ibid*., pp. 119-39.

[42] Spiegel, *op. cit*., p. 122.

presented in the Osiris myth, the world-system of the primitive gods, and similar constructs; these complexes themselves later coalesced. Further development is typified by a mixture of realism and fantasy, employment of the motifs of cunning and magic, the formation of etiological myths, and, formally, by the use of all the artifices of the developing art of narrative. Among these later works, many of which have a didactic purpose, we may mention especially the *Story of the Shipwrecked Sailor*,[43] the *Birth of the Kings of the fifth Dynasty* (which is legendary and has an introduction consisting of tales of magic), the *Story of Si-nuhe*[44] (a good example of Egyptian nationalism), the tales in the *Story of the Two Brothers*, as well as in the *Story of the Enchanted Prince* and the *Voyages of Un-amun*.

The situation is different once more in the case of the Hittites. In part they borrowed Mesopotamian poems, like the Gilgamesh Epic, in abbreviated form.[45] Other myths, especially those involving the god Kumarbi, derive from the Hurrians, who themselves took over Babylonian themes and made use of them in their own narratives.[46] Finally, there are mythic narratives originating in Asia Minor, which are probably pre-Hittite, such as the myth of Illuyankas (which provides the etiology for a festival) and the myth of the vanished god (the myth of Telipinu).[47]

The first Canaanite myths and epics, formerly known only from mere allusions or short quotations, are now accessible for the first time in the Ugaritic texts.[48] Besides the great cycle involving the gods Baal, Anat, and Mot, which is the most important,[49] we have such myths as the *Marriage of the Moon-God with the Goddess Nikkal* and the *Birth of the Gods Shahar and Shalim*. In addition, there are the epics of King Keret [50] and of Aqhat, the son of the

[43] W. Golénischeff, *Le conte du naufragé*, 1912; G. Lanczkowski, "Die Geschichte des Schiffbrüchigen," *ZDMG*, CIII (1953), 360-71.

[44] A. Alt, "Die älteste Schilderung Palästinas im Lichte neuer Funde," *PJB*, XXXVII (1941), 19-50; A. H. Gardiner, *Die Erzählung des Sinuhe und die Hirtengeschichte*, 1909; H. Goedicke, "The Route of Sinuhe's Flight," *JEA*, XLIII (1957), 77-85; H. Grapow, *Der stilistische Bau der Geschichte des Sinuhe*, 1952.

[45] H. Otten, "Die erste Tafel des hethitischen Gilgamesch-Epos," *Istanbuler Mitteilungen*, VIII (1959), 91 ff.; *idem*, "Zur Überlieferung des Gilgameš-Epos nach den Boğazköy-Texten," *Cahiers du Groupe François-Thureau-Dangin*, I (1960), 139 ff.

[46] M. Vieyra, "Le dieu Kumarbi et le syncrétisme religieux dans le Proche-Orient au second millénaire av. J.C.," *RHR*, CLV (1959), 138-39.

[47] J. G. MacQueen, "Hattian Mythology and Hittite Monarchy," *AnSt* IX (1959), 171-88.

[48] J. Aistleitner, *Die mythologischen und kultischen Texte aus Ras Schamra*, 2nd ed., 1964; G. R. Driver, *Canaanite Myths and Legends*, 1956; O. Eissfeldt, *El im ugaritischen Pantheon*, 1951; C. H. Gordon, *Ugaritic Literature*, 1949; J. Gray, *The Legacy of Canaan*, 2nd ed., 1965; E. Jacob, *Ras-Shamra-Ugarit et l'Ancien Testament*, 1960; A. Jirku, *Kanaanäische Mythen und Epen aus Ras Schamra-Ugarit*, 1962; A. S. Kapelrud, *Baʿal in the Ras Shamra Texts*, 1952; R. de Langhe, *Les textes de Ras Shamra-Ugarit et leurs rapports avec le milieu biblique de l'Ancien Testament*, 2 vols., 1945; M. H. Pope, *El in the Ugaritic Texts*, 1955.

[49] J. Obermann, *Ugaritic Mythology*, 1948.

[50] H. L. Ginsberg, *The Legend of King Keret*, 1946; J. Gray, *The Krt Text in the Literature of Ras Shamra*, 2nd ed., 1964; K.-H. Bernhardt, "Anmerkungen zur Interpretation des KRT-Textes von Ras Schamra-Ugarit," *WZGreifswald* V (1955/56), 101-21.

king Danel. Many concepts and motifs from the world of these myths and epics recur in the OT.

5. *Report in the ancient Near East.* The first attempt to comprehend the course of history[51] is the formal chronology,[52] which we first encounter in Mesopotamia in the form of the king list from the Akkad period. Such chronologies, in various forms, were constructed throughout the following centuries: at first the years were named after events, then simply given numbers; in Assyria, they were named after officials.[53] One great compilation is the Sumerian King List (dating from about 1760),[54] the prototype of many later lists, the most important of which is the great Assyrian King List (which goes down to 722).[55] The real roots of historical writing may be found in the building inscriptions and dedicatory inscriptions, some of which date back as far as 2600. The Vulture Stela of Eannatum is the first real historical document. The inscriptions contain a more or less detailed contemporary chronicle, describing the deeds of the ruler in power. While the Akkadian rulers describe their wars in bilingual documents, the Sumerian renaissance of the Ur III period avoids this practice until the time of Hammurabi, following instead the earlier tradition of describing the kings' peaceful acts.[56] The Akkadian practice was taken up once more by the Assyrians, who describe their campaigns in great detail in their annals, list in geographical order in their inscriptions the nations they have conquered, and summarize their military campaigns without regard for historical sequence in their military reports, some of which take the form of letters to the god Ashur.[57] The corresponding literary type in Babylonia during this period is the chronicle, represented in Assyria only by the so-called Synchronistic History, which deals with the period 1420–1160. These chronicles are systematic summaries of historical events; they cover considerable periods of time, going back some two thousand years, in decidedly impersonal style. Among them are the so-called Chronicle of Nabopolassar, the so-called Chaldean Chronicle, and the chronicle of Nabonidus and Cyrus.[58] It is hard to find any unifying purpose or dominant idea in these chronicles. It appears, however, that while the Sumerians simply set down the sequence of historical periods, the Babylonians understood history as the consequence of human deeds

[51] *AOT*, pp. 80-107, 331-90; *ANET*, pp. 227-322; cf. also D. O. Edzard, "Neue Inschriften zur Geschichte von Ur III unter Šūsuen," *AfO*, XIX (1959/60), 1-82; F. R. Kraus, "Altbabylonische Quellensammlungen zur altmesopotamischen Geschichte," *ibid.*, XX (1963), 153-55.

[52] F. Schmidtke, *Der Aufbau der babylonischen Chronologie*, 1952.

[53] S. Mowinckel, "Die vorderasiatischen Königs- und Fürsteninschriften," in *Gunkel-Festschrift*, I (1923), 278-322.

[54] T. Jacobsen, *The Sumerian King List*, 1939.

[55] E. Weidner, "Die grosse Königsliste aus Assur," *AfO*, III (1926), 66-77.

[56] L. W. King, *Chronicles Concerning Early Babylonian Kings*, 1907.

[57] T. Bauer, *Das Inschriftenwerk Assurbanipals*, 1933; R. Borger, *Die Inschriften Asarhaddons, Königs von Assyrien*, 1956; E. Weidner, "Die neue Königsliste aus Assur," *AfO*, IV (1927), 11-17; *idem*, "Die Königslisten aus Chorsabad," *ibid.*, XIV (1944), 362-69; *idem*, *Die Inschriften Tukulti-Ninurtas I. und seiner Nachfolger*, 1959.

[58] D. J. Wiseman, *Chronicles of Chaldaean Kings*, 1956.

and actions rewarded or punished by the gods. The fictitious royal inscriptions of the Late Sumerian period probably served the purpose of didactic historiography. Formally, the dominant narrative type is first-person description by the king himself.

In Egypt, too, in the so-called year tables of the First Dynasty, the regnal years of the kings were at first named for events; from the Second Dynasty on, this practice is superseded by simple enumeration. Annal writing, the first major form of Egyptian historiography, follows the pattern of the year tables. This form looks upon history not as a process of development or as a continuity, but as an endless summary of isolated facts. One may speak of a constantly repeated temporal cycle, in which the reigns of the kings follow upon each other as manifestations of the creation of the world.[59] Extracts from the annals make up the king lists (such as the Turin Papyrus[60]) and the military annals of Thut-mose III;[61] the Palermo Stone contains a collection of considerable size.[62] The king lists in Greek are a continuation of annal writing (Manetho, Eratosthenes). The second major form of Egyptian historiography is the "royal novella," [63] whose purpose is to describe a single event, depicting it as a deed of the divine king carrying out the will of the gods. The first instance of this literary type is the account of how Sesostris I (Twelfth Dynasty) built the temple of Atum at Heliopolis; it continues in use until the late period, when it loses its religious associations. The narrative format begins with the occasion of the king's deed (e.g., his accession or a dream), then tells how he announces his plan to the court and the officials, and finally describes the deed itself, which is usually cultic and cultural. Other forms include historical inscriptions on temples and stelae, hymnlike poems celebrating a royal deed, like the poem describing the battle of Kadesh under Ramses II, and historical descriptions of past events embellished with fantastic details, like the fragmentary narratives of King Apophis and Sekenenre and the conquest of Joppa. The nonroyal biographical inscriptions also deserve mention, most of which describe dignitaries and officials. They are found at first in tombs, then upon stelae, and finally in temples; they are usually written in the first person and placed in the mouth of the dead man, the memory of whose life they are to preserve. These inscriptions contain two parts: first, a so-called ideal biography (rules of conduct that the dead man declares he has followed), and second, a biographical outline of his life. Especially in the late period, which lays down ethical rules as the absolute norm for conduct, these biographies acquire a didactic purpose.[64]

[59] E. Otto in *Handbuch der Orientalistik*, I (1952), 140.

[60] G. Farina, *Il papiro dei Re restaurato*, 1938; cf. also A. H. Gardiner, "Regnal Years and Civil Calendar in Pharaonic Egypt," *JEA*, XXXI (1945), 11-28; E. Meyer, *Ägyptische Chronologie*, 1904; R. A. Parker, *The Calendars of Ancient Egypt*, 1951.

[61] H. Grapow, *Studien zu den Annalen Thutmosis' III.*, 1949.

[62] H. Schäfter, *Ein Bruchstück altägyptischer Annalen*, 1902.

[63] A. Hermann, *Die ägyptische Königsnovelle*, 1938; S. Herrmann, "Die Königsnovelle in Ägypten und in Israel," *WZLeipzig*, III (1953/54), 51-62.

[64] E. Otto, *Die biographischen Inschriften der ägyptischen Spätzeit*, 1954.

Egypt is the home of the pictorial narrative, which presents an event in relief in one or more scenes; in addition, there is also monumental art of a historical nature and representation of historical persons. We find this type of art only in the period of centralizing absolutistic governments, imperialistic international politics, and a secularized concept of the kingship. In Egypt it is limited to the period 1317–1165, in Mesopotamia to the period 883–626 (Moscati).

The Hittites accomplished some of their most impressive achievements in the realm of historiography.[65] The most true-to-life accounts come from the period of the Old Kingdom. Even though the two centuries of the Empire furnish the most highly developed examples of annals and autobiography, fixed forms of historical report developed very early, and events are described according to a unifying point of view.[66] This is true both of the bilingual inscription of Hattusilis I, discovered in 1957, with its annal-like description of military campaigns in literary form,[67] and of the introduction to the Decree of Telipinu, which puts forward harmony within the royal house and among the leading families as the guiding principle for the history of the land. The autobiography of Hattusilis III in addition allows us to see into the mind of the writer, presenting his personal history as election and guidance by his tutelary deity.[68] Among the Hittites, too, historiography means basically the description of contemporary events and royal autobiography; in contrast to the rest of the ancient Near East, however, the Hittites have an acute sense of history, a vision of the continuity of events, and exceptional literary ability.

From Syria, we can but mention at least the account given by King Idrimi of Alalakh of his flight, his life in exile, and his return to the throne.[69]

6. *Letters in the ancient Near East.* It will suffice merely to mention in passing the numerous letters found in the Near East: the Akkadian letters from Nimrud,[70] Mari,[71] Alalakh,[72] and Amarna;[73] the letters from Ugarit,[74] Some in Akkadian and some in Canaanite; and the Hittite letters.[75]

[65] A. Goetze, "Hittite and Anatolian Studies," in *The Bible and the Ancient Near East*, 1961, pp. 316-27; H. G. Güterbock, "Die historische Tradition und ihre literarische Gestaltung bei Babyloniern und Hethitern bis 1200," *ZA*, XLII (1934), 1-91; XLIV (1938), 45-145; A. Kammenhuber, "Die hethitische Geschichtsschreibung," *Saeculum*, IX (1958), 136-55; A. Malamat, "Doctrines of Causality in Hittite and Biblical Historiography," *VT*, V (1955), 1-12.

[66] H. Otten in H. Schmökel, *Kulturgeschichte des Alten Orient*, 1961, p. 413.

[67] F. Cornelius, "Die Annalen Ḫattušiliš I.," *Or*, XXVIII (1959), 292-96.

[68] A. Goetze, *Ḫattušiliš*, 1924; *idem*, *Neue Bruchstücke zum grossen Text des Ḫattušiliš*, 1930.

[69] S. Smith, *The Statue of Idri-mi*, 1949.

[70] H. W. F. Saggs, "The Nimrud Letters," *Iraq*, XVII (1955), 21-56, 126-154; XVIII (1956), 40-56; XX (1958), 182-212; XXI (1959), 158-79.

[71] *ANET*, pp. 482-83; *ARM;* J. Bottéro, "Lettres de la Salle 110 du Palais de Mari," *RA*, LII (1958), 163-76.

[72] D. J. Wiseman, *The Alalakh Tablets*, 1953.

[73] *AOT*, pp. 371-79; *ANET*, pp. 483-90; J. A. Knudtzon, *Die El-Amarna Tafeln*, 1907-15.

[74] C. H. Gordon, *Ugaritic Manual*, 1955: nos. 18, 26, 32, 54, 89, 95, 101, and others; *idem*, *Ugaritic Literature*, 1949, pp. 116-19; J. Nougayrol in *CRAI*, 1952, pp. 181-91; 1953, pp. 40-51; 1954, pp. 30-41; 1960, 163-71; PRU III-IV, 1955-56.

[75] E. Laroche, "Lettre d'un préfet du roi hittite," *RHA*, XVIII (1961), 81-88; H. Otten,

Later on, there are the letters of the Neo-Babylonian and Persian periods,[76] mostly written in Aramaic, and the Greek letters of the Hellenistic period.[77] The Israelite epistolary style is almost identical with contemporary style elsewhere.

7. *Israel.* The forms customarily used in Israel for law and instruction, narrative and report, obviously are basically identical with or similar to those employed elsewhere in the ancient Near East. Many of the literary types found in the historical and legal books are not typical of the OT, but of the ancient Near East in general. It is therefore all the more important to notice where changes or innovations have taken place and to inquire whether they have come about through the influence of Yahwism or for some other reason. This is especially true for historical narrative and historiography, which departs quite far from the first-person account of the king that is the dominant form elsewhere in the ancient Near East. Does a different conception of history stand behind this development? Even more noteworthy is the absence of many forms that are associated with prognostication, incantations, and magic: this is doubtless due to the rejection of such practices by Yahwism. Thus the study of rhetorical and literary types leads directly to the question of the uniqueness of the OT against its ancient Near Eastern environment.

§8 The Directive Literary Types and Their Traditions

A. Alt, *Die Ursprünge des israelitischen Rechts,* 1934 (= *Kleine Schriften,* 1953, pp. 278-332 [Eng. *Essays on Old Testament History and Religion*]); R. Bach, *Die Aufforderungen zur Flucht und zum Kampf im alttestamentlichen Prophetenspruch,* 1962; K. Baltzer, *Das Bundesformular,* 2nd ed., 1966; J. Begrich, "Berit," *ZAW,* LX (1944), 1-11 (= *Gesammelte Studien zum Alten Testament,* 1964, pp. 55-66); H. J. Boecker, *Redeformen des Rechtslebens im Alten Testament,* 1964; H. A. Brongers, *Oud-Oosters en Bijbels Recht,* 1960; D. Daube, *Studies in Biblical Law,* 1947; *idem,* "Rechtsgedanken in den Erzählungen des Pentateuchs," in *Von Ugarit nach Qumran, Eissfeldt-Festschrift,* 1958, pp. 32-41; *idem, The Exodus Pattern in the Bible,* 1963; A. Eberharter, *Der Dekalog,* 1929; K. Elliger, "Das Gesetz Leviticus 18," *ZAW,* LXVII (1955), 1-25; I. Engnell, *Israel and the Law,* 2nd ed., 1954; Z. W. Falk, *Hebrew Law in Biblical Times,* 1964; F. C. Fensham, "The Possibility of the Presence of Casuistic Legal Material at the Making of the Covenant at Sinai," *PEQ,* XCIII (1961), 143-46; *idem,* "Clauses of Protection in Hittite Vassal-Treaties and the Old Testament," *VT,* XIII (1963), 133-43; C. Feucht, *Untersuchungen zum Heiligkeitsgesetz,* 1964; G. Fohrer, "Der Vertrag zwischen König und Volk in Israel," *ZAW,*

"Hethitische Schreiber in ihren Briefen," *MIOF,* IV (1956), 179-89; Liane Rost, "Die ausserhalb von Boğazköy gefundenen hethitischen Briefe," *ibid.,* pp. 328-50.

[76] *AOT,* pp. 450-62; *ANET,* pp. 491-92; A. Cowley, *Aramaic Papyri of the Fifth Century B.C.,* 1923; G. R. Driver, *Aramaic Documents of the Fifth Century B.C.,* 1954; E. Hammershaimb, "Some Observations on the Aramaic Elephantine Papyri," *VT,* VII (1957), 17-34; E. G. Kraeling, *The Brooklyn Museum Aramaic Papyri,* 1953.

[77] O. Roller, *Das Formular der Paulinischen Briefe,* 1933 (esp. pp. 34-91).

LXXI (1959), 1-22; *idem*, "Das sogenannte apodiktisch formulierte Recht und der Dekalog," *Kerygma und Dogma*, XI (1965), 49-74; H. G. Gehman, "Natural Law and the Old Testament," in *Alleman-Festschrift*, 1960, pp. 109-22; E. Gerstenberger, *Wesen und Herkunft des sogenannten apodiktischen Rechts im Alten Testament*, Disseration, Bonn, 1961; H. Gese, "Beobachtungen zum Stil alttestamentlicher Rechtssätze," *ThLZ*, LXXXV (1960), 147-50; S. Gevirtz, "West-Semitic Curses and the Problem of the Origins of Hebrew Law," *VT*, XI (1961), 137-58; E. M. Good, "The 'Blessing' on Judah, Gen. 49,8-12," *JBL*, LXXXII (1963), 427-32; A. H. J. Gunneweg, "Über den Sitz im Leben der sog. Stammessprüche," *ZAW*, LXXVI (1964), 245-55; G. Heinemann, *Untersuchungen zum apodiktischen Recht*, Dissertation, Hamburg, 1958; J. Hempel, "Bund. II. Im AT," *RGG*, 3rd edition, I (1957), 1513-16; *idem*, *Das Ethos des Alten Testaments*, 2nd ed., 1964; R. Hentschke, *Satzung und Setzender*, 1963; F. Horst, "Recht und Religion im Bereich des Alten Testaments," *EvTh*, XVI (1956), 49-75 (= *Gottes Recht*, 1961, pp. 260-91); A. Jepsen, "Die 'Hebräer' und ihr Recht," *AfO*, XV (1945-51), 55-68; *idem*, "Berith," in *Rudolph-Festschrift*, 1961, pp. 161-79; A. Jirku, *Das weltliche Recht im Alten Testament*, 1927; W. Kessler, "Die literarische, historische und theologische Problematik des Dekalogs," *VT*, VII (1957), 1-16; R. Kilian, "Apodiktisches und kasuistisches Recht im Licht ägyptischer Analogien," *BZ*, NF VII (1963), 185-202; H.-J. Kittel, *Die Stammessprüche Israels*, Dissertation, Berlin, 1959; L. Köhler, "Der Dekalog," *ThR*, NF I (1929), 161-84; R. Kraetzschmar, *Die Bundesvorstellung im Alten Testament in ihrer geschichtlichen Entwicklung*, 1896; J. G. Leovy and G. M. Taylor, "Law and Social Development in Israel," *AThR*, XXXIX (1957), 9-24; N. Lohfink, "Die Bundesurkunde des Königs Josias," *Bibl*, XLIV (1963), 261-88, 461-98; D. J. McCarthy, *Treaty and Covenant*, 1963; G. E. Mendenhall, *Law and Covenant in Israel and the Ancient Near East*, 1955; S. Mowinckel, *Le Décalogue*, 1927; *idem*, "Zur Geschichte der Dekaloge," *ZAW*, LV (1937), 218-35; M. Noth, *Die Gesetze im Pentateuch*, 1940 (= *Gesammelte Studien zum Alten Testament*, 1957, pp. 9-141 [Eng. *The Laws in the Pentateuch, and Other Studies*, 1966]); *idem*, "Das alttestamentliche Bundschliessen im Lichte eines Mari-Textes," in *Mélanges Isidore Lévy*, 1955, pp. 433-44 (= *Gesammelte Studien zum Alten Testament*, pp. 142-54); W. Nowack, "Der erste Dekalog," in BZAW, XXXIII (1918), 381-97; M. J. O'Connel, "The Concept of Commandment in the Old Testament," *ThSt*, XXI (1960), 109-22; J. Pedersen, *Der Eid bei den Semiten*, 1914; J. J. Petuchowsky, "A Note on W. Kessler's 'Problematik des Dekalogs'," *VT*, VII (1957), 397-98; J. van der Ploeg, "Studies in Hebrew Law," *CBQ*, XII (1950), 248-59, 416-27; XIII (1951), 28-43, 164-71, 296-307; W. Preiser, "Vergeltung und Sühne im altisraelitischen Strafrecht," in *E. Schmidt-Festschrift*, 1961, pp. 7-38; G. Quell, "Der at.liche Begriff ברית," *ThW*, II (1935) 106-27; K. Rabast, *Das apodiktische Recht im Deuteronomium und im Heiligkeitsgesetz*, 1949; G. von Rad, *Der Heilige Krieg im alten Israel*, 3rd ed., 1958; H. Graf Reventlow, *Gebot und Predigt im Dekalog*, 1960; *idem*, "Kultisches Recht im Alten Testament," *ZThK*, LX (1963), 267-304; H. H. Rowley, "Moses and the Decalogue," *BJRL*, XXXIV (1951/52), 81-118 (= *Men of God*, 1963, pp. 1-36); R. Sauber, *Die Abstraktion im israelitischen Recht*, 1950 (microfilm); H. Schmidt, "Mose und der Dekalog," in *Gunkel-Festschrift*, I (1923), 78-119; H. Schmökel, *Das angewandte Recht im Alten Testament*, 1930; *idem*, "Biblische 'Du sollst'-Gebote und ihr historischer Ort," *Zeitschrift der Savigny-Stiftung für Rechtsgeschichte*, XXXVI (1950), 365-90; R. Smend, *Jahwekrieg und Stämmebund*, 1963; *idem*, *Die Bundesformel*, 1963; J. M. P. Smith,

The Origin and History of Hebrew Law, 1931; J. J. STAMM, *Der Dekalog im Lichte der neueren Forschung,* 1958, 2nd ed 1962; *idem,* "Dreissig Jahre Dekalogforschung," *ThR,* NF XXVII (1961), 189-239, 281-205; E. TÄUBLER, "Die Spruch-Verse über Sebulon," *MGWJ,* LXXXIII NF, XLVII (1939, 1963), 9-46; T. C. VRIEZEN, "Litterairhistorische vragen aangaande de Dekaloog," *NThSt,* XXII (1939), 2-24, 34-51; C. F. WHITLEY, "Covenant and Commandment in Israel," *JNES,* XXII (1963), 37-48; G. WIDENGREN, "King and Covenant," *JSS,* II (1957), 1-32; H. W. WOLFF, "Jahwe als Bundesvermittler," *VT,* VI (1956), 316-20; E. WÜRTHWEIN, "Der Sinn des Gesetzes im Alten Testament," *ZThK,* LV (1958), 255-70; W. ZIMMERLI, "Das Gesetz im Alten Testament," *ThLZ,* LXXXV (1960), 481-98; H.-J. ZOBEL, *Stammesspruch und Geschichte,* 1965.

1. *The formulas and sayings of everyday life.* By way of introduction to the other literary types, we shall first discuss briefly the formulas and sayings used by the individual and the group, with the exception of those that have optative form. To a large extent the formulas of everyday Israelite life are preserved only because they were appropriate to certain contexts in the books and narratives of the OT. In many cases this fact may have affected their form. There were certainly many more such stereotyped formulas than have come down to us.

The birth of a child, especially a son, gave the parents or relatives occasion for various sayings. Sayings related to the individual situation naturally have not survived, but we do possess stereotyped formulas such as that used to encourage the mother: "Fear not; for now you will have another son" (Gen. 35:17), and the similar expression used in I Sam. 4:20. We also have the mother's exclamation, "I have gotten a man" (Gen. 4:1). The legal formula "You are my son, today I have begotten you" (Ps. 2:7), from which Isa. 9:5 (Eng. 9:6) probably derives, was not employed for adopting but for legitimizing a child (e.g., one born of a slave).[1]

The formulas used at betrothal and marriage are echoed by the declaration of relationship with which the man receives the woman formed from his rib (Gen. 2:23). In the later period, the directive formula with which a father handed over a woman to her husband apparently might run, "Here receive her according to the law of Moses" (Tob. 7:13). For divorce, there was the formula inserted as a gloss in Hos. 2:4 (Eng. 2:2): "She is not my wife, and I am not her husband."[2] At a person's death, a saying like Job 1:21*b* might be used: "Yahweh gave, and Yahweh has taken away; blessed be the name of Yahweh." This saying is based on the legal principle that possession (of life, in this case) is by lease or grant.

Other common formulas refer to Israelite groups or their representatives.

[1] Cf. G. Fohrer, "*huiós*," ThW, VIII 344-45, 351; on so-called adoption, see M. David, "Adoptie in het oude Israel," *MAA,* XVIII 4 (1955), 85-103.

[2] L. Dürr, "Altorientalisches Recht bei den Propheten Amos und Hosea," *BZ,* XXIII (1935), 150-57; C. H. Gordon, "Hos. 2:4-5 in the Light of New Semitic Inscriptions," *ZAW,* LIV (1936), 277-80; C. Kuhl, "Neue Dokumente zum Verständnis von Hosea 2:4-15," *ibid.,* LII (1934), 102-9.

In the so-called Blessings of Jacob and Moses (Gen. 49; Deut. 33), for example, we have two series of originally independent sayings referring to the different tribes; these were later joined together and provided with a frame. Kittel and Gunneweg have recently studied these passages from the standpoint of form criticism and traditio-historical criticism; Zobel has examined them primarily for their historical significance. Other sayings were employed by the Song of Deborah (Judg. 5) and applied to the situation at hand. Another tribal saying is woven into the birth narrative of Ishmael (Gen. 16:11-12). The earlier poems of Balaam represent sayings developed in poetic form. One look at the sayings of the two major series shows that they are based on animal metaphors and puns. In Gen. 49:14-15, for example, Issachar is compared to an ass, while the following statement about his forced labor involves a pun on *'îš śākār*, "day laborer." The animal metaphor amounts in fact to an identification: Issachar is the lazy ass. The pun is intended to explain the nature or destiny implicit in the name: Issachar is destined to servitude as a result of his name. The same holds true for the other sayings, in which animal metaphor and pun have regulatory or directive power.

The animal metaphors point to a period not far distant from the (semi) nomadic way of life of the Israelite tribes; some of them may have originated in this period, and in any case soon after the occupation of Canaan. The puns are of somewhat later date. The expansions of the sayings above and beyond the two forms just discussed are even later. Those in Genesis 49 for the most part serve the purpose of the frame, which is to ascribe primacy to Judah; those in Deuteronomy 33 help give the collection its secondary character as a "blessing." The tribal sayings, then, are early material; their *Sitz im Leben* is not a tribal league's cultic worship of Yahweh,[3] but the scornful or admiring description of related groups or tribes in the (semi) nomadic environment. All reference to Yahwism is lacking in the early sayings; it occurs only in the later form of Deuteronomy 33. The first compilation in Genesis 49 took place under the control of the pan-Israelite ideal, with emphasis on the leadership of Judah; it forms a part of the Yahwistic source of the Pentateuch.

Particularly in the premonarchic period, when there was no standing army of professional soldiers, the conduct of war could be associated with religious ideas and customs, which are connected with the attempt to gain victory and avoid defeat by means of divine aid. This gave rise to more or less well established sayings. After a favorable oracle, Yahweh's decree was announced in the first or third person: "See, I have given into your hand Jericho" (Josh. 6:2), or "Yahweh has given you the city" (Josh. 6:16). Hence the command "Fear not" (Exod. 14:13) and the sayings in Num. 10:35-36, which now refer to the picking up and setting down of the ark before and after battle, but are in fact later liturgical formulas. Or men might be summoned to have courage, as in II Sam. 10:12. There were also general stereotyped forms for summoning men to battle or to flight; these can be recovered from the oracles against

[3] This is Weiser's* theory, in which he is followed by Gunneweg.

the foreign nations in the book of Jeremiah (Bach). Just as victory was proclaimed with the words, "Yahweh has put the enemy under our feet" (cf. I Kings 5:17 [Eng. 5:3], Pss. 18:39 [Eng. 18:38]; 110:1), so also the command "To your tents, O Israel" (cf. II Sam. 18:17; 19:9 [Eng. 19:8]; 20:22; I Kings 12:16) rang out when the militia were dispersed, either in defeat or in revolt against a hated leader. From the period of the monarchy comes the acclamation ". . . is king," with which the representative of all the people was hailed upon his accession as ruler (II Sam. 15:10).

Finally, the previously mentioned formula "Fear not," which at times is meant only to calm and encourage (I Sam. 28:12-13), also can take on the character of a summons or a directive. This is especially true when Yahweh or his angel appears (Judg. 6:23), in the context of battle, or when a powerful man promises protection to another (I Sam. 22:23).

2. *Rules of conduct in apodictic form.* Alt has termed all the sayings in this category apodictically formulated legal maxims; according to him, they are transmitted primarily in short or long series of maxims with parallel structure; they are uniquely Israelite and Yahwistic, and their categorical directives correspond to their intimate association with the divine will. This type of law has sometimes been called, somewhat incautiously, divine law. Meanwhile, a considerable number of scholars have attacked Alt's position.[4] In particular, the thesis that we are dealing here with truly indigenous Israelite law closely associated with Yahweh is denied by those who assume a non-Israelite origin for it in the Hittite vassal treaties, brought to Israel by way of Shechem (Heinemann), or else a common Semitic origin in kinship associations, grounded on the authoritative directives of the elders of the kinship group or the family (Feucht, Gerstenberger). Now the apodictic style—"Do this!" or "Do not do that!"—is a primitive form of directive; it is found everywhere. The compilation of series of formally identical commands and prohibitions, usually composed of ten (sometimes twelve) members so as to be memorized more easily, is probably a product of the (semi)nomadic milieu in the ancient Near East. Such a series provides the basis for Leviticus 18, as Elliger has shown.[5] The commandments of this passage, which was once a decalogue, are found in vss. 7-12, 14-16; one has been lost following the present vs. 9. All possess the primitive form "You shall not uncover the nakedness of . . . ," followed by the designation of the person. These rules derive from the situation of the (semi)nomadic extended family, whose common life had to be protected and guarded by an ethical code dealing with sexual activity.[6] The material and form of the apodictic series are therefore not legal in origin,[7] but moral and

[4] B. Landsberger, "Die babylonischen Termini für Gesetz und Recht," in *Symbolae Paulo Koschaker,* 1939, p. 223; T. J. Meek in *ANET,* p. 183 n. 24; see also Gese, Fensham, Fohrer, Gerstenberger, Gevirtz, and Kilian.

[5] Cf. the more recent commentaries and monographs dealing with the Holiness Code.

[6] The series has been secondarily expanded to form a dodecalogue, made to refer to Yahweh, and finally given the status of "law."

[7] There is therefore no term corresponding to the apodictic laws, since *ḥōq,* "*ordinance,*" is not used for them (Hentschke).

ethical; it came into being in the milieu of pre-Yahwistic nomadism.[8]

The series of prohibitions and commandments in Exod. 20:1-17, also referred to as the Decalogue in the stricter sense, is such a series of directives. Unlike the series in Leviticus, however, it came into being within the Yahwistic milieu and is the secondary product of several original series. Several attempts have been made to construct a proto-Decalogue of ten formally identical commandments, either by reduction to a minimum form consisting of two words only[9] or by arriving at a uniform longer pattern by expanding the short prohibitions and altering the commandments.[10] Such attempts, however, must be rejected because they demand major arbitrary emendations in the text. The commandments of the Decalogue in fact probably derive from three other series:

a) Five prohibitions derive from a series of commandments, each having four beats; these deal with duties toward Yahweh and toward one's neighbor:

I You shall have no 'other god.'[11]
II You shall not make yourself a graven image.
III You shall not take the name of Yahweh your God in vain.
IX You shall not bear false witness against your neighbor.
X You shall not covet your neighbor's house.

b) Three prohibitions derive from another series of commandments, each having two beats (cf. also Jer. 7:9; Hos. 4:2; Josh. 7:11; Lev. 19:11):

VI You shall not kill.
VII You shall not commit adultery.
VIII You shall not steal.

c) Two positive commandments derive from a series of commandments, each having three beats:

IV Remember the sabbath day.
V Honor your father and your mother.

Although prohibitions I–III could derive from the Mosaic period and other directives might even come from the pre-Yahwistic period,[12] the secondary character of the present series means that it cannot go back to Moses. A more likely assumption is that the Decalogue was assembled for the Elohistic source of the Pentateuch; the preface in verse 1 was added to give it the character of a divine directive. A cultic origin or purpose is out of the question; neither do we have here a piece of legislation. The Elohist himself proclaimed the Decalogue as a rule of conduct of Israel; as soon as he presents it, he has all

[8] Cultic recital of the law is not a necessary assumption and is difficult to visualize, the more so because Deuteronomy 27, generally cited as evidence, is a late text describing a fictitious cultic act.

[9] B. Couroyer, *L'Exode*, 1952, p. 97.

[10] Besides Alt and Rabast, see also E. Sellin, *Geschichte des israelitisch-jüdischen Volkes*, 2nd ed., I (1935), 83-84.

[11] The "before me" or "besides me" that now concludes the sentence is a later expansion.

[12] For a bibliography on the studies, mostly exegetical, devoted to the individual commandments, see the references and discussions in Stamm.

the people undertake to obey all the words that Yahweh has spoken, a decision that is ratified by a covenant ceremony (Exod. 24:3 ff.).

Another secondary series of rules of conduct is to be found in the so-called cultic decalogue of the Yahwist (Exod. 34:14-26),[13] which consists of four positively formulated apodictic directives referring to certain days of the year (vss. 18*aα*, 21*a*, 22*aα*, 26*a*) and six negatively formulated apodictic directives, four of which deal with questions involving the sacrificial system (vss. 20*bβ*, 25*a*, 25*b*, 26*b*), while the two remaining directives (vss. 14*a*, 17) correspond to the first two prohibitions in Exodus 20. The first two groups may derive from Judean sanctuary regulations, especially since they presuppose the environment of Canaanite Palestine (vss. 18*aα*, 22*aα*, 26). The Yahwist probably first compiled this decalogue, since it can hardly have existed as an independent entity and was certainly not intended for cultic recitation.

Tertiary series include the "plural decalogue" in Lev. 19:3-12, formed after the pattern of Exodus 20 (Mowinckel), and the decalogue in Exod. 23:10-19, which is dependent on Exodus 34. Most of the shorter series, containing less than ten commandments,[14] must be considered secondary and tertiary series, like those already discussed. A fourth stage is found at a later period: additional series were constructed artificially after the pattern of the earlier series. These include the "singular decalogue" in Lev. 19:13-18 (Mowinckel); the priestly torah employed in Ezek. 18:5-9; the guides for self-examination (*Beichtspiegel*)[15] regulating admission to the cult, which are employed in Isa. 33:14-16; Pss. 15; 24:3-6; the wisdom instruction employed in Job 31; and the mixed imitations in Ezek. 22:6-16 and Neh. 10:31-40 (Eng. 10:30-39).

3. *Legal maxims and decisions*. A. The realm of legal practice exhibits a variety of customs and legal maxims. The latter appear to refer primarily to murder or the death penalty; their metrical form and use of assonance frequently make them solemn and impressive, e.g., Gen. 9:6: "Whoever sheds the blood of man, / by man shall his blood be shed." If the murderer remained unknown, according to Deut. 21:7 the elders of the city had to say, "Our hand did not shed this blood, / neither did our eyes see it shed." I Kings 21:13 appears to contain a formula of accusation: "He cursed God and the king." There were also legal maxims employed in civil law; for instance, the widow who removes the sandal from the foot of the man refusing to perform the duty of levirate marriage is to spit at him and say, "So shall it be done to the man who does not build up his brother's house" (Deut. 25:9).

B. In addition, legal decisions were formed after the pattern of the series of apodictic rules. These briefly set out the crime and the punishment, and therefore differ considerably from the casuistic laws to be discussed below. Two examples are preserved: (*a*) the so-called *môt-yûmāt* series, which is scattered through

[13] H. Kosmala, "The So-called Ritual Decalogue," *ASTI*, I (1962), 31-61; R. H. Pfeiffer, "The Oldest Decalogue," *JBL*, XLIII (1924), 294-310; J. G. Torralba, "Decálogo ritual, Ex 34, 10-26," *EstBibl*, XX (1961), 407-21.

[14] For details, see Alt, Elliger, and Rabast.

[15] K. Galling, "Der Beichtspiegel, eine gattungsgeschichtliche Studie," *ZAW*, XLVIII (1929), 125-30.

the Book of the Covenant and the Holiness Code (Exod. 21:12, 15-17; 22:18-19 [Eng. 22:19-20]; Lev. 20:2, 9-13, 15-16, 27; 24:16); the sentences of this series are constructed in participial style, e.g., "Whoever curses [literally, 'one cursing'] his father or his mother shall be put to death"; (*b*) the series of curses in Deut. 27:15-26; here each sentence begins with the threat of punishment "Cursed be . . . ," followed by a statement of the crime in participial style. The dependence of this latter series on Leviticus 18, the *môt-yûmāt* series, and the socio-ethical ideas of Deuteronomic theology suggests that it may well have been framed during the period when Deuteronomic theology was most influential.

C. We come next to the casuistic laws. These follow precisely the usual style of ancient Near Eastern law, elucidating in detail various legal questions in order to regulate daily life and the performance of the cult. Their content, too, is for the most part borrowed from ancient Near Eastern law, particularly Canaanite law; the influence of Yahwism, however, has not rarely occasioned changes. This process began immediately after the occupation of Canaan; in the course of time, numerous other laws of this sort came into being as a result of changing conditions. At first the borrowing and framing of laws was in the hands of the elders, the heads of the families and tribes. The priests shared in this activity and continued it. Later, the process passed to *tôpᵉśê hattôrâ,* "those who administer the law" (i.e., those who, like the scribes in the period of early Judaism, apply the law to the case at hand), and the monarchy.

The casuistic laws are assembled by interpolation or by combination (Hempel*). Exod. 21:12-17 is an example of interpolation: between two apodictic laws of the *môt-yûmāt* series is inserted the rule governing asylum, which relates to the first law concerning manslaughter:

> But if he did not lie in wait for him . . . , then I will appoint for you a place to which he may flee. But if a man willfully attacks another to kill him treacherously, you shall take him from my altar, that he may die.

When laws are assembled by combination, all possibilities relating to a particular case are brought together; only the alternation between second and third person, as in Exod. 21:2-4, reveals the principle of composition:

> When you buy a Hebrew slave, he shall serve six years, and in the seventh he shall go out free, for nothing. If he comes in single, he shall go out single; if he comes in married, then his wife shall go out with him. If his master gives him a wife and she bears him sons or daughters, the wife and her children shall be her master's and he shall go out alone.

D. Finally, we come to the etiological legal narrative, which is connected with the legal material proper. These narratives derive legal practices from things done by Israel's ancestors; their function at some time was certainly to regulate conduct, and they must have had the character of directives. Such narratives can determine cultic practices; Exod. 12:27, for example, institutes a Passover custom, and Exod. 13:14-15 justifies the sacrifice of the firstborn. In addition, such narratives sometimes relate legal cases and decisions; in these instances the real purpose of the narrative is made quite clear, as in Numbers 9, which directs that those who are unclean or away on a journey are to celebrate the Passover later; Num. 15:32-36, which describes the stoning of a man who had violated the sabbath; and Numbers 27 and 36, which guarantee the right of a daughter to inherit.

4. *Rhetorical forms in legal proceedings.* Numerous forms that are frequently employed in the discourses of the prophets are associated with legal proceedings. Boecker mentions (*a*) the forms used in the dispute before court action: the summons to hand over the accused, the formulas of accusation and appeasement used in the pretrial dispute, the forms intended to avert the trial, the appeals of the accused and the plaintiff, and the form introducing an arraignment. Then follow (*b*) the rhetorical forms used in the trial itself: the accusations, the defenses (both personal and on behalf of others), the formulas of admission, and the settlement proposals. These are followed by (*c*) the concluding forms: the various forms of verdict and sentence. In addition, we can isolate (*d*) the forms used in civil law, in cases having to do with family and property, especially as everywhere in the ancient Near East the courts performed the functions of a notary. This category includes particularly invitations to purchase property and the procedure formally termed "purchasing a bride." [16] All these forms show how greatly legal procedures influenced the life of an Israelite.

5. *Treaties and contracts.* In Israel, as throughout the entire ancient Near East, treaties and contracts played an important role. The OT, however, usually describes the concluding of a treaty or contract without relating its content. Formally, we may distinguish four kinds of contract (Hempel): (*a*) the mutual contract between equal partners, which, especially in the earlier period, expresses a reciprocal relationship of solidarity with all the rights and duties that this implies for the contracting parties, so that they are linked together by a common bond (Pedersen); (*b*) the treaty or contract by which a powerful person binds himself, placing himself in a relationship toward a weaker party according to which he undertakes to perform certain conditions, while the weaker party has no active significance (Begrich); (*c*) the suzerainty or vassal treaty, in which certain obligations are placed upon the weaker party, while the powerful party restricts himself to general pledges of loyalty; the treaties made by the Hittites with their vassals fall into this category (Mendenhall); (*d*) the treaty or contract that a third party establishes between two others, like that found in one of the Mari letters (Noth), without mention of the obligations imposed on the parties to the treaty. When such treaties or contracts are concluded, not only are the conditions stipulated, but many kinds of ritual are also performed,[17] such as a mingling of the parties' blood or sprinkling with blood (Exod. 24:8), a handclasp (Ezek. 17:18), exchange of personal property (I Sam. 18:3-4), setting up a stela (Josh. 24:26), an oath (Gen. 21:22-24),

[16] W. Plautz, "Die Form der Eheschliessung im Alten Testament," *ZAW*, LXXVI (194), 298-318.

[17] Cf. D. J. McCarthy, "Three Covenants in Genesis," *CBQ*, XXVI (1964), 179-89.

a meal (Exod. 24:11), or the process described in Gen. 15:9-11, whereby whoever violates the contract calls down a curse upon himself (Jer. 34:18).

With regard to the persons or groups between which such treaties or contracts are concluded in the OT, we once more find four types:

A. Treaties are concluded between political entities or their representatives, such as that between Solomon and the king of Tyre (I Kings 5:16-26 [Eng. 5:2-12]; this passage probably follows the formulation of the treaty itself). The treaties of Abraham and Isaac with Abimelech of Gerar (Gen. 21: 22-33; 26:26-30), of Jacob with Laban (Gen. 31:44-50), and of Joshua with the people of Gibeon (Josh. 9:15) are to be understood in the same way. The text of a treaty is preserved in I Macc. 8:22 ff.

B. When a king is chosen or appointed, treaties are concluded between the future ruler and the people or their representatives,[18] as in the case of David (II Sam. 5:3), Joash (II Kings 11:17), and Josiah (II Kings 23:1-3). I Kings 12 gives us a glimpse of the customary proceedings, which in this case, however, come to a negative conclusion. I Sam. 10:11; 10:21*b*-27*a*; Hos. 6:7-11*a*; 10:3-4 also presuppose or mention a royal treaty.

C. There is frequent reference to contracts between individuals, such as that between Abraham and Ephron for the purchase of the cave of Machpelah (Genesis 23), that made by Jeremiah for the purchase of a field (Jeremiah 32), and that made by Boaz for Ruth (Ruth 4). The proceedings are described in detail; Jeremiah 32 mentions the two copies of the contract. The content of such contracts, however, is scarcely mentioned; Gen. 23:16-17 may contain a quotation from one of them. Tobit 7:16 mentions a marriage contract, Jer. 3:8, a deed of divorce.

D. Finally, the treaty or contract form was extended to the relationship between God and man (Abraham) or God and Israel, although the prophets prefer personal categories and use kinship terminology to define this relationship. The use of such legal metaphors under these circumstances is not without theological difficulties. Of course the Sinai covenant is based on the primitive treaty relationship, which forges a common bond between the two parties and places them in a common milieu. Later, apparently, the royal treaty provided the pattern (Fohrer). Recently the Hittite vassal treaties have been cited and parallelism has been established between their formulation and one type of covenant document, the "covenant formulation" (Baltzer), especially in the decalogues Exodus 20 and 34, as well as Deuteronomy 4; 29–30, and Joshua 24. The pattern runs as follows: opening formula, events leading up to the making of the treaty, declaration of purpose, individual stipulations, list of witnesses, blessings and curses. Seen from this point of view, the form of the covenant appears constant from the earliest period down to the latest. The connection between the Exodus and Sinai traditions, which recent analysis of the Pentateuch

[18] There is no antithesis between election and the charismatic principle. The election is not an election in the democratic sense, but signifies recognition of a demonstrated charisma.

has frequently cast doubt upon, would then be grounded in a treaty formulation as the original form-critical unit and in the Decalogue as a formal and objective unit. This derivation of the covenant form from the vassal treaties may be attractive, but there are many objections to it.

In this connection we shall mention only three points:

a) McCarthy bases his study not only on the Hittite vassal treaties but also on the earlier, pre-Hittite material of the ancient Near East, the treaties from Syria and Assyria, and the Hittite parity treaties. He arrives at a common treaty-form that was used for international agreements throughout almost the entire history of the ancient Near East in the pre-Hellenistic period; the Syrian-Assyrian and Hittite forms show a few idiosyncrasies. The mere appearance of the treaty-form therefore does not provide any point of reference for dating. The OT texts using the treaty-form need not go back to the original appearance of the literary type (the Hittite Empire), but could be linked with any contemporary events.

b) The Sinai covenant does not follow the treaty pattern. Even the historical question of how this is supposed to have taken place in the desert wilderness of northern Arabia is difficult to answer—all the more so if we are to restrict ourselves to Hittite vassal treaties. The existing parallels are more likely due to later editing and reshaping of the narratives. Even the alleged parallels themselves are dubious, as a few examples show: the first-person introduction "I am Yahweh" (Exod. 20:2) is not formally equivalent to "Thus [says] the sun Mursilis"; the corresponding parallel is rather "Thus says Yahweh." Neither can the mention of the deliverance from Egypt, Israel's basic confession of faith, be equated with the ancient Near Eastern recitation of events leading up to the treaty (e.g., "Although you were sick, I, the sun, have set you in the place of your father."). The relationship of Israel to Yahweh does not correspond to the bond between a vassal and his lord. Furthermore, Exod. 20:2 is not even an original part of the text; it is a Deuteronomistic expansion (Schmidt, Fohrer).

c) In point of fact, from the pre-Deuteronomic period there is little reference to a divine "covenant" (treaty) with Israel. The first sources to speak frequently of such a covenant are those representing Deuteronomic theology, the Priestly source of the Pentateuch, and other late texts (Jepsen). There is a lacuna of centuries between the Sinai covenant, conceived in nomadic terms, and covenant theology proper. The texts cited for the "covenant formulation" have been subjected to Deuteronomic or Deuteronomistic redaction. It is therefore not true that there was at the outset a strict, legalistic conception, which was later transformed and qualified on the basis of theological reservations. It is more accurate to say that, starting with Deuteronomic theology, when the covenant idea came to the fore, it was to some extent formulated in legalistic terms on the basis of the royal treaty. The "covenant formulation" was never completely realized; even in Deuteronomy and the Priestly source we find only a certain degree of approximation to the treaty concept of the ancient Near East.

§ 9 The Requesting and Wishing Literary Types and Their Traditions

H. C. Brichto, *The Problem of "Curse" in the Hebrew Bible,* 1963; F. C. Fensham, "Malediction and Benediction in Ancient Near Eastern Vassal Treaties and the Old Testament," *ZAW,* LXXIV (1962), 1-9; J. Hempel, "Die israelitischen Anschauungen von Segen und Fluch im Lichte altorientalischer Parallelen," *ZDMG,* LXXIX (1925), 20-110 (= *Apoxysmata,* 1961, pp. 30-113); F. Horst, "Segen und Segenhandlungen in der Bibel," *EvTh,* VII (1947/48), 23-37 (= *Gottes Recht,* 1961, pp. 188-202); *idem,* "Der Eid im Alten Testament," *ibid.,* XVII (1957), 366-84 (= *Gottes Recht,* pp. 292-314); I. Lande, *Formelhafte Wendungen der Umgangssprache im Alten Testament,* 1949; S. Mowinckel, *Psalmenstudien V: Segen und Fluch in Israels Kult- und Psalmdichtung,* 1924; *idem, The Psalms in Israel's Worship,* II, 1962, pp. 44-52; M. Noth, " 'Die mit des Gesetzes Werken umgehen, die sind unter dem Fluch'," in *Bulmerincq-Gedenkschrift,* 1938, pp. 127-45 (= *Gesammelte Studien zum Alten Testament,* 1957, pp. 155-71 [Eng. *The Laws in the Pentateuch, and Other Studies,* 1966]); J. Pedersen, *Der Eid bei den Semiten,* 1914; H. Schmidt, "Grüsse und Glückwünsche im Psalter," *ThStKr,* CIII (1931), 141-50.

1. *Request and wish.* The request was no less common in the life of the Israelite than among other peoples, even when we except for the time being requests directed to Yahweh, which were especially frequent in laments (§39.3). In daily life men ask for little things like bread (Gen. 47:15) or water (I Kings 17:10), as well as a woman (Judg. 14:3) or a favor that may mean life or death (Gen. 12:13). One can also address a request to the king (II Sam. 14:4: "Help, O king"), because it is his duty to provide such help and deliverance.[1] The imperative form of the verb usually expresses the request for a desired action (e.g., "Help!"). The written context shows here that we are dealing with a request and not a command; on the occasion of an actual request, the intonation naturally shows the same thing. In order to give the request a more polite and at the same time more urgent form, the speaker may begin, "Be pleased to . . . " (Judg. 19:6; II Kings 6:3). The phrase "to find favor in the eyes of someone" also serves to express politeness; it sometimes merely corresponds to "please" appended to a request (Gen. 18:3; 47:29). In addition, without an overt expression of a request, this same phrase may imply the wish that what has been asked for in secret may be granted (II Sam. 15:25). It may also express the request of a dependent or weak person that a promise made to him be fulfilled (II Sam. 16:4) or that permission for something be granted (Ruth 2:2, 10).

Like the request, the wish permeates all of life; on special occasions, it can take on the character of a benediction. Such a wish accompanies the woman who leaves her parental house (Gen. 24:60); we find a similar wish in Ruth 4:11. At the accession of a king, a wish rings out on behalf of the king's life: "Long live the king!" (I Sam. 10:24).

[1] On the meaning of this verb, cf. G. Fohrer in *ThW,* VII, 907-81.

The contrary-to-fact wish is usually introduced by the formula *mî yittēn,* "who gives?" in the sense of "who could give?" or "who might give?" It is directed to a person or power from whom one can receive what he wishes—primarily, therefore, to God. Lande has traced the development of this formula through a wealth of examples: from a simple question (Job 31:31) through a question expressing a wish (Judg. 9:29; Ps. 55:7 [Eng. 55:6]), it gradually turns into a precatory particle through the addition of a verb (Exod. 16:3; Job 6:8) and finally becomes a mere particle without any addition (Deut. 5:26 [Eng. 5:29]; Job 19:23).

2. *Formulas of salutation.* All salutations have the form of wishes. They are based originally on the concept of the efficacious spoken word, so that they impart what they express to the person addressed.

We come first to *šālôm,* "success, prosperity, well-being," which is wished in the ancient salutation formula *šālôm lᵉkā,* "May you have prosperity." By means of this formula, the speaker establishes a state of harmony and peace with the person addressed, who can then feel secure. The wish can be extended to family and property (I Sam. 25:6) or reduced to a mere "How do you do?" (II Sam. 20:9). Its formulaic employment in II Sam. 8:10 appears to signify a recognition of political dependence. The expression can also be used as a farewell formula: "Go prosperously [RSV: 'Go in peace']," as in Exod. 4:18; as an official formula of dismissal (II Sam. 15:9); or as a formula to cut off discussion, in the sense of "Enough!" (II Kings 4:23).

In addition, the verb "to bless" can be used for salutation, especially in the formula "Blessed be you in Yahweh [or: ' . . . as far as Yahweh is concerned']," which wishes blessing on the person addressed and imparts it to him (I Sam. 15:13). This is the usual form of greeting when the speaker is grateful to the addressee for a favor or wants to praise him. It is a salutation expressing special recognition or a more than normal measure of politeness.

Finally, we come to the salutation "Yahweh is [or: 'be'] with you" (Judg. 6:12; Ruth 2:4), which is also ambiguous: it can be either a statement of fact or a wish.

3. *Blessings and curses.* Those sayings and formulas that wish or impart a blessing or a curse possess efficacious power to an even greater degree, the more so because they derive from the realm of magic, with its belief in efficacious and irrevocable words; their effect is increased by their metrical form, repetition, and accompanying action. A curse can be placed upon a land (Deut. 11:29), affect a city (Josh. 6:26), consume a house (Zech. 5:4), and determine the fate of whole nations (Gen. 9:25), provided God does not transform its power into blessing (Numbers 22–24) or turn it upon the curser himself (Gen. 12:3). A blessing is usually introduced by *bārûk,* "Blessed (be) . . . ," a curse by *'ārûr,* "Cursed (be) . . . ." A curse consists of motivation clause, curse-formula, and a description of its consequences, e.g., Gen. 3:14. Curses are found in the legal milieu: as a conditional curse referring to a single or repeated action (Josh. 6:26; Deut. 27:15-26), as an oath (Job 31), or, in attenuated form, as a prayer against enemies (Ps. 109:6-20). A blessing often contains

imperatives. We find a blessing in conditional form combined with a ceremony of blessing in Gen. 27:27-40 and a cultic blessing in Num. 6:24-26; blessings also are associated with salutations, with meals, and with other occasions.

A. Theoretically any man can pronounce a blessing or a curse, most efficaciously when he is on the point of death. The purpose may be to reward good or evil deeds (Ruth 2:20; Prov. 11:26), inflict punishment upon an animal (Gen. 3:14-15) or a man (Gen. 4:11; 9:25-27), or transform a curse into a blessing (Judg. 17:2). There are also general blessings, e.g., at harvest time (Ps. 129:8; Ruth 2:4), on the occasion of a departure (I Sam. 20:42), or to express favor (Gen. 43:29). Sometimes a speaker may seek to avoid an actual curse by paraphrase, e.g., by using the sentence "May God do so to you and more also" (I Sam. 3:17) or by substituting the verb "to bless" for "to curse" (Job 1:5; RSV translates "curse"). The word *'āmēn* ("So be it") serves to ratify a blessing or a curse (Jer. 11:5).

B. The blessings and curses addressed to the patriarchs (Gen. 12:1-3; 14:19; 22:16-18; 28:13-15) or placed in their mouths (Gen. 27:27-29, 39-40; 48:15-16, 20) were thought to have particular power. The Blessing of Moses (Deuteronomy 33) in its present form is also a blessing composed of tribal sayings (§8.1); Genesis 49 and II Samuel 23 are similar. The sayings are directed primarily to the ancestors of the people blessed by God or to the groups and tribes considered their descendants, whose later fortunes are thus traced back to the early period.

C. A priest in particular has authority to bless and curse. By "putting the name of Yahweh upon the people of Israel," he gives effect to God's blessing (Num. 6:27), thereby transforming the originally magical formulas "Blessed (be) . . ." and "Cursed (be) . . ." into wishes referring to Yahweh: "Blessed [or: 'Cursed'] be . . . by [or: 'in the presence of'] Yahweh." This form then leads to the form of priestly intercession. Blessing and cursing also become cultic acts, which the community ratifies with its "Amen," affirming its adherence to what has been proclaimed (Deut. 27:13-26). Above all, it is a priest's duty to confer blessing, using, for example, the form of the so-called Aaronic blessing, Num. 6:24-26.

D. The formula "Blessed [or: 'Praised'] be Yahweh" took on the character of a thanksgiving, to be followed by a statement of the reason: Yahweh's favor, which is the cause for rejoicing and for which he is praised. The speaker may thank Yahweh for a favor shown him personally (I Sam. 25:32), for a favor shown the person he is addressing (Ruth 4:14), or for favors shown a third party (I Kings 5:21 [Eng. 5:7]).

4. *Oaths*. In a certain sense, the oath formula is a kind of curse. The speaker binds himself to do or not to do something, or swears that he has done or not done something, and to vouch for the accuracy of his statement pledges his own life (Num. 14:21), the life of the person addressed (I Sam. 1:26), or the life of Yahweh (I Sam. 14:39); in Gen. 42:15 he pledges the life of the king. An unfulfilled oath then has the effect of a curse. "As I live" means: "I will not remain alive if I have [or: 'have not'] done this or that."

§10 The Proclaiming and Instructing Literary Types and Their Traditions

J. Begrich, "Das priesterliche Heilsorakel," *ZAW*, LII (1934), 81-92 (= *Gesammelte Studien zum Alten Testament*, 1964, pp. 217-31); *idem*, "Die priesterliche Tora," in BZAW, LXVI (1936), 63-88 (= *Gesammelte Studien zum Alten Testament*, pp. 232-60); S. H. Blank, "The Curse, the Blasphemy, the Spell, and the Oath," *HUCA*, XXXIII (1950/51), 73-95; K. Elliger, "Zur Analyse des Sündopfergesetzes," in *Rudolph-Festschrift*, 1961, pp. 39-50; K. Galling, "Der Beichtspiegel," *ZAW*, XLVII (1929), 125-30; E. Grant, "Oracle in the Old Testament," *AJSL*, XXXIX (1922/23), 257-81; K. Koch, "Tempeleinlassliturgien und Dekaloge," in *Von Rad-Festschrift*, 1961, pp. 45-60; F. Küchler, "Das priesterliche Orakel in Israel und Juda," in BZAW, XXXIII (1918), 285-301; I. Lande, *Formelhafte Wendungen der Umgangssprache im Alten Testament*, 1949; J. Lindblom, "Lotcasting in the Old Testament," *VT*, XII (1962), 164-78; A. Lods, "Le rôle des oracles dans la nomination des rois, des prêtres et des magistrats chez les Israélites, les Égyptiens et les Grecs," in *Mélanges Maspéro*, I (1934), 91-100; G. Östborn, *Tora in the Old Testament*, 1945; R. Press, "Das Ordal im alten Israel," *ZAW*, LI (1933), 121-40, 227-55; R. Rendtorff, *Die Gesetze in der Priesterschrift*, 1954; E. Robertson, "The 'Urīm and Tummīm," *VT*, XIV (1964), 67-74.

1. *Oracles*. Notwithstanding the discovery that cult prophets as well as priests could carry on their activities at the various sanctuaries (§ 52), the priestly oracle is probably distinct from that spoken by the cult prophet. Its origin does not lie in unusual experiences, perhaps even of esctatic nature; it is characterized instead by the use of standard oracular techniques and liturgical formulas. In the preexilic period, the offering of sacrifice is only a minor function of the priest; his major function is, when people visit the sanctuary with requests and inquiries, to communicate to them the divine response, which will determine their destiny, and the divine instruction, which will regulate their lives. In addition, many of the oracles to be discussed here were obtained by laymen.

A. With respect to the techniques employed, we find occasional reference or allusion to practices current in the ancient Near East: the obtaining of omens by observation of the flight of birds (Gen. 15:11) or of water in a cup (Gen. 44:5), the discovery of God's decision from plants or rods that sprout and turn green in the sanctuary (Num. 17:16-26 [Eng. 17:1-11]) and the changing sound of the wind in the trees (II Sam. 5:22-24), by means of oracular staffs (Hos. 4:12) or spending the night in the sanctuary (incubation; Gen. 28:10-22; I Samuel 3; I Kings 3:5-15). In addition, although prohibited, necromancy was practiced and defended (I Sam. 28:7-25; Isa. 8:19). Foreign techniques such as hepatoscopy and divination by arrows are also known (Ezek. 21:26 [Eng. 21:21]).

The most important form of divination in Israel is the casting of lots by means of Urim and Thummim. A question that could be answered with *yes* or *no* would be brought before the deity; if the former oracle appeared, the answer was negative (*'ûrîm*, "cursed"); if the latter, the answer was positive (*tummîm*, "innocent [?]"). The original meaning of the expressions suggests that this oracle was first used to settle legal disputes.

B. In the casting of lots, the form of the oracle is a positive or negative answer to the question asked, especially in the period of Saul and David (I Sam. 23:2, 11). Alternatively, we may find the use of a fixed liturgical formula, which does not discuss the particular situation in detail: "Go in peace, and the God of Israel grant your petition which you have made to him" (I Sam. 1:17). This simple form is sometimes insufficient; more precise instructions are needed, like those given in II Sam. 5:23-24. In such cases, the oracle can take on metrical structure, like the oracle given to Rebecca (Gen. 25:23), which follows the pattern of a priestly pronouncement. The full form of the later positive oracle, the priestly oracle of favor (*Heilsorakel*), can be reconstructed by analogy to the prophetic words of favor and salvation used by Deutero-Isaiah (§53.4): it probably comprised a promise of divine intervention on behalf of the person seeking help, a statement of the expected consequences of this divine intervention, and a statement of the purpose behind Yahweh's favorable response. Some of the psalms presuppose oracles of this type, which are the reason for the abrupt transition from lament to thanksgiving (§39.3).

C. The oracle itself, which comes from Yahweh, is frequently in the first person, representing the *ipsissima verba* of God. On occasion Yahweh is spoken of in the third person (Pss. 20:7 [Eng. 20:6]; 85:9-14 [Eng. 85:8-13]). In addition, we find references to God's appearance in a theophany (Gen. 17:1; 26:24; 28:13; 46:3); on the assumption that such an appearance always produces fear and terror in the person addressed, it is followed by the admonition "Fear not."

2. *Judgment by ordeal.* Another task entrusted primarily to the priests is the investigation of doubtful situations. God's judgment is determined through an ordeal. An unknown criminal can be discovered by casting lots (Josh. 7:14-21). The guilt of an accused man can be ascertained through a technical procedure, e.g., an ordeal by drinking, such as that used in cases of suspected marital infidelity (Num. 5:11-31). In an ordeal of this type the curse pronounced becomes effective in the case of an actual transgression, revealing God's judgment of guilt or innocence. Finally, it is possible to prove one's innocence through an oath of purgation and voluntary acceptance of a curse—in the belief, once more, that the curse will be effective in case of guilt (Ps. 7:4-6 [Eng. 7:3-5]). For this purpose the oath formula is employed, which contains an abbreviated self-curse.

3. *Torah.* Torah is instruction, delivered orally; it is the information and advice concerning a specific question or situation given by a priest to a layman, e.g., to help him avoid actions that would make him accursed and perform actions that will bring blessing. The activity of the priests in this field was of the greatest significance.

A. Cultic torah provides instruction in questions involving cultic procedures, e.g., the distinctions between clean and unclean, sacred and profane. Haggai, for example (albeit for his own purposes), obtains the torah of the priests on the question whether cultic cleanness and uncleanness are infectious (Hag. 2:10-14). In Zech. 7:1-3; 8:18-19, a related question is asked of the priests and cult prophets: should the fast in memory of the conquest of Jerusalem be observed in the future? Zechariah undertakes to answer this question himself. There are also prophetical imitations of such torah, e.g., Isa. 1:10-17; 33:14-16; Mic. 6:6-8; the introduction in Isa. 1:10 probably is based on a common formula, but with the mention of Israel replaced by that of Sodom and Gomorrah:

Hear the word of Yahweh,
you rulers of Sodom!
Give ear to the teaching of our God,
you people of Gomorrah!

B. The entrance torah or torah liturgy investigates whether the necessary conditions for admission to the sanctuary have been fulfilled; for this purpose it may employ a "guide for self-examination" (*Beichtspiegel*), as is clearly the case in Pss. 15 and 24:3-6, where the lists of conditions are for the most part ethical.[1] Psalm 15 probably exhibits the typical pattern: a question asked of the priest by the arriving worshiper, the priest's reply (torah), a statement of assurance given by the priest. The instructions concerning the conditions of the relationship between Yahweh and Israel in Psalms 50, 81, and 95, communicated within a semiliturgical framework, are constructed according to this model. A late derivative of this literary type is the warning affixed to the Jerusalem temple in the late period prohibiting non-Jews from entering.

C. It is certain that the priests also provided information and instruction in general legal questions, so that it is proper to speak of legal torah. The priest would instruct the ignorant or resolve a difficult and obscure case. The decisions arrived at in this way could even develop into new law, as was common elsewhere in the ancient Near East.

4. *Cultic regulations and priestly professional lore.* Cultic regulations and the technical knowledge of priestly professional lore are resources constantly drawn upon by the priests in their work; among their major purposes is the training of young priests.

A. Cultic regulations like those drawn upon in the books of Numbers and Leviticus provide instruction concerning the work of a priest or lay down the criteria by which he must reach his decisions. Among other material they contain rules governing the various kinds of sacrifices, the recognition and treatment of skin ailments, and clean and unclean animals or conditions. They are easily stripped of their disguise as Yahweh's words to Moses. Removal of the corresponding introductory formula and transformation of the direct address or second person pronoun into the third person in most cases restores the original form. Furthermore, many superscriptions or subscriptions have been introduced, which make it easier to separate the various units, e.g., Lev. 6:2, 7, 18 (Eng. 6:9, 14, 25). In this fashion we arrive at a whole series of instruc-

[1] On the series of ten items, cf. §8.2.

tions for priestly service that derive from the living practice of the cult and preserve at least a nucleus dating from the preexilic period.

B. There are also other kinds of information and instruction distinct from the cultic regulations in that they represent small isolated units joined together in collections without any formal or material unity. They are also meant for the priesthood, and are in fact excerpts from the professional lore of the priests. Leviticus 11–15, for example, contains material of this sort.

5. *Approval, rejection, rebuke.* We must mention, finally, the formulas of daily life that express approval, rejection, or rebuke or else give instruction in this realm. A statement of approval, declaring that a thing is appropriate and well-conceived, can be made by a simple "Good!" (Gen. 1:31; Isa. 41:7); approval of a suggestion can be expressed by the phrase "The thing is good" (Deut. 1:14). Such a statement may mean only that success is expected (II Sam. 15:3). In addition, however, we find ethical judgment expressed in statements of disapproval using the forms "This thing is not good" (I Sam. 26:16) and "Such a thing ought not to be done" (Gen. 34:7). The latter form may include the phrase ". . . in Israel" (II Sam. 13:12) or be expanded (Gen. 20:9).

Questions, variously formulated, demanding an implied negative reply, can communicate definite rejection, particularly the question "What have I to do with you?" (II Sam. 16:10; translated incorrectly Judg. 11:12; I Kings 17:18). This form can also express rejection of all association with someone or something (II Sam. 16:10; II Kings 9:18-19).

The questions "What are you doing?" or "What have you done?" express rebuke. Originally they were meant to be instructive. A person asks the question, perhaps pointing at the same time to a poorly executed piece of work, in order to alert the person addressed to his mistake and urge him to reflect on it. With this as its point of departure, the idiom gradually became a general form of rebuke (Num. 23:11; Judg. 8:1).

§11 The Communicating Literary Types and Their Traditions

D. R. Ap-Thomas, "Some Notes on Old Testament Attitude to Prayer," *SJTh*, IX (1956), 422-29; G. Beer, "Zur israelitisch-jüdischen Briefliteratur," in BWAT, XIII (1913), 20-41; S. H. Blank, "Some Observations Concerning Biblical Prayer," *HUCA*, XXXII (1961), 75-90; P. A. H. de Boer, *De Voorbede in het Oude Testament*, 1943; A. Greiff, *Das Gebet im Alten Testament*, 1915; F. Hesse, *Die Fürbitte im Alten Testament*, Dissertation, Erlangen, 1949; B. Hornig, "Das Prosagebet der nachexilischen Literatur," *ThLZ*, LXXXIII (1958), 644-46; P. J. Huijser, "Prediking in het Oude Testament," *GThT*, XLII (1941), 165-82, 193-208, 241-55; N. B. Johnson, *Prayer in the Apocrypha and Pseudepigrapha*, 1948; I. Lande, *Formelhafte Wendungen der Umgangssprache im Alten Testament*, 1949; J. Marty, "Contribution à l'étude de fragments épistolaire antiques, conservés principalement dans la Bible Hébraïque," in *Mélanges Syriens Dussaud*, II (1939), 845-55; J. Naveh, "A Hebrew Letter from the Seventh Century B.C.," *IEJ*, X (1960), 129-39; O. Plöger, "Reden und Gebete im deuteronomistischen und chronistischen Geschichtswerk," in *Dehn-Festschrift*, 1957, pp. 35-49; G. von Rad, "Die levitische Predigt in den Büchern der Chronik," in *Procksch-Festschrift*, 1934, pp. 113-24; H. Torczyner *et al.*, Lachish I: *The Lachish Letters*, 1938; E. Vogt, "Ostracon Hebraicum saec. 7 a. C.," *Bibl*, XLI (1960), 183-84; XLII (1961), 135-36; A. Wendel, *Das israelitisch-jüdische Gelübde*, 1931; *idem*, *Das freie Laiengebet im vorexilischen Israel*, 1932; S. Yeivin, "The Judicial Petition from Meẕad Ḫashavyāhū," *BiOr*, XIX (1962), 3-10.

1. *Conversation.* In the literature of the OT, as in the life of ancient Israel, conversations play an important role. They begin with a series of relatively fixed idioms and motifs. First of these may be the salutation when the participants in the conversation first meet (§9.2). If a person notices someone else to whom he would like to speak but who is unaware of the person's presence, he may call or address the other person. One calls a person who is at a considerable distance; the person of higher rank merely uses the name of the person of lower rank (Gen. 21:17). The form of address may be the traditional terms of relationship with pronominal suffix, e.g., "my father" (Gen. 48:18), the mere name of the person of lower rank (I Sam. 17:55), the general title of respect "my lord" (Gen. 23:6), a title, or a term of rank or position (II Kings 6:26; 9:5). Conversation often begins with the reply "Here I am." Conversations are frequently introduced by such formalized expressions as the demonstrative particle "Behold!" the imperative "See," or the condensed idiom "*bî*, my lord," i.e, "Upon me, my lord, [let fall any unpleasant or detrimental outcome of our conversation]." The beginning of a conversation may also include questions of origin and destination. A stranger may be asked his name, what family he belongs to and from what land he comes, what his business is or where he is heading; he may then be invited to dinner or to spend the night. There is a corresponding form with which the stranger introduces himself; this form was also applied to Yahweh. An acquaintance may be asked where he is coming from, where he is going, and what he intends to do.

Independent of the conversation's content, there is also a relatively fixed framework within which it continues. After the introductory formulas, it is continued by "and now," "and then," or mere "and"; it may be enlivened by the imperatives "see," "hear," by verbal summons in the sense of "now then," or by "as you well know." To emphasize a point or enhance the conversation, the speaker may place the subject before the predicate, use the independent pronouns, mention the sense organs involved in an action (Jer. 26:11), or use the negative instead of or in addition to the positive expression of an idea (II Kings 20:1). Especially when using court syle, the speaker may refer to himself as the "slave [RSV: 'servant']" (II Sam. 11:21) or "son" (I Sam. 25:8) of the person addressed, employ derogatory terms for himself (I Sam. 24:15 [Eng. 24:14]), or, in solemn contexts, use his own name and speak of himself in the third person (II Sam. 24:23).

Single divisions of a conversation can be concluded by repeating an important sentence (I Kings 18:11-14). The whole conversation is sometimes ended—in agreement or disagreement—with "enough" (Gen. 45:28; §9.2). When the situation calls for it, a standard "good-bye" may be used.

2. *Formal speeches.* It is safe to assume that Israel had some formal art of rhetoric and that speeches had fixed forms. For instance, the speaker begins with a summons, calling people to assemble. He calls for silence and demands attention, names the persons he is addressing, and indicates the importance of his theme; only then does he begin his actual exposition. His goal, of course, differs somewhat from that of the modern speaker. He does not seek to convince his hearers by means of theoretical and rational arguments; he tries instead to achieve his purposes by influencing their wills directly. His argumentation therefore consists of repetition and assurances. At the same time, he gives full rein to the suggestive power of his words, into which he pours all his energy and enthusiasm, until he finally exhausts whatever resistance his hearers may have had and they deny what they previously had believed, as Job nearly succumbs to the speeches of his friends (Job 19:2). In a rhetorical contest the victor is he who can put the most power in his words, regardless of whether his reasoning is sound or not. It should not be forgotten, of course, that behind this propagandistic rhetoric lies the firm assurance that the truth, when presented, is capable of convincing others. This holds true also for speeches before a court of law (§8.4) and the dialogic disputes of the wisdom teachers (§50.9).

A. The political speech, therefore, is frequently used to wean away the supporters of a political opponent and to weaken a foreign enemy by shaking his followers' confidence in his leadership. Jotham, for instance, attempts to persuade the men of Shechem by means of his famous fable (Judg. 9:7-20; §47.6); the Assyrian ambassador makes a similar attempt to persuade the besieged Jerusalemites to cease resistance (II Kings 18:17-35). To achieve their purpose, such speeches condemn the conduct of the present leaders and depict its devastating consequences, then go on to praise the new leadership as "all sunshine and flowers" (Eissfeldt*).

B. Before a battle, the leader delivers a speech showing the necessity for fighting; he makes reference to Yahweh and the ancestral heritage, which must be preserved. He then expresses his confidence in a successful outcome and exhorts to the courage that prefers death to defeat. The proverbial statement that a living dog is better than a dead lion (Eccles. 9:4) seems to have enjoyed wide acceptance in its practical consequences. We find speeches, often quite brief, in the words of Joab before the double battle against the Ammonites and Arameans (II Sam. 10:12) and those of Jehoshaphat before the battle against the Ammonites and Moabites (II Chron. 20:20), and later in the speeches of the Maccabees (I Macc. 9; 13). The enemy, on the other hand, are urged to retire from the hopeless battle (II Sam. 2:25-26; II Chron. 13:4-12).

Deut. 20:5-8 contains a summons of a very different sort to be addressed to the army: certain categories of persons are to return home—those that have built a new house and not yet dedicated it, those that have planted a vineyard and not yet enjoyed its harvest, those that have betrothed a wife and not yet married her, together with those that are fearful and fainthearted. This dispensation ultimately goes back to demonic conceptions, which required the exclusion of certain taboo persons from the general levy.[1]

C. The farewell address of the spiritual or political leader, with which he takes his leave of his supporters or his people before his death or before undertaking a new task, looks back upon history to urge the hearers to remain faithful to the heritage of their fathers, and at the same time points to duties performed or tasks yet to be undertaken. We have such speeches from Joshua (Josh. 23–24) through Samuel (I Sam. 12) and David (I Kings 2) down to the Maccabees (I Macc. 2). None of these speeches, however, is extant in its original form; all have been subjected to later theological revision, or, under the influence of preaching, have been given a quite unhistorical form.

3. *Preaching*. The preaching of the priests and Levites, as religious discourse, is a composite literary type. It is influenced by priestly and liturgical torah; historical retrospection, like that in Psalms 78 and 106, transforms it into exhortation with a historical background. In addition, it has been influenced by the political speech and by prophetical and wisdom discourse. For these reasons, it is obviously a late type. We find it first in the framework of Deuteronomy and in the Deuteronomistic sections of Joshua–Kings. It is characterized by exhortation linked with reference to history, in which the past is presented as a chain of God's gracious acts placing Israel under a constant debt of gratitude (Eissfeldt*).

There are no sermons preached by the prophets, not even Jeremiah and Ezekiel; for their words are metrical, while preaching is always in prose. This literary type did influence the proclamation of the prophets in one way, however: many of Jeremiah's and Ezekiel's discourses are unusually large in scope and are modeled after the style of spontaneous speech.

4. *Prayers*. Apart from poetic types found in the psalms, which are in fact mostly prayers, we also find prose prayers, which vary from short aphoristic requests to prolix expositions. We may follow Eissfeldt* in calling the three most important forms petition, penitence, and thanksgiving.

A. The most important elements of the prayer of petition, which can be found in Judg. 16:28, are the address to Yahweh (including predication as God), the request, and the motivation or statement of purpose. We find an additional element in I Kings 3:6-9: God is reminded of his former gracious acts. This element especially is developed in much greater detail in later prayers, becoming, like the rest of the prayer, more verbose (cf. III Macc. 6:2 ff.).

A related form of the prayer of petition is the prayer of intercession, in which the person praying brings someone else's concern before God and entreats God to bless the other person, or else places himself in the position of another person that is culpable in some way (Hesse). Such intercession is ascribed to Abraham, who is referred to as a prophet (Gen. 20:7); we find it frequently in the

[1] Cf. W. Herrmann, "Das Aufgebot aller Kräfte," *ZAW*, LXX (1959), 215-20.

prophetical books (Amos 7:1-6), to the extent that God does not forbid it (Jer. 11:14).

B. The prayer of penitence is a special type of petition; the petitioner prays for forgiveness of his offense and remission of the threatened or decreed penalty. The prayer may consist of a mere confession of guilt (Judg. 10:10), or it may include a request for deliverance (Judg. 10:15) and a vow of thanks (I Sam. 12:10). In the late period, prayers of penitence can also include historical retrospection and grow quite prolix (Ezra 9; Daniel 9).

C. There are no extant examples of pure prayers of thanksgiving; the beginnings of the prayers of Jacob (Gen. 32:10-13 [Eng. 32:9-12]) and David (II Sam. 7:18-29), however, probably represent such prayers. The basic elements appear to be an address to Yahweh and a declaration of one's own unworthiness to receive God's grace (indirect thanksgiving). In its complete form, the prayer undoubtedly also contained direct thanksgiving.

Prayer can be cultic, with fixed forms, or non-cultic, with more flexibility. Postures for prayer include prostration on the ground, kneeling, and standing with outstretched arms, hands facing toward God or the sanctuary in the manner of a suppliant. Prayer at regular hours is first mentioned in Dan. 6:11, 14 (Eng. 6:10, 13).

5. *Letters.* The origin of the letter can be seen in II Kings 19:9-14. This passage speaks of the messengers of the Assyrian king, who are told, "Thus shall you say to Hezekiah"; according to vs. 14, a letter containing the message was handed over at the same time. The letter is therefore an extension of a messenger's oral communication; the written form served the purposes of attestation, examination, and preservation.

Of the earlier Israelite letters the most important section or sentence is preserved, e.g., the so-called Uriah letter of David (II Sam. 11:15), the letters of the king of the Arameans to the king of Israel (II Kings 5:5-6), of Jehu to the rulers of Samaria (II Kings 10:2-3), and of Jezebel to the elders of Israel (I Kings 21:8-10). A complete letter from Jeremiah to the exiles in Babylonia is preserved in a secondarily expanded form (Jer. 29:1-14); two other fragmentary letters are contained in Jer. 29:24-32. Israelite epistolary style is dependent on Babylonian style; the two are in fact practically identical. The introduction comprises the name of the sender and of the addressee together with a formula of salutation or loyalty. Then follow the body of the letter, perhaps introduced by *wᵉ ʿattâ,* "and now," as in the letter of Jehu, and a concluding formula.

From the Persian period we have letters to the Persian king and his replies (Ezra 4–6). Noncanonical Jewish literature contains other letters from the Hellenistic and Roman period; they are for the most part historically unreliable, but they do illustrate the form used for letters in the period of their composition. They accordingly contain Persian and Hellenistic formulas reflecting the chancery style of the royal courts, since they are mostly diplomatic correspondence. Letters from the time of Bar Kochba, some of them from him personally, were discovered a few years ago in the desert of Judah. The find rightly caused considerable sensation.

6. *Epistles*. An epistle, unlike a letter, does not spring from a particular situation; neither does it have a historical sender and addressee. It is rather a treatise, intended for the general public, that has been cast in a kind of epistolary form without introductory or concluding formulas. The only examples contained in the OT are the supposed edict of Nebuchadnezzar (Dan. 3:31–4:34 [Eng. 4:1-37])—a story permeated with hymnic motifs contrasting the transitory earthly kingdom with God's eternal kingdom—and the festival letter (Esther 9:20-22) enjoining the celebration of Purim. The epistle is therefore a very late literary type. Its origin lies in the Greek world, where, after its use by Herodotus (fifth century B.C.) and Gorgias (*ca.* 480–375), we find its full development in Isocrates (436–338). Its use in the OT is a sign of Greek and Hellenistic influence.[2]

§12 The Narrative Literary Types and Their Traditions

J. Barr, "The Meaning of 'Mythology' in Relation to the Old Testament," *VT*, IX (1959), 1-10; W. Baumgartner, "Israelitisch-Griechische Sagenbeziehungen," *Schweiz. Archiv für Volkskunde*, XLI (1944), 1-29 (= *Zum Alten Testament und seiner Umwelt*, 1959, pp. 147-78); E. Bethe, *Märchen, Sage, Mythus*, 2nd ed., 1922; E. Buess, *Die Geschichte des mythischen Erkennens*, 1953; B. S. Childs, *Myth and Reality in the Old Testament*, 1960; G. H. Davies, "An Approach to the Problem of Old Testament Mythology," *PEQ*, LXXXVIII (1956), 83-91; O. Eissfeldt, "Stammessage und Novelle in den Geschichten von Jakob und seinen Söhnen," in *Gunkel-Festschrift*, I (1923), 56-57 (= *Kleine Schriften*, I [1962], 84-104); *idem*, *Die Genesis der Genesis*, 2nd ed., 1961; *idem*, "Achronische anachronische und synchronische Elemente in der Genesis," *JEOL*, XVII (1963), 148-64; *idem*, *Stammessage und Menschheitserzählung in der Genesis. Wahrheit und Dichtung in der Ruth-Erzählung*, 1965; J. Fichtner, "Die etymologische Ätiologie in den Namengebungen der geschichtlichen Bücher des Alten Testaments," *VT*, VI (1956), 372-96; J. Gray, "Canaanite Mythology and Hebrew Tradition," *Transactions of the Glasgow University Oriental Society*, XIV (1953), 47-57; H. Gressmann, "Sage und Geschichte in den Patriarchenerzählungen," *ZAW*, XXX (1910), 1-34; H. Gunkel, *Schöpfung und Chaos in Urzeit und Endzeit*, 2nd ed., 1921; *idem*, *Elias*, 1906; *idem*, *Genesis*, 3rd edition 1910, 6th ed. 1964, VII-C ("Die Sagen der Genesis" [Eng. *The Legends of Genesis*, 1964]); *idem*, *Das Märchen im Alten Testament*, 1917; *idem*, *Geschichten von Elisa*, 1922; A. Heidel, *The Gilgamesh Epic and the Old Testament*, 2nd ed., 1954; J. Hempel, "Glaube, Mythos und Geschichte im Alten Testament," *ZAW*, LXV (1953), 109-67; C. A. Keller, " 'Die Gefährdung der Ahnfrau'," *ibid.*, LXVI (1954), 181-91; *idem*, "Über einige alttestamentliche Heiligtumslegenden," *ibid.*, LXVII (1955), 141-68; LXVIII (1956), 85-97; H.-J. Kraus, "Gedanken zum theologischen Problem der alttestamentlichen Sage," *EvTh*, VIII (1948/49), 319-28; J. L. McKenzie, "Myth and the Old Testament," *CBQ*, XXI (1959), 265-82; S. Mowinckel, *Tetrateuch-Pentateuch-Hexateuch*, 1964, pp. 78-86 (Excursus: "Das

[2] H. Peter, *Der Brief in der römischen Literatur*, 1901.

ätiologische Denken"); *idem* and W. F. ALBRIGHT, "The Babylonian Matter in the Predeuteronomic Primeval History (JE) in Gen 1–11," *JBL*, LVIII (1939), 87-103; L. ROST, "Theologische Grundgedanken der Urgeschichte," *ThLZ*, LXXXII (1957), 321-26; H. SCHMIDT and P. KAHLE, *Volkserzählungen aus Palästina*, 1918-30; I. L. SEELIGMANN, "Aetiological Elements in Biblical Historiography," *Zion*, XXVI (1961), 114-69; J. A. SOGGIN, "Kultätiologische Sagen und Katechese im Hexateuch," *VT*, X (1960), 341-47; L. E. TOOMBS, "The Formation of the Myth Patterns in the Old Testament," *JBR*, XXII (1961), 108-12; C. WESTERMANN, "Arten der Erzählung in der Genesis," in *Forschung am Alten Testament*, 1964, pp. 9-91; G. WIDENGREN, "Early Hebrew Myths and Their Interpretation," in *Myth, Ritual, and Kingship*, 1959, pp. 149-203; *idem*, "Myth and History in Israelite-Jewish Thought," in *Radin-Festschrift*, 1961, pp. 467-95.

1. *Their common relationship.* The narrative literary types have this in common: myth and fairy tale, saga and legend, all originate as forms of storytelling. They differ in that a myth is usually set in a long past primordial time and a fairy tale takes place outside the framework of time and space, while saga and legend take as their point of departure the individuality and importance of unique facts or events in space and time. Although one might be tempted to make a basic distinction between these narrative forms, the boundaries cannot be drawn precisely. In theory, of course, the saga, with its definite temporal and spatial content, referring for the most part to historical figures, events, or sites, is quite distinct from the myth, which describes an event in the divine realm of crucial importance for human existence, and also from the fairy tale, which moves in a world of fantasy. In practice, however, the boundaries are fluid.[1] This is especially true of the relationship between saga and legend, because the latter is in fact only a special form of the former, referring to persons and places, periods and institutions, that are religiously significant or sacred. We shall therefore treat them together.

One must also note that there was no sharp distinction between the individual narrative forms, or even between the narrative forms and the reportorial forms (§13), in the ancient Near East and in Israel. Past events were narrated or reported in every possible fashion, on the assumption that they took place as recounted. There are therefore sagas with mythical content, like the story of the marriages contracted between the heavenly beings and human women (Gen. 6:1-4), the story of the Deluge (Gen. 6:5–9:28), the story of how a city and a tower were built (Gen. 11:1-9), and other parts of the so-called Primal History. There are mythical overtones to all the narratives in which God appears upon earth and associates in human form with human beings, sharing in human emotions and needs, and performing human actions.[2] We are in a mythical world when Yahweh speaks to heavenly beings, to animals (like the serpent in the garden of God), and to men—all the more so when he lodges, eats, and drinks with Abraham. Similarly, sagas and legends not

[1] C.-M. Edsman in *RGG*, 3rd ed., V (1961), 1300.

[2] J. Lindblom, "Die Vorstellung vom Sprechen Jahwes zu den Menschen im Alten Testament," *ZAW*, LXXV (1963), 263-88.

infrequently take on features of the fairy tale, as in the case of Moses' miraculous rod (Exod. 4:1-9) and Elijah's mantle that can part water (II Kings 2:8). It is therefore scarcely correct to say that myth has been historicized in the OT (Weiser*); neither is history mythologized.[3] Contrary to such modernizing interpretations, Israel obviously did not distinguish clearly between the different narrative forms, but drew in equal measure upon mythological and fairy-tale motifs, as well as saga, legend, and reportorial forms.[4]

2. *Myth.* Myth takes place in the world of the gods, who have at least a determining voice in the events narrated. These events are not unique but typical; though constantly recurring, they are presented in the form of unique events in the primeval period. They are visualized and made concrete by means of personification and through portrayal of the destinies of gods and heroes, which are experienced as the origin of certain understandings and aspects of existence. Myth is based upon polytheism. In part, to the extent that it is associated with ritual, it is based upon the idea of a magical cult, in which typical events are realized and evoked by the performance of rituals and the reciting of myths.

No Israelite myth is known to exist, either *in toto* or by allusion. Apparently Israel never produced a myth, although it was undoubtedly no less capable of doing so than the other peoples of the ancient Near East. The descriptions of God's appearance in theophanies show that the possibility was there (Exod. 19; 33:19-22; Judg. 5:4-5; Ps. 18:8-16 [Eng. 18:7-15]). The necessary conditions for mythologizing—polytheism and magic—are not present, however, in Yahwism. Since Yahweh alone has the right to claim men's worship, and since besides Yahweh in the earlier period the existence of only less powerful, subordinate gods is assumed, and from the time of Jeremiah and particularly from the time of Deutero-Isaiah no other gods at all, there is no way for a myth to come into being. The mythological material we find in the OT has all been borrowed by Israel, mostly from Mesopotamia and Canaan. A distinction must also be made between the appearance of this material in narratives and its appearance in eschatological prophecy and psalms.

a) In narratives, we find mythological material almost exclusively in the so-called Primal History, Genesis 1–11, which represents a collection of sagas with mythological content, intended to portray events of fundamental significance. In the first creation account, Gen. 1:1–2:4*a*, the mythological background is shown by the mention of darkness and water as features of the primordial state of chaos, the birth of the cosmos through the division of the primeval flood, the orderly structure of the world, and the seven days of creation. In the second creation account, with the story of Paradise (Gen. 2:4*b*–3:24), we see the mythological background in the creation of man out of dust, the strange association between the fashioning of woman from a rib

[3] H. Ringgren, *Israelitische Religion*, 1963, p. 102.

[4] Cf. K.-H. Bernhardt, "Elemente mythischen Stils in der alttestamentalichen Geschichtsschreibung," *WZRostock*, XII (1963), 295-97. The intimate association between myth and history is discussed in detail by R. A. F. MacKenzie, *Faith and History in the Old Testament*, 1963.

and her designation "the mother of all living," the life-giving food, the temptation of man by woman, the sacred grove guarded by heavenly beings, and man's failure to gain equality with God. There is no extant parallel to the short account of how marriages between heavenly beings and human women produced the giants (Gen. 6:1-4), although there is obviously a myth in the background. The Mesopotamian origin of the Deluge story (Gen. 6:5–9:17), however, has been recognized for over ninety years; the similarity extends to minute details. The story of the building of a tower and a city at Babel is probably also based on a myth.

The general framework of these narratives, which is generally considered the work of the biblical narrator, is modeled after the epic of Atraḫasis, the "most wise," which was also the original setting of the Deluge story. Ashurbanipal's library clearly contained several copies of this epic, which can be traced through an Old Babylonian version (*ca.* 1550) back to the earliest and shortest Sumerian version (*ca.* 1700).[5] It begins with the creation of man, undertaken by the mother goddess with the help of Ea at the suggestion of the great gods Anu, Enlil, and Ea. Civilization begins with the founding of five cities (cf. Gen. 4:17), in which, according to the Sumerian King List, eight kings reigned before the Deluge (cf. Genesis 5). But when mankind begins to multiply, their noise bothers the god Enlil and disturbs his sleep. To reduce their numbers, the gods decree a six-year famine. When this does not suffice, they send the Deluge to exterminate the detested human race. Ea, however, betrays the secret to his protégé, who builds a boat and escapes with his family. It is easy to see that this epic, which probably included further episodes, narrates the events from creation to the Deluge in the same sequence as Genesis 1–9. Not only do isolated narratives in the Primal History have corresponding Mesopotamian prototypes, but even the sequence and structure of the whole agrees with the Mesopotamian original.

Israel did not borrow mythological narratives and motifs unchanged, but incorporated them into Yahwism and thereby transformed them. They are dissociated from polytheism and adapted so as to apply to the one God of Israel; the cosmogonic myth, for example, is subordinated to belief in God's act of creation. This belief, however, is itself associated with the relationship between God and man, to the extent that it depicts God's action in the life and destiny of mankind and the nations. The myth is accordingly not "historicized," but rather applied to the personal relationship between God and man instead of to polytheism.

b) Outside the Primal History, mythological motifs are used, in texts that can be dated, only from the time of Ezekiel on, especially in eschatological prophecy and in psalms of the exilic and postexilic period. The appearance of such traditions can therefore serve as a criterion for the late dating of the texts, the more so because it seems the product of a state of mind influenced by, if

[5] Cf. J. Lassøe, "The Atrachasis Epic: a Babylonian History of Mankind," *BiOr*, XIII (1956), 90-102; W. G. Lambert, "New Light on the Babylonian Flood," *JSS*, V (1960), 113-23.

not actually brought about by, the deportation and conditions in the Diaspora. Deutero-Isaiah, for example, can refer at the beginning of a passage to the mythical battle with chaos and at its conclusion to the miraculous parting of the sea during the Exodus, i.e., a historical event, while the connecting verse provides a transition (Isa. 51:9-10): he does not distinguish between the two motifs. Isolated mythological motifs are used when Yahweh's deeds are portrayed analogously to those of other gods, e.g., his battle with the chaos monsters (Isa. 27:1; Job 3:8), or when natural processes are described poetically (Ps. 19:5-7 [Eng. 19:4-6]).

The significance of such mythological motifs is merely subordinate and ancillary. They represent correlative images intended to visualize and interpret eschatological events, because at the eschaton something utterly unheard of and scarcely conceivable will take place. Events of the mythical primordial age can be referred to, moreover, because Yahweh's original actions will be repeated; what Yahweh did once makes his future conduct comprehensible.

3. *Fairy tale.* Fairy tales are set on earth, in the human world. Only inferior divinities appear, in direct relationship to man, either friendly or hostile. A fairy tale does not adhere to space and time, and is not bound by the laws of causality. Fantasy is reality. One could almost say that a fairy tale is a myth with a happy ending, whose scene is the earthly world of human beings.

Israel seems no more to have created any fairy tales than to have created myths; it appears, however, to have borrowed considerable fairy-tale material. The motif of the lewd woman who seeks to seduce a young man and then hates him and seeks to destroy him when, out of gratitude to her husband, he does not give in to her is of Egyptian origin (Gen. 39:7-20). Of Indian origin is the story of Solomon's judgment in the case of the child claimed by two women (I Kings 3:16-28). The Apocryphal story of Tobit draws on the widespread fairy tale of the grateful dead.

It should be noted, however, that no borrowed fairy tale is preserved in its pure form. Either it is worked into the context of a large-scale saga or historical account, like those mentioned in the preceding paragraph, or else we find merely the influence and survival of fairy-tale motifs in other literary types. In particular, motifs from the following types of fairy tale were employed (Hempel*): Motifs from the tale of magic include Moses' miraculous rod (Exod. 4:1-5), Elijah's mantle, which is able to part water (II Kings 2:8), and the inexhaustible and never empty meal jar and oil cruse (I Kings 17:16; II Kings 4:1-7). The transformation of Lot's wife into a pillar of salt (Gen. 19:26) is typical of metamorphosis tales. We find motifs of the occupational tale in the story of Cain and Abel (farmer and herdsman) and the story of Jacob and Esau (herdsman and hunter), which tell of enmity or deception (Gen. 4:1-16; 25:27-34; 27). As in the tale of good fortune, we hear of Saul, a peasant's son, who finds his father's asses and a royal crown (I Samuel 9), and of that other peasant lad who for a bag of gold and the king's daughter slays a giant (I Samuel 17). From the animal tale comes Balaam's talking ass (Num. 22:28-30). The distantly related animal and plant fable will be treated with the literary types belonging to wisdom literature (§47.6).

4. *Novella.* Like the fairy tale, the novella recounts the fate of a particular individual against his historical background. The story is the kind that can take place again and again; it does not survive as a historical reminiscence, but runs its course ever and again in typical fashion. In contrast to the fairy tale, the novella does not view the world and man through the glasses of desire and miracle, but rather depicts them realistically, as the narrator knows them by personal experience. It accentuates the events themselves and their effects upon human beings, while protraying people as quite passive, reacting to their destiny. The best example is the story cycle concerning Joseph and his brothers (Genesis 37; 39–48; 50). In addition, we may mention the book of Ruth and the narrative constituting the framework for the book of Job.

5. *Anecdote.* Unlike the literary types discussed up to this point, the anecdote is linked to specific facts and persons. In contrast to the novella, it portrays men intervening actively in history by word or deed and mastering their situation. It characterizes the man who acts decisively or speaks pertinently and cleverly. Some of the Samson stories can be termed anecdotes in this sense: his chasing the foxes with torches tied to their tales into the fields of the Philistines and his removing the doors from the gate of Gaza (Judg. 15:1–16:3). The same is true of the stories about David's magnanimous conduct toward Saul (I Samuel 24; 26) and the deeds of his mighty men (II Sam. 23:8-23).

6. *Saga and legend.* Sagas and legends make up the bulk of the narrative literary types in the OT. They can be classified into six major categories:

A. The geographical sagas include the story of how a tower and a city were built at Babylon (Gen. 11:1-9); this account, which represents a transformed myth, is intended to explain the origin of the enormous city with its towering ziggurat and the meaning of its name. The Sodom narrative (Genesis 19) is intended to explain the origin of the southern half of the Dead Sea along with the sterility and desolation of the region, as well as individual details like a pillar of salt in human shape on the slopes to the southwest. The narrative of Abraham's treaty with Abimelech of Gerar (Gen. 21:22-31) contains two references to the name of the city Beer-sheba, since the first part of the name refers to a well (*bᵉʼēr*) whose ownership is disputed, while the second part is explained both on the basis of the solemn oath (*šbʻ*) ratifying the treaty putting an end to the dispute and on the basis of the seven (*šebaʻ*) lambs set apart by Abraham. *Beer-sheba* is therefore to be interpreted as "Well of the Oath" or "Seven Wells."

B. Sanctuary legends also deal with specific sites; they are intended to explain why these sites are considered sacred. They include the narratives of the revelation of El Roi to Hagar at Beer-lahai-roi (Gen. 16:7-14), the revelation to Jacob at Bethel (Gen. 28:10-22), Jacob's nocturnal struggle at Penuel (Gen. 32:25-33 [Eng. 32:24-32]), his building of altars at Shechem and Bethel (Gen. 33:18-20; 35:1-7). The account usually describes a revelation or other appearance of the deity dwelling at the site, so that the person in question learns that the place is sacred and that the local divinity desires to be worshiped there in the future. Such legends (*hieroì lógoi*) were once told of all ancient sanctuaries. The later theory that the Jerusalem Temple alone was the proper place for worship led to the eradication or at least reinterpretation of many of them. For example, the building of an altar on Gerizim, the mountain of blessing, was transferred to Ebal, the mountain of cursing (Deut. 27:5-7); the cultic symbol of the state sanctuary of Northern Israel at Dan was made out to be the product of a double theft (Judg. 17–18).

C. Cult legends are intended to justify a particular cult or ritual: the serpent image installed in the Jerusalem Temple until *ca.* 700 B.C., representing a demon with curative powers, is traced back to an event from the time of Moses (Num. 21:4-9); circumcision is traced back to actions performed by Abraham (Genesis 17), Moses' wife (Exod. 4:24-26), and the Israelites entering the territory west of the Jordan (Josh. 5:2-9). The special position of the Jerusalem Temple results in the fire upon its altar being traced through the centuries: from the fire that came down upon the altar in the tent of meeting in the time of Moses (Lev. 9:24), through its installation in the Temple of Solomon (I Kings 8:4) and its concealment in a cistern by the priests after the destruction of the city by the Babylonians, down to the time of Nehemiah, who orders that it be rekindled (II Macc. 1:19-21), so that it continues to burn until the final destruction of the Temple.

D. The tribal and national saga is particularly characteristic of Israel. It is based on the assumption that a tribe or nation has an ancestor whose character and destiny represents, determines, or reflects that of the group. This kind of saga is therefore associated with a particular figure, historical or invented. This is particularly true of the narratives of the patriarchal period. It is often easy to see that these narratives refer in reality to tribes or nations, as in the blessing and cursing of Noah's sons (Gen. 9:25-27), the conception and birth of Ammon and Moab (Gen. 19:30-38), and Jacob's adoption of Ephraim and Manasseh (Genesis 48). The same is true also of extended saga cycles, such as the narratives concerning Hagar and Ishmael, Jacob and Esau, and Jacob and Laban.

E. The most important form after the tribal and national saga is the hero saga, which begins with the time of Moses. We may mention, for example, the victory over the Amalekites (Exod. 17:8-16) and the destruction of the tables containing the Decalogue (Exodus 32). The classic age of this form of saga is the period of the conquest of Palestine and of self-assertion against Canaanites, Philistines, and other enemies: in other words, the period from Joshua to David; cf. Joshua 10; Judges 3–16; I Samuel 11; 13–14; I Kings 22:34-35. Many of the narratives relating to this period have the formal character of sagas, though this statement should not be taken as implying a negative estimate of their historicity.

F. Personal legends focus on priests, prophets, and martyrs as religious figures. The few legends concerning priests either are hostile to the priesthood, like the narrative of the ungodliness of Eli's sons (I Samuel 1–3), or are the product of priestly circles in support of certain rights and prerogatives, like the narrative of Korah's rebellion against Moses and Aaron and the proof of Aaron's priestly prerogatives through the sprouting of a rod (Numbers 16–17). The books of Samuel, Kings, and Chronicles contain numerous legends of prophets. Besides prophets mentioned only once, Elijah, Elisha, and Isaiah are the classic figures; they are portrayed in part as active forces in politics, in part as deliverers and miracle workers. The martyr legend is the product of the late period, particularly after the Seleucid rulers' suppression and persecution of the Jewish religion. Several legends of this type, though with a happy ending, lie behind various narratives of the book of Daniel, which came into being in this period.

Not a few sagas and legends (the major exception being the hero legend) have the purpose of explaining the origin and cause of something presently existing; that is to say, they are etiological. In particular, they explain: (*a*) natural phenomena, such as the desolation of the region around the Dead Sea; (*b*) geographical and personal names, such as the name "Beer-sheba" or "Moses" (Exod. 2:10, which connects the name with the verb *māšâ*, "I drew him out [of the water]"); (*c*) cultic sites, practices, or objects, such as the image of the bronze serpent; (*d*) characteristics of a tribe or nation, such as the location of the Ishmaelites, explained by the flight of Hagar. It has long been demonstrated conclusively that a great part of the traditions concerning Israel's early history are etiological (Gressmann, Gunkel). Discussion continues, however, over whether etiology has the power actually to create a saga and whether it is possible to arrive at a "real" historical event after removing etiological features.[6] Did etiologies evoke and create the sagas embodying them, so that they must be considered *ipso facto* historically unreliable? Or is it possible on the contrary to remove the etiological features so as to arrive at a historical narrative? It is probably necessary to distinguish more precisely between etiological elements appended to narratives and narratives that are totally etiological. The explanation of the name "Moses" in the narrative of his birth and discovery is an example of the former; the explanation surely did not produce the whole narrative, but was rather appended to it. Gen. 21:22-32 is an example of the latter: its whole purpose is to explain the name "Beer-sheba"; the etiology is developed in the course of the narrative, so that the narrative came into being to fulfill this purpose. As a general rule, we may conclude that appended etiologies did not produce narratives, but were rather added to narratives already in existence. Narratives that came into being by growing out of etiologies are etiological throughout, and develop their explanation in the course of their presentation.

If we inquire further into the traditio-historical background, many sagas and legends turn out to be non-Israelite in origin. The narrative of the exposure and rescue of the infant Moses follows a widespread pattern whose essential

[6] Cf., for example, J. Bright, *Ancient Israel in Recent Historical Writing*, 1956; M. Noth, "Der Beitrag der Archäologie zur Geschichte Israels," *VTSuppl*, VII (1960), 262-82; also on this problem, see S. Mowinckel, *Tetrateuch-Pentateuch-Hexateuch*, 1964, pp. 78-86.

points are found as early as the birth story of Sargon, king of Akkad (*ca.* 2350). Some geographical and nature sagas, like the narrative about Sodom, and above all many sanctuary and cult legends were borrowed by Israel from the Canaanites. A whole series of sanctuaries such as Bethel and Shechem, Beersheba and Hebron–Mamre, were sacred sites for the Canaanites before they were for the Israelites, as archaeology frequently shows. The legends passed with the sanctuaries into the hands of the Israelites, who substituted their God Yahweh for the earlier Canaanite deities that revealed themselves at these sites. They transferred the revelation to figures from their own prehistory; the patriarchs especially came to be interpreted as recipients of revelations and founders of cults. Of course many sagas and legends came into being within Israel itself, especially the tribal and national sagas dealing with groups of Israelites.

In the course of a long and complex process of transmission, both the borrowed and the indigenous sagas and legends were revised many times. Four principles guided this revision:

a) The sagas and legends were "personalized" and adapted to the personal element in Yahwism. The sanctuary legend of Bethel consequently appears as a personal experience of Jacob. In the narrative of the rape of Dinah and the subsequent revenge (Genesis 34), Shechem, who is in love with the girl, the brothers enraged at her disgrace, and Jacob, who suspects trouble, are depicted so graphically as individuals that the reader scarcely realizes that the story deals with national or tribal groups.

b) The sagas and legends were made to refer to Israel, its ancestors and its tribes, to whatever extent was necessary. In other words, they were "nationalized." The Joseph novella describes the Egyptian background for the most part with great accuracy, and may even have been constructed on the basis of an Egyptian narrative. But the whole story has been made to serve the presentation of the history of Israel and Israel's ancestors.

c) The sagas and legends, to the extent necessary, were made to refer to Yahweh, the God of Israel. Thus, after his dream experience at Bethel, Jacob declares, "Surely Yahweh is in this place; and I did not know it." Then follows the explanation of the place-name: "He called the name of that place Bethel ['house of El']." This means that the sanctuary was once dedicated to the god El and named for him; when the narrative was made to apply to Jacob, "Yahweh" came to replace "El" except in the fixed place-name.

d) The sagas and legends were increasingly given religious significance, i.e., they were "theologized." Almost always God plays a role, often the central one. The presentation becomes more profound. While the Atraḫasis epic tells how the gods decreed the deluge because the noise of the human race disturbed Enlil's sleep, the Yahwist gives as the reason God's divine wrath occasioned by the wickedness of man, because "every imagination of the thoughts of his heart was only evil continually" (Gen. 6:5-7).

7. *Historical and theological significance.* Finally, in our study of the narra-

tive literary types, we come to the question of their historical and theological significance.

a) In the case of myth, fairy tale, and novella, the answer to the first question is automatically negative. Geographical and nature sagas, sanctuary and cult legends, though certainly based on facts in need of an explanation, are also unable to claim historical reliability for their explanatory narratives. Tribal and national sagas, hero sagas, and personal legends, on the other hand, often have a historical nucleus. Wherever they occur, they allude to history; and wherever historical events have taken place, stories have been told about them and handed down. Such sagas and legends can therefore easily contain an echo of historical reminiscence. Whether and to what extent the historical event can be determined is a problem that must be settled for each individual case. Two similar narrative complexes can differ in historical value; in addition, the recovered historical basis may turn out to be different from what was expected.[7]

It is impossible to determine whether the various narrators and redactors during the long process of growth and revision leading from the original narrative units to the present-day historical books were convinced of the historical reliability of the narrative. In fact, this is a modern question, which did not concern them because they did not aim at portraying or writing "history." For the earliest narrators, the purpose of their presentation was to justify Israelite claims to the settled areas and their sanctuaries, to legitimize their possession and the use of certain cultic practices. For the later narrators, for example the authors of the Pentateuch sources, everything was subordinated to the viewpoint of a dominant theological conception, which differs from author to author. This was their interest, not "history."

b) The theological significance of the narrative literary types is connected with their adaptation to Yahwism. Notwithstanding their *Sitz im Leben*, it consists in this: Religious statements are made about Yahweh and Israel, God and man, for which the narratives provide the raw material. What determines their continuing influence is not reminiscences of past events but rather the firm belief in a constant relationship between God and man. Being applied to Israel or to individual figures out of Israel's history, they are intended to portray the relationships between Yahweh and Israel in both good and evil, Yahweh's treatment of Israel within the framework of the international world, and the obedience or disobedience toward God of Israel or individual Israelites.

There is also a further viewpoint, especially in the case of the tribal and national sagas (Eissfeldt*). The process of redaction emphasized those elements that are universally human, giving the narratives a relevance that extends beyond the boundaries of Israel. They appear not only as descriptions of Israel's fate at a particular moment in the past, but also as descriptions of ever recurring human fates and attributes. Above all, they portray man within the context of his family ties.

[7] Cf. G. Fohrer, *Elia*, 1957; *idem*, *Das Buch Jesaja*, II (1962), on Isaiah 36–39; *idem*, *Überlieferung und Geschichte des Exodus*, 1964.

Finally, the process of theological revision turned the patriarchal figures of Genesis into examples of universal human attitudes toward life. Abraham exemplifies the man of faith, even though his faith fails on one occasion; Isaac exemplifies the patient and accepting man; Jacob exemplifies the man of steadfast hope, who at first tries to realize his expectations in all too human fashion, but is later portrayed as the man who hopes and trusts in God. The Joseph novella shows even more clearly Joseph's spiritual development from pride to humility. In this way the narratives achieve a significance far surpassing their original meaning; they apply to man in every age.

§13 The Reportorial Literary Types and Their Traditions

M. Adinolfi, "Storiografia biblica e storiografia classica," *RivBibl,* IX (1961), 42-58; W. F. Albright, "The List of Levitic Cities," in *Ginzberg Jubilee Vol.,* I (1945), 49-73; A. Alt, "Israels Gaue unter Salomo," in BWAT, XIII (1913), 1-19 (= *Kleine Schriften,* I [1953], 76-89 [Eng. *Essays on Old Testament History and Religion,* 1955]); *idem,* "Judas Gaue unter Josia," *PJB,* XXI (1925), 100-16 (= *Kleine Schriften,* II [1953], 276-88); *idem,* "Eine galiläische Ortsliste in Jos 19," *ZAW,* XLV (1927), 59-81; *idem,* "Bemerkungen zu einigen judäischen Ortslisten des Alten Testaments," *ZDPV,* LXVIII (1959), 193-210 (= *Kleine Schriften,* II [1953], 289-305); *idem,* "Festungen und Levitenorte im Lande Juda," in *Kleine Schriften,* II (1953), 306-15; *idem,* "Die Deutung der Weltgeschichte im Alten Testament," *ZThK,* LVI (1959), 129-37; W. Brandenstein, "Bemerkungen zur Völkertafel der Genesis," in *Debrunner-Festschrift,* 1954, pp. 57-83; A. Caquot, "Les songes et leur interprétation selon Canaan et Israël," in *Les songes et leur interprétation,* 1959, pp. 99-124; B. Dinur, "The Biblical Historiography of the Period of the Kingdom," in A. Malamat, ed., *The Kingdoms of Israel and Judah* (Hebrew), 1961, pp. 9-23; H. Duhm, "Zur Geschichte der alttestamentlichen Geschichtsschreibung," in *Plüss-Festschrift,* 1905, pp. 118-63; E. L. Ehrlich, *Der Traum im Alten Testament,* 1953; O. Eissfeldt, *Geschichtsschreibung im Alten Testament,* 1948; *idem, Die Genesis der Genesis,* 2nd ed., 1961; K. Elliger, "Die dreissig Helden Davids," *PJB,* XXXI (1953), 29-75; H. Gese, "Geschichtliches Denken im Alten Orient und im Alten Testament," *ZThK,* LV (1958), 127-45; M. Haran, "Studies in the Account of the Levitical Cities," *JBL,* LXXX (1961), 45-54, 156-65; G. Hölscher, *Die Anfänge der hebräischen Geschichtsschreibung,* 1942; E. Jacob, *La tradition historique en Israël,* 1946; *idem,* "Histoire et historiens dans l'Ancien Testament," *RHPhR,* XXXV (1955), 26-35; *idem,* "L'Ancien Testament et la vision de l'histoire," *RThPh,* VII (1957), 254-65; A. Jepsen, *Die Quellen des Königsbuches,* 2nd ed., 1956; R. Kittel, *Die Anfänge der hebräischen Geschichtsschreibung im Alten Testament,* 1896; B. Maisler, "Ancient Israelite Historiography," *IEJ,* II (1952), 82-88; G. Misch, *Geschichte der Autobiographie, I: Das Altertum,* 3rd ed., 1950; S. Mowinckel, "Die vorderasiastischen Königs- und Fürsteninschriften," in *Gunkel-Festschrift,* I (1923), 278-322; *idem,* "Hat es ein israelitisches Nationalepos gegeben?" *ZAW,* LVII (1935), 130-52; *idem, Studien zu dem Buche Ezra-Nehemia,* I–II, 1964; III, 1965; M. Noth, *Das System der zwölf Stämme Israels,* 1930; *idem,* "Studien zu den historisch-geographischen Dokumenten des Josuabuches," *ZDPV,* LVIII (1935), 185-255; *idem,* "Der Wallfahrtsweg zum

Sinai," *PJB*, XXXVI (1940), 5-28; G. von Rad, "Der Anfang der Geschichtsschreibung im alten Israel," *AfK*, XXXII (1944), 1-42 (= *Gesammelte Studien zum Alten Testament*, 1958, pp. 148-88 [Eng. *The Problem of the Hexateuch, and Other Essays*, 1966]); *idem*, "Die Nehemia-Denkschrift," *ZAW*, LXXVI (1964), 176-87; R. Rendtorff, "Geschichte und Überlieferung," in *von Rad-Festschrift*, 1961, pp. 81-94; *idem*, "Geschichte und Wort im Alten Testament," *EvTh*, XXII (1962), 621-49; A. Resch, *Der Traum im Heilsplan Gottes*, 1964; W. Richter, "Traum und Traumdeutung im Alten Testament," *BZ*, NF VII (1963), 202-20; N. H. Ridderbos, "Het Oude Testament en de Geschiedenis," *GThT*, LVII (1957), 112-20; LVIII (1958), 1-9; H. Schmidt, *Die Geschichtsschreibung im Alten Testament*, 1911; I. L. Seligmann, "Menschliches Heldentum und göttliche Hilfe," *ThZ*, XIX (1963), 385-411; J. Simons, "The 'Table of Nations' (Gen 10)," *OTS*, X (1954), 155-84; *idem*, *The Geographical and Topographical Texts of the Old Testament*, 1959; C. A. Simpson, "Old Testament Historiography and Revelation," *Hibbert Journal*, LVI (1957/58), 319-32; J. A. Soggin, "Alttestamentliche Glaubenszeugnisse und geschichtliche Wirklichkeit," *ThZ*, XVII (1961), 385-98; *idem*, "Geschichte, Historie und Heilsgeschichte im Alten Testament," *ThLZ*, LXXXIX (1964), 721-36; E. A. Speiser, "The Biblical Idea of History in Its Common Near Eastern Setting," *IEJ*, VII (1957), 201-16; E. Täubler, "Die Anfänge der Geschichtsschreibung," in *Tyche, Historische Studien*, 1926, pp. 17-74, 213-23; A. Weiser, *Glaube und Geschichte im Alten Testament*, 1931 (also in the collection with the same title, 1961, pp. 99-182); G. E. Wright, "Cult and History," *Interpr*, XVI (1962), 3-20.

1. *Lists*. The OT preserves numerous lists of different kinds, which may be classified into three groups.

A. The first group comprises the lists of nations and persons, among which the genealogical lists are of primary importance. We may cite the following examples: two lists of nations brought together in Genesis 10; the list of Nahor's descendants in Gen. 22:20-24; Keturah's in Gen. 25:1-4; Ishmael's in Gen. 25:12-16; the descendants of Esau–Seir–Edom in Genesis 36; the major portion of I Chronicles 1–9; and, last but not least, the several lists of Jacob's children, the ancestors of Israel, which differ from each other at several points (Genesis 49; Num. 1:5-15; 26). These latter lists, like the lists of non-Israelite tribes, are based on the highly developed genealogical concepts of the nomads. Contrary to the assumption that they represent sacral tribal leagues analogous to the Greco-Italian amphictyonies (Noth), for which there is no evidence in the ancient Near East, these lists represent popular summaries of larger genealogies. In addition, there are lists of officials and heroes (II Sam. 8:16-18; 20:23-26; 23:8-39), among which the list of Solomon's administrative officers deserves special mention (I Kings 4:7-19; 5:7-8 [Eng. 4:27-28]). From a much later period come the lists in Ezra–Nehemiah: the national census in Ezra 2, the list of those helping to build the wall in Nehemiah 3, the list of Ezra's companions in Ezra 8:1-14, the list of mixed marriages in Ezra 10:18, 20-44*a*, the list of the population of Judah and Jerusalem in Neh. 11:3-36 and of the priests and Levites in Neh. 12:1-16.

B. Historico-geographical lists contain the names of cities and towns (e.g., along a boundary), fortresses, and Levitical cities. Several such lists seem to have been brought together in Joshua 15–19. Numbers 33 contains an itinerary; another, earlier, itinerary seems to have been drawn upon in Exod. 13:20; 14:1-2; 15:22-23, and elsewhere.

C. Among the lists of material objects are lists of votive offerings, etc. (Exod. 35:21-29; Ezra 2:68-69) and of captured cattle and slave girls, together with their manner of distribution (Num. 31:32-47).

The present location of these lists says nothing about how old they are or whether they have preserved their original form. Some of them are undoubtedly ancient and belong to the period suggested by their place in the OT, e.g., the lists of Solomon's administrative officers and of those that helped Nehemiah rebuild the wall of Jerusalem. Others, especially the historico-geographical lists, reflect the situation of later periods than the time to which they are ascribed. Still others are artificial productions, constructed for specific purposes on the model of real lists, even though they may have used some earlier factual items, e.g., Numbers 33.

2. *Annals and chronicles.* The term "annals" refers to records (usually official) of important events arranged by year. They were intended to preserve the memory of these events, and were therefore stored in archives. They represent a true reportorial literary type. Annals were recorded since the earliest times, especially at the royal court, less commonly at sanctuaries. To be sure, they have not been preserved; only isolated notices in the books of the OT can be derived with a high degree of probability from them, e.g., those telling about Solomon's administrative officers and fortresses (I Kings 9:15-23) and the shrines he built for his foreign wives (I Kings 11:7), or the account of Pharaoh Shishak's attack upon Judah in the time of Rehoboam (I Kings 14:25-28). They are in the present narrative because the authors of the books of Kings found them in the history books that they allude to, which they used as sources. Since the Jerusalem Temple was actually a royal chapel, the passages relating to it may also come from court annals, e.g., the account of how Solomon built the Temple (I Kings 6–8), the description of the chest that Jehoiada the priest constructed to contain the money belonging to the Temple (II Kings 12:10-13 [Eng. 12:9-12]), and the reform of King Josiah (II Kings 22–23), particularly since the latter was also a political enterprise. This does not exclude the possibility that temple annals were kept in Judah and Israel, although there is little evidence for such annals in the ancient Near East.

In addition, we must assume the existence of chronicles in the two states of Israel and Judah; like their ancient Near Eastern prototypes, these would contain the dates of the various kings together with short notices describing their deeds and their fates. As in the case of annals, there is no direct evidence for this literary type; but its use may possibly be inferred from the books of Kings. Jepsen assumes that there was a synchronistic chronicle for both Judah and Israel; this remains dubious despite the Babylonian parallel, which is based on different political presuppositions. It is perhaps better to think in terms of separate Judahite and North Israelite chronicles, which the author of the books of Kings combined. This assumption would explain many wrong dates, which make it difficult to construct a chronology for the period of the monarchy.

3. *Historical narrative and historiography.* Israelite historiography serves more for general public and private purposes than for official purposes, the more so because royal autobiography, which elsewhere in the ancient Near East plays the central role in the recording and transmission of history, is completely lacking in Israel. This absence and the peculiarities of the royal psalms (§39.5) suggest that Israel's concept of kingship differed from that of the environment. The sole exception is I Kings 3:4-15, which seems to be modeled after the Egyptian royal novella.

At the beginning of our list of historical literary types we may put the self-contained narrative, whose purpose is to describe in more or less detail what a particular event was and how it took place. Examples include the account of Abimelech's kingship in Shechem (Judges 9) and the account of how Saul delivered the city of Jabesh in Gilead (I Samuel 11).

Another type of historical account is suggested by the allusions of the authors of the books of Kings to other compendia of data: the Book of the Acts of Solomon (I Kings 11:41) and the Book of the Chronicles of the Kings of Israel (I Kings 14:19) and of Judah (I Kings 14:29). These three books obviously contained extracts from the court annals; they must have been accessible to the general public, however, because otherwise it would have been senseless to refer to them. Apparently they did not constitute deliberately constructed literary works, but were compendia of separate incidents covering a long period of time. They described the wars of Jeroboam I and his reign (I Kings 14:19), the victories of Asa and Baasha (I Kings 15:23; 16:5), the conspiracy of Zimri (I Kings 16:20), Ahab's building of cities and an ivory palace (I Kings 22:39), the battle between Joash of Israel and Amaziah of Judah (II Kings 13:12; 14:15), the wars of Jeroboam II (II Kings 14:28), the conspiracy of Shallum (II Kings 15:15), the victories of Hezekiah and the measures he undertook to provide Jerusalem with water (II Kings 20:20), and the sin of Manasseh (II Kings 21:17). The references often state briefly that the historical books mentioned describe all that the kings did, including, therefore, the accounts in the present books of Kings.

In addition to the self-contained narratives and the compendia, there was also historiography proper: literary compositions devoted to a specific period, which link the materials both internally and externally and form them into a unified whole by means of an imposed structure—beginning with the period of awakening national consciousness based on the religious foundation of Yahwism during and after the reign of David (Weiser*). The very first production of this sort, the so-called Court History of David, is a masterly accomplishment (§32).

Further steps toward more comprehensive continuous treatments are found in the earlier sources of the Pentateuch or Hexateuch. These sources survey all of history from the creation of the world to Israel's occupation of Palestine; they are, however, less interested in "history" than in the presentation of their theological system, based on and illustrated by historical material (§12.7). These are followed, with a somewhat different accent, by the school of Deuteronomistic historiography, which is particularly apparent in the structuring of the period of the Judges and the monarchy. In the postexilic period, the tendency of Deuteronomistic historiography to omit secular material as much as possible is intensified; the writers concentrate instead on a religious view of history or a kind of "church history," as in the Priestly material and the Chronicler's History.

4. *Biography*. In biography the author seeks to portray his own conduct or that of others; his purpose may be to preserve what he describes for later recollection, to justify it in the eyes of his contemporaries or of posterity, or to consecrate it to God.

Biographical elements are found less in Israelite historiography than in prophetical accounts, e.g., the description of Amos' banishment from Bethel (Amos 7:10-17). Here, too, the biographical interest is not primary, as Baruch's account of Jeremiah, which seeks to prove that he is a true prophet of Yahweh, shows (§59.4).

Other prophetical accounts have autobiographical traits, e.g., Hosea's account describing the symbolic action of his second marriage (Hosea 3). They are no more autobiographies, however, than are the memoirs of Nehemiah, which exhibit many similarities to the votive style of the real or fictitious "autobiographies" of Egyptian dignitaries and officials (§ 7.5). They are biographical accounts dedicated to the memory of their "heroes," intended as memorials for them and as offerings dedicated to God, to be preserved in the temple.

5. *Dream-narrative*. Because of their autobiographical nature, dream-narratives, whether original or fictitious, are usually put in the first person, as in the narratives within the framework of the Joseph novella (Gen. 37:5-11; 40–41) and in the story of Gideon (Judg. 7:13). That dreams played an important role among cult prophets as means of receiving a revelation is shown by Jeremiah's polemic (Jer. 23:25-32) and the harsh measures described in Deut. 13:2-6 (Eng. 13:1-5), which apparently are directed against a borrowed Canaanite custom. The interpretation that often follows a dream-narrative is usually not in the first person, since it is given by a different party. It can take the form of direct address to the narrator or simply straightforward exposition (Judg. 7:14).

§14 Other Literary Types and Influence on Other Books

1. *Other literary types*. Besides the rhetorical and written forms just described, other literary types also occur in the historical and legal books. These derive from other areas of life and literature, and will be discussed in their proper place. Some common types of song, for example, are represented several times: work song (Num. 21:17-18; Neh. 4:4 [Eng. 4:10]), taunt

song (Num. 21:14-15, 27-30; cf. Judg. 5:15-17, 28-30), war and victory song (Exod. 17:16; Josh. 10:12-13; Num. 22–24*; Exod. 15:21; 16:23-25; I Sam. 18:7; Judg. 5), and dirge (II Sam. 1:19-27; 3:33-34). In addition, psalms have been interpolated at several points (Exod. 15:1-18; Deuteronomy 32; I Sam. 2:1-10; §39.7). Among the literary types belonging to wisdom literature (§ 47) we find proverbs (I Sam. 16:7; 24:14; II Sam. 5:8; I Kings 20:11), riddles (Judg. 14:14), parables (II Samuel 12), and fables (Judg. 9:8-15; II Kings 14:9).

2. *Influence on other books.* Conversely, several of the literary types just discussed appear in other books of the OT or have given rise to imitations. We find priestly torah and blessing in Pss. 15; 24:3-6; 133:3; 134:3. The prophetical accounts often have biographical or autobiographical features. The prophets especially imitated various literary types in their preaching, particularly torah, legal discourse, and historical survey.

§15 Compilation and Transmission

O. Eissfeldt, "Die kleinste literarische Einheit in den Erzählungsbüchern des Alten Testaments," *ThBl*, VI (1927), 333-37 (= *Kleine Schriften*, I [1962], 123-49); H. Gressmann, "Ursprung und Entwicklung der Joseph-Sage," in *Gunkel-Festschrift*, I (1923), 1-55; H. Gunkel, "Die Komposition der Joseph-Geschichten," *ZDMG*, LXXVI (1922), 55-71; J. Hempel, *Geschichten und Geschichte im Alten Testament bis zur persischen Zeit*, 1964; C. Kuhl, "Die Wiederaufnahme—ein literarkritisches Prinzip?" *ZAW*, LXIV (1952), 1-11; R. H. Pfeiffer and W. G. Pollard, *The Hebrew Iliad*, 1957; I. L. Seeligmann, "Hebräische Erzählung und biblische Geschichtsschreibung," *ThZ*, XVIII (1962), 305-25.

1. *Legal codes.* The process of compilation and transmission that brought the legal dicta into their present form of legal codes, some dependent and some independent, was long and complicated. Originally, the legal dicta were for the most part transmitted orally and in isolation for help in reaching a legal decision. The same holds true for the series of rules regulating conduct; grouping by ten, which was especially popular, was intended at least in part as a mnemonic device (for counting on one's fingers).

Interpolation and combination of the separate legal dicta brought the first small compilations into being (§8.3). Further unification turned these small compilations into larger ones, such as the section Exod. 21:1–22:16 (Eng. 21:1–22:17), which is set off by the heading *mišpāṭîm*, "ordinances" (cf. also Leviticus 11–15; 20–21; Deuteronomy 21–25). If, as elsewhere in the ancient Near East, we must think in terms of written transmission of these compilations, the same must apply all the more to the great composite legal codes. Of these large-scale works, the so-called Covenant Code (Exod. 20:22–23:9) and the Holiness Code (Leviticus 17–26) can be termed dependent law codes, because they have been absorbed into extensive literary works, while the law code of Deuteronomy together with its framework constitutes an independent work; the Priestly source of the Pentateuch, including the legal sections it has absorbed, also represents an independent unit. One must always remember that these compilations and law codes do not develop systematically the entire body of law obtaining at any one time; instead, like other works of this type in the ancient Near East, they contain new ordinances, judgments, or decisions intended to alter or replace traditional customary law, which is never recorded. This purpose affected the very process of transmission and often left traces in alterations, revisions, or supplementations of the basic text, which had to be adapted to a new situation or redefined to apply to the present. The basic text of Leviticus 23, for instance, was revised in this fashion even after it had been absorbed into the Priestly source; vss. 18*aβ*-19*a* were added from Num. 28:27-30 (Eissfeldt*). Leviticus 18, which at first consisted of a series of ten rules of conduct (§ 8.2), exhibits several stages of revision: (1) expansion into a dodecalogue by the addition of vss. 13 and 17*a*, and at the same time elevation to the status of Yahweh's ordinance by means of vs. 6, with the purpose of prohibiting certain degrees of consanguinuity in order to strengthen the matrimonial bond; (2) incorporation into a general law against unchastity by the addition of vss. 17*b*-23, in order to preserve the cultic holiness of the congregation of Yahweh; (3) inclusion in a framework of exhortations, vss. 2*b*-5, 24-30.[1] This and many other instances illustrate clearly the continual process of reinterpretation and adaptation to changing conditions, which in turn shows the original purpose of codification: the establishment of new laws through alteration of traditional customary law.

2. *Narrative and historical sections.* With few exceptions, the process of compilation, revision, and redaction of the narrative and historical sections of the books in question begins with the isolated individual narrative or account, no matter what literary type these sections may belong to. In innumerable instances these units can still be recognized. At first they were certainly transmitted by oral tradition. The simplest means of linking several stories was juxtaposition by means of connecting phrases such as "it came to pass" or "after this"; the resultant discrepancies or contradictions were only partially resolved. We may call this procedure "combination." In addition, we find interpolation, the insertion of brief notes or narratives into a context already present. It can often be recognized through the fact that the last sentence before the interruption is cited literally or with minor variations after the interpolation, e.g., Gen. 37:36 and 39:1; II Sam. 3:1 and 3:6*a*. A further stage is represented by the construction of small or large narrative cycles, like those that grew up around Jacob and Esau, Jacob and Laban, Elijah, or Elisha. Even the Court History of David, which appears to be a deliberately structured work, can be understood in this light, because it employed a series of individual narratives. In the case of such narrative cycles, we must at times think in terms of written transmission.

Besides this process of gradual growth coupled with simultaneous revision,

[1] Cf. K. Elliger, "Das Gesetz Leviticus 18," *ZAW*, LXVII (1955), 1-25.

in the course of which the individual narratives were personalized, nationalized, theologized, and applied to Yahweh (§12.6), we may also observe the growth of transmission through use of literary sources. While such a use can only be inferred for the Primal History (Genesis 1–11; §12.2), the mention of the book of the Wars of Yahweh and the book of the Upright (§42) is direct evidence for written sources. This holds true even more obviously for the historical works cited by the authors of the books of Kings and the sources mentioned in the Chronicler's History (§34). We are therefore dealing with a process of compilation and selective transmission of material lying ready to hand.

Both processes—compilation of narratives or narrative cycles and utilization of sources—resulted, after additional intermediate stages, in the formation of more extensive works. These include first of all the basic narrative of the Pentateuch or Hexateuch, which was then subject to further revision; it appears in various final forms in the different sources. Mention must also be made of the pre-Deuteronomistic drafts of the books of Judges, Samuel, and Kings, and the Chronicler's History. At the end of the long road that began with the individual narratives and the first written sources we come, then, to extensive presentations.

3. *Later historical and legal books.* Later historical and legal books that were not included in the OT include III Ezra (a translation of the conclusion of Chronicles, Ezra, and a small section of Nehemiah, plus three additional sections), the three books of Maccabees (I–II Maccabees constitute historical narrative, II Maccabees having a more "edifying" approach; III Maccabees is legendary), Tobit (a fairy tale or novella), Judith (historical romance), the narratives of Susanna and of Bel and the Dragon (additions to Daniel with fairy-tale and saga motifs, in part of foreign origin), the Letter of Jeremiah (a polemic against the worship of images, based on Jeremiah 29), the Letter of Aristeas (a legend concerning the origin of the LXX), the book of Jubilees (a legendary reworking of Genesis 1–Exodus 12), the Martyrdom and Ascension of Isaiah (a prophetical legend with two Christian supplements), the Testaments of the Twelve Patriarchs (parenesis), as well as some of the Qumran documents, such as the so-called Manual of Discipline (1QS, together with the supplements $1QS^a$ and $1QS^b$), the partially related Damascus Document, the so-called War Scroll (1QM, containing military regulations), the so-called Genesis Apocryphon (1QGenAp, containing a legendary reworking of parts of Genesis), and fragments of other documents, perhaps including the much-debated Copper Scroll.

CHAPTER TWO: THE PENTATEUCH

§16 Terminology and Content

ATD: G. von Rad, Genesis, 5th ed., 1958 (Eng. 1961); *idem,* Deuteronomy, 1964 (Eng. 1966); M. Noth, Exodus, 2nd ed., 1959 (Eng. 1962); *idem,* Leviticus, 1962 (Eng. 1965). COT: W. H. Gispen, Leviticus, 1950; *idem,* Numbers I, 1959, Numbers II, 1964. HAT: G. Beer and K. Galling, Exodus, 1939; K. Elliger, Leviticus, 1965; HK: H. Gunkel, Genesis, 3rd ed., 1910, 6th ed., 1964; B. Baentsch, Exodus–Numbers, 1903; C. Steuernagel, Deuteronomy, 2nd ed., 1923. HS: P. Heinisch, Genesis, 1930; *idem,* Exodus, 1934; *idem,* Leviticus, 1935; *idem,* Numbers, 1936; H. Junker, Deuteronomy, 1933. IB: C. A. Simpson, Genesis, 1952; J. C. Rylaarsdam, Exodus, 1952; N. Micklem, Leviticus, 1953; J. Marsh, Numbers, 1953; G. E. Wright, Deuteronomy, 1953. ICC: J. Skinner, Genesis, 2nd ed., 1930 (1951); G. B. Gray, Numbers, 1903 (1955); S. R. Driver, Deuteronomy, 3rd ed., 1902 (1952). KAT: O. Procksch, Genesis, 2nd and 3rd ed., 1924; E. König, Deuteronomy, 1917. KeH: A. Dillmann, Genesis, 6th ed., 1892 (Eng. 1897); *idem,* Numbers, 2nd ed., 1886; *idem,* Deuteronomy, 2nd ed., 1886; *idem* and V. Ryssel, Exodus–Leviticus, 3rd ed., 1897. KHC: H. Holzinger, Genesis, 1898; *idem,* Exodus, 1900; *idem,* Numbers, 1903; A. Bertholet, Leviticus, 1901; *idem,* Deuteronomy, 1899. SAT; H. Gunkel, Genesis, 2nd ed., 1921; Gressmann, Exodus–Deuteronomy, 2nd ed., 1922. SZ: H. Strack, Genesis, 2nd ed., 1905; *idem,* Exodus–Numbers, 1894; S. Oettli, Deuteronomy, 1893. ZBK: W. Zimmerli, Genesis 1-11, 2nd ed., 1957. Individual commentaries: Franz Delitzsch, Genesis, 1887 (Eng. 1888-99); E. König, Genesis, 2nd and 3rd ed., 1925.

1. *Terminology.* Judaism gave the general name "Torah" to the first five books of the OT on account of the "instruction" or "law" contained in them, the obligatory basis for life and conduct. The term also appears in compounds: *hattôrâ,* "The Law"; *tôrat mōšeh,* "The Law of Moses"; *sēper tôrat mōšeh,* "The Book of the Law of Moses." It seems that these terms were applied originally only to the legal codes or compilations in the five books, as several passages in the OT suggest (II Kings 14:6; II Chron. 25:4; 30:16; 35:12; Ezra 6:18; 10:3; Neh. 8:3; 13:1); Mark 12:26 and Matt. 5:17, however, refer to the entire contents of the books.

The Pentateuch was divided into five books in order to obtain divisions of approximately equal length, each of which would fit on one of the usual book scrolls. This division took place in the fourth century B.C. at the latest; the LXX is already familiar with it. The earliest known term expressing this division is Greek; we find it in Tertullian (second century C.E.): *hē pentáteuchos* [*bíblos*], "the book of five scrolls." Soon afterward we find it in the latinized masculine form *pentateuchus,* from which the term "Pentateuch" is derived. The Hebrew term "The Five Fifths of the Torah" appears to be later.

On analogy with the term "Pentateuch," scholars have coined additional terms, which are used in the literature:

Genesis–Numbers: Tetrateuch
Genesis–Joshua: Hexateuch
Genesis–Judges: Heptateuch
Genesis–Samuel: Octateuch
Genesis–Kings: Enneateuch

In Hebrew, the names for the five individual books were chosen from their initial words; in Greek, however, from which the latinized or Latin terms and the scholarly terms derive, the names describe their essential content:

1) *b^{e}rē'šît–génesis:* Genesis ("Beginning")
2) *w^{e}'ēlleh š^{e}môt–éxodos:* Exodus ("Departure")
3) *wayyiqrā'–leuitikón:* Leviticus ("Levitical Law")
4) *way(y)^{e}dabbēr* or *b^{e}midbār–arithmoí:* Numbers ("Census")
5) *'ēlleh hadd^{e}bārîm–deuteronómion:* Deuteronomy ("Second Law")[1]

2. *Content.* Despite its enormous scope, the content of the Pentateuch can be summarized in a few sentences. The presentation begins on a universal scale with the creation of the world and the subsequent primal history down to the division of mankind and the origin of the various peoples and nations. Then the narrative focuses on Abraham. Other characters are eliminated, and the story shifts to Isaac and Jacob. Beginning with Jacob's sons, the growth of Israel is depicted, from the sojourn in Egypt and the Exodus through the stay at Kadesh and the mountain of Yahweh and on through the period of wandering in the desert down to the death of Moses in Transjordan before the entry of the Israelites into the settled country west of the Jordan. It should be noted at once that the appointment of Joshua as Moses' successor furnishes the transition to the book of Joshua, so that the reader might be inclined to see the story of the Pentateuch continued into the beginning of the book of Judges. In the course of the narrative the legal codes and similar compilations have been interpolated at various points, according to their supposed historical origin.

Gen. 1–11 Primal History
12–50 Patriarchal History[2]

12–23	25:1-10, 12-18				Abraham
24	25:11, 19-20	26:1-33	35:27-29		Isaac
	25:21-34	26:34-35; 27–33	35:1-4, 6-20	36	Jacob
		34	35:5, 21-26	37–50	Joseph

Exod. 1:1–15:21 Oppression in Egypt and Exodus
1:1–2:10 Oppression of the Israelites and Birth of Moses
2:11–4:31; 6:2–7:7 Call of Moses

[1] This is based on a misunderstanding of Deut. 17:18, where the Hebrew does not speak of a "repetition" but of a "copy" of the law.

[2] The various narrative cycles are bracketed together in Genesis 25 and 35; the frame around the passages in the table is intended to indicate this close association.

5:1–6:1; 7:8-13 Negotiations with Pharaoh
7:14–13:16 Plagues and Release of the Israelites
13:17–14:31 Persecution and Deliverance
15:1-21 Victory Songs
15:22–40:38 Journey to the Mountain of God and Covenant
15:22–18:27 Wandering
19–24 Sinai Revelation, Decalogue, Covenant Code, Conclusion of Covenant
25–31 Regulations Establishing the Cult ("Tabernacle")
32–34 Transgression of the Covenant and New Covenant
35–40 Carrying out of Instructions in 25–31

Lev. 1–7 Sacrificial Regulations
8–10 First Priests and Sacrifices
11–15 Precepts Concerning Cleanness and Uncleanness
16 Purification Ritual for the Great Day of Atonement
17–26 Holiness Code
27 Rules Concerning Vows

Num. 1:1–10:10 Rules Concerning Levites and Order in Camp
10:11–20:13 From Sinai to Kadesh
10:11–12:16 Revolt and Opposition
13–14 Spies Sent to Canaan
15 Various Precepts
16–17 Revolt of Korah, Dathan, and Abiram
18 Rights and Duties of Priests and Levites
19 Precepts Concerning Purification
20:1-13 Murmuring of the People and Moses' Failure
20:14–36:13 Entry into Transjordan
20:14–21:35 Wandering and Battles
22–24 Balaam
25 Idolatry and Atonement
26 Organization and Census of the People
27 Rules Concerning Inheritance and Appointment of Joshua
28–30 Rules Concerning Sacrifices and Vows
31 Campaign Against the Midianites
32 Allotment of Territory West of the Jordan
33:1-49 List of Campsites
33:50–34; 29 Instructions for the Occupation of Canaan
35 Levitical Cities and Cities of Refuge
36 Supplementary Rules Concerning Inheritance

Deut. 1–11 Introductory Discourses
1–3 Events after Departure from Horeb
4:1-43 Exhortations and Warnings
4:44–5:33 Events at Horeb and Decalogue
6 Exhortation to Worship Yahweh
7 Future Relationship with the Canaanites
8:1–9:6 Exhortation to Obedience
9:7–10:11 The "Golden Calf"
10:12–11:32 Exhortation to Obedience
12–26 Deuteronomic Law Code
12:1–16:17 Regulations Primarily Concerning the Cult

16:18–21:9 Regulations Primarily Concerning Administration of Justice
21:10–26:19 Regulations Primarily Concerning Civil Law
27–30 Concluding Discourses
31–34 End of the Mosaic Period
31 Appointment of Joshua, Preservation and Recitation of the Law
32 Song of Moses
33 Blessing of Moses
34 Moses' Death

§17 History of Pentateuchal Studies

H. Bardtke, "Henning Bernhard Witter," *ZAW*, LXVI (1954), 153-81; A. Bea, "Der heutige Stand der Pentateuchfrage," *Bibl*, XVI (1935), 175-200; A. Bentzen, "Bemerkungen über neuere Entwicklungen in der Pentateuchfrage," *ArOr*, XIX (1951), 226-32; J.-P. Bouhot and H. Cazelles, "Pentateuque," in *Supplément au Dictionnaire de la Bible*, VII, pp. 687-858, 1964; O. Eissfeldt, *Die ältesten Traditionen Israels*, 1950; *idem*, "Die neueste Phase in der Entwicklung der Pentateuchkritik," *ThR*, NF XVIII (1950), 91-112, 179-215, 267-87; *idem*, *Die Genesis der Genesis*, 2nd ed., 1961; H. Holzinger, *Einleitung in den Pentateuch*, 1893; P. Humbert, "Die neuere Genesis-Forschung," *ThR*, NF VI (1934), 147-60, 207-28; E. König, *Ist die moderne Pentateuchkritik auf Tatsachen begründet?* 1933; A. Lods, *Jean Astruc et la critique biblique au XVIIIe siècle*, 1924; C. R. North, "Pentateuchal Criticism," in *The Old Testament and Modern Study*, 1951, pp. 48-83; J. de Savignac, "L'oeuvre et la personnalité de Jean Astruc," *NC*, V (1953), 138-47; D. C. Simpson, *Pentateuchal Criticism*, 2nd ed., 1924; R. Smend, Jr., *W. M. L. De Wettes Arbeit am Alten und Neuen Testament*, 1958; *idem*, "De Wette und das Verhältnis zwischen historischer Bibelkritik und philosophischem System im 19. Jahrhundert," *ThZ*, XIV (1958), 107-19; J. Steinmann, *Richard Simon et les origines de l'exégèse biblique*, 1960; F. Stummer, *Die Bedeutung Richard Simons für die Pentateuchkritik*, 1912; R. de Vaux, "A propos du second centenaire d'Astruc, Réflexions sur l'état actuel de la critique du Pentateuque," *VTSuppl*, I (1953), 182-98.

1. *Tradition*. In the postexilic period, Moses was considered the mediator or author of the Pentateuchal law, which had been given by God. The Deuteronomic law already represented a step in this direction. There is evidence for this view from the fifth century on (Mal. 3:22 [Eng. 4:4]; Ezra 3:2; 7:6; II Chron. 25:4; 35:12). The NT presupposes that he wrote the entire Pentateuch (Matt. 19:7-8; Mark 12:26; John 5:46-47; Acts 15:21; Rom. 10:5). Explicit references to this theory are found in Josephus, Philo, and the Talmud. The church borrowed this Jewish tradition that Moses was the author of the Pentateuch; until well into the seventeenth century it was only rarely disputed. It is true that occasional doubts were expressed throughout the entire period, but it is impossible to speak of critical scholarship. Origen countered the objections of Celsus to the unity and Mosaic authorship of the Pentateuch; others of the church fathers attacked similar views of various Gnostics. Several major figures disputed the Mosaic authorship on the grounds of isolated observations: in the Middle Ages, Isaac ben Jesus

(who pointed out that Gen. 36:31 presupposes the Israelite monarchy), Ibn Ezra (§1.2), and others; later, Karlstadt, Masius, Pereira, Bonfrère, and Hobbes; finally, Peyrère,[1] Spinoza,[2] Simon,[3] and Clericus.[4] No coherent and constructive observations were made. Various persons merely noticed conspicuous details without establishing a controlling principle.

The Pentateuch in fact turns out to be an anonymous work without any suggestion as to its author and without even any indirect hint that Moses was responsible for its total contents; tradition therefore claims more than does the Pentateuch itself about its origin. Only a few sections are ascribed specifically to Moses; even this limited claim is not necessarily correct. These sections are: the account of the battle against the Amalekites (Exod. 17:14); the so-called Covenant Code (Exod. 24:4); the so-called cultic decalogue (Exod. 34:27); the desert itinerary (Num. 33:2); Deuteronomy (Deut. 1:5; 4:45; 31:9, 24); the Song of Moses (Deut. 31:30). The great bulk of the Pentateuch, on the other hand, makes no claim to Mosaic authorship; neither does it claim to have been handed down by oral tradition since the time of Moses. That this negative conclusion agrees with the actual circumstances has been demonstrated since the eighteenth century by a wealth of studies and by convincing arguments of the most various sorts. For the present we shall mention a few of the many passages that point to the post-Mosaic period:

a) Some passages presuppose Israel's occupation of Palestine: "At that time the Canaanites were in the land" (Gen. 12:6; 13:7). Canaan is called "the land of the Hebrews" (Gen. 40:15). Transjordan is referred to from the point of view of a writer west of the Jordan as "beyond the Jordan" (Gen. 50:10-11; Num. 22:1; Deut. 1:1, 5).

b) Some passages show that the author lived later than the Mosaic period: the formula "to this day" (Deut. 3:14; 34:6; and *passim*); "And there has not arisen a prophet since in Israel like Moses" (Deut. 34:10).

c) Some passages presuppose the political situation of a later period: the use of *Dan* as a place name, which dates at the earliest from the Israelite settlement in the period of the Judges (Gen. 14:14; Deut. 34:1); "before any king reigned over the Israelites" (Gen. 36:31); the law concerning the king (Deut. 17:14-20).

2. *Attempts to solve the problem.* If the Pentateuch does not derive from Moses, the question then arises how in fact it came into being. The attempts

[1] In his anonymously published *Praeadamitae* (1651), I. de Peyrère suggests that Moses made use of certain sources and that portions of the Pentateuch derive from him.

[2] In the *Tractatus theologico-politicus* (1670), B. Spinoza thinks in terms of a tradition comprising several strands, and a final redaction on the part of Ezra bringing together many fragments.

[3] In his *Histoire critique du Vieux Testament* (1678), R. Simon considers only the laws Mosaic, deriving everything else from inspired annalists.

[4] In his *Sentiments de quelques théologiens de Hollande* etc. (1685), J. Clericus assumes a late origin for many parts of the Pentateuch, and a final redaction by the priest mentioned in II Kings 17:27-28 in the period following the fall of the Northern Kingdom of Israel.

to answer this question have given rise to Pentateuchal study and criticism, which have always constituted a significant portion of OT scholarship. It must be said at once that the question is justified and necessary and that attempts to answer it as precisely as possible are inevitable. The exegesis and theology of the OT cannot do without them.

The efforts to isolate the individual components that go to make up the Pentateuch and to determine their date and purpose have led to several hypothetical solutions. This critical study has two forerunners, who were soon forgotten and had no lasting effect. Pastor B. Witter, of Hildesheim,[5] used as his primary criterion for differentiation the alternation of the divine names "Yahweh" and "Elohim" in Genesis and recognized the existence of two different creation stories; he did not, however, extend his study to the entire book of Genesis. J. Astruc[6] likewise took the two divine names as his point of departure, distinguishing in Genesis two primary and ten secondary sources used by Moses.

a) The earlier documentary hypothesis (Eichhorn*, Ilgen) considered the Pentateuch (of which for the most part Genesis alone was studied) to be made up of various sources.[7] These sources are coherent narratives, which the final author or redactor used and combined as fixed documents. Difficulties of course arise as soon as one studies the legal codes (§18.3).

b) The fragment hypothesis (Geddes, Vater, and in part de Wette) took the legal codes of the Pentateuch as its point of departure. These give the impression of representing several sections of varying compass, which are independent of each other; they appear to have been juxtaposed in the Pentateuch without any internal continuity. Starting from this observation, various scholars attempted to understand the growth of the entire Pentateuch as a redactional linking of such legal and narrative "fragments." When this hypothesis is applied to the narrative sections, however, it becomes difficult to explain the deliberate structure and careful arrangement of the whole, including the chronology that accompanies this structure.[8]

c) The supplement hypothesis (Ewald [in part];[9] Bleek; Tuch; Franz Delitzsch) sought to solve this problem by assuming that one source constitutes the nucleus of the Pentateuch: the homogeneous so-called Basic Elohistic Source, which was later supplemented by Yahwistic sections. Ewald, whose approach was actually that of the early documentary hypothesis, soon dissociated himself from the supplement hypothesis and followed others in assuming two Elohistic sources, which were combined and supplemented by

[5] B. Witter, *Jura Israelitorum in Palaestinam terram Chananaeam Commentatione* etc., 1711.

[6] J. Astruc, *Conjectures sur le mémoires dont il paroit que Moyse s'est servi* etc., 1753.

[7] Eichhorn distinguished two major sources, an Elohist and a Yahwist; Ilgen distinguished two Elohists and a Yahwist (long referred to as "Jehovist" because of the misreading of *Yahweh*).

[8] A. Geddes, an English priest, assumed (1792, 1800) numerous fragments from the period of Solomon, deriving from two circles of writers (recognizable through the use of *Yahweh* and *Elohim*); J. S. Vater developed the theory that the Pentateuch was composed of 39 independent pieces with Deuteronomy as the nucleus.

[9] H. G. A. Ewald first supported this hypothesis in a review in *ThStKr, IV* (1831), 595-606.

a Yahwist. He thus produced a sort of combination documentary and supplement hypothesis (like that of Schrader).

d) The later documentary hypothesis (Hupfeld, Riehm, Dillmann, Franz Delitzsch) assumed the existence of three originally independent continuous sources: two Elohistic sources and a Yahwistic source, combined by a redactor. In addition, Riehm gained almost universal acceptance of de Wette's thesis that Deuteronomy is an independent work, distinct from the other books of the Pentateuch; thus a basis was laid for literary criticism, which thought in terms of four primary components set in a specific chronological order. Using the abbreviations common today, we have the sequence P (Priestly Source)—E (Elohist)—J (Yahwist)—D (Deuteronomy).[10]

e) Further study soon brought about major revision of the assumed chronological sequence of the sources. Reuss* and Vatke proposed to date the component designated by the siglum P not earliest but very late; the thorough studies of Graf, Kuenen*, and Wellhausen* won general acceptance for this position. The new theory went as follows: J is the earliest document in the Pentateuch; P does not stand at the beginning of the history of Yahwism, but belongs instead to a much later stage. The result is the sequence J—E—D—P. This theory was generally accepted by subsequent scholarship along with its suggested dating, though the dating has fluctuated somewhat and there has recently been a tendency to date the sources earlier: J (ninth century), E (eighth century), D (seventh century), and P (fifth century).

The major opponents of this theory are: König, Orelli, Strack, *et al.*, who considered E to be the earliest source and often assumed a much earlier dating: E about 1200, J about 1000, D about 700–650, and P about 500 B.C.; Dillmann, Graf Baudissin*, *et al.*, who suggested the sequence E—J—P—D, also involving an earlier dating in some cases: E 900–850, J 800–750, P 800–700, and D 650–623 B.C.; Kaufmann, with the thesis that P is the earliest source.[11]

f) Besides the numerous OT scholars who share the views of Graf, Kuenen, and Wellhausen, there is no lack of scholars who reject or modify it and seek to replace the later documentary hypothesis with a different theory. The following are the major schools of thought:

Many attempts have been made to retain the literary unity and Mosaic authorship of the Pentateuch; those supporting this view include Möller,[12] MacDonald,[13] Jacob,[14] Aalders,[15] Young*, and Rabast;[16] Levy[17] and

[10] Scholars since Hupfeld have also assumed the presence of a special redactor.

[11] Y. Kaufmann, *The Religion of Israel from the Beginnings to the Babylonian Exile*, 1960 (an abridged translation by M. Greenberg of the Hebrew original in eight volumes).

[12] W. Möller, *Die Einheit und Echtheit der fünf Bücher Mosis*, 1931.

[13] D. B. MacDonald, *The Hebrew Literary Genius*, 1933.

[14] B. Jacob, *Das erste Buch der Tora*, 1934.

[15] G. G. Aalders, *A Short Introduction to the Pentateuch*, 1949.

[16] K. Rabast, *Die Genesis*, 1951.

[17] I. Lewy, *The Growth of the Pentateuch*, 1955.

Wiseman[18] also seek grounds for maintaining the tradition.[19] Despite individual observations and comments that are frequently acute, these views contribute nothing toward answering the question of the origin of the Pentateuch. They are the inevitable defensive reactions against critical scholarship. Klostermann[20] and Robertson[21] represent a kind of crystallization hypothesis (Eissfeldt*), according to which the rest of the Pentateuch gradually grew up around the basic Mosaic law in the course of its public recitation.

Eerdmans[22] and Dahse[23] reject the variation between divine names as a criterion[24] and the hypothesis of continuous sources, representing instead a kind of supplement hypothesis.[25]

Löhr[26] assumes that Ezra assembled ancient material, part of which goes back to Moses, and composed the Pentateuch from it, thus in a sense reviving the fragment hypothesis.

On the basis of Pedersen's contributions to our knowledge of the Semitic mentality,[27] Engnell[28] and others assume a long chain of oral tradition lasting well into the postexilic period; they consider source analysis irrelevant or impossible. In this traditio-historical approach, too, apart from the arbitrary theories concerning history of religion associated with it, there is an unmistakable attempt to support tradition against critical opposition.[29]

Volz and Rudolph[30] reject the assumption of an E source. While Volz considers E and P to be merely redactors of J, Rudolph acknowledges the independence not only of P, but also of certain E sections, which, however, he understands as isolated interpolations in J.[31] Mowinckel,[32] too, has recently opposed the assumption of an independent E source; he prefers to interpret the E material as later supplements to and redactions of J based on variants

[18] J. Wiseman, *Die Entstehung der Genesis,* 1957.

[19] Cf. also M. H. Segal in *Scripta Hierosolymitana,* VIII (1961), 68-114; J. Liver, *ibid.,* pp. 189-217.

[20] A. Klostermann, *Der Pentateuch,* 1893.

[21] E. Robertson, *The Old Testament Problem,* 1950.

[22] B. D. Eerdmans, *Alttestamentliche Studien,* 4 vols., 1908-12; *idem,* "The Composition of Numbers," *OTS,* VI (1949), 101-216. Eerdmans assumes four strata: a polytheistic book of Adam, prior to 700 B.C. (Jacob recension); a polytheistic historical work prior to 620 (Israel recension); a monotheistic revision of both about 620; and definitely monotheistic passages from the postexilic period.

[23] J. Dahse, *Textkritische Materialien zur Hexateuchfrage,* 1912, which distinguishes ancient narrative material, a prophetical revision, and a priestly revision.

[24] The contrary view is represented by J. Skinner, *The Divine Names in Genesis,* 1914, and Driver*.

[25] See O. Eissfeldt in *ZDMG,* LXXXV (1931), 172-95, and in *ThR,* X (1938), 224-91.

[26] M. Löhr, *Untersuchungen zum Hexateuchproblem,* I (1924).

[27] J. Pedersen, *Israel,* 1926-40.

[28] I. Engnell, esp. in *Bibliskt Uppslagsverk,* 2nd ed., 1962-63.

[29] For the contrary view, see esp. Bentzen* and North.

[30] P. Volz and W. Rudolph, *Der Elohist als Erzähler, ein Irrweg der Pentateuchkritik?* 1933.

[31] For the contrary view, see O. Eissfeldt, "Die Komposition von Exodus 1–12," *ThBl,* XVIII (1939), 224-33.

[32] S. Mowinckel, *Tetrateuch-Pentateuch-Hexateuch,* 1964.

that grew up in the course of time, turning the *Jahwista invariatus* into a *variatus*.

According to Winnett,[33] the books of Exodus and Numbers contain a continuous North Israelite tradition without separate sources, which was subject to a preexilic (Deuteronomic) and a postexilic (P) revision.

Cassuto[34] supports a kind of fragment hypothesis. The Pentateuch constitutes a homogeneous work of the preprophetical period; in it a portion of the numerous separate Israelite traditions were used and revised so often that the multiplicity grew into a unity.

None of the views described means anything more than an admonition to confirm once more the soundness and reliability of the principles established by the later documentary hypothesis for analysis of the Pentateuchal sources.

3. *New approaches*. Meanwhile, Pentateuchal studies have proceeded along many different lines. Without calling the basis or principles of source analysis into question, they have on the one hand led to attempts to refine the methodology, and on the other have yielded new observations and insights that force us to redefine the concepts of "hypothesis" and "document."

a) In the realm of literary criticism we may notice efforts to refine the analysis. The sources no longer appear homogeneous, but are composed of several strata or strands. We shall discuss the various analyses of D in §25, and shall speak here only of the analysis of J, E, and P.

Schrader,[35] Budde,[36] and Bruston[37] made the first beginnings at separating J into several narrative strands, though in effect they weakened the documentary hypothesis by giving up the assumption of a single author working according to a deliberate plan. Smend[38] then took the crucial step of assuming that the traditional J source was neither homogeneous nor a basic source plus supplements, but rather consisted of two independent sources, both using the divine name "Yahweh." He termed them J^1 and J^2 and arrived thereby at five Pentateuchal sources: in chronological order, J^1—J^2—E—D—P. This theory has been followed, albeit with considerable variation, by several scholars, including Eichrodt,[39] Holzinger,[40] Meinhold,[41] Eissfeldt,[42] Simpson,[43] and Fohrer.[44] Eissfeldt substitutes the term "Lay Source" (L) for "J^1" in

[33] F. V. Winnett, *The Mosaic Tradition*, 1949.

[34] U. Cassuto, *La questione della Genesi*, 1934; *idem*, *The Documentary Hypothesis and the Composition of the Pentateuch*, 1961.

[35] E. Schrader, *Studien zur Kritik und Erklärung der biblischen Urgeschichte*, 1883.

[36] K. Budde, *Urgeschichte*, 1883.

[37] C. Bruston, "Les quatre sources des lois de l'Exode," *RThPh*, XVI (1883), 329-69; *idem*, "Les deux Jéhovistes," ibid., XVIII (1885), 5-34, 429-528, 602-37.

[38] R. Smend, *Die Erzählung des Hexateuch auf ihre Quellen untersucht*, 1912.

[39] W. Eichrodt, *Die Quellen der Genesis von neuem untersucht*, 1916.

[40] H. Holzinger in E. Kautzsch and A. Bertholet, ed., *Die Heilige Schrift des Alten Testaments*, 4th ed., I, 1922.

[41] J. Meinhold, "Die jahwistischen Berichte in Gen 12–50," *ZAW*, XXXIX (1921), 42-57.

[42] O. Eissfeldt, *Hexateuch-Synopse*, 1922.

[43] C. A. Simpson, *The Early Traditions of Israel*, 1948.

[44] G. Fohrer, *Überlieferung und Geschichte des Exodus*, 1964.

order to suggest what distinguishes this source from the cultic and priestly interests of P, while Fohrer prefers for it the siglum N on account of its pronounced nomadic character. Independently of Smend, Morgenstern[45] assumes a Kenite source (K) that came into being about 900 B.C. in southern Palestine, while Pfeiffer[46] assumes that the earliest source (S) came into being in the tenth century B.C. in Seir or southern Palestine. Hölscher,[47] on the contrary, has led the attempts to demonstrate once more the homogeneity of J. He is forced, however, to remove from J as doublets a series of sections that appear early and are in complete harmony with the characteristics of his J, while ascribing to J other sections that interrupt the progress of the narrative and do not fit into their J environment.

Procksch[48] has suggested a division of E into a source E^1 written in the Northern Kingdom and a form E^2, an expanded form of E^1 composed in Judah after the fall of the Northern Kingdom. In this case, though, it would be more accurate to speak of expansions in the sense of the supplement hypothesis.

The composite nature of P has long been recognized, especially with regard to the gradual growth of the legal complexes (Wellhausen). Von Rad's thesis,[49] however, goes well beyond the assumption of a basic source later expanded by various additions: he holds that P consists of two parallel strands, P^A and P^B, the latter exhibiting the more pronounced priestly and cultic character and going further in listing persons and dates. The question remains, though, in view of the legal material, whether the supplement and fragment hypothesis does not offer a more suitable explanation.

b) Form-critical study and motif analysis, first used on a large scale by Gunkel and Gressmann, have somewhat altered the concept of "documents." Attention no longer focuses on the individuality of the sources and their authors, but on the separate narratives and other materials, in order to comprehend their preliterary stage, the growth of oral tradition with its *Sitz im Leben* and place in the religion of the people. Seen from this point of view, the sources do not appear as deliberate compositions of great authors but as collections of ancient traditional popular material, assembled not by individuals but by schools. This approach recognizes correctly that all sources, even the more recent, contain early material, and therefore represent entities considerably more complex than had formerly been assumed. This has been particularly true since the discovery, in ever growing quantity, of the comparable traditions elsewhere in the ancient Near East. The study of the legal system and of historiography especially has led to notable, if not universally accepted, results, and will continue to increase our knowledge.

[45] J. Morgenstern, "The Oldest Document of the Hexateuch," *HUCA*, IX (1927), 1-138.

[46] R. H. Pfeiffer, "A Non-Israelite Source of the Book of Genesis," *ZAW*, XLVIII (1930), 66-73.

[47] G. Hölscher, *Die Anfänge der hebräischen Geschichtsschreibung*, 1942; *idem*, *Geschichtsschreibung in Israel*, 1952.

[48] O. Procksch, *Das nordhebräische Sagenbuch. Die Elohimquelle*, 1906.

[49] G. von Rad, *Die Priesterschrift im Hexateuch*, 1934.

There is also traditio-historical study, which, in contrast to Engnell's tradition-history, maintains the usual source analysis, but seeks to go back beyond this stage and examine the gradual growth of the present narrative tradition through the course of its long history. To this end one must pursue the various spheres of tradition, determining their age, their mutual relationship, and their reciprocal influence. On this basis, Noth,[50] in a fashion that is admittedly quite schematic, thinks in terms of five primary traditional themes, which were mutually independent: Exodus, occupation of Palestine, promise to the fathers, guidance in the desert, and revelation at Sinai. The thematically determined framework was filled out with narrative material, e.g., the plagues in Egypt and the Passover, Baal-Peor and Balaam, Jacob in Transjordan. A further process of external association and the addition of separate traditions such as the Joseph novella and various genealogies gradually produced a coalescence of the different themes.

All this focuses our attention on the prehistory of the sources; we come to see more and more how they grew through various stages. As a result Pentateuchal studies have become so complex that the period of the "hypotheses" can only be considered its beginning. It is, to be sure, a necessary beginning, the point at which everyone who studies the Pentateuch must begin afresh, only to confront the question of how the sources of the Pentateuch themselves came into being.

§18 Methods, Results, and Problems

C. H. W. Brekelmans, "Het 'historische Credo' van Israel," *Tijdschrift voor Theologie*, III (1963), 1-10; G. Fohrer, "Tradition und Interpretation im Alten Testament," *ZAW*, LXXIII (1961), 1-30; S. Mowinckel, *Le Décalogue*, 1927; *idem*, "Die vermeintliche 'Passahlegende' Ex 1–15 in Bezug auf die Frage: Literarkritik und Traditionskritik," *StTh*, V (1951), 66-88; M. Noth, *Überlieferungsgeschichte des Pentateuch*, 1948; J. Pedersen, "Passahfest und Passahlegende," *ZAW*, LII (1934), 161-75; *idem*, *Israel*, III–IV, 1940, pp. 384-415, 728-37; G. von Rad, *Das formgeschichtliche Problem des Hexateuch*, 1938 (= *Gesammelte Studien zum Alten Testament*, 1958, pp. 9-86 [Eng. *The Problem of the Hexateuch, and Other Essays*, 1966]); L. Rost, "Das kleine geschichtliche Credo," in *Das kleine Credo und andere Studien zum Alten Testament*, 1965, pp. 11-25; J. A. Soggin, "Kultätiologische Sagen und Katechese im Hexateuch," *VT*, (1960), 341-47; A. S. van der Woude, *Uittocht en Sinaï*, n.d. (1961).

1. *Results of previous studies.* In order to account for the nonhomogeneity of the Pentateuch, which comprises many kinds of material, scholars have proposed the documentary hypothesis, the supplement hypothesis, and the fragment hypothesis. The results of their studies are as follows:

a) None of these so-called hypotheses can be accepted to the exclusion of the others. In actual practice, none has ever been employed by itself; rather

[50] M. Noth, *Überlieferungsgeschichte des Pentateuch*, 1948.

one or another has been preferred, while other hypotheses have served to explain individual problems. Certainly in the present situation it is no longer possible to proceed narrow-mindedly.

b) The so-called hypotheses actually refer to various methods that contributed to the growth of the Pentateuch. It is therefore appropriate to speak, not of hypotheses, but of methods, each of which was used in its own place: the addition method (for the documentary hypothesis), the supplement method (for the supplement hypothesis), and the composition method (for the fragment hypothesis).

c) The continuous sources or narrative strands of the Pentateuch cannot be termed documents. They are more stratified and complex, often less tangible in wording and, on account of the use of ancient material, less the exclusive work of a single author than the term "document" suggests. The word "source" also fails to describe the situation accurately, while the phrase "narrative strand" leaves the legal material out of account. We shall therefore speak of "source strata."

d) In addition to the mere analysis of the source strata, we must also discuss the questions of form criticism and traditio-historical criticism, inquiring into the growth of the source strata and their *Sitz im Leben*. Attention must also be given to the redactio-historical question of their compilation as the Pentateuch.

2. *The addition method*. The addition method played the principal role in the growth of the Pentateuch. This is particularly true for the Pentateuch considered as a whole, in which three or more source strata, largely parallel in content, have been united by a process of addition and combination that took place in several stages. To give an example, the present Deluge narrative (Gen. 6:5–9:17) is made up of two originally independent presentations, each of which recounts the whole story with striking differences. They can easily be distinguished. If they are then compared to other narratives, they turn out not to be isolated fragments: they presuppose preceding narratives and are themselves continued by narratives that follow. Proceeding in this fashion, subsequent analysis yields two coherent source strata, which were later combined.

The following are the most important criteria for recognizing and distinguishing the source strata:

a) A series of texts or fragments of texts occurs, with certain alterations, two or more times. Entire sections that are parallel but separated by considerable intervals tell how the wife of one of the patriarchs was endangered (Genesis 12; 20; 26) or recount the Decalogue of the Mosaic period (Exodus 20; 34). In other instances the parallel presentations are no longer separated, but have been woven together to form a common narrative; the classic examples are the Deluge narrative (Gen. 6:5–9:17), the Joseph novella (Genesis 37; 39–48), and the Balaam narrative (Numbers 22–24).

b) The parallel sections exhibit differences and contradictions that show them to be mutually independent texts.

The two creation narratives, Gen. 1:1–2:4*a* and 2:4*b*-25, exhibit the following differences, among others:

Original state a watery chaos	—a barren steppe
Order of creation: plant—animal—man	—man—plant—animal
Creation of man and woman simultaneously	—successively

In the Deluge narrative, several differences are immediately apparent:

Deluge forty days of rain	—a second chaos
Duration 40 plus 21 days	—twelve months plus ten days
Rescue of seven pair of unclean animals, one pair of clean	—one pair of all animals

c) Similar discrepancies are found in the legal ordinances. Exod. 20:24 requires the building of an altar at every place where God reveals himself; Deut. 12:14 restricts this to a single site. Exod. 28:1 restricts the offering of sacrifice to Aaron's descendants; Deut. 18:7 extends the privilege to all Levites. Deut. 16:13 fixes a period of seven days for the Feast of Booths; Lev. 23:36 requires eight days.

d) The alternation of divine names, which Witter and Astruc took as their point of departure, is not insignificant, because, despite subsequent redaction, the varying usage is well preserved. J and the other source stratum which is partially distinguished (J^1, L, N) use the name "Yahweh" from the outset, whereas E and P at first use "Elohim" (P also uses "Shaddai") and introduce the name "Yahweh" only when God reveals himself to Moses (Exod. 3:15; 6:6).

e) Linguistic usage differs in the various source strata. The changing terminology for places, persons, and objects, turns out upon closer examination not to be random; it agrees instead with other distinguishing characteristics. Driver* and Steuernagel* present detailed tables. The differences between J and E especially suggest divergent forms of the ancient traditions in different parts of the country.

f) Finally, there are striking differences in point of view. The list of nations employed in Gen. 9:20-27 is restricted to Syria-Palestine; the two lists combined in Genesis 10 include a much larger territory, which is broken down in further detail. In addition, the separation between God and man is seen in different ways. In the story of Hagar (Genesis 16), the angel of Yahweh dwells upon earth; in Genesis 21 he calls down from heaven. In the story of the call of Moses (Exodus 3), one account portrays Moses as being forward and having to be warned; the other account portrays him as being fearful. Ethical differences, too, can be discerned: Gen. 12:10-16 simply records Abraham's lie that Sarah was his sister; Genesis 20, on the other hand, mitigates the deception by explaining that Sarah really was Abraham's half-sister. The source strata D and P especially exhibit well-defined theological positions that distinguish each from the other and from the earlier source strata.

On the basis of Pentateuchal studies we may therefore conclude with absolute assurance that there were once several source strata that came into being at different times. They extended from the period of the primal history or the patriarchal period to the death of Moses or Israel's occupation of Palestine; these were later added or combined, probably in several stages.

3. *The supplement method.* The addition method fails completely or in part to account for the legal codes, because these codes are not composed of two or more continuous strata. In these cases the supplement method comes into its own. The discrepancies within the Deuteronomic law code (Deuteronomy 12–26) are most easily explained by assuming that a basic complex received supplementary additions; similarly, the major portion of Deuteronomy constitutes an independent entity that has been inserted into its present framework, from which it differs distinctly. This is precisely the situation contemplated by the supplement method. The other portions of the Pentateuch, too, have received individual supplements, some of which were inserted in the source strata while they were still independent, others of which were inserted while the source strata were being combined or afterward.

4. *The composition method.* We come finally to the composition method, which refers to the mosaic-like joining of individual parts to form a greater whole. One cannot, of course, follow the so-called fragment hypothesis in assuming that a single author composed the Pentateuch out of a great number of unconnected individual fragments or even out of collections of intermediate size, because both the individual fragments and the collections are linked together in many and diverse ways. This method probably does describe the origin of the source strata quite accurately. In them ancient popular lore and material in written form, numerous individual fragments handed down by oral tradition and large-scale saga cycles have all been combined. The collections of laws, too, were often formed in this fashion.

5. *Motives and forces.* The question remains of the motives and forces that led to the growth of the Pentateuchal tradition. It is unquestionably not simply a historical work in the modern sense; that is, it is not the product of a scholarly interest in the recording of past events and figures for the use of an educated class (Weiser*). Of course this point of view cannot be completely disregarded, since we now realize that the ancient Near Eastern environment of Israel had a more highly developed historical consciousness and produced various forms of historical literature in much greater quantity than had formerly been assumed (§7.5).

Here, too, we find the didactic point of view, which also must have played a certain role in the growth of the Pentateuchal tradition, especially since later passages mention or presuppose questions addressed by children to their fathers. These questions resemble catechisms and are based on a corresponding system of domestic instruction.

In addition, we must not forget the pronounced pleasure Orientals derive from telling and listening to stories; this is surely one motive for the growth and transmission of these narratives.

These three points of view conflict directly with a one-sided cultic explanation, which finds the roots of the Pentateuchal tradition exclusively in the cult of ancient Israelite festivals. Of course the cult also played a role; the use of sanctuary and cult legends shows this. But it does not constitute the sole explanation. One can assume that individual narratives or even narrative complexes were employed in the cult. One can perhaps determine that a narrative is structured after the pattern of a cultic action. Mowinckel, for instance, calls the Sinai narrative the "description" or "reproduction" of a cultic festival. Such explanations demand detailed scrutiny, however, since the preexilic cult consisted more of sacrificial worship than of rhetoric. Any attempt, however, to view the Pentateuchal tradition in whole or in part as the outcome and product of the cult or, conversely, to interpret it as the norm and legitimation of the cult in the form of the festival legend behind a cultic observance must be rejected as not demonstrable from the texts.

Pedersen, for example, has interpreted the whole of Exodus 1–15 as the festival legend of the Passover on the basis of chapters 12–13; Noth has agreed with regard to chapters 1–13. In opposition, it must first be noted[1] that the actual regulations concerning Passover, the Feast of Unleavened Bread, and the consecration of the firstborn (Exod. 12:1-20, 24-27*a*; 13:3-16) belong to the late source strata D and P, which were composed at a time when the basic narrative had long been extant. Furthermore, it is not correct to say that the firstborn of the animals were sacrificed at the Passover; it is therefore impossible to derive the idea of the protection of the firstborn of the Israelites and the destruction of the firstborn of the Egyptians from the Passover, and the Passover cannot be considered the cultic nucleus of the narrative of the plagues. Finally, it is unlikely that the Passover was historicized and made to refer to the Exodus narrative before Deut. 16:1-8; this is true only for the Canaanite Feast of Unleavened Bread, which was originally independent of the Passover (Exod. 23:15; 34:18). Of course Exod. 12:21 contains a reference to the Passover, because the narrative source stratum needed a nomadic blood ritual to explain the protection of the Israelites from the "destroyer," and chose a Passover ritual for this purpose. It uses this ritual, however, because blood was needed, not out of interest in the Passover, as 12:21-23 unambiguously demonstrates. This argument shows at the same time that the separation of the Exodus and Sinai traditions, which rests on the derivation from the Passover, is untenable; traditio-historical considerations also show this separation to be erroneous.[2] Only Moses' victory song (Exod. 15:1-19), a later interpolation, gives the impression of a major break between the Exodus and subsequent events; in fact, we are

[1] Cf. the detailed discussion in G. Fohrer, *Überlieferung und Geschichte des Exodus,* 1964 pp. 79-97.

[2] On the Exodus narrative, see Fohrer, *op. cit.;* on the Sinai narrative, see W. Beyerlin, *Herkunft und Geschichte der ältesten Sinaitraditionen,* 1961 (Eng. *Origins and History of the Oldest Sinaitic Tradition,* 1965).

not dealing with two "themes" (Noth) but with one total complex.

Von Rad has also accepted Mowinckel's thesis concerning the Sinai narrative, but has altered it by suggesting that the narrative is the festival legend of the autumn covenant renewal festival at Shechem. He separates the tradition of the occupation, whose earliest form he finds in the so-called Short Historical Credo (Deut. 26:5-10), the festival legend of the Feast of Weeks at the sanctuary of Gilgal. The first assumption is contradicted, however, by the original connection between the Exodus tradition and the Sinai tradition. Furthermore, there is no evidence for the postulated festival; it cannot be derived from Exodus 19, Josh. 8:34; 24, and Deuteronomy 27, texts that are late (Deuteronomy 27) or have been subject to later revision (Joshua 24). With regard to the second assumption, it is certainly true that the occupation tradition, at least as contained in the book of Joshua, was not connected originally with the Moses and Sinai narrative but rather represented an autonomous complex. It did not, however, grow out of a cultic credo, any more than did the Hexateuch as a whole. New studies of Deut. 26:1-11 and, in part, of similar passages by Brekelmans, Rost, Weiser*, and van der Woude have demonstrated this in detail. In Deut. 26:1-11 there is no mention of any festival in connection with the offering of the first of all the fruit of the ground, at which the so-called Credo is to be recited; the different days on which harvest may come preclude such a possibility. Furthermore, the text is more like a prayer or catechism, intended to incorporate the agricultural rite into the historical traditions of Yahwism—a process that in no wise can go back to the earliest period. In addition, the text assumes a knowledge of the historical traditions; it is not their nucleus but their secondary summary, intended for teaching and learning. That it mentions the Exodus and occupation but says nothing of the events at Sinai is no more remarkable than failure of the Sinai tradition to appear in other passages. The reference to the deliverance from Egypt constitutes Israel's basic confession of faith, which for obvious reasons is repeated again and again. The Exodus event had several consequences, of which one was the Sinai covenant, another the occupation of Canaan. The occupation was the most important, because it meant attainment of the goal set by the Exodus. Failure to mention the Sinai tradition does not mean that the texts are unacquainted with it, but rather that the covenant concluded there did not play the role for them that today is ascribed to the covenant concept.

Finally, Weiser* takes as his point of departure the assumption that the linking of the revelation at Sinai, the tradition of the Exodus, and the (originally independent[3]) tradition of the occupation was not the work of J, but had already taken place before him and was a tradition that lay ready to hand. But Weiser understands this whole—the revelation of Yahweh's will and nature—as essential components of a cultic festival: the Covenant Festival that takes place, probably in the autumn, at the central sanctuary of

[3] Despite Weiser's arguments, this tradition must be considered independent.

the sacral tribal league, whose institutions Weiser claims continued on into the period of the monarchy. The Pentateuch and its sources are therefore to be understood as the fixed record of traditions deriving immediately from the cult and still having a living relationship to it, traditions meant for cultic recitation, a kind of lectionary, in fact, for the use of a cultic official. In this hypothesis nearly everything is brought together and linked with the postulated Covenant Festival: the tradition of *Heilsgeschichte,* the laws and regulations of the covenant, the historicization of other festivals, the pan-Israelite ideal, and much more, down to the Torah reading of the synagogue. The elevation of a single cultic action to the status of the sole explanation for a history lasting at least a thousand years is, however, suspect from the very outset in view of the multiplicity of the data. Furthermore, it presupposes additional hypotheses, on which it is based: a cultic tradition of the sacral Yahweh league, preserved at a central sanctuary, which had as its subject the revelation and realization of salvation in the representation and reenactment of *Heilsgeschichte* and the covenant renewal (Weiser*). This sentence contains several items of pure speculation: (1) the assumption of a sacral tribal league, which is nowhere mentioned, especially since the lists of Jacob's children probably represent genealogies (§13.1), and whose existence is contradicted by the course of history during the so-called period of the Judges;[4] (2) the assumption of a common central sanctuary, which is by no means a necessary conclusion from the preservation of the ark;[5] (3) the assumption of a Covenant Festival with a specific cultic tradition, which is nowhere mentioned;[6] (4) the assumption of a special type of cult with revelation and realization of salvation as its theme, which contradicts all the explicit statements of the OT about cultic actions; (5) the assumption of representation and reenactment in the cult, alluding to a cultic theophany whose purported occurrence in the Psalms has nothing to do traditio-historically with the original theophany at Sinai.[7] All these speculations are assembled in an additional hypothesis to explain the growth of the source strata of the Pentateuch. In reality, nothing is explained; the primary role is ascribed to a completely speculative process.

This listing does not exhaust the motives leading to the growth of the Pentateuchal tradition. One essential point—which was probably crucial in the earliest period—remains to be mentioned: the original tradition complexes are traditions having to do with the occupation or claiming of territory; they are intended to buttress the religious and legal claim of Israelite groups and tribes upon the settled territory and its shrines. This is true for the first narrative series, consisting of at least three tradition complexes, which presents the claims, based on God's promise, of the Abraham, Isaac, and

[4] Cf. the strictures of S. Herrmann, "Das Werden Israels," *ThLZ,* LXXXVII (1962), 561-74; R. Smend, *Jahwekrieg und Stämmebund,* 1963.

[5] J. Maier, *Das altisraelitische Ladeheiligtum,* 1965.

[6] For a detailed discussion, see E. Kutsch, *Das Herbstfest in Israel,* Dissertation, Mainz, 1955.

[7] C. Westermann, *Das Loben Gottes in den Psalmen,* 1953, pp. 69-72.

Jacob groups and their incipient realization. It is also true for the second series, containing the traditions of the Israelite host under Moses, making their way from Egypt by way of the mountain of God and through the desert to the borders of Canaan. It is true, finally, for the third series, connected with the figure of Joshua, which is handed down outside the Pentateuch in a portion of the book of Joshua. The divine basis for the territorial claims and the promise to the descendants involves a corresponding claim of Yahweh upon the Israelites, so that once more event and commandment, history and law, can be linked together. While the traditions were being fused and while they were being linked by the Joseph novella and the appointment of Joshua as Moses' successor, the individual portion of the growing whole came to appear in a different light, but this is only to be expected. This linking took place for the most part through living oral tradition within the total framework of religious and secular life in the course of many decades and even centuries.

§19 The Growth of the Historical Traditions

A. Alt, *Der Gott der Väter*, 1929 (= *Kleine Schriften*, I, 1953, pp. 1-78 [Eng. *Essays on Old Testament History and Religion*]); W. Beyerlin, *Herkunft und Geschichte der ältesten Sinaitraditionen*, 1961 (Eng. *Origins and History of the Oldest Sinaitic Traditions*, 1966); D. O. Edzard, "Mari und Aramäer?" *ZA*, NF XXII (56) (1964), 142-49; H. Eising, *Formgeschichtliche Untersuchung zur Jakobserzählung der Genesis*, 1940; G. Fohrer, "Tradition und Interpretation im Alten Testament," *ZAW*, LXXIII (1961), 1-30; *idem, Überlieferung und Geschichte des Exodus*, 1964; H. Gressmann, "Ursprung und Entwicklung der Joseph-Sage," in *Gunkel-Festschrift*, I (1923), 1-55; H. Gunkel, "Die Komposition der Joseph-Geschichten," *ZDMG*, LXXVI (1922), 55-71; J. Hoftijzer, *Die Verheissungen an die drei Erzväter*, 1956; A. Jepsen, "Zur Überlieferungsgeschichte der Vätergestalten," *WZ Leipzig*, III (1953/54), 265-87; O. Kaiser, "Stammesgeschichtliche Hintergründe der Josephsgeschichte," *VT*, X (1960), 1-15; C. A. Keller, "Grundsätzliches zur Auslegung der Abraham-Überlieferung in der Genesis," *ThZ*, XII (1956), 425-45; S. Mowinckel, "Hat es ein israelitisches Nationalepos gegeben?" *ZAW*, LIII (1935), 130-52; *idem*, " 'Rachelstämme' und 'Leastämme'," in *Von Ugarit nach Qumran, Eissfeldt-Festschrift*, 1958, pp. 129-50; M. Noth, *Überlieferungsgeschichte des Pentateuch*, 1948; *idem, Die Ursprünge des alten Israel im Lichte neuer Quellen*, 1961; G. von Rad, "Verheissenes Land und Jahwes Land im Hexateuch," *ZDPV*, LXVI (1943), 191-204 (= *Gesammelte Studien zum Alten Testament*, 1958, pp. 87-100 [Eng. *The Problem of the Hexateuch, and Other Essays*, 1966]); idem, "Josephsgeschichte und ältere Chokma," *VTSuppl*, I (1953), 120-27 (= *Gesammelte Studien zum Alten Testament*, pp. 272-80); L. Rost, "Die Gottesverehrung der Patriarchen im Licht der Pentateuchquellen," *VTSuppl*, VII (1960), 346-59; H. Seebass, *Mose und Aaron, Sinai und Gottesberg*, 1962; *idem, Der Erzvater Israel und die Einführung der Jahweverehrung in Kanaan*, 1966; J. Steinmann, *Les plus anciennes traditions du Pentateuque*, 1954; R. de Vaux, "Les Patriarches Hébreux et l'Histoire," *Studii Biblici Franciscani Liber Annuus*, XIII (1962/63), 287-97; A. Vergote, *Joseph en Égypte*, 1959; A. S. van der Woude, *Uittocht en Sinaï*, n.d. (1961).

1. *The patriarchs.* Before the historical narratives of the Pentateuch achieved their final form in the source strata, they went through a long process of transmission and formation, whose outlines are gradually becoming discernible. This is true first of all for the traditions about the so-called patriarchs in Genesis. It must not be overlooked that, in their present form, these very traditions contain a wealth of originally extraneous material that has been added in the course of centuries. If one disregards the expansions made by the addition of the primal history (Genesis 1–11) at the beginning and the Joseph novella at the end to provide a transition to the Moses traditions and then eliminates the extraneous, non-Israelite material from the present corpus of traditions, it shrinks down to a few brief notes and stories. The question is whether we can discover in these and perhaps in other features a nucleus of ancient tradition.

We come first to personal names corresponding to the non-Akkadian type, which are known from Mesopotamian texts of the first half of the second millennium B.C. These are primarily sentence-names made up of a verb in the imperfect and a divine name, like the name "Israel," or abbreviated names without a theophorous element, like Isaac. Names like Abraham and Jacob are well attested for this period, and for it alone.

In addition, Noth believes he can find in the texts from Mari (a site on the middle Euphrates, whose royal house and upper class were among the bearers of non-Akkadian names that entered the area during the twentieth –eighteenth centuries B.C.) both words and idioms deriving from the milieu of nomadic herdsmen, with their tribal organization and peculiar institutions, as well as legal theories and customs corresponding to what we know of ancient Israel. One may disagree with Noth on the basis of Edzard's arguments; but OT tradition is familiar with a Mesopotamian origin for certain early Israelite groups, and Gen. 24:4, 10 refers to their homeland as "Aram Naharaim," the land of the Arameans on the two rivers, i.e., the Euphrates and one of its tributaries (perhaps the Belikh). This region is suggested by the name "Haran," the city from which Abraham is said to have set out for Palestine and to which Jacob flees from Esau, as well as the names of Abraham's ostensible kinsmen: *Nahor* corresponds to the name of the city Naḫur in the vicinity of Haran; *Serug* corresponds to the name of the city Sarugi, between Haran and the Euphrates; and *Terah* corresponds to the name Til Turaḫi in the valley of the Belikh.

Further points of contact are provided by the texts from Nuzi, east of the middle Tigris,[1] dating from the somewhat later period around 1500 B.C. These exhibit a legal system of Hurrian origin; the same system is to be postulated for the Hurrians in the Euphrates region. A series of patriarchal narratives reflects their legal customs and practices. Since these are never found again in Palestinian law or narratives outside the patriarchal traditions,

[1] C. H. Gordon, "Biblical Customs and the Nuzi Tablets," *BA*, III (1940), 1-12; R. de Vaux, *Die hebräischen Patriarchen und die modernen Entdeckungen*, 1960 (originally published in French in *RB* LIII, LV, and LVI).

they probably contain ancient reminiscences of life in the region of the middle Euphrates in the sixteenth century. The legal practices include the intention of appointing a slave as heir and then the revoking of the appointment upon the birth of a son (Genesis 15),[2] use of a slave to bear children (Genesis 16; 30),[3] temporary hesitation about casting out the slave and her son (Gen. 21:8-14), fratriarchal authority within the patriarchal family (Gen. 24:50-51; 34:5-18), sale of the right of primogeniture (Gen. 25:29-34), and the role played by possession of the household gods (Gen. 31:19).[4] Of course this does not mean that the narratives with these family-law motifs are historical accounts. The motifs themselves, however, are original features of the tradition.

A bit later (fifteenth–fourteenth centuries) we find the term "Ḫapiru" or " 'Apiru,"[5] which first came to light in the Amarna Letters, the correspondence between certain rulers of Palestinian city-states and the Pharaohs, and has now turned up throughout the entire ancient Near East. It probably originated as a sociological term meaning "persons without family"; it then came to refer to the legally inferior aliens within a given state. The Hebrew term *'ibrî*, which derives from this word, characterizes the Israelites of the patriarchal period as groups of legally inferior aliens. In actual practice they must be thought of as nomadic herders of sheep and goats, tied to regions and routes with sources of water close together and sufficiently abundant pasturage, who continually alternate between steppe and settled territory, and are in constant contact with civilization. It is surely no accident that this is how the patriarchs are usually portrayed: as wandering owners of sheep and goats, interested in defending their claims to wells, who occasionally come to possess land and even begin to combine a bit of agriculture with their livestock raising. This, too, agrees with a specific early stage of development, probably even the situation of the so-called patriarchs themselves. Tradition depicts the patriarchs neither as camel bedouin[6] (despite their

[2] A. Caquot, "L'alliance avec Abram (Genèse 15)," *Semitica*, XII (1962), 51-66; O. Kaiser, "Traditionsgeschichtliche Untersuchung von Genesis 15," *ZAW*, LXX (1958), 107-26; H. Seebass, "Zu Genesis 15," *WuD*, VII (1963), 132-49; L. A. Snijders, "Genesis XV," *OTS*, XII (1958), 261-79.

[3] S. Kardimon, "Adoption as a Remedy for Infertility in the Period of the Patriarchs," *JSS*, III (1958), 123-26.

[4] A. E. Draffkorn, "*Ilāni/Elohim*," *JBL*, LXXVI (1957), 216-24; M. Greenberg, "Another Look at Rachel's Theft of the Teraphim," *ibid.*, LXXXI (1962), 239-48.

[5] R. Borger, "Das Problem der 'apīru ("Ḫabiru"), *ZDPV*, LXXIV (1958), 121-32; J. Bottéro, *Le problème des Habiru à la 4ème rencontre assyriologique internationale*, 1954; A. de Buck, "De Hebreeën in Egypte," in *Varia Historica*, 1954; M. Greenberg, *The Ḫab/piru*, 1955.

[6] B. Brentjes, "Das Kamel im Alten Orient," *Klio*, XXXVIII (1960), 23-52; W. Dostal, "The Evolution of Bedouin Life," in *L'antica società beduina*, 1959, pp. 11-34; J. P. Free, "Abraham's Camels," *JNES*, III (1944), 187-93; H. Klengel, "Zu einigen Problemen des altvorderasiatischen Nomadentums, *ArOr*, XXX (1962), 585-96; W. G. Lambert, "The Domesticated Camel in the Second Millenium, Evidence from Alalakh and Ugarit, *BASOR*, CLX (1960), 42-43; A. Pohl, "Das Kamel in Mesopotamien," *Or*, XIX (1950), 251-53; *idem*, "Nochmals das Kamel in Mesopotamien," *ibid.* XXI (1952), 373-74; *idem*, "Zur Zähmung des Kamels," *ibid.* XXIII (1954), 453-54; R. Walz, "Zum Problem der Domestikation der

ostensible possession of camels) nor as caravaneers in the Negeb[7] nor as settled farmers, but as seminomads under the influence of settled life while themselves just beginning the process of settling down. Here we probably have another ancient feature of the tradition.

Alt has put his finger on the actual nucleus of the patriarchal tradition. The figures of the "fathers" are described as historical persons for the sake of the "God of the fathers" or the gods of these fathers, to whom long after the occupation a continuing cult was devoted at a series of ancient sanctuaries.[8] We are dealing here with tribal gods, whether we prefer to call them the gods of the fathers or the nomadic form of an El religion. They were accepted and worshiped on the basis of a revelation received by the founder or leader of a tribe. They gave to the tribes the promise of possession of land in the settled areas and descendants, which lies at the very heart of the tradition. The promise to turn the group related by blood (*'am*, "people") into a great nation (*gôy*) conceived in territorial and political terms corresponds to the promise of possession of the land (Gen. 12:2, 7; 17:5, 8). The original nucleus is the designation of the patriarchs as recipients of revelations and promises, as founders of cults, and as charismatic leaders of their tribes within an undifferentiated and nonspecialized culture. They are leaders of different tribes; the relationships between the patriarchs are a secondary development. The story returns over and over again to accounts of theophanies associated with blessings and promises of territorial possession and descendants, but also to disputes with the previous possessors of the land. At one time there were probably many such ancestral traditions, since we must think in terms of a considerable number of Israelite tribes or groups infiltrating gradually into Palestine. Only a few of these traditions, however, became or were drawn into the common lore of all Israel.

And so the traditions found in Genesis of the Abraham tribe, the Isaac tribe, and the Jacob tribe, as we may call them for the sake of simplicity, drawing on earlier Mesopotamian and Hurrian features, establish the religious and legal claims of the tribes upon the settled territory. Since the presentation

---

altweltlichen Cameliden," *ZDMG*, CI (1951), 29-51; *idem*, "Neue Untersuchungen zum Domestikationsproblem der altweltlichen Cameliden," *ibid.*, CIV (1954), 48-87; *idem*, "Beiträge zur ältesten Geschichte der altweltlichen Cameliden under besonderer Berücksichtigung des Problems des Domestikationszeitpunktes," in *Actes IVe Congrès Anthropologique*, III (1956), 190-204.

[7] W. F. Albright, "Abram the Hebrew: A New Archaeological Interpretation," *BASOR*, CLXIII (1961), 36-54; *idem*, "Some Remarks on the Meaning of the Word *SḤR* in Genesis," *ibid.*, CLXIV (1961), 28; E. A. Speiser, "The Word *SḤR* in Genesis and Early Hebrew Movements," *ibid.*, pp. 23-28; for still another view, see C. H. Gordon, "Abraham and the Merchants of Ura," *JNES*, XVII (1958), 28-31.

[8] Cf. also O. Eissfeldt, "El and Yahweh," *JSS*, I (1956), 25-37; B. Gemser, *Vragen rondom de Patriarchenreligie*, 1958; V. Maag, "Der Hirte Israels," *Schweiz. Theol. Umschau*, XXVIII (1958), 2-28; L. Rost, "Die Gottesverehrung der Patriarchen im Lichte der Pentateuchquellen," *VTSuppl*, VII (1960), 346-59; C. Steuernagel, "Jahwe und die Vätergötter" in *Beer-Festschrift*, 1935, pp. 62-71.

shows them in various stages of their relationship to the settled territory—from fleeting contacts to the beginnings of permanent settlement—we are also dealing here with traditions about the way the first Israelite groups occupied the land in Palestine. Here we have the nucleus, in both form and content, of the patriarchal narratives: the independent narratives embodying the territorial claims and describing the territorial occupation of several Israelite groups with charismatic founders or leaders of tribes and based on promises made by the tribal gods. This also describes the historical background of these narratives.

The individual traditions about Abraham and Isaac center around sites in the territory of the tribes in the mountains of Judea and in the Negeb. They came into being and were first elaborated in this region. Genesis 15 and 26:2-3 probably represented the point of departure; in the course of time, however, considerable portions of the Isaac tradition were transferred to the figure of Abraham, and the Isaac tradition itself atrophied. The tradition about Jacob centers around sites in the territory of the tribes in central Palestine (Shechem and Bethel); it was first elaborated there. Whether the figure of Jacob was brought by Ephraimitic settlers into the colonial territory of the land of Gilead east of the Jordan and underwent further development in the Jacob-Esau and Jacob-Laban cycles to meet the demands of the new situation (Noth) or whether one must instead distinguish between two independent Jacob figures, one west of the Jordan, the other east of the Jordan (Eissfeldt), cannot be definitely decided. It is more reasonable to suppose that the tradition east of the Jordan goes back to an Israel group that had already laid a claim to specific regions in Transjordan and that their ancestor Israel is equated with Jacob in Gen. 32:29 (Eng. 32:28) and 35:10. One must always remember that no story or statement about the patriarchs is extant in its original form; all have been subject to considerable revision and expansion.

2. *Moses*. The tradition about Moses is essentially no different from the patriarchal traditions. The combined elements of theophany, oracle of favor, cult, and leadership in the story of the call of Moses parallel the nucleus of the patriarchal narratives. Like those ancestors, Moses appears as the recipient of revelation, charismatic leader, and cult founder for a group living in primordial circumstances, which for simplicity's sake will be called the "Moses host." In him all functions, including the priestly and prophetical, are still combined. While the motif of the increase in numbers of the Israelites in Egypt is definitely not original, but serves the secondary purpose of linking the story of Moses with the patriarchal traditions, the promise of territory given to the Moses host (Exod. 3:8; 13:17) represents an original traditio-historical element. Like the promises of territory and descendants in Genesis, it belongs to the very core of the tradition. This agrees also with the actual historical situation (the gradual settling of seminomadic groups in the built-up areas of Palestine during the fourteenth–twelfth centuries B.C.) and with the further traditions of the Moses host, which deal with their penetration into Palestine. That we are dealing with a promise of territory distinct from

the promises of Genesis is shown by the description of the land as "flowing with milk and honey," which occurs first in Exod. 3:8. This may be an ancient phrase used by the Israelites dwelling in Egypt, who imagined a rich land similar to the circumstances in Egypt. This also explains their subsequent disappointment in the period of living in the steppes and desert after the flight from Egypt.

Seen from this point of view, the original traditions of the Moses host turn out to be, like the patriarchal traditions, a narrative of territorial claims and territorial occupation. As in the patriarchal narratives, the claim of a host of Israelites to the settled territory of Palestine is given a religious basis. As in the patriarchal narratives, this is done by reference to an explicit promise of the deity to whom the host has turned at the instigation of their leader and who makes this promise the basis of his relationship to the host. The purpose of the Moses tradition is therefore to show that the host led by Moses out of Egypt to the borders of Palestine has as good a claim to a portion of the settled territory west of the Jordan as the Abraham, Isaac, and Jacob tribes and groups, or any other. Only the thought of such future territorial possession makes sense of the flight out of Egypt. This, too, as the ancient Song of Miriam (Exod. 15:20-21) shows, takes place in the name of Yahweh, just as the promise of territory comes from Yahweh. The success of this endeavor, ascribed to Yahweh, is one good reason why Mosaic Yahwism did not remain a mere variety of tribal religion.

The Exodus tradition is not an isolated complex made up out of disconnected individual sagas (Gressmann), or woven out of a single element of Israel's basic confession of faith, namely, deliverance by Yahweh. Neither can it be called the festival legend of a cultic observance (§18.5). In point of fact, the subsequent narrative also contains original elements of tradition that are connected with those of the Exodus. The connection is made clear from the very outset by the relationship between the call of Moses and Sinai or the mountain of God,[9] by the goal given the Exodus through the promise of territory, and by the itinerary that begins with the account of the flight and continues after the Song of Miriam. Conversely, the connection is reinforced once more by the Sinai narrative. This means that the Exodus and Sinai (or mountain of God) traditions never had an independent existence, but rather constituted a unity from the very beginning (Beyerlin, Fohrer, Van der Woude).

Like the narrative of the introduction of a judicial system by Moses' father-in-law (Exodus 18),[10] the Sinai tradition, which has been subject to much expansion and revision, contains a nucleus that is traditio-historically

[9] O. Eissfeldt, "Lade und Gesetztafeln," *ThZ,* XVI (1960), 281-84; M. Haelvoet, "La théophanie du Sinaï," *ETbL,* XXIX (1953), 374-97; W. Rudolph, "Der Aufbau von Ex 19-34," in BZAW, LXVI (1936), 41-48.

[10] C. H. W. Brekelmans, "Exodus XVIII and the Origins of Yahwism in Israel," *OTS,* X (1954), 215-24; R. Knierim, "Exodus 18 und die Neuordnung der mosaischen Gerichtsbarkeit," *ZAW,* LXXIII (1961), 146-71.

ancient, from which the figure of Moses can no more be eliminated than it can from the nucleus of the Exodus tradition. The essential elements dealing with the treaty concluded between Yahweh and the Moses host seem to have been employed in Exodus 19 and 24. It is clear that the event had no constitutive significance but rather, as the consolidation of a relationship that had already begun, was one of several consequences of the deliverance from Egypt. The continuation of the narrative in Numbers may contain additional elements of tradition pointing to an approach to Palestine through Transjordan, which had just been resettled by groups of Arameans. The original character of the Kadesh traditions is still in doubt.

All in all, we can make out an original totality: the narrative about the territorial claims and territorial occupation of the Moses host. This narrative comprises the ancient traditional elements of the initial situation in Egypt, the Exodus, the alliance with Yahweh at Sinai and subsequent wandering until arrival in Transjordan, the death there of the charismatic leader, and probably at one time also the account of settlement in the built-up territory west of the Jordan. This narrative, which parallels the traditions of other Israelite tribes and groups, is intended to justify the religious and legal claims of the Moses host to the settled territory of Palestine. It does this in the fashion that is at least in part typical of the OT, linking together faith in God and the account of his dealings with men and nations in past, present, and future.

3. *Other narratives of territorial occupation.* The tradition of how the Moses host settled in the territory west of the Jordan is not preserved. In the present course of the narrative, its place is taken by the Joshua tradition, found in the book of the same name. Joshua originally appeared only in the narrative of the occupation of the territory west of the Jordan; his presence in the Pentateuch is historically and traditio-historically secondary. It is nevertheless clear that the Joshua tradition is yet another narrative of territorial occupation. Even this does not exhaust the list of originally independent traditions of this type. Numbers 13–14 is also an occupation story, telling how the tribe of Caleb occupied the Canaanite city of Hebron in the mountains of Judah. The story of Sihon (Num. 21:21-31) goes back to reminiscences of how the tribe of Gad occupied their territory. Num. 32:1-38 tells of the distribution of territory east of the Jordan to Gad and Reuben, while Num. 32:39-42 contains brief notes about other groups. It is still a question whether the traditions centered about the oasis of Kadesh are not based on yet another occupation narrative, in which Aaron (not yet a priestly figure) played a role (Exod. 17:10). A detailed analysis of the Pentateuch will discover further traces and allusions.

4. *The development of the groundworks.* The nucleus of the Pentateuch, as well as of the Joshua traditions, is made up of the narratives supporting the territorial claims and the territorial occupation of various Israelite groups and tribes; a good part of them, at least, contain the explicit statement,

"Yahweh has given all the land into our hands." [11] Subsequent redaction of these narratives, which certainly took place in the course of oral tradition, did not lead directly to the source strata of the Pentateuch. At first, as Noth has demonstrated, it produced a common groundwork (G). This is shown by the similarities between J and E, which are definitely independent of each other. If we think in terms of a third early source, we must distinguish between a first and second basic narrative or groundwork.

The path leading from the original separate traditions to the comprehensive groundwork or groundworks cannot be traced in detail; its general features, however, can be made out. At this state especially it is cultic and didactic forces, as well as pleasure derived from elaborating a narrative, that influenced the formation of the tradition. The motif of territorial claims, which to all intents and purposes had been satisfied, diminished in importance, while interest in description of the actual course of history does not yet predominate.

a) An important step leading toward G was the genealogical linking of the patriarchal narratives. The process can be thought of in this fashion: First the Jacob narrative gained general recognition and acceptance and became part of the developing Pentateuchal tradition, so that the most natural way to introduce the preliminary material dealing with Isaac and Abraham was to extend the genealogical series backward and make them ancestors of Jacob (Noth). This argument of course presupposes a certain stock of Pentateuchal traditions. Since this assumption is uncertain, one can ask instead whether the Abraham narrative did not constitute the point of departure, to which were then appended the Isaac narrative (thus accounting for the way in which the Abraham narrative has undermined the Isaac narrative) and then the Jacob (Israel) narrative. In any event, the narratives and the complex made up out of them became the common property of all Israel at a relatively early date. The connection with the subsequent narratives resulted in increased emphasis being placed upon the promise of territorial possession and descendants, while the motif of realization of these promises became less significant.

In addition, the patriarchal and Mosaic traditions became linked, at first without the intervening Joseph novella. Apparently the narrative immediately went on to describe how Jacob and his family wandered to Egypt, as Deut. 26:5 still presupposes, where the "Aramean" probably refers to Jacob (cf. Gen. 24:4 ff.; 31:24).

Finally, a simple early form of the Joshua tradition must have been appended at an early date, leading to the introduction of the figure of Joshua into the Pentateuch. For P's account of Joshua's appointment as Moses' successor (Num. 27:15-23; Deut. 34:9), which does not harmonize with the subsequent occupation narrative of this source stratum, points to an earlier tradition, which the other source strata also presuppose with

[11] S. Wagner, "Die Kundschaftergeschichten im Alten Testament," *ZAW*, LXXVI (1964), 255-69.

their mention of Joshua and, in part, of his appointment as Moses' successor (Exod. 17:8-13; 24:13-15; 32:17-18; 33:11; Num. 11:28-29; Deut. 31:14, 23).

We must therefore assume that even in its earliest form G had completed the process of linking the Abraham-Isaac-Jacob tradition with the Moses tradition and the early Joshua tradition to form a continuous narrative. In this narrative the patriarchal tradition emphasized the element of territorial promise, while the Joshua tradition was henceforth to be the primary vehicle for representing the realization of the promise. The complex of the Moses tradition, including the Exodus and the events at Sinai, took on the significance of justifying Yahweh's claim upon Israel and representing Israel's obligations toward Yahweh.

b) In the course of its development, G absorbed many other ancient traditions. These include lists, like the list of the kings of Edom (Gen. 36:31-39) and genealogical lists (Gen. 22:20-24; 25:1-6), and narratives reflecting the history of various tribes and groups (Gen. 16:4-14; 19:30-38; 21:8-21; 25:21-26*a*, 29-34; 29–30;[12] 38:27-30). The story of the rape of Dinah (Genesis 23)[13] also belongs in this category. In addition, there are various sayings and songs, such as the legal maxim in Gen. 9:6, the oracle delivered to Rebecca (Gen. 25:23), and the blessings pronounced by Isaac (Gen. 27:27-29, 39-40). Less frequently, we find nature sagas such as the story of the destruction of Sodom (Genesis 19),[14] the story of the manna and the quails (Exodus 16; Numbers 11), or the miraculous springs (Exodus 17; Numbers 20).[15] There are, on the other hand, numerous sanctuary and cult legends, which not uncommonly are of Canaanite origin. They portray the revelation of El Roi (Genesis 16), the replacement of human sacrifice by animal sacrifice at a sanctuary no longer named (Gen. 22:1-19), the discovery of the sacred sites at Bethel (Gen. 28:10-22) and Penuel on the Jabbok (Gen. 32:25-33 [Eng. 32:24-32]),[16] the building of altars at Shechem and Bethel (Gen. 33:18-20; 35:1-4)—just as the cults of Beer-sheba and Hebron and their environs frequently play an important role—the burning bush (Sinai; Exodus 3), the bronze serpent (Num. 21:4-9), and the institution of circumcision (Genesis 17;

[12] S. Lehming, "Die Erzählung von der Geburt der Jakobsöhne," *VT*, XIII (1963), 74-81.

[13] S. Lehming, "Zur Überlieferungsgeschichte von Gen 34," *ZAW*, LXX (1958), 228-50.

[14] M. Haller, "Die Blüemlialpsage religionsgeschichtlich gesehen," in *Bertholet-Festschrift*, 1950, pp. 208-21; J. P. Harland, "Sodom and Gomorrah," *BA*, V (1942), 17-32; VI (1943), 41-54.

[15] S. Lehming, "Massa und Meriba," *ZAW*, LXXIII (1961), 71-77.

[16] O. Eissfeldt, "Non demittam te, nisi benedixeris mihi," in *Mélanges Robert*, 1957, pp. 77-81; J. L. McKenzie, "Jacob at Peniel: Gn 32,24-32," *CBQ*, XXV (1963), 71-76; J. Schildenberger, "Jakobs nächtlicher Kampf mit dem Elohim am Jabok (Gen 32,23-33)," in *Miscellanea Biblica Ubach*, 1953, pp. 69-96; H. J. Stoebe, "Der heilsgeschichtliche Bezug der Jabbok-Perikope," *EvTh*, XIV (1954), 466-74; E. Täubler, "The First Mention of Israel," *PAAJR*, XII (1942), 115-20; F. van Tright, "La signification de la lutte de Jacob près du Yabboq, Genèse XXXII 23-33," *OTS*, XII (1958), 280-309.

Exod. 4:24-26;[17] Josh. 5:2-9). Novella-like materials, such as the endangering of a patriarch's wife (Gen. 12:10-20; 20; 26) or the wooing of a wife (Genesis 24) are also included.

c) The latter category can also be included among the new narratives that came into being in the course of G's development, either woven out of the material ready to hand or appended as a kind of midrash. These include the description of the working conditions laid down for the Israelites (Exod. 5:5-21), the accounts of the first nine Egyptian plagues (Exod. 7:14–10:19),[18] of the worship of the bull image (Exodus 32),[19] of Moses' shining face (Exod. 34:29-35),[20] of the inspiration of the elders (Num. 11:14-30), or of the rebellion of Korah, Dathan, and Abiram (Numbers 16–17),[21] to name only a few characteristic examples.

5. *The two groundworks.* Between the source strata JE on the one hand and N (J^1, L) on the other there exist both many points of agreement and significant differences. In the first place, these differences may be traced back to the fact that G developed in different ways; the narrative strands culminating in JE and in N diverged at many points. In similar fashion, divergent tradition in Southern and Northern Israel produced the discrepancies between J and E. In the second place, the differences can be traced back to the fact that N was formed from an earlier stage of G with the addition of nomadic traditions, while JE grew out of a later stage, in which G was supplemented primarily by the material not represented in N. In this context we may disregard the source strata P and D. In any event, comparison of the three earlier source strata shows that we must think in terms of two groundworks: an earlier one (G^1) and a later one (G^2).

[17] Y. Blau, "Der Ḥatan Damim," *Tarbiz,* XXVI (1956/57), 1-3; J. de Groot, "The Story of the Bloody Husband (Exodus IV, 24-26)," *OTS* II (1943), 10-17; J. Hehn, "Der "Blutsbräutigam"," *ZAW,* L (1932), 1-8; H. Junker, "Der Blutbräutigam," in *Nötscher-Festschrift,* 1950, pp. 120-28; H. Kosmala, "The 'Bloody Husband'," *VT,* XII (1962), 14-28; G. Richter, "Zwei alttestamentliche Studien: I. Der Blutbräutigam," *ZAW,* XXXIX (1921), 123-28; F. Sierksma, "Quelques remarques sur la circoncision en Israël," *OTS,* IX (1951), 136-69.

[18] G. M. Camps, "Midraš sobre la historia de les plagues," in *Miscellanea Biblica Ubach,* 1953, pp. 97-113; H. Eising, "Die ägyptischen Plagen," in *Junker-Festschrift,* 1961, pp. 75-87; H.-P. Müller, "Die Plagen der Apokalypse, eine formgeschichtliche Untersuchung," *ZNW,* LI (1960), 268-78; strange theories concerning the historicity of the plagues have recently been proposed by G. Hort, "The Plagues of Egypt," *ZAW,* LXIX (1957), 84-103; LXX (1958), 48-59; E. Stechow, "Santorin-Katastrophe und 'Ägyptische Finsternis'," *FF,* XXVI (1950), 174; I. Velikovsky, *Worlds in Collision,* 3rd ed., 1952.

[19] S. Lehming, "Versuch zu Ex 32," *VT,* X (1960), 16-50; I. Lewy, "The Story of the Golden Calf Reanalysed," *ibid.,* IX (1959), 318-22; M. Noth, "Zur Anfertigung des goldenen Kalbes," *ibid.,* pp. 419-22; J. J. Petuchowski, "Nochmals "Zur Anfertigung des 'goldenen Kalbes' "," *ibid,* X (1960), 74.

[20] F. Dumermuth, "Moses strahlendes Gesicht," *ThZ,* XVII (1961), 240-48; J. de Fraine, "Moses' 'cornuta facies' (Ex 34,29-35)," *Bijdragen,* XX (1959), 28-38; S. Schulz, "Die Decke des Moses," *ZNW,* XLIX (1958), 1-31.

[21] G. Hort, "The Death of Qorah," *ABR,* VII (1959), 2-26; S. Lehming, "Versuch zu Num 16," *ZAW,* LXXIV (1962), 291-321; H. S. Nyberg, "Koraḥ's uppror (Num 16 f.)," *SEÅ,* XII (1947), 230-52.

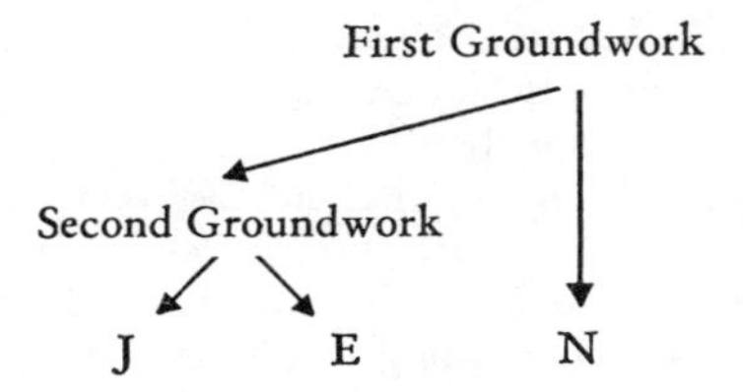

It is probably safe to assume that G^1 was current only as oral tradition, while G^2 was extant in written form at the time of the division of the kingdom after the death of Solomon. This form may well have developed in Jerusalem, where the further expansion and first codification of historical tradition would harmonize with the national consciousness of the era of David and Solomon, with its increasing historical consciousness. After the division of the kingdom, G^2 branched into a northern and a southern form.

a) Analysis of the Pentateuch indicates that G^1 recounted essentially the following events; their original order is not always clear:

Abraham's (and Lot's) departure from their homeland
Promise of territory and descendants to Abraham
Destruction of Sodom and deliverance of Lot
Announcement of the birth of Isaac
Endangering of Sarah
Casting out of Hagar
Birth of Isaac
Promise to Isaac
Jacob–Esau
Jacob–Laban
Jacob's return and stay at Shechem or Bethel
Wives and descendants of Esau
Jacob's emigration to Egypt
Oppression of the Israelites in Egypt and plan to exterminate them
Introduction of Moses
Moses' stay in Midian and his marriage
Call of Moses in Midian and return to Egypt
Slaying of the Egyptian firstborn and departure of the Israelites
Pursuit and deliverance at the Red Sea
March to the mountain of God (Sinai/Horeb)
Sinai covenant (descent of Yahweh or ascent to Yahweh)
Apostasy and command to depart
Desert wandering
Provision of water (mostly miraculous springs)
Manna and quails
Rebellion of Aaron and Miriam or Dathan and Abiram
Spying out of the land (Caleb) and its consequences
Edom denies permission to pass
Further wandering and victory over the Amorites
Repeated murmuring and apostasy of the people
Death of Moses

This is followed by the corresponding simple early groundwork of the book of Joshua (§30.2).

b) The following narratives are the primary additions in G^2:

Wooing of Rebecca
Jacob's reconciliation with Esau
Joseph novella
Moses' first negotiations with the Pharaoh
The preliminary Egyptian plagues
Introduction of a judicial system upon advice of Moses' father-in-law
Story of Balaam
Apportionment of territory to Gad and Reuben
Appointment of Joshua as Moses' successor

The addition of the Joseph novella and the story of Balaam are particularly important. The former is an accretion taken over from the territory of the "house of Joseph" in central Palestine (Genesis 37; 39–48; 50). Though it draws upon originally independent individual narratives, it represents a deliberately constructed whole with its own clear purpose; its unity is apparent from the very beginning. It is improbable, however, that the novella goes back to an ancient Israelite story of the Ramesside era, as Vergote proposes. The justification for the migration of the Israelites to Egypt and for the rise of the "house of Joseph," as well as the eclipsing of Manasseh by Ephraim, are closely connected with it. On these grounds it is possible to date the origin of the novella to around 1100 B.C.; in view of the Egyptian material, we may perhaps also assume that the narrative represents a revised Israelite version of a Late Egyptian tale. This may explain the features that are unmistakably reminiscent of wisdom literature.

The origin of the Balaam story (Numbers 22–24)[22] is very complex. A clear distinction must be drawn between the songs and the narrative. Mowinckel is undoubtedly right in assuming that the two songs of Numbers 24 were originally independent and that the songs of Numbers 23 are dependent on them, and also in assuming that they presuppose no acquaintance with the present narrative. The narrative of E, however, is not dependent on that of J; instead, both go back to G^2, in which a Balak tradition has been added describing an altercation between Israelites and Moabites. There was, however, a Balaam saga, as the song of Numbers 24 as well as Num. 31:8-16 and Josh. 13:22 presuppose. He seems to have been portrayed

[22] W. F. Albright, "The Home of Balaam," *JAOS,* XXXV (1915), 386-90; *idem,* "The Oracles of Balaam," *JBL,* LXIII (1944), 207-33; M. Burrows, *The Oracles of Jacob and Balaam,* 1938; O. Eissfeldt, "Die Komposition der Bileam-Erzählung," *ZAW,* LVII (1939), 212-41; *idem,* "Sinai-Erzählung und Bileamsprüche," *HUCA,* XXXII (1961), 179-90; M. Löhr, "Num 22,2–24,25," *AfO,* IV (1927), 85-89; S. Mowinckel, "Der Ursprung der Bilʿāmsage," *ZAW,* XLVIII (1930), 233-71; L. Pákozdy, "Theologische Redaktionsarbeit in der Bileam-Perikope," in *Von Ugarit nach Qumran, Eissfeldt-Festschrift,* 1958, pp. 161-76; V. Vermès, "Deux traditions sur Balaam. Nombres XXII 2-21 et ses interprétations midrashiques," *Cahiers Sioniens,* IX (1955), 289-302.

as a charismatic functionary of the shrine of Baal Peor, east of the Jordan, endowed with the power of magical words. The development of this figure leads from his portrayal as a malevolent foe to a description of how God overcomes his evil power and finally to his being compelled by God to pronounce, not a curse, but an efficacious blessing upon Israel. This final stage provides the basis for the songs in Numbers 24, which J added to his presentation (§22.2).

The primal history (Genesis 1–11) did not yet constitute a part of G². J was the first to add to his narrative this introduction, whose structure follows the epic of Atraḫasis (§12.2). This approach was then followed by N—though in large part drawing upon different narratives or motifs and therefore not dependent on a common original—and later by P, which is considerably less independent.

§20 The Origin of the Dependent Legal Collections and Codes

J. G. Aalders, *De verhouding tussen het Verbondsboek van Mozes en de Codex Hammurabi,* 1959; B. Baentsch, *Das Bundesbuch,* 1892; *idem, Das Heiligkeits-Gesetz,* 1893; W. Caspari, "Heimat und soziale Wirkung des alttestamentlichen Bundesbuches," *ZDMG,* LXXXIII (1929), 97-120; H. Cazelles, "L'auteur du code de l'alliance," *RB,* LII (1945), 173-91; *idem, Études sur le Code de l'Alliance,* 1946; K. Elliger, "Das Gesetz Leviticus 18," *ZAW,* LXVII (1955), 1-25; *idem,* "Heiligkeitsgesetz," *RGG,* 3rd ed., III (1959), 175-76; L. E. Elliott-Binns, "Some Problems of the Holiness Code," *ZAW,* LXVII (1955), 26-40; C. Feucht, *Untersuchungen zum Heiligkeitsgesetz,* 1964; G. Fohrer, *Die Hauptprobleme des Buches Ezechiel,* 1952, pp. 144-48; A. Jepsen, *Untersuchungen zum Bundesbuch,* 1927; R. Kilian, *Literarkritische und formgeschichtliche Untersuchung des Heiligkeitsgesetzes,* 1963; B. Kipper, "De origine mosaica 'Libri Foederis'," *VD,* XXIX (1951), 77-87, 159-71; A. Klostermann, "Beiträge zur Entstehungsgeschichte des Pentateuchs," *ZLThK,* XXXVIII (1877), 401-45 (= *Der Pentateuch,* I [1893], 368-418); K. Koch, *Die Priesterschrift von Exodus 25 bis Leviticus 16,* 1959; W. Kornfeldt, *Studien zum Heiligkeitsgesetz,* 1952; S. Küchler, *Das Heiligkeitsgesetz, Lev. 17–26,* Dissertation, Königsberg, 1929; J. L'Hour, "L'Alliance de Sichem," *RB,* LXIX (1962), 5-36, 161-84, 350-68; A. Menes, *Die vorexilischen Gesetze Israels,* 1928; J. Morgenstern, "The Book of the Covenant," *HUCA,* V (1928), 1-151; VII (1930), 19-258; VIII/IX (1931/32), 1-150, 741-46; XXXIII (1962), 59-105; *idem,* "The Decalogue of the Holiness Code," *ibid.,* XXVI (1955), 1-27; S. Mowinckel, "Zur Geschichte der Dekaloge," *ZAW,* LV (1937), 218-35; M. Noth, *Die Gesetze im Pentateuch,* 1940 (= *Gesammelte Studien zum Alten Testament,* 1957, pp. 9-141); W. Nowack, "Das Bundesbuch" in BZAW, XXXIV (1920), 132-40; R. H. Pfeiffer, "The Transmission of the Book of the Covenant," *HThR,* XXIV (1931), 99-109; K. Rabast, *Das apodiktische Recht im Deuteronomium und im Heiligkeitsgesetz,* 1948; G. von Rad, *Deuteronomium-Studien,* 2nd ed., 1948, pp. 16-24 (Eng. *Studies in Deuteronomy,* 1963); R. Rendtorff, *Die Gesetze in der Priesterschrift,* 1954; H. Graf Reventlow, *Das Heiligkeitsgesetz formgeschichtlich untersucht,* 1961; A. van Selms, "Die Bondsboek en die reg van Gosen," *HTSt,* XVI (1961), 329-43; J. A. Thompson, "The Book of the Covenant Ex 21–23 in the Light of Modern Archaeological Research,"

ABR, II (1952), 97-107; L. WATERMAN, "Pre-Israelite Laws in the Book of the Covenant," *AJSL*, XXXVIII (1921/22), 36-54; A. C. WELCH, *Deuteronomy, The Framework to the Code*, 1932; P. WURSTER, "Zur Charakteristik und Geschichte des Priesterkodex und des Heiligkeitsgesetzes," *ZAW*, IV (1884), 112-33.

1. *Survey*. Besides the historical traditions, some of the source strata of the Pentateuch include other material, which is usually termed "law." The OT, however, does not contain any systematically constructed legal works, but only collections of laws and law codes. The selection of material treated in these collections appears haphazard at first glance; as elsewhere in the ancient Near East, however, it is probably determined by their intent and purpose. In any case, they do not furnish even a relatively complete picture of the Israelite legal system, because the customary law obtaining at any time was for the most part transmitted orally. Most of the collections of laws and law codes, all of which were originally independent, have been absorbed by the source strata of the Pentateuch and should therefore now be termed dependent. Before they served as materials for the source strata, they had their own prehistory, which must be traced for each individual case. Collections of ordinary ("secular" or "social") laws and collections of cultic laws will be treated in the same fashion. Although the two types differ significantly in content, they have become interlocked and mutually supplementary.

The dependent legal collections and codes include above all the so-called Covenant Code and the so-called Holiness Code, together with additional collections or groupings that have been absorbed into P. The Deuteronomic law, on the other hand, can always be considered an independent legal code (§25).

2. *The Covenant Code*. The Covenant Code, sometimes called the Book of the Covenant and designated by the siglum C, received its name from its present association with Exod. 24:7, which states that Moses "took the book of the covenant and read it in the hearing of the people." Since it is stated that the people themselves listened to the Decalogue (Exod. 20:2-17), the phrase "book of the covenant," like the expression "all the words of Yahweh and all the ordinances," can refer only to Exod. 20:22–23:19. This literary framework, however, is the product of a late stage in the development of the Pentateuch. In reality, C is a secondary interpolation in the Sinai narrative, in which the term "book of the covenant" originally referred to the Decalogue (Exod. 20:2-17) as the basis of the covenant between Yahweh and Israel.

C is usually described as running from Exod. 20:22 to 23:33. Three qualifications must be stated at once, however. In the first place, 20:22-23 is distinguished by its plural form of address from the rest of the section, which uses the singular almost exclusively; these two verses represent a secondary introduction by the hand of the writer that incorporated C into the Sinai narrative, using 20:22-23 to provide a transition. Furthermore, the tertiary series of apodictic laws in 23:10-19 is closely connected with the so-called cultic decalogue of J (Exodus 34; §8.2). Within this passage, too, a decalogue can be distinguished, later expanded by the addition of regulations concerning the sabbatical year (vss. 10-11) and the three annual feasts (vs. 14). Its fourth through tenth commandments follow precisely the sequence of the decalogue of J, which also contains its first through third commandments. The dependence of 23:10-19 on the decalogue of J is shown unambiguously by the fact that the sequence follows, not the original form of J's decalogue, but its expanded text, and presupposes at least the additions in 34:22-23. Exod. 23:10-19 is therefore a late supplement to C. Finally, 23:20-33 has nothing at all to do with C. It contains portions of a dismissal by Yahweh, which should be assigned to the source strata J and E. Its original position was following Exodus 33 or 34.

For C, then, we are left with the complex Exod. 20:24–23:9, organized as follows:

(20:22-23	Secondary introduction)
20:24-26	Altar law
21:1–22:16	"Ordinances" (21:1—*mišpāṭim*)
	21:2-11 Slave law
	21:12-17 Capital crimes
	21:18-36 Bodily injury
	21:37–22:16 (Eng. 22:1-17) Property offenses
22:17-30	Religious offenses and duties
23:1-9	Administration of justice
(23:10-19	Supplement)

We shall inquire first into the origin of the separate sections, which did not belong together from the outset, as is shown by the position of the superscription (21:1) following the altar law and by the different forms of law.

A. The altar law (20:24-26) requires the piling up of earth or unhewn stones to form an altar whenever God gives occasion that he be cultically invoked at a particular place.[1] In content, at least, this law derives from the early period when Israelite nomads were settling in Canaan. This of course does not exclude the possibility that at a late date it was used for polemic against the building of splendid and luxurious altars (Eissfeldt*), a practice attacked in Hos. 10:1.

B. The collection in 21:1–22:16 (Eng. 21:1–22:17), referred to as "ordinances," does not represent a unitary legal code; it is composed of several individual collections.

a) The slave law in 21:2-11 is a piece of detailed casuistic legislation.[2] Although the boring through of the ear as a sign of slavery after the slave has been brought before God or to the door of the house is very archaic and is described in terms of a household god, the regulations presuppose settled

[1] E. Robertson, "The Altar of Earth (Exodus XX 24-26)," *JJS*, IV (1948), 12-21; J. J. Stamm, "Zum Altargesetz im Bundesbuch," *ThZ*, I (1945), 304-305.

[2] P. Heinisch, "Das Sklavenrecht in Israel und im Alten Orient," *StC*, XI (1934/35), 201-18.

life in a permanent civilization and already restrict the treatment of a slave as a piece of property.

b) The list of capital crimes (21:12-17) contains a portion of the *môt-yûmāt* series (§8.3). These are laws setting forth the crime and its punishment, which have been constructed according to the model of the series of apodictic rules of conduct. This is a late form-critical type, and the series has been distributed among various law codes; these observations suggest that this section is later than the preceding. We are not dealing with sacral law recited on cultic occasions. On the contrary—quite apart from the fact that even the ordinary casuistic law is considered God's gift—the form, which approximates that of the apodictic series, seems to reflect legislation framed in popular style for ease in memorization.

c) The regulations dealing with bodily injury, whether fatal or not (21:18-36), are mostly casuistic laws, most of which follow the principle of compensating the damage caused. Archaic material is also to be found, however, like the principle of precise revenge expressed in the *lex talionis* (vss. 23-25),[3] the taboo conception of the goring ox (vs. 28),[4] and the evaluation of a slave as a piece of property (vs. 32). Settled life within a permanent civilization is presupposed throughout.

d) The section dealing with property offenses (21:37–22:16 [Eng. 22: 1-17]) is casuistic legislation, which discusses primarily questions of cattle stealing (not only compensation, but also punishment) and theft in general (21:37–22:3 [Eng. 22:1-4]), goods given in security (22:6-12 [Eng. 22:7-13], vs. 8 [Eng. vs. 9] exhibiting a very archaic approach), animals given in security (22:9-12 [Eng. 22:10-13]; possibly of Israelite origin), hiring of animals (22:13-14 [Eng. 22:14-15]), and the rape of an unbetrothed virgin (22:15-16 [Eng. 22:16-17]). These laws, too, presuppose life in settled territory, where possession of cattle plays an important role for the individual Israelite.

C. The ordinances concerning religious offenses and duties (22:17-30 [Eng. 22:18-31]) comprise for the most part laws formulated after the model of apodictic rules of conduct. There are also statements having a different form. Like the alternation between singular and plural address, this points to a gradual composition and redaction of this section. In detail, vss. 17-19 (Eng. 18-20) discuss religious offenses, vss. 20-26 (Eng. 21-27) discuss the protection of the legally, socially, and economically weak,[5] and vss. 27-29 (Eng. 28-30) discuss duties toward God and the tribal ruler, as well as cultic offerings, while vs. 30 (Eng. 31), demanding holi-

[3] Cf. A. Alt, "Zur Talionsformel," *ZAW*, LII (1934), 303-5 (= *Kleine Schriften*, I [1953], 341-44); A. S. Diamond, "An Eye for an Eye," *Iraq*, XIX (1957), 151-55.

[4] A. van Selms, "The Goring Ox in Babylonian and Biblical Law," *ArOr*, XVIII 4 (1950), 321-30.

[5] F. C. Fensham, "Widow, Orphan, and the Poor in Ancient Near Eastern Legal and Wisdom Literature," *JNES*, XXI (1962), 129-39; I. Lewy, "Dating of Covenant Code Sections on Humaneness and Righteousness (Ex XXII 20-26; XXIII 1-9)," *VT*, VII (1957), 322-26.

ness, is a late conclusion. This section bears the particular stamp of Yahwism most strongly.

D. The basic laws pertaining to the administration of justice (23:1-9) are formulated apodictically, so that all free Israelites, who constitute the local legal entity, may impress them upon their memory. They have been revised and supplemented to show the impact of Yahwism. For the rest, they presuppose settled life in the towns of the civilized region.

It turns out that the individual collections of C, with the exception of the altar law, presuppose settled life in a permanent civilization. Their often striking similarity to other legal codes of the ancient Near East, not least the Code of Hammurabi, is not based on literary dependence; it is the result of the borrowing by the Israelites, as they became settled, of the legal theories of the Canaanite city-state civilization of Palestine (Pfeiffer). Just as the Canaanite legal theories were influenced particularly by Mesopotamian concepts, though resting at least in part upon further local Canaanite development, so Israel appropriated the legislation suitable to settled life, frequently permeating it with the spirit of Yahwism.

What does C represent as a whole? Is it a haphazard conglomeration of material or a higher literary unit? The latter view, supported especially by Merx, is probably closest to the truth, as comparison with other legal codes will show. The Holiness Code and Deuteronomy are similarly structured, so that an introductory cultic directive is followed by various laws pertaining to the administration of justice, social welfare, religion, and ethics. The selection and composition of the smaller collections therefore probably took place deliberately, and C most likely represents a consciously assembled law code, even though Morgenstern's and Waterman's assumption of artistic structure in decads and pentads will not stand up.

The intent and purpose of the collection can be seen from the situation obtaining in the ancient Near East. Small collections of individual judgments or decisions, such as existed in various cities, were drawn upon and supplemented by means of additional sections comprising laws formulated apodictically. The altar law at the beginning was added to give the whole a polemic tone. The end result was a legal code intended not to present the customary law in force at the time but to support a legal reform, in which new ordinances or judgments framed as laws altered earlier decisions. Beer is essentially right in seeing in C a guide for the reformation of justice (*Exodus*, p. 125). Despite the borrowing of Canaanite law, there is an unmistakable tendency to oppose Canaanite culture and permeate it with the forces of Yahwism (Weiser*).

The dating of C must probably be differentiated from the dating of the individual collections. We must note first that it lays no claim to having been proclaimed to Moses on Sinai and that it cannot derive from Moses, as Caspari, Cazelles, Sellin*, and Welch (Kadesh) assume. Most of its regulations presuppose life in a permanently settled region; even the more archaic altar law serves new purposes. Neither is it likely to have come into being soon after the Israelite conquest, in the premonarchic period (Jepsen, Noth, Sellin-Rost*), because the mention of the tribal rulers in 22:27 suggests at most an isolated earlier ordinance; in general, the laws pertain to an advanced stage of settled life. Furthermore, the dispute with the Canaanite way of life began very gradually. The lower limit is fixed in any case by the fact that C was incorporated into the source stratum E (*pace* Noth) and is earlier than Deuteronomy. It seems most likely that C originated in the early period of the monarchy, about the ninth century. This conclusion agrees with the dating of Menes, who sees in C the legal deposit of Jehu's revolution, and of Morgenstern, who, on the basis of the altar law, prefers to connect it with Rechabite circles or the followers of Elisha. These two scholars are also correct in their assumption that C almost surely did not come into being in Judah (Reuss*) but rather in the Northern Kingdom of Israel, the home of E (Steuernagel* *et al.*). In accordance with the usual practice in the ancient Near East, though, it was probably created as a royal code of legal reform, even if it was not actually the law of the land (Caspari).

We may therefore distinguish the following stages in the growth and redaction of C: (1) origin of the individual collections; (2) combination of the individual collections 21:2–22:16 (Eng. 22:17) under the superscription in 21:1*a*; (3) association with other material to form a royal law code (20:24–23:9); (4) incorporation into E in a place different from that presently given it (§21:2); (5) insertion into the Sinai narrative.

3. *The Holiness Code.* The Holiness Code (H), Leviticus 17–26, received its name from Klostermann on account of the frequently recurring formula "You shall be holy; for I Yahweh your God am holy" and its variants (e.g., Lev. 19:2; 20:7). In fact, its distinguishing characteristic is the demand for holiness in the sense of cultic and ethical purity that it makes of the people. This marks it as an originally independent entity, which has been incorporated into P and adapted to suit this source stratum (§21.2). No superscription occurs; only internal continuity shows that it begins with chapter 17. On the other hand, 26:3-45, together with the formal subscription in vs. 46, provides a distinct conclusion.

At first glance, H does not seem to exhibit any logical organization or deliberate structure, as a summary of the content shows:

17	Slaughtering of animals and eating their flesh
18	Sexual intercourse
19	Religious and ethical regulations
20	Capital offenses, sexual and otherwise
21	Holiness of priests
22	Holiness of cultic offerings and sacrifices
23	Calendar of feasts
24:1-9	Details of worship in the sanctuary
24:10-23	Israelite law applies to aliens

25:1–26:2 Sabbatical Year and Jubilee Year
26:3-46 Declaration of reward and punishment

H does not constitute an original self-contained unit. Even after elimination of the additions and changes that were intended to adapt H to P, we are left with a series of repetitions: e.g., 17:12=19:26*a*; 19:3*b*=19:30*a* and 26:2*a*; 19:27-28=21:5; 19:31=20:6; 19:34=24:22. This suggests that H, like C, represents the combination of several individual collections that were once autonomous. It is by no means clear, however, how many individual collections are involved and where they begin and end. Therefore many discussions content themselves with stating that H was composed on the basis of several independent units and collections (Elliott-Binns), but that their number can no longer be ascertained (Sellin-Rost *).

Baentsch assumes three strata, viz., 18–20+23–25; 21–22; 17, which were put together by the final redactor of 26. The first two strata are themselves composites of smaller collections. Bertholet thinks in terms of twelve independent sections combined to form H; Eissfeldt * proposes five collections, each concluding with general exhortations to keep the commandments (17–18; 19; 20; 21–22; 23+25 [24 being mostly a later addition]). Elliger suggests a considerably more complicated course of development: the earliest literary stratum, a kind of legal basis for the community, is contained in the nucleus of 17–19+25–26 (Ph_1), which was expanded by a later redactor and supplemented by the addition of 21:1-15; 20 (Ph_2), with the intent of placing these obligations upon the individual and not merely upon the community as such; Ph_2 was then supplemented twice, first by the addition of 21:16-24; 22:17-22; 23 * (Ph_3), then by the addition of 22:1-16, 26-33; 24; and the expansions in 23 (Ph_4). Kilian sees a Proto-Holiness Code in portions of 18–25, in which various sources, some independent, some already joined in larger units (18–20*), were brought together prior to 586 B.C., while a second redactor created the pre-P form of H, including 26; after this, he assumes a P-redactor and further supplements (17). Feucht, too, assumes a Proto-H formed from 18–23A and a few verses from Numbers (from the pre-Deuteronomic period), 25 (625–609 B.C.), and 26 (exilic); these sections are themselves in turn composed of a multiplicity of sources and fragments.

Such complicated explanations are not very convincing. This is especially true of Reventlow's form-critical analysis, according to which the basis of 17–20 is the so-called apodictic law, which grew up around a decalogue in 19. This basis is then said to have grown to its present form in a long process of continuous development involving various stages and strata, which included not only material expansions and changes but also a considerable amount of torah material and preaching, as well as priestly law in 21–25. Essentially the same course of development is assumed for 21–26, with the difference that 21, for example, is based on priestly professional lore. The nucleus of the whole (the decalogue in 19) derives from Sinai; other sections, too, go back to the Sinai and desert situation. From the very outset, according to this theory, H was connected with the cult, the ancient Israelite Covenant Festival, and was a liturgical document.

It would be more accurate to say that H is clearly the product of a loose juxtaposition, possibly in several stages, of extant complexes of precepts (Noth), the more so because in general the individual chapters constitute reasonably unified sections, treating quite different material.

A. The ordinance concerning the slaughtering of animals (17:1-7) presupposes that the Deuteronomic requirement of a single cultic center was in force, so that the nucleus (vss. 3-4), and certainly the detailed expansions, derive from the post-Deuteronomic period, albeit they make use of cultic traditions that are in part very ancient. The supplement (17:8-16), which is introduced by a new superscription, contains a few expansions, followed by the prohibition against eating blood and carrion. Here we are dealing with conceptions that are in part ancient but have been subject to later reformulation and revision.

B. Leviticus 18 is based on a decalogue containing rules of conduct going back to the nomadic period, intended to regulate sexual activity in the extended family (§8.2), which has been revised in several stages (Elliger). It was first expanded to form a dodecalogue, proclaimed as the ordinance of Yahweh, and made to refer to marriage. It was then incorporated into a general law against unchastity, which was intended to guarantee the holiness and cultic acceptability, not of the family, but of the community. This law belongs to a later period. The whole was finally placed in a parenetic framework.

C. In 19:3-12, after the introduction, a decalogue in the plural can be discerned or surmised (Mowinckel). The first four commandments and the last four can be identified without any trouble; the middle two, however, in vss. 5-8 and 9-10, are more difficult to determine. The various apodictic forms show that we are dealing with a series of rules of conduct, but not with an original series. The commandments are instead framed after the pattern of those in the Decalogue of Exodus 20 (a tertiary series); they are influenced by the socio-ethical requirements of Deuteronomy and are more recent than the latter book. This decalogue might be called a domestic "catechism." It is followed in 19:13-18 by a decalogue in the singular, which is form-critically late. It was simply constructed after the pattern of earlier series, and represents a kind of freely composed "catechism" concerning proper life and behavior. Its ethical requirements protecting the weak and the "neighbor" from injustice in daily life and in court are based on the theology of the prophets and Deuteronomy. Lev. 19:19 contains a three-part series prohibiting the combination of things of two different kinds; in content, this series may be pre-Israelite. Vss. 20-22 then contain a casuistic discussion of a special case in marital law; vss. 23-25, a commandment, perhaps pre-Israelite, concerning the harvesting of fruit from newly planted trees; vss. 26-31, various individual ordinances against idolatrous and superstitious practices; vs. 32, the requirement that older persons be honored; vss. 33-34, the prohibition against exploitation of a stranger; and vss. 35-36, the requirement of honesty in buying and selling. Despite the appearance of ancient concepts, therefore, the whole section is a motley assortment dating from a late period, more concerned with rules of conduct than with actual law.

D. The content of 20 is largely identical with that of 18, except that the description of the transgression is followed at once by threat of the death penalty. The nucleus (vss. 7-21) consists of a list of capital sexual offenses made up of laws from the *môt-yûmāt* series (§8.3; 20:2), i.e., casuistic legal precedents formulated apodictically (vss. 9-13, 15-16); these have undergone various kinds of expansion. They are preceded by a similarly formulated law against "Moloch" worship,[6] with expansions (vss. 1-6), and followed by the formally equivalent addendum in vs. 27, which comes after a concluding exhortation (vss. 22-26). As in C, the nucleus goes back to the early preexilic period.

E. Chapter 21 contains two sections, each introduced by a superscription. The first (vss. 1-15) comprises regulations prohibiting the priests from exposing themselves to certain types of cultic uncleanness. The second (vss. 16-24) is a list of the defects that make it impossible to exercise priestly office. Since this is all part of priestly professional lore, its use in cultic recitation is quite out of the question. As Noth has shown in detail, none of the ordinances antedates the early exilic period.

F. The cultic regulations concerning offerings and sacrifices (22) may be grouped in several subdivisions (vss. 1-9, 10-16, 17-25, 26-33), but these subdivisions are no more unitary than the whole. Just as a great variety of stylistic forms succeed one another, so all kinds of regulations of various origin have been juxtaposed, interpreted, expanded, supplemented, and connected with other portions of H (especially 17 and 21). If one assumes several stages in the growth of H, 22 was added in one of the latest.

G. The festival calendar (23) is also not a real unit, but rather a composition of two traditions. The first, like Ezek. 45:21-25, tersely describes the vernal and autumnal festivals, probably following the tradition of the Jerusalem Temple. The other presents at greater length the ordinances pertaining to the three agricultural and harvest festivals, which Israel borrowed from the Canaanite cult. There is much to recommend the view that H seeks to combine the two series of festivals (Noth); this necessitates dating the calendar in the exilic period.

H. The ordinances concerning the lamps and shewbread in the sanctuary

[6] E. Dhorme, "Le dieu Baal et le dieu Moloch dans la tradition biblique," *AnSt*, VI (1956), 57-62; K. Dronkert, *De Molochdienst in het Oude Testament*, 1953; O. Eissfeldt, *Molk als Opferbegriff im Punischen und Hebräischen und das Ende des Gottes Moloch*, 1935; J.-G. Février, "Molchomor," *RHR*, CXLIII (1953), 8-18; J. Hoftijzer, "Eine Notiz zum punischen Kinderopfer," *VT*, VIII (1958), 288-92; W. Kornfeld, "Der Moloch," *WZKM* LI (1952), 287-313.

(24:1-9) probably constitute a supplement to H, as does the etiological legal narrative 24:10-23 (with its interpolated laws).

I. The precepts concerning the Sabbatical Year, to be observed every seven years, and the Jubilee Year, to be observed every fifty years[7] (25:1-55, supplemented by 26:1-2), also reached their present form by means of a long course of development. The precepts concerning the Sabbatical Year (vss. 1-7, 17-25, 35-40*a*, 42-43, 47-49, 53, 55) may have constituted the foundation; but the juxtaposition of singular and plural address shows that they, too, do not form a unit.

K. Chapter 26 proclaims reward in the case of obedience (vss. 3-13) and punishment in the case of disobedience (vss. 14-39), along with the promise of mercy when punishment is accepted contritely (vss. 40-45). This section has its own separate history, as is shown in vss. 3-39 by the juxtaposition of Yahweh speech in the first person and impersonal formulations and in vss. 40-45 by the transition from direct address to Israel to the third person. Traditio-historically, the proclamation of reward and punishment at the end of a legal code has a long history behind it. Even the Code of Hammurabi ends with a brief blessing for the maintenance of justice and a series of curses, developed *in extenso*, upon those who scorn the code. The list of calamities that God will send is also a motif that follows ancient Near Eastern models. The last portion of the chapter especially presupposes the catastrophe that befell the state of Judah and the deportations to Babylonia.

When H was assembled out of once independent individual collections and complexes, chapter 17, with its cultic ordinances, especially those concerning the slaughtering of animals (17:1-7), was placed at the beginning, after analogy to the structure of C. This explains its isolated position. On the other hand, the sequence presenting the holiness of the community (18), of the priests (21), of offerings and sacrifices (22), of the festival calendar (23), and of the Sabbatical and Jubilee Years (25), followed by the concluding proclamations (26), can be interpreted as a deliberate and orderly structure. Only the interpolation of the motley assortment of ordinances in 19 and the capital offenses in 20 breaks the sequence; it can be explained, however, by observing that this order brings together in 18–20 all the ordinances pertaining to the everyday life of the community. Despite the diverse material, then, the structure of H is more highly developed than that of C.

Like C, H is basically a legal code, although it includes extralegal regulations in 19 and bits of priestly professional lore in 21. As a whole, it follows the practice of the ancient Near Eastern legal codes, defining the kind of justice that is to prevail by taking over and extending or changing old ordinances and introducing new ones; its guiding principle is cultic and ethical purity ("holiness"). It is intended to provide the legal basis for a community whose political and governmental powers are obviously very restricted.

[7] For a discussion of both, see E. Kutsch in *RGG*, II[3] (1958), 568-69; III[3] (1959), 799-800 (with bibliography).

Some of the individual collections or complexes must be dated in the post-Deuteronomic or exilic period; this also fixes an upper limit for the origin of H, making it impossible to date the Holiness Code in the pre-Deuteronomic period (Elliott-Binns). All the evidence suggests instead that H was codified during the period of the Babylonian Exile (sixth century). Any attempt to date it more precisely must take into account the similarities between H and the exilic prophet Ezekiel, which are too extensive to be fortuitous. Reventlow's proposed solution—to consider H the ritual for a cultic observance whose material Ezekiel also draws upon—is impossible, because H represents a legal code and some of the individual collections within it are very late. But serious objections can also be raised against the assumption that H is earlier than Ezekiel and that Ezekiel is dependent upon H, or, conversely, that Ezekiel or one of his disciples was the author or redactor of H. These same objections apply to the more detailed theory of Kilian, that Ezekiel is dependent on "Proto-H," while the redactor of the pre-P version of H is dependent in turn upon Ezekiel. It is instead most likely that Ezekiel and the redactor of H, each independently of the other, take as their point of departure at least extant or developing individual collections and complexes, if not a first combined edition. The latter might have come into being toward the end of the preexilic period and been known to the prophet, who belonged to the priestly circles of the Temple, while he was still in Jerusalem. Its further revision and final codification as H, however, did not take place until the Exile.

We may therefore postulate the following stages in the growth and redaction of H: (1) the growth of the individual collections and complexes through a gradual process, sometimes lasting very long, involving manifold expansion and revision; (2) a first combined collection, made at Jerusalem toward the end of the preexilic period; (3) final redaction as the legal code H during the Exile; (4) incorporation in the source stratum P, with supplements and changes.

4. *Other collections of laws.* We shall refer only briefly to the other dependent collections, the more so because for the most part they do not represent law in the strict sense, but rather cultic regulations and priestly professional lore (§10.4).

Leviticus 1–7 contains instructions pertaining to the sacrificial system. The first section (1–5) is made up of cultic regulations, with the emphasis partially on reproduction of the ritual (1–3), partially on the occasion and effect of the sacrifices (4–5). The core of 1–3 appears to derive from the Jerusalem of the late preexilic period; that of 4–5 seems more likely to come from the exilic or postexilic period. Chapters 6–7 record the priestly professional lore necessary for the performance of the sacrifices, above and beyond the ritual; originally, this knowledge was undoubtedly transmitted orally, and may have been committed to writing after the destruction of the Temple in 587 B.C. The whole collection came into being during the exilic or postexilic period, and was later incorporated into P.

The precepts regarding what is clean and what is unclean in Leviticus 11–15 are, for the most part, a collection (itself composed of several sections) of priestly professional lore concerning purity and impurity. There are regulations about clean and unclean animals (11), which are in part very ancient; these were added to well into the post-Deuteronomic period (cf. Deut. 14:3-21). Other regulations deal with the uncleanness resulting from giving birth (12) and from skin diseases (13–14); the instructions as to the proper measures to take are framed in the style of ritual. Still other regulations deal with uncleanness deriving from bodily discharges (15); these are in casuistic style. The pre-P collection was incorporated into P.

The situation is probably similar in the case of the quite diverse ordinances in Numbers 4–6; 15; 18:8-32; 19; and 28–30,[8] which now form part of P. It is scarcely possible, however, to assume that the source stratum P drew almost exclusively on ancient material, using a ritual collection as the basis for Exodus 25–Leviticus 16 (Koch).

The series of curses in Deut. 27:15-26 contains casuistic law formulated apodictically. It came into being in the Deuteronomic period (§8.3), and is therefore far from being the most archaic series of prohibitions in the OT.[9] The series rapidly lost its independent status, and came to serve the purposes of a fictitious cultic action within the framework of Deuteronomy.

The two decalogues in Exodus 20 and 34 are not mentioned in this context because they represent series of rules of conduct, and were brought together by E and J, respectively.

§21 The Growth of the Source Strata

1. *Further redaction of the groundworks.* The earlier source strata of the Pentateuch grew out of further redaction of G. In the process, J and E made use of the later presentation G^2, while N, after its conservative fashion, made use of G^1. P presupposes the combination JEN, albeit often going back, deliberately or by chance, to the earlier presentation G^1. In any case, the source strata rest upon the activity of individual authors, who exhibit various linguistic and stylistic forms. Traditio-critical analysis refutes the assumption that we are dealing with works deriving from "schools" of narrators, showing that the lack of formal uniformity, mentioned as an argument against individual authorship, should instead be understood as evidence of the author's dependence upon the long and complex history of transmission.

The motive forces behind the growth of the source strata cannot be sought in the cultic or didactic realm, or in simple pleasure in telling stories. We find instead two other motives: the intention of surveying and portraying a particular historical period important to one's own people, and the attempt

[8] L. Rost, "Zu den Festopfervorschriften von Numeri 28 und 29," *ThLZ*, LXXXIII (1958), 329-34.

[9] G. von Rad (ATD), p. 119.

to permeate this portrayal with religious concepts and understand events theologically.

Apart from their particular idiosyncrasies, the authors of the earlier source strata faithfully followed the traditions they used both as a whole and in detail. These traditions had already attained a form so fixed that few changes could be made in sequence or content; the final literary version was for the most part subject only to linguistic and stylistic revision. This probably holds true also for the special material of the source strata, not found in G, most of which does not represent a literary innovation but rather was formed out of other branches of the tradition.

The case of P is slightly different. This source stratum took the total presentation available (JEN) and made selections from it, abbreviated it, and added other traditions. Its author conceived the whole according to a new and independent plan, as well as formulating it as a literary work in his own peculiar linguistic and stylistic form. He nevertheless borrowed much material out of reverence for tradition, giving up thereby the chance for absolute consistency in his work. This holds true particularly in view of the observation that he has also used special material in his work, extended passages of traditions with their own prehistory, e.g., the creation account and the narrative in Genesis 23, which diverges widely from his usual manner of presentation.

2. *Inclusion of legal collections and codes.* While J and N restrict themselves to historical tradition, E and P have also incorporated legal collections or codes. Despite its narrative framework, Deuteronomy must be considered an independent legal code.

The original position within the source stratum of the Covenant Code, which was incorporated into E, remains unsure; the present location, at any rate, is secondary (§20.2). Weiser* assumes that it once followed Joshua 24, constituting the legal document embodying the covenant concluded at Shechem. Sellin-Rost *, on the other hand, assume that it came before the section Deut. 27:2, 8, 5-7*a* (thought to belong to E) and constituted the law given to Moses before the crossing of the Jordan and engraved upon a stone at Shechem. It was later displaced by Deuteronomy 12–26. Still others place C here, but consider it Moabite law. All these suggestions, however, are merely hypotheses; the original place of C within E can in fact no longer be ascertained. In any case, a Deuteronomistic redactor later incorporated it in the Sinai narrative, and Deuteronomic or Deuteronomistic hands are likewise responsible for the references to the altar law of C in Deut. 27:4-7 (Proto-Deuteronomy) and Josh. 8:30-35 (Deuteronomistic redaction). At the same time, in order to incorporate C, he took the description of the people's fear of Yahweh and Moses' approach alone to him (Exod. 20:18-21), which had originally referred to the Decalogue (Exod. 20:1-17), and placed it after the Decalogue to introduce C. In this way C found its final location in the Pentateuch.

A number of originally independent legal codes or collections have been incorporated into P; the most important of them is H (§20.3-4). These have all received various supplements and changes intended to adapt them to the views and other ordinances of P. The standard commentaries should be consulted for details.

3. *The nature and character of the source strata.* In this way, if we include D, four (or probably even five) source strata came into being, some of which are composed of narrative material only, while others contain both narrative and legal material in varying proportion. These source strata therefore represented independent historical accounts or historical and legal accounts. Their temporal sequence can be determined with some probability. Opinions may differ as to the relationship between J and E, so that E has sometimes been placed before J; all observations, however, suggest that J is the earlier source stratum. It is more difficult to date the additional source stratum that has recently been separated from J (J^1, L, N). Although it is usually considered the earliest stratum, there seems to be considerable evidence for the assumption that, although based on an earlier form of the common tradition than J (G^1), it was in fact assembled as a reply to the theological perspective of J. In this case, it can be placed between J and E. We therefore arrive at the sequence J—N—E—D—P. In addition, the Pentateuch contains some further material that does not belong to any of the source strata, but has been incorporated independently of them (§27).

The nature and character of the source strata are determined in the first place by the fact that they were not composed and written down all at once, but rather came into being in the course of a long and various history. Within this history, final literary redaction and definition by a single author mark an especially noteworthy stage; it is, however, only the latest (for the time being) of several stages. The growth of the source strata did not take place exclusively or even primarily as an act of literary creation, but rather as an extended process within a much more inclusive area of life. Secondly, the source strata are determined in part by the narrative material contained and incorporated in them, which was originally transmitted orally. Despite all revision, the ancient narratives have at times preserved so much of their peculiar quality that at first glance they do not seem to form part of a source stratum at all. In such cases, we must determine whether this is due to the peculiar character they have preserved or whether they are in fact incompatible with the source stratum. Purely literary criteria do not always suffice for this decision.

The source strata are both collections of ancient narrative and legal material and also artistic compositions. They grew up and were shaped through oral tradition; at the same time, however, they are literary works with a fixed written form. Their authors are both collectors and original writers. These facts explain many irregularities and inconsistencies within the source strata. Their later linking to form the Pentateuch has made it impossible to separate them in every case down to the last single word. Sometimes this separation can be made very precisely; sometimes one can say only that a particular section exhibits elements of two or more source strata.

§22 THE SOURCE STRATUM J

L. ALONSO SCHÖKEL, "Motivos sapienciales y de alianza en Gn 2–3," *Bibl,* XLIII (1962), 295-316; K. BUDDE, *Die biblische Urgeschichte,* 1883; G. H. DAVIES, "The Yahwistic Tradition in the Eighth-Century Prophets," in *T. H. Robinson-Festschrift,* 1950, pp. 37-51; O. EISSFELDT, "Stammessage und Novelle in den Geschichten von Jakob und seinen Söhnen," in *Gunkel-Festschrift,* I (1923), 56-77 (= *Kleine Schriften,* I [1962], 84-104); *idem, Geschichtsschreibung im Alten Testament,* 1948; *idem,* "Sinai-Erzählung und Bileam-Sprüche," *HUCA,* XXXII (1961), 179-90; B. L. GOFF, "The Lost Jahwistic Account of the Conquest of Canaan," *JBL,* LIII (1934), 241-49; H. HELLBARDT, *Der Jahwist und die biblische Urgeschichte,* Dissertation, 1935; M.-L. HENRY, *Jahwist und Priesterschrift,* 1960; G. HÖLSCHER, *Die Anfänge der hebräischen Geschichtsschreibung,* 1942; *idem, Geschichtsschreibung in Israel,* 1952; A. JEPSEN, "Zur Überlieferungsgeschichte der Vätergestalten," *WZ Leipzig,* III (1953/54), 265 ff.; B. LUTHER, "Die Persönlichkeit des Jahwisten," in E. MEYER, *Die Israeliten und ihre Nachbarstämme,* 1906, pp. 105-73; V. MAAG, "Jakob-Esau-Edom," *ThZ,* XIII (1957), 418-29; J. MEINHOLD, "Die jahwistischen Berichte in Gen 12–50," *ZAW* XXXIX (1921), 42-57; S. MOWINCKEL, *The Two Sources of the Predeuteronomic Primeval History (JE) in Gen 1–11,* 1937; *idem, Erwägungen zur Pentateuch Quellenfrage,* 1964; *idem, Tetrateuch-Pentateuch-Hexateuch,* 1964; M. NOTH, *Überlieferungsgeschichte des Pentateuch,* 1948; G. VON RAD, *Das formgeschichtliche Problem des Hexateuch,* 1938 (= *Gesammelte Studien zum Alten Testament,* 1958, pp. 9-86 [Eng. *The Problem of the Hexateuch, and Other Essays,* 1966]); H. SCHMÖKEL, "Zur Datierung der Pentateuchquelle J," *ZAW,* LXII (1950), 319-21; H. SCHULTZE, "Die Grossreichsidee Davids, wie sie sich im Werk des Jahwisten spiegelt," *ThLZ,* LXXXI (1956), 752-53; H. W. WOLFF, "Heilsgeschichte—Weltgeschichte im Alten Testament," *Der evangelische Erzieher,* XIV (1962), 129-36; *idem,* "Das Kerygma des Jahwisten," *EvTh,* XXIV (1964), 73-98 (= *Gesammelte Studien zum Alten Testament,* 1964, pp. 345-73).

1. *Terminology and content.* The name "Yahwist" applied to the author of the source stratum and the term "Yahwistic" applied to the source stratum itself derive from the fact that, in contrast to other presentations, they employ the divine name "Yahweh" from the very outset, and not merely after God's appearance to Moses.[1] This observation, which was made very early, turned out to be in one sense an obstacle to further analysis of the Pentateuch, since it seemed to argue against the division of the stratum originally termed J into two strata, although E and P are in an analogous relationship, both using the term "Elohim" to refer to God from the outset. It is therefore more accurate to say that J is one of the two source strata that use the name "Yahweh" even in the pre-Mosaic period.

By and large, the following sections can be assigned to J; they show the

[1] F. Horst, "Die Notiz vom Anfang des Jahwekultes in Genesis 4,26," in *Beiträge zur EvTh,* XXVI (1957), 66-74.

course of his presentation and its essential content (* signifies the presence in more or less important measure of material from the source strata indicated in parentheses in cases where it would have been too intricate to mention the individual verses or parts of verses):

Gen.	2:4*b*–3:24* (N)	Creation, Paradise, fall of man and curse placed on him
	4:1-16	Cain and Abel
	4:25-26	Seth
	6:5-8; 7:1–8:22* (P)	Deluge
	9:18-20, 28-29	Shem, Ham, and Japheth
	10:8-19, 21, 24-30	Table of nations
	11:28-30	Genealogy of Abraham
	15:1*b*β-2, 7-12, 17-18	Promise of land and descendants
	16:1*b*-2, 4-14	Hagar's flight and announcement of the birth of Ishmael
	18:1-15* (N)	Announcement of the birth of Isaac
	18:17–19:28* (N)	Sodom and Gomorrah
	21:1*a*, 2*a*, 7	Birth of Isaac
	22:20-24	Nahor's descendants (Rebekah)
	24* (E)	Wooing of Rebekah
	25:18	Ishmaelites
	25:27-28* (E)	Jacob and Esau
	26:1-3*a*, 6-11, 24-25	Blessing of Isaac, endangering of Rebekah at Gerar
	27:1-45* (E)	Jacob deceives Esau
	28:13-16, 19	Jacob's dream at Bethel
	29:1-14* (NE)	Jacob's arrival at Laban's home
	29:31–30:24* (EP)	Jacob's children
	30:25-43* (NE)	Jacob's agreement and wealth
	31:17-43* (NEP)	Jacob's flight
	31:44–32:1 (Eng. 31:44-55)* (NE)	Jacob's treaty with Laban
	32:2-22 (Eng. 32:1-21)* (E)	Prelude to meeting with Esau
	32:23-24*a* (Eng. 32:22-23*a*)*; 33:1-16* (E)	Jacob's meeting with Esau
	33:17	Jacob at Succoth
	36:2*b*, 9-39* (NE)	Descendants of Esau and Seir; Edomites
	37:3-36*; 39:1–46:5*; 46:28–48:2* (except 47:5*b*-6*a*, 7-11); 48:8-22*; 50:1-11, 14-26* (E)	Joseph novella
	49:1*b*-28*b*α	Blessing of Jacob
Exod.	1:6, 8, 10*b*, 12*a*	Oppression in Egypt
	1:22*; 2:1-10* (E)	Birth, exposure, and rescue of Moses
	2:11-14	Murder and flight to Midian
	2:15*b*β-22* (N)	Moses' marriage in Midian
	2:23*a*α; 3:1-20* (E); 4:18, 29, 31*b*	Moses' call

5:1–6:1* (E)	Negotiations with Pharaoh
7:14–10:29* (EP)	Plagues upon Egypt
11:4-8; 12:29-30, 32	Slaying of the firstborn and release of Israel
13:17–14:31* (NE)	Pursuit and deliverance of Israel
16* (NP)	Manna
17:1-7* (NE)	Miraculous spring at Massah and Meribah
18* (E)	Introduction of a judicial system
19:2-25* (NE)	Sinai and appearance of Yahweh
20:18-21* (NE)	Impression on the people
23:20-33* (E); 33:1-3*a*	Dismissal of the people
34:1-28	Decalogue
Num. 10:29-36* (N)	Departure
11:4-35* (NE)	Quails
13:17–14:45* (NEP)	Spying out of the land (Caleb)
16* (P)	Rebellion of Dathan and Abiram
20:14-20* (E)	Edom refuses permission to pass through
21:19-20* (E)	Route to Moab
21:21-35* (NE)	Victory over the king of the Amorites
22:2–24:25* (E)	Balaam
25:1-5* (N)	Intercourse with Moabite women
32:1-38* (E)	Dwelling places east of the Jordan for Gad and Reuben
Deut. 31:14, 16, 23* (E)	Announcement of Moses' death and appointment of Joshua
34:1*(EP)-6	Moses' death

2. *Extant tradition and the contribution of J.* J's presentation is based primarily on G², of which it is an editorial revision. The occasional correspondences with N alone are traceable either to the use of special Judahite material (Genesis 19) or the later omission of a corresponding narrative by E (Exod. 2:15-22). This brings us to the question of the relationship between the tradition already extant and J's own contribution. To answer this question, we must take into account the structure of the entire work. It begins with creation and the life of man in the Garden of God, but then describes at once how the course of man's life leads downward to sin and judgment:[2] from the fall of man and the curse placed upon him through Cain's murder and punishment[3] to the almost complete extermination of

[2] J. Begrich, "Die Paradieserzählung," *ZAW*, L (1932), 93-116 (= *Gesammelte Studien zum Alten Testament*, 1964, pp. 11-38); J. Dus, "Zwei Schichten der biblischen Paradiesgeschichte," *ZAW*, LXXI (1959), 97-113; P. Humbert, *Études sur le récit du paradis et de la chute dans la Genèse*, 1940; F. Hvidberg, "The Canaanite Background of Gen I-III," *VT*, X (1960), 285-94; J. L. McKenzie, "The Literary Characteristics of Gen 2-3," *ThSt*, XV (1954), 541-72; M. Metzger, *Die Paradieserzählung (Gen 2,4–3,24), die Geschichte ihrer Auslegung van J. Clericus bis W. M. L. de Wette*, Dissertation, Bonn, 1957 (1959); H. Schmidt, *Die Erzählung von Paradies und Sündenfall*, 1931; H. J. Stoebe, "Gut und Böse in der Jahwistischen Quelle des Pentateuchs," *ZAW*, LXV (1953), 188-204.

[3] I. Engnell, "Kain och Abel," *Svenska Jerusalems Föreningens Tidsskrift*, XLVI (1947), 92-102; S. H. Hooke, "Cain and Abel," *Folklore*, L (1939), 58-65 (= *The Siege Perilous*, 1956, pp. 66-73).

sinful man by the Deluge, after which mankind, still without any prospect for improvement, begins to multiply and cover the earth once more.[4] This dark background places the new beginning of the patriarchal narrative in even sharper relief. At the outset the path narrowed from all mankind to Abraham; now, with an occasional glance at other offspring of the fathers, it gradually expands again, from the three patriarchs through the children of Jacob to the beginnings of the nation in the Mosaic period. This is not, however, simply an account of *Heilsgeschichte*. God's promises of territory and descendants and his helping intervention are met time and time again by human failures and threatened disaster.[5] The situation is identical in the time of Moses: from his childhood and call, from the oppression and deliverance of the people, and from the revelation at Sinai and the relationship established there through the long period of wandering down to arrival at the borders of the promised land. Here, though, the basic idea becomes clearer: the victory of God's dominion in the face of the nation's enemies and Israel itself, as well as the establishment and preservation of a close relationship with God despite all Israel's rebellions.

In all this J largely follows the extant tradition of G^2, in which he found ready to hand not only the unity between the Exodus and Sinai traditions (which had been there from the beginning), but also the linking of these traditions with the story of the patriarchs by means of the Joseph novella. In addition, J included some earlier material, particularly the Blessing of Jacob (Genesis 49) as an oracle applying to all Israel (§8.1), the liturgical formulas of Num. 10:35-36, made secondarily to refer to the ark (§8.1), and the Balaam songs in Numbers 24 (§19.5). The so-called cultic decalogue (Exod. 34:14-26) probably represents J's own creation based on earlier material (§8.2).

Of course J revised and interpreted the borrowed (and occasionally expanded) tradition in his own fashion. The way various aspects of history are emphasized, described above, which distinguishes J from E, must probably be considered J's own contribution; we shall study it more closely in the following paragraphs. In particular, the so-called primal history, the preliminary matter of Genesis, comes from J's hand. Even though he composes this primal history after the pattern of a Mesopotamian prototype (§12.2), he uses it to trace history back to its beginnings, interpreting all events from the standpoint of sin, the dissolution of fellowship with God, and of judgment, the victory of God's dominion over the sinner.

3. *Characteristic content.* Among the distinctive marks of J, we may mention first his positive attitude toward agricultural civilization and the Yahweh cult that goes with it (Eissfeldt *). The so-called cultic decalogue,

[4] R. Rendtorff, "Genesis 8,21 und die Urgeschichte des Jahwisten," *Kerygma und Dogma*, VII (1961), 69-78.

[5] C. A. Keller, "Die Gefährdung der Ahnfrau," *ZAW*, LXVI (1955), 181-91; E. H. Maly, "Genesis 12,10-20; 20,1-18; 26,7-11 and the Pentateuchal Question," *CBQ*, XVIII (1956), 255-62.

with its ordinances concerning the three harvest festivals, is typical for the recognition of this indissoluble unity. It is linked also with a positive attitude toward national power, the state, and kingship (Eissfeldt*). Quite apart from such verse as Gen. 27:29, this attitude finds expression in the Balaam songs of Numbers 24, whose presence in J is more than accidental: vss. 3-9 extol the fertility of the land and the invulnerability of Israel under Saul; vss. 15-19 are a retrospective exaltation of David (both passages in the form of pronouncements concerning the future). Starting with Exod. 3:8, it is J that applies to Palestine the phrase "flowing with milk and honey," which may be very ancient. It is easy to understand that, in his account, the people gladly depart from Sinai and set out joyfully for the civilized land and that Yahweh accompanies them in order to dwell in this land.

One should also note the extent to which individual events are placed in a larger context and subordinated to overall points of view, and how the broad perspective forges history out of stories (Weiser*). This is illustrated by the structure of the work as a whole, with the addition of the primal history, and by J's particular placing of emphasis. The mixture of nationalistic ideas, mentioned above, with universalistic ideas is striking. At the outset, all mankind is supposed to stand in a special relationship with God; but this is abolished by the judgment of the Deluge, with God's final statement of resignation in Gen. 8:21. This paves the way for the election of Israel, by means of which the other peoples are to be blessed as well. First Israel itself is to be the people blessed above all others, to whom is assigned the crucial position on earth. Then the other peoples can and may share in Israel's blessing, so that their fate depends on their attitude toward Israel. This is the inseparable unity characteristic of nationalistically inclined Yahwism, with its assumption that salvation is given *ex hypothesi* for Israel. While later so-called written prophecy takes basic issue with this point of view, J seems to have been influenced by the earlier form of prophecy, as when he depicts the call of Moses as a kind of prophetical call.

4. *Theology*. Our discussion has already touched on certain basic characteristics of J's theology. One point of departure is the insight into the nature of man expressed in the introductory matter of the primal history: man lives the life of one who wants "to be like God," and therefore refuses to obey God, denying his dominion and withdrawing from his fellowship. In man "every imagination of the thoughts of his heart [is] only evil continually," as J puts it, probably in his own words, in the introduction to the Deluge narrative (Gen. 6:5). God nevertheless preserves man for childbearing and manual labor (Gen. 3:16-17), even protecting the life of the fratricide against blood vengeance (Gen. 4:15).[6] After the Deluge, God guarantees the continued existence of the world, because the punishment inflicted shows no prospect of making man any better (Gen. 8:21-22). Mankind will

[6] O. Sauer, "Bemerkungen zum Kainszeichen," *Antonianum*, XXXIII (1958), 45-56; B. Stade, "Beiträge zur Pentateuchkritik 1," *ZAW*, XIV (1894), 250-318.

nevertheless be preserved from destruction, so that first Israel and then, through Israel, the rest of mankind can share in God's blessing. Despite all human resistance—including that of Israel—God's dominion and fellowship with God will be realized upon earth.

The decision made by each human individual can be of crucial importance, as Abraham's apparent "haggling" with God over the fate of Sodom shows (Gen. 18:22*b*-33). The state of the individual is admittedly not completely linked with that of the group; Sodom will perish as a whole or be saved as a whole. But this very outcome is made to depend on a small number of inhabitants. J is therefore well on the way from corporate to individual responsibility and liability, like that formulated by Ezekiel 18.

The second point of departure builds on the general awareness on the part of ancient Near Eastern man that his life is dominated and controlled by divine powers, adding the statement of who this all-controlling deity is. J seeks to show, not least when opposing the temptations offered by other religious ideas, that from the moment of creation it has been Yahweh that has determined, and still determines, the fate of mankind and of Israel. Yahweh's desire is to dominate in all of life; at the same time, he seeks fellowship with man through his presence in the world and in earthly events. Not even for a moment does he forsake sinful mankind. The anthropomorphic conceptions, too, indicate that the transcendent God is near to man and speaks with him. In this situation, man, if he makes the right decision, becomes a man of faith like Abraham, a man of patient acceptance like Isaac, a man of hope and expectation like Jacob, or a man of humility like Joseph.

. *Origin.* It is hard to say when J was composed, because it lacks any unambiguous reference to contemporary events. The datings most often proposed are either in the era of David and Solomon (Noth, Sellin-Rost*, Weiser*) or in the ninth century (Hölscher); scholars have occasionally even suggested the period around 800 or a bit later (Jepsen, Mowinckel). The lower limit is set by the characteristics mentioned in 3. above: delight in agriculture and cult, in national power, the state, and the kingship. After the catastrophe of the Northern Kingdom, which affected Judah as well, we do not expect to find these qualities as highly developed as they are in J. But there is already general agreement that J should not be dated after 722 B.C. The question is, what is the upper limit?

It has recently been common to date J in the era of David and Solomon, but the long prehistory of its composition raises serious objections to deriving it from this period. The traditions J draws upon could not have been borrowed and developed to such a degree in the south until after David had forged an "Israelite" tribe of Judah out of various groups. G^2 is all we can assign to the period of David and Solomon. Furthermore, if E is not dependent on J but is rather an outgrowth of G^2, this means with respect to E, which was probably composed in the Northern Kingdom, that at the time of the division of the Kingdom after Solomon's death J was not yet extant, but only the later form of G, and that G² underwent separate development in the south and in the north before reaching its final form in J and E. Even J's idea of "all Israel" finds its true significance only in the post-Solomonic period; after the political schism, it stresses Israel's intellectual and political unity and grounds this unity in history. We may therefore assign the origin of J to the decades between 850 and 800 B.C., after the anti-Canaanite religious policies of Asa and Jehoshaphat and at the beginning of the recovery, under Amaziah, of the ideals of a national religion and a political unit embracing all Israel.

Most scholars agree that J came into being in the territory of Judah. More precisely, we may think in terms of Jerusalem and the royal court, especially because J judges the Davidic kingship so favorably. Mowinckel is probably right in calling J a court historiographer, a "wise" (i.e., literate and erudite) man who had gone through the scribal school at court. There are several traces of such erudition, including his Table of Nations[7] with its list of cities founded by Nimrod (Gen. 10:8-12) and his statement that Hebron was founded seven years before Zoan in Egypt. After the presentation of G², which is no longer extant, J's composition is the earliest presentation of the beginnings of Israel's history.

§23 The Source Stratum E

Cf. the bibliography to § 22; K. Budde, *Deuteronomium 33*, 1922; O. Eissfeldt, "Die Komposition von Ex 1–12," *ThBl*, XVIII (1939), 224-33; J. Morgenstern, "The Elohist Narrative in Exodus 3,1-15," *AJSL*, XXXVII (1920/21), 242-62; O. Procksch, *Das nordhebräische Sagenbuch. Die Elohimquelle*, 1906; W. Rudolph, *Der "Elohist" von Exodus bis Josua*, 1938; P. Volz and W. Rudolph, *Der Elohist als Erzähler ein Irrweg der Pentateuchkritik?* 1933.

1. *Terminology and content.* The name "Elohist" applied to the author of this source stratum and the term "Elohistic" applied to the source stratum itself derive from the observation that, in contrast to J, they at first avoid the name "Yahweh" and use instead the divine appellative "Elohim." The name "Yahweh" is first revealed to Moses in Exod. 3:14-15; from this point on, E uses both Yahweh and Elohim in his presentation. As in the case of J, the term "E" is not a happy choice, because P, too, uses the divine appellative "Elohim" at the beginning; earlier scholars sometimes spoke of two E sources (§17.2). It is therefore more accurate to say that E is one of the two source strata that use the divine appellative "Elohim" at the beginning of their presentation.

While the existence of J is recognized almost without dispute, the situation

[7] W. Brandenstein, "Bemerkungen zur Völkertafel der Genesis," in *Debrunner-Festschrift*, 1954, pp. 57-83; J. Simons, "The 'Table of Nations' (Gen X): its General Structure and Meaning," *OTS*, X (1954), 155-84; D. J. Wiseman, "Genesis 10: Some Archaeological Considerations," *Journal of the Transactions of the Victoria Institute London*, LXXXVII (1955), 12-24.

with respect to E is more difficult. Some deny the existence of such a source stratum altogether; others think in terms of redaction of an E groundwork; still others assume only a fragmentary complex of traditions. Before discussing these questions, we shall list the sections that should probably be ascribed to E, which characterize the course of his presentation and its essential content (* signifies the presence in more or less important measure of material from the source strata indicated in parentheses in cases where it would have been too intricate to mention the individual verses or parts of verses):

Gen.	15* (J)	Promise of territory and descendants to Abraham
	20	Endangering of Sarah at Gerar
	21:1*b*, 6	Birth of Isaac
	21:8-21	Casting out of Hagar and Ishmael
	21:22-34	Abraham's treaty with Abimelech
	22:1-19	Abraham's call to sacrifice Isaac
	24* (J)	Courtship of Rebekah
	25:11*a*; 26:3*b*-5	Blessing of Isaac
	25:27*; 27:1-45* (J)	Jacob deceives Esau
	28:10-12, 17-18, 20-22	Jacob's dream at Bethel
	29:1-14* (JN)	Jacob's arrival at Laban's home
	29:31–30:24* (JP)	Jacob's children
	30:25-43* (JN)	Jacob's agreement with Laban
	31:1-16* (N)	Jacob's wealth and command to return
	31:17-43* (JNP)	Jacob's flight
	31:44–32:1 (Eng. 31:44-55)* (JN)	Jacob's treaty with Laban
	32:2-22 (Eng. 32:1-21)* (J)	Prelude to meeting with Esau
	32:24*a* (Eng. 32:23*a*); 33:1-16* (J)	Jacob's meeting with Esau
	33:18-20* (NP)	Jacob at Shechem
	34* (N)	Murder of Shechem
	35:1-4, 6-7* (P)	Altar at Bethel
	35:8, 14	Death of Deborah
	35:16-20	Birth of Benjamin, death of Rachel
	36:2*b*, 9-39* (JN)	Descendants of Esau and Seir; Edomites
	37:3-36*; 39:1–46:5*; 46:28–48:2 (except 47:5*b*-6*a*, 7-11); 48:8-22*; 50:1-11, 14-26* (J)	Joseph novella
Exod.	1:12*b*	Oppression in Egypt
	1:22*; 2:1-10* (J)	Birth, exposure, and rescue of Moses
	2:15* (JN)	Moses' flight to Midian
	3:1-15* (J); 4:10-31* (JN)	Moses' call
	5:1–6:1* (J)	Negotiations with Pharaoh
	7:14-25* (JP); 9:13-35* (J); 10:12-27* (J)	Plagues upon Egypt
	11:1; 12:31, 39*b*	Slaying of the firstborn and release of Israel

13:17–14:31* (JN)	Pursuit and deliverance of Israel
17:1-7* (JN)	Miraculous spring at Horeb
18* (J)	Introduction of a judicial system
19:2-20* (JN)	Arrival at the mountain of God, encounter with God
20:1-17* (D)	Decalogue
20:18-21* (JN)	Impression on the people
20:22–23:19	Covenant Code
23:20-33* (J)	Dismissal of the people
24:3-8	Obligation of the people
24:12-18* (NP); 31:18*b*	Moses receives the tables of stone
32* (N)	Worship of the bull image
33:5-11	Tent of revelation
Num. 11:4-35* (JN)	Manna, inspiration of the elders
12* (N)	Rebellion of Aaron and Miriam against Moses
13:17–14:25* (JNP)	Spying out of the land (Caleb)
20:1*b*	Death of Miriam
20:14-21* (JN)	Edom refuses permission to pass through
21:4-9	Bronze serpent
21:10-19, 20* (J)	Route to Pisgah
21:21-35* (JN)	Victory over Sihon
22:2–24:25* (J)	Balaam
32:1-38* (J)	Dwelling places east of the Jordan for Gad and Reuben
Deut. 31:14-17, 23* (J)	Preparation for the appointment of Joshua
33	Blessing of Moses
34:1* (JP)	Moses' death

2. *Other views and variations.* Besides the assumption that a source stratum E, with the scope just outlined, can be recognized in the Pentateuch, there are other views and variations.

a) Since E frequently appears in intimate association with parts of J, which at times it seems more to supplement than to parallel, it is understandable that Volz and Rudolph went a step further and denied the very existence of E. In their view, we are dealing instead solely with expansions and parallel traditions to J, of varying age and authorship. Eissfeldt in particular, on the basis of his study of Exodus 1–12, has rightly rejected this view. The pieces assigned to E are frequently genuine doublets to J and not infrequently contradict the latter source stratum. In addition, the pieces share certain linguistic and stylistic idiosyncrasies, as well as similar ideas and conceptions. In combination they constitute a large-scale whole with a definite external and internal structure.

It is likewise impossible to follow Mowinckel in excluding the source stratum E by assuming that, besides a "*Jahwista invariatus*," there was also a "*variatus*," which represents a later development of the former and to which the pieces usually ascribed to E belong. E cannot be analyzed into a mass of variants that have arisen in the course of time. The doublets and parallels of many narrative complexes that are traditionally divided into J and E are too unequivocal to be explained by assuming merely the further development of traditions, as the parallelism between Genesis 20 and 26:1-3*a*, 6-11 and the interweaving of various presentations in Genesis 37 and Exodus 3 show.

b) Others have perceived certain tensions within the content of E, and to explain them have assumed both an Elohistic groundwork (E) and a later redaction (E^1) (Kuenen) or attempted to show a division into one form that originated in the Northern Kingdom and another that was expanded in the Southern Kingdom (Procksch). This assumption has rightfully been disputed. There is no proof in any passage that E has been revised or supplemented; the source stratum exhibits instead a strong internal unity. There is no contradiction, as some have asserted, between the sanctuary legend with its approval of the local incubation oracle (Gen. 28:10-22) and the attack on the local cult of the bull image (Exodus 32); different cultic actions are referred to, one of which is approved, the other disapproved.

c) It is likewise incorrect to assume that the preserved form of E is more fragmentary than that of J (Noth, Weiser*), if this assumption is meant as a wholesale judgment. It is, of course, sometimes true that the narratives of E, when combined with J, were drawn upon only to the extent that they differ from J, or were limited to brief notes, e.g., Exod. 1:12*b*. Even the beginning of E is missing, as will be shown presently. There are, however, many contrary examples, in which E has been drawn upon quite as extensively as J. Above all, E has been completely preserved in those passages where it has introduced new narratives from oral tradition, e.g., Gen. 21:22-34; 22:1-19; Num. 21:4-9, or where it departs widely from J, e.g., Genesis 20. Considered as a whole, E must be viewed as an originally independent source stratum, most of which is preserved.

3. *Extant tradition and the contribution of E.* The presentation of E, like that of J, is based primarily on G^2, of which it is a redaction. E contains more special material, however, than does J. To answer the question of the relationship between extant tradition and E's own contribution, we must once more turn first to the structure of the whole.

It is noteworthy that E now begins (Gen. 15:1) abruptly with the words, "After these things. . . ." The phrase used implies that other remarks or narratives originally preceded the present account. We can hardly assume, of course, that E narrated a primal history, parts of which may even be preserved (Dillmann, Hölscher). The introductory material is clearly the work of J, whom E did not follow in this respect. E followed tradition and began with the Abraham narrative. One may argue from Joshua 24:2-13 that, before Genesis 15, E told of Abraham's migration to Palestine from the pagan environment of Mesopotamia. God's promise to Abraham is followed by a very few further narratives concerning him, most of which actually concern the heir of the promise, especially Isaac. The narratives concerning Jacob and his twelve sons, in the second part of Genesis, are particularly detailed. The same is true of the Moses tradition, which includes considerable special material: besides the Decalogue, the narrative concerning the worship of the bull image (Exodus 32), the Covenant Code in a location that can no longer be determined (§21.2), and the Blessing of Moses (Deuteronomy 33).

A survey of the outline and sequence of the narratives shows unmistakably that E parallels the source stratum J from the Abraham narrative on, a phenomenon explained by their common dependence on G^2. In addition, E exhibits considerable additional fixed material. We may mention especially: the quotation from the book of the Wars of Yahweh (Num. 21:14-15); the so-called Song of the Well (Num. 21:17-8); and the taunt song against Sihon, King of the Amorites (Num. 21:27-30; §40); not to mention the Book of the Covenant and the Blessing of Moses (Deuteronomy 33), a collection of tribal oracles in the overall form of a blessing (§8.1), which parallels J's Blessing of Jacob (Genesis 49).

It is an unmistakable fact, however, that E has given the tradition a new interpretation. A certain amount of theological reflection is generally evident. The realistic, lifelike, and vivid narrative of J stands in contrast to a theological rationalism that is sometimes dull (Weiser*). E marks the beginning of a systematic articulation of history, which P later develops further. Despite the identification of the God of the patriarchs with Yahweh (Exod. 3:14), the use of different names for God in the period before and after Moses divides it theologically into two sections, preceded according to Josh. 24:2 by yet another period, that of the ancestral fathers, who served other gods. This is in line with a certain "erudition" that shows up in the recounting of details such as Gen. 35:8, 19; Exod. 13:18, or in the mention of earlier sources, such as Num. 21:14, 17, 27.

E's individuality is expressed in a series of further traits of his presentation (Weiser*): First, many of the special Judahite traditions concerning Lot and Sodom are left out, as are similar traditions about Abraham. The figure of the latter, in fact, is much less significant than in J; Jacob instead occupies the foreground, so that Jacob and Joseph become the major figures of the patriarchal period. Second, there is a parallel interest in the North Israelite sanctuaries of Bethel and Shechem. This is not at variance with the attention paid to Beer-sheba, in the south, because Amos 5:5 and 8:14 presuppose a close relationship between the Northern Kingdom and this pilgrimage sanctuary. Third, the importance of Moses is emphasized more strongly than in J (a tendency developed further by D and P), e.g., through the revelation of Yahweh's name to him and through the ascription of the Covenant Code and the tribal oracles of the Blessing of Moses to him. Finally, E is more closely related to the prophetic tradition than is J. Abraham is called a prophet (Gen. 20:7); Moses especially is referred to as a prophet—inspired by Yahweh, proclaiming Yahweh's will, endowed with power, and practicing intercession. Num. 11:29 even has Moses express the wish that the entire people of Yahweh might consist of prophets endued by God with his spirit.

4. *Characteristic content and theology.* The characteristic content and theology of E must be treated together (Eissfeldt*, Weiser*). They include, first, a marked emphasis on the distance separating God from the world and from man. God does not wander about upon the earth, but dwells in heaven. He thence approaches man through the mediation of his messengers (Gen. 21:17; 28:12) and reveals himself during the night in a dream or vision (Gen. 20:3, 6; 28:12; 31:11). The image of God is thus dematerialized and spiritualized; at the same time, the anthropomorphic conceptions retreat. In the presence of the mighty God man is not importunate, but filled with fear and awe (Exod. 3:6).

There is also a corresponding refinement of ethical principles. In J, Abraham lies by saying that Sarah is his sister; E diminishes the lie by explaining that Sarah is in fact Abraham's half-sister. Jacob's herds increase, not through deceitful shepherds' tricks, but through God's intervention; they belong to Jacob by right as the withheld inheritance of his wife. E is primarily responsible for portraying the patriarchs as exemplary individuals, presented in edifying and admonishing fashion and depicted with human emotions, like Abraham's pity for the slave woman (Gen. 21:11) or his grief when required to sacrifice his son (Gen. 22:1-19).

Israel's self-understanding in E likewise differs from that in J. The religio-theological aspect takes priority over the nationalistic. The idea of Yahweh as king (Num. 23:21-22; contrast 24:7, 18-19, from J) corresponds to this tendency. The blessing of Abraham, which is transferred to Isaac (Gen. 22:17-18), is interpreted in such a way as to emphasize the religious aspect of Israel's election more strongly. This election, however, loses its positive significance for the other peoples: Israel will possess the gate of its enemies, and the nations will merely use the name of Israel in their blessings. The universal perspective of J falls victim to a religious and nationalistic concentration upon Israel. God's dominion and fellowship are essentially restricted to Israel (a tendency developed further by D and P).

As a result, the separation of Israel that follows from its election becomes seclusion, and the world of the nations becomes the world of paganism; as the Song of Balaam puts it (Num. 23:9*b*): "Lo, a people dwelling alone, / and not reckoning itself among the nations!" It follows that foreign gods are to be put away (Gen. 35:2), their worship is censured as apostasy from Yahweh (Exodus 32), and human sacrifice is rejected (Gen. 22:1-19), while the Canaanite massebahs are merely reinterpreted as memorial pillars and funerary monuments, or the like (Gen. 28:18-22; 35:20).

More markedly than in J, historical events are seen from the standpoint of divine judgment upon human sin. This holds true both for the Amorites (Gen. 15:16) and for Israel itself. By constructing and worshiping the bull image at the mountain of God, Israel breaks the covenant with God while Moses is in God's presence. The incident ends discordantly and menacingly:

God rejects Moses' intercession and commands him to lead the people away from the real dwelling place of God, the mountain of God, "to the place of which I have spoken to you" (Exod. 32:34)—these words, "spoken almost as an aside" (Eissfeldt*), refer to Canaan, toward which, in J, Israel sets out joyfully. In the same breath, the future course of history is proclaimed: "In the day when I visit, I will visit their sin upon them." The apostasy from God is not forgiven because of Moses' intercession; God will requite it in his own good time. Despite the connections between E and the earlier prophetic tradition, this is certainly not to be equated with the threats of an Amos and Hosea; it does not refer to the totality of the nation and its end, but rather the necessary expiation of apostasy by the desert generation. Afterward, the basic state of salvation in which E, too, sees Israel to be will be restored. Once rejection of God's dominion has been requited, Israel can continue to live in fellowship with God.

5. *Origin.* Most scholars assume that E originated in the Northern Kingdom. Noth, however, following Smend and Hölscher, has argued for Judah; and Eissfeldt * has expressed doubts about the Northern Kingdom as the homeland of E. Since J and E both derive from a common basis of traditions embracing all Israel, it is not easy to reach a decision. Precisely because of its derivation from G^2, those features of E that, in contrast to J, point to the Northern Kingdom are most conspicuous: the prominence of Jacob and Joseph, with the preference shown the latter in the Blessing of Moses at the expense of Abraham and Isaac; the emphasis on the Moses tradition, upon which Jeroboam I based his cultic measures (I Kings 12:28-33), which, however, are criticized at the same time (Exodus 32). Furthermore, E takes special interest in the sanctuaries of Bethel and Shechem, which, along with Beer-sheba in the south, were associated with the Northern Kingdom; he also mentions the graves of the ancestors in the Northern Kingdom (Gen. 35:8, 19-20; probably also Josh. 24:30-33). In addition, we must note the influence of E upon the prophet Hosea, whose home was in Northern Israel, and upon Deuteronomy, which in its original form probably came into being there. All these observations suggest that E came into being in the Northern Kingdom as a counterpart to J. Just as their common basis explains the parallelism to J, so, too, the separate development of G^2 in the north and the political, intellectual, and cultic opposition between north and south explain the differences.

If this view is correct, E's origin must fall between the division of the kingdom after the death of Solomon and the catastrophe of the Northern Kingdom in 722 B.C.; more precisely, it probably came into being after J. The exilic period (Hölscher) is certainly out of the question. If we take into account the connection between E and the prophetic tradition, and the apparently peaceful situation of the people under the monarchy (Num. 23:21; Deut. 33:13-17), we can follow Weiser* in dating E in the period of Jeroboam II, before the middle of the eighth century.

§24 The Problem of a Third Early Source Stratum (J^1, L, N)

Cf. the bibliography for §17.3 (notes 26-36) and §22.

1. *The assumption of a third stratum.* Even more difficult and problematic than the existence and state of preservation of the source stratum E is the question of a third preexilic source stratum besides J and E. Ever since the pioneering analysis of Smend, not a few attempts have been made to demonstrate the existence of such a source stratum (§17.3). The divergence in detail between these attempts is no argument against the undertaking itself, but is due rather to the transmission of the text, which, more than two thousand years after the redactional combination and revision of several originally independent works, presents considerable difficulties to analysis. It is certainly understandable, therefore, that many reject the assumption of a third early source stratum. This rejection is based on the reasoning that J—for the use of the divine name "Yahweh" from Gen. 2:4*b* on means that only J is in question—incorporated quite diverse traditions in his work, transmitted them with great fidelity, changed them very little, and did not iron out the discrepancies completely (Sellin-Rost *; Weiser*). Of course if one follows Noth in assuming a common basis for J and E, which their analysis shows to be an extremely likely hypothesis, it is very striking that only J and not E should have employed a series of blocks of ancient material, which, in addition, are out of harmony with J's usual presentation, which parallels the source stratum E, if they do not in fact interrupt it completely.

In fact, a series of observations supports the assumption of a third preexilic source stratum. The narratives of the primal history, after the pieces belonging to P have been removed, exhibit two completely divergent tendencies. According to one series of passages, assigned in §22 to J, the path taken by man after creation leads downward in a straight line to sin and judgment. The other series, on the contrary, exhibits a regular rhythm of positive events, a violent or arrogant advance on the part of man, followed by repulse. We have here two mutually exclusive conceptions, not just unassimilated material.

Furthermore, several narratives or motifs occur thrice (after elimination, once more, of the P sections): Abraham is promised territory and descendants not only in Genesis 15 (JE) but also in Gen. 13:14-18; the patriarch's wife is endangered not only in Genesis 20 and 26 (JE), but also in Gen. 12:10-20; Esau sells his birthright (Gen. 25:29-34) as well as being deceived by Jacob (Gen. 27:1-40) (JE); Yahweh is called the God of the Fathers not only in Exod. 3:15-16 (JE), but also in Exod. 4:5; Yahweh commands Moses to return to Egypt not only in Exod. 3:10, 16 (JE), but also in 4:19, according to which he takes his wife and sons with him (4:20), while according to JE they were brought to him later by his father-in-law (Exod. 18:5-6); the command to slaughter the Passover lamb and smear its blood on the lintel and doorposts does not agree with the command in JE.[1]

In other cases, it is clear that several narratives have been woven together but analysis into J and E will not suffice. In Genesis 18–19, for example, where E is not present, two narratives have been combined; in one, it is Yahweh that visits Abraham and Sodom, in the other it is three of his messengers. The narrative concerning the manna (Exodus 16) also divides into two strata, in addition to which we have the E narrative in Num. 11:4-9. We frequently encounter a fusion of three narratives, as in the Jacob narratives (Gen. 29:1-14; 30:25-43; 31:17-43; 31:44–32:1 [Eng. 31:44-55]) and the Sinai narrative.[2] In these and other instances we find narrative features that can neither be assigned to the presentations of J or E nor be understood as isolated fragments or additions, whether early or late, because they constitute a logical continuity.

Finally, there is linguistic evidence for a third source stratum, of which at least one example should be cited: Moses' father-in-law, whom E simply introduces anonymously in this fashion (Exod. 18:8) and J refers to as a "priest of Midian" named Jethro (for which *Jeter* is an error or by-form) (Exod. 3:1), is also called Hobab ben Re'uel, the Kenite (Exod. 2:18; Num. 10:29; Judg. 1:16).[3]

2. *Terminology and content*. We may conclude, then, that it is advisable to think in terms of a third preexilic source stratum, which, like J, uses the divine name "Yahweh" even in the pre-Mosaic period. There is so far no agreement on what to call this source stratum. The siglum J^1, which was used at first, can too easily lead to the incorrect idea of a close parallelism or relationship with the Yahwist (J^2). The term "Lay Source," with the siglum L (Eissfeldt*), is inaccurate, because the source stratum exhibits a theology as highly developed as that of J or E, and is certainly not typical of the laity. Since its basic attitude, in contrast to the positive evaluation of civilized life on the part of J and E, is determined by the concepts of (semi)nomadic Israelite groups, we here suggest the term "Nomadic Source Stratum" (N).

In broad outline, the following sections can be assigned to N; they show the course of his presentation and its essential content (* signifies the presence in more or less important measure of material from the source strata indicated in parentheses in cases where it would have been too intricate to mention the individual verses or parts of verses):

Gen.	2:8-9* (J); 3:18-19*aα*, 21, 22*b*, 24	Man in Eden, tree of life, banishment
	4:17-24	Kenites and civilization
	6:1-4	Origin of the giants

[1] Cf. in detail G. Fohrer, *Überlieferung und Geschichte des Exodus*, 1964, pp. 82-83.
[2] O. Eissfeldt, "Die älteste Erzählung vom Sinaibund," *ZAW*, LXXIII (1961), 137-46.
[3] Cf. the demonstration by O. Eissfeldt, *Hexateuch-Synopse*, 1922, pp. 59-61.

9:21-27	Noah and his vineyard
11:1-9	Tower of Babel; dispersal of mankind
12:1-2, 4*a*	Departure of Abraham and Lot; blessing
12:6-9	Altars at Shechem and Bethel
12:10-20	Endangering of Sarah in Egypt
13:1-5, 7-11*a*, 12*b*-13	Separation of Abraham and Lot
13:14-18	Promise of territory and descendants
18:1-15* (J)	Promise of Isaac's birth
18:16, 22*a*	Visitors set out for Sodom
19:1-28* (J)	Sodom and Gomorrah
19:30-38	Origin of Moabites and Ammonites
25:1-6	Descendants of Abraham and Keturah
25:11*b*	Dwelling place of Isaac
25:21-26	Birth of Esau and Jacob
25:29-34	Esau sells his birthright
26:12-23, 26-33	Isaac's wealth and treaty with Abimelech
29:1-14* (JE)	Jacob's arrival at Laban's home
29:15-28*a*, 30	Jacob's marriage to Leah and Rachel
30:25-43* (JE)	Jacob's agreement with Laban
31:1, 3	Command to return
31:17-43* (JEP)	Jacob's flight
31:44–32:1 (Eng. 31:44-55)* (JE)	Jacob's treaty with Laban
32:24*b*-33 (Eng. 32:23*b*-32)	Jacob's struggle at Penuel
33:18-20* (EP)	Jacob at Shechem
34* (E); 35:5	Rape of Dinah; murder of Shechem
35:21-22*a*	Reuben's disgraceful act
36:2*b*, 9-39* (JE)	Descendants of Esau and Seir; Edomites
38	Judah and Tamar
Exod. 1:7*, 9, 10*a*, 11, 14*a** (P)	Oppression in Egypt [4]
2:15*bβ*-22* (J)	Moses' marriage in Midian
3:21-22; 4:1-9, 19-20*a*, 24-26, 30*b*-31*a*	Moses' call
11:2-3; 12:21-23, 27*b*	Preparation for slaying of the firstborn
12:33-37*a*, 38-39*a*	Departure of Israel
13:17–14:31* (JE)	Pursuit and deliverance of Israel
15:20-21	Song of Miriam
15:22-27	March to Marah and Elim
16* (JP)	Manna
17:1*bα*	Arrival at Rephidim
17:8-16	Victory over the Amalekites
19:2-25* (JE)	Sinai and appearance of Yahweh
20:18-21* (JE)	Impression on the people
24:1-2, 9-11	Covenant meal with Yahweh
24:13*a*, 14-15*a*	Moses and Joshua on the mountain
32:17-18, 25-29	Licentiousness of the people and punishment

[4] The order to slay the male children (Exod. 1:15-21) is probably made up on the basis of a statement in N.

33:3*b*-4	Command to depart
Num. 10:29-36* (J)	Departure
11:1-3	Rebellion at Taberah
11:4-35* (JE)	Quails
12* (E)	Rebellion of Aaron and Miriam against Moses
13:17–14:45* (JEP)	Spying out of the land (Caleb)
20:1*a*, 2-13* (P)	Miraculous spring at Meribah
20:21	Edom refuses permission to pass
21:1-3	Defeat of the Canaanites
21:21-35* (JE)	Victory over the king of the Amorites
25:1-5* (J)	Worship of Baal of Peor and punishment
32:39-42	Conquests of the sons of Machir, Jair, and Nobah east of the Jordan

3. *Extant tradition and the contribution of N.* N reflects an earlier stage of tradition than do J and E. The primal history diverges so widely from J that it must be considered N's own work, imitating the introductory material of J; apart from this the most important differences are the absence of the Joseph novella, which in fact belongs to a later stage of tradition, and the absence of the Egyptian plagues preceding the slaying of the firstborn. In addition, the Jacob-Esau and Jacob-Laban narratives stand in isolation: after selling his birthright, Esau moves to Edom and never appears again, so that Jacob, who has not fled from him, does not meet him again after returning from Laban. In other words, the two narrative cycles are not yet completely fused.

The outline and sequence of the whole nevertheless parallels the presentations of J and E so closely, and the divergences mentioned point so unequivocally to an earlier stage in the redaction of the common tradition, that we must conclude that N is dependent neither on J nor on E, nor did N employ a tradition completely different from them. The account is based instead upon an earlier form of the common basis of J and E, namely G^1.

Apart from the special interpretation of the primal history, N's own contribution is to be found mostly in the incorporation of archaic narrative material with nomadic traits, which can be assigned to three groups.

a) The material of a more general nature includes the Noah-oracles concerning Shem, Japheth, and Canaan (Gen. 9:25-27);[5] Ham has been added in Gen. 9:18, 22. These oracles obviously refer to a specific historical situation. While Gunkel sought to derive them from the middle of the second millennium, the period of David is more probable, since David—as here predicted—subjugated the Canaanites. Since the Canaanites represent civilization, N can view this with approval. Japheth then would stand for resident Indo-Aryan or Hittite tribes, or, more generally, those portions of Palestine's population that came from the north, possibly including the Philistines, especially since

[5] L. Rost, "Noah der Weinbauer," in *Alt-Festschrift,* 1953, pp. 169-78.

the legendary Greek figure Japetos appears to come from Asia Minor. Shem would refer to the immigrant tribes, including the Israelites.

The Song of Miriam (Exod. 15:20-21) is a song to accompany a victory dance, which contains a summons to the hearers to extol the victor, a general motivation for the summons, and a description of the victory. It probably came into being directly after the event celebrated, so that it may well derive from the Moses host and represent one of the earliest texts of the OT.

The so-called Song of the Banner (Exod. 17:16) is an ancient oath sworn upon the pole of the banner, declaring war forever against the Amalekites in the name of Yahweh.

The narrative in Exod. 24:1-2, 9-11 reflects the ancient custom of preparing for or carrying out the conclusion of a treaty or covenant by means of a meal shared by the various parties. This predominantly nomadic custom corresponds to the settled custom of a banquet to celebrate victory over the enemies of the deity, the banquet inaugurating a new era of peace and well-being in Canaanite mythology, and the coronation banquet of the earthly king on the occasion of his proclamation as king or his enthronement. There is also the general custom of cultic meals.

b) The narratives and briefer notices dealing with the history of peoples and tribes include especially the offensive story of the origin of the Moabites and Ammonites (Gen. 19:30-38), which probably was originally intended to make a positive point, characterizing the peoples concerned as unmixed races; the list of the nomadic groups descended from Abraham and Keturah (Gen. 25:1-6); and the narratives describing the misdeeds of Jacob's sons Simeon, Levi, Reuben, and Judah (Gen. 34; 35:21-22; 38).

c) The archaic or nomadic material includes first of all the Song of Lamech (Gen. 4:23-24), a song boasting of blood vengeance carried to its extreme limit. It may be of non-Israelite origin, possibly deriving from the milieu of the nomadic Kenites, who settled in southern Judah and were later absorbed into Judah.

Other ancient material includes the narrative of Jacob's nocturnal struggle (Gen. 32:25-33 [Eng. 32:24-32]) with its cultic saga and the brief narrative of Yahweh's nocturnal ambush of Moses (Exod. 4:24-26), which justifies circumcision of children in place of adult circumcision.[6] Also typical of nomadic thought are the brief notices concerning the robbing of the Egyptians (Exod. 3:21-22; 11:2-3; 12:35-36) and the statement that on first contact with civilization the Israelites at once succumbed to temptation and deserted Yahweh for Baal (Num. 25:1-5).

4. *Characteristic content and theology.* Our description has already touched on the characteristic content and theology of N. It begins at the very beginning, using the primal history to set the tone. Time after time man enters the situation of a settled civilization or achieves similar progress: he lives in the Garden of God, creates a nomadic civilization with musicians

[6] For details, cf. Fohrer, *op. cit.* (note 1), pp. 45-48, with additional bibliography.

and smiths, discovers viniculture, and builds a city and a ziggurat. Time after time the unruly creature goes astray or is put in the position of overstepping his limits, appropriating divine powers, or taking heaven by storm: the tree of life in Eden, the marriage of heavenly creatures with human women, the building of the city and tower. Time after time God must intervene and curb his creature, banishing man from the garden, shortening his life-span, or scattering mankind, now become numerous, throughout the earth. It is especially the achievements of civilizations that make man presumptuous and necessitate punishment. In contrast to J and E, N exhibits an unmistakable hostility toward the milieu of settled civilization.

At his best, as a true man of faith, man is a nomad. The very first human beings are depicted as nomads: the genealogy of Cain seems unacquainted with other ways of life, and the narrative of the building of the city and tower thinks of undivided mankind as a wandering group of nomads. In Egypt, not only the manufacture of brick but also work in the fields appears as harsh oppression. The poor nomads are well aware that the Egyptian civilization is superior, but they boast of having robbed the Egyptians with artful cunning. These and many other features of the narratives are comprehensible only from the nomadic point of view.

This also explains the author's attitude toward the departure from the mountain of God. As a result of the Israelites' licentiousness, their stay there ends disastrously. Their further advance is neither a joyful migration to the promised land of civilization, as in J, nor an awaiting of the punishment to come on account of their apostasy, as in E, but the consequence of their ill-fated dismissal from the presence of Yahweh, who stays behind upon his mountain. Israel was actually supposed to have stayed there with him. N looks upon the settled land with its sanctuaries as an imperfect substitute for the true homeland of Yahweh and Israel: the desert and the mountain of God (Eissfeldt*). Throughout the narrative there echoes criticism of Palestinian Yahwism, which has been influenced by Canaanite religion.

The God of the desert, who can be worshiped truly only in the milieu of the nomadic way of life, exhibits strikingly anthropomorphic traits. In the primal history especially Yahweh is concerned for his power; for this reason he banishes man from the Garden of God and scatters mankind throughout the earth. The narratives of Jacob's wrestling and the ambush of Moses, which have been applied to Yahweh, could also occur in no other source stratum.

5. *Origin.* It is difficult to fix the time of N's origin. Eissfeldt* considers the work the earliest narrative stratum, dating it between 950 and 850. The use of early material and the presence of archaic features do not necessarily mean, however, that N is the earliest source stratum. It is, of course, based on the earlier form of the groundwork; but this fact means only that G^1 was familiar—perhaps as oral tradition—in the environment of N. This environment, however, is shot through with the nomadic attitude toward life, such as we know or assume to have existed in southern Judah, including

the Negeb, or among the Rechabites, who remained a separate group from the time of Jehu down to the days of Jeremiah.

The relationship between N and J may give us one clue to the dating. N has used an earlier form of G than that used by J; but in the introductory matter of the primal history N seems to follow essentially the model of J, although the author rejects J's connection with the traditions of Mesopotamian civilization and goes his own way. The whole presentation, in fact, can best be understood as a reaction and reply on the part of conservative nomadic circles to J's enthusiasm for settled civilization. These circles produced practically nothing on their own initiative. If J came into being in the decades between 850 and 800, N should be placed slightly later, around 800 or soon after; it is therefore a bit earlier than E.

Interpretation of N as a reaction against J suggests the southern part of Judah as its place of origin; there the nomadic way of life was preserved longest, and cattle raising was more important than agriculture. The author of this source stratum comes from the milieu of a cattle-raising society faithful to Yahweh, which opposed or rejected Canaanite civilization and the Palestinian civilization of Israel with its Canaanite traits.

§25 The Source Stratum D

A. Alt, "Die Heimat des Deuteronomiums" in *Kleine Schriften,* II (1953), 250-75 (Eng. *Essays in Old Testament History and Religion,* 1966); O. Bächli, *Israel und die Völker,* 1962; W. Baumgartner, "Der Kampf um das Deuteronomium," *ThR,* NF I (1929), 7-25; A. Bentzen, *Die josianische Reform und ihre Voraussetzungen,* 1926; G. R. Berry, "The Date of Deuteronomy," *JBL,* LIX (1940), 133-39; J. A. Bewer, "The Case for the Early Date of Deuteronomy," *JBL,* XLVII (1928), 304-79; L. B. Paton, "The Case for the Postexilic Origin of Deuteronomy," *ibid.;* G. Dahl, "The Case for the Currently Accepted Date of Deuteronomy," *ibid.;* H. Breit, *Die Predigt des Deuteronomisten,* 1933; R. Brinker, *The Influence of Sanctuaries in Early Israel,* 1946; K. Budde, "Das Deuteronomium und die Reform König Josias," *ZAW,* XLIV (1926), 177-224; A. Causse, "La transformation de la notion d'alliance et la rationalisation de l'ancienne coutume dans la réforme deutéronomique," *RHPhR,* XIII (1933), 1-29, 289-323; R. Dobbie, "Deuteronomy and the Prophetic Attitude to Sacrifice," *SJTh,* XII (1959), 68-82; F. Dornseiff, "Die Abfassungszeit des Pentateuchs und die Deuteronomiumsfrage," *ZAW,* LVI (1938), 64-85; F. Dumermuth, "Zur deuteronomischen Kulttheologie und ihren Voraussetzungen," *ZAW,* LXX (1958), 59-98; W. Eichrodt, "Bahnt sich eine neue Lösung der deuteronomischen Frage an?" *NkZ,* XXXII (1921), 41-51, 53-78; J. A. Emerton, "Priests and Levites in Deuteronomy," *VT,* XII (1962), 129-38; K. Galling, *Die israelitische Staatsverfassung in ihrer vorderorientalischen Umwelt,* 1929; H. Gressmann, "Josia und das Deuteronomium," *ZAW,* XLII (1924), 313-37; J. Hempel, *Die Schichten des Deuteronomiums,* 1914; G. Hölscher, "Komposition und Ursprung des Deuteronomiums," *ZAW,* XL (1922), 161-255; F. Horst, *Das Privilegrecht Jahwes,* 1930 (= *Gottes Recht,* 1961, pp. 17-154); J. H. Hospers, *De numerus-wisseling in het boek Deuteronomium,* 1947; A. R. Hulst, *Het Karakter van den cultus in Deuteronomium,* 1938; A. Jirku, *Das weltliche Recht im Alten*

Testament, 1927; M. G. KLINE, *Treaty of the Great King,* 1963; E. KÖNIG, "Deuteronomische Hauptfragen," *ZAW,* XLVIII (1930), 43-66; J. L'HOUR, "Une législation criminelle dans le Deutéronome," *Bibl,* XLIV (1963), 1-28; N. LOHFINK, *Das Hauptgebot,* 1963; *idem,* "Die Bundesurkunde des Königs Josias," *Bibl,* XLIV (1963), 261-88, 461-98; M. LÖHR, *Untersuchungen zum Hexateuchproblem II: Das Deuteronomium,* 1925; V. MAAG, "Erwägungen zur deuteronomischen Kultzentralisation," *VT,* VI (1956), 10-18; B. MAARSINGH, *Onderzoek naar de Ethiek van de Wetten in Deuteronomium,* 1961; G. T. MANLEY, *The Book of the Law,* 1957; A. MENES, *Die vorexilischen Gesetze Israels,* 1928; G. MINETTE DE TILESSE, "Sections 'tu' et sections 'vous' dans le Deutéronome," *VT,* XII (1962), 29-87; W. L. MORAN, "The Ancient Near Eastern Background of the Love of God in Deuteronomy," *CBQ,* XXV (1963), 77-87; J. M. MYERS, "The Requisites for Response," *Interpr,* XV (1961), 14-31; M. NOTH, *Die Gesetze im Pentateuch,* 1940 (= *Gesammelte Studien zum Alten Testament,* 1957, pp. 9-141 [Eng. *The Laws in the Pentateuch, and Other Studies,* 1966]); G. ORMANN, "Die Stilmittel im Deuteronomium," in *Baeck-Festschrift,* 1938, pp. 39-53; T. OESTREICHER, *Das Deuteronomische Grundgesetz,* 1923; A. PUUKKO, *Das Deuteronomium,* 1910; G. VON RAD, *Das Gottesvolk im Deuteronomium,* 1929; *idem, Deuteronomium-Studien,* 2nd ed., 1948 (Eng. *Studies in Deuteronomy,* 1963); D. W. B. ROBINSON, *Josiah's Reform and the Book of the Law,* 1951; H. SCHMIDT, "Das deuteronomische Problem," *ThBl,* VI (1927), 39-48; M. H. SEGAL, "The Book of Deuteronomy," *JQR,* XLVIII (1957/58), 315-51; C. A. SIMPSON, "A Study of Deuteronomy 12–18," *AThR,* XXXIV (1952), 247-51; W. STAERK, *Das Deuteronomium,* 1894; *idem, Das Problem des Deuteronomiums,* 1924; *idem,* "Noch einmal das Problem des Deuteronomiums," in *Sellin-Festschrift,* 1927, pp. 139-50; C. STEUERNAGEL, *Der Rahmen des Deuteronomiums,* 1894; *idem, Die Entstehung des deuteronomischen Gesetzes,* 2nd ed., 1901; M. WEINFELD, "The Source of the Idea of Reward in Deuteronomy," *Tarbiz,* XXX (1960/61), 8-15; *idem,* "The Origin of Humanism in Deuteronomy," *JBL,* LXXX (1961), 241-47; *idem,* "The Change in the Conception of Religion in Deuteronomy," *Tarbiz,* XXXI (1961/62), 1-17; A. C. WELCH, *The Code of Deuteronomy,* 1924; *idem, Deuteronomy, the Framework to the Code,* 1932.

1. *Terminology, scope, structure, and style.* The name of the source stratum D and the book of Deuteronomy is based on a misinterpretation of Deut. 17:18, where the LXX rendered the Hebrew expression meaning a *copy* of the law as a *repetition* of the law (*deuteronómion*). This source stratum is represented hardly at all in the books Genesis–Numbers. Besides a few supplementary or redactional notes, such as those in the Decalogue (Exod. 20:1-17), one can assign to it the regulations concerning the Passover, the Feast of Unleavened Bread, and the firstborn (Exod. 12:24-27*a*; 13: 3-16). These few sentences will not be treated in the following discussion. For the rest, we have to do primarily with the book of Deuteronomy, most of which belongs to D. This is true at least for Deuteronomy 1–30 and a few verses of 31–32. The bulk of 31–34 consists either of expansions of the basic material or of continuations of the other source strata found in Genesis–Numbers. This shows that the D portion of Deuteronomy once constituted an independent entity, which could be supplemented by expansions but was then drawn into the already extant Pentateuch tradition.

Apart from the sections belonging to other source strata (Deut. 31:14-17, 23; 33–34), the book purports to be the testament and farewell address of Moses directly before his death and also the basis of a new covenant concluded between Yahweh and Israel after the first covenant had been broken at the mountain of God in the desert. This is the covenant in Moab mentioned in Deut. 28:69 (Eng. 29:1). The introductory discourses (1–11) lead up to the legislation with historical reminiscences and exhortations to obedience. The nucleus (12–26) contains the statutes and ordinances of the supposed covenant in Moab. The concluding discourses (27–30, and a few verses in 31–32) exhort once again to obedience toward the law, pronounce blessings and curses, and finally conclude with the Song of Moses (32).

Just as external evidence distinguishes this complex as a separate unit within the Pentateuch, so also its style shows it to be a literary work distinct from the other source strata. Apart from a verbose and impressive prolixity, which is connected with its hortatory purpose, the style is characterized primarily by certain typical phrases, e.g., "the word [or 'commandment'] which I command you this day" (4:2; 12:28; 15:15; and *passim*); "with all your heart and with all your soul" (4:29; 6:5; 10:12; and *passim*); "the place which Yahweh will choose, to make his name dwell there" (12:11; 14:23; 16:2; and *passim*). It is quite possible to speak of a Deuteronomic style, which, with its facile solemnity and fervor, appealing to the emotions (Sellin-Rost*), was extremely effective. Apart from the activity of the Deuteronomistic editors or authors of the books Joshua–Kings, this style appears again in Jeremiah and Ezekiel, and even as late as the postexilic prophets Haggai, Zechariah, and Malachi.

2. *Connection with Josiah's reformation.* The so-called reformation of King Josiah constitutes the point of departure for questions concerning D. This reformation probably began after the death of the last important Assyrian king, Ashurbanipal, in 626 B.C., and ended about 622. The report of this reformation in II Kings 22–23 mentions a lawbook, which Chrysostom, Jerome, and Athanasius,[1] and later Hobbes and Lessing,[2] identified with Deuteronomy. The basic hypothesis was that proposed by de Wette: Deuteronomy is a different work from the earlier books of the Pentateuch; it comes from the hand of a later author and was composed not long before its discovery in the days of Josiah.[3] Especially after the support given it by Riehm,[4] this view gained almost universal acceptance; it has been modified only by the recognition that the source stratum P should be placed temporally not before D but after it, and that it presupposes D.

Of course, as in the case of the rest of the OT, there is no lack of divergent views. Some scholars defend Mosaic origin (Kline, Robinson) or

[1] E. Nestle, "Das Deuteronomium und 2 Könige 22," *ZAW*, XXII (1902), 170-71, 212-13.

[2] J. Hempel, *ZAW*, LI (1933), 299 n. 1.

[3] W. M. L. de Wette, *Dissertatio critico-exegetica, qua Deuteronomium a prioribus Pentateuchi libris diversum, alius cuiusdam recentioris auctoris opus esse monstratur,* 1805.

[4] E. K. A. Riehm, *Die Gesetzgebung Mosis im Lande Moab,* 1854.

at least an origin in the Mosaic period (Löhr), although the same objections arise as against the derivation of the entire Pentateuch from Moses, and the legal ordinances of D belong to a significantly later period than those of C. Others have assumed at least a considerably earlier date than the period of Josiah. Oestreicher, for instance, denies that the idea of cultic centralization in Jerusalem belongs either to Deuteronomy or the reformation of Josiah; having put aside this connection, he dates Deuteronomy in a much earlier period. Budde and König have rightly opposed this view. There is also no evidence to support the view of Welch, who places the original Deuteronomy in the period of the early monarchy or the Judges, or the view of Brinker, who suggests that it was composed by Samuel for the sanctuary at Shechem. Finally, other exegetes have derived Deuteronomy from the exilic or post-exilic period, making it later than the reformation of Josiah. Hölscher especially has supported this view with arguments based on the utopian character of Deuteronomy and the continuation of the abuses prohibited by Deuteronomy into the time of Jeremiah and Ezekiel. These, however, are not sufficient grounds on which to base a late dating, as Budde, Gressmann, and Noth, among others, have shown.

There are convincing reasons for seeing a connection between Deuteronomy and the lawbook of Josiah's reformation. The "reformation" was certainly not induced by Deuteronomy. In reality, we have to do with a long-term plan on the part of the king, conceived at the beginning of the decline of the Assyrian Empire, to free himself from Assyrian vassalage, restore his own sovereignty, and even recreate the empire of David. The measures taken included putting a stop to the cult of the state gods of Assyria in the national sanctuary at Jerusalem. This had all been planned or begun before the discovery of Deuteronomy. This lawbook, however, led to additional measures, which are required only there and are mentioned in the report of the reformation: the removal of all sanctuaries apart from the central shrine of the Jerusalem Temple, the abolishing of all alien cults in this shrine, and the celebration of the Passover in the Temple. The following correspondences illustrate these principles:

Cultic centralization	II Kings 23:8-9, 19	Deut. 12:13-18
Abolition of the astral cult	23:11-12	17:3
Removal of the cult prostitutes	23:7	23:18
Extirpation of the necromancers	23:24	18:11-12
Prohibition of child sacrifice	23:10	18:10
Celebration of Passover in the Temple	23:21-23	16:1-8

By contrast, there is only one discrepancy: instead of being placed on an equal footing with the Jerusalem priests (Deut. 18:6-7), the priests of the forbidden local sanctuaries are given a subordinate place (II Kings 23:8-9). Assuming that the regulations in fact belonged to Proto-Deuteronomy, this measure is due to the understandable efforts of the Jerusalem priesthood to avoid carrying out the ordinance, which would have been unfavorable to them.

If Deuteronomy brought about or influenced certain of Josiah's reforms, in trying to answer the question of its origin we must note the information given by the report of the reformation, which states that Hilkiah, the high priest, found it in the Temple. This statement admits of various explanations. Fraud on the part of the priests (Cornill*, H. Schmidt*) is certainly out of the question. More likely is a "discovery" analogous to the legendary accounts of the origin of sacred writings, intended to provide divine legitimation for newly composed books; Egyptian works, for example, were traced back in this fashion to Thoth or Osiris.[5] This assumes, of course, that Deuteronomy had just been composed at that time. Since this is unlikely, as remains to be shown, we must probably assume instead that a book was actually discovered that had long been deposited and preserved in the Temple. This could be a result of the custom of depositing documents in the Temple on account of their importance (I Sam. 10:25; Deut. 31:26; II Kings 19:14), or, like the memoirs of Nehemiah, as a votive offering. If, however, the original Deuteronomy came into being in the Northern Kingdom, then it was rescued along with other documents after the fall of the Northern Kingdom, brought to Jerusalem, preserved in the Temple, and—perhaps in connection with the first reform measures—discovered again by chance.

This brings us finally to the questions of how and where the law code of Josiah's reformation, which is connected with Deuteronomy, came into being, whether it is identical with the present form of the book, and, if not, how the book came to be in its present form.

3. *Scope and content of Proto-Deuteronomy.* The question as to the scope and content of the law code of Josiah's reformation, which is usually referred to in brief as Proto-Deuteronomy, arises from the observation that the present book cannot simply be equated with the original form.

The following evidence may be cited: (*a*) The account in II Kings 22:8, 10, according to which the book was read or recited several times in a single day, suggests a work of no great length. (*b*) II Kings 22:8 calls it "the book of the law," a term that presupposes less narrative material than Deuteronomy 1–11, 27–33. (*c*) The discourses of the framework contain repetitions and doublets: two superscriptions followed by introductory discourses (1:1–4:43;[6] 4:44–11:32); at the end, multiple ceremonies of blessing and cursing (27:11-13, 14-26; 28[7]), and multiple exhortations.[8] Several

[5] Cf. J. Hermann, "Ägyptische Analogien zum Funde des Deuteronomiums," *ZAW*, XXVIII (1908), 291-302; also the prescript of *Papyrus Carlsberg nr. VII*, ed. E. Iversen, 1958.

[6] N. Lohfink, "Darstellungskunst und Theologie in Dtn 1,6–3,29," *Bibl*, XLI (1960), 105-34; E. Mørstad, "Deuteronomium 4,25-28 og 29-40," *NTT*, LX (1959), 34-45.

[7] I. Lewy, "The Puzzle of Dt XXVII: Blessings Announced, but Curses Noted," *VT*, XII (1962), 207-11; E. Mørstad, "Overveielser til Dtn 28," *NTT*, LX (1959), 224-32; *idem, Wenn du der Stimme des Herrn, deines Gottes, gehorchen wirst. Die primären Einführungen zu Dtn 28,3-6 und 16-19*, 1960; M. Noth, "Die mit des Gesetzes Werken umgehen, die sind unter dem Fluch," in *Bulmerincq-Gedenkschrift*, 1938, pp. 127-45 (= *Gesammelte Studien zum Alten Testament*, 1957, pp. 155-71).

[8] N. Lohfink, "Der Bundesschluss im Land Moab," *BZ*, NF VI (1962), 32-54.

sections have undergone later redaction, primarily in the exilic period. Evidence of priestly origin is even present (1:3; 4:41-43). (*d*) The same situation obtains in the legal portion. The requirement of cultic centralization is present in three forms (12:2-7, 8-12, 13-19). The cultic regulations in 16:21–17:7 interrupt the continuity between 16:20 and 17:8. Some sections are later additions from the exilic period and are easily recognizable as such; for example, the list of clean and unclean animals (14:1-21) and the regulations concerning prophecy (18:15-22). (*e*) Finally, the juxtaposition of sections or sentences with address in the singular or plural suggests a gradual process of growth, however it is to be explained.

It is difficult, however, to determine exactly the extent of Proto-Deuteronomy, defining it neither too broadly nor too narrowly. Several proposals proceed too schematically: the simple excision from the present Deuteronomy of everything that is out of keeping with the period of Josiah (Bertholet), ascribing to Proto-Deuteronomy only what is mentioned in II Kings 22–23 (Puukko), or assuming an original stratum in the singular (Steuernagel). Neither is it satisfactory to assume, thinking of C and H, that Proto-Deuteronomy comprised only the legal section without any framework (Eissfeldt*: without any historical introduction), because the terror occasioned by its recitation before the king is incomprehensible without the explicit derivation from Moses and the concluding exhortations with their blessings and curses. The scope of Proto-Deuteronomy can probably be determined only in broad outline; its exact wording is no longer accessible, because later redaction has been very thoroughgoing.

A. The legal portion comprised at least the following groups of ordinances, which exhibit material or formal similarities:

a) the ordinances concerning cultic centralization, which are characteristic of D: 12; 14:22-29; 15:19-23; 16:1-17; probably also 17:8-13; 26:1-15;

b) the casuistically framed ordinances concerning "civil" justice in the nucleus of 21–25;

c) the abomination laws, whose concluding formula declares that such and such an action is an abomination to Yahweh: 16:21–17:1; 18:9-14; 22:5; 23:19 (Eng. 23:18); 25:13-16; perhaps also 22:9-12;

d) the so-called humanitarian laws: 22:1-4; 23:16-17, 20-21 (Eng. 23:15-16, 19-20); 24:6–25:4; this category perhaps includes the military laws: 20; 21:10-14; 23:10-15 (Eng. 23:9-14), all of which have been put in group (*b*);

e) finally, the ordinances developed from C, to the extent that they are not embodied in the groups already mentioned, e.g., 15:1-11, 12-18; 16:18-20; 19:1-13, 16-21.

The following probably did not belong to Proto-Deuteronomy: the statements concerning temptation and idolatrous apostasy (13); the parenetic statements in 17:2-7; the royal law (17:14-20);[9] the law concerning the

[9] A. Caquot, "Remarques sur la 'loi royale' du Deutéronome (17,14-20)," *Semitica*, IX

priests (18:1-8); the laws concerning removal of landmarks and statements of witnesses (19:14-15); the parenetic conclusion (26:16-19); and the later additions (14:1-21; 18:15-22).

A certain structure within the legal portion is discernible, to the extent that regulations concerning the cult, the judicial system, and "civil" law occur primarily in that order. This places the Deuteronomic law code not only temporally but structurally between C (with no clear structure) and H (structured according to a recognizable plan). Most important, the basic cultic requirement stands at the beginning, as in the other two law codes.

B. Unlike C and H, the Josianic Proto-Deuteronomy probably included a framework with introductory and concluding discourses. Many attempts have been made to isolate this framework on the basis of a distinction between the passages with singular address and those with plural; Steuernagel even thought he was able to distinguish three strata in 1–11, two using the plural address and the third the singular, while only the third stratum turns out to have a concluding discourse of some size. This analysis is much too uncertain, however, to gain general assent. Neither is it possible to ascribe the sections with plural address to the redactor of the so-called Deuteronomistic Historical Work (Minette de Tilesse), because the variations in address occur even within the individual sections. The explanation that "confusion of number" is a stylistic device (Lohfink) must also be rejected, especially because it results in a very far-fetched interpretation. Probably the juxtaposition and intermingling of singular and plural forms is due to the editing of Proto-Deuteronomy; in any case, it provides no clue for determining the introduction and conclusion of the framework.[10]

In fact, however, Deuteronomy 1–11 does consist of two introductions, which can be distinguished. The first introduction includes, after the superscriptions in 1:1-5, the narrative concerning the golden bull (9:7–10:11; now displaced), seven additional narratives of the Mosaic period linked by "we" sections (1:6–3:29), and the nucleus of the introduction to the recitation of the law (4:1-43). The second introduction begins with the superscriptions in 4:44-49, followed by the legitimation of the law code as Yahweh's will, revealed to Moses on the mountain of God (5:1–6:3), parenetic exposition (6:4–9:6), and emphatic exhortations to obey the ordinances (10:12–11:32). There can be no doubt that this second introduction (4:44–11:32) constitutes the original introduction to Proto-Deuteronomy, giving it legitimation and authority.

The concluding chapters contain the following corresponding sections: the command to write the law upon large stones on Mount Gerezim and to build an altar (27:1-8), and the pronouncement of blessings or curses, depending on whether Yahweh's ordinances are obeyed or not (27:9-10;

(1950), 21-33; K. Galling, "Das Königsgesetz im Deuteronomium," *ThLZ*, LXXVI (1951), 133-38.

[10] Even Exod. 12:24-27*a*; 13:3-16 contain both singular and plural forms.

28:1-68). The sections that repeat the latter ceremony thrice (27:11-13, 14-26) are plainly later additions, the more so because they interrupt the continuity of the pronouncement of blessings and curses. The first introduction has as its corresponding passages the discourses concerning the covenant in Moab (29–30), together with their introduction (28:69 [Eng. 29:1]). All other passages are later additions: Joshua's appointment and the regulations concerning the writing down of the law and its recitation every seven years (31:1-13), the preservation of the law (31:24-30), the exhortation (32:45-47), and the prediction of Moses' death (32:48-52).

The following passages, then, represent the extent of Proto-Deuteronomy, though in edited form:

Introduction 4:44–11:32 (omitting 9:7–10:11);
Law code 12; 14:22-29; 15:1-11, 12-18, 19-23; 16:1-17, 18-20, 21-22 + 17:1; 17:8-13; 18:9-14; 19:1-13, 16-21; 20; 21–25; 26:1-15;
Conclusion 27:1-8; 27:9-10 + 28:1-68.

4. *Growth of the Proto-Deuteronomic law code*. The growth of the Proto-Deuteronomic law code was a complicated process, as is shown above all by its relationship to other traditions.

a) Hempel has discussed in detail the traditio-historical problems and the problems connected with the history of the legal material itself. He sees in Josiah's lawbook the ancient Jerusalemite temple rule, revised at the time of Hezekiah or Manasseh to support cultic centralization; it was expanded at the same time by the addition of social ordinances and a historical introduction. Still later, according to Hempel, an "abomination-source" was incorporated. Horst assumes instead a decalogue embodying "Yahweh's legal privileges" as the pre-Deuteronomic basis of 12–18; this was edited and expanded three times, the last time in support of cultic centralization.

In contrast to these theories, we must note first the long-familiar relationship with C, which can be described under three aspects. First, the Proto-Deuteronomic law code has considerable material in common with the final form of C, as the following table shows:

Deut.		Exod.	Deut.		Exod.
15:1-11	—	23:10-11	22:28-29	—	22:15-16 (Eng. 22:16-17)
15:12-18	—	21:2-11			
15:19-23	—	22:28-29 (Eng. 22:29-30)	23:20-21 (Eng. 23:19-20)	—	22:24 (Eng. 22:25)
16:1-17	—	23:14-17			
16:18-20	—	23:2-3, 6-8	24:7	—	21:16
19:1-13	—	21:12-14	24:10-13	—	22:25-26 (Eng. 22:26-27)
19:16-21	—	23:1			
22:1-4	—	23:4-5	24:17-18	—	23:9
			24:17-22	—	22:20-23 (Eng. 22:21-24)
			26:2-10	—	23:19*a*

Closer comparison shows that the Deuteronomic version is later and modernizes the version of C. Deut. 15:1-11, for example, extends the regulations concerning the agrarian Year of Release (Exod. 23:10-11) to the laws concerning debt, as befits the increasing importance of a monetary economy in the history of economic development. While Exod. 21:2-11 presupposes the purchase of slaves and regulates the length of their service, Deut. 15:12-18 discusses the case of the enslavement of a previously free man for economic reasons, as well as the similar situation of a bondwoman, since women had in the meantime acquired the right of inheritance. The regulations concerning the cities of refuge in Deut. 19:1-13 are intended to expand and update the earlier regulations of Exod. 21:12-14. Second, we may note a conflict between the Proto-Deuteronomic law code and C, expressed primarily in the rejection of a multiplicity of cultic sites and the requirement of cultic centralization, which leads in turn to the necessity of changing quite a few of the earlier cultic ordinances. Finally, about half the ordinances of C are skipped over and omitted. This does not mean that the law code goes back to an unknown collection of laws rather than C, but rather, as elsewhere in the ancient Near East, that the unmentioned ordinances are considered as continuing in force. In accordance with the ancient Near Eastern models of such law codes, we may conclude that the Proto-Deuteronomic law code was not intended to supplant the earlier C and replace it (Eissfeldt*), but rather to improve and supplement it.

In addition, it made use of material deriving from various periods, probably handed down by oral tradition. For example, the regulations concerning the procedure to be followed in case of murder by person or persons unknown (Deut. 21:1-9) and the law of the assembly (Deut. 23:2-9)[11] are very archaic, at least *in nucleo*. The "military laws" (20; 23:10-15 [Eng. 23: 9-14]) are later; they can only have come into being during the period of the monarchy, although the regulations concerning exemption from military service are based on archaic conceptions.[12] The use in part of international legal norms is in harmony with the origin of many other Israelite ordinances. It is therefore not surprising that parallels exist with the Egyptian wisdom book of Amen-em-opet, and that Deut. 25:13-16 (dealing with false measures) corresponds to Amen-em-opet 16, or Deut. 19:14 (concerning shifting of boundaries) to Amen-em-opet 6. There are likewise parallels to other ancient Near Eastern texts.[13]

The Proto-Deuteronomic law code is also influenced by the Elohistic tradition with its rejection of foreign gods and pagan practices; this influence is illustrated by the incorporation of the Decalogue (Deut. 5:6-21), the em-

[11] K. Galling, "Das Gemeindegesetz in Deuteronomium 23," in *Bertholet-Festschrift*, 1950, pp. 176-91.

[12] M. du Buit, "Quelques contacts bibliques dans les archives royales de Mari," *RB*, LXVI (1959), 576-81; S. B. Gurewicz, "The Deuteronomic Provisions for Exemption from Military Service," *ABR*, VI (1958), 111-21; W. Herrmann, "Das Aufgebot aller Kräfte," *ZAW*, LXX (1958), 215-20.

[13] C. H. Gordon, "A New Akkadian Parallel to Deuteronomy 25,11-12," *JPOS*, XV (1935), 29-34; *idem*, "An Akkadian Parallel to Deuteronomy 21,1 ff.," *RA*, XXXIII (1936), 1-6; for a Ugaritic parallel, cf. H. Cazelles, *VT*, VIII (1958), 105.

phasis on Moses as lawgiver, and the parenetic-hortatory style. Finally, it is also influenced by the prophetic tradition with its emphasis on social ethics and by the views of the rural priesthood, which was less affected by religious syncretism than were the national sanctuaries.

b) Form-critically, a large portion of the Proto-Deuteronomic law code falls into the category of casuistic law. Such laws introduce the case with an "If . . . ," sometimes define it more precisely, lay down the exact procedure and judgment, and on occasion fix the penalty (§8.3). Typical examples are 15:12-18; 21:15-17; 22:13-21; 24:1-4; 25:1-3.

Occasionally there are also laws formulated apodictically (15:1; 16:19; 16:21–17:1; 23:2-8 [Eng. 23:1-7]). Series of these apodictic laws originally served to express extralegal rules of conduct (§8.2); individually, however, they occur in ancient Near Eastern and Israelite law, and, in a form-critically secondary stage, they were joined to form legal series.

All this is in harmony with what is observed elsewhere in the ancient Near East and the OT. In addition, the Josianic law code exhibited at least the rudiments of a parenetic and hortatory exposition. In the section dealing with the Year of Release (15:1-11), for example, an apodictic law and a legal interpretation are followed by such hortatory and didactic material, addressing the layman directly; the same kind of material follows an apodictic law in the section dealing with the firstborn (15:19-23). We here find a characteristic rhetorical form, which is augmented in the course of further redaction, and in the later additions (13:1-6 [Eng. 12:32–13:5]; 17:14-20; 18:15-22) even appears without being introduced by a law. The earlier state of affairs is most likely to be found in 23 ff.; these chapters exhibit a less parenetic form than the preceding, and were not subjected to as much later editing as the earlier chapters.

Closely related are the parenetic passages in the introductory discourses, especially 6:4–9:6, in which the Deuteronomic style gradually unfolds. Von Rad has cogently pointed out not only the direct address to the individual but also its rationalistic and didactic nature, which serve in large measure to derive solutions for new problems from the ancient traditions, which are invested with an almost canonical authority.

5. *The development from the original lawbook to the present book of Deuteronomy*. Proto-Deuteronomy, the lawbook of Josiah's reformation, constitutes a certain point of departure, from which, looking both backward and forward, we can reconstruct the history of the development of Deuteronomy, tracing the several stages leading from the original lawbook to the present book.

a) The question of the first stage is connected with that of the place and date of origin. Contrary to Reuss* and the many scholars who followed him the second half of the nineteenth century, Deuteronomy can hardly have been written just prior to its discovery, perhaps by the high priest Hilkiah. Judah at the time of Hezekiah or Manasseh is probably also out of the question. More to the point is the evidence cited by Welch, Alt, and others in support of Northern Israel as the place of origin of part of the laws. It is doubtful, however, that the nucleus of the book came into being among Yahwistic circles in Northern Israel as a "restoration program" after the fall of the Northern Kingdom in 722 (Alt); neither is it likely to have come into being in Judah at the time of Hezekiah through collaboration between refugees from Northern Israel and prophetic and Levitical circles (Sellin-Rost *). The relationship with C shows plainly that Deuteronomy was conceived as a revision and expansion of the former law code. In this case, the original Deuteronomic law code must have come into being in Northern Israel before its fall, i.e., probably not later than the first half of the eighth century. The great prosperity of the kingdom under Jeroboam II could have provided the occasion.

By analogy with C, we must also assume that this North Israelite law code contained only new and modernizing legislation, as Eissfeldt * assumes for all of Proto-Deuteronomy. It accordingly began like C (and later H) with the basic cultic requirement. In line with its purpose, it showed no traces of parenesis. It was a royal law code of the type that is amply attested in the ancient Near East.

b) After the fall of the Northern Kingdom, it was brought to Jerusalem along with other Israelite literature. There an initial redaction must soon have taken place. We may follow Sellin-Rost* in thinking of a cooperative effort at the time of Hezekiah, the outcome of which was deposited in the Temple after 701 in consequence of the king's political downfall. The situation during the reign of Manasseh could also have instigated the growing reform movement to carry out this work. At this stage the book was put in the form discovered by Hilkiah in the Temple. This means that the legal portion was revised in parenetic-hortatory style and provided with an initial framework, consisting of the introduction 4:44–9:6; 10:12–11:32 and the conclusion 27:1-10; 28:1-68. The law code retained its character, since there are other legal codes in the ancient Near East exhibiting an introduction and a conclusion, such as the Code of Lipit-Ishtar and the Code of Hammurabi. This provides the clue for answering the question of the book's *Sitz im Leben*, not the model of a cultic ceremony such as a hypothetical Covenant Renewal Festival (von Rad) or the formularies of the Hittite vassal treaties.

c) In this form the book was discovered by Hilkiah and used to support the further measures of Josiah. This could only come about by ascribing constitutional authority to the book. In fact, according to II Kings 23:1-3, the king entered into a new treaty with the people through their representatives, who had been summoned to Jerusalem. Both parties undertook an equal obligation to obey the new law. The actual wording states unequivocally that we are dealing not with a covenant between Josiah and the people on the one hand and Yahweh on the other, nor with a covenant between Yahweh and the people mediated through Josiah, but with a treaty between the king and his people.[14] The Deuteronomic law code was thereby made the basis for the relationship between king and people, i.e., the system of government; the law therefore took on the nature of a constitution (Galling). Josiah's successors were of course not bound by this covenant, so that Jehoiakim could simply ignore it.

d) Further redaction probably began as early as the time of Josiah. First, it reinforced the parenetic-hortatory features. Second, this stage most likely represents the source of the warlike spirit that pervades the earlier introduction and the legal portion, which von Rad associates, probably correctly, with the Levitical priests of the Josianic period as supporters of a warlike revival movement and militant piety. It is connected with the reorganization of the army, in which, after the disbanding of the standing army following the catastrophe of the year 701, recourse was had to the original form of the militia composed of all free citizens.[15] The revival of the warlike spirit of ancient Yahwism is in line with this reorganization.

e) Later still, probably in the exilic period, the second framework was added, consisting of the introduction 1:1–4:43; 9:7–10:11 and the conclusion 28:69 (Eng. 29:1); 29–30. It serves to incorporate Deuteronomy into the Pentateuchal tradition by taking as its point of departure the breaking of the covenant entered into by Yahweh and Israel at the mountain of God through the bull cult (9:7–10:11) and introducing a supposed covenant in Moab (28:69 [Eng. 29:1]) based on Deuteronomy. At the same time, the book took on the character of the testament or farewell address of Moses just before his death, of which there can have been no hint in the earlier stages.

Finally, the supplements (31:1-13; 31:24-30; 32:45-47; 32:48-52) were added to the later conclusion.

A further supplement, which presupposes the incorporation of Deuteronomy in the Pentateuch and the following narrative of Moses' death, as recounted by the other source strata, is the Song of Moses (32:1-43) together with its framework (31:19-22; 32:44). Since it belongs to none of the source strata but is instead an independent entity, it will be discussed in §27.4.

In view of the course of development just outlined, which in reality was even more complex, the hitherto quite summary explanations will not hold up. Some have assumed that the present book came into being through gradual supplementation of the Josianic lawbook or an earlier prototype (Hempel, Horst, and above all Hölscher). Others have assumed that two or more editions of the Josianic Proto-Deuteronomy have been combined (Wellhausen, Staerk, Steuernagel). As stated, neither view is accurate. The legal portion of the book furnishes no evidence for assuming several parallel portions or parallel editions, which were combined by addition. Instead, there was always just one legal portion, which was supplemented by redaction and

[14] G. Fohrer, "Der Vertrag zwischen König und Volk in Israel," *ZAW*, LXXI (1959), 1-22, 13-14.

[15] E. Junge, *Der Wiederaufbau des Heerwesens des Reiches Juda unter Josia*, 1937.

expansion. On the other hand, two framework narratives were composed successively, the later of which was added to the earlier and made to mesh with it by the transference of 9:7–10:11. Thus the growth of the legal portion is explained by the supplement method, that of the framework by the addition method.

6. *Deuteronomy within the Pentateuch*. Not only is Deuteronomy incorporated externally in the Pentateuch and made a part of it by the appearance of other source strata in the final chapters, but also the later framework narrative is linked to the Pentateuch internally and materially. This framework constitutes a coherent whole; 1–3 cannot be removed from it and viewed as the beginning of the so-called Deuteronomistic Historical Work (Noth). It incorporates Deuteronomy in the Pentateuchal tradition through the assumption of a covenant concluded in Moab after Israel's transgression of the covenant concluded at the mountain of God. In the exilic period, then, Deuteronomy was already an integral part of the nascent Pentateuch. Furthermore, interpolations from the Priestly source stratum (1:3; 4:41-43) show that Deuteronomy remained a part of the Pentateuch from that time on. Both observations speak against dissociating it from the Pentateuch and connecting it with the books that follow.

7. *Theology*. The theology of Deuteronomy can be summarized under three headings: the unique cultic center, which is a consequence of the uniqueness of God and is intended to combat the tendency toward a pluralistic concept of God brought about by a multiplicity of sanctuaries; Yahweh's jealousy, directed against Israel's worship of other gods, and especially against Canaanite influences; and the love of God, who with inexplicable grace has shown favor to Israel since the time of the fathers, requiring in return the love of Israel toward both God and fellow man, so that, as in the time of Moses, Israel lives in a present of decision.

All life is brought within God's loving will. This represents an attack upon the secularization of the state and of life in general that accompanied cultural progress. In this respect Deuteronomic theology constitutes a revival of the earlier cultic attitude and religious nationalism, at the same time tacitly parting company with rationalistic, "enlightened," and "secular" wisdom. The dominion of God is once again the goal; it is symbolized materially by the central sanctuary with its cultic ceremonial involving huge crowds. The way of life God wills for Israel is given a firm foundation by being linked to the written revelation of God's will, so as to avoid human guilt and the consequent judgment threatened by the prophets. For even the prophetical criticism of the view that Israel is essentially on a right footing with God is taken up in Deuteronomy. Unlike the prophetic tradition, however, which generally took quite a negative view of Israel's prospects for the future, Deuteronomic theology seeks to deliver the people as a whole from the threatened judgment of destruction, without in any way detracting from the seriousness of the situation. This attempt to achieve a synthesis between prophetical theology on the one hand and cultic theology and religious nationalism on the other is a considerable theological accomplishment.

The keynote is struck by the concept of election,[16] for which Deuteronomic theology employs the verb *bāḥar* as a technical term, giving it first place so as to be able to summon the entire nation to a new life. The reference to election proclaims and requires real fellowship between Israel and God as the practical basis for faith and life. The concrete expression of this election is God's covenant with Israel, which also begins to assume a central position. In addition, Deuteronomic theology addresses the individual sinful human being. Through the personal decision of every individual for God the entire nation is to be delivered. If the conversion takes place, the election will remain in force; the threatened rejection will not come to pass, and the prophetical prediction of judgment will go unfulfilled.

Of course we must not overlook the fact that Deuteronomy, with its interest in the codified will of Yahweh, was moving in the direction of a canon with authoritative recognition. In late additions, Deuteronomy is itself already understood as "Scripture" (17:18; 28:58, 61; 29:19-20 [Eng. 29: 20-21); this marks the beginning of the development of a "Religion of the Book," a faith that can be taught and learned (cf. 7:6-16; 30:11-20).

§26 The Source Stratum P

Cf. the bibliography to § 22; E. Auerbach, "Die babylonische Datierung im Pentateuch und das Alter des Priester-Kodex," *VT*, II (1952), 334-42; *idem*, "Der Wechsel des Jahres-Anfangs in Juda," *ibid*., IX (1959), 113-21; K. Elliger, "Sinn und Ursprung der priesterlichen Geschichtserzählung," *ZThK*, XLIX (1952), 121-43; P. Grelot, "La dernière étape de la rédaction sacerdotale," *VT*, VI (1956), 174-89; S. Grill, "Die religionsgeschichtliche Bedeutung der vormosaischen Bündnisse (Gen 9,9-17; 17,9-14)," *Kairos*, II (1960), 17-22; M. Haran, "Shilo and Jerusalem; The Origin of the Priestly Tradition in the Pentateuch," *JBL*, LXXXI (1962), 14-24; J. Hempel, "Priesterkodex," in Pauly-Wissowa, *Realencyclopädie der classischen Altertumswissenschaft*, XXII, 1954, pp. 1943-67; P. Humbert, "Die literarische Zweiheit des Priester-Codex in der Genesis," *ZAW*, LVIII (1940/41), 30-57; Y. Kaufmann, "Der Kalender und das Alter des Priesterkodex," *VT*, IV (1954), 307-13; K. Koch, "Die Eigenart der priesterschriftlichen Sinaigesetzgebung," *ZThK*, LV (1958), 36-51; *idem*, *Die Priesterschrift von Exodus 25 bis Leviticus 16*, 1959; S. R. Külling, *Zur Datierung der "Genesis-P-Stücke," namentlich des Kapitels Genesis XVII*, 1964; M. Löhr, *Untersuchungen zum Hexateuchproblem I: Der Priesterkodex in der Genesis*, 1924; B. Luther, "Ḳāhāl und ʿedāh als Hilfsmittel der Quellenscheidung im Priesterkodex und in der Genesis," *ZAW*, LVI (1938), 44-63; G. von Rad, *Die Priesterschrift im Hexateuch*, 1934; R. Rendtorff, *Die Gesetze im Priesterschrift*, 1954; J. Roth, "Thèmes majeurs de la tradition sacerdotale dans le Pentateuque," *NRTh*, XC (1958), 696-721; E. A. Speiser, "Leviticus and the Critics," in *Kaufmann Jubilee Volume*, 1960, pp. 29-45; L. Waterman, "Some Repercussions from Late Levitical Genealogical Accretions in P and the Chronicler," *AJSL*, LVIII (1941), 49-56; W. Zimmerli,

[16] T. C. Vriezen, *Die Erwählung Israels nach dem Alten Testament*, 1953; P. Altmann, *Erwählungstheologie und Universalismus im Alten Testament*, 1964.

"Sinaibund und Abrahambund," *ThZ*, XVI (1960), 268-88 (= Gottes Offenbarung, 1963, 205-16).

1. *Terminology and content.* The term "Priestly Document" (or "Priestly Code") is based on the interest this source stratum shows in cultic and ritual institutions and priestly regulations. Some of these are supported by narratives; others are preserved in collections or complexes, both large and small. P's individuality distinguishes it from its environment at least as clearly as D. It exhibits a formal style (influenced by D and Ezekiel), a characteristic use of language, a love for genealogies and numbers, an interest in cultic and priestly matters, an emphasis upon cultic purity and holiness, an avoidance of anthropomorphisms. There is less emphasis on cultic sites, the priesthood, and the cult in the pre-Mosaic period, during which, as in E, the name "Yahweh" is not used. For these reasons P was the first individual stratum to be identified and distinguished, though it was long thought to be the earliest and most reliable presentation and was not dated correctly until the nineteenth century.

Scholars generally ascribe the following sections to P; they characterize the course of its presentation and its essential content (* signifies the presence in more or less important measure of material from the source strata indicated in parentheses in cases where it would have been too intricate to mention the individual verses or parts of verses):

Gen.	1:1-2:4*a*	Creation
	5	Forefathers (Seth's genealogy)
	6:9–8:22* (J)	Deluge
	9:1-17	Covenant with Noah
	10:1-7, 22-23, 31-32	Table of nations
	11:10-27, 31-32	Genealogies of Shem, Terah, and Abraham
	12:4*b*-5	Departure of Abraham and Lot
	13:6, 11*b*-12*a*	Separation of Abraham and Lot
	16:1*a*, 3, 15-16	Birth of Ishmael
	17	Covenant with Abraham; prediction of Isaac's birth
	19:29	Destruction of the cities
	21:2*b*-5	Birth and circumcision of Isaac
	23	Death and burial of Sarah
	25:7-10	Death and burial of Abraham
	25:12-17	Genealogy of Ishmael
	25:19-20	Genealogy of Isaac
	26:34-35; 27:46–28:9	Jacob sent to Paddan-aram
	29:28*b*-29	Jacob's marriage with Rachel
	30:4*a*, 9*b*	Bilhah and Zilpah
	31:18*b*; 33:18*aβ*	Jacob's return and arrival at Shechem
	35:6*a*, 9-13, 15	Blessing and renaming of Jacob
	35:22*b*-26	Jacob's sons
	35:27-29	Jacob's arrival at Hebron; death and burial of Isaac

36:1-2*a*, 4-8	Esau's migration to Seir
36:40-43	Chiefs of Esau
37:1-2	Jacob and Joseph
46:6-7 (8-27)	Jacob's departure to Egypt
47:5*b*-6*a*, 7-11; 48:3-7; 49:1*a*, 28*b*β-33; 50:12-13	Jacob and his sons in Egypt
Exod. 1:7, 13-14* (N)	Oppression in Egypt
2:23*a*β-25; 6:2–7:7	Call of Moses
7:8-13	Negotiations with Pharaoh
7:14–9:12* (JE); 11:9-10	Plagues upon Egypt
12:1-20, 28, 40-51; 13:1-2	Celebration and departure of the Israelites
16* (JN)	Quails and manna
19:1	Arrival at Sinai
24:15*b*-18*a*; 31:18*a*	Yahweh and Moses meet on Sinai
25:1–31:17	Regulations inaugurating the cult ("Tabernacle")
34:29-35	Moses' descent from Sinai
35–40	Carrying out of the instructions in 25–31
Lev. 1–7	Sacrificial regulations
8–10	The first priests and sacrifices
11–15	Ordinances concerning purity
16	Ritual for the Day of Atonement
17–26	Holiness Code
27	Regulations concerning vows
Num. 1:1–10:10	Regulations concerning Levites and camp order
10:11-28	Departure from Sinai and order of march
13:1–14:45* (JNE)	Spying out of the land (Caleb)
15	Various ordinances
16* (J); 17	Rebellion of Korah and his followers
18	Rights and duties of the priests and Levites
19	Ordinances concerning purification
20:1*a*, 2-13* (N)	Miraculous spring; punishment of Moses and Aaron
20:22-29	Death of Aaron; appointment of his successor
22:1	Route to the Jordan Valley
25:19; 26	Organization and census of the people
27	Regulations concerning inheritance; appointment of Joshua
28–30	Regulations concerning sacrifices and vows
31	Campaign against the Midianites
33:1-49	List of campsites
33:50–34:29	Instructions for the occupation of Canaan
35	Levitical cities and cities of refuge
36	Supplement to the regulations concerning inheritance
Deut. 34:1* (JE), 7-9 (10-12)	Death of Moses (other P sections are Deut. 1:3; 4:41-43)

2. *Extant tradition and the contribution of P.* For the question of the relationship between extant tradition and P's own contribution, it is of fundamental importance to note that the source stratum P presupposes the combined strata JNE as the basis of the Pentateuch, as, for example, the narrative of the call of Moses shows. In addition, D had already been incorporated with the rest, as the influence of Deuteronomic style, the expansion of the D material in Exodus 12–13, and the P passages Deut. 1:3; 4:41-43 suggest. Although P parallels the earlier source strata, it is equally evident that P has treated the material quite arbitrarily, and, in particular, has abbreviated it greatly. The Sodom narrative shrinks to a single sentence; the Jacob-Laban and Jacob-Esau narrative cycles vanish almost entirely; and there is almost no mention of Joseph in Egypt. The narrative becomes more detailed when it treats matters of cultic interest (Genesis 17), anticipates the occupation of the land (Genesis 23), or discusses historical periods.

These features set the tone for P from the very outset. It begins with an account of the primal history, which is concerned primarily with creation,[1] the Deluge,[2] and the covenant with Noah. For the rest, as in the history of the patriarchs, P restricts itself to mere genealogies, which link the individual narratives and brief notices. Having listed the rest of mankind in the table of nations,[3] it concentrates on the prehistory of Israel, leaving sin out of account whenever possible and leading up to the Moses tradition, which receives the major emphasis. Thus the primal history and patriarchal history, and even the narrative of the deliverance from Egypt, are reduced to a mere introduction to the revelation on Sinai, with which nearly all the important material is linked. With the exception of the Sabbath, dietary laws, circumcision, and Passover, all the important ordinances are traced back to this revelation or the period immediately following, through the mediation of Moses. This produces a picture very different from that of the earlier source strata, completing the concentration on the Mosaic era that had begun in E, D, and H.

At the same time, P incorporated both early and late material that had previously been independent. We may mention especially the so-called Blessing

[1] J. B. Bauer, "Die literarische Form des Heptaemeron," *BZ*, NF I (1957), 273-77; *idem*, "Der priesterliche Schöpfungshymnus in Gen 1," *ThZ*, XX (1964), 1-9; H. Gunkel, *Schöpfung und Chaos in Urzeit und Endzeit*, 2nd ed., 1921; S. Herrmann, "Die Naturlehre des Schöpfungsberichtes," *ThLZ*, LXXXVI (1961), 413-23; P. Humbert, "La relation de Genèse 1 et du Psaume 104 avec la liturgie du Nouvel-An israélite," *RHPhR*, XV (1935), 1-27 (= *Opuscules d'un Hébraïsant*, 1958, pp. 60-82); F. Hvidberg, "The Canaanite Background of Gen I-III," *VT*, X (1960), 285-94; C. A. Keller, "‚Existentielle' und ‚heilsgeschichtliche' Deutung der Schöpfungsgeschichte (Gen 1,1–2,4)," *ThZ*, XII (1956), 10-27; J. Morgenstern, "The Sources of the Creation Story—Genesis 1,1–2,4," *AJSL*, XXXVI (1919/20), 169-212; E. W. Nieboer, *Opmerkingen over Gen 1*, 1955; N. H. Ridderbos, *Beschouwingen over Genesis I*, 1954; L. Rost, "Der Schöpfungsbericht der Priesterschrift," *CuW*, X (1934), 172-78; W. H. Schmidt, *Die Schöpfungsgeschichte der Priesterschrift*, 1964; C. F. Whitley, "The Pattern of Creation in Genesis, Chapter 1," *JNES*, XVII (1958), 32-40.

[2] A. R. Hulst, "*Kol baśar* in der priesterlichen Fluterzählung," OTS, XII (1958), 28-68.

[3] Cf. the bibliography in § 22 note 7.

of Aaron (Num. 6:24-26), which undoubtedly comes from the preexilic period; the list of the heads of the Israelite tribes or clans (Num. 1:4-16; 7:12-83; 13:4-16), whose distribution among the postulated twelve tribes may be P's own contribution, while the names themselves often go back to the earliest period of Israel's history; the list of families (Num. 26:5-51) and the list of campsites (Numbers 33), which can hardly have been invented by P, but merely edited by him. P also made use of the law code H and the collections or complexes Leviticus 1–7; 11–15; Numbers 4–6; 15; 18:8-32; 19; 28–30 (§20.3-4).

Finally, there were other traditions for P to draw upon. The creation narrative and, to an even greater degree, the list of ancestors and the Deluge narrative are based on mythological traditions, mostly of Mesopotamian origin. Special material of Palestinian provenience includes the narrative concerning the purchase of the cave of Macpelah (Genesis 23).[4] All this material, however, has been digested and subordinated to the individual biases of P.

3. *The problem of literary unity.* Although P constitutes an independent intellectual unit, there remains the problem of its literary unity. The enormous mass of borrowed material, which not infrequently interrupts the continuity and thus reveals its special nature, raises doubts, which the repetitions and contradictions reinforce. The tracing of the Sabbath to creation, certain dietary laws to the time of Noah, and circumcision to the time of Abraham, as well as the mention of the purchase of the cave, do not belong in this category. They are connected in part with the periodic interpretation of history (cf. 4), in part with the promise of territory. The situation in the case of the laws is different:

Exodus 27–29; Leviticus 8–9 describe the altar of burnt offering; Exod. 30:1-10; 35–40 also mention the altar of incense.

Exod. 28:41; 30:30; and *passim* mention the anointing of all priests; Exod. 29:7, 29; Lev. 4:3, 5, 16; and *passim* mention only Aaron.

Lev. 4:14 specifies a young bull as a sin offering; Lev. 9:3; Num. 15:24 specify a male goat.

Num. 4:3-15, 23-28 specify thirty years as the age when a Levite becomes eligible for service; Num. 8:23-26 specifies twenty-five years.

To explain this situation, Wellhausen divided P into three strata, and others have followed his lead. In similar fashion, von Rad considers P as composed of two continuous source strata together with a "Book of Generations." Besides Eissfeldt, who has dealt at length with this latter "Book,"[5] Humbert and Weiser* particularly attack this assumption, partially for reasons of literary criticism, partially on account of the resulting chronological difficulties and the dominant internal uniformity. Noth seeks another

[4] M. R. Lehmann, "Abraham's Purchase of Machpelah and Hittite Law," *BASOR*, CXXIX (1953), 15-18.

[5] K. Budde, "Ellä toledoth," *ZAW*, XXXIV (1914), 241-53; XXXVI (1916), 1-7; O. Eissfeldt. "Biblos geneseōs," in *Fascher-Festschrift*, 1958, pp. 31-40; *idem*, "Toledot," in *Klostermann-Festschrift*, 1961, pp. 1-8.

explanation, arguing that P was originally a purely narrative work with the establishment of the national and cultic community at Sinai as its focus, into which the legal portions were inserted later. More precisely, Elliger interprets the narrative work as a book of consolation written during the Exile. This theory is contradicted by the close connection between the historical narrative and the law that results from the link between the schema of historical periods and the law given on Sinai (cf. 4). Hempel, who sees the origin of the individual ancient traditions in the scenes of a cultic drama, takes a different tack, thinking in terms of a complex course of development through oral tradition, whose stages cannot be recognized by literary analysis, but only by their content.

In any case, P is not to be understood as a literary unit, but as a literary composite. We must think first in terms of a basic written document growing out of the new redaction of the Pentateuchal material, in which the ancient narrative traditions were incorporated at the same time. The legal portions, originally independent, were added gradually, but were apparently updated again and again, until the final redaction of the Pentateuch was complete. Neither at this stage nor at any other were the various traditions harmonized. The various expansions include, e.g., Exod. 6:13-30; 12:42*b*, 43-51;13:1-2; 27:20-21; 30:1-18; 31:1-11; 35–40*; Leviticus 27; Num. 7:1-88. Considered as a whole, P achieved its present form by means of the supplement method.

4. *Characteristic content.* Among the specific characteristics of P, first and foremost is the close connection between historical narrative and law. Both are linked together inextricably. Within the context of the narrative Yahweh decrees each set of ordinances, which apply first to the situation at hand and then stand as eternal decrees from generation to generation. The narrative provides the foundation for the eternal law, and the eternal law justifies the presentation of the narrative. For this reason, the narrative material is far from homogeneous. When it is not associated with divine ordinances, it seldom goes beyond genealogies or short notices, which serve to link the whole together. On the other hand, P becomes downright verbose when cultic institutions are to be derived from the story (Gen. 1:1–2:4*a*; 6:9–9:17; 17). The scope of the narrative material and of the legal material are directly proportional.

A further characteristic is the chronology that is imposed upon the whole.[6] The reckoning of time begins with creation and is continued with precision. The method follows ancient Near Eastern prototypes. Diverging slightly from the Mesopotamian royal inscriptions, P gives his dates according to the ages (rather than the regnal years) of the representatives of each generation.

History is structured not only by the genealogies but also by the formula "These are the generations of *N*.," which is used as a superscription except in Gen. 2:4*a* (Gen. 6:9; 10:1; 11:10, 27; 25:12, 19; 36:1, 9; 37:2; Num. 3:1), as well as "This is the book of the generations," which precedes the list of ancestors (Gen. 5:1). It is used where the narrative is restricted to an

[6] A. Jepsen, "Zur Chronologie des Priesterkodex," *ZAW*, XLVII (1929), 251-55.

entity of moderate size, and marks the gradual transition from the history of the world and mankind to the history of Israel and its most select elite (Eissfeldt *).

E had begun to divide history into great periods; P completes this process by distinguishing several stages in God's revelation and a series of covenants. The first stage begins with the creation of the world; in an unexpressed covenant God gives man dominion over the world, decrees vegetarian diet as an ordinance of the covenant, and institutes the Sabbath as a sign of the covenant. He concludes the second covenant after the Deluge, with Noah; the Noachian laws are the ordinances of the covenant, and its sign is the rainbow. The third covenant is concluded with Abraham, with the commandment and sign of circumcision; the fourth and last is the Sinai covenant, involving the entire cultic program. P seeks at least in part to mark these stages by using various divine appellatives: Elohim (I–II), El Shaddai (III), Yahweh (IV).

In all this we see a kind of priestly erudition, which also finds expression in various numerical and other data, which usually do not correspond with reality. More than 600,000 men cannot possibly have assembled in the courtyard of the Tabernacle; neither could 2,500,000 persons live for a considerable period in the desert of Sinai, not to mention having with them the number of sheep used for the Passover. In fact, the number of fighting men was calculated from the numerical value of letters by means of gematria. First the numerical values of *b-n-y y-ś-r-ʾ-l* are added; the result is then multiplied by 1000. To this figure is added the simple numerical value of the words *k-l r-ʾ-š*. The result is 603,551, which, rounded off to 603,550, is the number of fighting men given in Num. 1:46; 2:32.

5. *Theology*. These observations have already told us much about the theology of P. This theology also includes the new purpose of the entire work. What P narrates and the ordinances he records not only held true in the past, but also and above all hold true in the present and the future. P contains a program for the divinely willed reconstruction of the community after the Exile or for a reformation of the community in the postexilic period. This program is retrojected into the past in order to legitimize it and give it authority. Because God decreed his ordinances long ago, for the most part on Sinai, as eternal legislation, they must be accepted unquestioningly in the present.

This God, according to P, is absolutely transcendent. He does not reveal himself in his own form, neither in reality nor in dreams. Only his *kābôd*, his *glory*, is revealed; and even it is hidden, to be looked upon by Moses alone. This tendency leads P to emphasize the idea of the tent-sanctuary at the expense of the ancient idea, connected with settled life in civilization, that God dwells and is present in the temple.[7] The transcendent God does not

[7] M. Haran, "The Ark and the Cherubim," *IEJ* IX (1959), pp. 30-38, 89-98; *idem*, "The Nature of the 'ʾOhel Môʿēdh' in Pentateuchal Sources," *JSS*, V (1959), 50-65; *idem*, "Shilo and Jerusalem: The Origin of the Priestly Tradition in the Pentateuch," *JBL*, LXXXI (1962),

dwell in the tent-sanctuary, but rather appears in it from time to time in a cloud with his *kābôd*.

This emphasis on God's transcendence involves a different relationship between God and man, which is illustrated by the camp order in Numbers 2.[8] Here the priests and Levites encamp as a kind of separating and protecting wall between the sanctuary and the people. It is no longer possible to approach God directly; one must instead go through the clergy, who act as mediators. In similar fashion, God no longer speaks directly to the people, but rather through Moses and Aaron. The life of the people is encompassed by the ritual law and secured by propitiation, which is the primary purpose of the cult.

6. *Origin.* In answering the question of the date of P, we may say quite generally—despite the use of earlier material—that we are dealing with the latest source stratum of the Pentateuch. Wellhausen quite correctly objected to a dating in the preexilic period: "But if the Priestly Code is in fact to be dated this early, then the king must have had no part in the cult and must in general have been a quite superfluous figure in the community; Israel must even then have been a church and not a state. But the evidence is all to the contrary. . . ."[9] P is later than D. P presupposes as self-evident D's requirement that the cult be centralized at a single place. P's cultic regulations are later; the agricultural character of the festivals, which is still recognizable in D (and in H), is obliterated, and they are determined instead by the calendar. Josiah's terror following the discovery of the Deuteronomic law code and the report of the reforms carried out subsequently would be incomprehensible if the much stricter P had already been in effect as law. Furthermore, P is later than H, which was incorporated as it was found, and than Ezekiel, who makes no mention of a high priest, and predicts (Ezekiel 44) the degradation of the Levites to the status of temple servants, which P presupposes. Finally, the prophets Deutero-Isaiah, Haggai, Zechariah, and Malachi are clearly familiar with Deuteronomy, but not with P. Only Chronicles, written some time after the middle of the fourth century, shows the influence of P. All these arguments show that P came into being in the fifth century.

As the place of origin, we may assume the Babylonian Diaspora. This follows primarily from the observation that P was the law brought to Jerusalem by Ezra with the authorization of the Persian king (Ezra 7:1-10), which formed the basis for Ezra's reformation. Though he was not the author of P, despite the term "scribe of the law of the God of heaven," he imposed it upon the Jerusalem community (Nehemiah 8–9), as the relationships between Neh. 8:13-15 and Lev. 23:40; Neh. 8:18 and Lev. 23:36

14-24; L. Rost, "Die Wohnstätte des Zeugnisses," in *Baumgärtel-Festschrift,* 1959, pp. 158-65; R. de Vaux, "Arche d'alliance et Tente de réunion," in *Mémorial Gelin,* 1961, pp. 55-70.

[8] A. Kuschke, "Die Lagervorstellung der priesterschriftlichen Erzählung," ZAW, LXIII (1951), 74-105.

[9] J. Wellhausen, *Prolegomena zur Geschichte Israel,* 2nd ed., IV, 1883.

show. It remains to ask whether the book of the law brought by Ezra was not actually the entire Pentateuch, expanded by the addition of P (§28.1).

§27 Passages Not Belonging to the Source Strata

W. F. Albright, "Šhinar-Šangār and its Monarch Amraphel," *AJSL*, XL (1923/24), 125-33; *idem*, "The Historical Background of Genesis XIV," *JSOR*, X (1926), 231-69; *idem*, "Abram the Hebrew: A New Archaeological Interpretation," *BASOR*, CLXIII (1961), 36-54; I. Benzinger, "Zur Quellenscheidung in Gen 14," in BZAW, XLI (1925), 21-27; F. M. T. Böhl, "Die Könige von Genesis 14," *ZAW*, XXXVI (1916), 65-73; *idem*, "Tud'alia I, Zeitgenosse Abrahams, um 1650 v. Chr.," *ibid.*, XLII (1924), 148-53; F. Cornelius, "Genesis XIV," *ibid.*, LXXII (1960), 1-7; H. del Medico, "Melchisédech," *ibid.*, LXIX (1957), 160-70; L. R. Fisher, "Abraham and his Priest-King," *JBL*, LXXXI (1962), 264-70; H. W. Hertzberg, "Die Melchisedek-Traditionen," *JPOS*, VII (1928), 169-79 (= *Beiträge zur Traditionsgeschichte und Theologie des Alten Testaments*, 1962, pp. 36-44); K. Jaritz, "Wer ist Amraphel in Genesis 14?" *ZAW*, LXX (1958), 255-56; R. Lack, "Les origines de ʿElyôn, le Très-Haut, dans la tradition cultuelle d'Israël, *CBQ*, XXIV (1962), 44-64; G. Levi della Vida, "El ʿElyon in Genesis, 14,18-20," *JBL*, LXIII (1944), 1-9; J. Meinhold, *I. Mose 14*, 1911; H. H. Rowley, "Melchizedek and Zadok (Gen 14 and Ps 110)," in *Bertholet-Festschrift*, 1950, pp. 461-72; N. A. van Uchelen, *Abraham de Hebreeër*, 1964; L.-H. Vincent, "Abraham à Jérusalem," *RB*, LVIII (1951), 360-71.

A. Bender, "Das Lied Exodus 15," *ZAW*, XXIII (1903), 1-48; F. M. Cross, Jr., and D. N. Freedman, "The Song of Miriam," *JNES*, XIV (1955), 237-50; N. Lohfink, "De Moysis epinicio (Ex 15,1-18)," *VD*, XLI (1963), 277-89; K. G. Rendtorff, "Sejrshymnen i Exodus 15 og dens forhold till tronbestigelssalmerna," *DTT*, XXII (1959), 65-81, 156-71; M. Rozelaar, "The Song of the Sea," *VT*, II (1952), 221-28; H. Schmidt, "Das Meerlied," *ZAW*, XLIX (1931), pp. 59-66; R. Tournay, "Recherches sur la chronologie des psaumes," *RB*, LXV (1958), 321-58; J. D. W. Watts, "The Song of the Sea—Ex XV," *VT*, VII (1957), 371-80.

J. B. Bauer, "Könige und Priester, ein heiliges Volk (Ex 19,6)," *BZ*, NF II (1958), 283-86; W. Caspari, "Das priesterliche Königreich," *ThBl*, VIII (1929), 105-10; R. J. Faley, *The Kingdom of Priests*, 1960; G. Fohrer, " 'Priesterliches Königtum', Ex 19,6," *ThZ*, XIX (1963), 359-62; R. Klopfer, "Zur Quellenscheidung in Exod 19," *ZAW*, XVIII (1898), 197-235; R. Martin-Achard, "Israël, peuple sacerdotal," *Verbum Caro*, XVIII (1964), 11-28; W. L. Moran, "A Kingdom of Priests," in *The Bible in Current Catholic Thought*, 1962, pp. 7-20; H. Wildberger, *Jahwes Eigentumsvolk*, 1960.

W. F. Albright, "Some Remarks on the Song of Moses in Deuteronomy XXXII," *VT*, IX (1959), 339-46; E. Baumann, "Das Lied Mose's (Dt XXXII 1-43) auf seine gedankliche Geschlossenheit untersucht," *ibid.*, VI (1956), 414-24; K. Budde, *Das Lied Moses*, 1920; O. Eissfeldt, *Das Lied Moses Deuteronomium 32,1-43 und das Lehrgedicht Asaphs Psalm 78 samt einer Analyse der Umgebung des Moseliedes*, 1958; A. Klostermann, *Der Pentateuch*, 1893, pp. 223-367; R. Meyer, "Die Bedeutung von Deuteronomium 32,8 f. 43 (4Q) für die Auslegung des Moseliedes," in *Rudolph-Festschrift*, 1961, pp. 197-209; W. Moran, "Some Remarks on the Song of Moses," *Bibl*, XLIII (1962), 317-27; E. Sellin, "Wann wurde das Moselied Dtn 32 gedichtet?" *ZAW*, XLIII (1925), 161-73; P. W. Skehan, "The Structure of the Song of Moses in Deuteronomy (Deut 32,1-43)," *CBQ*, XIII (1951), 153-63; G. E. WRIGHT, "The Lawsuit of God: a Form-Critical Study of Deuteronomy 32," in *Essays Muilenburg*, 1962, pp. 26-67.

1. *Genesis 14.* Genesis 14 does not belong to any of the source strata; it came into being in isolation and was incorporated into the Pentateuch. The narrative tells how four mighty kings attack Palestine, vanquishing, among others, the city-kings of Sodom and Gomorrah. Lot, who has been dwelling in Sodom, they take away captive. Abraham with his 318 servants follows the victorious army, conquers it, frees Lot, and upon his return dedicates to Melchizedek, the priest-king of "Salem," a tenth of the booty and shows generosity to the king of Sodom.

The narrative has frequently been cited to support an early dating for Abraham, through an identification of Amraphel, one of the hostile kings, with Hammurabi of Babylon, which would mean, by the old chronology, that Abraham lived around 1900 B.C. The popularity of this view has waned, however, since the new chronology constructed on the basis of the Mari texts places Hammurabi about 1700. It has recently been argued on the basis of this narrative that Abraham was a princely merchant from the city of Ura in Asia Minor in the fourteenth century.

All attempts to draw historical conclusions from Genesis 14 founder on the observation that we are dealing here with a late text, which presupposes the existence of the Pentateuch. It is dependent on the narratives involving Lot (Genesis 12–13; 18–19 [N's contribution]), and has points of contact with E and, in language, with P. It also shares with P the use of gematria, since the number of Abraham's servants is calculated from the name of Abraham's servant Eliezer (Gen. 15:2 [J]). The use of the pseudonym "Salem" for Jerusalem, which is supported by Ps. 76:3 (Eng. 76:2) and column 22.13 of the so-called Genesis Apocryphon from Cave One at Qumran, also points to a late date. We must therefore follow Steuernagel*, Procksch, and many others (*pace* Sellin) in calling Genesis 14 a late midrash. It has parallels in the legends of Daniel and in the book of Judith, and is intended to glorify Abraham and gain recognition for the high priest at Jerusalem. It provides no historical information about Abraham, since his figure is a late addition to the other material of the narrative.

Nevertheless, the learned author obviously had ancient accounts or notices at his disposal. Two of them go back to the second millenium, though they probably derive from oral tradition, rather than a cuneiform document in the Temple archives (Steuernagel *).

a) One tradition describes the victorious raid of peoples from the east; it contains the name of the four kings, which, however, cannot be associated with historical persons belonging to the same period. Amraphel of Shinar (Mesopotamia) can no longer be equated with Hammurabi; among the more recent suggestions, which even include a Syrian king, the derivation of the name from Amar-pi-el, appears reasonable. The second name, "Arioch of

Ellasar," could go back to the form "Arriwuk," in which case it would be a Hurrian form; it turns up as the name of a son of Zimri-Lim, king of Mari. The third name, "Tidal of Goiim," corresponds to the form "Tudḫalias," the name of several Hittite kings. The fourth name, "Chedorlaomer of Elam," has a corresponding form in the Elamite name "Kutir-Lagamar," although this name is not found in the Elamite king list. In view of the long history of transmission, it is no longer possible to illuminate the assumed historical situation.

b) An ancient reminiscence is also connected with the name of Melchizedek, in whom we may see a Canaanite city-king of Jerusalem. If his priestly functions, according to Ps. 110:4, were transferred to the Davidic line as the later city-kings of Jerusalem, we may surmise that David conquered the city during the reign of Melchizedek.

2. *Exod. 15:1-19.* Exod. 15:1-19 contains in vss. 1*b*-18 a song that the superscription in vs. 1*a* places in the mouth of Moses and the Israelites after their deliverance at the Reed Sea; vs. 19 is an explanatory note incorporating the song into the context. It begins with a slightly altered form of the text of the Song of Miriam (Exod. 15:21), and then goes on to describe further events from the period of desert wandering and the occupation of Canaan that are among Yahweh's "glorious acts." This basic purpose, expressed in vss. 2-3, accounts for the themes selected, so that the absence of any reference to the events at Sinai does not justify drawing any conclusions.

There is an extreme divergence of opinions with respect to the literary type and basic purpose of the song. It is often called a Passover hymn or psalm (e.g., Beer, Rozelaar, Sellin-Rost*), although it neither makes reference to the festival nor mentions any of the events that would be important from this point of view (the slaying of the Egyptian firstborn while the Israelites were protected). Others think in terms of a song for the autumnal New Year's Festival, the so-called Enthronement Festival of Yahweh (cf. §39.2), or the alleged Covenant Festival (e.g., Bentzen*, H. Schmidt, Weiser*), although the text makes no reference to any festal circumstances. Others conjecture a complex process of cultural development behind the growth of the song (Watts), a harmonization of hymnic elements and a "historical ballad" (Rylaarsdam), or a homiletical and pious paraphrase of the Song of Miriam (Pfeiffer). Form-critically, the song is a hymn, whose "I" can represent the community, expanded by formal elements of the victory song and thanksgiving song. It represents a poetic praise of Yahweh for his deliverance at the Reed Sea and subsequent saving acts. It dates from a period when the motif of deliverance at the sea was popular.[1]

Opinions as to the song's date are also as widely divergent as possible. They extend from the Mosaic period[2] through the period of the Judges (Sellin, Cross-Freedman: material from the twelfth century, written form

[1] A. Lauha, "Das Schilfmeermotiv im Alten Testament," *VTSuppl*, IX (1963), 32-46.
[2] W. F. Albright, *The Archaeology of Palestine*, 1949, p. 233.

from the tenth),[3] the period of the monarchy (Rozelaar), and the Deuteronomic period (Beer, Tournay) to the postexilic period (Bender, Pfeiffer). Vss. 17-18 provide a point of reference: the idea that Yahweh has prepared for himself a dwelling place in Jerusalem, the Temple, so as to be able to reign as king for ever, can be expected, at the earliest, in the late preexilic period.[4] In addition, the introductory words of vss. 18, "It is Yahweh that reigns as king," which takes the perfect tense of the introduction to a few psalms, influenced by Deutero-Isaiah, and turns it into an imperfect (§39.2), together with the motif of deliverance at the sea, point to the postexilic period.

3. *Exod. 19:3b-8*. Exod. 19:3*b*-8 is a short independent section in the Sinai narrative, belonging to none of the source strata. It demands obedience toward Yahweh's commandment, which will make Israel Yahweh's own possession. Israel is to be a priestly kingship and a holy nation. These latter phrases have been interpreted in many ways. Recent studies seem to show, however, that "*gôy*" refers to the *nation* as a political entity, ruled by a king, while "*mamlākâ*" can mean not only "kingdom" but also "kingship" or "king." This is in fact the meaning of the word in association with "nation" from I Kings 18:10; Jer. 18:7; 27:8 on. And so the nucleus of the section states that Yahweh intends to create a holy nation, consecrated to him, with a priestly kingship or king. On the basis of the late association between "kingship" and "nation," the long recognized influence of Deuteronomic language, and the connection, in both language and ideas, with H, which goes back to preexilic traditions (§20.3), we may conclude that Exod. 19:3*b*-8 derives from priestly circles in Jerusalem toward the end of the Judahite monarchy.

4. *Deuteronomy 32*. It is most unlikely that Deut. 32:1-43, the Song of Moses, together with its narrative framework 31:19-22; 32:44 describing Moses' recitation of the song, belonged to the source stratum E and led to the incorporation of the Deuteronomic law code in its position immediately preceding. It is instead an interpolation, laboriously disguised by means of the framework, and constitutes a kind of parallel to the Blessing of Moses, Deuteronomy 33 (Budde). *Pace* Weiser*, it does not presuppose a cultic situation, since vss. 3, 7, 15, and 43 do not point in this direction; neither is it based on a fixed pattern of liturgical proclamation, all the more so because it is a mixture of various formal elements: it begins and ends with hymnic elements, for the rest drawing on elements of historical reflection, prophetical proclamation, and wisdom instruction. Considered as a whole, the Song of Moses (which even after being incorporated in the Pentateuch continued to circulate as an independent unit in the Qumran literature) is a "testament" or "last will of Moses" (Meyer); especially in the postexilic period, literature of this type was produced in great quantity.

This raises the difficult question of the song's date. Quite apart from the

[3] For arguments against an early date, see especially S. Mowinckel, *VT*, V (1955), 27-28.
[4] Cf. G. Fohrer, "Zion-Jerusalem im Alten Testament," *ThW* VII, 307-308.

language and intellectual milieu, vss. 7, 10, 13-18 make Mosaic authorship impossible, since they imply that Israel had already a long history in Palestine. Eissfeldt thinks that the historical reflection extends only to the occupation of Canaan, the resulting apostasy, and the appearance of the Philistines as the instrument of God's punishment; he therefore derives the song from the middle of the eleventh century, possibly from Samuel. Others, however, interpret the "no people" of vs. 21 as the Arameans of the ninth century, the Assyrians of the eighth (Sellin-Rost*), the Babylonians of the seventh or sixth (Budde), or the Samaritans of the fifth (Sellin).

The entire description in the vicinity of vs. 21 points so unequivocally to the catastrophe of the state of Judah brought about by the attack of the Babylonians, while vss. 32-43 predict catastrophe for these enemies and renewed vindication for Israel, that it is a real question why the exilic origin of the song was ever in doubt. In addition, the echoes of Isa. 63:7–64:11 (Eng. 63:7–64:12), which comes from the same period, and above all the extremely pervasive influence of the ideas of Ezekiel, suggest that the song was composed around or shortly after the middle of the sixth century. An even later date is quite unlikely, although Meyer assumes the period of the universal Persian monarchy about 400 B.C. on the basis of his interpretation of the new text of vss. 8-9 and 43 found in the important fragment from the Fourth Cave at Qumran.

§28 The Growth of the Pentateuch

The Pentateuch (or Hexateuch) as a whole did not come into being in a single great process of combining all the source strata that had long existed independently side by side. It was instead built up gradually. D, for example assumes the combination JNE; P also assumes the incorporation of D. The stages in this process of compilation are called redactions, and the persons who undertook them are called redactors. They are referred to by the siglum R, to which is added the siglum for the source strata incorporated in each case. For example, the redaction that added the source stratum P to the body of material already in existence is called R^{P}.

This terminology gives the impression that the gradual growth of the Pentateuch from the individual source strata was essentially a literary process. This impression is quite accurate. The history of the growth of the Pentateuch as a whole is not traced by form-criticism, but by redaction-history. The amalgamation of the source strata was not a cultic process (Weiser*) but a literary process (Noth), whose goal was to incorporate all the historical traditions. If the process had been cultic, it would be hard to understand why the earlier tradition should have been preserved side by side with the later tradition, which would have replaced it in cultic recitation. During the latter part of the Israelite monarchy, there was in the ancient Near East a strong tendency to assemble collections of literature. This tendency was also at work in Israel. The growth of the Pentateuch took place against this ancient Near Eastern background. There can hardly be any doubt that a work of this sort found an audience and proved useful to many people; we may think primarily of the scribal schools and wisdom schools. The histories of Solomon and the kings of Judah and Israel, which were used as sources for the books of Kings, are further evidence for this interest in historical works. Only after Deuteronomic theology lent its support to a "religion of the book" and the altered cultic situation of the Exile led to a word-centered worship did liturgical use of the largely complete Pentateuch (or Hexateuch) begin.

It is admittedly impossible at the present time to present the redaction-history of the Pentateuch in detail. It is impossible even to answer the question of the order in which the source strata were joined together with assurance. It is possible that J and E were the first to be combined. Ps. 78:44-51, however, follows J exclusively in its descriptive list of the Egyptian plagues, preferring the cruder account of E only for the first plague; if this psalm derives from the end of the preexilic period, J and E seem to have been still separate at this time. Much evidence can be cited for a preliminary combination of J and N. The Deuteronomic additions in Exodus 12–13, for example, admit the conclusion that JN must have been available in combination to the author of the additions. For the present, much remains obscure.

It is easier to grasp the methods of redaction. In some cases, it retained the parallel accounts side by side and joined them together, e.g., the narratives concerning the creation, the endangering of the patriarch's wife, and most of the Egyptian plagues. In other cases, it interwove the accounts, e.g., the narratives concerning the Deluge and the two forms of the Joseph novella, where the source strata appear alternately. Still another procedure was followed with the narratives of Moses' birth and the deliverance of the Israelites at the sea: the presentation of one or two source strata provides the foundation, and is merely supplemented by features from an additional source stratum. Finally, the editorial process can lead to a complete coalescence of the source strata so that they can no longer be distinguished, as in Exod. 2:15-22, or it can consist in redactional expansion of a brief notice into an account of some size, as in Exod. 1:15-21. The latest source stratum, P, was frequently placed as a framework about the already extant material, as in the Deluge narrative (albeit following the general remarks of J), the Table of Nations, the description of the oppression in Egypt (Exod. 1:7-14), and the story of the call of Moses. This method probably seemed the simplest procedure in view of the already fixed combination of the earlier source strata, into which P was inserted only rarely.

In the course of redaction, individual portions of a source stratum were frequently misplaced in their new context. Depending on what order of combination is assumed, for example, in Exodus 4, either vss. 19-20*a*, 24-26,

30*b* or 27-28, 30*a* have fallen out of order.[1] In addition, larger sections were sometimes shifted; C is probably the best example.

All in all, the process of redaction made the presentation more complicated and confused, but added considerable depth to the total impression of the Pentateuch.

The question arises when the Pentateuch (or Hexateuch) finally was extant as a combination of JNEDP. In answering it, we must refer once more to Ezra's reformation (cf. §26.6). It has been pointed out that several of its measures are not based upon P: Neh. 10:31; 13:1-3 are based on Exod. 34:16; Deut. 7:2-5 and Neh. 10:32 on Deut. 15:2. This means that the Pentateuch as a whole provided the basis for Ezra's reformation and was probably brought by him from Babylonia. It follows that the Pentateuch must have come into being there shortly after the composition of P, by the addition of P to the material already extant. This dating is supported by the fact that the Samaritans took over the Pentateuch in the fourth century, obviously as an officially recognized foundation for their religion.

The process is further complicated by the observation that the source strata may have concluded by recounting the story of the occupation of Canaan by Israel under the leadership of Joshua. We must therefore look for a continuation of the source strata in the book of Joshua. If this is the case, then the entire complex Genesis–Joshua, referred to as the Hexateuch, came into being in Babylonia, after which the book of Joshua was separated once more from the rest so that the remaining Pentateuch, without the large-scale territorial claims, could gain the approval of the Persian officials as religious law. Later on, additions of various size were included, such as Genesis 14, and the Pentateuch was divided into five books.

TRANSITION

§29 The Assumption of Larger Works

1. *Hypotheses.* We have several times raised the question of the total scope of the source strata, but have not answered it. Did the source strata end with the death of Moses, recounting the promise of territorial possession but not the realization of the promise? How is the contents of the book of Joshua related to the source strata? May there even be literary strands going as far as the books of Kings? The simple view holds that the source strata are limited to the Pentateuch. The following hypotheses represent departures from this view—apart from the extreme simplification that, after a long procession

[1] Cf. G. Fohrer, *Überlieferung und Geschichte des Exodus*, 1964, p. 54.

of oral transmission, the whole historical tradition was committed to fixed written form in a P-work and a D-work in the postexilic period:

a) The early source strata of the Pentateuch or Hexateuch continue on into the books Judges–Samuel or Judges–Kings. After the first suggestions along this line, Budde (§31) and Cornill (§32) presented the evidence in detail. The theory was supported by Benzinger and Hölscher (§33) for the source strata J and E; Smend, Eissfeldt, and Simpson (§31) also added the third early source stratum (J^1, L). In the last analysis, then, we should assume a single comprehensive historical work.

b) The source strata go only as far as the end of Numbers, so that there was never a Pentateuch but only a Tetrateuch as a literary entity. The books Deuteronomy–Kings constitute a second work, which Noth has called the Deuteronomistic History (§30). Independently of Noth, Jepsen (§33) has proposed a similar theory. According to Noth, the author of the Deuteronomistic History combined into a single work what had previously been independent units and added passages of his own exposition. This took place during the Exile. Later, interpolations of considerable size were made. According to this theory, we should think in terms of two great historical works: the Tetrateuch and the Deuteronomistic History. Variations are of course possible. Hempel, for instance, considers Judg. 2:6-10 as the earlier beginning of the Deuteronomistic History and Joshua 23 as the later beginning. Far from creating a comprehensive presentation of Israel's history, including oral and written traditions, the Deuteronomistic History actually prevented such a presentation from coming into being by interrupting, through its treatment of the sources used for the book of Kings, the ongoing "organic" development of an overall picture.

c) The source strata of the Pentateuch continue on through the book of Joshua and into the beginning of the book of Judges, so that we can speak of the Hextateuch as an inclusive historical work made up out of these source strata. The subsequent books, on the other hand, are not made up of continuous sources; neither are they to be understood as a single unified work. Each came into being independently through the composition method (§18.4), applied to individual fragments or complexes (Kittel: bibliography to §31).

2. *Criticism*. The hypotheses described under (*a*) and (*b*) above, which think in terms of one or two comprehensive historical works, are certainly impressive attempts to solve the extremely difficult problems of the growth and composition of the books Joshua–Kings. Our presentation in §30–33 does not follow them, however, because weighty arguments tell against them.

a) No attempt to assign the material in the books Judges–Kings to two or three narrative strands and to equate these strands with the source strata of the Pentateuch has been even remotely successful. Despite occasional doublets, which can be explained otherwise than through assignment to continuous sources, the alleged narrative strands in the books Judges–Kings are represented very meagerly and are subject to stylistic change. In contrast to the originality of JNE, they are limited from the book of Judges on for the most part to the mere compilation and juxtaposition of various traditions, neither intending nor achieving a clear order and intellectual consistency. This hypothesis leaves open more questions than it solves.

b) Several observations argue against the assumption of a Deuteronomistic History. In the first place, Deuteronomy became an integral part of the Pentateuch after a period as an independent work, as the supplements show. This is demonstrated by the continuation of the source strata J, E, and P at the end of the book (Deut. 31:14-17, 23; 33–34), the incorporation of verses from P (Deut. 1:3; 4:41-43), and the present position of the book (§25.6). Furthermore, there are significant connections between the Pentateuch and the book of Joshua that are not based upon redactional interference but were already present in the preexilic source strata, such as the reference to the removal of Joseph's bones (Exod. 13:19 [E]) and its carrying out (Josh. 24:32), and the introduction of the figure of Joshua (Exod. 17:8-14 [N]; 24:13-15 [N]; 32:17-18 [N]; 33:11 [E]; Num. 11:28-29 [E]; Deut. 31:14, 23 [JE]). This agrees with the observation that the source strata of the Pentateuch continue through the book of Joshua and into the book of Judges, as close examination shows. In the book of Joshua, Noth constantly eliminates certain material, mostly E, as alleged editorial additions, without examining the relationships of these "editorial additions" to each other and to the stratum E in the Pentateuch. This approach oversimplifies the situation. In addition, it is incomprehensible that the source strata should not have contained a final account of the occupation or that this account should later have been omitted, since both the ancient narrative nuclei and the presentation as a whole lead up to the occupation of Canaan. Finally, it is impossible to think of the books Judges–Kings as parts of a work composed by a Deuteronomistic author or redactor. The book of Judges has certainly been subject to Deuteronomistic editing, as the framework passages surrounding the narratives show; the result is a cyclic course of history with a constantly repeated series: apostasy—punishment—repentance—deliverance. The books of Kings, on the other hand, which were not edited but composed by the Deuteronomist, present a course of history that leads downward in a straight line to destruction. In the books of Samuel, again, only slight Deuteronomistic influence is observable. Procedure and perspective are so different that the books cannot be derived from a single author or redactor.

3. *The development of the historical books*. The presentation in §30–33 follows essentially the Hexateuch hypothesis described under (*c*) above. The development of the historical books may therefore be described roughly as follows:

a) Gradual combination of the source strata JNE produced a Proto-Hexateuch, comprising the material from the source strata as found in Genesis–Numbers, at the end of Deuteronomy, in the book of Joshua, and at the beginning of the book of Judges.

b) Next, D was incorporated and the book of Joshua was edited deuteronomistically to join it securely to Deuteronomy.

c) P was added later, completing the Hexateuch, from which the book of Joshua was soon dropped for political reasons.

d) In the period of stage (*b*), the books of Judges, Samuel, and Kings, edited or composed deuteronomistically, came into being essentially in their present form. It should be noted that they are the product of various hands working in various ways. Secondary changes resulted in the end of the Hexateuch being transferred to the beginning of the book of Judges and the end of the History of David being transferred to the beginning of the books of Kings.

In summary, we may say:

1. The Hexateuch once existed as a literary entity, albeit only for a short time in its complete form (including P).
2. When the book of Joshua was dropped, the Pentateuch came into being as a truncated literary work; it became the foundation for the Jewish community from the time of Ezra on.
3. There never was a Tetrateuch, Heptateuch, Octateuch, or Enneateuch.
4. There never was a Deuteronomistic History as a unified literary entity; instead, we have a series of books Deuteronomy—Kings, each composed or edited in a different way.
5. Finally, there is general agreement that, as the last stage in the process, the Chronicler's history came into being; it is usually thought of as comprising Chronicles, Ezra, and Nehemiah.

CHAPTER THREE: JOSHUA THROUGH KINGS (THE FORMER PROPHETS)

§30 The Book of Joshua and Judg. 1:1–2:5

ATD: H. W. Hertzberg, 2nd ed., 1959. BOT: B. J. Alfrink, 1952. HAT: M. Noth, 2nd ed., 1953. HK: C. Steuernagel, 2nd ed., 1923. HS: A. Schulz, 1924. IB: J. Bright, 1953. KeH: A. Dillmann, 2nd ed., 1886. KHC: K. Holzinger, 1901. SAT: H. Gressmann, 2nd ed., 1922. SZ: S. Oettli, 1893. Individual commentaries: L. Roussel (chapters 1–12), 1955.

Y. Aharoni, "The Province-List of Judah," *VT*, IX (1959), 225-46; W. F. Albright, "The List of Levitic Cities," in *Ginzberg Jubilee Volume*, I (1945), 49-73; A. Alt, "Judas Gaue unter Josia," *PJB*, XXI (1925), 100-16 (= *Kleine Schriften*, II [1953], 276-88 [Eng. *Essays on Old Testament History and Religion*, 1966]); *idem*, "Das System der Stammesgrenzen im Buche Josua," in *Sellin-Festschrift*, 1927, pp. 13-24 (= *Kleine Schriften*, I [1953], 193-202); *idem*, "Eine galiläische Ortsliste in Jos 19," *ZAW*, XLV (1927) 59-81; *idem*, "Josua," in BZAW, LXVI (1936), 13-29 (= *Kleine Schriften*, I [1953], 176-92); *idem*, "Bemerkungen zu einigen judäischen Ortslisten des Alten Testaments," *Beiträge zur biblischen Landes- und Altertumskunde*, LXVIII (1951), 193-210 (= *Kleine Schriften*, II [1953], 389-305); *idem*, "Festungen und Levitenorte im Lande Juda," in *Kleine Schriften*, II (1953), 306-15; K. Budde, "Richter und Josua," *ZAW*, VII (1887), 93-166; F. M. Cross, Jr., and G. E. Wright, "The Boundary and Province Lists of the Kingdom of Judah," *JBL*, LXXV (1956), 202-26; O. Eissfeldt, "Die Eroberung Palästinas durch Altisrael," *WdO*, II (1955), 158-71; M. Haran, "Studies in the Account of the Levitical Cities," *JBL*, LXXX (1961), 45-54, 156-65; E. Jenni, "Zwei Jahrzehnte Forschung an den Büchern Josua bis Könige," *ThR*, NF XXVII (1961), 1-32, 97-146; Z. Kallai-Kleinmann, "The Town Lists of Judah, Simeon, Benjamin and Dan," *VT*, VIII (1958), 134-60; *idem*, "Note on the Town Lists of Judah, Simeon, Benjamin and Dan," *ibid.*, XI (1961), 223-27; Y. Kaufmann, *The Biblical Account of the Conquest of Palestine*, 1953; C. A. Keller, "Über einige alttestamentliche Heiligtumslegenden, II," *ZAW*, LXVIII (1956), 85-97; J. Maier, *Das altisraelitische Ladeheiligtum*, 1965; A. Malamat, "Traditions Concerning Early Israelite History in Canaan," in *Scripta Hierosolymitana*, VIII (1961), 303-34; K. Möhlenbrink, "Die Landnahmesagen des Buches Josua," *ZAW*, LVI (1938), 238-68; S. Mowinckel, *Zur Frage nach dokumentarischen Quellen in Josua* 13–19, 1946; *idem*, *Tetrateuch-Pentateuch-Hexateuch*, 1964; M. Noth, "Studien zu den historisch-geographischen Dokumenten des Josuabuches," *ZDPV*, LVIII (1935), 185-255; *idem*, *Überlieferungsgeschichtliche Studien*, I, 1943; *idem*, "Überlieferungsgeschichte zur zweiten Hälfte des Josuabuches," in *Nötscher-Festschrift*, 1950, pp. 152-67; G. Schmitt, *Der Landtag von Sichem*, 1964; K.-D. Schunck, *Benjamin*, 1963; G. E. Wright, "The Literary and Historical Problems of Joshua 10 and Judges 1," *JNES*, V (1946), 105-14.

1. *Terminology, content, source strata.* The book takes its name from its primary figure. There is a Talmudic tradition that Joshua also wrote it, but

this is contradicted by its character as an anonymous work as well as by observations similar to those that contradict the Mosaic origin of the Pentateuch.

In content, the book tells how the oft-repeated promise to the fathers that the land would be given to their numerous descendants came to be realized. The Pentateuch itself tells how the land east of the Jordan was distributed to Israelite tribes, a theme taken up again by Josh. 13:15-32. The book of Joshua goes on to tell how Israel conquered and distributed the land west of the Jordan in the period between Moses and the death of Joshua. The section Judg. 1:2–2:5, which Judg. 1:1 places after the death of Joshua and which has been secondarily transferred to the beginning of the book of Judges, represents the conclusion of the narrative. It is alien to the book of Judges and is intimately connected with the first part of the book of Joshua.

1–12 Conquest of the land west of the Jordan under Joshua's leadership
- 1 Preparation
- 2 Reconnaissance of Jericho
- 3–4 Crossing of the Jordan
- 5 Israel at Gilgal
- 6 Conquest of Jericho
- 7 Achan's theft; defeat at Ai
- 8 Conquest of Ai; altar built on Mount Ebal
- 9 Deception by the Gibeonites
- 10 Battle at Gibeon; conquests in the south
- 11 Battle at Merom; conquests in the north
- 12 List of defeated kings

13–22 Distribution of the land
- 13 Command; distribution of land east of the Jordan
- 14–19 Distribution of land west of the Jordan
- 20 Cities of refuge
- 21 Cities for the priests and Levites
- 22 Altar built east of the Jordan

23–24 Two farewell addresses of Joshua

Judg. 1:1–2:5 Battles and incomplete conquests

If we are to understand the history of the book's development, we must reject Noth's oversimplified analysis, which, for example, in 2–6 eliminates the verses to be ascribed to E and other doublets as later editorial additions, and take instead as our point of departure the observation, which has long been recognized, that the source strata of the Pentateuch continue through Judg. 2:5. The views as to which verses are to be assigned to the various strata are admittedly more divergent than in the case of the Pentateuch, as the analyses of Eissfeldt, Hölscher, Mowinckel, Smend, and Weiser* show. There are two basic reasons for this divergence: first, the thorough editorial revision on the part of the Deuteronomists, who were particularly interested in the history of the post-Mosaic period; and second, the transmission-history of 1–11, which has created an independent occupation narrative in fixed form. It may be possible to approximate its nucleus by analyses like those of Dus and Maier. The earliest presentation, which corresponds to the groundwork G[1], is found in Judg. 1:1–2:5; it belongs to N. Following the pattern of G[1], G[2] took its place and was used by JE to provide the pre-Deuteronomistic material of Joshua 1–11 and a few additional passages. P furnishes primarily the bulk of 12; 13:15–21:42. In addition, there are the passages to be ascribed to the Deuteronomistic revision, most of which came into being independently.

2. *N*. The striking passage Num. 32:39-42 (in which vs. 40 serves only to provide continuity with the surrounding narrative), which tells of conquests east of the Jordan, has been assigned to the source stratum N. It is out of place in its immediate environment, which presupposes the conquest of the territory east of the Jordan by Moses. It takes instead as its point of departure the notion that the groups mentioned crossed over from west of the Jordan and gained dwelling places for themselves by conquest. Other short passages of similar type, which are distinguished from their environment stylistically and materially as well as by their religiously and ethically archaic evaluation of persons and actions, are to be found in the book of Joshua: 11:13, concerning northern Palestine; 15:13-19, concerning southern Palestine; 15:63, concerning the continued residence of the Jebusites in Jerusalem; 16:10, concerning the failure to conquer Gezer; 17:11-13, concerning the Plain of Jezreel; and 19:47, concerning the migration of the Danites. In addition, the anecdotal narrative 17:14-18 concerning the distribution of Gilead probably belongs in this context. None of these passages was originally located in its present position. Their source is instead Judges 1, where they occur as parts of a larger whole:

Josh.		Judg.
15:13-19	—	1:10-15
15:63	—	1:21
16:10	—	1:29
17:11-13	—	1:27-28
19:47	—	1:34-35

The individual passages have been removed from this original context and distributed throughout the book of Joshua, where they are found a second time. The only reasonable time at which this can have taken place is the postexilic period, after Judg. 1:2–2:5 was removed from the Hexateuch and placed at the beginning of the book of Judges.

Wellhausen was the first to recognize that Judges 1, to which the nucleus of Judg. 2:1-5 also belongs, was an occupation narrative and a parallel to the main narrative of the book of Joshua. Meyer[1] marshaled more evidence and ascribed the report to J, Budde corrected the theory by pointing out that the report begins after the conquest of Jericho, and Smend ascribed it to the source stratum J[1] (N). Mowinckel has recently supported this view, which is shared by others, rejecting in particular the theses that Judges 1 is a separate document independent of the Pentateuchal sources, a list of the

[1] E. Meyer, "Kritik der Berichte über die Eroberung Palästinas," *ZAW*, I (1881), 135.

territorial claims of the various tribes, or a conglomerate of early tradition fragments (Noth). In fact, the entire section is a compact narrative consisting mostly of etiological anecdotes. It resembles the royal inscriptions of the ancient Near East both in its terse, schematic listing of historical actions and events and in its occasional more extended anecdotal treatment of individual events. Although Num. 32:39-42 should be included among these passages, it is not a complete report, but rather represents a fragment taken from a larger context. At the outset of the narrative, the Israelites are located during Joshua's lifetime in the Jordan Valley, whence—divided into tribes—they "go up" into the land east and west of the Jordan to conquer it. In this fashion we are given a brief survey of the territories occupied by the tribes; those cities that could not be conquered are expressly mentioned. The author wrote, not a history of how the occupation took place, but a survey of the results of the occupation in narrative form.

The narrative is organized not chronologically but geographically—and this not according to the map, but according to the presupposed historical situation. It begins with the campaign against the hill country of Ephraim, which is the region most accessible to the Jordan Valley, then directs its attention to the south, and finally once more to central and northern Palestine; the description of the occupation runs from south to north. The narratives of JE also follow this pattern, which constitutes the connecting link between the brief narrative G^1 and the more detailed G^2.

The southern tribes occupy the center of interest; Judah, for instance, is said to have been the first tribe to set out on the conquest. This fact probably points to the territory of Judah, where the source stratum N came into being. The presentation presupposes the situation of the Davidic and Solomonic period (subjugation and compulsory labor of Canaanite subjects) and was written considerably after the time of Solomon (Mowinckel), observations that agree with what we have seen in the Pentateuch.

The source stratum N does not depict the conquest of Palestine as a single process under the leadership of Joshua, but as several separate campaigns, only partially successful, on the part of the individual tribes or groups of tribes. In this regard it presents the historical situation more accurately than do the other source strata.

3. *G^2*. The occupation narrative of J and E is based on G^2. This form of the groundwork is based on G^1, but is given a distinctive form by a series of originally separate narratives. The connection with G^1 can be seen first of all in 14:6-15 (E), which represents a legendary and edifying revision of 15:13-19 (N). Furthermore, Mowinckel has rightly pointed out that the presentation (which he calls the source of the Deuteronomistic History, Noth's "compiler") follows the geographical pattern of G^1 (N), according to which Palestine is conquered in three major battles: first central Palestine, then southern Palestine, and finally northern Palestine.

This shows the continuity between G^1 and G^2. In addition, the latter presentation has incorporated two groups of narratives, transforming the sequence of a geographical survey of the results of the occupation into a temporal sequence of historical events.

A. We are dealing mostly with etiological sagas, which were originally not connected with the figure of Joshua. These were individual sagas, some probably of Canaanite origin, which attempted to trace conspicuous objects and circumstances back to events in the past.

2 and the conclusion of 6: the permission granted the clan of Rahab, from Jericho, to dwell in Israelite territory, which may have been connected with sacral prostitution at a Canaanite sanctuary.[2]

3:1–5:1: the circle of stones at Gilgal and, secondarily, the twelve stones set up in the Jordan, which are associated with a crossing of the Jordan depicted like a procession and patterned after the deliverance at the Sea of Reeds.[3]

5:2-9: the place-name "Hill of the Foreskins," given to the place where once the local community undertook the ancient ritual of circumcision.

5:13-15: the sacredness of an unnamed site to be found in the vicinity of Jericho and Gilgal (a sanctuary legend).[4]

6: the curse attaching to the site of Jericho (conquest by means of a magic circle), which probably is pre-Israelite, the more so because, despite all efforts, no archaeological evidence has been found for a conquest of the city during the period of the Israelite occupation of Canaan.

7: a large heap of stones in the Valley of Achor near Jericho, for which the name "Achan" (or, more correctly, "Achar") is cited in explanation.

8:1-29; the ruined tell of Ai, with a heap of stones at the city gate; excavations have shown that the city was last conquered many centuries before the Israelite occupation of Canaan.

9: the treaty between Gibeon and its adjacent cities, which were not conquered by the Israelites, and their Israelite surroundings.[5]

Half of these etiological sagas are located at the sanctuary of Gilgal; the others probably referred to points along the road taken by pilgrims from the hill country to the sanctuary of Gilgal. It is likely, therefore, that this is where the sagas were joined to form a cycle. More precisely, we may observe that the sagas 2 + 3:1–5:1 + 6 themselves form a unified composition, to which the others are loosely joined. Since Gilgal lay in the territory of Benjamin,

[2] F.-M. Abel, "L'anathème de Jéricho et la maison de Rahab," *RB*, LVII (1950), 321-30; G. Hölscher, "Zum Ursprung der Rahabsage," *ZAW*, XXXVIII (1919/20), 54-57; J. A. Soggin, "Giosué 2 alla luce di un testo di Mari," *RSO*, XXXIX (1964), 7-14.

[3] B. J. Alfrink, "De litteraire compositie van Jos 3 en 4," *StC*, XVIII (1942), 185-202; J. Dus, "Die Analyse zweier Ladeerzählungen des Josuabuches (Jos 3-4 and 6)," *ZAW*, LXXII (1960), 107-34; H.-J. Kraus, "Gilgal—ein Beitrag zur Kulturgeschichte Israel," *VT*, I (1951), 181-99; P.-P. Saydon, "The Crossing of the Jordan: Jos chaps. 3 and 4," *CBQ*, XII (1950), 194-207.

[4] A. George, "Les récits de Gilgal en Josué 5,2-15," in *Mémorial Chaine*, 1950, pp. 169-86.

[5] J. M. Grintz, "The Treaty with the Gibeonites," *Zion*, XXVI (1961), 69-84; F. C. Fensham, "The Treaty between Israel and the Gibeonites," *BA*, XXVII (1964), 96-100; M. Haran, "The Gibeonites, the Nethinim and the Sons of Solomon's Servants," *VT*, XI (1961), 159-69; J. Liver, "The Literary History of Joshua IX," *JSS*, VIII (1963), 227-43.

Benjamin belonged to the Central Palestinian group of tribes, and Joshua came from this group, his introduction into the sagas is understandable. With the introduction of the figure of Joshua, the etiological sagas became an occupation narrative for the Central Palestinian group of tribes and, as a consequence of the political and military significance of these tribes, the common property of all Israel.

B. The reason why the figure of Joshua was introduced into the etiological sagas can be deduced from the hero sagas associated with them:

11:1-9, concerning the battle at the waters of Merom, originally connected with sites in northern Palestine and deriving from that region.
10:1-11, 15, together with the song fragment 10:12-14, concerning the battle between Gibeon and Aijalon; this passage is indissolubly connected with the figure of Joshua, and depicts him as a warlike tribal leader. Likewise the statements in 17:14-18, which probably belong to N (G^1), according to which the Central Palestinian group of tribes turns to Joshua in order to expand their territory, seem to presuppose that he was a tribal leader of this kind.
24 appears to contain the nucleus of an ancient saga. In its present form the narrative is Deuteronomistic, as earlier criticism properly recognized and Mowinckel has recently stressed. Nevertheless, the present form is based upon an earlier source, which, like the other sagas, presupposes the unity of all Israel under the leadership of Joshua. In its earliest form it goes back to a tribal narrative in which a historical background with the figure of Joshua can be recognized: not a Covenant Festival regularly celebrated at Shechem, but Joshua's unique commitment of his own tribe to Yahweh, in whose name he had achieved his successes. This gives us the final reason for the introduction of Joshua into the etiological sagas and the growth of G^2's history of the occupation of Canaan.

4. *J and E.* Taking G^2 as their basis, the two source strata J and E gave the following account, for the most part in parallel except for the introductory sentences (1:1-2, 10-11) in E:

2	Reconnaissance of Jericho
3:1–5:1	Crossing of the Jordan
6	Conquest of Jericho
7	Defeat at Ai (Achan's theft)
8:1-29	Conquest of Ai
9	Treaty with Gibeon
10:1-15	Battle between Gibeon and Aijalon
11:1-9	Battle at the waters of Merom
18:2-10	Distribution of the land among seven tribes (following the distribution of the land east of the Jordan and omitting the distribution to Judah and Joseph).

It should be noted that individual parts of verses, verses, or groups of verses in 2–6 and 8–11 belong to the Deuteronomistic recensions or P; these are listed, insofar as possible, in 5. and 6.

All the narratives exhibit numerous doublets, which plainly suggest two narrative strands. Detailed analysis is made quite difficult by the revision to which the presentation was subject after J and E had been combined. In addition, each source stratum contains some special material:

J 5:2-9	Circumcision at Gilgal (vss. 4-7 in Deuteronomistic recension)
5:13-15	Appearance of the commander of the army of Yahweh
19:51*b*; 21:43-45	Concluding notice (21:44 in Deuteronomistic recension)
A mention of the death of Joshua has dropped out.	
E 14:6-15	Hebron given to Caleb
24:1-27*	Joshua's farewell address (in Deuteronomistic recension)
24:28-30	Death of Joshua
24:32	Burial of the bones of Joseph
24:33	Death of Eleazar

Both source strata, closely following fixed tradition, have essentially the same idea of the course of the occupation. After the reconnaissance of Jericho, the crossing of the Jordan, and the conquest of Jericho, all Israel under the leadership of Joshua marches into central Palestine and takes it, after an initial abortive attempt, through the battle of Ai. Then Joshua defeats the Canaanites to the south and to the north in two additional battles, while the region around Gibeon voluntarily becomes subject to Israel through a treaty. The distribution of the land east of the Jordan had already taken place (Num. 32:1-38). It only remains for Joshua to distribute the land west of the Jordan. According to a report that has been left out, Judah and Joseph first received their portions; then the rest of the land was assigned by lot to the other seven tribes. No hint remains of further battles and the incompleteness of the conquest. Instead, J declares that Yahweh gave to the Israelites the entire land in which they settled, so that all the promises were realized. And E documents the final possession of the land through the graves that contain Joseph, Joshua, and Eleazar.

5. *Deuteronomistic redaction.* The original book of Joshua, made up of JNE, went through two Deuteronomistic recensions. It is not always possible to tell what is to be ascribed to the first recension and what to the second. That a difference in fact exists can be seen from the fact that we encounter both entire Deuteronomistic passages and also isolated sentences or fragments. It also follows from the observation that to the Deuteronomistic section 1:7-8 additional material has been added (1:3-6, 9, 12-18), which comes from Deuteronomy.[6] The Deuteronomistic recensions include particularly:

1:3-9	Yahweh's command to cross the Jordan
1:12-18	Commitment of the tribes east of the Jordan to obedience
8:30-35	Altar built on Mount Ebal
10:16-43	Defeated kings and conquered cities in the south
11:10-20	Conquered cities in the north; retrospect of the conquest
22:1-8	Dismissal of the tribes east of the Jordan

[6] N. Lohfink, "Die deuteronomistische Darstellung des Überganges der Führung Israels von Moses auf Josue," *Scholastik*, XXXVII (1962), 32-44.

23 Joshua's farewell address
24* (E) Deuteronomistic recension of Joshua's farewell address according to E.[7]
Judg. 2:6-10 is linked to Joshua 23 in order to furnish an introduction for the Deuteronomistic recension of the book of Judges, which was still without N's occupation narrative (Judg. 1:1–2:5).

Besides the passages listed, the text contains short notices deriving from the Deuteronomistic recensions, e.g., Josh. 2:10-11; 5:4-7; 8:1*a*, 2*a*, 13*a*; 9:27*b*; 10:1*, 3*, 5*; 11:1*, 8*, 21-23; 21:24. These generally did not alter the substance of the earlier narratives. The Deuteronomists had no quarrel with the existing presentation of the swift and complete conquest of the land, accomplished by the aid of divine miracles, and the destruction of the Canaanites.

After the Deuteronomistic recensions, then, the book of Joshua consisted of 1–11 (apart from a few later notices and sections); 14:6-15; 18:2-10; 19:51*b*; 21:43-45; 22:1-8; 23–24; Judg. 1:1–2:5.

6. *P*. It is impossible to determine with assurance whether the source stratum P is represented in the first part of the book. We may assume, nevertheless, that P possessed an occupation narrative, however brief and summary, and was not content with the lists in Joshua 12–22. Although the giving of the Law on Sinai constitutes the fourth and last stage in the history of God's revelation, it remained to tell of the occupation of the land in which Israel could live its life according to the divine ordinances. In fact, Num. 13:2; 20:12; 22:1; 27:12-23 and the instructions concerning the division of the land, the Levitical cities, and the cities of refuge in Numbers 34–35 look forward to the occupation of Canaan. This material is not simply left hanging in the air; neither was it made up out of whole cloth on the basis of some supplements to the book of Joshua and interpolated into the Pentateuch.

In the book of Joshua, some traces can be found of P in a few narratives where motifs occur three times: in the narrative of the crossing of the Jordan (3–4), since the twelve stones are set up not only at the lodging place (4:8) and at Gilgal (4:20), but also in the midst of the Jordan (4:9), in the narrative of the conquest of Jericho (6), which contains in addition to the double narrative strand with its two commands to spare Rahab (6:17, 22) a third narrative strand that does not mention the woman, according to which the conquest of Jericho, like the crossing of the Jordan, took place after the fashion of a priestly procession; and also in 9:15*b*, 17-21, sentences characteristic of P. P's account of the distribution of the land is found in 12; 13:15-33; 14–19*; 21:1-42; 22:9-34.

The list of kings defeated by Israel (12) certainly did not belong to the Deuteronomistic book of Joshua, because it lists kings and cities that were not mentioned in the rest of the book and contains a conception of the conquest of the land that does not agree with the account in 1–11: Palestine

[7] C. H. Giblin, "Structural Patterns in Jos 24,1-25," *CBQ*, XXVI (1964), 50-69; J. L'Hour, "L'Alliance de Sichem," *RB*, LXIX (1962), 5-36, 161-84, 350-68.

was ruled by thirty kings, whom Joshua defeated one after another. This is P's "erudite" history of the conquest.

The distribution of the land begins (13:15-33) with the land east of the Jordan (already described by JNE in Numbers 32). The distribution of the land west of the Jordan follows in the major portion of 14–19 (omitting the notices taken from Judges 1 and the sections 14:6-15; 18:2-10; 19:51*b*, which belong to JE). Then, following the instructions in Numbers 35, there follows the appointment of cities of refuge and Levitical cities (20; 21:1-42).[8]

Following Alt, Noth assumes that three lists provide the basis for 13–19; 21, which he does not assign to P but considers rather as interpolations made by a later redactor of his Deuteronomistic History. These lists are: (1) for 15, a list of the cities and towns in the state of Judah after its division into twelve administrative districts in the time of King Josiah, while Kallai-Kleinmann thinks in terms of the period of Hezekiah; (2) for 19, a "system of tribal boundaries" with a list of points determining the boundaries of the individual tribal territories in the period of the Judges; (3) for 21, a list of the Levitical cities that reflects the cultic centralization of Josiah (Alt) or else is very late (Noth), but which Albright dates to the time of David. Mowinckel has raised serious objections to this view, which are generally valid.

a) The data for Judah certainly reflect the period of its greatest expansion, and can only refer to the historical situation under Josiah. If there was ever an official list of this sort, it must have been kept in the court archives and been destroyed with the rest of the archives when the Babylonians destroyed Jerusalem. The data in Joshua 15 can only be based on an idealized reminiscence of the glorious period under Josiah.

b) The data concerning the tribal boundaries are a theoretical construction that cannot possibly date from the period of the Judges, as Mowinckel has demonstrated in detail. Ezekiel 48 presents a similar theory.

c) The data concerning the Levitical cities are likewise purely theoretical; even Haran admits the presence of utopian features. The number of the cities is set schematically at 48, according to the principle that four cities are to be located in each of the twelve tribal territories. The postexilic perspective of the author is evident from his neglect of the north, which had long been separated from Judah. We may agree with Noth in saying that the entire theory came into being quite late.

P concludes with 22:9-34, which recounts the dismissal of the tribes from east of the Jordan that had taken part in the occupation of the land west of the Jordan and the altar built by these tribes beside the Jordan. The warning against illegitimate forms of cult and cultic sites constitutes a concluding admonition characteristic of P.

P diverges from the earlier presentations in paying less attention to the incomplete (N) or complete (JE) conquest of the land, concentrating instead

[8] M. David, "Die Bestimmungen über die Asylstädte in Jos 20," *OTS*, IX (1951), 30-48; J. Simons, "The Structure and Interpretation of Josh XVI–XVII," *Orientalia Neerlandica* 1948, pp. 190-215.

on its distribution together with a description of the boundaries of the individual tribal territories and a list of their cities. It gives us a history of Israel's occupation of Palestine that is less narrative than enumerative, and belongs in the category of "learned literature" (Mowinckel). In conformity with P's general purpose, the plan for the distribution of the land is, like Ezekiel 48, a program for the future such as was conceived in the Babylonian Diaspora in the fifth century.

7. *Separation from the Pentateuch.* Apart from the considerable Deuteronomistic editing, the growth of the book of Joshua resembles that of the Pentateuch. The combination of the source strata now found in all six books in the course of time produced the Hexateuch. But the link between the Joshua section and the Pentateuch was soon broken. The separation was made following the report of the death of Moses, the mediator of the law. In order that the book of Joshua, now independent, might conclude with the report of Joshua's death, a part of it was separated and placed at the beginning of the books of Judges. Later, in addition to 5:10-12 and 13:1-14, the notices from Judges 1 were interpolated into the book of Joshua.

The separation of the book of Joshua from the Pentateuch took place after the incorporation of P, and should probably be associated with Ezra's reformation. The Persian king's recognition of the Law as the foundation for the Israelite community demanded that P's politically intolerable program for the distribution of the land be relinquished. The separation took place at the latest when Ezra was given his commission, probably around 400 B.C.

§31 The Book of Judges

ATD: H. W. Hertzberg, 2nd ed., 1959. BOT: J. de Fraine, 1956. EH: V. Zapletal, 1923. HK: W. Nowack, 1902. HS: A. Schulz, 1926. IB: J. M. Myers, 1953. ICC: G. F. Moore, 2nd ed., 1898, reprinted 1949. KeH: E. Bertheau, 2nd ed., 1883. KHC: K. Budde, 1897. SAT: H. Gressmann, 2nd ed., 1922. SZ: S. Oettli, 1893. Individual commentaries: C. F. Burney, 2nd ed., 1920.

L. Alonso Schökel, "Erzählkunst im Buche der Richter," *Bibl*, XLII (1961), 143-72; E. Auerbach, "Untersuchungen zum Richterbuch," *ZAW*, XLVIII (1903), 286-95; LI (1933), 47-51; W. Böhme, "Die älteste Darstellung in Richt 6,11-23 und 13,2-24 und ihre Verwandtschaft mit der Jahveurkunde des Pentateuch," *ZAW*, V (1885), 251-74; K. Budde, *Die Bücher Richter und Samuel*, 1890; F. Dornseiff, "Das Buch Richter," *AfO*, XIV (1941-44), 319-28 (= *Kleine Schriften*, I, 2nd ed., 1959, pp. 340-63); O. Eissfeldt, *Die Quellen des Richterbuches*, 1925; G. Hölscher, *Geschichtsschreibung in Israel*, 1952; E. Jenni, "Vom Zeugnis des Richterbuches," *ThZ*, XII (1956), 257-74; *idem*, "Zwei Jahrzehnte Forschung an den Büchern Josua bis Könige," *ThR*, NF XXVII (1961), 1-32, 97-146; R. Kittel, "Die pentateuchischen Urkunden in den Büchern Richter und Samuel," *ThStKr*, LXV (1892), 44-71; E. C. B. MacLaurin, *The Hebrew Theocracy in the Tenth to the Sixth Centuries B.C. An Analysis of the Books of Judges, Samuel and Kings*, 1959; M. Noth, *Überlieferungsgeschichtliche Studien*, I, 1943; W. Richter, *Traditionsgeschichtliche Untersuchungen zum Richterbuch*, 1963; E. Robertson, "The Period of the Judges,"

BJRL, XXX (1946), 91-114; K.-D. SCHUNCK, *Benjamin,* 1963; C. A. SIMPSON, *Composition of the Book of Judges,* 1957; R. SMEND, "JE in den geschichtlichen Büchern des AT," hrsg. von H. Holzinger, *ZAW,* XXXIX (1921), 181-217; B. STADE, "Zur Entstehungsgeschichte des vordeuteronomischen Richterbuches," in *Baumgärtel-Festschrift,* 1959, pp. 192-96; K. WIESE, *Zur Literarkritik des Buches der Richter,* 1926; H. WINCKLER, "Der bericht über die ehud-sage," in *Alttestamentliche Untersuchungen,* 1892; *idem,* "Quellenzusammensetzungen der Gideonerzählungen," in *Altorientalische Forschungen,* I, 1893; A. H. VAN ZYL, "The Relationship of the Israelite Tribe to the Indigenous Population of Canaan According to the Book of Judges," in *OuTWP* (1959), 51-60; *idem,* "The Message Formula in the Book of Judges," *ibid.,* pp. 61-64.

1. *Terminology and content.* The book of Judges takes its name from the term applied to the central figures of its narratives, although narratives of a different sort are found at the beginning and at the end. These narratives are intended to account for the period between the death of Joshua and the appearance of Samuel. The book is anonymous. Talmudic tradition considers Samuel the author, but this tradition is contradicted by the gradual growth of the book, which can be traced from the original isolated narratives through a first compilation to a Deuteronomistic recension, together with a few late additions.

The content of the books falls into four large sections. Of these, 1:1–2:5 was discussed in §30.2 as the occupation narrative of the Hexateuchal source stratum N and will not concern us.

1:1–2:5	Prelude: the incomplete occupation	
2:6–3:6	Introduction	
	2:6-10	Linking to the book of Joshua
	2:11–3:6	Characteristics of the period of the Judges
3:7–16:31	Narratives concerning the Judges	
	3:7-11	Othniel, from southern Judah
	3:12-30	Ehud, from Benjamin
	3:31	Shamgar, from Beth-anath in Galilee (1:33?)
	4–5	Deborah, from Ephraim; Barak, from Naphtali
	6–8	Gideon, from Manasseh
	9	Abimelech, from Shechem
	10:1-2	Tola, at Shamir
	10:3-5	Jair, in Gilead
	10:6–12:7	Jephthah, from Gilead
	12:8-10	Ibzan, at Bethlehem
	12:11-12	Elon, at Aijalon
	12:13-15	Abdon, at Pirathon
	13–16	Samson, from Dan
17–21	Supplements	
	17–18	Founding of the sanctuary at Dan
	19–21	Crime and punishment of the Benjaminites at Gibeah

2. *The "Judges."* Because the narratives concerning the Judges are of such unequal length, it has become customary to use two different terms for the

Judges. The heroes of the detailed narratives are called the "major" Judges: Othniel, Ehud, Deborah (and Barak), Gideon (and Abimelech), Jephthah, and Samson; those that are merely mentioned in brief notices are called the "minor" Judges: Shamgar, Tola, Jair, Ibzan, Elon, and Abdon. Within the framework of the presentation, they all appear to exercise their judgeship over the entire nation as regents of Israel and forerunners of the kings. The narratives themselves still show the inaccuracy of this interpretation. As in the Hexateuch, figures that appeared and events that took place in a small portion of Israel have been made to refer to the entire nation.

More precisely, we can distinguish two types of figure included under the Hebrew term "judge," which actually means "executor of justice," "helper," "ruler." A first group comprises warlike heroes, be they leaders of tribal militias, tribal heroes, or individuals about whom we lack sufficient information:

Othniel	Gideon
Ehud	Abimelech
Shamgar	Jephthah
Deborah	Samson

A second group, with data concerning the length of time the person in question judged Israel, his family, and his burial place, obviously represents a different type.[1] Some scholars have wanted to see in this type the central amphictyonic office of "Judge of Israel," appointed to exercise judgeship over the entire tribal league, to whom "God's law" in apodictic form was entrusted. Quite apart from the hypothesis of the amphictyony, this interpretation is rendered dubious by the fact that the series of apodictically formulated regulations did not originally represent legal dicta but rather rules of conduct (§8.2). It is a more likely assumption that through the activity of these men, to the extent that they were engaged in the administration of justice, there was an influx of Canaanite law into Israel. Richter's study in particular has shown that their function, though not military, comprised more than judicial administration. The latter is to be thought of as one part of the work of government. The notices concerning these Judges are patterned after the earlier form I Sam. 13:1 and the form found in the books of Kings (e.g. I Kings 11:41-42). The Judges of the second group are not associated with tribes. Their temporal sequence is secondary, so that they may have ruled at the same time in different cities or regions. They therefore constitute the transition from tribal to city government. Possibly the trend toward the formation of small city-

[1] A. Alt, *Die Ursprünge des israelitischen Rechts,* 1934 (= *Kleine Schriften* I [1953], 278-332, esp. 300-302); F. C. Fensham, "The Judge and Ancient Israelite Jurisprudence," *OuTWP* 1959, pp. 15-22; O. Grether, "Die Bezeichnung 'Richter' für die charismatischen Helden der vorstaatlichen Zeit," *ZAW,* LVII (1939), 110-21; H. W. Hertzberg, "Die Kleinen Richter," *ThLZ,* LXXIX (1954), 285-90; H.-J. Kraus, *Die prophetische Verkündigung des Rechts in Israel,* 1957; M. Noth, "Das Amt des 'Richters Israels'," in *Bertholet-Festschrift,* 1950, pp. 404-17; A. van Selms, "The Title 'Judge'," *OuTWP,* 1959, pp. 41-50; W. Vollborn, "Der Richter Israels," in *Rendtorff-Festschrift,* 1958, pp. 21-31; W. Richter, "Zu den 'Richtern Israels'," *ZAW,* LXXVII (1965), 40-72.

states, which can be observed since the Hyksos period, was also at work among the Israelites. According to statements in the book of Judges, the following are among the city or district rulers:

Gideon	Ibzan
Tola	Elon
Jair	Abdon
Jephthah	

Two figures are common to both groups: Gideon and Jephthah. Both are central figures in hero narratives; in addition, isolated statements about them follow the ruler pattern. Both groups may be included under the Hebrew expression "judge" because the working of divine charisma was seen in the activity of both warriors and rulers. If the traditions of the book of Judges are to be understood, however, the two groups must be distinguished. The narratives concerning hero figures constitute the major portion of the book and around them the nucleus of the book came into being. The notices concerning city or district rulers were added later.

3. *The traditions concerning the hero figures.* Each of the traditions concerning the hero figures came into being as a separate entity. For a considerable period they were independent narratives within the individual tribes. To the extent that several narratives were current concerning a particular hero, like Gideon or Samson, we must probably think in terms of an early growth of narrative cycles in oral tradition, in which several rhetorical types were joined together. The next step was to make the heroes and their deeds refer to all Israel. This most likely took place in the period of David and Solomon, especially because "Israel" represents a political entity. At this stage the narratives or narrative cycles concerning the individual heroes were not yet linked together.

A. The traditional basis for the narrative about Othniel (3:7-11)[2] is and remains enigmatic. While 1:12-15 (N) establishes the right of his clan to possess Kiriath-sepher, in 3:7-11 only his name and the name of his opponent Cushan-rishathaim derive from an early tradition, which can no longer be determined. The narrative, by contrast, is schematic and purely Deuteronomistic. Only with serious reservations, therefore, can we include this section among the hero stories.

B. The narrative concerning Ehud and his murder of Eglon,[3] king of the Moabites, originally comprised 3:15*aβ*-26; it was later expanded to include all Israel by the addition of 3:27-29.

C. The short notice concerning Shamgar (3:31),[4] who must probably be

[2] A. Malamat, "Cushan Rishathaim and the Decline of the Near East around 1200 B.C.," *JNES*, XIII (1954), 231-42; E. Täubler, "Cushan-Rishathaim," *HUCA*, XX (1947), 137-42.

[3] O. Glaser, "Zur Erzählung von Ehud und Eglon (Ri 3,15-26), *ZDPV*, LV (1932), 81-82; E. G. H. Kraeling, "Difficulties in the Story of Ehud," *JBL*, LIV (1935), 205-10.

[4] E. Danelius, "Shamgar ben 'Anath," *JNES*, XXII (1963), 191-93; F. C. Fensham, "Shamgar ben 'Anath," *ibid.* XX (1961), 197-98; A. van Selms, "Judge Shamgar," *VT*, XIV (1964), 294-309.

considered a non-Israelite from Galilee (cf. 1:33), recounts his battles with the Philistines' associates, who had settled on the fringe of the Plain of Jezreel. The mention of Ehud in 4:1*b* means that the account of Shamgar is a late addition.

D. The early narrative concerning Barak and the charismatic (prophetess) Deborah is to be found in 4:4*a*, 5*, 6-10, 12-16. Sisera, their opponent, has been associated secondarily with Jabin of Hazor, although Josh. 11:10-15 already tells of the city's destruction. The anecdote concerning Jael, who breaks the law of hospitality and slays the foe, was originally an independent tradition.

E. The Song of Deborah,[5] contained in chapter 5, probably came into being soon after the events it depicts; it may well be among the earliest Israelite songs that have been preserved (*ca.* 1200 B.C.). By literary type it is a victory song (§40.5). Although it would be incorrect to call it a psalm, it is not completely secular, but is rather a religious victory song. It exhibits a hymnlike beginning and conclusion; the description of the time of distress before the war of liberation can be compared to the narrative that forms a part of a thanksgiving song. The censure of the cowardly, the curse invoked upon the disloyal allies, and the taunting of the defeated foe all have a magico-religious basis. We may assume that the song was sung at a victory celebration held at a sanctuary after the battle (Oettli) or was structured after the pattern of such a celebration (Richter).

Pace Bentzen*, who like many others interprets the song as a thanksgiving psalm, Seale points out its relationship to nomadic war songs, from which Judges 5 differs only in being permeated with religious sensitivity. The same observation applies to the theory of Weiser, who considers the song a liturgical composition intended for the cultic celebration of the amphictyony, accompanying a cultic drama. Richter, removing vss. 1-5 and 31, terms it a propaganda song.

F. With Gideon, whose real name was Jerubbaal, are linked a series of narratives, etiological traditions, anecdotes, and a brief notice.[6] Judg. 7:11*b*,

[5] P. R. Ackroyd, "The Composition of the Song of Deborah," *VT*, II (1952), 160-62; W. F. Albright, "The Song of Deborah in the Light of Archaeology," *BASOR*, LXII (1936), 26-31; J. Blenkinsopp, "Ballad Style and Psalm Style in the Song of Deborah," *Bibl*, XLII (1961), 61-76; G. Gerleman, "The Song of Deborah in the Light of Stylistics," *VT*, I (1951), 168-80; O. Grether, *Das Deboralied*, 1941; T. Piatti, "Una nuova interpretazione metrica, testuale, esegetica del Cantico di Debora Giudici 5,2-31," *Bibl*, XXVII (1946), 65-106, 161-209; M. S. Seale, "Deborah's Ode and the Ancient Arabian Qasida," *JBL*, LXXXI (1962), 343-47; E. Sellin, "Das Deboralied," in *Procksch-Festschrift*, 1934, pp. 149-66; I. W. Slotki, "The Song of Deborah," *JThSt*, XXXIII (1932), 341-54; A. Weiser, "Das Deboralied," *ZAW*, LXXI (1959), 67-97.

[6] L. Alonso Schökel, "Heros Gedeon. De genere litterario et historicitate Jdc 6–8," *VD*, XXXII (1954), 3-20, 65-76; W. Beyerlin, "Geschichte und heilsgeschichtliche Traditionsbildung im Alten Testament (Richter VI–VIII)," *VT*, XIII (1963), 1-25; S. A. Cook, "The Theophanies of Gideon and Manoah," *JThSt*, XXVIII (1926/27), 368-83; D. Daube, "Gideon's Few," *JJS*, VII (1956), 155-61; Y. Kaufmann, "The Gideon Stories," *Tarbiz*, XXX (1960/61), 139-47; E. Kutsch, "Gideons Berufung und Altarbau Jdc 6,11-24," *ThLZ*, LXXXI (1956),

13-21 (expanded by the addition of *7:9-11a,* 12, 22) contains a hero saga telling of a surprise attack upon a Midianite camp; 8:5-9, 13-21*a* (expanded by the addition of 8:4, 10-12) contains a saga cycle about Gideon's deeds east of the Jordan, with his blood vengeance upon two Midianite chiefs as the focus. A further saga concerning the slaying of two other Midianite chiefs, with etiologies for the names "Raven Rock [RSV: 'rock of Oreb']" and "Wolf Winepress [RSV: 'wine press of Zeeb']," is linked with statements reflecting enmity between Ephraim and Gilead (7:25–8:3). There are three additional cult legends, which are in part etiological: first, 6:11-24, a legitimation of the altar of Ophrah, which is linked with a call narrative after the fashion of Exod. 3:10-22; Jer. 1:5-12; second, 6:25-31*aα*, which describes the destruction of the altar of Baal and the change to Yahweh worship (at Ophrah?), together with an etiological note concerning the name "Jerubbaal"; and third, 8:21*b*, 24-27*a*, which describes the making of an ephod at Ophrah. In addition, the anecdotes concerning the dew-oracle (6:33-34*, 36-40) and the selection of three hundred warriors (7:2-8) have been woven into the narrative. The latter of these anecdotes extends the traditions so that it applies to all Israel. The entire section is brought to its conclusion by 8:30, 32, a short notice with characteristics like those concerning the city rulers (expanded by the addition of vs. 31, to link it to chapter 9).

G. The tradition concerning Abimelech was preserved because his father Jerubbaal was equated with Gideon. It constitutes a narrative cycle. Chapter 9:1-7, 16*a*, 19*b*-21, 23-24 tells of Abimelech's kingship at Shechem[7] and the defection of the citizens from him; 9:26-40 tells of Gaal's attack and defeat; 9:41-45 and 9:46-49 contains two parallel traditions of Abimelech's vengeance upon Shechem; 9:50-54 tells of his death at the hands of a woman. The Fable of Jotham has been woven into the cycle[8] (§47.6). The concluding remarks in 9:55-57 are pre-Deuteronomic.

H. The ancient Jephthah tradition, introduced in 10:17-18, contains a long narrative concerning Jephthah's war against the Ammonites (11:1-29, 32*b*-33*a*) together with a concluding ruler notice (12:7) which corresponds to the introduction. To this basic stratum three pieces have been added: first, the

---

75-84; A. Malamat, "The War of Gideon and Midian: A Military Approach," *PEQ*, LXXXV (1953), 61-65; E. Nestle, "Das Vlies des Gideon," *ARW*, XII (1909), 154-56; W. Schultz, "Das Flies des Gideon," *OLZ*, XIII (1910), 241-51; S. Tolkowsky, "'Gideon's 300' (Judges VII and VIII)," *JPOS*, V (1925), 69-74; V. L. Trumper, "The Choosing of Gideon's 300 Judges 7,5.6," *ibid.*, VI (1926), 108-109; C. F. Whitley, "The Sources of the Gideon Stories," *VT*, VII (1957), 157-64.

[7] E. F. Campbell, Jr., "Excavation at Shechem, 1960," *BA*, XXIII (1960), 102-110; A. D. Crown, "A Reinterpretation of Judges IX in the Light of Its Humour," *Abr-Nahrain*, III (1961/62), 90-98; E. Nielsen, *Shechem*, 1955; E. Sellin, *Wie wurde Sichem eine israelitische Stadt?* 1922.

[8] E. H. Maly, "The Jotham Fable—Anti-Monarchical?" *CBQ*, XXII (1960), 299-305; U. Simon, "The Parable of Jotham (Judges IX,8-15): The Parable, Its Application and the Narrative Framework," *Tarbiz*, XXXIV (1964/65), 1-34.

narrative of efforts to pass through the territory of Moab (11:12-28), the nucleus of which is dependent on Numbers 20–21 (this section is a later addition); second, the etiological legend explaining a cultic practice on the basis of the lament for Jephthah's daughter (11:30-31 [32*a*], 34-40); third, a combination like that found in 7:25–8:3 of a note concerning the enmity between Ephraimites and Gileadites and the shibboleth episode between Ephraimites and Gileadites (12:1-6).

I. The Samson tradition[9] consists of a series of self-sufficient narratives and anecdotes, which were loosely linked together and later incorporated into the book of Judges in two stages. The first group consists of: 13:2-25, Samson's birth; 14, Samson's marriage and riddles; 15:1-8, Samson burns the grain of the Philistines; 15:9-19, Samson slays the Philistines with the jawbone of an ass (in part etiological). The Deuteronomistic concluding formula in 15:20 is followed by a second group, which was apparently later appended to the first: 16:1-3, Samson at Gaza; 16:4-22, Samson and Delilah; 16:23-31*a*, Samson's death, 16:31*b*, the new concluding formula.

The traditions concerning the Judges are partially made up out of individual fragments and are partially expansions of a basic narrative. This explains the occasional parallels and discrepancies. It is an unlikely assumption, however, to think in terms of two or three continuous narrative strands, not to mention equating these with the source strata of the Hexateuch, as Richter's detailed analysis has once more confirmed. In chapter 4, for example, the Jabin tradition is only attached superficially to the Sisera tradition, and does not form a part of the early narrative. In the Gideon tradition, the campaign against the Midianite chiefs Zebah and Zalmunna, undertaken for reasons of blood vengeance, is an original element of the narrative; the mention of the two other chiefs is based only on etiological motives. The basic narrative concerning Jephthah, who fights against the Ammonites as a tribal leader summoned from exile, has also been expanded by the addition of a cult legend and the late passage 11:12-28.

Kittel and Pfeiffer*, while assuming two continuous sources, are hesitant about relating them to the Hexateuch. While Kittel admits considerable affinity to J and E, though without equating his sources with them, Pfeiffer considers it probable that they have nothing to do with the Hexateuchal sources. In contrast, Budde, Cornill *, Eissfeldt*, Sellin*, Simpson, and Smend not only assume that the book of Judges contains two or three parallel traditions, but consider these the continuation of the Hexateuchal sources. It is impossible, however, to analyze the narrative into two or three sources: after the composite sections have been broken down into their individual traditions and the supplements added to a basic narrative have been determined, there are no variants left of any importance.

4. *The pre-Deuteronomistic book of Judges.* At a time that can no longer be fixed but must have been during the early or middle period of the monarchy,

[9] J. Blenkinsopp, "Structure and Style in Judges 13–16," *JBL*, LXXXII (1963), 65-76; H. Gunkel, "Simson," in *Reden und Aufsätze*, 1913, pp. 38-64.

the traditions concerning the hero figures, consisting of individual narratives and narrative cycles, were joined together to form a pre-Deuteronomistic book of Judges. Without placing particular emphasis on the term, this book can be called a book of heroes or deliverers. It was a loose and disorganized compilation, in which the narratives followed one another without external or internal connection. The narrative cycles were created by the incorporation of parallel and supplementary accounts, to the extent that this had not already taken place in the course of oral tradition. Most important, the tradition was given literary form. No geographical organization (Sellin-Rost*) is discernible. The extension of the events so as to refer to all Israel had already taken place; further religious elaboration was yet to follow.

It may be possible to distinguish two stages in the growth of the book of heroes or deliverers. On the one hand, the farewell address of Samuel (I Samuel 12), after which the period of the monarchy begins with the superscription in 13:1, mentions the following "Judges" in vs. 11: Jerubbaal (the real name of Gideon), Jephthah, Samuel, and the unknown Bedan (not to be changed to Barak). On the other hand, the Samson narratives, quite apart from the later appendixes to the book of Judges, appear to have been added to the tradition at two different times, just as I Samuel 1–6 does not belong to the early Samuel tradition. It is therefore possible that the first form of the pre-Deuteronomic books of heroes or deliverers to come into being comprised the narratives of Jerubbaal (Gideon), Bedan, Jephthah, and Samuel. In a second stage the narratives of Jerubbaal (Gideon) and Jephthah were included with other accounts of deliverers, while the narrative of Bedan was dropped completely and that of Samuel, whose figure was linked with the Saul tradition, almost completely.

5. *The Deuteronomistic book of Judges.* The loose compilation that was the pre-Deuteronomistic book underwent a revision—probably in the period of the Exile—out of which the Deuteronomistic book of Judges emerged.[10] More precisely, we must think in terms of a twofold revision and an additional expansion by a third hand.

A. The first and basic revision produced the framework in which the individual complexes are set and which, through multiple repetition, forges them into one great whole; this revision can hardly be termed pre-Deuteronomistic (Beyerlin). In addition to the narrative of Othniel (3:7-11), all of which is constructed according to this pattern, the framework comprises: 3:12-15*aα*, 30; 4:1*a*, 2, 3*a*, 23-24 + 5:31*b*; 6:1, 6*b* + 8:27*b*, 28, 33-35*; 10:6-10*a*, 16 + 11:33*b*; 13:1 + 15:20. The description of the period of the Judges each time begins with the statement that Israel deserted Yahweh and thereby aroused his anger, which expressed itself through Yahweh's allowing enemies to attack and oppress Israel as a form of punishment. Moved by Israel's

[10] W. Beyerlin, "Gattung und Herkunft des Rahmens im Richterbuch," in *Weiser-Festschrift*, 1963, pp. 1-29; W. Frankenberg, *Die Composition des deuteronomistischen Richterbuches (Richter II,6–XVI), nebst einer Kritik von Richter XVII–XXI*, 1895; E. O'Doherty, "The Literary Problem of Judges 1,1–3,6," *CBQ*, XVIII (1956), 1-7.

subsequent conversion and appeal for help, Yahweh each time raised up a deliverer who conquered the enemies, so that Israel could live in peace until the death of the deliverer. According to this pattern, there is an ever repeated cycle of apostasy, punishment, conversion, and deliverance. Since this takes place at regular intervals, it is based on a cyclic conception of history. The hortatory expansions in 6:7-10; 10:10*b*-15 and Gideon's refusal of the kingship (8:22-23) may also derive from this revision.

At the same time, the statement of the number of years in each period sets the narratives in a chronological order, which had been lacking in the pre-Deuteronomistic book. It is based on the Deuteronomistic calculation of the period between the Exodus from Egypt and Solomon's building of the Temple, 480 years (I Kings 6:1). Since—apart from the section 1:1–2:5, which belongs to the Hexateuch—neither the notices concerning the city rulers nor chapters 17–21 were included in this pattern, they must not have formed a part of the Deuteronomistic book of Judges.

B. A second Deuteronomistic hand added an introduction (2:11-19), which differs from the framework just described in that it does not mention Israel's appeal for help and conversion, presenting Yahweh's intervention on Israel's behalf as an act of pure grace. The expansion 6:2-6*a* seems to pursue the same basic idea. In the course of this second revision, additional Samson narratives (chapter 16) were added, as well as the concluding formula 16:31*b*.

C. Finally, to provide a link with the period of Joshua and a new characterization of the period of the Judges as a time of testing for Israel, a third hand added 2:6-10 and 2:20–3:6 as a framework surrounding the Deuteronomistic introduction 2:11-19.

After the entire Deuteronomistic revision, the book of Judges—apart from 1:1–2:5—comprised the complex 2:6–16:31, minus only the notices concerning the city rulers.

6. *Later additions*. Presumably in the postexilic period, there were added three sections that had previously been transmitted independently. They did not belong to the Deuteronomistic book of Judges, because they are left out of the chronological pattern. It is most unlikely that they formed part of the pre-Deuteronomistic book of Judges, were omitted by the Deuteronomistic revision, and later were incorporated once more.

A. The first section to be added comprises the notices about city or district rulers (10:1-5; 12:8-15); these do not derive from a "list," but were formed after the pattern of similar royal notices (cf. 2). Only the names and the cities may be based on early tradition. They were added in order to make up a list of twelve "Judges" to correspond to the canonical number of the tribes.

B. The second section to be added (17-18) comprises the originally independent narrative of the origin of the sanctuary in Dan; several doublets in this narrative suggest a considerable history of transmission and revision.[11] As an appendix to the book of Judges, it serves as a connecting link between the premonarchic period, when "there was no king in Israel" and "every man did what was right in his own eyes" (17:6), and the beginnings of the monarchy. Previously, toward the end of the monarchic period, it had been revised so as to depict the discreditable circumstances—a double theft—to which the sanctuary in Dan owed its origin. This form probably goes back to the claim of Jerusalem to be the only true sanctuary. We may assume that the original narrative was a Danite tradition describing the migration of the tribe within Palestine; in it there was of course no mention of any theft.

C. The third section to be added (19–21) tells how the Benjaminites of Gibeah ravished the concubine of a Levite and how Israel punished them.[12] The original form of this narrative also came into being before Israel became a state. It is most unlikely that the story was a tradition of the tribal league (Noth); more likely it was a Benjaminite tribal narrative, which, like so many such narratives, was later extended to apply to all Israel (Eissfeldt). In the course of its transmission it took on a decided bias against the kingship of Saul, who came from Gibeah, so that this recension probably came into being in Judah, the territory of the Davidic dynasty in the preexilic period. Finally, in the late postexilic period, the narrative was expanded like a midrash by a redactor influenced by P.

7. *Retrospect*. The book of Judges in its present form seems therefore to have come into being as follows: At the beginning we have the independent hero narratives together with the Song of Deborah. Some were soon combined with other narratives to form narrative cycles; during the time of David and Solomon, they were all made to refer to all Israel. The oral tradition gave rise, possibly in two stages, to a pre-Deuteronomistic book of heroes or deliverers with a fixed written form. Deuteronomistic revision gave to this loose compilation a firm structure with chronological and material continuity. In the postexilic period were added the notices about the city or district rulers, the appendixes, and the conclusion of the Hexateuchal narrative. The final revision of 19–21 should probably be dated in the fifth century, at which time the book of Judges received its final form.

8. *Historical reliability and theological characteristics*. The book has considerable historical value, even though it only gives us information about details. In this respect, however, it is a valuable source, providing insights into the political and religious situation during the initial period of settlement in Canaan. As the Israelite tribes began to consolidate their position in various

[11] J. A. Bewer, "The Composition of Judges, Chaps. 17, 18," *AJSL*, XXIX (1912/13), 261-83; C. Hauret, "Aux origines du sacerdoce danite, à propos de Jud 18,30-31," in *Mélanges Robert*, 1957, pp. 105-13; M. Noth, "The Background of Judges 17–18," in *Essays Muilenburg*, 1962, pp. 68-85.

[12] J. A. Bewer, "The Composition of Judges, Chaps. 20, 21," *AJSL*, XXX (1913/14), 149-65; O. Eissfeldt, "Der geschichtliche Hintergrund der Erzählung von Gibeas Schandtat," in *Beer-Festschrift*, 1935, pp. 19-40.

areas and towns and come to terms with the Canaanites, both groups had to defend themselves against new neighbors and intruders. Theologically, the book is important because it is characteristic, in the various stages of its growth, of the ever changing interpretation of historical tradition, illustrating the interpenetration of historical presentation and theological interpretation.

§32 The Books of Samuel

ATD: H. W. Hertzberg, 2nd ed., 1960 (Eng. 1964). BOT: A. van den Born, 1956. COT: C. J. Goslinga, I, 1948. EH: A. Schulz, 1919/20. HK: W. Nowack, 1902. HS: H. A. Leimbach, 1936. IB: G. B. Caird, 1953. ICC: H. P. Smith, 1912, reprinted 1953. KAT: W. Caspari, 1926. KeH: O. Thenius and M. Loehr, 3rd ed., 1898. KHC: K. Budde, 1902 (Eng. 1894). SAT: H. Gressmann, 2nd ed., 1921. SZ: A. Klostermann, 1887.

K. Budde, *Die Bücher Richter und Samuel,* 1890; R. A. Carlson, *David, the Chosen King,* 1964; W. Caspari, "Literarische Art und historischer Wert von II Sam 15–20," *ThStKr,* LXXXII (1909), 317-48; C. H. Cornill, "Ein elohistischer Bericht über die Entstehung des israelitischen Königthums in I Samuelis 1–15 aufgezeigt," *ZKWL,* VI (1885), 113-41; *idem,* "Zur Quellenkritik der Bücher Samuelis," in *Königsberger Studien,* 1 (1887), 25-89; *idem,* "Noch einmal Sauls Königswahl und Verwerfung," *ZAW,* X (1890), 96-109; O. Eissfeldt, *Die Komposition der Samuelisbücher,* 1931; C. J. Goslinga, "De parallele teksten in de boeken Samuel en Kronieken," *GThT,* LXI (1961), 108-16; G. Hölscher, *Geschichtsschreibung in Israel,* 1952; I. Hylander, *Der literarische Samuel-Saul-Komplex (I. Sam 1–15),* 1932; E. Jenni, "Zwei Jahrzehnte Forschung an den Büchern Josua bis Könige," *ThR,* NF XXVII (1961), 1-32, 97-146; R. Kittel, "Die pentateuchischen Urkunden in den Büchern Richter und Samuel," *ThStKr,* LXV (1892), 44-71; T. Klaehn, *Die sprachliche Verwandtschaft der Quelle K der Samuelisbücher mit der Quelle J des Heptateuch,* Dissertation, Rostock, 1914; E. C. B. MacLaurin, *The Hebrew Theocracy in the Tenth to the Sixth Centuries B.C.,* 1959; J. Maier, *Das altisraelitische Ladeheiligtum,* 1965; F. Mildenberger, *Die vordeuteronomische Saul-Davidüberlieferung,* Dissertation, Tübingen, 1962; M. Noth, *Überlieferungsgeschichtliche Studien,* I, 1943; H.-U. Nübel, *Davids Aufstieg in der Frühe israelitischer Geschichtsschreibung,* Dissertation, Bonn, 1959; R. H. Pfeiffer, "Midrash in the Books of Samuel," in *Quantulacumque Lake,* 1937, pp. 303-16; O. Plöger, *Die Prophetengeschichten der Samuel- und Königsbücher,* Dissertation, Greifswald, 1937; R. Press, "Der Prophet Samuel," *ZAW,* LVI (1938), 177-225; L. Rost, *Die Überlieferung von der Thronnachfolge Davids,* 1926; K.-D. Schunck, *Benjamin,* 1963; R. Smend, "JE in den geschichtlichen Büchern des AT," hrsg. von H. Holzinger, *ZAW,* XXXIX (1921), 181-217; H. Tiktin, *Kritische Untersuchungen zu den Büchern Samuelis,* 1922; T. C. Vriezen, "De Compositie van de Samuël-Boeken," *Orientalia Neerlandica,* 1948, pp. 167-89; G. Wallis, "Die Anfänge des Königstums in Israel," *WZ Halle-Wittenberg,* XII (1963), 239-47; A. Weiser, *Samuel,* 1962.

1. *Terminology and content.* The name of the two books of Samuel might derive from the Jewish tradition that they were composed by Samuel or by Samuel, Nathan, and Gad, as I Chron. 29:29 obviously presupposes. Since there is no basis for this theory, it would be more correct to say that the books are

named after the first figure that plays a major role in them; admittedly, Saul and (in II Samuel) above all David have at least an equal right to be considered. But the two books were originally a single unit within the canon; the division into two parts is found in Hebrew manuscripts and printed editions only from 1448 on. The LXX, followed by the Vulgate, had already undertaken the division, though at the same time preserving a larger unity. It lumped the books of Samuel and Kings together under the name "Kingdoms"; this larger unit it then divided into four books, numbered consecutively, the first two corresponding to I–II Samuel, the latter two corresponding to I–II Kings. The division between I and II Samuel, which occurs after the death of Saul, follows a principle that we have observed elsewhere (Genesis ends after the death of Jacob and Joseph, Deuteronomy after the death of Moses, and Joshua after the death of Joshua); but the conclusion of the David story has been included, less aptly, at the beginning of the following book (I Kings 1–2).

In content, the books of Samuel are linked to the book of Judges. For their first section, in fact, there may once have been a formal connection, if there existed an early book of deliverers including Samuel (§31.4). The books tell the story of the origin of the Israelite monarchy and of the first two kings, Saul and David.

I 1–7	Samuel	
	1–3	Boyhood
	4–6	History of the ark in the Philistine period
	7	Samuel's war against the Philistines
I 8–15	Samuel and Saul	
	8–11	Origin of the monarchy
	12	Samuel's farewell adress
	13–14	Wars of Saul
	15	Rejection of Saul
I 16–31	Saul and David	
	16	Anointing of David; service at court
	17	David and Goliath
	18–20	David's relationship to Saul, Jonathan, and Michal; his flight
	21–27	David's life as refugee, adventurer, and client of the Philistines
	28	Saul and the witch of Endor
	29–30	David in southern Palestine
	31	Saul's death after the battle of Gilboa
II 1–8	Rise of David	
	1	Lament for Saul and Jonathan
	2–4	David as king over Judah
	5	David as king over Israel; conquest of Jerusalem
	6	Transfer of the ark to Jerusalem
	7	Nathan's prophecy
	8	David's military successes and his officials
II 9–20	Court history of David	
	9	David's magnanimity toward Jonathan's son

	10–12	Ammonite war; adultery with Bathsheba
	13–18	Absalom's rebellion and David's flight
	19	David's return to Jerusalem; hostility between Judah and Israel
	20	Rebellion of the Benjaminite Sheba
II 21–24	Appendixes	
	21:1-14	Famine and blood vengeance of the Gibeonites
	21:15-22	David's heroes in the Philistine wars
	22	Psalm of David (Psalm 18)
	23:1-7	The last words of David
	23:8-39	David's heroes
	24	Census and pestilence

2. *Continuous sources or independent fragments?* As in the case of other books, the question arises whether the books of Samuel are the product of continuous sources or independent fragments. Examination of their content shows that they do not constitute a single literary unit. The tensions, repetitions, and parallels, the interweaving of various narratives, and the differences between the views or biases expressed point unequivocally in the opposite direction. For example, there are several presentations of the origin of the monarchy: on the one hand, Samuel anoints Saul at the command of Yahweh (I Sam. 9:1–10:16); on the other, the people express their desire for a king and Samuel reluctantly consents, holding that a king represents rebellion against the sole kingship of Yahweh (I Sam. 8; 10:17-27). Twice Saul is rejected (I Sam. 13:8-14; 15:10-31). Twice David is introduced to Saul: as a lyre player (I Samuel 16) and as the opponent of Goliath (I Samuel 17). Twice he engages himself to serve the Philistines (I Sam. 21:11-16 [Eng. 21:10-15] and 27); twice he shows magnanimity to Saul, who is pursuing him (I Samuel 24; 26). These are a few examples; others could be cited as well.

These observations have led to the assumption that the books of Samuel are made up of two or three continuous sources and that these sources can be equated with those of the Hexateuch. Budde in particular, after many earlier attempts (Eichhorn*, Thenius [1842 edition], Wellhausen*), expounded this thesis systematically, dividing the narrative material between the source strata J and E. According to Budde, these source strata were combined, and the resulting book severely abbreviated through a Deuteronomistic redaction, to be expanded once more by a later hand. Cornill* and Hölscher, among others, followed Budde, while Steuernagel* traced the two source strata only through II Samuel 8. Smend and Eissfeldt apply the three-source theory and think of the books as a combination of three parallel narrative strands, probably the continuations of L, J, and E.

Gressmann, on the other hand, sought to explain the books as a loose compilation of individual narratives of varying scope. Noth, Sellin-Rost*, Weiser*, and others assume in similar fashion that large and small narrative complexes have been brought together, i.e., in part interwoven, in part strung out one after another, sometimes linked very loosely. Weiser thinks in terms of a long process of utilization and elaboration of tradition on the basis of a prophetical interpretation of history. Noth (like Sellin-Rost), following his thesis of a Deuteronomistic History, holds that the Deuteronomistic redaction linked the independent pieces together for the first time (to the extent that they do not actually derive from the Deuteronomist). In this case, of course, it is hard to understand why the contradictory views and biases were not at least in part subordinated to a new controlling principle by means of framework passages, as in the book of Judges and the books of Kings.

Both attempted explanations raise doubts. The same arguments as in the book of Judges apply against any division into source strata, perhaps even more than in the earlier book (Weiser*): the authors of the source strata would have had to limit themselves almost entirely to a mere compiling and superficial linking of the traditions, while in the Hexateuch taking materials at least equally fixed in form and treating them with considerable independence and individuality. In addition, the narrative strands that some have claimed to find do not constitute consistent presentations, but rather comprise narratives so different in style, structure, and content that they appear completely fragmented and do not represent literary units.

The other attempted explanation is therefore right in assuming that in the books of Samuel traditions quite heterogeneous and deriving from various circles have been juxtaposed and linked together without any attempt to harmonize their differences. This atomistic view, however, does not explain all the phenomena. Some supplements, for instance, probably presuppose an earlier compilation of narrative complexes; other narratives can be thought of as constituting a supplementary stratum.

We may distinguish in all five stages in the growth of the books of Samuel: (*a*) a linking together of what were originally independent narratives and more comprehensive presentations, partially popular, partially deriving from the royal court, to form a basic narrative stratum, depicting imperfectly and without continuity the origin of the monarchy and the empire from the perspective of religious nationalism; (*b*) the incorporation of some supplements into the basic stratum; (*c*) the addition of a supplementary stratum with a prophetical perspective, producing the most important parallels and contradictions; (*d*) a Deuteronomistic redaction; (*e*) a few later supplements.

3. *The basic stratum.* The basic stratum, characterized by religious nationalism, comprises four narratives or narrative complexes. It did not yet include any link with the period of the Judges (or any formal connection with the book of Judges); neither did the figure of Samuel, who is characterized at times as a "Judge," at times as a prophet, and at times—according to the Qumran fragments—as a Nazirite, as yet play a significant role. The account starts with the Philistine troubles (and the fate of the ark), then turns at once to Saul and David, who gradually alleviated this and other troubles, and then describes the up-and-down career of David, concluding with the appointment of his successor.

A. In style, vocabulary, and general purpose the so-called ark narrative (I Sam. 4:1–7:1; II Sam. 6; 7) appears to be a self-contained tradition recounting the fate of the ark from the time of its capture by the Philistines through the events in Philistine territory down to David's transfer of the ark to Jerusalem.[1] Samuel plays no role at all in this account. II Samuel 6 should not be removed from the narrative complex and assigned to the story of David (as Nübel, Schunck, and Vriezen do). The narrative as a whole, however, is probably based upon three early presentations that at first had no literary connection.

a) I Sam. 4:1–7:1 is based on an early report from the pre-Davidic period; it recounted briefly and soberly the fate of the ark, which had been brought into their camp by the Israelites (4:1*b*-4*a*), fell into the hands of the Philistines (4:10-11*a*), and was carried by them through their cities as the spoils of war (5:1-2, 10), after which it gradually fell into oblivion. To this report have been added extensive expansions, including Deuteronomistic notices.

b) II Sam. 6:1-12, 14, 20-23 is based on another report from the Davidic or early Solomonic period. The role of the Gittite Obed-edom supports the historicity of the account, but the details of the ark's transfer have been obscured to some extent, as the etiology of the place-name Perez-Uzzah shows.

c) Finally, II Sam. 7:1-7, 17 recounted how David was prevented from building the temple he had planned; in the course of further revision, this section furnished the conclusion to the ark narrative. It later went through another revision, which removed it from the ark narrative (cf. D).

The narratives were compiled and revised by a Jerusalemite priest, who expanded them by the addition of legends (the triumphal procession of the ark), particularly in I Samuel 5–6, so that a continuous literary complex came into being during the Solomonic period or shortly afterward. Its purpose was to legitimize Jerusalem and magnify its importance as the home of the ark; in order to do this, it placed great emphasis on the ark's power.

B. The narrative of Saul's rise and end (I Sam. 9:1–10:16; 11; 13–14; 31) consists of individual early narratives that have been compiled to form a loose cycle. The following narratives are involved (Weiser*): (*a*) Saul's encounter with Samuel, who anoints him king (9:1–10:16), a popular saga with motifs of fairy tale and miracle story;[2] (*b*) Saul's victory over the Ammonites and proclamation as king (11), a hero saga, which does not presuppose 9–10;[3] (*c*) Saul's Philistine wars (13:1–14:46), a historical narrative with saga motifs, which came into being in a warlike or military

[1] A Bentzen, "The Cultic Use of the Story of the Ark in Samuel," *JBL*, LXVII (1948), 37-53; G. R. Driver, "The Plague of the Philistines (1 Samuel V,6–VI,16), *JRAS*, 1950, pp. 50-52; J. Dus, "Der Brauch der Ladewanderung im alten Israel," *ThZ*, XVII (1961), 1-16; E. Nielsen, "Some Reflections on the History of the Ark," *VTSuppl*, VII (1960), 61-74; J. R. Porter, "The Interpretation of 2 Samuel VI and Psalm CXXXII," *JThSt* NS, V (1954) 161-73.

[2] M. Bič, "Saul sucht die Eselinnen (1 Sam IX)," *VT*, VII (1957), 92-97; H.-J. Stoebe, "Noch einmal die Eselinnen des *Ḳîš*," ibid., pp. 362-70.

[3] K. Möhlenbrink, "Sauls Ammoniterfeldzug und Samuels Beitrag zum Königtum des Saul," *ZAW*, LVIII (1940/41), 57-70.

milieu, and which did not originally include the rejection of Saul (13:7b-15*ba*); (*d*) the summary of Saul's wars (14:47-48, 52), which was intended to furnish the conclusion of the compilation; (*e*) Saul's tragic end (31), a supplement to the compilation, permeated by the same spirit as the other narratives:[4] respect for the king, awareness of the difficulty of his position, and admiration for the occasional successes that he nevertheless achieved. It is quite conceivable that the whole account came into being in Benjamin, Saul's home.

C. The narrative of the rise of David (I Sam. 16:14–II Sam. 5*; II Sam. 8:1-15) is of a different sort (Weiser*); it is by and large a continuous presentation, without gaps. While in contrast to the Benjaminite narrative it describes Saul in quite negative terms, on the grounds that the spirit of Yahweh had left him, it is not guilty of extravagance with respect to David. It follows the course of David's life from the time Saul receives him at court through his persecution by the king, his life as an adventurer, his vassalage in service of the Philistines, and finally the death of Saul and Ishbaal, which opens the way for him to become king over Judah and over Israel.[5] It has quite rightly been stressed that the author observes in close contact with reality, has a sense of historical and religious coherence, shows familiarity with the events he narrates, and is literarily gifted. It is likely that he also borrowed the lament for Saul and Jonathan (II Sam. 1:17-27)[6] and for Abner (II Sam. 3:33-34) from a reliable tradition. He probably belonged to the intelligentsia at the court of David and Solomon. His presentation ends with II Sam. 5:10, 12, a statement that the goal has been achieved: Yahweh has established David as king. While II Sam. 5:13-16 should be considered a later addition, 5:17-25 (David's victories over the Philistines) originally followed 5:3; 8:1-15 (David's military successes) was appended to round off the narrative.

In its present form the narrative is not a unit; it exhibits parallel recensions. Besides the expansion in I Samuel 17, taken from the prophetical supplementary stratum, the most important doublets include the different versions of David's flight (I Samuel 20), his joining the Philistines (21:11-16 [Eng. 21:10-15];

[4] J. Schelhaas, "De ondergang van Israëls verworpen koning en de handhaving van het koningschap," *GThT*, LVIII (1958), 143-52, 161-70.

[5] A. Alt, "Jerusalems Aufstieg," *ZDMG*, LXXIX (1925), 1-19 (=*Kleine Schriften*, III [1959], 243-57); M. Bič, "La folie de David," *RHPhR*, XXXVII (1957), 156-62; O. Eissfeldt, "Ein gescheiterter Verusch der Wiedervereinigung Israels (2. Sam 2,12–3,1)," *NC*, III (1951), 110-27; *idem*, "Noch einmal: Ein gescheiterter Versuch der Wiedervereinigung Israels," *ibid.*, IV (1952), 55-59; G. Fohrer, "Zion-Jerusalem im Alten Testament," *ThW*, VII (1961), 291-318; G. Lanczkowski, "Die Geschichte vom Riesen Goliath und der Kampf Sinuhes mit dem Starken von Retenu," *MDAI Kairo*, XVI (1959), 214-18; J. Morgenstern, "David and Jonathan," *JBL*, LXXVIII (1959), 322-25; M. Noth, "Jerusalem und die israelitische Tradition," *OTS*, VIII (1950), 28-46 (=*Gesammelte Studien zum Alten Testament*, 2nd ed., 1960, pp. 172-87); H.-J. Stoebe, "Die Goliathperikope 1 Sam XVII 1–XVIII 5 und die Textform der Septuaginta," *VT*, VI (1956), 397-413; R. de Vaux, "Les combats singuliers dans l'Ancien Testament," *Bibl*, XL (1959), 495-508.

[6] C. H. Goslinga, "Davids klaaglied over Saul en Jonathan," *GThT*, L (1950), 53-70.

27), and his magnanimity toward Saul (24; 26). It is hard to decide how these doublets originated. In each case one of the versions may derive from the supplementary stratum. Nübel gives another explanation worth mentioning, including II Samuel 9; 10–12 in the account. He assumes two pre-Deuteronomistic strata: (*a*) a basic stratum whose text was later added to and displaced; this stratum begins with I Sam. 16:1 and ends with II Samuel 8–9 and the original form of II Samuel 7; its purpose is to give a vivid account of Yahweh's incomprehensible support of David; (*b*) a revised document written about 800 by a priest, turning each narrative of David's successful projects into a story of his successful probation. Deuteronomistic revision is limited almost exclusively to II Samuel 7. The historical consequences of this theory—e.g., the conclusion that David's kingship at Hebron and Saul's administration were contemporaneous—cast doubts upon the correctness of Nübel's analysis.

D. Not rarely the so-called Nathan prophecy (II Samuel 7)[7] is viewed as a single self-contained unit dating from the period of the events described or the Deuteronomistic period. On the contrary, we must hold to the view that this narrative is made up of an earlier basic block of material and later expansions. II Sam. 7:1-7, 17, the conclusion of the ark narrative, originally told only how David was prevented from building the temple he had planned. This narrative was expanded by the addition of the core of 7:8-16, 18-29, and the whole was subjected once more to Deuteronomistic revision. The introductory formula in 7:8 marks the new beginning; in what follows, the ark and the projected temple no longer occupy center stage, but only the figure of David himself. The interpolation is made possible by the ambiguity of the word "house," which can mean a "house" as the dwelling place of Yahweh and also "house" in the sense of "kingship" or "dynasty." As soon as "house" is used in the latter sense, we hear no more of the ark. The interpolation was also assisted by familiarity with the Egyptian royal novella (§7.5), which Solomon employed to legitimize his kingship (I Kings 3:4-15) and whose major themes are temple building and royal theology. What in I Kings 3 referred only to the person of Solomon is extended by the "Davidic Covenant" (II Sam. 7:8-16, 18-29) so as to apply to the entire dynasty. This divine legitimation of the dynasty must be later than I Kings 3, which would otherwise have been superfluous; it most

[7] G. Ahlström, "Der Prophet Nathan und der Tempelbau," VT, XI (1961), 113-27; H. van den Bussche, "Le Texte de la prophétie de Nathan sur la dynastie Davidique," *EThL*, XXIV (1948), 354-94; A. Caquot, "La prophétie de Nathan et ses échos lyriques," *VTSuppl*, IX (1963), 213-24; H. Gese, "Der Davidsbund und die Zionserwählung," *ZThK*, LXI (1964), 10-26; E. Kutsch, "Die Dynastie von Gottes Gnaden," *ibid.*, LVIII (1961), 137-53; J. L. McKenzie, "The Dynastic Oracle: II Sam 7," *ThSt*, VIII (1947), 187-218; S. Mowinckel, "Natanforjettelsen 2. Sam Kap. 7," *SEÅ*, XII (1947), 220-29; M. Noth, "David und Israel in 2 Samuel 7," in *Mélanges Robert*, 1957, pp. 122-30 (=*Gesammelte Studien zum Alten Testament*, 2nd ed., 1960, pp. 334-35; M. Simon, "La prophétie de Nathan et le temple," *RHPhR*, XXXII (1952), 41-58; M. Tsevat, "Studies in the Book of Samuel III," *HUCA*, XXXIV (1963), 71-82.

likely took place in the time of Rehoboam, Solomon's immediate successor.

E. The narrative referred to as the Court History of David (II Samuel 9–20; I Kings 1–2) is also a self-contained whole. We may observe, following the studies of Rost, that the narrative exhibits the following characteristics: It places major emphasis on conversations, developing each as a brief independent scene; it rarely mentions God as the actual cause of events; and it relegates the priesthood and cult to the background.

The most important analysis along different lines is that of Carlson, who considers II Samuel a Deuteronomistic work based on a David epic, in which chapters 2–7 describe David under the blessing and 9–24 describe David under the curse. Carlson completely rejects the assumption of a Court History culminating in the succession to the throne, interpreting 9–24 as a commentary on the second half of the Davidic period that views the figure of David and the events of the period from the perspective of the Deuteronomistic ideology. In detail: 10–12 originally followed the pattern of the Ugaritic Legend of King Keret; 13–21:14 (consisting of two seven-year cycles, 13–14 and 15–21:14) was structured to correspond to the series of laws in Deut. 23:13 ff. (10–12 = Deut. 22:22; 13–14 = Deut. 22:28-29; 15–20 = Deut. 23:1 [Eng. 22:30]; 21–24 is an artfully composed Deuteronomistic appendix (using the technique of composition found in Deuteronomy 32–33). This attempt to demonstrate Deuteronomistic redaction and ideology cannot be considered successful.

The presentation of the Court History of David, which is a historical source equal in importance to the narrative of David's rise, has rightly been rated an unequaled masterpiece of ancient Near Eastern historiography. Besides the realistic and true-to-life portrayal of people and events, the artful and dramatic structure of the narrative contributes much to its success. The author was undoubtedly an eyewitness to the events and a member of the royal court. He wrote the work in the time of Solomon to justify Solomon's succession to the throne; the conclusion of the narrative, I Kings 2:46, is a statement in support of Solomon's kingship. It may well have been written between the third (I Kings 2:39) and the fourth year of Solomon's kingship, since it does not mention the future temple (cf. I Kings 6:1). It is impossible to identify the author precisely; the various suggestions include Ahimaaz, Solomon's son-in-law (Klostermann, Budde), and Abiathar, David's priest (Duhm).

4. *The formation of the basic stratum and its supplements.* When the basic stratum was assembled and the supplements added to it, the narratives just described were loosely linked together. The nationalistic religion and historical consciousness that followed upon the achievements of the Davidic period gave rise in the post-Solomonic period to a specific account of the course of history from the Philistine troubles to the Davidic and Solomonic empire.

In the process, several sections were transferred to a new position, where they belong chronologically: the conclusion of the ark narrative (II Sam.

6; 7:1-7, 17) was placed after David's conquest of Jerusalem; the narrative of Saul's death (I Samuel 31) was placed in its present position.

In addition, supplementary material was interpolated to complete the picture. This consists primarily of lists and anecdotes, all of which probably derive from the time of Saul or David:

I Sam. 14:49-51	Saul's family and court
II Sam. 8:16-18	David's court
II Sam. 21:15-22	Anecdotes concerning David's heroes
II Sam. 23:8-39	Anecdotes and lists of the three heroes and the thirty heroes[8]

We also find two other narratives: that of the Gibeonites' blood vengeance upon Saul's sons during a famine (II Sam. 21:1-14)[9] and that of David's census and the ensuing pestilence (II Samuel 24)[10]; these were related to each other by the person responsible for the supplements or by a later redactor through the addition of 24:1. The former narrative clearly associates historical reminiscences with the etiology of a Canaanite harvest practice. The second narrative associates a priestly etiological account of the building of a sacrificial altar on the threshing floor of Araunah after the census and pestilence with a Canaanite etiological account of how the threshing floor of Araunah was consecrated as the site for a sanctuary (the Temple mountain).

5. *The supplementary stratum.* To the basic stratum with its supplements was added a supplementary stratum, which has largely determined the appearance of the books of Samuel. It is not a unified whole in the sense of constituting a continuous narrative strand; it is distinguished less by its literary form than by its content. Within its narratives, at least some of which go back to an ancient traditional nucleus,[11] prophetical thought comes to grips with the early history of the monarchy and its traditions, so that the narratives parallel or even contradict the popular tradition and the religious-nationalistic tradition of the court. These narratives deal primarily with Samuel and Saul.

A. The so-called story of Samuel's boyhood (I Samuel 1–3) is a distinct narrative complex, but is the end product of a considerable prehistory.[12] The following elements can be recognized: (*a*) the narrative of Samuel's birth and dedication to the service of Yahweh at Shiloh, which is probably unhistorical and originally did not apply to Samuel (Hylander); the major portion of this narrative is found in chapter 1, and continues in 2:11,

[8] K. Elliger, "Die dreissig Helden Davids," *PJB,* XXXI (1935), 29-75.

[9] H. Cazelles, "David's Monarchy and the Gibeonite Claim," *PEQ,* LXXXVII (1955), 165-75; J. Dus, "Gibeon—eine Kultstätte des Šmš und die Stadt des benjaminitischen Schicksals," *VT,* X (1960), 353-74; A. S. Kapelrud, "King and Fertility," *NTT,* LVI (1955), 113-22; A. Malamat, "Doctrines of Causality in Hittite and Biblical Historiography: a Parallel," *VT,* V (1955), 1-12.

[10] W. Fuss, "II Samuel 24," *ZAW,* LXXIV (1962), 145-64.

[11] Cf. the provisional analysis by H. Seebass, "Traditionsgeschichte von I Sam 8; 10:17 ff. und 12," *ZAW,* LXXVII (1965).

[12] M. Noth, "Samuel und Silo," *VT,* XIII (1963), 390-400.

18-21 (the dedication may itself involve two traditions, one as Nazirite, the other as priest); (*b*) an appended psalm depicting the victory of the faithful and the destruction of the wicked (2:1-10); mention of the king in vs. 10 means that the psalm is preexilic; vs. 5*b* accounts for its use here;[13] (*c*) the two anecdotes concerning the sons of Eli (2:12-17, 22-25), which, according to Noth, constitute together with vss. 27-36 a unified narrative directed against the sanctuary of Shiloh, an unlikely theory; their purpose is instead to set up an antithesis to Samuel; (*d*) the deuteronomistically edited threat of an anonymous man of God against the house of Eli (2:27-36), which presupposes the existence of the Temple of Solomon and legitimizes it vis-à-vis Shiloh;[14] (*e*) the narrative of God's revelation of himself to Samuel (I Samuel 3), which presupposes the existence of traditions (*a*), (*c*), and (*d*), and takes them as a point of departure in supporting Samuel's prophetical office. The author of (*e*) assembled the traditions to form the story of Samuel's boyhood.

B. The narrative of Israel's conversion and Samuel's victory over the Philistines (I Sam. 7:2-17) has been revised according to the Deuteronomistic pattern of the book of Judges, especially in its first part. It depicts Samuel as a kind of "Judge," more specifically as a warlike tribal leader and city ruler like Jephthah. Material from an earlier book of Judges may have gone into this account. As a whole the account is unhistorical; the story of Saul contradicts the statement that Israel was untroubled by the Philistines during the lifetime of Samuel (7:13).

C. A narrative describing Saul's elevation to the kingship is to be found in I Sam. 8; 10:17-27.[15] It tells how the people demand that Samuel give them a king; the person of Saul is arrived at by lot. This version has a critical attitude toward the monarchy, although in 10:21*bβ*-27*a* it employs a fragment of an earlier narrative, according to which Saul, whose stature made him stand out from the rest of the people, was selected by oracle to be king. From this fragment comes the motif of the "prerogatives of kingship," which the narrator discusses proleptically in 8:11-18 as an anticipation of "royal prerogatives."

D. Samuel's farewell address (I Samuel 12) is closely associated with C. It has been subjected to later Deuteronomistic revision. In it, following the selection of a king by lot, Samuel relinquishes his office, which is not described in detail.

E. The later version of Saul's rejection by Samuel is found in I Sam. 13:7*b*-15*bα*, which already represents priestly interests and bases the rejection upon Saul's improper sacrificial procedure.

F. The earlier version of Saul's rejection is found in I Samuel 15. The reason given here is that Saul did not carry out the military ban completely.

[13] G. Bressan, "Il cantico di Anna," *Bibl*, XXXII (1951), 503-21; XXXIII (1952), 67-89.

[14] M. Tsevat, "Studies in the Book of Samuel I," *HUCA*, XXXII (1961), 191-216.

[15] I. Mendelsohn, "Samuel's Denunciation of Kingship in the Light of the Akkadian Documents from Ugarit," *BASOR*, CXLIII (1956), 17-22.

The narrative is based on an early tradition of Saul's campaign against the Amalekites.

G. The narrative of how Samuel anointed David king (I Sam. 16:1-13) is colored by the prophetical viewpoint, but is not critical of or hostile toward the kingship. Like II Samuel 7, it legitimizes the Davidic kingship vis-à-vis other claims.[16]

H. The expansion of the narrative concerning David's victory over Goliath (I Samuel 17) should probably also be assigned to the prophetical supplementary stratum; this is suggested above all by the theological exposition in vss. 45-47.

I. The narrative of Saul's visit to the medium at Endor (I Samuel 28), which has been incorporated into the context by the addition of vss. 1-2, is also hostile toward Saul, who is described as sinning against Yahweh. It is not impossible, however, that it goes back to an early tradition.[17]

The narratives are based throughout upon such a theological view of history as one might expect from prophetical circles. This view of history comes out strongly opposed to the kingship, which followed its own nationalistic interests by means of power politics, and emphasizes the conflict between earthly power and divine power, a conflict found even more markedly in the Elijah narratives.

6. *The Deuteronomistic redaction.* The traces of Deuteronomistic revision, which the books of Samuel underwent, are less in evidence than in the books of Joshua and Judges. Apart from the chronological notices in I Sam. 4:18*b* and II Sam. 5:4-5, we find only the revision of the threat against the house of Eli (I Sam. 2:22-36), the narrative of Israel's conversion and Samuel's victory over the Philistines (I Samuel 7), Samuel's farewell discourse (I Samuel 12), and the prophecy of Nathan (II Samuel 7). In these sections the Deuteronomistic historical ideology could find expression.

7. *Conclusion.* The growth of the books of Samuel was brought to an end by three additions, of which the psalm in I Sam. 2:1-10 has already been mentioned (5A). The psalm in II Samuel 22 is identical with Psalm 18; it is a combination of an individual song of thanksgiving and a royal song, which gives thanks for a victory that has been won. The so-called last words of David (II Sam. 23:1-7) are in fact a description of the ideal ruler in a mixture of prophetical and wisdom language.[18] The latter two additions have turned the appendixes (II Samuel 21–24) into a motley assortment of material; this in turn abetted the separation of the books of Samuel and

[16] C. J. Goslinga, "Het geheim der verwachting van Davids konigschap," *GThT*, LVII (1957), 6-12.

[17] I. Trencsényi-Waldapfel, "Die Hexe von Endor und die griechisch-römische Welt," *AcOr* Budapest, XII (1961), 201-22; F. Vattioni, "La necromanzia nell' Antico Testamento, 1 Sam 28:3-25," *Augustinianum*, III (1963), 461-81.

[18] S. Mowinckel, " 'Die letzten Worte Davids' II Sam 23,1-7," *ZAW*, XLV (1927), 30-58; O. Procksch, "Die letzten Worte Davids," in *Kittel-Festschrift*, 1913, pp. 113 ff.

the transfer of the conclusion of the succession narrative from the Court History of David to I Kings 1–2.

The text of the books of Samuel was still in a state of flux for a considerable period after this; various versions were current. The text used in the Chronicler's History differs from the Masoretic text. So also does the Septuagint, whose textual form has been shown to be an independent version by the Hebrew fragments discovered in the fourth cave at Qumran.[19] The Septuagint text may represent the Palestinian form, the Masoretic text the Babylonian.

8. *Historical reliability and theological characteristics.* The historical value of the books of Samuel differs greatly from section to section. The David narratives, which are based on a detailed knowledge of the events, are the most reliable; several parts of the appendixes are in the same category. The narratives from the period of Saul's reign bear the mark of saga more pronouncedly, though an essentially accurate picture can probably be recovered from them. The traditions concerning Samuel are contradictory and frequently unhistorical; they characterize Samuel as Nazirite, priest, prophet, and Judge. The same is true of the traditions concerning the origin of the monarchy and Samuel's part in it.[20]

The views of Weiser and Wallis show how uncertain many points remain. According to Weiser, I Sam. 7:2-6, 15-17, which depicts Samuel as a Judge, originated at Mizpah; 8 is based on reminiscences of Samuel's close associates at Ramah; and 9–12 comprise four different traditions concerning the origin of the monarchy: 9:1–10:16, a relatively late account of Saul's anointing; 10:17-26, the narrative, originating in Mizpah, of Saul's selection by lot according to the sacral tradition of the tribal league; 10:27–11:15, a parallel tradition from the sanctuary of Gilgal, which is closest to the historical events; and 12, likewise from Gilgal, written from the perspective of the covenant tradition. All the traditions can be characterized as three literarily heterogeneous narrative series, each exhibiting approximately the same biases. They all point to the decisive influence of Samuel during the transition to monarchy. Wallis, on the other hand, assumes that there are three reports concerning the origin of Saul's kingship: I Samuel 11, telling how he was acclaimed king at Gilgal; 9:1–10:16, telling how he was anointed *nāgîd* in Ephraim; and 8 + 10:17-27*, telling how he was chosen by lot at Mizpah. These are independent reports, which means that Saul was not made king

[19] For examples from I Samuel 1–2; 23 see W. H. Brownlee, *The Meaning of the Qumrân Scrolls for the Bible,* 1964, pp. 12-18.

[20] W. Beyerlin, "Das Königscharisma bei Saul," *ZAW,* LXXIII (1961), 186-201; M. Buber, "Das Volksbegehren," in *Lohmeyer-Gedenkschrift,* 1951, pp. 53-66; G. Fohrer, "Der Vertrag zwischen König und Volk in Israel," *ZAW,* LXXI (1959), 1-22; W. A. Irwin, "Samuel and the Rise of the Monarchy," *AJSL,* LVIII (1941), 113-34; M. Newman, "The Prophetic Call of Samuel," in *Essays Muilenburg,* 1962, pp. 86-97; E. Robertson, "Samuel and Saul," *BJRL,* XXVIII (1944), 175-206; J. A. Soggin, "Charisma und Institution im Königtum Sauls," *ZAW,* LXXV (1963), 54-65; H. Wildberger, "Samuel und die Entstehung des israelitischen Königtums," *ThZ,* XIII (1957), 442-69.

over all Israel at once, but was elevated to that status by the free decision of individual tribes (Benjamin, Ephraim, Gilead).

Theologically, part of the narratives reflect the awakening of religious nationalism, such as was represented first by the royal court at Jerusalem and later was given literary form above all by the source stratum J of the Hexateuch. In this regard, the religious legitimation of the Davidic dynasty also plays an important role. Other narratives bear witness to internal conflict with this interpretation of history on the basis of a prophetical theology, leading to a more profound conception.

§33 The Books of Kings

BK: M. Noth, 1964. BOT: A. van den Born, 1958. EH: A. Sanda, 1911/12. HK: R. Kittel, 1902. HS: S. Landersdorfer, 1927. IB: N. H. Snaith, 1954. KeH: O. Thenius and M. Löhr, 3rd ed., 1898. KHC: I. Benzinger, 1899. SAT: H. Gressmann, 2nd ed., 1921. SZ: A. Klostermann, 1887.

I. Benzinger, *Jahvist und Elohist in den Königsbüchern*, 1921; G. Hölscher, "Das Buch der Könige, seine Quellen und seine Redaktion," in *Gunkel-Festschrift*, I (1923), 158-213; *idem*, *Geschichtsschreibung in Israel*, 1952; E. Jenni, "Zwei Jahrzehnte Forschung an den Büchern Josua bis Könige," *ThR*, NF XXVII (1961), 1-32, 97-146; A. Jepsen, *Die Quellen des Königsbuches*, 2nd ed., 1956; E. C. B. MacLaurin, *The Hebrew Theocracy in the Tenth to the Sixth Centuries B.C.*, 1959; J. A. Montgomery, "Archival Data in the Book of Kings," *JBL*, LIII (1934), 46-52; M. Noth, *Überlieferungsgeschichtliche Studien*, I, 1943; O. Plöger, *Die Prophetengeschichten der Samuel- und Königsbücher*, Dissertation, Greifswald, 1937; R. Smend, "JE in den geschichtlichen Büchern des AT," hrsg. von H. Holzinger, *ZAW*, XXXIX (1921), 181-217; H. Winckler, "Beiträge zur Quellenscheidung der Königsbücher," in *Alttestamentliche Untersuchungen*, 1892, pp. 1-54.

1. *Terminology and content.* The books of Kings take their names from the fact that they present the history of the Judahite and Israelite kings. Like the books of Samuel, they originally constituted a single book; in the LXX, they and the books of Samuel together constituted the books of Kingdoms. The division into two books, which was first adopted by the LXX and then in turn by the Vulgate, has been adopted since 1448 by the Hebrew manuscripts and printed texts as well. The secondary nature of this division is clear from the observation that it disrupts the history of King Ahaziah. The story of Solomon's succession, the conclusion of the Court History of David, has been transferred from the books of Samuel to the beginning of the history of Solomon.

The content of the books can be given only in rough outline:

I Kings 1-11	History of Solomon
	1–2 Appointment as king and measures to secure the throne
	3–10 Glory of his reign
	11 Dark side of his reign
I Kings 12–II Kings 17	History of the Judahite and Israelite kings from the di-

	vision of the kingdom to the catastrophe of Israel, the Northern Kingdom
II Kings 18–25	History of the Judahite kings to the destruction of Jerusalem and the liberation of Jehoiachin

In the second and third sections, the presentation has been organized chronologically in such a way that the accounts of the individual kings occur in the order of their accession.

2. *The formation of the books.* To the question of how the books of Kings came into being, various answers have been proposed. The view of the Talmud that Jeremiah was the author can be disregarded. There remain three other views to discuss.

a) The existence of a pre-Deuteronomistic book of Kings is often assumed; this is thought to have come into being primarily through the addition of two or three of the source strata found in the Hexateuch. How many such narrative strands are to be assumed remains a disputed question, as does their scope and therefore the scope of the pre-Deuteronomistic book of Kings.

Benzinger believes he can trace the source stratum J as far as II Kings 17:3-4 (reaching its final form in the time of Hezekiah) and E as far as II Kings 22–23 (finished in the time of Josiah); in addition, according to Benzinger, the actual author of the books of Kings made use of the History of Solomon, the History of the Kings of Judah, and the History of the Kings of Israel. According to Hölscher, J runs only as far as the division of the kingdom (I Kings 12); all the rest—to the extent that it does not derive from the Deuteronomistic author or later editors—belongs to E (after 587 B.C.). Smend and Eissfeldt* analyze the pre-Deuteronomistic book of Kings as a combination of the three sources L (J^1), J, and E; these scholars restrict themselves to determining isolated sections belonging to the sources and make no attempt to reconstruct the narrative strands in detail.

Nevertheless, the state in which the tradition is found makes the assumption of continuous narrative strands even less likely than in the books of Judges and Samuel, not to mention associating them with the source strata of the Hexateuch. We do not find parallel traditions such as would require assignment to two or three sources; neither do we find passages exhibiting characteristic content or theology throughout the books, which would suggest such a source division.

b) Jepsen follows a different line, thinking in terms of a pre-Deuteronomistic book of Kings and a gradual formation of the entire complex. The basic narrative is the synchronistic chronicle in I Kings 2:10–II Kings 18:8. It was composed after a Babylonian model toward the end of the eighth century on the basis of material from the royal archives; its purpose was, without theological reflection, to contrast the stability of the Davidic dynasty to the frequent upheavals in the Northern Kingdom. Additional material comes not from several different historical sources but from a single annalistic source, composed among priestly circles at Jerusalem in the first half of the seventh century; this source surveyed the period from Solomon to Manasseh. A first redaction, along priestly lines, took place at Jerusalem about 580, combining the two basic narratives and adding a few supplementary passages, e.g., II Kings 23:4-15. A second redaction, from the perspective of the *nᵉbî'îm*, introduced the prophet legends and evaluated the history according to "Deuteronomistic" categories; this redaction was undertaken at Mizpah after 561 (cf. II Kings 25:27-30) by a disciple of Jeremiah.

Despite the ancient Near Eastern model, the existence of a synchronistic chronicle including both Judah and Israel is a dubious assumption, the more so because the corresponding statements concerning the later Judahite kings cannot simply be explained as redactional additions. The serious chronological discrepancies that the data of the books of Kings yield are best explained as the result of using two independent chronicles. The various designations for the sources and the references to one of them even in the case of the later Judahite kings argue against a single annalistic work. In place of the two suggested redactions, it is more satisfactory to assume the work of two Deuteronomistic hands.

c) We may therefore incline toward Noth's thesis of a Deuteronomistic History, at least with respect to the books of Kings; according to this view, in the middle of the sixth century a Deuteronomistic author collected ancient material, sifted it, and arranged it according to the principles of a theology of history. Although this does not in fact hold true for Deuteronomy and the book of Joshua, the book of Judges has been subjected to considerable Deuteronomistic editing (mostly in the framework sections) and the books of Samuel much less so. For the books of Kings, we should not think in terms of a pre-Deuteronomistic recension. They are instead the work of Deuteronomistic authors (Weiser*), and differ thereby both from the source strata of the Hexateuch and from the books following the Hexateuch. Basic to this argument is the framework; unlike the framework of the book of Judges, which was placed around narrative material already extant, the framework of the books of Kings was created at the same time the narrative material of the sources was forged into a whole, so that the author of the framework is none other than the author of the books of Kings. In the books of Kings, then, we have a work planned and composed by a Deuteronomistic hand; in the following paragraphs we shall discuss the various components.

3. *The framework.* The reports concerning the individual kings are set in a framework that gives the work its characteristic stamp. This framework consists of recurring introductory and concluding passages. The introductions contain: (*a*) a synchronistic dating of the king's accession; (*b*) his place of residence; (*c*) the length of his reign; (*d*) an evaluation of his religious attitude. In the case of the Judahite kings, the introductions contain also: (*e*) the king's age at his accession; and (*f*) the name and occasionally the home of the king's mother.[1] The conclusions contain: (*a*) a reference to the

[1] H. Donner, "Art und Herkunft des Amtes der Königinmutter im Alten Testament," in *J. Friedrich-Festschrift*, 1959, pp. 105-45; G. Molin, "Die Stellung der Gebira im Staate Juda," *ThZ*, X (1954), 161-75.

historical sources to be discussed below, frequently with observations concerning their content; (*b*) a mention of the king's death and his place of burial; and (*c*) the name of his successor.

For David, Solomon, and Jeroboam I, we find only the concluding formula; for Solomon we also have part of the introduction. We encounter the complete framework from I Kings 14 on, though without synchronism in the case of Rehoboam (I Kings 14:21-22, 29-31):

> Rehoboam was forty-one years old when he began to reign, and he reigned seventeen years in Jerusalem. . . . His mother's name was Naamah the Ammonitess. And 'he' did what was evil in the sight of Yahweh, and 'he' provoked him to jealousy with 'his' sins which 'he' committed, more than all that 'his' fathers had done.[2]
>
> Now the rest of the acts of Rehoboam, and all that he did, are they not written in the Book of the Chronicles of the Kings of Judah? . . . And Rehoboam slept with his fathers and was buried . . . in the city of David. . . . And Abijam his son reigned in his stead.

The partial or complete absence of the framework in the case of some of the later kings is due to the particular course of their lives. There is no concluding formula for Joram and Ahaziah because they were murdered by Jehu (II Kings 9:22-23). There is no introductory formula for the revolutionary Jehu (II Kings 11:34-36). Both are missing in the case of Athaliah, because II Kings 11 gives the same information in different fashion. The concluding formula is also not given for the kings that were deposed by the enemy: Hoshea, of Israel; and Jehoahaz, Jehoiachin, and Zedekiah, of Judah.

Besides the information concerning the length of the kings' reigns, the synchronisms and the evaluations of the kings are especially important.

a) During the period of the two kingdoms Judah and Israel, the accession of each king is dated synchronistically by the regnal year of the ruler in the other kingdom, e.g. (I Kings 15:1): "Now in the eighteenth year of King Jeroboam the son of Nebat, Abijam began to reign over Judah." Often, it is true, these data do not agree with the numbers of the regnal years, and at times both are at odds with the real chronology as determined from extrabiblical sources. Scholars have proposed various explanations of this state of affairs, but none of the systems they have developed has gained general recognition.[3]

[2] The sentence has been secondarily expanded so as to refer to all Judah.

[3] W. F. Albright, "The Chronology of the Divided Monarchy of Israel," *BASOR*, C (1945), 16-22; *idem*, "Further Light on Synchronisms between Egypt and Asia in the Period 935-685 B.C.," *ibid.*, CXLI (1956), 23-27; J. Begrich, *Die Chronologie der Könige von Israel und Juda,* 1929; A. Carlier, *La chronologie des rois de Juda et d'Israël*, 1953; J. Finegan, *Handbook of Biblical Chronology,* 1964; D. N. Freedman and E. F. Campbell, Jr., "The Chronology of Israel and the Ancient Near East," in *Essays Albright,* 1961, pp. 203-28; A. Jepsen and R. Hanhart, *Untersuchungen zur israelitisch-jüdischen Chronologie,* 1964; J. Lewy, *Die Chronologie der Könige von Israel und Juda,* 1927; P. van der Meer, *The Chronology of Ancient Western Asia and Egypt,* 3rd ed., 1963; S. Mowinckel, "Die Chronologie der israelitischen und jüdischen Könige," *AcOr* Copenhagen, X (1932), 161-277; C. Schedl, "Juda," *VT*, XII (1962), 88-116; E. R. Thiele, *The Mysterious Numbers of the Hebrew Kings*, 1951; *idem,* "The Synchronisms

b) The criterion by which the kings are judged is whether or not they permitted or encouraged various cults besides that of the Jerusalem Temple. If they did so, they are considered evil; if not, they are considered good. By this reasoning, only Hezekiah and Josiah are approved of unreservedly;[4] Asa, Jehoshaphat, Joash, Azariah, and Jotham are accorded a lesser degree of approval. All other kings of Judah, and the Israelite kings without exception, are condemned. This evaluation is clearly based on the Deuteronomic law concerning cultic centralization and Josiah's reformation, which are applied retrospectively as the norm for the entire period of the monarchy.

4. *The historical sources.* In the conclusion passages of the framework, the author expressly mentions the historical sources he employed. These comprise three books: the Acts of Solomon (I Kings 11:41), the Chronicles of the Kings of Israel (I Kings 14:19–II Kings 15:31), and the Chronicles of the Kings of Judah (I Kings 14:29–II Kings 24:5). We have said what there is to say about these sources in §13.3.

For the history of Solomon,[5] the Deuteronomistic author (who is also responsible for the major portion of I Kings 8 and 11:1-13) not only selected the material from the historical source, but also arranged it in a definite pattern: a royal novella legitimizing Solomon's rule (3:4-15), his wise judgment (3:16-28), his administration (4:1–5:8 [Eng. 4:1-28]), his wisdom (5:9-14 [Eng. 4:29-34]), the building of the palace and temple (5:15–9:14 [Eng. 5:1–9:14]), fortifications (9:15-24), Solomon's wealth and wisdom (9:25–10:29), his apostasy under the influence of his wives and the ensuing punishment (11:1-40). In the description of Solomon's building operations, the temple characteristically occupies the foreground,[6] although it was only

of the Hebrew Kings—a Re-Evaluation," *Andrews University Seminary Studies*, I (1963), 121-38; II (1964), 120-36; for the last years of Judah, see D. J. Wiseman, *Chronicles of Chaldaean Kings (626–556 B.C.) in the British Museum*, 1956, and the literature referring to it.

[4] P. Buis, *Josias*, 1958; F. Horst, "Die Kultusreform des Königs Josia," *ZDMG*, LXXVII (1923), 220-38; A. Jepsen, "Die Reform des Josia," in *Baumgärtel-Festschrift*, 1959, pp. 97-108; O. Procksch, "König Josia," in *Zahn-Festschrift*, 1928, pp. 19-53; H. H. Rowley, "Hezekiah's Reform and Rebellion," *BJRL*, XLIV (1961/62), 395-431 (=*Men of God*, 1963, pp. 98-132); E. W. Todd, "The Reforms of Hezekiah and Josiah," *SJTh*, IX (1956), 288-93.

[5] F. C. Fensham, "The Treaty between Solomon and Hiram and the Alalakh Tablets," *JBL*, LXXIX (1960), 59-60; A. W. Heathcote, *Israel to the Time of Solomon*, 1960; B. Rothenberg, "Ancient Copper Industries in the Western Arabah," *PEQ*, XCIV (1962), 5-71; J. Schreiden, "Les entreprises navales du roi Salomon," *AIPhHOS*, XIII (1955), 587-590; F. Thieberger, *Le roi Salomon et son Temps*, 1957; G. E. Wright, "More on King Solomon's Mines," *BA*, XXIV (1961), 59-62; S. Yeivin, "Did the Kingdom of Israel Have a Maritime Policy?" *JQR*, L (1959/60), 193-228.

[6] P. L. Garber, "Reconstructing Solomon's Temple," *BA*, XIV (1951), 2-24; H. W. Hertzberg, "Der heilige Fels und das Alte Testament," *JPOS*, XII (1932), 32-42 (=*Beiträge zur Traditionsgeschichte und Theologie des Alten Testaments*, 1962, pp. 45-53); W. Kornfeld, "Der Symbolismus der Tempelsäulen," *ZAW*, LXXIV (1962), 50-57; J. L. Myres, "King Solomon's Temple and other Buildings and Works of Art," *PEQ*, LXXX (1948), 14-41; A. Parrot, *Le Temple de Jérusalem*, 1954 (English: *The Temple of Jerusalem*, 1955); H. Schmidt, *Der heilige Fels in Jerusalem*, 1933; H. Schult, "Der Debir im salomonischen Tempel," *ZDPV*, LXXX (1964), 46-54; L.-H. Vincent, *Jérusalem de l'Ancien Testament*, II–III, 1956.

the royal chapel. It is also characteristic of the author that he regards Solomon's diplomatic marriages with foreign women and his building of cultic sites for them as a sin and the reason for his failures. Such parallel passages as 4:20 + 5:1 (Eng. 4:20-21) and 5:4-5 (Eng. 4:24-25); 5:6-30 (Eng. 4:26–5:16) and 10:23-26 + 9:10-23, as well as comparison of the Masoretic text with that of the Septuagint, show that the text fluctuated for a long time and that the Masoretic text, Codex Vaticanus, and the Lucianic recension of the Septuagint should probably be considered composites of various textual forms.

For the history of the kings of the post-Solomonic period, the Deuteronomistic author generally took only brief notices from his two historical sources, referring the reader back to the sources for details. He draws upon them at greater length only in the case of Athaliah and Joash (II Kings 11–12)[7] and Josiah's reformation (II Kings 22–23).[8]

5. *The narrative complexes.* The narrative complexes used by the author include a few royal traditions and a series of prophet legends of varying scope.

A. The royal traditions include first of all the narrative of the division of the kingdom (I Kings 12:1-19), for which Rehoboam bears most of the blame, and the story of Jehu's revolution (II Kings 9*–10). In addition, I Kings 20:1-34 and 22, with their narratives of the wars and death of Ahab, represent the remnants of an independent Ahab tradition, which is closely associated with the events described and probably derives from the ninth century.[9] In chapter 22, this tradition is linked with a prophet legend concerning Micaiah ben Imlah. It honors the greatness of this clever, ambitious, magnanimous, and courageous king (20:4, 7-9, 33; 22:35), who, however, will not hear the words of Yahweh's prophet. Because of his negative evaluation of Ahab, the Deuteronomistic author used only a part of this tradition.

B. The Elijah tradition consisted originally of six individual narratives (I Kings 17–19; 21; II Kings 1:1-17):[10]

1. Drought and gift of rain (I Kings 17:1; 18:1$a\beta$-2a, 16-17, 41-46)
2. Judgment on Mount Carmel (I Kings 18:19-40)[11]

[7] W. Rudolph, "Die Einheitlichkeit der Erzählung vom Sturz der Atalja," in *Bertholet-Festschrift*, 1950, pp. 473-78.

[8] R. Meyer, "Auffallender Erzählungsstil in einem angeblichen Auszug aus der 'Chronik der Könige von Juda'," in *Baumgärtel-Festschrift*, 1959, pp. 114-23.

[9] E. Haller, *Charisma und Ekstasis*, 1960.

[10] A. Alt, *Der Stadtstaat Samaria*, 1954 (=*Kleine Schriften*, III [1959], 258-302); *Élie le prophète*, 1956-57; G. Fohrer, *Elia*, 1957; H. Gunkel, *Elias, Jahve und Baal*, 1906; C. A. Keller, "Wer war Elia?" *ThZ*, XVI (1960), 298-313; B. D. Napier, "The Omrides of Jezreel," *VT*, IX (1959), 366-78.

[11] A. Alt, "Das Gottesurteil auf dem Karmel," in *Beer-Festschrift*, 1935, pp. 1-18 (=*Kleine Schriften*, II [1953], 135-49); D. R. Ap-Thomas, "Elijah on Mount Carmel," *PEQ*, XCII (1960), 146-55; O. Eissfeldt, *Der Gott Karmel*, 1953; K. Galling, "Der Gott Karmel und die Ächtung der fremden Götter," in *Alt-Festschrift*, 1953, pp. 105-25; H. Junker, "Der Graben um den Altar des Elias," *Trierer ThZ*, LXIX (1960), 65-74; H. H. Rowley, "Elijah on Mount

3. Theophany on Horeb (I Kings 19:3*b*, 8*b**, 9-12, 13*)
4. Call of Elisha (I Kings 19:19-21)[12]
5. Judicial murder of Naboth (I Kings 21:1-9, 11-20)
6. Ahaziah's oracle (II Kings 1:2-8, 17*a*)

Except for the third, all these narratives have a historical nucleus. The first, second, and fifth narratives take place against the background of Ahab's neutral policy toward the Israelite and Canaanite population, giving equal status to both, and his attempted introduction of an absolute monarchy. The last narrative shows that Elijah could not bring the royal house over to his views.

At various stages in the transmission of these narratives, six anecdotes were added:

1. Elijah fed at the brook Cherith (I Kings 17:2-6)
2. Elijah fed at Zarephath (I Kings 17:7-16)
3. Restoration of the widow's son (I Kings 17:17-24; 18:1*aα*)
4. Encounter with Obadiah (I Kings 18:2*b*-15*)
5. Sustenance provided by an angel (I Kings 19:4*a*, 5-8*)
6. Attempted arrest of Elijah (II Kings 1:9-16)

The growth and development of the tradition, in the course of which the verses not mentioned above were added, began soon after the historical events and came to a temporary conclusion toward the end of the ninth century. Not long after this tradition had assumed a fixed written form, it was divided into two sections:

a) The first section comprises the novella I Kings 17–19, in which narratives and anecdotes (with the exception of those in [*c*] below) were linked by means of the historically inappropriate motifs of Ahab's polytheism and the persecution of the prophets of Yahweh. This section introduces Elijah by name, occasionally calls him a prophet, links his active intervention with miraculous events, and characterizes him as a second Moses. It is influenced by the Elisha tradition, to which it has been adjusted.

b) The second section comprises I Kings 21 and II Kings 1:2-8, 17*a*. In it the prophet is called "Elijah the Tishbite" and his antagonist "the king of Samaria"; Elijah is merely the messenger entrusted with Yahweh's message.

c) There is also a third element, comprising the two anecdotes I Kings 17:17-24; 18:1*aα*; and II Kings 1:9-16, which introduce Elijih as a "man of God" and exaggerate the miraculous events to the level of the superhuman. These anecdotes presuppose the two narrative sections just mentioned, and represent a link between them.

C. The Elisha tradition occurs as a reasonably continuous whole in II Kings

---

Carmel," *BJRL*, XLIII (1960/61), 190-219 (=*Men of God*, 1963, pp. 37-65); R. de Vaux, "Les prophètes de Baal sur le Mont Carmel," *BMB*, V (1941), 7-20; E. Würthwein, "Die Erzählung vom Gottesurteil auf dem Karmel," *ZThK*, LIX (1962), 131-44.

[12] A. Alt, "Die literarische Herkunft von I Reg 19,19-21," *ZAW*, XXXII (1912), 123-25.

2; 3:4-27; 4:1-8, 15; 9:1-10; 13:14-21.[13] We are dealing here with an independent complex of traditions, distinct from the Elijah tradition in both form and content, although there has been mutual influence and adaptation.

a) The first strand comprises a continuous narrative cycle of popular miracle stories, linked together by being related to Gilgal. The anecdotes constituting this cycle were originally independent, either reflecting real deeds of power on the part of Elisha or applying common motifs to him. After the introductory narrative (II Kings 2:1-18), which is intended to depict the beginning of Elisha's activity, come the following passages: 2:19-22, 23-25; 4:1-7, 8-17, 18-37, 38-41, 42-44; 6:1-7. Chapter 8:1-6, which presupposes Elisha's death, was written by the compiler as a conclusion to the miracle stories. The isolated tradition in II Kings 13:20-21 belongs here only by virtue of its content.

b) A second strand of tradition comprises a series of individual narratives that remained independent until being joined to the first group. Considered as a whole, they are rather like historical narrative; individually, however, they exhibit varying characteristics. The features of miracle story, legend, or saga are found in 5; 6:8-23; 8:7-15. The passages 3:4-27; 6:24–7:20 resemble the narrative type found in the Ahab tradition. Chapter 9:1-10 has been absorbed into the report of Jehu's revolution; 13:14-19 reports a symbolic action. What these narratives have in common is their reference to the political and historical importance of Elisha. In some of them he is hostile to the ruling dynasty, so that he sides with the Arameans in order to bring about its downfall (3:4-27; 8:7-15). This points to the time of Joram, the last king belonging to the dynasty of Omri. The turning point is the revolution of Jehu, which numbers Elisha among its spiritual authors. In the other narratives, which derive from the period of the dynasty of Jehu, Elisha is friendly to the ruling dynasty and hostile to the Arameans (5; 6:8-23; 6:24–7:20; 13:14-19).

D. The Isaiah tradition (II Kings 18:13; 18:17–20:19 [combined with 18:14-16, a notice from the historical source]) was later also incorporated into the book of Isaiah (=Isa. 36–39). It comprises four narratives, the first two of which are interwoven.

a) Two narratives of the Assyrians' threat to Jerusalem during the reign of Hezekiah and its miraculous deliverance are found in II Kings 18:13, 17–19:37.[14] The first narrative begins with an introduction (18:13) and then continues in 18:17–19:9*a*, where it breaks off abruptly so that the second narrative can be appended, and finally returns in 19:36-37. The second narrative (19:9*b*-35) has therefore been interpolated into the first. Both exhibit similar structure, and can be divided into four sections:

[13] K. Galling, "Der Ehrenname Elisas und die Entrückung Elias," *ZThK*, LIII (1956), 129-48; H. Gunkel, *Geschichten von Elisa*, 1922; J. Heller, "Drei Wundertaten Elisas," *CV*, I (1958/59), 61-70; W. Reiser, "Eschatologische Gottessprüche in den Elisa-Legenden," *ThZ*, IX (1953), 327-38.

[14] These narratives do not refer to two different campaigns, a view repeated recently by J. Bright, *A History of Israel*, 1959.

Sennacherib demands capitulation	18:13, 17-37	19:9*b*-13
Hezekiah's reaction	19:1-5	19:14-19
Isaiah's promise	19:6-7	19:20-34
Retreat of the Assyrians	19:8-9*a*, 36-37	19:35

In the first, second, and fourth sections, the second narrative presents a simpler and briefer account, which, however, bears a more marked theological stamp. Since in this narrative the Assyrian attack is directed against God himself, in the third section the original oracle of Yahweh has been replaced by three extended prophecies (vss. 21-28, 29-31, 32-34). In the first two sections of the first narrative, on the contrary, the account is bipartite and more detailed. Although there are echoes of historical reminiscences, we are dealing here not with historical narratives but with legends, which are meant for the edification of the reader. That the actual course of events was different can be seen from the notice in 18:14-16 and the report of Sennacherib. Furthermore, the interpolated prophecies are dependent on Isa. 14:4-32 and Deutero-Isaiah, so that they date from the late exilic period at the earliest. The legends contribute nothing to our understanding of Isaiah.

b) The narrative of Hezekiah's sickness and miraculous recovery (20: 1-11) was not originally linked to a specific time during his reign. The introduction and the addition of vs. 6 have associated it with the months of the Assyrian threat.

c) The narrative of the envoys sent by Merodach-baladan of Babylon (20:12-19) reflects what was originally an episode in the preparations for Hezekiah's revolt against the Assyrians. Later, on the basis of the interpolated prophecies, it was reinterpreted to apply to the Babylonian Exile.

E. Additional prophet legends, besides the narrative concerning Micaiah ben Imlah that has been incorporated into I Kings 22, include the following:

I Kings 11:29-39; 12:15; 14:1-18; 15:29, concerning Ahijah of Shiloh; this narrative was later made to serve the purposes of the Deuteronomist;
I Kings 12:21-24, concerning Shemaiah;
I Kings 12:32–13:32, concerning the appearance of an anonymous prophet attacking the altar at Bethel, with an appended narrative of his disobedience and punishment, which has at times been considered the popular tradition concerning Amos;[15]
II Kings 21:7-15, an anonymous prophecy against the King Manasseh.

6. *The Deuteronomistic books of Kings*. The author or authors of the Deuteronomistic books of Kings created the framework for the accounts of the individual kings and selected the suitable material, both historical and narrative, from the extant traditions. It is clear that they did not intend to provide a detailed presentation of historical events and therefore did not do justice to the actual significance of the monarchy and its representatives. Their goal was a religious survey of history, with emphasis on the Jerusalem

[15] Most recently O. Eissfeldt, "Amos und Jona in volkstümlicher Überlieferung," in *Barnikol-Festschrift*, 1964, pp. 9-13.

Temple and the prophets and the relationship of the kings to the Temple. Those kings whose reigns were uneventful in this respect were represented by the barest minimum of data; for example, Omri, who is of extraordinary historical importance, is dismissed in six verses.[16] For additional information, the reader could be referred to the historical sources, which were still at his disposal.

Since the framework with its evaluation of the kings presupposes the Deuteronomic law of cultic centralization and the reformation of Josiah, the Deuteronomistic books of Kings might have been written after 622 B.C. The last date given (II Kings 25:27) is the year 561, which must therefore constitute the upper limit for the time of origin. The presence of two Deuteronomistic hands can often be shown, however, so that we must think in terms of two authors or an author and a supplementor. The "author" wrote the major portion of the books soon after 622 and is the real creator of the work. Since he is unfamiliar with the Babylonian Exile and Josiah's death in battle (II Kings 22:20), he must have completed his work before 609. The "supplementor" extended and finished it during the Exile. From him come the references to the Exile and other supplementary material, as well as the conclusion of the books (II Kings 23:25*b*–25:30). He concludes with the release of Jehoiachin,[17] but knows nothing of the end of the Exile (538 B.C.).

7. *Later additions*. Like other books, the Deuteronomistic books of Kings have acquired some later addition. Apart from short remarks and glosses, these include: the expansion of Solomon's prayer at the dedication of the Temple (I Kings 8:23-26, 41-51) and the theophany (I Kings 9:1-9), an anonymous prophet legend (I Kings 20:35-43), the expansion of the reason for the destruction of the Northern Kingdom (II Kings 17:7-20, 29-40). Both in the history of Solomon and elsewhere the text of the books was long in a state of flux and subject to change; it did not become fixed until later, when the books were canonized.

8. *Historical reliability and theological purpose*. The historical value of the books of Kings derives from their authors' use of reliable historical sources as well as prophetical traditions that at least in part have a historical basis. The authors preserved valuable notices, even though they selected their data tendentiously and, in the history of Solomon, arranged it in unhistorical order. Much more, however, fell victim to the Deuteronomistic revision of history and was irretrievably lost with the ancient historical sources.

The theological purpose of the authors derives from their historical situation. The "author," who lived in the time of Josiah, judges history according to the relationship between the king and the Jerusalem Temple, the true sanctuary

[16] H. Parzen, "The Prophets and the Omri Dynasty," *HThR*, XXXIII (1940), 69-96; C. F. Whitley, "The Deuteronomic Presentation of the House of Omri," *VT*, II (1952), 137-52.

[17] W. F. Albright, "King Joiachin in Exile," *BA*, V (1942), 49-55; E. Weidner, "Jojachin, König von Juda, in babylonischen Keilschrifttexten," in *Mélanges Syriens Dussaud*, II (1939), 923-35.

of Yahweh, and the prophets, those who proclaim Yahweh's word. Everywhere he seeks parallels to the situation of his own time. He is concerned with the struggle against pagan and syncretistic religious abuses and the victory of pure Yahwism as the last chance for deliverance from inward decay and outward destruction as shown by the record of history. The "supplementor," who worked during the Exile, sees in the situation of the deported Israelites proof of their earlier sins, and looks upon the destruction of Israel and Judah as the judgment proclaimed by the prophets. The events of the past determine the duties of the present. History is to be a lesson and a warning for the present generation, confronted with a new decision; this generation must find its way back to the sources of its faith if it and Yahwism are not to perish.

CHAPTER FOUR: THE CHRONICLER'S HISTORY

§34 The Chronicler's Work
(I–II Chronicles, Ezra, Nehemiah)

ATD: K. Galling, 1954, reprinted 1958. BOT: A. van den Born, 1960; J. de Fraine, 1961. HAT: W. Rudolph, 1955; *idem*, 1949. HK: R. Kittel, 1902 (Eng. 1895); K. Siegfried, 1901. HS: J. Goettsberger, 1939; H. Schneider, 4th ed., 1959. IB: W. A. L. Elmslie, 1954; R. A. Bowman, 1954. ICC: E. L. Curtis and A. A. Madsen, 1910, reprinted 1952; L. W. Batten, 1913, reprinted 1949. KAT: J. W. Rothstein and J. Hänel, I, 1927. KeH: E. Bertheau, 2nd ed., 1873; *idem* and V. Ryssel, 2nd ed., 1887. KHC: I. Benzinger, 1901; A. Bertholet, 1902. SAT: M. Haller, 2nd ed., 1925. SZ: S. Oettli, 1889.

1. *Unity, transposition, division.* It is generally recognized that I–II Chronicles, Ezra, and Nehemiah were fashioned as a literary unit, which is called the Chronicler's History. It provides a survey of Israel's total history and prior events from the creation of the world to the time of Ezra and Nehemiah. The uniformity of language, style, and procedure, the constant intellectual milieu, which focuses on the Temple and the cult, the law, the Levites, and the Davidic dynasty, indicate that one author, the Chronicler, was responsible for the whole. In addition, the original unity can still be seen from the fact that the conclusion to the books of Chronicles (II Chron. 36:22-23) agrees almost word for word with Ezra 1:1-3. This observation at the same time confirms that the correct sequence of the books, in contrast to that found in the Hebrew canon (Ezra–Nehemiah–Chronicles), must be: Chronicles–Ezra–Nehemiah. Two circumstances are responsible for their present transposition and division.

a) I–II Chronicles are divided from Ezra–Nehemiah because the latter books were the first to receive canonical status. Unlike Chronicles, whose content parallels that of the books Genesis–Kings, Ezra–Nehemiah recount hitherto unrecorded events of special significance for the Jews. Since Chronicles was not recognized as canonical until later, its place in the canon was after Ezra–Nehemiah.

b) Within the canon, Chronicles and Ezra–Nehemiah at first each constituted one book. As in the case of Samuel and Kings, the LXX separated each of these into two books; the first evidence for the division of Ezra–Nehemiah is found in Origen, in the first half of the third century C.E. The division passed from there into the Latin translations, and, from 1448 on, into the Hebrew manuscripts and printed editions.

2. *Terminology.* Chronicles, whose name goes back to Jerome (*chronicon totius divinae historiae*), was called in Hebrew [*sēper*] *dibrê hayyāmîm,*

"[The Book of] the Days' Events," i.e., "Annals." In the LXX, it was called *paraleipómena,* "Things Passed Over, Omitted." The entirety of the books Ezra–Nehemiah was named after Ezra, even in the LXX. After their division, they were named in the Hebrew tradition after their two major figures.

Since the LXX counts the apocryphal book of Ezra as the first book by this name, we have the following confusing terminology in the Masoretic text, the LXX, and the Vulgate:

Ezra	— *Esdras b*	— Esdras I
Nehemiah	— *Esdras g*	— Esdras II
III Ezra (apocryphal Ezra)	— *Esdras a*	— Esdras III
IV Ezra (Ezra Apocalypse)	— *Esdras ho prophḗtēs* (*Esdra apokálupsis*)	— Esdras IV

In the KJV and RSV, the books are called Ezra, Nehemiah, I Esdras, and II Esdras.

3. *Content and purpose.* The content of the books, which we can only give in rough outline, reveals the purpose of the work: to show that, in contrast to the godless Northern Kingdom, the Kingdom of Judah, with the Davidic dynasty and the Jerusalem Temple, is the true Israel and the representative of God's dominion, realized in the Kingdom of David. Its legitimate heir is the postexilic cultic community at Jerusalem, which preserves and continues this tradition, not the Samaritan community, which was then coming into being.

I Chronicles	1–9	From Adam to Saul (genealogical lists)
	10–29	Saul's death and David
II Chronicles	1–9	Solomon
	10–36	From the division of the kingdom (apostasy of the "ten tribes") to the end of the Exile
Ezra	1–6	From the reconstituting of the community to the building of the Temple
Ezra 7–Nehemiah 13		Reconstitution and consolidation under Ezra and Nehemiah

4. *Origin.* In dating the Chronicler's History, we must remember that it shows familiarity with the entire Pentateuch, including the incorporated Priestly Code. Furthermore, it presupposes the work of Nehemiah and Ezra; their work must in fact lie in the rather distant past, since the Chronicler could treat the tradition concerning it quite arbitrarily. To be sure, the activity of the two men is assigned to quite different dates. If—as seems most likely (§35.6)—Nehemiah was active in years 445–432 and Ezra from 398 B.C. on, the earliest possible date for the Chronicler is the second half of the fourth century. Since, despite the earlier opposition of the Jerusalem community to Samaria, the Chronicler directs his attack concretely against the Samaritan community that came into being after 350, we must date the creation of his History more precisely to the period around 300. The presentation makes it perfectly clear that it was written in Jerusalem.

§35 The Formation and Nature of the Chronicler's Work

F. Ahlemann, "Zur Esra-Quelle," *ZAW*, LIX (1942/43), 77-98; W. F. Albright, "The Date and Personality of the Chronicler," *JBL*, XL (1921), 104-24; J. P. Asmussen, "Priesterkodex und Chronik in ihrem Verhältnis zueinander," *ThStKr*, LXXIX (1906), 165-79; A. Bea, "Neuere Arbeiten zum Problem der biblischen Chronikbücher," *Bibl*, XXII (1941), 46-58; A. Bentzen, "Sirach, der Chronist und Nehemia," *StTh*, III (1950/51), 158-61; G. J. Botterweck, "Zur Eigenart der chronistischen Davidgeschichte," *ThQ*, CXXXVI (1956), 402-34; A.-M. Brunet, "Le Chroniste et ses sources," *RB*, LX (1953), 481-508; LXI (1954), 349-86; *idem*, "La théologie du Chroniste," *BEThL*, XII (1959), 384-97; K. Budde, "Vermutungen zum 'Midrasch des Buches der Könige'," *ZAW*, XII (1892), 37-51; H. van den Bussche, *Het probleem van Kronieken*, 1950; H. Cazelles, "La mission d'Esdras," *VT*, IV (1954), 113-40; D. N. Freedman, "The Chronicler's Purpose," *CBQ*, XXIII (1961), 436-42; K. Galling, *Studien zur Geschichte Israels im persisschen Zeitalter*, 1964; H. H. Grosheide, "De dateering van de Boeken der Kronieken," *GThT*, XXXVI (1935), 170-82; *idem*, "Een geschrift van Tabeël?" *ibid.*, L (1950), 71-79; C. J. Goslinga, "De parallele teksten in de boeken Samuël en Kronieken," *GThT*, LXI (1961), 108-16; J. Hänel, "Das Recht des Opferschlachtens in der chronistischen Literatur," *ZAW*, LV (1937), 46-67; A. S. Kapelrud, *The Question of Authorship in the Ezra-Narrative*, 1944; M. W. Leeseberg, "Ezra and Nehemia: A Review of the Return and Reform," *Concordia Theological Monthly*, XXXIII (1962), 79-90; B. Luther, "Ḳāhāl und ʿedāh als Hilfsmittel der Quellenscheidung im Priesterkodex und in der Chronik," *ZAW*, LVI (1938), 44-63; F. Mezzacasa, "Esdras, Nehemias y el Año Sabático," *RevBibl*, XXIII (1961), 1-8, 82-96; S. Mowinckel, *Ezra den Skriftlärde*, 1916; *idem*, *Statholderen Nehemia*, 1916; *idem*, "Erwägungen zum chronistischen Geschichtswerk," *ThLZ*, LXXXV (1960), 1-8; *idem*, " 'Ich' und 'Er' in der Ezrageschichte," in *Rudolph-Festschrift*, 1961, pp. 211-33; *idem*, *Studien zu dem Buche Ezra-Nehemia*, I–II, 1964; III, 1965; R. North, "Theology of the Chronicler," *JBL*, LXXXII (1963), 369-81; M. Noth, *Überlieferungsgeschichtliche Studien*, I, 1943; G. von Rad, *Das Geschichtsbild des chronistischen Werkes*, 1930; *idem*, "Die levitische Predigt in den Büchern der Chronik," in *Procksch-Festschrift*, 1934, pp. 113-24 (= *Gesammelte Studien zum Alten Testament*, 1958, pp. 248-61 [Eng. *The Problem of the Hexateuch, and Other Essays*, 1966]); *idem*, "Die Nehemia-Denkschrift," *ZAW*, LXXVI (1964), 176-87; H. H. Schaeder, *Esra, der Schreiber*, 1930; *idem*, *Iranische Beiträge*, I, 1930; R. Smend, *Die Listen der Bücher Esra und Nehemia*, 1881; W. F. Stinespring, "Eschatology in Chronicles," *JBL*, LXXX (1961), 209-19; C. C. Torrey, *The Composition and Historical Value of Ezra-Nehemia*, 1896; *idem*, *Ezra Studies*, 1910; *idem*, *The Chronicler's History of Israel. Chronicles-Ezra-Nehemiah Restored to Its Original Form*, 1954; A. C. Welch, *The Work of the Chronicler, Its Purpose and Date*, 1939.

1. *Sources for the preexilic period.* The Chronicler did not frame a completely new and independent presentation; for the most part he drew upon extant sources, always selecting the material that served his purposes. He thus continued the procedure begun by the Deuteronomistic authors of the books of Kings. His sources for the preexilic period (I–II Chronicles) in any case included the books Genesis–Kings, which his presentation largely parallels. This can be seen from their analogous outline and correspondences, in part word

for word. While he drew upon Genesis for the genealogies of the patriarchs from Adam to Jacob and the descendants of Esau (Edomites), which he records in I Chronicles 1, the list of the sons of Jacob, which in the Chronicler's account comprised only a few verses of I Chronicles 2–9 (Noth), was based on the notices in Numbers 26, supplemented by a genealogy of David and the high priests. For the entire period of the monarchy, in which after the division of the kingdom the author mentions only the kings of Judah and ignores the kings of Israel completely, the primary sources at least are the books of Samuel and Kings.

In addition, like the author of the books of Kings, the Chronicler concludes the accounts of the individual kings by mentioning specific sources in which additional material about the kings can be found. The question is therefore whether these sources were accessible to him and provided a portion of his material (Eissfeldt* *et al.*), or whether we are dealing with nothing more than a literary imitation of the statements in the books of Kings (Galling, Noth, Torrey, *et al.*).

The sources mentioned fall into two groups:

a) Some sources are said to deal with the kings, but no author is mentioned:
The Book of the Kings of Israel and Judah (II Chron. 27:7; 35:27; 36:8);
The Book of the Kings of Judah and Israel (II Chron. 16:11; 25:26; 28:26; 32:32);
The Book of the Kings of Israel (II Chron. 20:34);
The Chronicles [or: Words] of the Kings of Israel (II Chron. 33:18);
The Midrash on the Book of Kings (II Chron. 24:27).
b) Other sources are described as the "words," "prophecy," "vision," or "midrash" of specific prophets:
Samuel, Nathan, and Gad for the history of David (I Chron. 29:29);
Nathan, Ahijah, and Iddo for Solomon (II Chron. 9:29);
Shemaiah and Iddo for Rehoboam (II Chron. 12:15);
Iddo for Abijah (II Chron. 13:22);
Jehu for Jehoshaphat (II Chron. 20:34);
Isaiah for Uzziah (II Chron. 26:22) and Hezekiah (II Chron. 32:32);
"The Seers" for Manasseh (II Chron. 33:19).

The very number and multiplicity of these supposed sources raise doubts as to whether we are dealing with independent works available to the Chronicler. The various designations for sources concerning the kings probably refer one and all to the Deuteronomistic books of Kings. The same is true for the prophetical sources, whose "authors" all are found in the books of Samuel and Kings, so that we may think of the sources ascribed to them as the relevant sections of these books, all of which in the late period were thought to have been written by prophets.

Chronicles does, however, contain a series of notices that are undoubtedly early and reliable but are not found in the books of Kings. These include at least the following:

II Chron.	11:5*b*-10*a*	List of Rehoboam's fortifications
	26:6-8*a*	Wars of Uzziah

26:9, 15*a*	Uzziah's fortifications at Jerusalem
27:5	Jotham's Ammonite campaign
28:18	Cities lost to the Philistines by Ahaz
32:30	Hezekiah's Shiloah tunnel
33:14*a*	Manasseh's fortifications
35:20-24	Josiah's death in battle

Other notices concerning fortifications and defense works may have been used in II Chron. 14:5-7; 17:2*a*, 12*b*-19; 25:5; 27:3-4. The same situation seems to obtain in the two battle accounts II Chron. 13:3-20 and 14:8-14 (Eng. 14:9-15). The Chronicler must have taken all these data concerning military installations (which include the Shiloah tunnel) and the military operations of the Judahite kings from a further source, about which we can say only that it contained notices concerning such matters. Oral traditions (Bentzen*, Engnell*) are most unlikely.

2. *Sources for the postexilic period.* The books of Ezra and Nehemiah make no mention of the sources drawn upon, unless one interprets the references in Neh. 1:1; 7:5; and 12:23 in this fashion. It is nevertheless clear that the Chronicler had access to and made use of several sources for the postexilic period.

A. In Ezra 1:1–4:5, which tells of the return of the deportees, the first construction work on the Temple, and the opposition of some to this work,[1] at least 1:2-4, 8-11*a;* and 2 come from early sources. It is impossible to say with assurance whether the entire section represents such a source (Eissfeldt*) or is the Chronicler's own narrative (Noth, Rudolph, Schaeder) based on the fragments mentioned and the books of Haggai and Zechariah.

B. Ezra 4:6–6:18 is based on an Aramaic source: an account, supported by official documents, of the difficulties encountered in building the Temple and the city walls during the reigns of Darius I, Xerxes, and Artaxerxes I.[2] It is not chronologically accurate, because it recounts the events that took place under Darius I (4:24–6:18) after those that occurred later under Xerxes and Artaxerxes (4:6-23). This has been explained on the grounds that we are dealing with a vindication directed to Artaxerxes by the Jews to prove their political loyalty, which therefore begins with the most recent period (Kittel, Klostermann, Schaeder), although the text makes no reference to such a purpose. Some have assumed that we have here an account of the reconstruction of the city and the Temple from the period around 300 B.C., when the actual events lay far enough in the past that the whole affair seemed

[1] E. J. Bickermann, "The Edict of Cyrus in Ezra 1," *JBL*, LXV (1946), 249-75; 249-75; K. Galling, "Der Tempelschatz nach Berichten und Urkunden im Buche Esra," *ZDPV*, LX (1937), 177-83 (="Das Protokoll über die Rückgabe der Tempelgeräte," in *Studien zur Geschichte Israels im persischen Zeitalter*, 1964, pp. 78-88); H. L. Ginsberg, "Ezra 1,4," *JBL*, LXXIX (1960), 167-69; L. Rost, "Erwägungen zum Kyroserlass," in *Rudolph-Festschrift*, 1961, pp. 301-7.

[2] K. Galling, "Kyrosedikt und Tempelbau," *OLZ*, XL (1937), 473-78; R. de Vaux, "Les décrets de Cyrus et de Darius sur la reconstruction du Temple," *RB*, XLVI (1937), 29-57.

one single project, culminating in the building of the Temple (4:24 ff.) (Noth). It is more likely that the Chronicler himself transposed the sections so that 4:6-16 would document the hostility of the ruling class in Samaria (4:1-5) (Rudolph).

C. The so-called Memoirs of Ezra constitute another source. Their use of the first person can hardly be termed a fiction, with the explanation that they go back to an unknown eyewitness to the events (Mowinckel); neither can the entire presentation be ascribed to the Chronicler (Hölscher, Kapelrud, Noth, Torrey). Even though revision by the Chronicler is very probable, the basic account probably does go back to Ezra. The Memoirs undoubtedly include Ezra 7:11–9:5 (in addition to the late list in 8:1-14, the prayer in 9:6-15 should also be considered a late addition, *pace* Schaeder). It is debatable, however, whether Ezra 10, which is in the third person, also derives from the Memoirs of Ezra and was later changed from the first to the third person (Budde, Rudolph), especially since a large part of the chapter is a later addition. The same question also arises with regard to Neh. 8:1–9:5, in which Ezra is also the major figure (the mention of Nehemiah in 8:9 is a gloss). With respect to its chronology and content, the narrative falls between Ezra 8:32-36 and 9:1; but it is also in the third person. From these observations we may conclude that Ezra 7:11–9:5 is a part of the Memoirs of Ezra, revised by the Chronicler; Ezra 10* and Neḥ. 8:1–9:5, on the contrary, were composed by the Chronicler after the pattern of the Memoirs (*pace* Schaeder, the prayer in Neh. 9:6-37 must also be called an addition[3]).

D. The Memoirs of Nehemiah, a unitary work in votive style bearing its own definite stamp, which was written as a votive offering to God (§7.5, 13.4), are found in Neh. 1:1–7:5 (omitting the list in 3:1-32); 11:1-2; 12:27–13:31.[4] They report primarily how the city wall was rebuilt despite all opposition, as well as the social and cultic measures taken by Nehemiah. At first they may not have belonged to the Chronicler's History; they may have been added a century later by the "Second Chronicler" (Bright, Galling) or linked during the Maccabean period to the story of Ezra by a post-Chronistic redactor (Hölscher, Mowinckel). It is nevertheless quite reasonable to ascribe their use and the linking of the work of Ezra and Nehemiah to

[3] L. J. Liebreich, "The Impact of Nehemiah 9,5-37 on the Liturgy of the Synagogue," *HUCA*, XXXII (1961), 227-37; M. Rehm, "Nehemias 9," *BZ* NF, I (1957), 59-69; A. C. Welch, "The Source of Nehemiah 9," *ZAW*, XLVII (1929), 130-37.

[4] A. Alt, "Judas Nachbarn zur Zeit Nehemias," *PJB*, XXVII (1931), 66-74 (=*Kleine Schriften*, II (1953), 338-45); *idem*, "Die Rolle Samarias bei der Entstehung des Judentums," in *Procksch-Festschrift*, 1934, pp. 5-28 (=*ibid.*, pp. 316-37); M. Avi-Yonah, "The Walls of Nehemiah," *IEJ*, IV (1954), 239-48; M. Burrows, "The Topography of Nehemiah 12,31-43," *JBL*, LIV (1935), 29-39; *idem*, "Nehemiah's Tour of Inspection," *BASOR*, LXIV (1936), 11-12; F. M. Cross, Jr., "Geshem the Arabian, Enemy of Nehemiah," *BA*, XVIII (1955), 46-47; H. H. Rowley, "Sanballat and the Samaritan Temple," *BJRL*, XXXVIII (1955/56), 166-98 (=*Men of God*, 1963, pp. 246-76); C. C. Torrey, "Sanballat 'The Horonite'," *JBL* XLVII (1928), 380-89.

the Chronicler himself. The nucleus of Nehemiah 10,[5] however, which later was further expanded, may be an addition.

E. Finally, the Chronicler either employed or composed several lists. These include:

The census list in Ezra 2,[6] which records the composition of the Judean community about 400 B.C., and may have formed a part of the hypothetical sources 1:1–4:5.

The list of those accompanying Ezra (Ezra 8:1-14), which the Chronicler constructed artificially on the basis of Ezra 2. The list of those engaged in the reconstruction (Neh. 3:1-32),[7] which may not have formed a part of the Memoirs of Nehemiah; if so, however, the Chronicler probably took it from another document.

3. *Expansions and later additions.* The Chronicler's History has received considerable expansions and additions, which we shall describe here for completeness' sake. Apart from brief notices, most of this material consists of lists.

The genealogy in I Chronicles 2–9 has been supplemented by the addition of the following sections: 2:18–4:23; 4:25-43; 5:1-2, 4-10, 11-26, 27-41 (Eng. 6:1-15); 6:5-33, 39-66 (Eng. 6:20-48, 54-81); 7:2-11, 15-19*, 21-40; 8:5–9:44.[8]

Other additions include the lists of David's heroes and warriors (I Chronicles 12), the priests and Levites (15:4-10, 16-24; 16:5-38, 41-42 [including the psalm]), and the Temple personnel, (23:3–27:34); the artificial list of mixed marriages in Ezra 10:18, 20-44; the list in Neh. 7:6-72, copied from Ezra 2; the list of names in Neh. 10:2-28, 38*b*-40*a* (made up of names occurring elsewhere in Ezra–Nehemiah); the lists of the inhabitants of Jerusalem and Judah (Neh. 11:3-36) and the priests and Levites (Neh. 12:1-26; based on the archival records of the Temple).

In addition, the long prayers in Ezra 9:6-15 and Neh. 9:6-37 also represent later expansions.

[5] A. Jepsen, "Nehemia 10," *ZAW*, LXVI (1954), 87-106.

[6] A. L. Allrik, "The Lists of Zerubbabel (Nehemiah 7 and Ezra 2) and the Hebrew Numeral Notation," *BASOR*, CXXXVI (1954), 21-27; K. Galling, "The 'Gōla-List' according to Ezra 2 // Nehemia 7," *JBL*, LXX (1951), 149-58 (="Die Liste der aus dem Exil Heimgekehrten," in *Studien zur Geschichte Israels im persischen Zeitalter*, 1964, pp. 89-108); *idem*, "Von Nabonid zu Darius," *ZDPV*, LXIX (1953), 42-64; LXX (1954), 4-32 (= "Politische Wandlungen in der Zeit zwischen Nabonid und Darius," *ibid.*, pp. 1-60).

[7] M. Burrows, "Nehemiah 3,1-32 as a Source for the Topography of Ancient Jerusalem," *AASOR*, XIV (1934), 115-40.

[8] A. Alt, "Bemerkungen zu einigen judäischen Ortslisten des Alten Testaments," *ZDPV*, LXVIII (1951), 193-210 (=*Kleine Schriften*, II [1953], 289-305); H. J. Katzenstein, "Some Remarks on the Lists of the Chief Priests of the Temple of Solomon," *JBL*, LXXXI (1962), 377-84; A. Lefèvre, "Note d'exégèse sur les généalogies des Qehatites," *RSR*, XXXVII (1950), 287-92; B. Mazar, "Gath and Gittaim," *IEJ*, IV (1954), 227-38; K. Möhlenbrink, "Die levitischen Überlieferungen des Alten Testament," *ZAW*, LII (1934), 184-231; M. Noth, "Eine siedlungsgeographische Liste in 1. Chr 2 und 4," *ZDPV*, LV (1932), 97-124; L. Waterman, "Some Repercussions from Late Levitical Genealogical Accretions in P and the Chronicler," *AJSL*, LVIII (1941), 49-56.

This means that the Chronicler's History has been subject to more expansion than other historical books. Similar observations have led some scholars to think in terms of a gradual process of growth. Rothstein sought to distinguish two redactions, the first dependent on the Priestly Code and the earlier material in the history of the monarchy, the second dependent on the entire Pentateuch. This distinction cannot be supported, however, because it can be shown that the entire history is dependent on the Pentateuch (von Rad). Galling takes a different approach, assuming two different authors and dating the "second Chronicler" around the beginning of the second century. It is doubtful, however, whether the expansions and additions really betray a single recension on the part of one man rather than deriving from several persons, each providing his own supplementary material.

4. *Use of sources.* At first glance, the Chronicler seems to have been faithful to his sources. He has preserved their text exactly whenever possible. The minor formal divergences are due to his adapting the material to the language and style of his day, altering of unintelligible passages (when he does not omit them altogether), and occasional interpolation of explanatory or supplementary notes.[9] His selection, however, is very free, and determined by the purpose of his presentation (§34.3). This principle led him to omit almost everything that took place prior to David (except the death of Saul) and outside Judah, and also to eliminate everything that would have made the few ideal Judahite kings appear in a bad light or replace it with a more favorable account. In this connection he also sometimes rearranged the narratives of his sources, so that events appear in a different light. This procedure can be recognized at once in the portrait of David. The Chronicler has selected from his sources the material that leads up to preparations for the building of the Temple and shows David to be a victorious and mighty king. In addition, the chronology of his decisive deeds is greatly condensed in order to link the different events as closely as possible. The succession narrative, on the other hand, is ignored, as is Solomon's construction of the palace. In the history of this latter king, the Chronicler has even turned the surrender of various places in Galilee to Tyre into a gift to Solomon (II Chron. 8:1-2). These observations arouse suspicion toward the way in which he has employed his sources for the postexilic period. In fact, the Chronicler not only undertook the transposition in Ezra 4:6–6:18, which has upset the chronology, but also broke up the Memoirs of Nehemiah and interpolated a section from the Memoirs of Ezra, so as to associate both men with the great events of the building of the city wall and the introduction of the law.

5. *The Chronicler's special material.* The treatment of sources that we have just described would not in itself have altered the picture of the history of the monarchy in comparison to that contained in the books of Samuel and Kings to the extent that actually took place. This alteration is due rather to the

[9] According to J. T. Milik, *Dix ans de découvertes dans le Désert de Juda,* 1957, p. 25 (English: *Ten Years of Discovery in the Wilderness of Judaea,* 1959), for I and II Samuel the Chronicler followed a form of the text represented by 4QSam[a].

Chronicler's special material, which constitutes nearly half the presentation (Torrey). In part it serves to correct the sources. This is especially true for the ascription to David of all preparations for the building of the Temple, so that nothing is left for Solomon but the actual construction. The situation is similar when the cultic measures mentioned in the Memoirs of Nehemiah (Neh. 13:4-31) are proleptically ascribed to Ezra. To some extent the Chronicler allows himself to be guided by the historical piety of his time. For instance, he no longer places the measures taken by the kings to reform the cult in their proper historical chronology, but instead places them as early as possible: as late as the third year of Jehoshaphat's reign (II Chron. 17:7), but in the first month of the first year of Hezekiah (II Chron. 29:3); Josiah's reforms begin when he is twenty, after four years of meditation (II Chron. 34:3). The Chronicler describes the measures taken by Hezekiah (II Chron. 29:3–31:21) and the Passover celebrated by Josiah (II Chron. 35:1-19) at length, basing his account on the life and institutions of his own time. He also expounds his views on how a military campaign conducted in the name of Yahweh should proceed (II Chron. 20:1-30).[10]

As opportunity presents itself, the Chronicler frequently interpolates speeches in his narrative; they are in the style of contemporary Levitical preaching (von Rad). Among the outstanding examples are David's speeches to Solomon, the "officials of Israel," and the assembled populace concerning the significance of the Jerusalem Temple (I Chron. 22:7-16; 28:2-10; 29:1-5), Abijah's speech to Jeroboam and the Israelites, and the prayer of Jehoshaphat before battle (II Chron. 13:4-12; 20:5-12). The latter are typical examples of the Chronicler's interpretation of history. In addition, the Chronicler frequently introduces prophets who preach repentance and apply the doctrine of retribution to the situation at hand (II Chron. 12:5-8; 15:1-7; 16:7-10; 19:2-3; 20:37; 29:9-11).

Last but not least, the Chronicler shows himself to be a skillful narrator, who knows how to paint for his readers a vivid picture of the persons and events of history. Much more than the Deuteronomistic author of the books of Kings, he elaborates details, as, for example, the narrative of Uzziah's leprosy shows (II Chron. 26:16-21).

6. *Historical reliability.* These observations allow us to judge the historical value of the Chronicler's History. In the books of Chronicles, the data concerning military installations and battles, which go beyond the books of Kings and come from an unknown source, may be considered reliable and trustworthy. There can also be no doubt concerning the importance of the Memoirs of Ezra and Nehemiah, especially because they contain not only unintentional portraits of the two figures but also important information about the postexilic period, which is for the most part historically obscure. The Aramaic documents in Ezra 4:6 ff. and the royal decree in Ezra 7:12-26 are probably

[10] M. Noth, "Eine palästinische Lokalüberlieferung in 2. Chr 20," *ZDPV*, LXVII (1945), 45-71.

genuine documents. In Ezra 1:1–4:5, ancient documentary material has at least been drawn upon.

The presentation is also valuable for the indirect light it throws on the period of the Chronicler. His account provides insights into the religious life and cultic institutions of his environment, its world view and interpretation of history, for which we have little other data at our disposal.

For the rest, however, the Chronicler's own material and the way in which he used his sources completely distorts the history of the monarchy. For the postexilic period, the interweaving of the Memoirs of Ezra and Nehemiah has made of the chronological sequence of the two figures a problem for which even today there is no unanimously accepted solution. Apart from the view that only Nehemiah is a historical figure, while Ezra is a legendary substitute for Nehemiah, corresponding to the ideas of a later period, there are three basic interpretations, which agree only in taking as their point of departure the dating of Nehemiah's activity in the years 445–432 (or a bit later), during the reign of Artaxerxes I:

a) Ezra and Nehemiah both worked in the period of Artaxerxes I, in the order given by the Chronicler: first Ezra, from 458 on, then Nehemiah.

b) Ezra and Nehemiah both worked in the period of Artaxerxes I. First the city wall was rebuilt under Nehemiah, who then departs because he recognizes the necessity for an internal reformation. Ezra undertakes this task, but is recalled because of the unrest following the law against mixed marriages. Nehemiah thereupon returns and sees to it that the law of Ezra is respected.

c) Nehemiah worked at Jerusalem in the period of Artaxerxes I, but Ezra under Artaxerxes II, from 398 on. When all the arguments are weighed, this view appears most probable.

7. *Theological character*. Von Rad has studied the Chronicler's theology most thoroughly. This theology is first of all characterized by a presentation of events patterned according to the doctrine of retribution, applied less to the people as a whole than to particular individuals. The Chronicler explains all the misfortunes that befell the kings as punishment for their sins, among which offenses against priests and prophets weigh especially heavily. In the case of Manasseh, whose long reign despite the enormity of his sins contradicts the doctrine of retribution, this leads to a remarkable correction of history (II Chronicles 33): after his deportation by the Assyrians, Manasseh was converted to Yahweh while at Babylon. In reality, Manasseh was summoned before the Assyrian ruler, and the outcome was anything but a conversion.

In addition, the Chronicler allows Yahweh to control history through miraculous intervention even more than do the source strata E, D, and P in the Hexateuch. The best example is the account of Jehoshaphat's victory (II Chron. 20:1-30). After a service of worship on the previous day, the army is drawn up, led by singers in holy array, who begin a song of thanksgiving. Thereupon the enemy, under the influence of God, massacre one another and are already dead when the Judahites come on the scene. All that remains is to spend three days collecting the booty.

This brings us to the Chronicler's high opinion of the cult at the Jerusalem Temple, the only legitimate sanctuary. The center of interest is the performance of the cult itself; the sacrifices are described at length. It is characteristic that only authorized cultic personnel are allowed access to holy places and permitted to perform holy actions, and that liturgical singing is reserved to the Levites.

Finally, there is a striking religious glorification of David, which is intimately linked with the Temple and its cult, for which David makes all the preparations. His age appears as a sought-after ideal. Yahweh's promises to the house of David and the unbreakable covenant between them are referred to again and again. We see here in the late period a nostalgic longing for the Davidic dynasty; the Chronicler probably hoped for a future restoration of the Davidic monarchy.

CHAPTER FIVE: OTHER BOOKS

§36 The Book of Ruth

ATD: H. W. Hertzberg, 2nd ed., 1959. BK: G. Gerleman, 1960. BOT: J. de Fraine, 1956. HAT: M. Haller, 1940. HK: W. Nowack, 1902. HS: A. Schulz, 1926. IB: L. P. Smith, 1953. KAT: W. Rudolph, 1939. KAT[2]: W. Rudolph, 1962. KeH: E. Bertheau, 2nd ed., 1883. KHC: A. Bertholet, 1898. SAT: H. Gressmann, 2nd ed., 1922. SZ: S. Oettli, 1889.

M. Burrows, "The Marriage of Boaz and Ruth," *JBL*, LIX (1940), 445-54; M. B. Crook, "The Book of Ruth—A New Solution," *JBR*, XVI (1948), 155-60; M. David, "The Date of the Book of Ruth," *OTS*, I (1942), 55-63; G. S. Glanzman, "The Origin and Date of the Book of Ruth," *CBQ*, XXI (1959), 201-7; H. Gunkel, "Ruth," in *Reden und Aufsätze*, 1913, pp. 65-92; P. Humbert, "Art et leçon de l'histoire de Ruth," *RThPh*, XXVI (1938), 257-86 (= *Opuscules d'un Hébraïsant*, 1958, pp. 83-110); A. Jepsen, "Das Buch Ruth," *ThStKr*, CVIII (1937/38), 416-28; O. Loretz, "The Theme of the Ruth Story," *CBQ*, XXII (1960), 391-99; J. Myers, *The Linguistic and Literary Form of the Book of Ruth*, 1955; H. H. Rowley, "The Marriage of Ruth," *HThR*, XL (1947), 77-99 (= *The Servant of the Lord*, 1952, pp. 161-86); J. Schoneveld, *De betekenis van de lossing in het boek Ruth*, 1956; S. Segert, "Vorarbeiten zur hebräischen Metrik, III," *ArOr*, XXV (1957), 190-200; W. E. Staples, "The Book of Ruth," *AJSL*, LIII (1936/37), 145-57.

1. *Terminology and content.* This small book takes its name from one of the three figures that play the major roles in it. From the very beginning it belonged to the third part of the Hebrew canon, the "Writings," although its canonicity was once in doubt, as can be seen from Talmud Bab. Megilla 7*a*. It was later used as a festival scroll for the Feast of Weeks, i.e., the festival of the wheat harvest. Since it purports to narrate a story from the period of the Judges, the LXX and other translations placed it after the book of Judges. In content, it is a continuous narrative.

1:1-6	Introduction: Emigration to Moab of a Judahite family from Bethlehem; death of the father, Elimelech; marriage of the sons to Moabite women; death of the sons; the mother Naomi's wish to return home.
1:7-22	Return of Naomi with her daughter-in-law Ruth ("where you go, I will go," referring to the mother-in-law); Orpah, the other daughter-in-law, remains behind.
2	Boaz, a wealthy relative of Ruth's husband, is attracted to the diligent and virtuous Ruth as she is reaping grain.
3	Ruth's mother-in-law advises her to go to Boaz at night and lie at his feet, to remind him of his duty as a relative to redeem her by marriage and urge him to perform it.
4:1-17	Another relative relinquishes his claim to Ruth; Boaz marries her; a son, Obed, is born to them.
4:18-22	Genealogy of David.

2. *Literary type and historical background.* The resemblance to popular saga suggests that the narrative is based on such a saga—like the framework narrative of the book of Job. Originally, it may even have had poetic form (Myers). In the dress of its present style, however, it conforms to the literary type of the novella, composed by an unknown author. He is responsible for the characterization of the major figures.

In its basic features, the narrative was a single unit from the outset. The suggestion that Naomi was originally the only woman involved or the most important figure (Gunkel, Haller, Jepsen) cannot be demonstrated and is unlikely. The only doubtful point is whether 4:17*b*, 18-22 belonged to the original narrative.

The ancient saga had a historical setting, particularly with respect to its date and locale. The formation of the names "Boaz" and "Elimelech" also fits in with the period of the Judges. "Naomi," too, is a common feminine name; but since it means "pleasant," it seems to have been chosen deliberately as a symbolic contrast to the bitter fate of the woman who bore it. Though it cannot be proved conclusively, it seems probable that the names of Naomi's two Moabite daughters-in-law have a certain symbolic significance: "Orpah" may mean "faithless" and "Ruth" may mean "companion." This is absolutely certain with respect to the names of the dead sons: "Mahlon" means "weakness" and "Chilion" means "consumption." Whether all these names occurred already in the popular saga or derive in part from the author of the novella cannot be determined. In any case, they are not related to any fertility cult at Bethlehem, whose myth is represented by the narrative (Staples).

3. *Connection with David.* The crucial problem for interpretation of the novella is its relationship to David (4:17*b*, 18-22). It is recognized almost universally that the genealogy of David, which derives either from I Chron. 2:2-15 or the same tradition, must be considered a later postscript. The genealogy, beginning with Perez (4:18-22), was added because of the nuptial good wishes addressed to Boaz (4:12), which mention Perez, and also because of the appearance of Boaz and Obed among the ancestors of David.

The question remains, however, whether the two clauses of 4:17*b* ("They named him Obed; he was the father of Jesse, the father of David") originally belonged to the narrative. Eissfeldt* has rightly denied their originality on grounds of form and content. Formally, the name of Ruth's child should either occur in 17*a*, where we now find the statement that "the neighborhood gave him a name," or be introduced in 17*b* with *therefore,* as in other examples. In terms of content, the explanation of the name, "A son has been born to Naomi [the pleasant one]," bears no relation to the name "Obed" ("servant, worshiper"). As others have accurately observed before, the child should have been named something like "Ibleam" or "Ben Noam" (Gunkel, Eissfeldt*). This means that 4:17 is not in its original form, but has at least been expanded by the addition of 17*b*, apart from possible alterations in 17*a*. The original name has been removed and the name "Obed" introduced in order to make the child David's grandfather, who, according to tradition, was named Obed. The narrative of the book, therefore, originally had no connection with David. It is out of the question that the book presupposes an ancient tradition of David's Moabite origin, which it attempts to gloss over and neutralize by judaizing David's ancestors and the heritage of his family (Gerleman). Instead, the book was transformed into a narrative concerning David's family after it was finished. This is in line with the interest the late period shows in David, which by no means must always take the form it does in the Chronicler's History. That we are dealing here with a secondary alteration can also be seen from the fact that the narrative does not reckon Elimelech or Boaz among the ancestors of David.

4. *Interpretation.* The significance of the novella, therefore, cannot be ascribed to its recounting the early family history of the house of David (Oettli *et al.*). Neither does it consist in a protest against the ruthless attitude of Ezra and Nehemiah in the question of mixed marriages (Weiser* *et al.*). Not a single sentence suggests such a purpose. Instead, like the Job legend, the purpose of the narrative from the very outset was edification. Just as Job proves equally faithful in good fortune and ill, so Naomi and Ruth pass the difficult tests to which they are subjected: the former is concerned for the good of her daughter-in-law rather than for her own good, while remaining faithful to the family of her husband; the latter attaches more weight to her obligations toward her mother-in-law than to her previous national and religious ties and her chances for personal happiness (Eissfeldt*). Boaz, however, who fulfills his ancient obligations, opens thereby a new way out of the trials. To fulfill one's traditional obligations when subjected to the trials and tests of life because this course leads to change of fortunes—such was the teaching even of the ancient saga.

The author of the novella gave it a more profound religious significance by connecting it with faith in Yahweh's beneficent providence, which guides history. Ruth's arrival in the proper field is due to Yahweh's guidance; the success of Naomi's plan is due to Yahweh's grace; and the blessing of a son bestowed upon the marriage with Boaz is due to Yahweh's kindness (Rudolph). What Boaz says to Ruth when they first meet expresses the religious content of the book: "Yahweh recompense you for what you have done, and a full reward be given you by Yahweh, the God of Israel, under whose wings you have come to take refuge." At the same time, we hear a similar magnanimity toward those who belong to another nation, like that expressed in the book of Jonah.

5. *Origin.* In dating the book, we must distinguish between the different stages in its formation. The novella did not originate in the late period of the monarchy (Haller, Rudolph), and certainly not in the period of the Solomonic enlightenment (Gerleman); this date is likely, however, for the popular saga. The author of the novella should be dated in the postexilic period; this conclusion is supported by the intellectual content of the book, its linguistic character, and its position in the third division of the canon. We must probably think in terms of the close of the fifth century or, even more likely,

the fourth century B.C. The alteration and expansion making the book refer to David must be dated even later.

§37 THE BOOK OF ESTHER

ATD: H. RINGGREN, 2nd ed., 1962. HAT: M. HALLER, 1940. HK: K. SIEGFRIED, 1901. HS: J. SCHILDENBERGER, 1941. IB: B. W. ANDERSON, 1954. ICC: L. B. PATON, 1908. KAT[2]: H. BARDTKE, 1963. KeH: E. BERTHEAU and V. RYSSEL, 2nd ed., 1887. KHC: G. WILDEBOER, 1898. SAT: M. HALLER, 2nd ed., 1925. SZ: S. OETTLI, 1889.

A. BEA, "De origine vocis פּוּר," *Bibl*, XXI (1940), 198-99; H. CAZELLES, "Note sur la composition de rouleau d'Esther," in *Junker-Festschrift*, 1961, pp. 17-29; V. CHRISTIAN, "Zur Herkunft des Purimfestes," in *Nötscher-Festschrift*, 1950, pp. 33-37; N. S. DONIACH, *Purim or the Feast of Esther*, 1933; W. ERBT, *Die Purimsage in der Bibel*, 1900; M. GAN, "The Book of Esther in the Light of the Story of Joseph in Egypt," *Tarbiz*, XXXI (1961/62), 144-49; T. H. GASTER, *Purim and Hanukkah in Custom and Tradition*, 1950; H. GUNKEL, *Esther*, 1916; P. HAUPT, *Purim*, 1906; J. HOSCHANDER, *The Book of Esther in the Light of History*, 1923; S. JAMPEL, *Das Buch Esther auf seine Geschichtlichkeit kritisch untersucht*, 1907; P. JENSEN, "Elamitische Eigennamen," *WZKM*, VI (1892), 47-70, 209-26; P. DE LAGARDE, *Purim*, 1887; J. LEWY, "The Feast of the 14th Day of Adar," *HUCA*, XIV (1939), 127-51; *idem*, "Old Assyrian puru'um and pūrum," *RHA*, V (1939), 116-24; A. E. MORRIS, "The Purpose of the Book of Esther," *ET*, XLII (1930/31), 124-28; H. RINGGREN, "Esther and Purim," *SEÅ*, XX (1956), 5-24; B. SCHNEIDER, "Esther Revised According to the Maccabees," *Studii Biblici Franciscani Liber Annuus*, XIII (1962/63), 190-218; R. STIEHL, "Das Buch Esther," *WZKM*, LIII (1956), 4-22; S. TALMON, " 'Wisdom' in the Book of Esther," *VT*, XIII (1963), 419-55; C. C. TORREY, "The Older Book of Esther," *HThR*, XXXVII (1944), 1-40; H. ZIMMERN, "Zur Frage nach dem Ursprunge des Purimfestes," *ZAW*, XI (1891), 157-69.

1. *Terminology and content.* This book, named after its real protagonist, comprises ten chapters of continuous narrative set at the court of the Persian king Ahasuerus or Xerxes (485–465). It tells how Esther, the foster-daughter of Mordecai, comes to replace Vashti, the rejected queen, while at about the same time Mordecai saves the life of the king by discovering a plot against him (1–2). Meanwhile Haman, the grand vizier and an enemy of the Jews, secures an edict decreeing the annihilation of the Jews on the thirteenth day of the twelfth month, Adar (February–March), a date determined by lot (*pûr*) (3). At the request of Mordecai, however, Esther risks her life and succeeds in persuading the king to retract his order. Haman, caught in suspicious circumstances, is hanged on the gallows intended for Mordecai; Esther inherits his property, Mordecai his office (4:1–8:2). At Esther's request, the king issues a decree allowing the Jews to destroy their enemies. This takes place on the thirteenth of Adar throughout the entire land, and again on the fourteenth of Adar in Susa itself. Then the fourteenth of Adar is declared a festival for the Jews in the province, the fifteenth for the Jews in the capital. This festival, the Feast of Purim, is inculcated by letters from Mordecai

and Esther (8:3–9:32). The book concludes with a reference to further accounts concerning the king and Mordecai in a historical work.

The book of Esther, which belongs to the third division of the Hebrew canon, was, like other books, of dubious canonicity according to Talmud Bab. Megilla *7a*. Its popularity prevailed, however, so that it finally became the festival scroll for the Feast of Purim.

2. *Literary type*. The book purports to be the festival legend for the Feast of Purim and to recount the historical circumstances of its origin. This is done so skillfully that the events described seem in fact to lead up to the celebration and institution of the festival and justify the obligation of repeating the festival faithfully each year. In line with the secular character of the festival, the narrative is also set in the popular and secular world where the conflicts between other peoples and the Jews broke out.

The narrator bends every effort to give his presentation the appearance of a historical narrative by citing dates and much circumstantial detail, purportedly historical. The book nevertheless contains a series of historical inaccuracies and errors. Furthermore, the account of the development of the Feast of Purim does not accord with historical reality. It is true that the narrator has some knowledge of the administration of the Persian Empire and the layout of the palace at Susa, just as he also used a historical event to depict the danger threatening the Jews. But he thinks of Xerxes as the immediate or almost immediate successor to Nebuchadnezzăr, i.e., about a century too early. Except for the king, the actors in the story are unknown from the available sources for Persian history. The resistance decree and the slaying of tens of thousands of Persians are historically incredible; many features of the narrative bear the mark of novella or fairy tale. When this is considered together with the general historical background, the book is most accurately termed a historical romance (Gunkel). This is in line with its kinship to the Hellenistic romance, a kinship long maintained and recently demonstrated once again (Stiehl).

3. *Origin of the narrative material and historical background*. In discussing the origin of the narrative material and its historical basis, we must disregard the Book of the Chronicles of the Kings of Media and Persia, mentioned as a source in 10:1-3. The reference can hardly refer to a genuine midrashic chronicle of the Jewish Diaspora in Persia. In fact, it is an imitation of the source references in the Deuteronomistic books of Kings, and probably represents a later addition.[1]

It is unlikely, however, that the book would have associated the Feast of Purim with the intended pogrom without some historical basis; the nucleus is probably to be found in a persecution and deliverance of the Jews in the eastern Diaspora during the Persian period. There is no basis in the text for the attempt to derive the book's origin from the persecutions under Antiochus IV Epiphanes and the Maccabean wars (Haupt, Pfeiffer*).

[1] D. Daube, "The Last Chapter of Esther," *JQR*, XXXVII (1946/47), 139-47.

Furthermore, the Feast of Purim is itself historical. Its name is derived from Haman's determination by *pûr* of the day on which the Jews were to be annihilated, but which became a day of destruction for their enemies. In 3:7 and 9:24-26, this "*pûr*" is glossed as a foreign word by the Hebrew word "*gôrāl*" ("lot"); this interpretation is confirmed by the Assyrian "*puru'um*" and "*pūrum*." The name therefore suggests that we are dealing with what was originally a non-Jewish festival, which the Jews borrowed in a Mesopotamian form. Since the determination of fortune by casting lots is associated with the turn of the year (Adar being the twelfth month), Purim may have been a New Year's festival. Some scholars have undertaken to trace the festival further back to a Persian origin. Suggestions have included the Persian feast of the dead, Farwardigan (de Lagarde), the Sakaia festival (Meissner [2]), and the Mithrakana festival (Ringgren). Gaster has sought to reconstruct the main features of the first of these by means of the material in the book of Esther. It is perhaps possible to speak of the *disiecta membra* of a festival pattern.

Less likely is the interpretation of the Feast of Purim as a battle between the Babylonian deities Mordecai (=Marduk) and Esther (=Ishtar) on the one hand and the Elamite gods Haman (=Uman) and Vashti (=Mashti) on the other, representing the struggle between the gods of light and the gods of darkness (Jensen, Zimmern).[3] There is also little to support a derivation of the persecution tradition from hostility between worshipers of Marduk and worshipers of Mithra, linked by another tradition with the casting of lots and the name "Purim" (Lewy).

The problems surrounding the Feast of Purim have to date not found a satisfactory solution. All we can say is that the festival may have originated in Persia and undergone further development in Mesopotamia, where the name originated, and was finally borrowed by the Jews—first of all in the Diaspora—and legitimized by means of the festival legend.

Apart from the historical data, the narrator apparently employed three narrative traditions. The first is the story of Vashti, a harem narrative of Persian origin well suited to depicting the royal milieu and the power of the kings. It is not closely linked with the remainder of the book. The second tradition, from the eastern Diaspora, tells the story of Mordecai, a Jew, and Haman, an aristocratic Persian, who were enemies. Haman, however, was unable to destroy Mordecai. On account of the service that Mordecai had shown the king, Haman had to reward him as the king instructed and be reduced in rank because he sought to attack a Jew; Mordecai was given Haman's former position at court. The third tradition, also of Jewish origin, tells the story of Esther, a Jew who was able to win the favor of the king and use her position when her religious compatriots were threatened with a

[2] B. Meissner, *ZDMG*, L (1896), 296 ff.

[3] The name "Mordecai" has been derived from a Babylonian name, "Mardukā" (A. Ungnad, *ZAW*, LVIII [1940/41], 243). The name "Esther" is probably neither Persian ("star") nor Old Indic ("young woman"); it derives from the Akkadian "Ishtar."

persecution, interceding with the king on their behalf. The inventive genius of the narrator has combined all these materials into a continuous absorbing story.

4. *Origin.* The characters in the story are not found in the panegyric on the fathers Ecclesiasticus 44–49; the book itself is not found at Qumran. These facts, however, are irrelevant for dating the book, being due rather to the secular character of the festival and the book. More significantly, the Feast of Purim is first alluded to in II Macc. 15:36-37 (*ca.* 50 B.C.), which means that by that time the festival had found its way to Palestine from the eastern Diaspora. The book of Esther, as the festival legend, must therefore have originated in the East quite a while before. The language of the book makes 300 B.C. the upper limit for its time of origin. To determine the date more precisely within the period between 300 and 50 B.C., it is probably wrong to rely on Pfeiffer's* association of the book with the period of the Maccabees or Steuernagel's* with the Day of Nicanor. We may note instead certain similarities to the books of Daniel and Judith, and above all its resemblance to a Hellenistic romance. On this evidence, an origin in the first half of the second century B.C. seems most likely.

5. *Supplement and later additions.* Esther 9:20-32 constitutes a supplement, distinguished from the rest of the book both by its ponderous style and by its content, since it prescribes that all Jews are to celebrate the Feast of Purim on the fourteenth and fifteenth of Adar, making no distinction between city and countryside (Bertheau, Pfeiffer*, Steuernagel*, *et al.*). Chapter 10: 1-3, with its reference to the Chronicles of the Kings of Media and Persia, also proves to be a later addition.

The LXX contains further additions, most of which expand on the present text: following 1:1, the dream of Mordecai and his discovery of the plot against Artaxerxes; following 3:13, Artaxerxes' edict concerning the annihilation of the Jews; following 4:17, the prayers of Mordecai and Esther; following 5:1-2, the account of Esther's reception by the king; following 8:12, Artaxerxes' edict in favor of the Jews; following 10:3, the interpretation of Mordecai's dream and the date on which the Greek translation of the book was brought to Egypt.

6. *Value.* While the book contains an absorbing narrative and characterizes its major figures artistically and accurately, its religious and theological value is doubtful. Up until 1542, Luther for the most part assessed it positively, criticizing it bitterly only in the context of his attitude toward contemporary Judaism. Apart from this, it is less a sacred document than a secular book; it never mentions God directly, referring to him only indirectly in 4:14. It is the product of a nationalistic spirit, seeking revenge upon those that persecute the Jews, which has lost all understanding of the demands and obligations of Yahwism, especially in its prophetical form. It is to this extent an indictment and an admonition, illustrating the effects of persecution within Judaism itself.

PART TWO

The Formation of the Poetic Books

CHAPTER ONE: GENERAL

§ 38 Lyric Poetry in the Ancient Near East and in Israel

J. Begrich, "Die Vertrauensäussergungen im israelitischen Klageliede des Einzelnen und in seinem babylonischen Gegenstück," *ZAW*, XLVI (1928), 221-60 (= *Gesammelte Studien zum Alten Testament*, 1964, pp. 168-216); A. M. Blackman, "The Psalms in the Light of Egyptian Research," in D. C. Simpson, *The Psalmists*, 1926, pp. 177-97; F. M. T. Böhl, "Hymnisches und Rhythmisches in den Amarna-Briefen aus Kanaan," *ThLBl*, XXXV (1914), 337-40 (= *Opera minora*, 1953, pp. 375-79, 516-17); G. Castellino, *Le lamentazioni individuali e gli inni in Babilonia e in Israele*, 1939; A. Causse, "Les origines de la poésie hébraïque," *RHPhR*, IV (1924), 393-419; V (1925), 1-28; J. Coppens, "Les parallèles du Psautier avec les textes de Ras-Shamra-Ougarit," *BHET* (1946), 113-42; C. G. Cumming, *The Assyrian and Hebrew Hymns of Praise*, 1934; E. R. Dalglish, *Psalm Fifty-One in the Light of Ancient Near Eastern Patternism*, 1962; J. J. A. van Dijk, *Sumerische Götterlieder*, II, 1960; F. Dornseiff, "Ägyptische Liebeslieder, Hoheslied, Sappho, Theokrit," *ZDMG*, XC (1936), 589-601 (= *Kleine Schriften*, I, 2nd ed., 1959, pp. 189-202); G. R. Driver, "The Psalms in the Light of Babylonian Research," in D. C. Simpson, *The Psalmists*, 1926, pp. 109-75; A. Erman, *Die Literatur der Ägypter*, 1923 (Eng. *The Literature of the Ancient Egyptians*, 1927); A. Falkenstein, *Sumerische Götterlieder*, I, 1959; *idem* and W. von Soden, *Sumerische und akkadische Hymnen und Gebete*, 1953; C. L. Feinberg, "Parallels to the Psalms in Near Eastern Literature," *BS*, CIV (1947), 290-321; K. Grzegorzewski, *Elemente vorderorientalischen Hofstils auf kanaanäischem Boden*, Dissertation, Königsberg, 1937; A. Hermann, *Altägyptische Liebesdichtung*, 1959; H. P. Hurd, *World's Oldest Love Poem. Hieroglyphic Text (Louvre C 100)*, 1954; A. Jirku, "Kanaʿanäische Psalmenfragmente in der vorisraelitischen Zeit Palästinas und Syriens," *JBL*, LII (1933), 108-20; S. N. Kramer, *Lamentation over the Destruction of Ur*, 1940; *idem*, "Sumerian Literature, a General Survey," in *Essays Albright*, 1961, pp. 249-66; *idem*, *The Sumerians*, 1963; W. G. Lambert, "Divine Love Lyrics from Babylon," *JSS*, IV (1959), 1-15; V. Maag, "Syrien-Palästina," in H. Schmökel, ed., *Kulturgeschichte des Alten Orient*, 1961, pp. 552-55; T. J. Meek, "Babylonian Parallels to the Song of Songs," *JBL*, XLIII (1924), 245-52; W. M. Müller, *Die Liebespoesie der alten Ägypter*, 1899; R. T. O'Callaghan, "Echoes of Canaanite Literature in the Psalms," *VT*, IV (1954), 164-76; W. O. E. Oesterley, *Ancient Hebrew Poems*, 1938; H. Otten, "Das Hethiterreich," in H. Schmökel, ed., *Kulturgeschichte des Alten Orient*, 1961, pp. 424-25; J. H. Patton, *Canaanite Parallels to the Book of Psalms*, 1944; H. W. Robinson, *The Poetry of the Old Testament*, 1947; H. Schmökel, *Heilige Hochzeit und Hoheslied*, 1956;

S. Schott, *Altägyptische Liebeslieder*, 1950; G. A. Smith, *The Early Poetry of Israel in its Physical and Social Origins*, 4th ed., 1913, reprinted 1927; J. Spiegel, "Poesie und Satire," in *Handbuch der Orientalistik*, I, III (1952), 158-69; F. Stummer, *Sumerisch-akkadische Parallelen zum Aufbau alttestamentlicher Psalmen*, 1922; G. Widengren, *The Accadian and Hebrew Psalms of Lamentation as Religious Documents*, 1936.

1. *Mesopotamia.* Apart from its own peculiarities, Israelite poetry forms one part of the voluminous poetic literature of the ancient Near East. In Mesopotamia, the Sumerian and Old Babylonian type of poetry begins about the middle of the third millennium at the latest and continues until around 1600 B.C.; it is succeeded, from about 1300 B.C. on, by a "refined" and canonized type, echoes of which continue into the Seleucid period. The texts handed down to us are almost exclusively sacral or religious; these are mostly hymns, penitential poems, and laments. Poetry based on everyday life is scarcer; there seems to have been little interest in its transmission and preservation.[1]

The hymns can be assigned to four groups: praise of the gods (including hymns in the first person, especially common from the mouth of the goddess Ishtar); praise of the king (mostly extravagant self-glorification); songs of praise to the gods with interpolated blessings and prayers for the kings; and poems glorifying Sumerian temples. The penitential poems and laments—apart from the lament over the destruction of Sumerian cities and city-states—represent for the most part public penitential liturgies connected with ceremonies of propitiation. They comprise a lament over sickness and suffering, at times a confession of sins, and then a request for healing and deliverance from the sins. In a wider sense, this category includes prayers for extispicy and royal prayers, as well as liturgical charms embodying individual requests, which begin with an address to the deity and a passage in praise of him, followed by the complaint, the request, and words of thanksgiving or blessing. Furthermore, the cultic love song developed as a literary type; only fragments of such songs are preserved, most of which are difficult or impossible to interpret. They seem to refer to love between gods or sacral marriage, praising the beauty and allure of the beloved or mourning his loss. Recently, dirges in which a man bewails the death of his father and his wife have been discovered.

The hymns and laments in particular follow a standard form quite closely. Almost all the countless gods are described with the same glowing epithets; prayer and thanksgiving are addressed to them without perceptible distinction. Later Babylonian poetry gives a less formulaic impression, but tends to elaboration and mannerism. This effect is heightened by the use of acrostic technique, which adorns a religious dictum or a royal name with laudatory epithets. But we also find verses of poetic beauty, echoes of deep personal religiosity and a profound awareness of sin and repentance.

The Sumerians were the first to classify their songs, sometimes according to the instruments for which they were composed ("Songs for the Lyre," i.e., songs of praise; "Songs for the Drum," i.e., songs concerning the gods), as well

[1] *AOT*, pp. 241-81; *ANET*, pp. 382-92, 455-63, 496.

as into such categories as "Long Songs" and "Hero Songs." The later period mentions several additional types, such as "Songs Sung with Lifted Hands," with conjurations and prayers for deliverance from sickness and misfortune, and "Songs of Appeasement," intended to placate angry deities.

There was also political poetry, including a poem probably commissioned by the Sumerian king Tukulti-Ninurta I concerning the relations between Assyria and Kassite Babylon during the fourteenth and thirteenth centuries; a poem in the form of a hunting song glorifying the battle fought by an Assyrian king (perhaps Tiglath-pileser I) against Murattash; and also a poem belittling Nabonidus, the last king of Babylon.

2. *Egypt.* Not much of the earlier poetry of Egypt has been preserved. Its character is for the most part inaccessible to us, because its phonetic pattern and rhythm were not recorded, although the poetry depended upon the beauty of the sonorous word and its internal structure upon the precise modulation of the words employed. It can be stated, however, that originally the Egyptian poets sought for each object of their experience a form of expression that would define its intrinsic nature and that this poetry gradually came to include the expression of ideas, emotions, and moods. There was also another type of poetry, making its first appearance in the New Kingdom, which took as its point of departure not the object of experience, but the person experiencing it (mostly love poetry).[2]

The most important literary type is the hymn addressed to a deity or a king. The hymn addressed to a god clearly derives from the cult. The earliest examples are in the form of litanies assigning to particular deities certain places, sacred precincts, and cult objects; these consist therefore merely of lists. Gradually, as in Mesopotamia, the poetry is adorned by a plethora of epithets. The invocations of the royal crowns are also connected with the cult and above all the Morning Song, with which the deity was greeted by morning worshipers in his temple, as was the king upon awakening in his palace. The litany-like hymn composed of names continues to be used in the later periods. Other hymns also came into being, which contain connected mythological narratives or passages of deep emotion. These include the Hymn to Amon, which depicts the god as the creator of the world and all the animals, describing his glorious appearance and great mythical deeds. The hymns to the sun, especially the hymn of Amenhotep IV, should be counted among the most valuable poetic texts in Egyptian literature.

The royal hymn is closely related in form and content to the hymn to a god, the more so because court custom demanded that the king be addressed with a hymn. Even the many decorative epithets are taken from hymns to gods. Besides the praises sung by the court poets, who in the Ramesside period obviously sought to outdo each other in glorifying the victories and deeds of the rulers, we find glorification of the royal power in the form of self-praise and dialogue between deity and king.

There were also laments and dirges; the lament prescribed for the mourning

[2] *AOT*, pp. 12-32; *ANET*, pp. 365-81, 467-71.

ritual of the Osiris cult provided a further opportunity for mythological narrative. In addition, there was poetry chanted or recited on the occasion of banquets in the tomb. As early as the archaic period we also find a series of work songs pertaining to various professions; from the New Kingdom there are numerous love songs, mostly forming parts of collections. These latter use numbers or the names of flowers to introduce plays on words, pretend to be the speech of trees in a garden, or take as their leitmotiv the birds and their capture in the reeds. In contrast to the earlier poetry, the choice of leitmotiv here replaces the fixed formulation of an object of experience with a playful attention to the situation of the moment. The poet uses the description of outward circumstances to characterize the mood of the person experiencing the event. In this way a decidedly subjective approach contrasts with the objectivity of earlier poetry.

3. *Elsewhere in the ancient Near East.* We may presuppose the existence of analogous poetic forms elsewhere in the ancient Near East, although much less of it has been preserved. As an example of Hittite popular poetry the so-called Soldiers' Song from an Old Hittite text has been cited. We also find hymns and prayers, some of which may count as literary compositions; they are often distinguished for the sincerity and profundity of their thought. In one hymn to the sun-god a Babylonian prototype can be clearly recognized.

The Canaanites, too, had cultic songs as well as other kinds, though so far few have been found among the Ugaritic texts. The most important categories are probably once more hymns, laments, and songs to accompany sacrifice. The use of such songs is illustrated by the ritual for a day of propitiatory sacrifice occasioned by a political disaster; the ritual contains the complete text of the laments composed for the occasion. Such a formulary may restrict itself to merely mentioning familiar cultic songs to be sung by quoting their incipits, a procedure familiar from Mesopotamian catalogs. All in all, we may safely assume a common poetic tradition throughout the entire Canaanite or Syro-Palestinian region, exhibiting only minor differences due to geographical separation, historical differentiation, and various foreign influences.

4. *Israelite poetry.* Israelite poetry is rooted in the soil of the abundant poetic literature of the ancient Near East, including that of Canaan. In particular, scholars have pointed out the close parallels between the Mesopotamian laments and the laments in the book of Psalms, between the Hymn to the Sun of Amenhotep IV and Psalm 104, and between Canaanite poetry and Psalm 29. Quite apart from the formal parallels, it has come to appear likely that the Canaanite religion at least exerted some influence upon the content of the Old Testament psalms, although Yahwism and Israel's unique concept of God and existence carried the day. Hempel* has provided the best summary of the individuality of the poetry found in the Old Testament, especially the various types of psalms, describing it under three heads: [3] a gradual religious spiritualization, which substitutes purely religious goals, above all the forgiveness of sins, for secular goals; the transcending of magical ritual and the magical purpose of hymns to God, ascribing responsibility for human suffering to Yahweh rather

[3] Hempel*, p. 38.

than the host of demons and witches; the religious restriction of all statements about the nature of the supernatural world to Yahweh alone, the God of the nation and of the individual. The details will be discussed in § 41, after we have examined the various poetic types.

It is hardly possible to distinguish between secular and religious (cultic) poetry. Songs dealing with the circumstances of everyday life can have every bit as much religious import as those that are intended for the cult. More significant is the distinction between those songs that refer to events in the life of the group or the individual, growing out of these events or having a function in them, and those that are intended as works of art for interested listeners, whose sole function is to provide a "concert." The former are overwhelmingly more common than the latter.

§ 39 The Literary Types of the Psalms and Their Traditions

G. W. Ahlström, *Psalm 89*, 1959; E. Balla, *Das Ich der Psalmen*, 1912; C. Barth, *Die Errettung vom Tode in den individuellen Klage- und Dankliedern des Alten Testaments*, 1947; E. Baumann, "Struktur-Untersuchungen im Psalter," *ZAW*, LXI (1949), 114-76; LXII (1950), 115-52; J. Begrich, "Die Vertrauensäusserungen im israelitischen Klageliede des Einzelnen und in seinem babylonischen Gegenstück," *ZAW*, XLVI (1928), 221-60 (= *Gesammelte Studien zum Alten Testament*, 1964, pp. 168-216); A. Bentzen, "Der Tod des Beters in den Psalmen," in *Eissfeldt-Festschrift*, 1947, pp. 57-60; K.-H. Bernhardt, *Das Problem der altorientalischen Königsideologie im Alten Testament*, 1961; H. A. Brongers, "Die Rache- und Fluchpsalmen im Alten Testament," *OTS*, XIII (1963), 21-42; A. Büchler, "Zur Geschichte der Tempelmusik und der Tempelpsalmen," *ZAW*, XIX (1899), 96-133, 329-44; XX (1900), 97-135; A. Causse, "L'ancienne poésie cultuelle d'Israël et les origines du Psautier," *RHPhR*, VI (1926), 1-37; K. R. Crim, *The Royal Psalms*, 1962; P. Descamps, "Pour un classement littéraire des Psaumes," in *Mélanges Robert*, 1957, pp. 187-204; A. Feuillet, "Les psaumes eschatologiques du règne de Yahweh," *NRTh*, LXXIII (1951), 244-60, 352-63; S. B. Frost, "Asseveration by Thanksgiving," *VT*, VIII (1958), 380-90; B. Gemser, "Gesinnungsethik im Psalter," *OTS*, XIII (1963), 1-20; H. Gressmann, "The Development of Hebrew Psalmody," in D. C. Simpson, *The Psalmists*, 1926, pp. 1-21; H. Gunkel and J. Begrich, *Einleitung in die Psalmen*, 1933; M. Haller, "Ein Jahrzehnt Psalmforschung," *ThR*, NF I (1929), 377-402; A. R. Johnson, "The Psalms," in *The Old Testament and Modern Study*, 1951, pp. 162-209; H.-J. Kraus, *Die Königsherrschaft Gottes im Alten Testament*, 1951; A. Lauha, *Die Geschichtsmotive in den alttestamentlichen Psalmen*, 1945; F. Mand, "Die Eigenständigkeit der Danklieder des Psalters als Bekenntnislieder," *ZAW*, LXX (1958), 185-99; S. Mowinckel, *Psalmenstudien*, I–VI, 1921-24, reprinted 1961; *idem*, "Traditionalism and Personality in the Psalms," *HUCA*, XXIII (1950/51), 205-31; *idem*, *Offersang og sangoffer*, 1951 (Eng. *The Psalms in Israel's Worship*, I–II, 1962); *idem*, *Zum israelitischen Neujahr und zur Deutung der Thronbesteigungspsalmen*, 1962; *idem*, "Psalm Criticism between 1900 and 1935," *VT*, V (1955), 13-33; R. E. Murphy, "A Consideration of the Classification 'Wisdom Psalms'," *VTSuppl*, IX (1963), 156-67; N. Nicolsky, *Spuren magischer Formeln in den Psalmen*, 1927; *Le Psautier, Études présentées aux XIIe Journées Bibliques*, ed. R. de Langhe, 1962; E. Pax, "Studien zum Vergeltungsproblem der Psalmen," *Studii Biblici Franciscani Liber Annuus,* XI (1960/61), 56-112; R. PRESS, "Der zeitgeschichtliche Hintergrund der Wallfahrtspsalmen," *ThLZ,* XV (1959), 401-15; G. QUELL, *Das kultische Problem der Psalmen,* 1926; G. VON RAD, "Erwägungen zu den Königspsalmen," *ZAW,* LVIII (1940/41), 216-22; *idem,* "'Gerechtigkeit' und 'Leben' in der Kultsprache der Psalmen," in *Bertholet-Festschrift,* 1950, pp. 418-37; N. H. RIDDERBOS, *Psalmen en Cultus,* 1950; L. SABOURIN, *Un classement littéraire des psaumes,* 1964; G. SAUER, *Die strafende Vergeltung Gottes in den Psalmen,* 1961 (from a dissertation, Basel, 1957); H. SCHMIDT, *Die Thronfahrt Jahwes,* 1927; *idem, Das Gebet der Angeklagten im Alten Testament,* 1928; *idem,* "Grüsse und Glückwünsche im Psalter," *ThStKr,* CIII (1931), 141-50; J. J. STAMM, "Ein Vierteljahrhundert Psalmenforschung," *ThR,* NF XXIII (1955), 1-68; P. VOLZ, *Das Neujahrsfest (Laubhüttenfest),* 1912; A. WEISER, "Zur Frage nach den Beziehungen der Psalmen zum Kult," in *Bertholet-Festschrift,* 1950, pp. 513-31 (= *Glaube und Geschichte im Alten Testament,* 1961, pp. 303-21); C. WESTERMANN, *Das Loben Gottes in den Psalmen,* 1953 (Eng. *The Praise of God in the Psalms,* 1965); *idem,* "Struktur und Geschichte der Klage im Alten Testament," *ZAW,* LXVI (1954), 44-80; *idem,* "Vergegenwärtigung der Geschichte in den Psalmen," in *Kupisch-Festschrift,* 1963, pp. 253-80 (= *Forschung am Alten Testament,* 1964, pp. 306-35); *idem,* "Zur Sammlung des Psalters," *Theologia Viatorum* VII (1961/62), 278-84 (= *Forschung am Alten Testament,* 1964, pp. 336-43); J. W. WEVERS, "A Study in the Form Criticism of Individual Complaint Psalms," *VT,* VI (1956), 80-96; H. ZIRKER, *Die kultische Vergegenwärtigung der Vergangenheit in den Psalmen,* 1964.

1. *Distinguishing the literary types.* Gunkel's studies paved the way for an analysis of the psalms into literary types. Previously, scholars had attempted to classify them according to their content; Gunkel grouped them instead according to their formal characteristics. Apart from a few demurrers this approach has been generally accepted, although certain criticisms have been made on points of detail: aesthetic judgments in the realm of literary history, theories concerning the religious life of the psalmists, and ambiguities in stating the relationship between the psalms and the cult. As a result of these criticisms Gunkel's methodology has been corrected and modified (Mowinckel; commentaries of Kissane and Kraus). In particular, the problem of the relationship between the cult on the one hand and the psalm types and extant individual psalms on the other has been vehemently debated many times. Sometimes, scholars have assumed the existence of an all-inclusive cultic action to which all the psalms can be assigned, a view that has tended to replace historical or eschatological interpretation, which used to be more popular. This development began with Mowinckel's thesis of an Enthronement Festival of Yahweh (*Psalmenstudien,* II). This theory was generally seconded by H. Schmidt and extended further by the Scandinavian school, which places maximum emphasis on the cultic principle (e.g., Engnell, Ahlström). Weiser*, too, with his hypothetical Covenant Festival Cult, comes near to this position. Above all, the cult functional interpretation, first suggested by Mowinckel, takes as its point of departure the theory that the psalms not only derive form-critically from early cultic poetry, but are in fact with few exceptions true cultic psalms, composed

for the cult and used in it. This theory implies also that they were not composed for or on the basis of a single occasion, but for regular use. The laments of the individual, for example, actually represent cultic formularies; other psalms actualize for the cult the so-called *Heilsgeschichte* traditions of Israel.

Now we may consider proved the thesis that all the psalm types once had their *Sitz im Leben* in the cult. This does not mean, however, that we may assume an all-inclusive cultic action for all the types, but rather various cultic ceremonies. Neither should we presume that the psalm types continued to remain closely linked to the cultic actions; we must reckon with the possibility that they became dissociated and achieved independent existence. The use of the cultic hypothesis just stated as a basic and unique principle of interpretation is a biased exaggeration, which wrongly equates religion and cult.[1] Other interpretive possibilities are equally justified: derivation from a unique historical event, just as Psalm 137 recalls the events of the Exile; eschatological interpretation, which is certainly preferable to a cult-drama interpretation for the conclusion of Psalm 46 with its proclamation of an end to war; and reading as the personal statement of the poet, which Psalms 51 and 73 suggest. The psalms, too, reflect the variety of religious life through the course of the centuries.

In classifying the psalms into various literary types, the primary criteria are formal questions of literary style; the content of the psalms is utilized only when absolutely necessary. Some scholars speak of major categories such as Zion songs or Songs of Yahweh's Enthronement, but this approach wrongly places major emphasis on questions of content; both categories actually belong to the literary type of the hymnic song. Likewise, whether the songs refer to an individual or the people as a whole should be utilized only as a secondary criterion. From the formal point of view there turn out to be three great psalm types, each comprising several subsidiary categories:

a) Hymnic songs
b) Laments
c) Songs of thanksgiving.

We shall examine a fourth group in isolation, although the psalms belonging to it can be assigned to the psalm types just mentioned:

d) Royal songs

e) Wisdom poetry and didactic poetry must be considered forms of wisdom instruction rather than a psalm type.

In classifying the psalms, the question arises of whom the "I" of the psalms refers to. The collective interpretation, which had previously been popular, was first rejected by Gunkel and Balla in favor of an individual interpretation. Then, in support of the earlier view, scholars pointed once more to the frequent

[1] For a criticism of this approach, cf. especially K.-H. Bernhardt, *Das Problem der altorientalischen Königsideologie im Alten Testament*, 1961.

personification of a group by means of a collective or ideal person, or the king as the "incarnation" of society. Some went so far as to assign all the psalms to the royal ritual and term them originally royal psalms. Though this approach is exaggerated,[2] it remains true that the line between "collective" and "individual" was more fluid in the ancient Near East than it is today (cf. Ps. 129:1—" 'Sorely have they afflicted me . . . ,' let Israel now say"). In short, the "I" must be determined in each case from the total context of the psalm, though in the majority of the psalms the individual interpretation seems the most likely.

Furthermore, objections can be raised against other principles of classification. Westermann distinguishes between "descriptive praise" (hymn) and "narrative praise" (thanksgiving), the latter pertaining to the nation or an individual. As we shall see, however, both these categories have diverse form-critical roots; and the distinction between praise and thanksgiving appears clearly in the psalms. Kraus brings together songs of lament, thanksgiving, and confidence, for both the individual and the nation, on the grounds that though formally distinct they point to a common *Sitz im Leben*. This is historically accurate, but in the OT these psalm types have long gone their separate ways and must be examined independently. Ahlström would prefer to classify the psalm types according to the terms occurring in the superscriptions of the psalms (e.g., *lamᵉnaṣṣēaḥ, lᵉdāwīd*), as in Mesopotamian poetry. But the Mesopotamian superscriptions in fact do not refer to literary types; they classify the songs according to their musical setting or content (§ 38.1). In addition, in the OT the same terms introduce quite diverse songs, so that they are useless for purposes of classification.

2. *Hymnic songs*. In Israel, a hymn is a song praising the greatness and majesty of Yahweh in his creation and governance of the destiny of men and nations. The most important Hebrew term is *tᵉhillâ*, "praise, song of praise." It first designated only hymnic songs; later its use was extended and the plural came to be used as a name for the entire psalter. The *Sitz im Leben* of these songs is the cult; their nucleus is the ritual ejaculation *hallᵉlû-yāh*. They are therefore primarily cultic songs, composed for use in the cult. Psalms 98 and 150 accordingly mention the musical instruments that accompanied the singing of the songs. The chanting was done by the temple singers, sometimes divided between precentor and choir on the one hand and congregation on the other, sometimes according to tribes or other divisions. Besides these, there are other songs originally composed by devout individuals to express their religious experiences; they were employed secondarily in the cult. These may be called religious songs. Finally, the hymnic style invaded other song types and various rhetorical forms.

In the structure of the hymnic songs we may distinguish introduction, body, and conclusion:

a) The introduction exhibits for the most part imperatives to praise Yahweh

[2] Cf. the survey and criticism in Bernhardt, *op. cit.*

or jussive and cohortative summonses to sing his praises. Because of the cultic situation, these forms are mostly in the plural. The intended persons or groups can be addressed or named and instructed in the manner in which the song is to be performed. The so-called Enthronement Songs of Yahweh and the Zion songs exhibit characteristic introductory motifs.

b) The body is linked to the introduction by a motivating "For . . . ," apposition, or a relative clause. The body itself is characterized primarily by participial style. In content, it lists the glorious attributes and deeds of Yahweh, often anthropomorphically referring to the parts of his body, and describes his creative power and his guidance of Israel in the past and in the present. This narration (*sipper*) can at times approximate confession. In one special form of the body, the introduction overwhelms the entire song and itself becomes a hymn listing the creatures or musical instruments called upon to join in the praise.

c) The conclusion often employs the same elements as the introduction. It may, in addition, contain a prayer for the gracious acceptance of the song ("dedication"), an intercession, a curse, or a blessing.

The hymnic songs can be classified into four subcategories:

A. The largest subcategory comprises the hymns proper. They are intended for the diverse occasions when the family or community would want to praise their God: the great annual festivals, sacrifices, processions, and other cultic celebrations. We meet first those hymns that praise God for his actions in the lives of men and nations; this type can expand to include (noncultic) didactic historical poems (Psalms 78; 105–106). Gradually there come also hymns in praise of the creator, leading to the development of creation psalms (Psalms 8, 104).

B. The so-called enthronement psalms or psalms of Yahweh as king are characterized by the formula *yhwh mālak*. They include Psalms 47, 93, and 96–99. Their meaning has been much discussed.[3]

According to Mowinckel, H. Schmidt, and Volz, they are to be interpreted as songs sung in the temple at the annual celebration of Yahweh's enthronement or at the New Year's festival, when this enthronement was celebrated. According to this view, they are related especially closely to Babylonian or Canaanite concepts. These scholars claim that Israel celebrated the constant renewal of Yahweh's first enthronement after his victory over the chaos monster and on New Year's Day represented dramatically the creation of the world as the great event of *Heilsgeschichte:* year after year Yahweh renews the struggle against his enemies, conquers them, and guarantees thereby the continued stability of the world. In opposition to this theory, the apparently eschatological nature of the songs has been pointed out (Gunkel), as well as the fact that only

[3] Cf. L. Köhler, "*Jahwäh mālak,*" *VT,* III (1953), 188-89; D. Michel, "Studien zu den sogennanten Thronbesteigungspsalmen," *ibid.,* VI (1956), 40-68; J. Morgenstern, "The Cultic Setting of the 'Enthronement Psalms'," *HUCA,* XXXV (1964), 1-42; L. I. Pap, *Das israelitische Neujahrsfest,* 1933; J. Ridderbos, "Jahwäh malak," *VT,* IV (1954), 87-89; N. H. Snaith, *The Jewish New Year Festival,* 1947.

from 604 B.C. on is there evidence for the existence of a parallel Babylonian festival (Snaith). In addition, the formula mentioned has been studied in detail. Köhler has pointed out that the word order (subject—predicate) differs from the usual word order in a sentence, emphasizing the subject. Michel has defined the meaning of the verb more precisely, showing that it means not "become king," but rather "be king" and especially "reign as king."

According to these studies, the formula should be translated "It is Yahweh [and no other god] that reigns as king." Now the royal title,[4] for which the earliest literary evidence is Isaiah 6, was probably applied to Yahweh since the building of the Solomonic temple; at that time it became an additional name, besides "Yahweh Sabaoth," for the God of the ark, to express his dominion over Israel. Yahweh's unique position in the world is also described in Ps. 47:3, 8 (Eng. 47:2, 7) by means of the title "(great) king of all the earth"; this title draws upon two ancient Near Eastern royal titles: "great king" (*šarru rabū*) and "king of the universe" (*šar kiššati*). Just as in the ancient Near East there is only one such king, the king of Assyria (and, in the period when these psalms came into being, the ruler of Persia), so there can be only one such God. After a few hints in Jeremiah, we first find this emphasis on the uniqueness of Yahweh stated explicitly by Deutero-Isaiah (cf. Isa. 44:6; 45:5). The psalms in question are therefore largely dependent on Deutero-Isaiah's message, notwithstanding the earlier application of the royal title to Yahweh. Everything is derived from Yahweh and snatched from the power of other gods: the creation and preservation of the world, Yahweh's universal dominion over all nations, the definition of a criterion of ethical order, and the protection of those that hold to it. The songs of Yahweh as king are not connected with the concept of an enthronement of Yahweh or with a festival; they proclaim his sole dominion. It is therefore best to term them monotheistic hymns, which may have been preceded by songs like Psalm 82, which is formally constructed as a forensic attack upon the other gods on the part of Yahweh.

C. A third subcategory comprises the Zion songs (Psalms 46, 48, 76, 84, 87, 122).[5] These praise the magnificence of Zion with its sanctuary, usually in connection with the greatness of Yahweh. Since they employ not a few ancient mythological motifs, many scholars have derived these traditions from a Jerusalemite cult tradition, dating the Zion songs from the early preexilic period; such derivation, however, is an error. Only from the time of the Exile on do we find this large-scale use of such motifs, which had long enjoyed an underground existence. The motif of the battle with the nations does not belong with the others; its origin is quite late. In short, the Zion songs cannot

[4] On the royal title of Yahweh, cf. especially A. Alt, "Gedanken über das Königtum Jahwes," in *Kleine Schriften,* I (1953), 345-57; O. Eissfeldt, "Jahwe als König," *ZAW,* XLVI (1928), 81-105; W. Schmidt, *Königtum Gottes in Ugarit und Israel,* 2nd ed., 1966.

[5] G. Wanke, *Die Zionstheologie der Korachiten in ihrem traditionsgeschichtlichen Zusammenhang,* 1966.

have been composed before the postexilic period, perhaps by the guild of Korahite singers.[6]

D. The pilgrimage songs, such as Psalms 15 and 24, were composed for a specific cultic situation: a visit to the sanctuary, a procession about Jerusalem, entry into the temple, or a procession about the altar. Some of them stress the shared experience in worship of longing for the sanctuary and joy in the nearness to God experienced there, so that they may reflect a deeply personal piety.

3. *Lament*. Next to hymns, the most frequent type of psalm in the Psalter is the lament. The original term for this type of song was probably *tᵉḥinnâ*. Their *Sitz im Leben* is once more the cult, their nucleus a cultic appeal, perhaps *ḥonnēnî yhwh*, "Have mercy on me, Yahweh." We are therefore dealing primarily with cultic laments, as is especially clear in the case of the communal laments. Lament and petition on the part of the community played an important role both in ceremonies of lamentation for times of special need (cf. I Kings 8:33-40; 21:9-12; Jer. 36:1-10), the course of which is suggested particularly by the book of Joel,[7] and on some of the regularly recurring annual festivals (Day of Atonement, New Year's Festival, days of penitence to commemorate catastrophes). The cultic roots of some of the individual laments are likewise clearly discernible. It is certainly incorrect to consider all these songs purely cultic, recited as part of a ritual (Mowinckel, H. Schmidt); many phrases seem to have metaphorical rather than realistic significance. But even in these cases—e.g., Ps. 51:9 (Eng. 51:7): "Purge me with hyssop!"—they presuppose the original existence of a ceremony. Finally, the laments suggest cultic use when their purpose is to obtain a divine oracle by lot or from a priest or cult prophet (such an oracle is preserved in Ps. 60:8-10 [Eng. 60:6-8]).

Besides these, many laments of the individual without reference to the cult seem to have been composed following the fixed pattern of the literary type as religious or devotional songs of devout individuals, especially when the situation presupposed is the domestic sickbed. Eissfeldt * correctly states that songs like Psalms 39, 51, and 130 are so personal in tone and profound in content that they must have been more than mere texts to accompany cultic ceremonies; such an origin is also most unlikely for the acrostic Psalm 25. There is no hint, however, of a developmental tendency; religious poetry made its appearance very early and continued to exist alongside cultic poetry.

Finally, we encounter formal imitations of laments, especially on the part of the prophets. The communal lament is echoed, for example, in Jer. 3:21-25; 14:7-9, 19-22; Hos. 6:1-3; 14:3*b*-4 (Eng. 14:2*b*-3); the lament of the individual is found in the confession-like laments of Jeremiah and in the book of Job. Not a few of these imitations follow the lament proper with a reply from Yahweh promising or refusing forgiveness and aid, conditionally or

[6] Other songs, like Psalms 122 and 134, in which the Jerusalem Temple plays an important role, are difficult to date. It is not impossible that Psalm 134 originated in the late preexilic period. During the Exile, too, as Ps. 137:3 shows, songs were composed on the theme of yearning for Zion.

[7] Cf. also H. W. Wolff, "Der Aufruf zur Volksklage," *ZAW*, LXXVI (1964), 48-56.

unconditionally. This corresponds to the oracle following the cultic lament, so that the original form is still preserved by the imitations.

In structure, the lament exhibits a series of typical characteristics:

a) The introduction usually begins with an invocation of God, often elaborated with various epithets; there follows a cry for help, a petition, or a reproachful question. Sometimes the song at the same time expresses confidence in Yahweh (Ps. 25:2), a motif that could be developed independently in a song of confidence.

b) Following the transition, the body may contain the following elements: an account of the distress in the form of lament (illness, legal accusation, persecution, desolation, etc.), interspersed with questions asking God "How?" and "How long?" and with attacks upon enemies, real or supposed; petitions for God's favor and aid, perhaps associated with requests or imprecations; reference to reasons for Yahweh's intervention (recollection of previous aid, appeal to Yahweh's honor, loss of a worshiper through death), as well as protestations of innocence and the motif of confidence; the vow of a thank-offering or song of thanksgiving, which at times even appears at the conclusion of the lament.

c) The conclusion frequently contains an expression of confidence that the request will be granted or a thanksgiving to Yahweh. The transition from despair to confidence, from fear to thanksgiving, takes place so suddenly and abruptly that the final verses have often been considered a later addition or a separate appended psalm. The situation is not the same in all cases; the optimistic conclusion can have three possible origins: (1) The thanksgiving verses look back upon aid that has already been granted; they were spoken on a later occasion, possibly at the thank offering, and transmitted along with the lament, e.g., Psalm 22. (2) Sometimes they express the confidence that comes to the speaker in the course of the lament and petition, e.g., Psalm 13. (3) Finally, we may assume that the lament was answered by an oracle, after which, if it was favorable, the worshiper at once expressed thanksgiving, e.g., Psalm 6. Since the oracle usually could not be transmitted along with the lament in liturgical use, as it might differ completely from case to case, many laments now contain a lacuna.

Following these considerations, we may outline the form of the as yet undifferentiated song types as follows:

Lament and petition (introduction and body of the present songs of lament);
Oracle, followed (if favorable) by
Song of thanksgiving.

The laments fall into three subcategories:

A. The communal lament, apart from prophetical imitations, remained almost always linked to the cult.

B. The lament of the individual, in accordance with its originally cultic character, can refer to two kinds of need and distress: (1) Since the sanctuary was a place where one might seek healing for illnesses and its priests were often thought to command healing powers, the psalms of illness arose. Since illness was considered a punishment for sin, they are at the same time penitential psalms, filled with acknowledgment of guilt, e.g., Psalms 6. (2) Since litigants also sought equitable judgment at the sanctuary, particularly in difficult cases or when the facts were unclear, seeking to obtain God's decision by oracle, there came into being the psalms of the accused (H. Schmidt), containing petitions for aid against hostile accusers and filled with protestations of innocence and integrity, and therefore psalms of innocence, e.g., Psalm 27 B.

The problem of the identity of the enemies of the individual in the psalms has had very diverse solutions proposed. The earlier derivation from the party structure of early Judaism has of course been completely dropped. Nicolsky and others, following Mowinckel's suggestion, have interpreted the enemies as magicians and sorcerers thought to be responsible for the illness of the worshiper. Birkeland, who considers that the laments were originally royal songs, has suggested interpreting the enemies as foreigners.[8] These interpretations, however, are possible only in isolated instances and cannot be generally valid. We are instead for the most part dealing with personal enmity of the kind that is not exactly uncommon in everyday life. At the same time, those attacked are always identified with the righteous and their enemies with the wicked. In addition, the "virtue of poverty" plays a significant role, contrasting the poor-humble-devout with the impious enemy.[9]

C. The motif of confidence, found in the introduction or body, took on independent existence in the song of confidence, which may be put in the mouth of the people (Psalms 125, 129) or the individual (Psalms 11, 16, 23).

4. *Thanksgiving.* We also find songs of thanksgiving, both of the people and of the individual. Like the thank offering, they are termed *tôdâ*. This in itself points to a cultic *Sitz im Leben,* an observation confirmed by other phrases referring to the sacrificial cult (Ps. 66:13) and by the votive stele of Yehawmelek, king of Byblos, which depicts him before the goddess Baalat with a libation bowl in his hand (cf. Ps. 116:13). As we saw in our examination of the lament, one root of the thanksgiving song is to be found in the thanksgiving pronounced in the sanctuary immediately upon receiving a favorable oracle. A second root lies in the presentation of a thank offering in performance of a vow after an actual improvement in circumstances. Besides the thank-offering song and the cultic song of thanksgiving, there is also a religious thanksgiving song divorced from the cult, in which the thanksgiving itself replaces the thank-offering.

In the structure of the thanksgiving songs we may note the following points:

[8] H. Birkeland, *Die Feinde des Individuums in der israelitischen Psalmenliteratur,* 1933; *idem, The Evildoers in the Book of Psalms,* 1955; cf. also G. Marschall, *Die "Gottlosen" des ersten Psalmenbuches,* 1929; A. F. Puukko, "Der Feind in den alttestamentlichen Psalmen," *OTS,* VIII (1950), 47-65; N. H. Ridderbos, *De "werkers der ongerechtigheid" in de individueele Psalmen,* 1939.

[9] Cf. generally J. Maier, *Die Texte vom Toten Meer,* II (1960), 83-87.

a) In the introduction, the worshiper states his purpose, frequently employing hymnic motifs.

b) Following references to the place and purpose of the song (in the great congregation, to instruct all nations), the body consists primarily of a narrative interwoven with expressions of confidence and confession, in which the connection with the lament of the individual can be clearly seen: description of the earlier need, the subsequent invocation of God and deliverance through him, by reason of which the worshiper confesses his faith in him. As in the songs of lament, the need can be depicted in two ways: brought about through the sin of the worshiper, which God has forgiven ("positive confession"), or through the wickedness of enemies, from which God has freed the innocent ("negative confession"). In connection with the narrative didactic elements often appear, rooted in the experience of Yahweh's aid: the worshiper seeks to express his thanksgiving by attempting to bring others to the same experience. In this way the forms of wisdom instruction penetrated into the Psalter, so that many thanksgiving songs are practically didactic poems (Psalms 32, 73).

c) As in the hymn, the conclusion recalls the praises of the introduction.

Formally and stylistically the thanksgiving songs are in many cases freer and less conventional than the other literary types; their language is sometimes far from exalted poetry. Such songs were certainly not composed by professional temple poets or singers, and could not have been claimed as cultic formularies. They probably come from persons that composed a song as a good and pleasing act, to accompany their thank offering.

We can distinguish two subcategories of thanksgiving song:

A. The communal thanksgiving song is very rare, because the community could express its thanksgiving in hymns, praising Yahweh for his mighty acts on Israel's behalf. In Psalm 136, for example, the first part of each verse contains a summons to thanksgiving or mentions an act of Yahweh; the second part contains the regular response "His steadfast love endures for ever!"

B. The thanksgiving song of the individual may involve positive or negative confession. Psalm 107 is a song of this type for a thanksgiving ceremony of four groups of persons; each group is called upon to give thanks for deliverance from its need (being lost in the desert, imprisonment, illness, peril at sea) and does so in its own verse.

5. *Royal songs*. The royal songs that have been preserved are religious and cultic in nature and can be assigned to the various literary types already mentioned. They deserve separate discussion, however, because they exhibit characteristic OT features. One portion of these songs, some of which probably belonged originally to the ritual of the King's enthronement, takes as its point of departure hymnic praise of Yahweh's power, from which the subordinate power of the king derives. The oracle form plays a significant role here. Psalm 2, for example, spoken by a king at his enthronement, refers to an oracle received from Yahweh. Psalm 110 mentions an oracle (or three oracles) delivered by a cult prophet for the king. Psalm 45 is an oracle of blessing on the occasion of a royal marriage. In Psalm 101, the king outlines the principles by which

he will rule; Psalm 72 contains a petition for a blessing upon the king. Psalm 21 may have been sung at an annual commemorative festival, Psalm 132 on the anniversary of the founding of the royal sanctuary at Jerusalem, emphasizing the close ties between the ruling dynasty and the temple. Another portion of the royal songs are laments or thanksgivings. Psalm 44 prays for divine aid in a coming war; Psalms 20 and 144 contain similar prayers. Psalm 89 B reproaches God for a military defeat; Psalm 18 B gives thanks for a victory.

In number these songs constitute a tiny fraction of the poetry that has been preserved, despite the four centuries of the monarchy. Although this is due in part to later selection, which eliminated quite a bit in the postmonarchic period and which meant impoverishment as well as uniformity, it is also due in large measure to the faith of the OT, in which Yahweh occupies the decisive position, and in whose cult the sacral ruler is less important than the people or the congregation worshiping before Yahweh. Despite the dependence of the royal songs on the oriental court style, with its emphasis on world dominion (adoption, election, legitimation, and guidance of the king by the deity; proclamation of a period of blessing and prosperity; permanence, righteousness, and victory), they remain securely rooted in Yahwism. Not the king, but God, stands in the foreground. There were apparently no songs glorifying the king, nor did the king boast of his own renown. By the same token, the royal songs in the cult speak less of the king's might and his accomplishments than of God's promises to him, the petitions he addresses to God, and the things for which he gives thanks to God.

6. *Other forms.* Other forms, most of which are found within individual psalms, belong to the sphere of the priests and cult prophets. In the entrance liturgies of Psalms 15 and 24, priestly torah outlines the requirements that must be met by those who visit the sanctuary; Psalm 132 proclaims the demands God makes upon the royal house. Psalm 134:3 contains a priestly blessing formula. In the case of oracles, it must often remain a moot question whether they derive from priests or cult prophets. Those in Psalms 2 and 110 probably come from cult prophets; in Psalm 81, too, we seem to hear a cult prophet.

Furthermore, the forms of wisdom literature have exerted some influence, producing wisdom poems and didactic poems. These will be discussed in § 47.5. They are not the product of the cult nor are they intended for cultic use, but are completely personal devotional poems from the postexilic period, in which wisdom instruction and devotion to the law frequently intermingle. It is uncertain whether the alphabetic form of some songs also derives from the influence of wisdom literature. This form has not turned up elsewhere in the ancient Near East, but does appear in Greek, Hellenistic, and Roman poetry, so that the cultured wisdom teachers may have borrowed it from this source.[10] These songs, of which Psalm 119 is an example, are meant to demonstrate the skill

[10] M. Löhr, "Alphabetische und alphabetisierende Lieder im Alten Testament," *ZAW*, XXV (1905), 173-98; R. Marcus, "Alphabetic Acrostics in the Hellenistic and Roman Periods," *JNES*, VI (1947), 109-15; P. A. Munch, "Die alphabetische Akrostichie in der jüdischen Psalmendichtung," *ZDMG*, XC (1936), 703-10.

of the writer, furnish a mnemonic device for the learner, and possibly express the idea of totality ("from A to Z"), although the requirements of the form interfere with logical progression and produce a disconnected effect. In these songs the initial letters of the verses or strophes follow the sequence of the Hebrew alphabet. The method varies in detail. Each verse can begin with a new letter (e.g., Psalms 25, 34, 111, 112), to be followed in some cases by one or more verses falling outside the pattern (e.g., Psalms 9/10, 37; Lamentations 1, 2, 4); or several verses may begin with the same letter (Psalm 119; Lamentations 3). Alphabetizing songs exhibit the same number of verses as the alphabet has letters (Psalms 33, 103; Lamentations 5).

Finally, we come to mixed types and the construction of liturgies. The former occur when a poetic type is expanded by the addition of elements drawn from a different type. For example, the introduction of a lament may have hymnic character or the element of the vow may already incorporate the thanksgiving. The influence of wisdom literature may lead to a complete transformation. A liturgy, by contrast, results from the linking of several literary types to form a larger composition, probably recited by several speakers or singers in a specific cultic situation. Each literary type is used in a fashion appropriate to its *Sitz im Leben*. Examples include entrance liturgies (Psalms 15 and 24) and thanksgiving songs (Psalms 66 and 107). Cult prophets also appear to have composed such liturgies, to be recited in the cult by themselves or by others. Examples include Isaiah 24–27, 33; Mic. 7:8-20; Habakkuk; and Joel. In addition, other prophets imitated such liturgies for their own purposes, as in Jer. 14:2–15:2; Hos. 5:15–6:6; 14:2-9. The litany, common in Babylonian psalms, with its frequent repetition of the same response by the congregation, is found in Psalm 136.[11]

7. *Psalms in other books of the OT*. Other books of the OT have incorporated individual psalms already extant as finished songs, using them at suitable places, e.g., Exod. 15:1-19; Deuteronomy 32; I Sam. 2:1-10; Isa. 38:10-20. It is true that their original significance was not always observed, as when Jonah in the belly of the sea monster is made to sing a thanksgiving song before his deliverance (Jonah 2:3-10 [Eng. 2:2-9]). The liturgies of the cult prophets, on the other hand, are genuinely fresh compositions. Even in the late period psalms continued to be written and songs were composed; the literary types themselves underwent further development.[12] This is shown by such evidence as the hymns from Qumran (1QH) and the book of the Psalms of Solomon.

The influence of the psalm types upon prophetical imitations of the songtypes or individual portions of them will be discussed when the prophets are examined in detail.

Finally, the stylistic influence of these songs can be seen in other passages. They have influenced the prayers found in prose literature, for example,

[11] Cf. also J. Obermann, "An Antiphonal Psalm from Ras Shamra," *JBL*, LV (1936), 21-44.

[12] G. Morawe, "Vergleich des Aufbaus der Danklieder und hymnischen Bekenntnislieder (1QH) von Qumran mit dem Aufbau der Psalmen im Alten Testament und im Spätjudentum," *RdQ*, IV (1963/64), 323-56.

Solomon's prayer at the dedication of the temple (I Kings 8), the confessions of sin in Ezra 9 and Nehemiah 9, and the penitential prayer in Daniel 9. In similar fashion certain formal elements, especially of the hymn and lament, enter into wisdom literature, for example in Proverbs 8, the book of Job, and Ecclesiasticus 24.

§ 40 The Song Types of Everyday Life and Their Traditions

K. Budde, "Das Volkslied Israels im Munde der Propheten," *PJ*, LXXIII (1893), 460-83; A. Causse, "Les origines de la poésie hébraïque," *RHPhR*, IV (1924), 393-419; V (1925), 1-28; M. E. Chase, *Life and Language in the Old Testament*, 1956; M. Cramer, *Die Totenklage bei den Kopten*, 1941; G. Gerleman, "Die Bildsprache des Hohenliedes und die altägyptische Kunst," *ASTI*, I (1962), 24-30; W. Herrmann, "Gedanken zur Geschichte des altorientalischen Beschreibungsliedes," *ZAW*, LXXV (1963), 176-97; F. Horst, "Die Formen des althebräischen Liebesliedes," in *Littmann-Festschrift*, 1935, pp. 43-54 (= *Gottes Recht*, 1961, pp. 176-87); H. Jahnow, *Das hebräische Leichenlied im Rahmen der Völkerdichtung*, 1923; P. Kahle, "Die Totenklage im heutigen Ägypten," in *Gunkel-Festschrift*, I (1923), 346-99; E. Littmann, *Abessinische Klagelieder*, 1949; P. Lohmann, *Die anonymen Prophetien gegen Babel aus der Zeit des Exils*, Dissertation, Rostock, 1910; *idem*, "Das Wächterlied Jes 21,11.12," *ZAW*, XXXIII (1913), 20-29; E. Lüddeckens, *Untersuchungen über religiösen Gehalt, Sprache und Form der ägyptischen Totenklagen*, 1943; H. W. Robinson, *The Poetry of the Old Testament*, 1947; G. A. Smith, *The Early Poetry of Israel in its Physical and Social Origins*, 4th ed., 1913 (reprinted 1927).

1. *Work song, harvest song, vintage song, watchman's song.* The earliest work songs come from ancient Egypt. The Song of the Well in Num. 21:17-18 appears to be such a song, sung while the tribal leaders dug a well on the steppe or in the desert. The scepter and staff represent symbols of power; the song is rooted in the idea that the poetic word is filled with a power that is frankly magical. It is therefore in fact an incantation pronounced by a man of God. Neh. 4:4 (Eng. 4:10) contains a lamenting work song that could almost be called a strike song, resembling the appeal of the oppressed that comes before Yahweh. The singing of work songs was common, although they have not been preserved. Jesus ben Sirach heard a farmer singing while plowing, but considered himself superior to such imprudent behavior (Ecclus. 38:25).

There were also harvest songs and vintage songs. The joyful shout *hêdād* during the bringing in of the harvest and the treading of the grapes may preserve the Hebrew term for such songs, but it may also have been a kind of incantation (cf. Ps. 65:14). Apart from the dominant mood of joy—"as with joy at the harvest" (Isa. 9:2) is practically a proverbial expression—harvest festivals were celebrated that were strongly influenced by Canaanite concepts and practices (cf. Judg. 9:27). The shout *hêdād* probably points to this fertility religion. For this very reason, none of the ancient harvest and vintage songs have been preserved; they were too strongly stamped with the mark of their

Canaanite origin and too little permeated by Yahwism. In their place we find a few songs of thanksgiving dedicated to Yahweh the giver (Psalms 65, 67).

Song of Sol. 3:3; 5:7 mentions the night watchman who kept watch in Israelite towns. Isa. 12:12 points to his song as a literary type. Here, of course, we are not dealing with a song sung regularly, but with an evasive answer to the question of how late it is.

2. *Drinking song*. The drinking songs sung at revels can also touch upon the religious sphere, as prophetical polemic (Isa. 5:11-13; Amos 6:4-6) shows, castigating self-confident disregard for Yahweh and oppression of the poor. Such songs, or better aphorisms, are cited in Isa. 22:13 and 56:12; both passages illustrate clearly the negative relationship to the demands of Yahwism.

3. *Taunt song*. The taunt song is often termed a *māšāl*, an efficacious verbal formula. Considered as a kind of incantation or imprecation, it could produce a powerful effect in the ancient world. It occurs in several forms.

A. It may refer to a particular individual; the only extant example, Isa. 23:15-16, taunts the forgotten harlot.

B. It usually refers to other tribes, cities, or nations. In it we hear scornful contempt for and imprecations upon the enemy, coupled with support of the singer's own interests. It can be understood as a political weapon and compared to journalistic propaganda (Eissfeldt*), but the undercurrent of magico-religious imprecation must not be ignored. Num. 21:14-15 is probably a fragment of a taunt song meant to list the territories won from the enemy. Num. 21:27-30 now refers to the victory of Sihon, king of the Amorites, over a king of Moab, but probably goes back originally to a victory of Israel over Moab. As the Song of Deborah shows, with its mockery of the tribes that did not join in the battle and its description of the contrast between the expectations of the mother of Sisera, the Canaanite general, and his pitiful death (Judg. 5:15-17; 28-30), victory songs can borrow motifs from taunt songs. Wisdom literature, too, has made use of such material, as in Isa. 44:12-20, which mocks idols together with those that manufacture and worship them.

C. The prophets give taunt songs a new function by referring to future events depicted in a taunt song as having already taken place. A typical example is the song about Babylon in Isaiah 47. For the most part, however, the prophets substitute threats against foreign nations for taunt poetry. Sometimes, as in the case of Nahum, this is done in the context of favorable oracles, so that proclamation of salvation for Israel is linked with the threat, which thereby serves the purposes of foreign policy. At other times, as in the case of Amos, Israel is included in the threat, so that the prophet bears witness to the universal majesty of God.

4. *Love song and epithalamium*. In Israel, the fall was the major time for love songs and epithalamia. Weddings usually took place after the harvest; then could be heard the "voice of the bridegroom and the voice of the bride," the shrill cries of the dancing women, and the monotonous rhythm of the drums. Such songs might be simple popular poetry or high poetic art; the Song of Solomon comprises a whole collection.

One should not be too quick to call these songs secular. In Psalm 45, the prophetical introduction and style, the religious terms in which the king is described, and the blessing all show that we are dealing with a cultic song recited by a cult prophet at the marriage of a ruler. Furthermore, several scholars have pointed out the similarities between these love songs and epithalamia and those supposed to have been sung during the ritual of the marriage of gods or the divine marriage of the sacral king.[1] There are two explanations for such similarities: On the one hand, the cultic songs depended on the style and vocabulary of the other love songs and epithalamia, and of course may have influenced them in turn; on the other, both kinds of song derived from one and the same situation. Materials borrowed by Israel from alien religions, however, were revised by being secularized.

Detailed examination reveals various minor literary types, which, with one exception, we need only list, following the analysis of Horst: song of admiration, e.g., Song of Sol. 1:9-11; comparison and allegory, e.g., 1:13-14; 6:2; song of description, e.g., 4:1-7; self-portrayal, e.g., 1:5-6; boasting song, e.g., 6:8-9; jesting dialogue, e.g., 1:7-8; description of an experience, e.g., 2:8-9; and song of longing, 2:4-5. The song of description has a long history, which Herrmann has sketched from the Sumerian period down to the description of Sarah in the Genesis Apocryphon from Qumran, and which continues on into the Arab period. Furthermore, Gerleman has shown that such descriptions began with the description of three-dimensional figures from the plastic art of Egypt, primarily images of gods. The descriptions in the Song of Solomon still show clear traces of this origin.

Portrayals of misfortune in love constitute the antithesis to these songs. We find such descriptions in the indicting parable of the disappointed man in Isa. 5:1-7 and the drastic allegories in Ezekiel 16 and 23, imitations of the original literary type.

5. *War song and victory song.* War songs and victory songs constitute a not insignificant portion of Israelite poetry. Apart from the victory song proper, analysis reveals several forms that are associated with war and battle.

A. Josh. 10:12 contains a remnant of an incantation. We read that almost by magic the leader of the host commanded sun and moon to stand still so that the Israelites might carry on the battle until the enemy were completely destroyed. The invocation of the banner of Yahweh (Exod. 17:16), whose power in war is called upon against the Amalekites, and Elisha's exclamation after the arrow shot by King Joash (II Kings 13:17) are to be interpreted similarly.

B. The *Sitz im Leben* of songs of blessing and cursing before battle is best illustrated by the Balaam narrative (Numbers 22–24). A man of God filled with divine power is called upon to bless his own side and curse the enemy

[1] H. Ringgren, "Hohes Lied und hieros gamos," *ZAW*, LXV (1953), 300-302; H. Schmökel, "Zur kultischen Deutung des Hohenliedes," *ibid.*, LXIV (1952), 148-55; *idem, Heilige Hochzeit und Hoheslied*, 1956; W. Wittekindt, *Das Hohe Lied und seine Beziehungen zum Istarkult*, 1927.

in order to guarantee the outcome of the contest. A similar purpose lay behind the curse songs or curses called down upon the enemy by a warrior like Goliath before single combat and the shouts of the attacking army, intended to be powerful cries effectively increasing their own strength and weakening that of the enemy. The semimagical use of mockery also belongs in this category.

C. The exciting war song proper had the same function as the later marches. Judg. 5:12 refers to such a song; Isa. 51:9-10 contains a prophetical imitation.

D. A victory song was frequently sung by the women upon the return of the victorious army or at a separate victory celebration, accompanied by music and dancing; we may see examples in Exod. 15:20-21; Judg. 11:34; I Sam. 18:6-7. The songs are very short, consisting of one or two long verses repeated alternately by the women in two groups. At the victory celebration of the Philistines, too, after their capture of Samson, a similar song with rhyming endings (Judg. 16:23-25) was sung. Outstanding in its dramatic vitality is the Song of Deborah (Judges 5), which, despite its subject, should not simply be dismissed as being secular (§ 31.3).

6. *Dirge*. The Hebrew term for "dirge" is *qînâ* or *nehî;* its *Sitz im Leben* is the house of mourning, where it was sung by the family and friends of the dead person or by professional mourners, invariably women, to the accompaniment of the flute. It can usually be recognized by its introductory *'êk* or *'êkâ*, "Ah, how. . . ." Lament for the dead constitutes a part of the obligatory mourning ritual; anyone neglecting this lament exposes himself to slander. Therefore the demand that Jeremiah and Ezekiel refrain from mourning (Jer. 16:5; Ezek. 24:15-24) is a harsh command, and the statement to someone living that none will lament him (Jer. 22:18-19) is a terrible threat.

In the dirge the secular world of everyday life once more comes in contact with religion and cult. In the first place, lament for the dead originally constituted a part of the cult of the dead, from which the professional status of the mourning women derives. These women must learn and teach the funeral songs (in Jer. 9:19-21 [Eng. 9:20-22] the prophet performs this function). The sarcophagus of King Ahiram of Byblos (*ca.* 1200 B.C.) depicts them striking their breasts and tearing their hair. There are many additional practices, including funeral dancing, funerary gifts, and the placing of food and drink in the tomb. In addition, the cultic origin of the funeral lament is further illustrated by the lament for the vegetation god, dead or hidden in the underworld. In Jeremiah's threat against Jehoiakim (Jer. 22:18-19), we find the inappropriate exclamation "Ah sister!" and according to the LXX Jeroboam's child is lamented with the phrase "Alas, lord" (I Kings 12:24m). These formulas still point to the lament for the divine lord, bewailed by his sister and beloved; there were at the same time appropriate exclamations and laments for her, as she went into the underworld. In the vegetation cults the gods are lamented like human beings. The separate existence of a noncultic dirge, independent of the dirge sung for the gods, has been demonstrated by Lüddeckens for the Egyptian Middle Kingdom and New Kingdom, and by Kahle for the more recent period.

Thus the stylistic forms and expressions of the Israelite dirge are rooted for the most part—though not exclusively—in the ancient Near Eastern dirge for the gods and cult of the dead. Yahwism, of course, had no place for either. Therefore the form and content of the borrowed dirges were largely secularized and separated from the cult, coming instead to express human emotions—love and hate, honor and mockery.

A. The form that remained closest to its original significance is the personal dirge following the death of a particular individual. Two such songs, rightly ascribed to David, are those upon the death of Saul and Jonathan (II Sam. 1:19-27) and of Abner (II Sam. 3:33-34). The former is a poetic masterpiece, and at the same time deeply emotional. The curse upon the battlefield (vs. 21) is of religious nature, while the phrase "my brother," with which Jonathan is addressed, accurately reflects the friendship between him and David despite its formulaic quality. The euphemistic vs. 23 is conventional.

B. The collective dirge refers to tribes, cities, or nations, whose downfall it echoes. It is best exemplified, though not in pure form, in a few passages from the book of Lamentations, which bewail the "death" of Jerusalem, portrayed as a woman, following its destruction by the Babylonians.

C. The prophetical dirge, too, refers generally to the community. It does not, however, bewail a real death and destruction, but rather death and destruction to come, which are portrayed as having already come to pass. This is true, for example, of Amos' lament for the virgin Israel (Amos 5:1-3). In this way the prophet intensified his threat of disaster: it is so sure to take place that its results can already be mourned.

A frequently employed variety is the mocking prophetical dirge, usually directed against a foreign power; the announcement of its imminent downfall awakes not pity or sadness, but derision and joyful satisfaction. Here we have a connection between dirge and taunt song, so that Isa. 14:4-21—unquestionably the most impressive example of this literary type, directed against a foreign ruler[2]—can be called a *māšāl,* a taunt song. Besides Nah. 3:18-19, against Assyria, the book of Ezekiel contains numerous examples of this sort: 26:15-18; 27; 28:11-19 (against Tyre); 31; 32:1-8, 17-32 (against Egypt); and 19:1-9, 10-14 (against Zedekiah, the king of Judah).

Finally the style of the dirge has affected the form of the oracle concerning the Servant of Yahweh in Isa. 52:13–53:12. In this case, however, the content is completely reversed: the description of need and the death of the Servant provide the basis for the salvation that has been achieved through him.

7. *Connection with historical events.* Some of the songs mentioned, like the Song of Deborah and the lamentations on the destruction of Jerusalem, were from the very outset linked to specific historical events. They were handed down and preserved because of the significance of these events. Other songs, however, were only later interpreted as referring to such events (e.g., Exod. 17:16; Num. 21:14-15, 17-18, 27-30). This makes these songs more difficult to understand,

[2] G. Quell, "Jesaja 14,1-23," in *Baumgärtel-Festschrift,* 1959, pp. 131-57.

but we must remember that only this association led to their being preserved. In other cases they led to the preservation of a narrative that could be associated with them. A large part of early Israelite song has simply vanished. The existence of additional songs can be inferred from some of the superscriptions of the psalms or from analysis of the content of other books. Ezek. 16:1-43, for example, presupposes a song (or fairy tale) telling of the exposure and rescue of a child; 17:1-10 presupposes a song concerning an eagle and a cedar twig; 19:1-9, a song concerning a lion; and 19:10-14, a song concerning a grapevine.[3]

§ 41 The Characteristics of the Old Testament Literary Types

1. *Adaptation of foreign material.* Our survey of the song types has shown how they used foreign forms and material and how their history casts light on the characteristics of the songs found in the OT.

The process by which foreign material was appropriated and adapted may be summarized in four points. First, such material was rejected when it could not be incorporated into Yahwism. This holds true especially for the harvest songs and vintage songs associated with the Canaanite cults, as well as the songs in praise of the king, which were at variance with the central significance of Yahweh. Second, songs deriving from foreign cults were secularized. This category includes love song and epithalamium, to the extent that these derived their content from the ritual of the vegetation cults, and the dirge, to the extent that it was rooted in the dirge for the dead god and the cult of the dead. Third, Yahwism appropriated for its own purposes songs that were primarily secular, above all the victory song, which now sings of Yahweh's triumphs (Judg. 5:11; Heb. *ṣidqôt,* "acts of righteousness"). Fourth, material belonging to alien religions, especially when of magical origin, was adapted to Yahwism: the hymn, whose original purpose was to guarantee and actualize the victorious power of the deity, now declares the worship and honor of God; the lament, which leaves the realm of conjuration and apotropaic magic and signifies instead prayerful submission to God, pointing to fellowship with God as the only possibility for meaningful human existence; and the royal song, formerly a part of the ritual of the divine king, which now becomes an acknowledgment of God's sovereignty.

2. *Adaptation of foreign forms.* The adaptation of foreign forms may be summarized in two points. First, their inadequacy produces tensions, best illustrated by the hymn. Throughout the ancient Near East the hymn praises a deity by piling up laudatory epithets and by comparison with other gods. The hymnic style of Israel contains remnants of this comparison, e.g., in the question "Who is like Yahweh?" But there is tension between this form and others that do more justice to the uniqueness of Yahweh, such as Ps. 96:4-5. Second, alterations were made and new forms were created. Babylonian laments have as their goal a favorable oracle and therefore seek to flatter the deity by descriptions of his glory. In place of these descriptions, the OT substitutes the motif of sure trust

[3] C. Kuhl, *Ältere Materialien im Buche Hesekiel,* Habilitationsschrift, Berlin, 1939.

as the basis for confidence. In addition, this motif achieved independent status, giving rise to the song of confidence.

3. *Development within Israel.* There are four important observations to make concerning the development of these song types within Israel. First, the form itself was not always rigorously preserved. In consequence of the partial separation from the cult and the growing consciousness of the individual, a loosening process sets in that leads to less strict adherence to the formal structure or even its disintegration. This can be seen in mixed styles and literary types—for example, in the book of Lamentations and in alphabetic songs. Second, the treatment of meter varies. Initially, there is a tendency to limit the great freedom of earlier poetry and make the meter uniform within a given piece. This tendency reaches a climax in the late preexilic period; Nahum and Habakkuk are examples. In the postexilic period a reverse tendency sets in, leading to metrical confusion. Third, there was from early times a tendency to compose noncultic songs alongside the cultic songs of a particular literary type, so that both kinds develop together and exist side by side. This happened, for example, in the case of hymns, laments, and thanksgivings. The situation is somewhat different in the case of taunt songs and dirges, where collective songs come into being alongside the individual songs. Fourth, we may note that the prophetical movement adopted most of the song types, utilized them, and imitated them. This tendency parallels the separation from the cult and the composition of collective songs, so that the reasons for this development lie for the most part in the prophetical message, with its criticism of the dominant cult and its appeal to the people and the nations. The question of the uniqueness of Israelite poetry vis-à-vis that of the rest of the ancient Near East leads us therefore to the prophetical faith as the driving force that makes all religious statements refer to the God that guides the destiny of men and nations; that acknowledges his all-pervasive power, superior to all magic, cult, or human self-glorification; that demands obedient and submissive trust in this God, a trust that acknowledges his authority and seeks his fellowship. Therefore the history of Israelite poetry is intimately linked with the faith of the prophets, the only basis that provides a satisfactory explanation. The worship of the synagogue, beginning during the Exile, substituted verbal expression for cultic action, thereby aiding the process of deepening and spiritualization. Beside the cultic religion of the postexilic Temple, the way remained open for personal faith and devotion.

§ 42 Compilation and Transmission

1. *Compilation and transmission.* By its very nature, a song comes into being and is employed as an independent unit. Songs can be learned one at a time and transmitted in the same way by oral tradition. Practical considerations, however, soon lead to their being collected and written down. This is especially true of the cultic songs, which were assembled in songbooks, like those of the guilds of Asaph and Korah in the Psalter.

The collections, which are most accurately termed anthologies, seem to have incorporated songs of similar or identical content. This is suggested by the titles of the earliest collections, now no longer extant: the Book of the Wars of Yahweh, cited in Num. 21:14, obviously a collection of songs recounting the victories of Yahweh and Israel and the defeats of their enemies; and the Book of Jashar or Book of the Upright, cited in Josh. 10:13 and II Sam. 1:18, obviously a collection of songs telling of heroes in battle.[1] From the late period, II Chron. 35:25 mentions a collection of laments that contained, among other things, songs on the death of King Josiah. This collection cannot have been identical with our book of Lamentations, and is therefore also no longer extant. The principle of compiling songs of similar or identical content is amply attested, however, by the Song of Solomon and the book of Lamentations.

The repetition of the same song, in whole or in part, in the Song of Solomon leads us to the further observation that smaller collections were first assembled and later combined to form a large collection. This is especially true of the Psalter, which is composed of a whole series of collections, several of which can still be discerned. It is quite possible for the final collection to have a different significance and purpose than its components possessed. In the case of the Psalter, the placing of Psalm 1 at the beginning makes this clear (cf. § 43.5).

2. *Later songs or songbooks.* Later songs or songbooks, not incorporated in the OT, include the Prayer of Manasseh (an individual lament), the Prayer of Azariah (a community lament found among the additions to the book of Daniel), the Song of the Three Children (a mixture of thanksgiving and hymn, also among the additions to Daniel), the book of Baruch (a penitential prayer in the style of a community lament, a didactic poem, and a cycle of poems), the Psalms of Solomon (eighteen psalms, including hymns, laments, thanksgivings, and didactic poems), as well as the Thanksgiving Scroll (1QH) and similar collections of songs and prayers from Qumran.

[1] The LXX of I Kings 8:53 probably refers to the same book when it speaks of the Book of Song (*yšr* corrupted or misread to yield *šîr*).

CHAPTER TWO: THE SONGBOOKS

§ 43 The Psalter

ATD: A. Weiser, 6th ed., 1963 (Eng. 1962). BK: H.-J. Kraus, 2nd ed., 1962. COT: J. Ridderbos, 1955-58. HAT: H. Schmidt, 1934. HK: F. Baethgen, 3rd ed., 1904. H. Gunkel, 4th ed., 1926. HS: H. Herkenne, 1936. IB: W. S. McCullough and W. R. Taylor, 1955. ICC: C. A. and E. G. Briggs, 1906-1967 (reprinted 1951-52). KAT: R. Kittel, 5th and 6th ed., 1929. KeH: J. Olshausen, 1853. KHC: B. Duhm, 2nd ed., 1922. SAT: W. Staerk, 2nd ed., 1920. SZ: H. Kessler, 2nd ed., 1899. Individual commentaries: B. Bonkamp, 2nd ed., 1956; J. Calès, 6th ed., 1936; B. D. Eerdmans, 1947; E. J. Kissane, 1953-54 (Eng. 1964); E. König, 1927; E. A. Leslie, 1949; W. O. E. Oesterley, 4th ed., 1953; N. Peters, 1930; E. Podechard, 1949-54; F. Wutz, 1925.

A. Arens, *Die Psalmen im Gottesdienst des Alten Bundes*, 1961; E. Baumann, "Struktur-Untersuchungen im Psalter," *ZAW*, LXI (1949), 114-76; LXII (1950), 115-52; M. Bič, "Das erste Buch des Psalters, eine Thronbesteigungsfestliturgie," *Supplements to Numen*, IV (1958), 316-32; P. E. Bonnard, *Le Psautier selon Jérémie*, 1960; A. Büchler, "Zur Geschichte der Tempelmusik und der Tempelpsalmen," *ZAW*, XIX (1899), 96-133, 329-44; XX (1900), 97-135; M. J. Buss, "The Psalms of Asaph and Korah," *JBL*, LXXXII (1963), 382-92; M. Buttenwieser, *The Psalms, Chronologically Treated*, 1938; A. G. Clarke, *Analytical Studies in the Psalms*, 1949; L. Delekat, "Probleme der Psalmenüberschriften," *ZAW*, LXXVI (1964), 280-97; P. Drijvers, *Les Psaumes: genres littéraires et thémes doctrinaux*, 1958 (Eng. *The Psalms, Their Structure and Meaning*, 1965); B. D. Eerdmans, "Essays on Masoretic Psalms," *OTS*, I (1942), 105-300; W. E. Farndale, *The Psalms in New Light*, 1956; H. J. Franken, *The Mystical Communion with JHWH in the Book of Psalms*, 1954: A. Gelin, *Les Psaumes de Yahvé*, 1953; F. Giesebrecht, "Über die Abfassungszeit der Psalmen," *ZAW*, I (1881), 276-332; C. Hauret, "L'interprétation des Psaumes selon l'école 'Myth and Ritual'," *RSR*, XXXIII (1959), 321-42; XXXIV (1960), 1-34; S. Holm-Nielsen, "Den gammeltestamentige salmetradition," *DTT*, XVIII (1955), 135-48, 193-215; D. Michel, *Tempora und Satzstellung in den Psalmen*, 1960; H. Möller, "Strophenbau der Psalmen," *ZAW*, L (1932), 240-56; W. O. E. Oesterley, *A Fresh Approach to the Psalms*, 1937; J. Paterson, *The Praises of Israel*, 1950; H. Ringgren, *The Faith of the Psalmists*, 1963; P. J. N. Smal, *Die Universalisme in die Psalms*, 1956; N. H. Snaith, "The Triennial Cycle and the Psalter," *ZAW*, LI (1933), 302-7; W. Staerk, "Zur Kritik der Psalmenüberschriften," *ZAW*, XII (1892), 91-151; A. Szörényi, *Psalmen und Kult im Alten Testament*, 1961; R.-J. Tournay, "Les Psaumes complexes," *RB*, LIV (1947), 521-42; LVI (1949), 37-60; *idem*, "Sur quelques rubriques des Psaumes," in *Mélanges Robert*, 1957, pp. 197-204; *idem*, "Recherches sur la chronologie des Psaumes," *RB*, LXV (1958), 321-57; LXVI (1959), 161-90; M. Tsevat, *A Study of the Language of the Biblical Psalms*, 1955; J. E. Viana, "Como se formó la primera parte del libro de los Salmos?" *Bibl*, XLIV (1963), 129-58; A. C. Welch, *The Psalter in Life, Worship and History*, 1926; C. Westermann, "Zur Sammlung des Psalters," *Theologia Viatorum*, VIII (1961/62), 278-84 (= *Forschung am Alten Testament*, 1964, pp. 336-43);

idem, "Vergegenwärtigung der Geschichte in den Psalmen," *Kupisch-Festschrift*, 1963, pp. 253-80 (= *Forschung am Alten Testament*, 1964, pp. 306-35); cf. also the bibliography to § 39.

1. *Terminology and enumeration*. While for a portion of the Psalter the term *tᵉpillôt*, "prayers" (Ps. 72:20), was chosen, a term referring primarily to the laments, as a name for the book as a whole, the preference went to the unusual plural form *tᵉhillîm*, "hymns," in the sense "collection of hymns, hymnal." In Greek, however, the earliest name, *psalmoí* (Luke 20:42; Acts 1:20—*bíblos psalmôn*), is based on the word *mizmōr*, "song." Some manuscripts, however, use the term *psaltērion*, which goes back to the Hebrew *nēbel*, a stringed instrument. The Greek has given us our words "psalm" and "psalter."

As it presently stands, the Psalter is divided into 150 psalms, but the enumeration of the Masoretic text differs from that of the LXX. The latter counts Psalms 9–10 and 114–115 as one psalm and divides Psalms 116 (1-9, 10-19) and 147 (1-11, 12-20) into two psalms. The enumeration of the LXX was followed by the Vulgate and by Luther when quoting the psalms. When looking up a psalm in the LXX, one must remember its enumeration, which may be summarized as follows:

	MT	LXX	MT	LXX
Psalms	1–8	1–8	116:10-19	115
	9–10	9	117–146	116–145
	11–113	10–112	147:1-11	146
	114–115	113	147:12-20	147
	116:1-9	114	148–150	148–150

In addition, the LXX preserves another psalm, number 151, which is identical with the first of five noncanonical Syriac psalms contained in the writings of a Nestorian bishop of the tenth century. These psalms go back to a Hebrew original, as the Hebrew text of Psalm 151 (Syriac I) and Syriac II–III in 11QPsᵃ shows.[1]

Only in its identification of Psalms 9–10 as one psalm (both parts in fact constitute a single song) is the LXX correct vis-à-vis the Masoretic text. The variations, however, suggest that even when the versions agree the psalms were not always divided correctly. Psalms 42–43, for example, constitute a single song, as the repeated refrain shows (42:6, 12 [Eng. 42:5, 11]; 43:5). Psalm 19 is a composite containing a fragment of a song and a poem in praise of the law (19:2-7, 8-15 [Eng. 19:1-6, 7-14]). We may assume that such inaccuracies occurred with some frequency.

2. *Significance of the superscriptions*. A large number of the psalms possess superscriptions, which purport to contain information concerning the composi-

[1] J. A. Sanders, "Ps 151 in 11QPss," *ZAW*, LXXV (1963), 73-86; *idem*, "Two Non-Canonical Psalms in 11QPsᵃ," *ibid.*, LXXVI (1964), 57-75; *idem*, *The Psalms Scroll of Qumran Cave* 11 (MQPsᵃ), 1965.

tion of the psalms and their cultic use.[2] Sometimes, following a practice whose first beginnings may be seen in a catalog of texts and authors from the library of Ashurbanipal, dating from the beginning of the first millennium,[3] they contain early attempts at literary criticism, ascribing the psalms to specific persons or furnishing data concerning the circumstances of their origin. Others give more precise names for the type of song, liturgical or musical notes, and references to the purpose of the psalms.

a) Among the names mentioned in the superscriptions, "Moses," "David," and "Solomon" are clearly intended to designate the authors of the psalms, while the mention of guilds of temple singers like Asaph and Korah should probably be understood as denoting particular collections, like the series notes of the Mesopotamian psalms.[4] A preconceived cultic theory lies behind the view that *lᵉdāwīd* originally designated those psalms that were recited in the temple cult by the king or were composed for a king of the Davidic dynasty. This interpretation is adopted, with minor differences, by Engnell, Mowinckel, and Weiser. It also presupposes the undemonstrated antiquity of the phrase, which is improbable in view of the close connection between the superscriptions of the psalms generally and the traditions of the Chronicler's History (Kraus). Although the introductory particle *lᵉ* is ambiguous and in Ugaritic texts specifies not the author but the protagonist of a poem (Baal, Aqhat, Keret), its interpretation

[2] L. Delekat, "Probleme der Psalmenüberschriften," *ZAW*, LXXVI (1964), 280-97; A. Guilding, "Some Obscured Rubrics and Lectionary Allusions in the Psalter," *JThSt*, NS III (1952), 41-55; R. Gyllenberg, "Die Bedeutung des Wortes Sela," *ZAW*, LXVIII (1940/41), 153-56; A. Jirku, *ibid.* LXV (1953), 85-86 (on Ps. 22:1); H. G. May, "ʿAl . . . in the Superscriptions of the Psalms," *AJSL*, LVIII (1941), 70-83; H. D. Preuss, "Die Psalmenüberschriften in Targum und Midrasch," *ZAW*, LXXI (1959), 44-54; N. H. Ridderbos, "Het bindend karakter van het *lᵉ Dâwîd* in de opschriften der Psalmen," *GThT*, LII (1952), 184-92; R. B. Y. Scott, "The Meaning and Use of *Selah* in the Psalter," *Bull. Canad. Soc. Bibl. Stud.*, V (1939), 17-24; N. H. Snaith, "Selah," *VT*, II (1952), 43-56; J. W. Thirtle, *The Titles of the Psalms*, 2nd ed., 1905.

[3] W. G. Lambert, "A Catalogue of Texts and Authors," *JCSt*, XVI (1962), 59-77.

[4] 1. The group of temple singers Asaph, which I Chron. 16:5 traces back to the time of David, at least returned as such from the Exile (Ezra 2:41; Neh. 7:44). Since the psalms associated with their name are of diverse types, this group probably did not compose them, but rather used them as their hymnal. 2. Ethan, referred to in I Kings 5:11 (Eng. 4:31) as a native Canaanite artist (a wise man and an Ezrahite), is mentioned as the composer of Psalm 89. There is reason for this identification, since the psalm is associated with the later group of singer Ethan (I Chron. 15:17 ff.), who probably recited and composed psalms. 3. Heman, too, is called an artist in I Kings 5:11 (Eng. 4:31), and possibly associated with the musicians' guild Mahol. According to Ps. 88:1 (Eng. 88 superscription), he was a native (Ezrahite) poet who composed the song, which was then borrowed by the Korahites. A postexilic group of temple singers bears his name (I Chron. 25:4 ff.). 4. Jeduthun is referred to as a poet (Ps. 39:1 [Eng. 39 superscription] and 62:1 [Eng. 62 superscription]), a singer (Ps. 77:1 [Eng. 77 superscription]), and a seer (II Chron. 35:15); several postexilic groups of singers bear his name. 5. For the group of Korah we may trace a historical development. Either it was at first responsible only for minor services in the Temple until a portion of its members succeeded in rising to the rank of a group of singers, or else the group of temple singers Korah came into being in the postexilic period and absorbed the aspiring doorkeepers. The final redaction of Numbers 16 is directed against their further rise to priestly privileges.

as *lamed auctoris* in the case of the Psalter is confirmed by the frequent mention of the circumstances under which David is said to have composed a psalm; it is highly unlikely that these represent later commentary. This view agrees with the ancient conception of David as a poet and singer. Ps. 72:20 and Song of Sol. 1:1 further confirm this interpretation.

b) In thirteen cases the circumstances given for the composition of the psalm (information frequently contained in the diwans of Arab poets) are events from the life of David (Psalms 3, 7, 18, 34, 51, 52, 54, 56, 57, 59, 60, 63, 142).

c) The names for the various types of song are not always intelligible. Those whose meanings are clear are *mizmōr* and *šîr*, "song"; *tᵉhillâ*, "hymn"; and *tᵉpillâ*, "prayer (of lament or petition)"; perhaps also *maśkîl*, "artistic song, didactic poem"; and *šîr hammaʿălôt*, "pilgrimage song" (interpreted by others as "serial song," "step song," or "travel song").[5] Other terms, such as *miktām* (Luther—"*gülden Kleinod*"; Mowinckel—"psalm of atonement") and *šiggāyôn* (perhaps from the Akkadian word for "lament") are scarcely intelligible.

d) The musical and liturgical notes include references to musical performance, such as *bingînôt*, "with stringed instruments"; references to tunes, like 22:1 (Eng. 22 superscription), "Hind of the Dawn," and 56:1 (Eng. 56 superscription), "A Dove on Far-off Terebinths." The phrase *ʿal haššᵉmînît*, "upon the eighth," may refer to vocal pitch or the string of an instrument. Of disputed meaning are the terms *lamnaṣṣēaḥ*, "for the choirmaster" or "musical performance," [6] and *selâ*, whose possible meanings are "musical interlude," "repetition (*da capo*)," and "bending in prayer." "Hallelujah" is a cultic refrain. Since singing accompanied by music or performed by a choir was most feasible at large sanctuaries like Jerusalem, all such references may perhaps derive from that source, to the extent that they are not postexilic additions, added at a time when the Jerusalem Temple was considered the only legitimate sanctuary.

e) Several superscriptions indicate the purpose of the psalms: Psalm 30, the dedication of the Temple; Psalms 38 and 70, the memorial or incense offering; and Psalm 100, the thank-offering. Later, certain psalms were sung at the regular morning burnt offering (*tāmîd*), and are therefore called *tamid* psalms. The versions give the following series for each day of the week, beginning with Sunday: 24 (LXX), 48, 82 (Talmud), 94 (LXX), 81 (Old Latin and Armenian), 93 (LXX), and 92. At Passover and on other feasts Psalms 113–118 were recited. Finally, the recitation of psalms and verses of psalms was associated with all types of days and prayers.

3. *Authorship and age.* The superscriptions, all of which are secondary, provide no clues as to the real authors and age of the psalms. At most, some of the psalms associated with guilds of singers may have been composed by these guilds. Otherwise, however, the superscriptions do not provide any reliable informa-

[5] Other suggestions include, for example, those of Delekat: *mizmōr* = poem (recited by an individual), *šîr* = a well-known song, *maśkîl* = a popular song, a hit.

[6] Among other views, Delekat, for example, suggests that (*la-*)*mᵉnaṣṣēaḥ* = the outstanding, distinguished one (David); in combination with *bingînôt* = of the one distinguished in songs (of the greatest one in the art of poetry).

tion, especially since the traditions vary in the Masoretic text and in the versions. In particular, David cannot possibly have composed or even heard the psalms that are labeled *lᵉdāwīd,* because many of them presuppose the Jerusalem Temple or even the Babylonian Exile, and others show a familiarity with a different stage in the development of Yahwism than that attested in the reliable sources for the Davidic period. The data added by the compilers do, however, reflect the correct awareness that the postexilic community not only composed their own songs but also preserved and employed songs deriving from an earlier tradition. The Psalter, like our hymnals, contains a selection of songs dating from several centuries.

Although the beginnings of Israelite cultic poetry can be dated as early as there were Israelites with their own cult, the earliest texts of the Psalter have been borrowed and made to refer to Yahweh: Psalm 19 A (a fragment of a creation hymn mentioning the sun-god), 29 (Canaanite), and 104 (Canaanite, composed in imitation of the sun hymn of Amenhotep IV). All these praise God's power and greatness in nature; the borrowing most likely took place in the postexilic period. Some of the psalms definitely date from the preexilic period. This holds true first of all for the royal psalms and the other psalms that presuppose an Israelite king as a real figure. It holds true also for certain other psalms that do not mention the king at all; exegesis must determine these psalms individually. It cannot be considered impossible that one psalm or another even dates back to the time of David, whose talent as a poet is attested by the dirge for Saul and Jonathan. A vastly greater number derive from the exilic period (echoed especially in Psalm 137) and the postexilic period, when, as the Chronicler's History shows, the singing of psalms played a particularly important role. The discoveries at Qumran have ruled out any dating from the Maccabean period in the second century B.C.[7] Since the psalms contain for the most part no specific historical references, or at most only veiled allusions, all attempts at dating can attain no more than a certain degree of likelihood. Comparative study of motifs and content against the background of the entire OT, an approach still in its infancy, can often provide more clues. Psalm 8, for example, seems to presuppose the creation narrative of P (Gen. 1:1–2:4*a*); 103, Deutero-Isaiah and Trito-Isaiah; 51, the material in Isaiah 1 and Ezekiel 36; and 119, the books of Malachi, Lamentations, Proverbs, and Job, as well as Trito-Isaiah. Such comparisons often make it possible to set an upper limit in dating the psalms. On the whole, one must resist the new conservative tendency automatically to ascribe all the psalms or at least the majority of them to the period of the early monarchy or even the preexilic period in general. The antiquity of songwriting in the ancient Near East and in Israel provides no grounds for an early dating of the individual psalms that have been preserved.

4. *Survey of literary types, origin, and cultic association of the psalms.* It is impossible to provide a detailed analysis of each psalm within the context of

[7] P. R. Ackroyd, "Criteria for the Maccabean Dating of Old Testament Literature," *VT,* III (1953), 113-32; E. Goossens, *Die Frage nach makkabäischen Psalmen,* 1914; C. D. Hassler, *Commentationes criticae de Psalmis Maccabaicis auos ferunt,* 1827-32.

this book. Nevertheless, it seems appropriate to give a kind of survey listing the literary type of each psalm, its approximate date, and its association with the cult. The following pages therefore give the results of an analysis in the briefest possible form, although these must necessarily remain subjective.

a) First, the literary type of each psalm is indicated by means of the following abbreviations:

H Hymn
H(M) Monotheistic hymn
H(Z) Zion song
H(P) Pilgrimage song
L(C) Community lament
L(I) Individual lament
C(C) Community song of confidence
C(I) Individual song of confidence
T(C) Community thanksgiving
T(I) Individual thanksgiving
R Royal psalm
WD Wisdom and didactic poetry

b) Second, the suggested date of each psalm is roughly indicated, to the extent that this is possible; in most cases the reason is briefly given. A question mark indicates a complete lack of clues as to the date.

c) With regard to cultic association, the only distinction made is between cultic and noncultic songs. There is no attempt to distinguish songs originating in the cult from those that were merely employed in the cult. In addition, those songs that attest a close association between their authors and the cult are labeled cultic. In many cases, precise distinctions are impossible or can be made only with serious reservations. Otherwise the number of purely cultic songs (those growing out of the cult or intended from the beginning for cultic use) would be significantly smaller than that given.

1 WD; postexilic (theological development); noncultic didactic poem.[8]
2 R; preexilic (§ 39.5); cultic (enthronement).[9]
3 L(I); preexilic?; cultic.[10]
4 L(I); ? ; cultic.[11]
5 L(I); ? ; cultic.[12]

[8] In the notes that follow, literature dealing with the individual psalms is cited without title. E. P. Arbez, *CBQ*, VII (1945), 398-404; P. Auvray, *RB*, LIII (1946), 365-71; G. J. Botterweck, *ThQ*, CXXXVIII (1958), 129-51; I. Engnell, in *Studia Orientalia Pedersen*, 1953, pp. 85-96; P. Haupt, *AJSL*, XIX (1903/04), 129-42; P. Joüon, *RSR*, XXVII (1937), 440-56; H.-J. Kraus, *EvTh*, (1950/51), 337-51; H. W. Wolff, *ibid.*, IX (1949/50), 385-94.

[9] G. E. Closen, *Bibl*, XXI (1940), 426-28; F. Hesse, *Luther-Jahrbuch*, XXV (1958), 23-41; R. Köbert, *Bibl*, XXI (1940), 426-28; R. Press, *ThZ*, XIII (1957), 321-34; A. Robert *RSR*, XXXIX (1951), 88-98; H. H. Rowley, *JThSt*, XLII (1941), 143-54; I. Sonne, *HUCA*, XIX (1945/46), 43-55.

[10] R.-J. Tournay, *RB*, LII (1945), 214-16.

[11] L. Dürr, *Bibl*, XVI (1935), 330-38; R.-J. Tournay, *RB*, LII (1945), 216-19.

[12] L. Krinetzki, *ThQ*, CXLII (1962), 23-46.

6 L(I); late preexilic or postexilic (similarity to 41 and 88); cultic.[13]
7 L(I); ? ; cultic.[14]
8 H; postexilic (presupposes Gen. 1:1–2:4*a*); noncultic song of universal type.[15]
9/10 T(I) and L(I); exilic—postexilic (similarity to Lamentations 3, tendency toward didacticism, alphabetic form); possibly cultic.[16]
11 C(I); preexilic?; personal song of a suppliant.[17]
12 L(C); postexilic (theological development); cultic.[18]
13 L(I); ? ; cultic origin not clear, may be understood as an expression of personal piety.
14 L(I); postexilic (theme, influence of prophecy and wisdom); cultic, possibly for synagogue worship.[19]
15 H(P); preexilic?; cultic (entrance liturgy).[20]
16 C(I); postexilic (reflects the situation of Trito-Isaiah); cultic.[21]
17 L(I); ? ; cultic.[22]
18:1-31 (Eng. 18:1-30) T(I); postexilic (language and thought); cultic.[23]
18:32-51 (Eng. 18:31-50) R; preexilic (§ 39.5); cultic (thanksgiving for a victory).
19:1-7 (Eng. 19:1-6) H; originally non-Israelite and very ancient, borrowed in the postexilic period, together with:
19:8-15 (Eng. 19:7-14) WD; postexilic (theological development); noncultic.[24]
20 R; late preexilic (end of the monarchy, Deuteronomistic influence: *šēm* theology); cultic (petition).
21 R; preexilic (§ 39.5); cultic (annual memorial celebration).[25]
22 L(I) and T(I); postexilic? (similarity to 41 and 88, T(I) presupposes Deutero-Isaiah, linguistically late expressions); L(I) on the surface not cultic, T(I) cultic.[26]

[13] J. Coppens, *HUCA*, XXXII (1961), 217-26.

[14] J. Leveen, *JRAS*, 1946, pp. 81-83; M. Löhr, *ZAW*, XXXVI (1916), 225-37.

[15] P. A. H. de Boer, *OTS*, II (1943), 171-93; J. Hempel, *FF*, XXXV (1961), 119-23; J. J. Koopmans, *ThT*, III (1948), 1-10; H. Kruse, *JSS*, V (1960), 343-47; C. J. Louis, 1946; J. Morgenstern, *HUCA*, XIX (1945/46), 491-523; S. Mowinckel, in *Studia Orientalia Pedersen*, 1953, pp. 250-62; C. Schedl, *FF*, XXXVIII (1964), 183-85; J. J. Stamm, *ThZ*, XIII (1957), 470-78.

[16] H. Junker, *RB*, LX (1953), 161-69; M. Löhr, *ZAW*, XXXVI (1916), 225-37.

[17] J. Morgenstern, *JBL*, LXIX (1950), 221-31; I. Sonne, *ibid.*, LXVIII (1949), 241-45.

[18] P. Wernberg-Møller, *ZAW*, LXIX (1957), 69-71.

[19] K. Budde, *JBL*, XLVII (1928), 160-83; C. C. Torrey, *ibid.*, XLVII (1927), 186-92.

[20] J. L. Koole, *OTS*, XIII (1963), 98-111.

[21] C. Schedl, *ZAW*, LXXVI (1964), 171-75; E. Zolli, *ThZ*, VI (1950), 149-50.

[22] D. Gualandi, *Bibl*, XXXVII (1956), 199-208; J. Leveen, *VT*, XI (1961), 48-54; R. Pautrel, *RSR*, XLVI (1958), 78-84; C. Schedl, *BZ*, NF VI (1962), 100-102.

[23] F. Asensio, *Gregorianum*, XXXIII (1952), 219-60, 566-611; F. M. Cross, Jr., and D. N. Freedman, *JBL*, LXXII (1953), 15-34.

[24] K. Budde, *OLZ*, XXII (1919), 257-66; L. Dürr, in *Sellin-Festschrift*, 1927, pp. 37-48; R. Eisler, *MVG*, XXII (1917), 21-70; H.-J. Kraus, *EvTh*, X (1950/51), 337-51; J. Morgenstern, *HUCA*, XIX (1945/46), 491-523; J. van der Ploeg, *JEOL*, XVII (1963), 193-201; O. Schröder, *ZAW*, XXXIV (1914), 69-70; R.-J. Tournay, in *Nötscher-Festschrift*, 1950, pp. 271-84; N. H. Tur-Sinai, *ArOr*, XVII (1949), 419-433; M. Weippert, *ZAW*, LXXIII (1961), 97-99.

[25] G. R. Driver, *AfO*, XVIII (1957), 129; F. C. Fensham, *ZAW*, LXXVII (1965), 193-202.

[26] F. Asensio, *Gregorianum*, XXXIII (1952), 219-260, 566-611; G. Beer, in *BZAW*, XLI (1925), 12-20; E. Courte, 1932; A. Feuillet, *NRTh*, LXX (1948), 137-49; S. B. Frost, *Canadian JTh* VIII (1962), 102-15; J. Magne, *Semitica*, XI (1961), 29-41; R. Martin-Achard, *Verbum Caro*, LXV (1963), 78-87; N. H. Ridderbos, *OTS*, XIII (1963), 43-76; C. Westermann, 1955.

23 C(I); postexilic? (theological development); associated with the temple.[27]
24 H(P); late preexilic? (theological development); cultic (entrance liturgy).[28]
25 L(I); postexilic (formally and linguistically); noncultic.[29]
26 L(I); ? (vs. 11 may suggest a date after Deutero-Isaiah); cultic.[30]
27:1-6 C(I); preexilic?; noncultic.
27:7-14 L(I); preexilic?; cultic.[31]
28 L(I); preexilic (cf. vss. 8-9); cultic.
29 H; originally Canaanite and very ancient, transferred to Yahweh in the postexilic period (combination of *kābôd* and *šēm* theology); cultic.[32]
30 T(I) with hymnic forms; preexilic (content); cultic.[33]
31:1-9 (Eng. 31:1-8) L(I) and T(I); late preexilic (theological development); cultic.
31:10-25 (Eng. 31:9-24) L(I) and T(I); late preexilic (theological development); cultic.
32 T (I); postexilic (wisdom influence); cultic.
33 H; postexilic (alphabetizing form); cultic.[34]
34 WD, mixture of T(I) and didactic poetry; postexilic (dependent on 51); cultic, more likely intended for synagogue worship than for the sacrificial cult.[35]
35 L(I); ? ; cultic.[36]
36 Mixture of L(I), H, and WD; postexilic (influence of contemplative wisdom poetry); cultic.[37]
37 WD; postexilic (theme and theological development); noncultic didactic poem.[38]
38 L(I); postexilic? (similarity to 41 and 88); possibly cultic.[39]
39 L(I); ? ; expression of personal piety.
40:1-12 (Eng. 40:1-11) T(I); postexilic (theological development); cultic.

[27] F. Asensio, *Bibl*, XL (1959), 237-47; J. Böhmer, *BZ*, XXIII (1935/36), 166-70; P. Haupt, *AJSL*, XXI (1905/06), 133-52; L. Köhler, *ZAW*, LXVIII (1957), 227-34; J. Morgenstern, *JBL*, LXV (1946), 13-24; D. Müller, *ZÄS*, LXXXVI (1961), 126-44; E. Vogt, *Bibl*, XXXIV (1953), 195-211; A. H. van Zyl, *OuTWP*, 1963, pp. 64-83.

[28] O. Eissfeldt, *WdO*, II (1954-59), 480-83; G. R. Deaver, Dissertation, Dallas, 1953; V. V. Hueso, *EstBibl*, XXII (1963), 243-53; R. Rendtorff, in *Rendtorff-Festschrift*, 1958, pp. 121-29; I. W. Slotki, *JBL*, LI (1932), 214-26; J. D. Smart, *ibid.*, LII (1933), 175-80; M. Treves, *VT*, X (1960), 428-34.

[29] S. Holm-Nielsen, *StTh*, XIV (1960), 45-48; N. H. Ridderbos, *OTS*, XIII (1963), pp. 43-76.

[30] L. A. Snijders, *OTS*, XIII (1963), 112-30; E. Vogt, *Bibl*, XLIII (1962), 328-37.

[31] H. Birkeland, *ZAW*, LI (1933), 216-21; I. W. Slotki, *JThSt*, XXXI (1929/30), 387-95.

[32] A. Caquot, *Syria*, XXXIII (1956), 36-41; H. Cazelles, in *Mémorial Gelin*, 1961, pp. 119-28; G. Cooke, *ZAW*, LXXVI (1964), 24-26; F. M. Cross, Jr., *BASOR*, CXVII (1950), 19-21; F. C. Fensham, *OuTWP*, 1963, pp. 84-99; K. Fullerton, *JBL*, XLVIII (1929), 274-90; E. Pax, *BZ*, NF VI (1962), 93-100; N. H. Ridderbos, *GThT*, LX (1960), 64-69; L. F. Rivera, *RevBibl*, XXIII (1961), 9-14; E. Vogt, *Bibl*, XLI (1960), 17-24.

[33] L. Krinetzki, *ZKTh*, LXXXIII (1961), 345-60.

[34] A. Deissler, in *Mélanges Robert*, 1957, pp. 225-33.

[35] B. Couroyer, *RB*, LVII (1950), 174-79; S. Holm-Nielsen, *StTh*, XIV (1960), 49-50; L. J. Liebreich, *HUCA*, XXVII (1956), 181-92; H. Wiesmann, *Bibl*, XVI (1935), 416-21.

[36] G. R. Driver, *ThZ*, IX (1953), 468-69; J. Magne, *RB*, LIV (1947), 42-53.

[37] L. A. F. le Mat, 1957.

[38] J. Allegro, *PEQ*, LXXXVI (1954), 69-75; P. A. Munch, *ZAW*, LV (1937), 36-46.

[39] R. Arconada, *VD*, X (1930), 48-56, 107-16.

40:14-18 (Eng. 40:13-17) L(I); ? ; cultic.[40] (Vs. 13 [Eng. vs. 12] is a late addition.)
41 T(I); postexilic (didactic tendencies); cultic.[41]
42/43 L(I); preexilic? (borrowed by the Korahites after the Exile); cultic.[42]
44 R; preexilic (§ 39.5); cultic (petition for God's assistance in battle).
45 R; preexilic (§ 39.5); oracle of a cult prophet on the occasion of a royal marriage.[43]
46 H(Z); postexilic (§ 39.2 C); cultic, with eschatological conclusion.[44]
47 H(M); postexilic (§ 39.2 B); cultic.[45]
48 H(Z); postexilic (§ 39.2 C); cultic.[46]
49 WD; postexilic (theological development); noncultic didactic poem.[47]
50 Judgment liturgy of a cult prophet; postexilic (theological development); cultic.[48]
51 L(I); exilic—postexilic (presupposes Ezek. 36.25 ff. and other passages, vss. 20-21 [Eng. 18-19] added prior to 515); noncultic song of personal piety.[49]
52 L(I) (a transformed prophetical invective); postexilic (theological development); cultic (vs. 11 [Eng. vs. 9]).[50]
53 =14.
54 L(I); late preexilic or later (*šēm* theology); cultic.
55 L(I); postexilic (language and style); possibly cultic, but no strong cultic associations.
56 L(I) and T(I); preexilic (images drawn from the sphere of the monarchy); cultic (vs. 13 [Eng. vs. 12]).
57 L(I); preexilic? (motifs drawn from the royal songs); cultic.[51]
58 L(?); postexilic (like 14); probably not cultic.[52]
59 L(I); preexilic?; cultic.
60 L(C); exilic? (following the defeat of Judah in 587?); cultic.
61 L(I); preexilic (prayer for the king); cultic.
62 C(I); postexilic (elements of wisdom instruction); cultic.[53]

[40] S. Cavaletti, *RSO*, XXXII (1957), 293-99.
[41] J. Coppens, *HUCA*, XXXII (1961), 217-26.
[42] H. Kruse, *JSS*, V (1960), 333-43; H. H. Rowley, *Bibl*, XXI (1940), 45-50.
[43] N. H. Ridderbos, *OTS*, XIII (1963), 43-76; C. Schedl, *VT*, XIV (1964), 310-18; R. Tournay, *VTSuppl*, IX (1963), 168-212.
[44] O. Eissfeldt, *ThBl*, I (1922), 54-59; H. Junker, *Bibl*, XLIII (1962), 197-201; L. Krinetzki, *Münchner ThZ*, XII (1961), 52-71; A. F. Puukko, *StTh*, I (1935), 29-33; H. Schmidt, *Luther-Jahrbuch*, 1926, pp. 98-119; M. Weiss, *Bibl*, XLII (1961), 255-302.
[45] A. Caquot, *RHR*, XXXIX (1959), 311-37; J. Muilenburg, *JBL*, LXIII (1944), 235-56; K.-H. Ratschow, *ZAW*, LIII (1935), 171-80.
[46] M. J. Dahood, *CBQ*, XVI (1954), 15-19; L. Krinetzki, *BZ*, NF IV (1960), 70-97; J. Morgenstern, *HUCA*, XVI (1941), 1-95.
[47] J. Lindblom, in *Horae Soederblomianae*, I (1944), 21-27; P. A. Munch, *ZAW*, LV (1937), 36-46; J. van der Ploeg, *OTS*, XIII (1963), 137-72; M. Stenzel, *ThZ*, X (1954), 152-54; P. Volz, *ZAW*, LV (1937), 235-64.
[48] P. Auvray, *RB*, LIII (1946), 365-71; W. Caspari, *ZAW*, XLV (1927), 254-66.
[49] R. Arconada, *VD*, XI (1931), 197-206; E. R. Dalglish, 1962; R. Galdos, *VD*, X (1930), 67-79; R. Press, *ThZ*, XI (1955), 241-49; C. Steuernagel, in *Sellin-Festschrift*, 1927, pp. 151-56; H.-J. Stoebe, 1958.
[50] A. M. Scharf, *VD*, XXXVIII (1960), 213-22; C. Schedl, *BZ* NF, V (1961), 259-60.
[51] R. Pautrel, *RSR*, XLIV (1956), 566-72; I. W. Slotki, *Journal of the Manchester Egyptian and Oriental Society*, XVIII (1933), 61-65.
[52] M. J. Dahood, *CBQ*, XVII (1955), 300-303.
[53] A. M. Honeyman, *VT*, XI (1961), 348-50.

63 T(I); late preexilic? (assuming that the prayer on behalf of the king in vs. 12*a* [Eng. vs. 11*a*] is original); cultic.
64 L(I); ? ; associated with the cultic community.[54]
65 T(C), with many hymnic forms; postexilic?; cultic.
66 Thanksgiving liturgy consisting of H, T(C), and T(I); postexilic (theological development); cultic (offering of vows).
67 T(C); postexilic (theological development); cultic (liturgy).[55]
68 Mixture of various forms and literary types, mostly hymnic; Canaanite and early Israelite song fragments made into a postexilic Jerusalemite song with cultic associations.[56]
69 L(I); postexilic (vss. 36-37 [Eng. vss. 35-36]); cultic.[57]
70 = 40 B.
71 L(I); postexilic (theological development); cultic.[58]
72 R; preexilic (§ 39.5); cultic (prayer for blessing).[59]
73 WD; postexilic (theme and theology); song of personal piety by a man of striking individuality, borrowing cultic expressions and using them in a new sense.[60]
74 L(C); exilic or early postexilic (after the destruction of the temple); cultic.[61]
75 T with an oracle of Yahweh and admonition; postexilic (theological development); based on the cult.[62]
76 H(Z); postexilic (§ 39.2 C); cultic elements in the style and summons.[63]
77:1-16 (Eng. 77:1-15) L(I); exilic (time of distress for Israel); song of personal meditation.
77:17-21 (Eng. 77:16-20) H; postexilic (theological development); cultic.[64]
78 WD; late preexilic (belongs to the Deuteronomistic school); noncultic poem for the instruction of the community.[65]
79 L(C); postexilic (presupposes the books of Jeremiah and Ezekiel, as well as Lamentations 5); cultic.[66]

[54] E. C. Dell'Oca, *RevBibl*, XXII (1960), 89-92; A. Strobel, *RB*, LVII (1950), 161-73.
[55] H. G. Jefferson, *VT*, XII (1962), 201-205.
[56] J. Aistleitner, *BZ*, XIX (1931), 29-41; W. F. Albright, *HUCA*, XXIII, 1 (1951), 1-39; F. C. Fensham, *JNES*, XLX (1960), 292-93; S. Grill, *ThZ* XVII (1961), 432-34; P. Haupt, *AJSL*, XXIII (1906/07), 220-40; S. Iwry, *JBL*, LXXI (1952), 161-65; S. Mowinckel, 1953. E. Podechard, *RB*, LIV (1947), 502-20; R.-J. Tournay, *ibid.*, LI (1942), 227-45.
[57] E. Vogt, *Bibl*, XLIII (1962), 79-82.
[58] R.-J. Tournay, in *Nötscher-Festschrift*, 1950, pp. 274-80.
[59] P. Grelot, *VT*, VII (1957), 319-21; R. E. Murphy, 1948; R. Pautrel, in *Mémorial Gelin*, 1961, pp. 157-64; P. W. Skehan, *Bibl*, XL (1959), 302-308.
[60] H. Birkeland, *ZAW*, LXVII (1955), 99-103; G. Kuhn, *ibid.*, LV (1937), 307-308; P. A. Munch, *ibid.*, p. 46; H. Ringgren, *VT*, III (1953), 265-72; E. Würthwein, in *Bertholet-Festschrift*, 1950, pp. 532-49.
[61] N. Liebschütz, *AJSL*, XL (1923/24), 284-87; XLI (1924/25), 279; F. Willesen, *VT*, II (1952), 289-306.
[62] A. González, *EstBibl*, XXI (1962), 5-22.
[63] O. Eissfeldt, *ThLZ*, LXXXII (1957), 801-808; S. Talmon, *IEJ* (1960), 174-80.
[64] E. C. Dell'Oca, *RevBibl*, XXII (1960), 89-92; H. G. Jefferson, *VT*, XIII (1963), 87-91; A. Weiser, *ThLZ*, LXXII (1947), 133-40.
[65] O. Eissfeldt, 1958; H. Junker, *Bibl*, XXXIV (1953), 487-500; J. W. Rothstein, *ZWTh*, XLIII (1900), 532-85; J. Schildenberger, in *Junker-Festschrift*, 1961, pp. 231-56.
[66] O. Glombitza, *NThT*, XIV (1960), 329-49.

80 L(C); late preexilic (possibly time of Josiah); cultic.[67]
81 Judgment liturgy of a cult prophet; late preexilic to postexilic (similarities to the Deuteronomistic message); cultic poem.
82 Judgment speech of Yahweh spoken by a cult prophet, with invective, admonition, and threat; preexilic (attack on the Canaanite pantheon); cultic poem.[68]
83 L(C); postexilic (motif of attack by the nations, "Assyria" as a symbol of the dominant world power); cultic.
84 H(Z); postexilic (§ 39.2 C); the song's piety is based completely on the temple cult.[69]
85 L(C) and oracle of Yahweh; postexilic (reference to deliverance from the Exile, presupposes Deutero-Isaiah); cultic (liturgy).[70]
86 L(I); postexilic (many borrowings); cultic.
87 H(Z); postexilic (§ 39.2 C); cultic.[71]
88 L(I); postexilic (similar in language to the book of Job); noncultic lament.[72]
89:1-19 (Eng. 89:1-18) H; preexilic (material and content); cultic.
89:20-53 (Eng. 89:19-52) R; preexilic (§ 39.5); cultic (after a military defeat).[73]
90 L(C); postexilic (meditative wisdom in a community lament); cultic.[74]
91 WD; postexilic? (theological development); didactic song, possibly intended for the cult.[75]
92 Mixture of H and T(I); postexilic (theological development); cultic.[76]
93 H(M); postexilic (§ 39.2 B); slight cultic association.[77]
94:1-11 L(C); postexilic (conceptual milieu); cultic.
94:12-23 T(I); postexilic (conceptual milieu); noncultic song.[78]
95 H and prophetical admonition; postexilic (content and theological development); cultic poem (liturgy).[79]
96 H(M); postexilic (§ 39.2 B); cultic.[80]
97 H(M); postexilic (§ 39.2 B; dependent on many other psalms); cultic association dubious, eschatological theology.
98 H(M); postexilic (§ 39.2 B); cultic.

[67] O. Eissfeldt, in *Alt-Festschrift*, 1953, pp. 65-78; *idem*, *WdO*, III (1964), 27-31; H. Heinemann, *JQR*, XL (1949/50), 297-302; A. Roiffer, *Tarbiz*, XXIX (1959/60), 113-24.

[68] G. Cooke, *ZAW*, LXXVI (1964), 29-34; A. Gonzalez, *VT*, XIII (1963), 293-309; C. H. Gordon, *JBL*, LIV (1935), 139-54; J. Morgenstern, *HUCA*, XIV (1939), 29-126; R. T. O'Callaghan, *CBQ*, XV (1953), 311-14; E. Podechard, in *Mémorial Chaine*, 1950, pp. 291-96.

[69] L. Grollenberg, *VT*, IX (1959), 311-12; R.-J. Tournay, *RB*, LIV (1947), 521-33.

[70] M. J. Dahood, *Bibl*, XXXVII (1956), 338-40; P. Nober, *VD*, XXXVIII (1960), 34-35.

[71] E. Beaucamp, *Studii Biblici Franciscani Liber Annuus*, XIII (1962/63), 53-75; R. G. Castellino, *VD*, XII (1932), 232-36; G. E. Closen, *ibid.*, XIV (1934), 231-40; A. Kaminka, *REJ*, LV (1908), 146-48.

[72] J. Hofbauer, *BEThL*, XII (1959), 504-10; P. Joüon, *RSR*, XXVII (1937), 440-56.

[73] G. Ahlström, 1959; G. Cooke, *ZAW*, LXXVI (1964), 26-29; O. Eissfeldt, in *Essays Muilenburg*, 1962, pp. 196-207; *idem*, *WdO*, III, 1/2 (1964), 27-31; W. B. Ward, *VT*, XI (1961), 321-39.

[74] J. Herrmann, in *Schmitz-Festschrift*, 1953, pp. 57-70.

[75] A. Caquot, *Semitica*, VIII (1958), 21-37; O. Eissfeldt, *WdO*, II (1954-59), 343-48; J. de Fraine, *Bibl*, XL (1959), 372-83.

[76] N. M. Sarna, *JBL*, LXXXI (1962), 155-68.

[77] H. G. Jefferson, *JBL*, LXXI (1952), 155-60.

[78] O. Glombitza, *NThT*, XIV (1960), 329-49.

[79] J. Finkel, *AJSL*, L (1933/34), 32-40.

[80] A. Caquot, *Syria*, XXXIII (1956), 36-41; R.-J. Tournay, *RB*, LIV (1947), 533-42.

99 H(M); postexilic (§ 39.2 B); cultic.
100 H; postexilic (theological development); cultic song for the thank offering.
101 R; preexilic (§ 39.5); cultic (outlines the basis of government).[81]
102 L(I); exilic–postexilic (possibly presupposes Deutero-Isaiah); personal noncultic song.
103 H; postexilic (presupposes Deutero-Isaiah, linguistic evidence); cultic style and language, but actually an individual imitation, a devotional song not composed for the cult.[82]
104 H; postexilic (theme and conception, but borrowing motifs of the Sun Hymn of Amenhotep IV); noncultic devotional song, although the author is immersed in the cultic milieu.[83]
105 WD; postexilic (presupposes the Pentateuch in its final form); cultic song for the instruction of the community (historical psalm).
106 WD with interpolations of penitence and petition; postexilic (post-Deuteronomistic, presupposes the Pentateuch in its final form); cultic (historical psalm).
107 Thanksgiving liturgy; postexilic (presupposes the Diaspora); cultic.
108 = 57:8-12 (Eng. 57:7-11) and 60:7-14 (Eng. 60:5-12); postexilic combination of lament, thanksgiving, and oracle; composed for liturgical purposes?
109 L(I); preexilic? (theological development); cultic.[84]
110 R (three fragments); preexilic (§ 39.5); oracles of a cult prophet for the king (vss. 1-3, 4, 5-7).[85]
111 T(I); postexilic (form and content); noncultic didactic song.[86]
112 WD; postexilic (postexilic theology); noncultic poem.[87]
113 H; postexilic (theological development; piety of the poor); cultic.
114 H; postexilic (post-Deuteronomistic); cultic.[88]
115 H/C(C); postexilic ("those who fear Yahweh"=proselytes); cultic (liturgy).
116 T(I); postexilic (aramaisms); cultic.[89]
117 H; postexilic (after Deutero-Isaiah); cultic.
118 T(C); postexilic? (theological development); cultic (thanksgiving liturgy).[90]

[81] O. Kaiser, *ZAW*, LXXIV (1962), 195-205.

[82] A. Jepsen, *Kerygma und Dogma*, VII (1961), 261-71; N. H. Parker, *Canadian JTh*, I (1955), 191-96.

[83] E. C. Dell'Oca, *RevBibl*, XXII (1960), 89-92; G. R. Driver, *JSS*, VII (1962), 12-22; O. Eissfeldt, *FF*, XXXIII (1959), 113-17; P. Humbert, *RHPhR*, XV (1935), 1-27; H. Kruse, *VD*, XXIX (1951), 31-43; G. Nagel, in *Bertholet-Festschrift*, 1950, pp. 395-403; A. van der Voort, *RB*, LVIII (1951), 321-47; M. Weiss, 1964.

[84] H. L. Creager, *JNES*, VI (1947), 121-23; E. J. Kissane, *Irish ThQ*, XVIII (1951), 1-8.

[85] A. Caquot, *Semitica*, VI (1956), 33-52; J. Coppens, 1955; *idem*, *Supplements to Numen*, IV (1958), 333-48; H. E. del Medico, *ZAW*, LXIX (1957), 160-70; E. R. Hardy, *JBL*, LXIV (1945), 385-90; H. G. Jefferson, *ibid.* LXXIII (1954), 152-56; E. J. Kissane, *Irish ThQ*, XXI (1954), 103-14; L. Krinetzki, *ThGl*, LI (1961), 110-21; J. Morgenstern, *JQR*, XXXII (1941/42), 371-85; H. H. Rowley, in *Bertholet-Festschrift*, 1950, pp. 461-72; J. de Savignac, *OTS*, IX (1951), 107-35; C. Schedl, *ZAW*, LXXIII (1961), 290-97; H.-J. Stoebe, in *Baumgärtel-Festschrift*, 1959, pp. 175-91; R.-J. Tournay, *RB*, LII (1945), 220-37; G. Widengren, 1941.

[86] S. Holm-Nielsen, *StTh*, XIV (1960), 35-37.

[87] *Ibid.*

[88] H. van den Bussche, *ColBG*, III, 1 (1957), 77-83.

[89] S. Daiches, in *Gaster Anniversary Vol.*, 1936, pp. 64-67; I. Lohr, in *Van der Leeuw-Festschrift*, 1950, pp. 317-21.

[90] J. Meysing, *VT*, X (1960), 130-37; H. Schmidt, *ZAW*, XL (1922), 1-14.

119 WD; postexilic (late devotion to the law, influenced by Deuteronomistic theology and wisdom instruction); noncultic didactic poem (anthology).[91]
120 L(I); ? ; personal noncultic song.
121 H(P); postexilic (theological development); cultic (dismissal liturgy).[92]
122 H(Z); postexilic (§ 39.2 C); cultic.[93]
123 L(C); exilic—postexilic (historical situation); cultic.
124 T(C); postexilic (aramaizing language); cultic.[94]
125 C(C); postexilic (style and conceptual milieu); cultic.
126 L(C); postexilic (reference to deliverance from the Exile); possibly cultic, but cultic associations only external.[95]
127 WD; postexilic?; two noncultic wisdom passages.
128 WD; postexilic (form and content); noncultic instruction and blessing.
129 C(C); postexilic (historical presuppositions); cultic.
130 L(I); postexilic (form and language); personal devotional song with no cultic associations.[96]
131 C(I); postexilic (theological development); personal devotional song (cultic reference in vs. 3).
132 R; preexilic (§ 39.5); cultic (for the anniversary of the founding of the royal sanctuary).[97]
133 WD; postexilic; noncultic wisdom passages with metaphors appropriate to everyday life.[98]
134 H and blessing; ? ; cultic associations.[99]
135 H; postexilic (theological development and use of tradition); cultic.
136 T(I); postexilic (use of tradition); cultic (litany).
137 L(C); postexilic (presupposes the end of the Exile); noncultic song expressing personal emotions.[100]
138 T(I); postexilic (presupposes the Diaspora); cultic.
139 L(I); ? ; cultic.[101]
140 L(I); postexilic (theological development); cultic.
141 L(I); postexilic (theological development); personal noncultic song by an author connected with the cult.[102]
142 L(I); ? ; personal song in cultic style.
143 L(I); postexilic (theological development); cultic.[103]
144 R; preexilic (§ 39.5); cultic (petition).

[91] A. Deissler, 1955; H.-J. Kraus, *EvTh*, X (1950/51), 337-51; A. Robert, *RB*, XLVIII (1939), 5-20.

[92] O. Eissfeldt, in *Lilje-Festschrift*, 1959, pp. 9-14; J. Morgenstern, *JBL*, LVIII (1939), 311-32; P. H. Pollock, *ibid.*, LIX (1940), 411-12.

[93] F. Horst, *EvTh*, XVI (1956), 53.

[94] I. W. Slotki, *JBL*, LI (1932), 214-26.

[95] J. Strugnell, *JThSt*, NS VII (1956), 239-43.

[96] R. Arconada, *VD*, XII (1932), 213-19; C. H. Cornill, in *BZAW*, XXXIV (1920), 38-42; S. Porúbčan, *VT*, IX (1959), 322-23; P. Volz, in *BZAW*, XLI (1925), 287-96.

[97] O. Eissfeldt, *WdO*, II (1954-59), 480-83; J. R. Porter, *JThSt*, NS V (1954), 161-73.

[98] H. Gunkel, in BZAW, XXXIV (1920), 69-74.

[99] W. F. Albright, *NTT*, LVI (1955), 1-12.

[100] O. Glombitza, *NThT*, XIV (1960), 329-49.

[101] E. Baumann, *EvTh*, XI (1951/52), 187-90; G. A. Danell, 1951; H. Hommel, *ZAW*, XLVII (1929), 110-24; E. Würthwein, *VT*, VII (1957), 165-82.

[102] R. Pautrel, *RSR*, XLIV (1956), 219-28; R.-J. Tournay, *VT*, IX (1959), 58-64.

[103] R. Arconada, *VD*, XIII (1933), 240-56.

145 H; postexilic (form, language, use of tradition); cultic.[104]
146 H; postexilic (form and language); cultic.
147 H; postexilic (after Deutero- and Trito-Isaiah); cultic.
148 H; postexilic; cultic.
149 H; postexilic (use of tradition); cultic.[105]
150 H; postexilic; cultic, for festival worship.

This survey yields the following statistics:

a) Date of the psalms:	
1. preexilic preexilic? late preexilic	23%
2. exilic exilic–postexilic	4.5%
3. postexilic postexilic?	62%
4. ?	8.5%
5. Special cases	2%
b) Cultic association of the psalms:	
1. Cultic	73.5%
2. Noncultic	18%
3. Doubtful or intermediate	8.5%

5. *Compilation and growth of the Psalter*. In its final form, as we have it today, the Psalter is divided into five books, each of which concludes with a doxology: Psalms 1–41, 42–72, 73–89, 90–106, and 107–150. This gives the impression that we are dealing with a homogeneous work, but this impression is erroneous. The division is only the last stage of a long and complicated course of development, modeled after the growth of the Pentateuch or later interpreted as an imitation of the Pentateuch. There is, however, no material correspondence to the books of the Pentateuch.[106] In reality, the Psalter is the end product of several different collections. This is suggested by 72:20 ("The prayers of David, the son of Jesse, are ended"), the superscriptions, the partial alternation of divine names, and the various doublets (14 = 53; 18 = II Samuel 22; 40:14-18 [Eng. 40:13-17] = 70; 57:8-12 [Eng. 57:7-11] + 60:7-14 [Eng. 60:5-12] = 108). In some cases, we can recognize the path leading from small collections through larger ones to the Psalter, which was not completed as a whole until the fourth century.

A. Psalms 3–41. The Davidic Psalter is the largest original collection. With the exception of Psalm 33, which has no superscription, all the songs bear the label *l^edāwīd;* in the case of a few psalms, we are even told the supposed occasion in the life of David to which the song refers. Psalm 2, a royal psalm, was obviously placed at the beginning of the collection because of the Davidic interpretation. Almost a third of the songs have nothing to associate them with

[104] S. Holm-Nielsen, *StTh,* XIV (1960), 35-37; L. J. Liebreich, *HUCA,* XXVII (1956), 181-92.

[105] H. Gunkel, in *Orientalische Studien Haupt,* 1926, pp. 47-57.

[106] Contrary to J. Dahse, *Das Rätsel des Psalters gelöst,* 1927; and Arens.

cultic use, so that the collection brings together both cultic and noncultic songs; it was intended as a kind of prayer book for private use and personal edification. This agrees with the observation that it comprises for the most part songs of the individual, especially laments.

B. Psalms 42–83. These psalms together with an appendix consisting of psalms 84–89 constitute the Elohistic Psalter, in which the divine name "Yahweh" is regularly replaced by the designation "Elohim." We are dealing here with a deliberate redaction, as Psalm 14 shows, which parallels Psalm 53 but uses the name "Yahweh." The grounds for this redaction are to be found in the increasing disinclination of Judaism to pronounce the name of God and in the emphasis on God's uniqueness provided by the universal designation "Elohim." The Elohistic Psalter comprises several separate collections, which exhibit evidence of cultic origin or use:

a) Psalms 42–49, together with the appendix 84–85, 87–88. These are the Korahite psalms, arranged according to the type of song each represents. They represented the repertory of the Korahites, a guild of temple singers that came into being in the postexilic period; some of them were probably composed by members of this guild, as the special Zion theology of some of the songs suggests. The appendix also includes Psalm 86, a David psalm.

b) Psalms 50, 73–83. These are the Asaph psalms, likewise the repertory of a guild of temple singers; this group returned from the Exile already constituted as such a guild.

c) Psalms 51–72. This is a second Davidic Psalter, in which only Psalms 66–67 lack the superscription *"l^{e}dāwīd,"* and Psalm 72 is ascribed to Solomon. Ps. 72:20 shows this group to be an independent collection. The psalms (mostly, like 3–41, songs of the individual, especially individual laments) are arranged according to the type of song each represents; almost all have musical or liturgical annotations. They were assembled for use in the cult, and some originally noncultic psalms were included in the process.

C. Psalms 90–149 constituted a third major collection. In contrast to the two others, the psalms in it have almost no musical or liturgical annotations; the mention of an author is also strikingly uncommon. It consists of four small collections, which have been skillfully joined together:

a) Psalms 90–104. No special distinguishing features, but characterized by the presence of most of the monotheistic hymns.
b) Psalms 108–110, 138–145. The remnants of a third collection of David psalms.
c) Psalms 120–134. The Book of Pilgrimage Songs (cf. 2*c*).
d) Psalms 105–107, 111–114, 116–118, 135–136, 146–149. The Hallelujah psalms, which now conclude the three collections just mentioned or their constituent parts:

a) Psalms 90–104 + 105–107
b^1) Psalms 108–110 + 111–114, 116–118
c) Psalms 120–134 + 135–136
b^2) Psalms 38–145 + 146–149
Psalms 115, 119, and 137 are late additions to the Psalter.

The individual collections were intended in part for private use (A), but mostly for the cult (most of the constituent parts of B and C). The earliest general title given to such a collection (72:20), which uses the term *t^e^pillôt*, was probably also meant to characterize the psalms as sung prayers, possibly for synagogue worship. The same is true for the title *t^e^hillîm*, which describes the Psalter as the hymnal of the postexilic community. This is in line with the character of Psalm 150, appended as a conclusion, which lists the musical instruments used in the praise of God. We must also not overlook the nature of Psalm 1, a wisdom song placed at the head of the entire collection. This psalm removes the Psalter from the realm of public worship, alienates it and many of the songs assembled in it from their original *Sitz im Leben*, and transforms it into a wisdom book for theological edification.

6. *Theological ideas.* When examining the theological ideas of the Psalter, one must remember that the earlier psalms represent a biased selection of Israel's poetic material. From the preexilic period, almost the only songs preserved were those deriving from Jerusalem or associated with its cult; all the songs that originated after Josiah's reformation presuppose the Jerusalem Temple as the only legitimate sanctuary. This leads to a concentration from the very outset upon sacral subjects and those associated with the court and later to a kind of sectarian attitude, so that the psalms whose content is thus restricted cannot be taken as representative of Yahwism in all its depth and variety. For this reason the sometimes exaggerated importance attached to Zion must be diminished.

This having been said, Jerusalem and its cult may be called one of the two foci of the faith exhibited by the psalms. For this faith the Temple is the place God has chosen to be present and reveal himself; from it blessing pours forth, and in it all the members of Israel have their citizenship. To be able to dwell in Jerusalem, the city of the Temple, is reason for thanksgiving and jubilation. To be able to enter the Temple and tarry there is a special grace, so that many psalms echo a real yearning for the Temple. Of course prayer and thanksgiving can substitute for the sacrificial cult (Ps. 50:14; 141:2); confidence and trust in God, expressed through humility and praise of his goodness, can be preferred to it (Ps. 40:7-9 [Eng. 40:6-8]; 51:17-19 [Eng. 51:15-17]).

The other focus of the faith expressed in the psalms is the law, which describes what God requires of man, because obedience calls forth God's gracious favor, while disobedience brings his punitive vengeance. This is the source of the recurrent distinction between the righteous or devout and the wicked or impious. This view of course led to grave difficulties, which Psalms 49 and 73 tried to resolve, each in its own way. The latter psalm, like the book of Job, finds the solution to the riddle in the experience of fellowship with God. These two ideas, then, that of God's dominion and that of fellowship with God, are the twin poles of the religion of the law and the cult.

§ 44 Lamentations

ATD: A. Weiser, 2nd ed., 1962. BK: H.-J. Kraus, 2nd ed., 1960. BOT: B. N. Wambacq, 1957. HAT: M. Haller, 1940. HK: M. Löhr, 2nd ed., 1906. HS:

T. PAFFRATH, 1932. IB: T. J. MEEK, 1956. KAT/KAT²: W. RUDOLPH, 1939, 1962. KeH: O. THENIUS, 1855. KHC: K. BUDDE, 1898. SAT: H. SCHMIDT, 2nd ed., 1923; W. STAERK, 2nd ed., 1920. SZ: S. OETTLI, 1889. Individual commentaries: H. G. A. EWALD, *Die Dichter des Alten Bundes,* I, 3rd ed., 1866; C. F. KEIL, 1872 (Biblischer Commentar) (Eng. 1880); G. RICCIOTTI, 1924; G. M. RINALDI, 1953; H. WIESMANN, 1954.

B. ALBREKTSON, *Studies in the Text and Theology of the Book of Lamentations,* 1963; J. BÖHMER, "Ein alphabetisch-akrostisches Rätsel und ein Versuch, es zu lösen," *ZAW,* XXVIII (1908), 53-57; C. FLÖCKNER, "Über den Verfasser der Klagelieder," *ThQ,* LIX (1877), 187-280; N. K. GOTTWALD, *Studies in the Book of Lamentations,* 1954; M. LÖHR, "Der Sprachgebrauch des Buches der Klagelieder," *ZAW,* XIV (1894), 31-50; *idem,* "Sind Thr IV und V makkabäisch?" *ibid.,* pp. 51-59; *idem,* "Threni III und die jeremianische Autorschaft des Buches der Klagelieder," *ibid.,* XXIV (1904), 1-16; H. MERKEL, *Über das alttestamentliche Buch der Klagelieder,* Dissertation, Halle, 1889; C. VAN DER STRAETEN, "La métrique des Lamentations," in *Mélanges de Philologie Orientale,* 1932, pp. 193-301; M. TREVES, "Conjectures sur les dates et les sujets des Lamentations," *Bulletin Renan* XCV (1963), 1-3; H. WIESMANN, "Die literarische Art der Klagelieder des Jeremias," *ThQ,* CX (1929), 381-428; *idem,* "Der geschichtliche Hintergrund des Büchleins der Klagelieder," *BZ,* XXIII (1935/36), 20-43; *idem,* "Der Verfasser der Klagelieder ein Augenzeuge?" *Bibl,* X (1936), 71-84; J. K. ZENNER, *Beiträge zur Erklärung der Klagelieder,* 1905.

1. *Terminology.* Hebrew manuscripts and printed editions call the book of Lamentations by the first word of chapters 1, 2, and 4, *'êkâ,* "Alas, how . . . ." This title, which usually introduces a dirge, is appropriate to the content of the songs. The earlier name, according to Talmud Bab. Baba bathra 15*a,* was *qînôt,* "dirges," corresponding to the name given in the translations: Greek *thrênoi,* Latin *lamentationes,* German *Klagelieder.* In most of the translations the title also ascribes the book to Jeremiah, after whose book it is placed. This view is probably based on II Chron. 35:25, although the laments for Josiah mentioned in this passage, one of which Jeremiah is said to have composed, cannot be identified with the book of Lamentations despite Lam. 4:20. The book serves as the festival scroll of the Ninth of Ab, the date of the destruction of Jerusalem.

2. *Literary type and style.* The book of Lamentations comprises five separate songs coterminous with the chapters. It is impossible to assign them to a specific literary type because in many instances we have a mixture of types. The poet's purpose was not to produce an exemplary poetic form but to embody certain specific ideas, to which the form had to accommodate itself.

Chapters 1, 2, and 4, as their initial word suggests, are dirges, more precisely collective dirges mourning perished Jerusalem. Nevertheless, the poet modulates into other literary types. In 1, in contrast to a dirge, Jerusalem herself addresses Yahweh in prayer, confessing her sins; vss. 12-16, 18-22 are composed in the style of an individual lament. In 2, also, the author departs from the dirge form: the poem focuses on Yahweh; after the lament over Jerusalem, the author speaks in his own person, and finally places a prayer in the mouth of the city. Chapter 4 begins as a dirge, but in vss. 17-20 a group speaks in the style of a community lament, and in vss. 21-22 the poet addresses Edom and Zion.

Chapter 3 is for the most part an individual lament, which passes into the style of a community lament in vss. 40-47 and then returns to the earlier form. In vss. 25-39 we find a meditation on the meaning of suffering. The conclusion contains a narrative of deliverance appropriate to a thanksgiving (vss. 55-62) and a prayer that God will curse the enemies; here we have the element of confidence that God will hear the lament and respond to it favorably. The "I" of the song, which alternates with a "we," has been interpreted as a personification of Jerusalem speaking as a sufferer (Eissfeldt*, Gottwald), as a representative speaking in the name of the whole community (Keil, Ewald, Ricciotti, Rinaldi), and as an individual who is merely describing his personal fate and not that of the community as a whole (Budde). It is probably more accurate to follow Rudolph in thinking in terms of an individual who feels himself singled out by God's wrath and presents himself as an example to his people. It is not necessary to draw the conclusion that the poet intends to place these words in the mouth of Jeremiah; he may quite well be speaking on the basis of his own experience.

Chapter 5 is a pure community lament, beginning with an invocation of Yahweh, continuing with a detailed lament over the present misery, and ending with a brief prayer for aid.

This analysis of literary types is followed by most scholars. Kraus, however, pointing to Mesopotamian laments over destroyed temples, particularly the Sumerian temple of Ur, postulates a new literary type, the "lament for the destroyed sanctuary," with a cultic lamentation ceremony as its *Sitz im Leben*. In Mesopotamia, though, such laments do not constitute an independent literary type (which would be quite peculiar as a sort of liturgical composite); they form a sub-category of the general class of laments. The analogous situation in Jerusalem is sufficient explanation for their similarity to the book of Lamentations; furthermore, the considerable differences should not be overlooked. Finally, the extreme mixture of literary types found in the OT songs and the peculiarity of their stylistic form (which will be discussed below) speak against the assumption made by Kraus.

Stylistically, the first four songs are structured as alphabetic songs. In 1 and 2, the first verse of each three-verse strophe begins with the letters of the alphabet in sequence. In 3, each verse of each strophe begins in this way, and in 4, the first verse of each two-verse strophe. In 2, 3, and 4, *pê* precedes *ʿayin*, which probably means that the order of the alphabet was not fixed at the time of composition. Chapter 5 is an alphabetizing song; it has as many verses as there are letters in the alphabet. As a consequence of the stylistic form, the intellectual structure of the songs is loose and the presentation somewhat disconnected.

3. *Occasion and content*. The songs depict and were occasioned by the misery and destruction of Jerusalem after its capture by the Babylonians. They were composed on the basis of meditation upon the reasons for this terrible catastrophe. We are dealing here primarily with expressions of personal feeling, albeit clearly intended to have a pastoral ministry toward the others whom disaster had befallen. It is most unlikely, however, that they were intended from the

outset for recitation at cultic lamentation ceremonies; such ceremonies are first mentioned in Zech. 7:1-7; 8:18-19, and were probably not introduced until years or decades after the events.[1] Above all, the alphabetic form argues against the assumption of an original cultic purpose; it characterizes the songs as elegies composed by a cultured man, meant primarily for reading and not for recitation.[2]

4. *Origin.* The date of the songs follows from their occasion and content: they presuppose the capture of Jerusalem. Rudolph prefers to date the first song in the time of the first occupation and deportation (597) and the others in the years following the final catastrophe (587). But even if the first song does not explicitly mention the destruction of the city and the temple, vss. 10, 17, 19-20 suggest the same situation as chapters 2–5. All the songs, therefore, probably were composed after the year 587, though we cannot fix a precise date for each of them. Chapters 2, 4, and (in part) 5 exhibit concrete details, while 1 and 3 are written in more general terms; but this is more likely due to the poet's intentions than to greater or lesser temporal proximity to the events. This alone can be safely stated: They were written by an eyewitness and before the situation was changed by Cyrus' emancipation edict in the year 538. To date 1 and 3–5 in the period 170–166 B.C. (Treves) is out of the question.

The place of origin cannot be determined with assurance. Gottwald thinks in terms of composition in Babylonia during the Exile; Sellin* places at least 1, 2, and 4 in Babylonia, while suggesting Jerusalem or Palestine for 3 and 5; Rudolph and Weiser* consider Palestine the place of origin for all the songs. There is no definite evidence for any of these assumptions, however. Since Palestine undoubtedly learned very quickly of Ezekiel's preaching, chapters 2 and 4 could quite easily have come under its influence there. On the other hand, one of the exiles could easily give the impression of having experienced the catastrophe of Jerusalem at firsthand. Therefore the question of where these songs originated must remain undecided.

The songs were probably brought together after the end of the Exile at Jerusalem, in the fifth century at the latest. They were collected for the practical purpose of assembling in one document the songs used for ceremonial commemoration of the destruction of Jerusalem.

5. *Authorship.* Jeremiah is out of the question as author of the songs, although recently Wiesmann has vigorously supported this position. After the catastrophe the prophet did not lament, but admonished the people to acknowledge the fate decreed by God and to obey the Babylonians; he may also have promised salvation to come, a promise contradicted by several verses of Lamentations (cf. 1:10; 4:17, 20*b*). Neither should the author or authors be sought among the official cult prophets (Kraus), whose guilt is recounted in 2:14 and 4:13 by someone not of their number.

[1] The pilgrimage to Jerusalem described in Jer. 41:5 does not bear witness to such observances, but rather to the continued existence of opportunity for cultic worship at Jerusalem; furthermore, it takes place before the Feast of Booths.

[2] Cf. Jahnow, p. 169.

Wiesmann and Rudolph, however, have shown the probability that all the songs were composed by a single author (*pace,* for example, Eissfeldt*). The evidence, despite the fact that *ʿayin* and *pê* have a different order in 1 than in 2–4, includes similarities of language and content, stylistic form, and the pastoral purpose and basic theological approach of the songs, all of which hold them together as a unity. If 4:17-20 reflects the personal experience and thoughts of the poet, he was among those that hoped for Jerusalem's deliverance to the very last, and appears to have fled Jerusalem with King Zedekiah. The stylistic form, too, suggests that he belonged to the cultured upper class. It does not necessarily follow that he was deported after the catastrophe; he might have been assigned to the circle around Gedaliah.

6. *Significance.* At any rate, the destruction of the state and its capital opened his eyes to the deeper significance of the events and led him to a profound appreciation of what had taken place, a receptiveness to the message of the prophets, and an attempt to help his fellow sufferers, caught in a crisis of faith (Weiser*). He sees God's wrath as the immediate cause of the disaster and attributes God's wrath to the sins of the people, with the priests and cult prophets foremost among the guilty. The only deliverance from misery and despair he sees to be prayer to God, who will be gracious and merciful to a repentant people.

§ 45 The Song of Solomon

ATD: H. Ringgren, 2nd ed., 1962. BK: G. Gerleman, 1963- . BOT: M. A. van den Oudenrijn, 1962. COT: G. C. Aalders, 1952. HAT: M. Haller, 1940. HK: K. Siegfried, 1898. HS: A. Miller, 1927. IB: T. J. Meek, 1956. KAT²: W. Rudolph, 1962. KeH: F. Hitzig, 1855. KHC: K. Budde, 1898. SAT: W. Staerk, 2nd ed., 1920. SZ: S. Oettli, 1889. Individual commentaries: A. Bea, 1953; H. G. A. Ewald, 1826; R. Gordis, 1954; L. Krinetzki, 1964; G. S. Pouget and J. Guitton, 1934 (Eng. 1948); G. Ricciotti, 1928; A. Robert, R. Tournay, and A. Feuillet, 1963.

W. F. Albright, "Archaic Survivals in the Text of Canticles," in *Driver-Festschrift,* 1963, pp. 1-7; D. Broadribb, "Thoughts on the Song of Solomon," *Abr-Nahrain,* III (1961/62), 11-36; A. Bruno, *Das Hohe Lied, Das Buch Hiob,* 1956; K. Budde, "Was ist das Hohelied?" *PJ,* LXXVIII (1894), 91-117; D. Buzy, "Un chef-d'oeuvre de poésie pure: le Cantique des Cantique," in *Mémorial Lagrange,* 1940, pp. 147-62; A. Feuillet, "Le Cantique des Cantiques et la tradition biblique," *NRTh,* LXXIV (1952), 706-33; *idem, Le Cantique des Cantiques,* 1953; C. Gebhardt, *Das Lied der Lieder,* 1931; P. Haupt, *Biblische Liebeslieder,* 1907; J. G. Herder, *Lieder der Liebe,* 1778; C. Kuhl, "Das Hohelied und seine Deutung," *ThR* NF, IX (1937), 137-67; G. Kuhn, *Erklärung des Hohen Liedes,* 1926; A. Lacocque, "L'insertion du Cantique des Cantiques dans le Canon," *RHPhR,* XLII (1962), 38-44; F. Landsberger, "Poetic Units Within the Song of Songs," *JBL,* LXXIII (1954), 203-16; T. J. Meek, "Canticles and the Tammuz Cult," *AJSL,* XXXIX (1922/23), 1-14; R. E. Murphy, "The Structure of the Canticle of Canticles," *CBQ,* XI (1949), 381-91; H. Ringgren, "Hohes Lied und hieros gamos," *ZAW,* LXV (1953), 300-302; A. Robert, "Le genre littéraire du Cantique des Cantiques," *RB,* LII (1945), 192-213; H. H. Rowley, "The Interpretation of the Song of Songs," *JThSt,* XXXVIII

(1937), 337-67 (= *The Servant of the Lord,* 1952, pp. 187-234); *idem,* "The Song of Songs: An Examination of Recent Theory," *JRAS* (1938), 251-76; H. Schmökel, "Zur kultischen Deutung des Hohenliedes," *ZAW,* LXIV (1952), 148-55; *idem, Heilige Hochzeit und Hoheslied,* 1956; M. H. Segal, "The Song of Songs," *VT,* XII (1962), 470-90; M. Thilo, *Das Hohelied,* 1921; L. Waterman, *The Song of Songs,* 1948; J. G. Wetzstein, "Die syrische Dreschtafel," *Zeitschrift für Ethnologie,* V (1873), 270-302; W. Wittekindt, *Das Hohe Lied und seine Beziehungen zum Istarkult,* 1927.

1. *Terminology.* The book takes its name from its first two words: *šîr haššîrîm* (LXX: *āsma âsmátōn;* Vulgate: *canticum canticorum*). This periphrastic superlative is intended to suggest that the book is "the most beautiful [*or* best] song of Solomon," who is reputed to have written 1005 songs (I Kings 5:12 [Eng. 4:32]). The association with Solomon is probably the real reason why the book became part of the Canon; its canonical status dates back to before the so-called Synod of Jamnia (*ca.* A.D. 100), nor was it questioned at that time. Subsequently, during the second century, doubts arose as to the propriety of its inclusion, but these were put to rest by the statement of Mishna Yadayim 3.5. Evidence for the use of the book as the festival scroll for Passover dates from the eighth century.

2. *History of interpretation.* The history of interpretation of the Song of Solomon is no feather in the cap of biblical exegesis.[1] As early as the first century C.E., accurate awareness that the book depicts and celebrates love between man and woman was forced to give way to allegorical or typological interpretation, then becoming dominant; to this approach has been added more recently a mythological and cultic interpretation.

a) The natural interpretation of the book as an expression of erotic love was the earliest and came about spontaneously. In *Ant.* viii. 7. 3, Josephus accepts it as being self-evident in his description of Solomon's glory; according to Mishna Ta'anit 4.8, the common people understood the book literally. Rabbi Aqiba's curse upon those who sing it in the marriage house indicates the same for the second century. Later, however, this interpretation was repressed; Theodore of Mopsuestia was posthumously condemned by the Fifth Council of Constantinople (553) for supporting it, and in 1545 Castellio was banished from Geneva for this and other heresies. Herder was the first to gain a hearing for such voices, and others of similar views but more cautious; he preferred to all other interpretations "the plain meaning of the words, rejected by all, the best of all exegetes." By his account of Syro-Palestinian marriage customs in his study of the Syrian threshing floor (1873), Wetzstein provided considerable support for the natural interpretation: On the eve of her wedding, the bride dances a sword dance to the rhythm of a song that praises her beauty and finery. During the first week following the wedding, the "royal week," the newly

[1] C. Kuhl, "Das Hohelied und seine Deutung," *ThR,* NF IX (1937), 137-67; D. Lerch, "Zur Geschichte der Auslegung des Hohenliedes," *ZThK,* LIV (1957), 257-77; F. Ohly, *Hohelied-Studien,* 1958; P. P. Parente, "The Canticle of Canticles in Mystical Theology," *CBQ,* VI (1944), 142-58; P. Vulliaud, *Le Cantique après la tradition juive,* 1925.

married couple play the roles of king and queen. Among the songs sung during this period we find another descriptive song. Since in this area conditions have changed very little among the common people throughout the centuries until very recently and the practices are very tenacious, we clearly have an echo of very ancient customs here. In addition, the designation of the married couple as king and queen is more widespread than Wetzstein realized, so that we actually have a broad basis for the practice (Rudolph).[2]

b) For centuries the dominant interpretation was allegorical or typological, an explanation that is still met even today. It sees the book as based upon a deeper spiritual meaning, originally in order to justify the inclusion of the book in the Canon despite occasional doubts. Within Judaism, such interpretations refer to Yahweh and Israel; in the Christian church, they refer to Christ and the church, the individual soul, or Mary.

While this interpretation gradually lost ground in Protestant exegesis from the end of the eighteenth century on, it is still dominant in Orthodox Judaism and in Catholic exegesis (e.g., Ricciotti, Buzy, Robert, Bea, Tournay, Feuillet, Krinetzki). Recently the Catholics have cited the marriage symbolism of the prophets to support their view. Rudolph provides a detailed refutation, while Herder constructed an ironic imitation of the allegory.[3]

c) The mythological or mythological and cultic interpretation sees the book as referring to a marriage ceremony between vegetation deities or the sacral marriage of the ancient Near Eastern sacral king. This line of thought begins with Erbt, who thought in terms of a marriage of the sun-god (Dôd) with his sister, the moon-goddess Ishtar (Šalmīt).[4] More recently, Meek, Haller, Wittekindt (a cycle of cultic songs for a Jerusalemite festival), and Schmökel have represented this view.

Schmökel seeks to reconstruct an original cultic drama with three scenes and thirty-eight songs by means of a mosaic regrouping of the verses constituting the text of the book. This drama furnished the liturgy for celebrating the sacral marriage of a pair of Palestinian deities. Apart from the disputed question of marriage between deities, which has not yet been settled, one asks in vain what could have induced the early Jewish theologians, despite the traditional antipathy of Yahwism toward vegetation and fertility cults, to borrow such a liturgy, undertake the labor of a thorough revision, only to end up with love songs and epithalamia necessitating allegorical interpretation. The only positive result of this approach is the insight that mythological and cultic language naturally conformed to the usual language of love poetry and conversely that mythological and cultic terminology probably influenced the language of lovers.

[2] For collections of modern Near East poetry, see G. Dalman, *Palästinischer Diwan,* 1901; S. Linder, *Palästinische Volksgesänge,* 1952-55; E. Littmann, *Neuarabische Volkspoesie,* 1902; G. Jacob, *Das Hohelied, auf arabische und andere Parallelen untersucht,* 1902; G. Musil, *Arabia Petraea,* III, 1908; S. H. Stephan, "Modern Palestinian Parallels to the Song of Songs," *JPOS,* II (1922), 199-278.

[3] J. G. Herder, in *Herders Sämmtliche Werke,* ed. B. Suphan, VIII (1892), 553-54.

[4] W. Erbt, *Die Hebräer,* 1906, pp. 196-202.

d) We may note in passing, finally, the historical interpretation, like that of Waterman, according to whom the book refers to Abishag the Shunamite, who, after the death of David, rejected Solomon's advances out of faithfulness to her rustic lover and was subsequently praised in the songs of Northern Israel.

3. *Love songs and epithalamia.* The Song of Solomon is a mixture of love songs and epithalamia. The connection with marriage cannot be completely denied (Rowley, Buzy); neither can the book be interpreted totally from this perspective and called the textbook for an Israelite wedding (Budde). The mention of the bride and the wedding shows that 3:6-11; 4:8, 9-11; 4:12–5:1 are epithalamia; to these must be added at least 1:2-4, 9-17; 7:1-6 (Eng. 6:13–7:5); and 8:5-7. Other songs are merely love poetry like that familiar from ancient Egypt or the modern Near East. All these songs sing of the magic of love, the yearning of the lovers to be together, their passion and devotion, their joy in their union. Fervently and sensuously they celebrate the love that brings a man and a woman into each other's arms with an overwhelming power that cannot be denied.

The songs breathe the atmosphere of pulsing life; they are also imbued with the vivid language of love poetry, which describes the charms of the woman under the images of vineyard, garden, and fountain, and the pleasures of love under the images of eating and drinking, pasturing, or gathering. This "pleasure-loving sensuousness" (Gerleman) even includes nature. Descriptions of nature provide the setting for the love scenes and are distinguished by their idyllic and secular character from the conception of nature found in the hymnic songs and in wisdom literature. The descriptive songs depict the persons represented after the manner of statues (§ 40.4); at the same time, the poems present the lovers or bridal pair in disguises or literary travesties, once more a borrowing from Egyptian poetry. Gerleman singles out for special mention the description in terms of "king" and "queen," calling it a "high" disguise, and that in terms of "shepherd" and "gardener," which belongs to a different sphere, calling it a "low" disguise. The former can still be found in the popular customs observed by Wetzstein.

4. *Literary form.* To explain the literary form of the Song of Solomon, many have supported the view that it is a love drama (Pouget-Guitton, Waterman, Bruno, *et al.*) or the Jewish equivalent of the Greek *mimos* (Gebhardt). Many difficulties attend this hypothesis: it misrepresents the travesties, encounters trouble in selecting the male protagonist ("king" or "shepherd"?), and must overlook the description of the woman first as a country girl and then as a city dweller. It is completely disproved by its inability to demonstrate any meaningful continuous action or any progress or goal of the story.

The same holds true for the assumption that the book represents a consistent, unified composition passing from first love through engagement and marriage to married life (Thilo) or repeatedly depicting in various dialogues and monologues the path that leads from admiration of the beloved to union (Buzy). There is no trace of such a progression of thought, nor can the frequent alternation of persons, ideas, and moods be unified in this fashion.

Instead, the Song of Solomon came into being as a collection of what were originally independent songs; we have similar collections of Egyptian love songs. In this respect the book resembles the other song collections of the OT, as well as a good number of the wisdom and prophetical books. Several repetitions suggest, furthermore, that the Song of Solomon comprises at least two subsidiary collections (1:15=4:1; 2:6-7=8:3-4; 2:17*a*=4:6*a*; 2:17*b*=8:14). Similarity of content occasionally determines the sequence of songs; in most cases, the use of catchwords provides the organizing principle.

5. *Formal literature.* The Song of Solomon is frequently termed popular poetry (Herder, Budde, Rudolph, *et al.*). Its strikingly literary character, however, speaks against this assumption, as do its artistry, verbal power, and aura of culture, none of which is appropriate to the style of a peasant village. Last but not least, there are the close associations with Egyptian poetry. All these arguments suggest that the book is formal literature in the strict sense of the word: compositions bearing the personal stamp of creative poets, composed deliberately and making conscious use of stylistic devices, permeated in their very sentence structure with lyric sensitivity. Even in this respect, however, the book is not a unity and does not go back to a single author. Similarities of vocabulary, imagery, external form, and content, however, suggest authorship by a homogeneous group of cultured writers familiar with Egyptian poetry.

6. *Origin.* As author of the songs, Solomon is out of the question. They cannot be dated in his period, or even in the preexilic period as a whole. The aramaisms in the language point unambiguously to the postexilic period, a date further supported by the Iranian loanword *pardēs* (4:13), which also occurs in Aramaic, and the Greek loanword *'appiryôn* (3:9).[5] The conception of love and the connection with Egyptian literature are quite as possible in this period as in the period of Solomonic humanism (Gerleman) or the ninth century.[6] The compromise position, that the songs are ancient but were aramaized in the postexilic period (Gordis, Rudolph), appears suspiciously to have been formulated for the purpose of maintaining the earlier date of the songs. The time of origin of the songs, soon after which they were collected, is best thought of as the fifth or fourth century. We may assume that they were composed and collected in Palestine; the numerous references to places and buildings evidence as detailed a knowledge of Jerusalem as of the wider Syro-Palestinian region.

7. *Significance.* The significance of the Song of Solomon for its own period may be seen in its rejection of the sacral divinization of sex rampant in the mythological fertility cults of the ancient Near East, but also in its refusal to devaluate or reject sex, a rejection originating primarily from a Jewish Christianity of Essene stamp and Platonic-Hellenistic mysticism. The Song of Songs declares that, if marriage is in accord with God's will, then so is its basis, sexual love.

[5] Cf. A. Jepsen, "Pardes," *ZDPV*, LXXIV (1958), 65-68; F. Rundgren, "אפריון 'Tragsessel, Sänfte'," *ZAW*, LXXIV (1962), 70-72.

[6] W. F. Albright, *Archaeology and the Religion of Israel*, 2nd ed., 1946, p. 182 n. 35.

PART THREE

The Formation of the Wisdom Books

CHAPTER ONE: GENERAL

§ 46 Wisdom in the Ancient Near East and in Israel

A. Alt, "Die Weisheit Salomos," *ThLZ*, LXXVI (1951), 139-44 (= *Kleine Schriften*, I [1953], 90-99 [Eng. *Essays on Old Testament History and Religion*, 1966]); R. Anthes, *Lebensregeln und Lebensweisheit der alten Äygpter*, 1933; W. Baumgartner, *Israelitische und altorientalische Weisheit*, 1933; *idem*, "Die israelitische Weisheitsliteratur," *ThR*, NF V (1933, 259-88; *idem*, "The Wisdom Literature," in *The Old Testament and Modern Study*, 1951, pp. 210-37; F. W. von Bissing, *Altägyptische Lebensweisheit*, 1955; P. A. H. de Boer, "The Counsellor," *VTSuppl*, III (1955), 42-71; H. Brunner, "Die Weisheitsliteratur," in *Handbuch der Orientalistik*, I (1952), 90-110; A. de Buck, "Het religieus karakter der oudste egyptische wijsheid," *NThT*, XXI (1932), 322-49; A. Causse, "Sagesse égyptienne et sagesse juive," *RHPhR*, IX (1929), 149-69; J. J. A. van Dijk, *La Sagesse suméro-accadienne*, 1953; L. Dürr, *Das Erziehungswesen im Alten Testament und im Antiken Orient*, 1932; A. Erman, *Die Literatur der Ägypter*, 1923, pp. 86-121, 238-302 (Eng. *The Literature of the Ancient Egyptians*, 1927); J. Fichtner, *Die altorientalische Weisheit in ihrer israelitisch-jüdischen Ausprägung*, 1933; *idem*, "Zum Problem Glaube und Geschichte in der israelitisch-jüdischen Weisheitsliteratur," *ThLZ*, LXXVI (1951), 145-50; G. Fohrer, "σοφία κτλ.; B. Altes Testament," *ThW*, VII, 476-96; T. H. Gaster, "Samaritan Proverbs," in *Studies Neuman*, 1962, pp. 228-42; H. Gese, *Lehre und Wirklichkeit in der alten Weisheit*, 1958; R. Gordis, "The Social Background of Wisdom Literature," *HUCA*, XVIII (1943/44), 77-118; E. I. Gordon, "A New Look at the Wisdom Literature of Sumer and Akkad," *BiOr*, XVII (1960), 122-52; H. Gressmann, *Israels Spruchweisheit im Zusammenhang der Weltliteratur*, 1925; P. Humbert, *Recherches sur les sources égyptiennes de la littérature sapientiale d'Israël*, 1929; J. Kázmér, *Wesen und Entwicklung des Weisheitsbegriffes in den Weisheitsbüchern des Alten Testaments*, 1950; S. N. Kramer, "Sumerian Wisdom Literature," *BASOR*, CXXII (1951), 28-31; W. G. Lambert, *Babylonian Wisdom Literature*, 1960; J. Lindblom, "Wisdom in the Old Testament Prophets," *VTSuppl*, III (1955), 192-204; J. Meinhold, *Die Weisheit Israels*, 1908; R. E. Murphy, "The Concept of Wisdom Literature," in *The Bible in Current Catholic Thought*, 1962, pp. 46-54; M. Noth, "Die Bewährung von Salomos 'Göttlicher Weisheit'," *VTSuppl*, III (1955), 225-37, W. O. E. Oesterley, *The Wisdom of Egypt and the Old Testament*, 1927; E. Otto, "Bildung und Ausbildung im alten Ägypten," *ZÄS*, LXXXI (1956), 41-48; J. Paterson, *The Wisdom of Israel*, 1960; G. von Rad, "Die ältere Weisheit Israels," *Kerygma und Dogma*, II (1956), 54-72; O. S. Rankin, *Israel's Wisdom Literature*, 2nd ed., 1954; H. Ringgren, *Word and Wisdom*, 1947; J. C.

RYLAARSDAM, *Revelation in Jewish Wisdom Literature*, 1947; *Les Sagesses du Proche-Orient ancien*, 1963; G. SAUER, *Die Sprüche Agurs*, 1963; W. VON SODEN, "Leistung und Grenze sumerischer und babylonischer Wissenschaft," *Die Welt als Geschichte*, II (1936), 411-64, 509-57; *idem, Zweisprachigkeit in der geistigen Kultur Babyloniens*, 1960; W. ZIMMERLI, "Zur Struktur der alttestamentlichen Weisheit," ZAW, LI (1933), 177-204.

1. *The concept*. In discussing the Hebrew stem *ḥākam* (Greek: *sophía, sophós*), OT studies speak of wisdom instruction and wisdom literature, but this does not do justice to the range of meanings of the Hebrew expression or to its real import. On the one hand, it can refer to such things as the ability of a craftsman (Exod. 31:3 and *passim*), the art of government (Jer. 50:35; Isa. 10:13), the art of magic and divination (Gen. 41:8; Isa. 44:25, and *passim*), and deceitful cunning (II Sam. 13:3; Job 5:13). On the other hand, the knowledge that it presupposes is not concerned with theoretical mastery of the problems of life and the universe, but with solutions of a practical nature to the problems confronting God or man. "Wisdom" is careful, deliberate, experienced, and adept action, by means of which a person can fit into the existing order of the universe so as to make himself master of it, solve the problems presented by life, and finally master life itself. Wisdom is concerned with life as a whole and affects all the areas of life, so that it means cleverness and experience devoted to practical ends. The word *lēb*, "heart," which is frequently added, shows that such cleverness and expertise can arise from an inner "sense" for proper action, action in accord with the order of the universe. This "sense" is promoted by knowledge of tradition, education, or personal experience. The antithetical notion, "folly," is a corresponding disorder in the very center of a man's life, which shows itself first in his behavior, then in recklessness and arrogance.[1]

2. *Mesopotamia*. In Mesopotamia there is no expression analogous to the Hebrew.[2] There came into being, however, an extensive wisdom literature, which—although for the most part preserved in Akkadian recension—goes back in large measure to Sumerian traditions.

Most of the extant Sumerian literature consists of a large number of proverb collections, for the most part arranged as school texts and commonly arranged according to the sign with which each proverb begins.[3] Later texts discuss

[1] Cf. also W. Caspari, "Über den biblischen Begriff der Torheit," *NkZ*, XXXIX (1928), 668-95.

[2] Van Dijk (pp. 17-21) assumes that Sumerian *ME* plays a central role, but the criticism of T. Fish in *JSS*, I (1956), 286-88, casts doubt on this assumption. The Babylonian word "*nēmequ*," "wisdom," and various adjectives are used to mean skill and accomplishment in magic and the cult, so that the text "I will praise the Lord of Wisdom" describes the god Marduk as being expert in the rites of exorcism; cf. Lambert, p. 1. The Akkadian word "*ḫakâmu*," "to comprehend, understand," is probably a loanword from West Semitic, borrowed as a technical term.

[3] E. I. Gordon, "The Sumerian Proverb Collections," *JAOS*, LXXIV (1954), 82-85; *idem*, "Sumerian Proverbs: 'Collection Four,' " *ibid.*, LXXVII (1957), 67-79; *idem*, "Sumerian Proverbs and Fables ('Coll. Five')," *JCSt*, XII (1958), 1-21, 43-75; *idem, Sumerian Proverbs*,

ethical questions and furnish practical suggestions for how to live in harmony with the universe and therefore successfully,[4] or else examine the problems arising from this order of the universe,[5] so that some have at times been looked upon as forerunners of the book of Job. In addition, the Mesopotamian fables, disputations, debates, and other texts whose literary type is often difficult to determine are traditionally placed with wisdom literature.[6]

The same circles of collectors to whom we owe the proverbs also began the construction of scholarly lists with their collections of concepts, which sought to bring systematic order to the whole world of objects and experiences. For practical applications in instruction, etc., this order was probably not interpreted in rational terms, but depicted vividly by the recounting of myths and other poems that told of the creation or restoration of such order out of chaos. As a consequence, the lists systematically supplemented the paradigmatic poems and sought to gain mastery over the world by reducing the names of things to a systematic order. In the course of constructing these lists, the Babylonians and Assyrians brought into being a whole new type of wisdom instruction, educational wisdom, which attained its final form above all in the series ḪAR-ra (*ḫubullu*), with twenty-four tablets and thousands of entries.[7]

3. *Egypt*. In Egypt the norm of conduct, which wisdom instruction is intended to secure, is described by the word *maʿat*, which is best translated "justice, rightness, primal order, order of the universe." [8] The goal of wisdom instruction is to prepare the way for this order, which derives from the deity and is valid for the entire world, by preserving knowledge of it, transmitting this knowledge, and applying it in new situations. Without neglecting personal

1959; S. N. Kramer, "Forty-eight Proverbs and their Translation," in *Troisième Rencontre Assyriologique*, 1954, pp. 75-84; Lambert, pp. 275-82. For arrangement according to the order of written signs, cf. Prov. 11:9-12 and the principles on which the alphabetic psalms are based (§ 39.6); these, of course, do not represent collections.

[4] These include the texts cited in chapters 4–5 of Lambert: The Teaching of Šuruppak, The Counsels of Wisdom, The Counsels of a Pessimist, Advice for a Prince, Hymn to Ninurta, Shamash Hymn.

[5] These include the texts cited in chapters 2–3 of Lambert: the Poem of the Righteous Sufferer (*ludlul bēl nēmeqi*), the Babylonian Theodicy, and perhaps also the Dialogue Concerning Pessimism (chap. 6).

[6] See, for example, the fables and disputes contained in Van Dijk, pp. 29-85, and Lambert, chapter 7. In addition, E. Ebeling, *Die babylonische Fabel und ihre Bedeutung für die Literaturgeschichte*, 1929; J. Johnston, "Assyrian and Babylonian Beast Fables," *AJSL*, XXVIII (1912), 81-100; J. Nougayrol, "Une fable hittite," *RHA*, XVIII (1961), 117-19; E. Weidner, "Zur Tierfabel-Sammlung aus Assur," *AfO*, XVI (1952/53), 80; for Egypt, see E. Brunner-Traut, "Der Katzenmäusekrieg im Alten und Neuen Orient," *ZDMG*, CIV (1954), 347-51; *idem*, "Ägyptische Tiermärchen," *ZÄS*, LXXX (1955), 5-11; *idem*, "Altägyptische Tiergeschichte und Fabel," *Saeculum*, X (1959), 124-85; R. Würfel, "Die ägyptische Fabel in Bildkunst und Literatur," *WZ Leipzig*, II (1952/53), 63-77.

[7] E. Chiera, *Sumerian Lexical Texts from the Temple School of Nippur*, 1929; F. C. Jean, *Lexicologie sumérienne*, 1931; L. Matouš, *Die lexikalischen Tafelserien der Babylonier und Assyrer in den Berliner Museen*, I, 1933; B. Meissner, "Ein Vokabularfragment aus Assur," *Archiv für Keilschriftforschung*, I (1923), 51 ff.

[8] Cf. R. Anthes, *Die Maat des Echnaton von Amarna*, 1952; also Brunner, pp. 83-96; Gese, pp. 11-21.

experience, which also plays an important role in OT wisdom instruction, the wise men of Egypt think of themselves as faithful transmitters of a rightness that has held true throughout the ages (cf. Isa. 19:11—"a student of wise men and kings of bygone ages"). Since *maʿat* is a changeless quantity and applies to every member of the social group in question equally and without alteration, man's duty is to accommodate and subject himself to it. The ideal of such a man is the "silent man" or the "correctly silent man," who acts according to *maʿat,* restrains himself under all circumstances, holds back, and avoids all excitement—in contrast to the "hot man," who is unrestrained and subject to his appetites. The outcome follows directly from human conduct: at times the success of an activity and its "inner truth" are viewed as a unity; at times the rules of conduct are justified by reference to advantage or detriment; at times these rules are presented as expressions of divine will, with consequent reward or punishment.

Since the concept of *maʿat* comprehends both the order of the cosmos and the order of human life, realms that are distinct in modern thought, we find two literary types of primary importance in wisdom literature: the scholarly lists of onomastica,[9] which were probably influenced by the Sumerian lists, and the "teachings" or "instructions" of fixed form,[10] seven of which are preserved whole or almost whole, five fragmentarily, and six or seven others only through mention of their titles.[11] In addition, there are a few documents that may be termed meditations or disputations.[12]

4. *Elsewhere in the ancient Near East.* Elsewhere in the ancient Near East, very little wisdom literature or none at all has been preserved.[13] Israel, however, was acquainted with the "wisdom" of other nations: the Edomites[14] (Jer. 49:7; Obadiah 8); the "peoples of the east" in the region of Ṣafa in the

[9] A. H. Gardiner, *Ancient Egyptian Onomastica,* 1947; H. Grapow, "Wörterbücher, Repertorien, Schülerhandschriften," in *Handbuch der Orientalistik,* I, 2 (1952), 187-93.

[10] The Egyptian word also means "education," "instruction," and theological doctrine. The title regularly reads: "The beginning of the teaching that A composed for his son (pupil) B."

[11] Cf. the description in Brunner, pp. 96-110 (with bibliography): Teaching of Imhotep, Teaching of Prince Djedefhor, Teaching for Kagemni, Teaching of Ptahhotep, Teaching for King Merikarē, Teaching for King Amenemhēt, Teaching of Cheti, son of Duauf, Teaching of Anii, Teaching of Amenemope, Teaching of Papyrus Insinger. See also B. Gemser, "The Instructions of ʿOnchsheshonqy and Biblical Wisdom Literature," *VTSuppl,* VII (1960), 102-28; G. Posener and J. Sainte Fare Garnot, "Sur une Sagesse égyptienne de basse époque," in *Les Sagesses du Proche-Orient ancien,* 1963, pp. 153-57.

[12] E. Otto, "Weltanschauliche und politische Tendenzschriften," in *Handbuch der Orientalistik,* I, 2 (1952), 111-19, includes also the Admonitions of a Sage, the Dialogue of One Tired of Life with his Soul, the Teaching for King Merikarē, the Prophecies of Nefer-rehu, the Laments of Cha-cheper-Re-seneb, the Laments of the Peasant, the Teaching for King Amenemhēt, Papyrus Harris I, and the so-called Demotic Chronicles.

[13] The Teaching of Ahikar, despite a Syriac and Aramaic version, probably goes back to an Assyrian prototype. *AOT,* pp. 454-62; *ANET,* pp. 427-30; B. Meissner, *Das Märchen vom weisen Achiqar,* 1917.

[14] Their influence on Israel has been exaggerated by R. H. Pfeiffer, "Edomitic Wisdom," *ZAW,* XLIV (1926), 13-25; *idem,* "Wisdom and Vision in the Old Testament," *ibid.,* LII (1934), 93-101.

northern part of Transjordan (I Kings 5:10 [Eng. 4:30]); and last but not least the Canaanites, who also in this field presumably exerted an influence upon Israel.[15] Ezek. 28:3, 17 speaks in general terms of the Phoenicians, Ezek. 27:8 Cn of *ṣemer,* referring probably to Ṣumra (north of Tripolis, not far from Arvad), and Zech. 9:2 of Sidon.

Beyond mere acquaintance and influence, the dependence of Israelite wisdom on that of the ancient Near East extends to actual texts found in the OT. Prov. 22:17–23:11 derives from the Egyptian Instruction of Amen-em-opet and 23:13-14 from the Teaching of Ahikar. Proverbs 30 and 31:1-9 derive from Syro-Palestinian peoples or tribes (§ 49.4, 7, 8).

5. *Israel.* Wisdom instruction in Israel therefore fits into the general ancient Near Eastern environment; its uniqueness, however, can be seen at various stages of its historical development.

From time immemorial there has been practical knowledge, based on experience, of certain laws governing the order of the universe and the activities of daily life. Man's need to make himself master of his environment and control his own life within it makes it necessary for him to seek order and regularity in the manifold phenomena and events he encounters so as to fit smoothly into them. This takes place above all in proverbs, which simply state the results of observation and experience and leave it to the individual to draw the appropriate conclusions for his own conduct (I Sam. 24:14 [Eng. 24:13]; Prov. 11:2*a*; 16:18; 18:12); the statement may involve a paradox (Prov. 11:24; 20:17; 25:15; 27:7). In this fashion one seeks to comprehend the framework and limits of the universal order, but without tracing the order back to a basic principle that is universally valid or creating a system. The importance of such proverbs can be seen from the way in which they were at times expanded subsequently by the addition of a second line stating an analogy applicable to human life (Prov. 25:23; 26:20; 27:20) and by the way Qoheleth uses them to reinforce his insights (§ 51.5).

Wisdom instruction in the strict sense was practiced during the reign of Solomon in connection with the development of the political machinery at the royal court and in the circles of the increasing numbers of officials, as well as in the wisdom school, whose existence we can assume at least in Jerusalem.[16] It follows that this official wisdom of the court must be distinguished from

[15] This influence, even if only linguistic, has been the subject of much investigation, with sometimes exaggerated conclusions: W. F. Albright, "Some Canaanite-Phoenician Sources of Hebrew Wisdom," *VTSuppl,* III (1955), 1-15; M. J. Dahood, "Canaanite-Phoenician Influence in Qoheleth," *Bibl,* XXXIII (1952), 30-52, 191-211; *idem,* "Some Northwest-Semitic Words in Job," *ibid.,* XXXVIII (1957), 306-20; *idem,* "Qoheleth and Northwest Semitic Philology," *ibid.,* XLIII (1962), 349-65; *idem, Proverbs and Northwest Semitic Philology,* 1963; *idem,* "Northwest Semitic Philology and Job," in *The Bible in Current Catholic Thought,* 1962, pp. 55-74; C. L. Feinberg, *Ugaritic Literature and the Book of Job,* Dissertation, Baltimore, 1945; G. Sauer, *Die Sprüche Agurs,* 1963; C. I. K. Story, "The Book of Proverbs and Northwest-Semitic Literature," *JBL,* LXIV (1945), 319-37.

[16] Reservations have been expressed by R. B. Y. Scott, "Solomon and the Beginnings of Wisdom in Israel," *VTSuppl,* III (1955), 262-79.

popular wisdom ("family wisdom"). The statement concerning Solomon in I Kings 5:12-13 (Eng. 4:32-33) gives us a more precise picture of court wisdom: "He also uttered three thousand proverbs; and his songs were a thousand and five. He spoke of trees, from the cedar that is in Lebanon to the hyssop that grows out of the wall; he spoke also of beasts, and of birds, and of reptiles, and of fish." Solomon therefore appears to posterity as the ideal wise man; but this passage ascribes to him personally the characteristics of his reign, and mistakenly connects the large numbers with proverbs and songs. If we take this into account, we can recognize the two types of wisdom instruction that can also be found in Mesopotamia and Egypt: (1) the construction of lists, suggested by the mention of flora and fauna, in this case two lists, one of 1005 items and the other of 3000; this is better termed educational wisdom than nature wisdom, because it includes more than mere natural phenomena; (2) the practical wisdom that provides rules of conduct, suggested by the two forms "proverb" and "song."

In the eighth century, too, "wisdom" represents the education and ethics of the governmental classes in the larger sense. In Jerusalem, life and government follow the principles of wisdom, as Isaiah's polemic against the "wise" shows, describing their apparently sagacious but actually pernicious activities (Isa. 5:20-21; 29:14; 31:1-3). The importance of wisdom instruction at that time for public life is shown by the superscription in Prov. 25:1. From the end of the seventh century on, the concept of wisdom is extended. In addition to the "wise" proper (Jer. 18:18), the term is applied to priests (Jer. 8:8-9), minor functionaries (Deut. 1:13, 15), and members of the judiciary (Deut. 16:19). This marks the beginning of a development which, in the postexilic period, saw wisdom instruction cease to represent the education and ethics of official circles and become the concern of more extensive groups. This also brought into being a separate class of wisdom teachers (Elihu in Job 32–37; Qoheleth). From the time of Solomon on, this teaching is based on an ideal of the education and training of the whole man, seeking to impart this ideal through knowledge of the laws and principles regulating both the world and human life. The ideal man is described as having "a cool spirit"—i.e., self-control (Prov. 17:27)—being "slow to anger" (Prov. 14:29), possessed of "a tranquil mind" and impervious to "passion" (Prov. 14:30); his opposite is the "hot-tempered man," who "has a hasty temper" (Prov. 15:18; 14:29).

In the postexilic period a final step was taken. The concept of wisdom was subjected to theological scrutiny and incorporated into a comprehensive theological system. Wisdom was understood as God's summons to man, a mediator of revelation, the schoolmistress of Israel and the nations, even as the principle implanted in the world at creation. The theological ideas were brought together and unified in the general concept of wisdom. This tendency may be observed especially in Proverbs 1–9 and Job 28 (probably drawing on a Gnostic myth),[17] by implication in the Elihu speeches of the book of Job, and quite plainly

[17] Cf. Fohrer, pp. 490-92, with additional bibliography on the question of personification or hypostatization of wisdom.

in the linking or equating of wisdom with the law in the didactic poems (§ 47.5) and Ecclesiasticus 24. Of course this system inevitably provoked criticism—not on account of its deficient theology of history, whose importance for Israel is often overestimated, but on account of the doctrine of retribution and, ultimately, the very existence of this system itself. The books of Job and Qoheleth bear witness to this criticism.

Two points distinguish Israelite wisdom instruction from that of the ancient Near East in general. In the first place, it was nationalized and made the common property of all Israel, so that it lost its connection with a particular class and became relevant to human life apart from all social restrictions, and at the same time was adapted in detail to the situation of Israel in Palestine. In the second place, it became ever more intimately associated with Yahwism, ceasing to be a compendium of worldly wisdom transcending particular religions and becoming instead a body of religio-ethical instruction, and even the framework of a theological system. For this reason the name "Yahweh" is frequently used in place of the general term "God" or "deity," and the religious attitude considers "fear of Yahweh" to be the beginning of wisdom.

6. *Significance of wisdom.* Notwithstanding the criticism leveled against the late theology of wisdom, the significance of wisdom instruction consists in its emphasis upon the value of morality vis-à-vis the superiority of the heavy fist or cunning, agile intelligence, and in its doctrine of retribution, which emphasizes the value of the law and of justice vis-à-vis the superiority of thoroughgoing hypocrisy or the contrivances of a suspicious mind. It represents practical religion in daily life, i.e., in the sphere of proper ethical conduct, in which the cult plays a minor role.[18] The order upon which the world and human life are based, in which man must find his place and according to which he must frame his life, is established and maintained by God. He therefore gives to the "wise" success and happiness as a blessing and a gift of grace, and to the "foolish" and wicked he brings disaster—not as an automatic and mechanical consequence, but on the basis of his retributive justice.

Of course this approach has its utilitarian and eudaimonistic side; not for nothing are the profits of religious devotion repeatedly mentioned (Job 22:2-3; 35:6-8). The cleverness and expertise of wisdom instruction not only derive from a certain basic attitude—an awareness of orderliness and regularity of divine nature—but also point toward a certain specific goal: mastery of the world and of life by submission to the order of the universe and discovery of one's proper place within it. This is the conduct that Job's friends repeatedly demand of him. In contrast to the approach of pure utilitarianism, there is no

[18] G. von Rad, *Theologie des Alten Testaments,* I, 1957 (4th ed., 1962), 431, argues that the person receiving instruction was nevertheless a member of the cultic community and that wisdom regulated his life outside the cultic sphere. This view depends on the unproved assumption that the wise man was part of the official structure of the cultic community. Furthermore, the attitude of wisdom instruction toward the cult, when in fact it mentions the cult at all, is mostly critical; cf. Prov. 15:8, 29; 20:25; 21:3, 27; 28:9; 30:12. It emphasizes the disposition of the cultic worshiper rather than the cultic act itself, and, finally, finds value in prayer rather than sacrifice. Cf. also Fichtner, pp. 41-42.

essential difference or antithesis between the "internal" value of an action, which resides in the behavior or conduct itself, and "external" success; they are both one and the same thing. Therefore the wise man who fears God may expect "plentiful success" (Job 26:3).

§ 47 The Literary Types of Wisdom and Their Traditions

G. Boström, *Paronomasi i den äldre Hebreiska Maschalliteraturen,* 1928; *idem, Proverbiastudien,* 1935; O. Eissfeldt, *Der Maschal im Alten Testament,* 1913; A. H. Godbey, "The Hebrew mašal," *AJSL,* XXXIX (1922/23), 89-108; A. S. Herbert, "The 'Parable' (māšāl) in the Old Testament," *SJTh,* VII (1954), 180-96; A. R. Johnson, "משל," *VTSuppl,* III (1955), 162-69; J. Pirot, "Le 'Māšāl' dans l'Ancien Testament," *RSR,* XXXVII (1950), 565-80; J. Schmidt, *Studien zur Stilistik der alttestamentlichen Spruchliteratur,* 1936.

1. *Mashal.* In wisdom instruction, the basic unit of rhetorical or literary form is the saying, either proverb or aphorism. The Hebrew term for both is *māšāl,* a very comprehensive expression that can apply to anything from a proverb to a didactic poem, from popular clichés to the discourses of the wise, from serious admonitions to taunt songs. Originally it may have meant "incantation" or "word of power." Therefore not every statement is a mashal, but only a statement having the power to create a new reality or gain recognition for an experience of the people or the wise and present it as a valid reality.[1]

2. *Proverb.* Like all the rest of the ancient Near East, Israel was familiar with proverbs and used them to record their experiences and insights concerning the regularity and order of the world and of human life. Proverbs are by no means peculiar to Israel; we may see something uniquely Israelite only when a proverb has become part and parcel of Yahwism. Numerous proverbs, immediately evident to the ear, express universal human experiences (I Sam. 24:14 [Eng. 24:13]); I Kings 20:11; Jer. 23:28; Eccles. 9:4). Sometimes a proverb derives from a specific historical situation and is introduced as a formula (II Sam. 5:8). Many proverbs are in prose, but in the course of time the rhythmic form won out (Ezek. 18:2). In content, utilization by Yahwism marks a great advance. A proverb may acquire religious overtones and illuminate religious situations (Prov. 10:6, 11), and can refer specifically to Yahweh (I Sam. 16:7). Of course those that rejected Yahwism could also use the proverb form to express their ideas (Zeph. 1:12).

3. *Riddle and numerical saying.* On the one hand, the riddle (Hebrew *ḥîdâ*) is connected with the popular proverb; on the other, it was borrowed by wisdom instruction. Prov. 1:6 practically equates riddles with the aphorisms of the wise.[2] In many cases riddles originally expressed the mystery of an

[1] Hempel*, p. 44.

[2] O. Eissfeldt, "Die Rätsel in Jdc 14," *ZAW,* XXX (1910), 132-35; J. R. Porter, "Samson's Riddle: Judges XIV,18," *JThSt* NS, XIII (1962), 106-109; H. Schmidt, "Zu Jdc 14," *ZAW,* XXXIX (1921), 316; N. H. Torczyner, "The Riddle in the Bible," *HUCA,* I (1924), 125-49.

association and its watchword, the secret of a superhuman being (e.g., the Sphinx), or, quite generally, a hidden power that becomes available to the person who solves them. We therefore find riddle contests as a kind of mortal combat or as an exhibition of power, the latter being appropriate to initiation ceremonies, courtship, and marriage. According to Judg. 14:14, Samson asked such a riddle in the course of a wedding celebration. The ancient significance of riddles explains why the queen of Sheba came to test Solomon with "hard questions" (I Kings 10:1). Later, the solving of riddles became merely a form of entertainment (cf. III Esdras 3–4; Letter of Aristeas § 178–300). The ability to solve riddles, however, is still considered a special power in the case of Daniel (Dan. 5:12); it enables him even to discover the content of a dream the king had forgotten.

The numerical saying is a form related to the riddle. It may be of Canaanite origin, as the Ugaritic text 51 iii. 17-21 and its absence elsewhere in the ancient Near East suggest. If so, it was borrowed and developed by Israel.[3] In it, the first member of a verse mentions a number and the second member the next higher number, followed by a list of objects corresponding in number to the latter. It seems reasonable to suppose that the numerical saying grew out of the riddle and that both the original question in the form of a riddle and the present numerical saying served first as mnemonic aids for educational wisdom. Later, practical wisdom made use of this form, which combines riddle and instruction. In the OT, we find such numerical sayings in Prov. 6:16-19; 30; Ps. 62:12 (Eng. 62:11); Job 5:19-22; expressions that are similar to numerical sayings occur in Amos 1:3–2:8 and Job 33:14-15.[4]

4. *Aphorism.* The aphorism or artificial wisdom saying, although it draws upon popular proverbial material and has rhythmical structure, is no longer a popular form of expression; it is an artistic and sometimes an artificial creation. It always has metrical form, as befits the original significance of the mashal as an expression of power; this form also made it easier for students to memorize. Such aphorisms were composed at least from the time of Solomon on. The existence of proverbs mentioning the king (Prov. 16:10; 22:29; 25:2; and *passim*) and the collection of proverbs made at the direction of Hezekiah (Prov. 25:1) point to the period of the Israelite monarchy. At that time, the "wise man" was, so to speak, the state official with an academic education; later, a class of wisdom teachers came into being alongside the priests and prophets (Jer. 18:18). They are the bearers of the practical wisdom expressed in aphorisms. As one might expect, this type of wisdom absorbed much foreign material, much of which was contributed by the foreigners in the king's

[3] A. Bea, "Der Zahlenspruch im Hebräischen und Ugaritischen," *Bibl*, XXI (1940), 196-98; D. Buzy, "Les machals numériques de la sangsue et de l'ʿalmah," *RB*, XLII (1933), 5-13; W. M. W. Roth, "The Numerical Sequence x/x+1 in the Old Testament," *VT*, XII (1962), 300-311; G. Sauer, *Die Sprüche Agurs*, 1963; W. B. Stevenson, "A Mnemonic Use of Numbers in Proverbs and Ben Sira," *Transactions of the Glasgow University Oriental Society* IX (1938/39), 26-38; F. Stummer, *Der kritische Wert der altaramäischen Aḥiḳartexte aus Elephantine*, 1914.

[4] Cf. also Ecclus. 23:16; 25:7-11; 26:5, 28; 50:25-26; and, in the Mishna, Pirke Aboth 5:1-15.

service and the Israelites that had returned home to Israel after service in other lands.

An aphorism can take the form of a statement (Prov. 10:1 ff.), an account of a personal experience (Prov. 24:30-34), an exhortation (Prov. 3:9), or a question (Prov. 6:27). In contrast to the proverb, which comprises only one line, the aphorism came to employ the long verse comprising two members as its dominant form (§ 5); most of the parallelism is antithetical (Prov. 10:2).[5] In cases of synonymous parallelism, the second member of the verse often emphasizes the "moral" of the first, more metaphorical, member (Ecclus. 13:1). In synthetical parallelism, the second member frequently resolves the image used in the first (Prov. 10:26). Sometimes the second member is so vague and inappropriate that its presence seems due solely to stylistic reasons (Prov. 12:11). In addition, an aphorism can be expanded by means of a motivation clause (Prov. 25:21-22) or even a series of similar statements that contribute little or nothing by way of new content (Prov. 6:20-21, 23). Qoheleth developed his own special form of aphorism (§ 51.5). Aphorisms make use of various literary devices, including synonymy (Prov. 17:21), listing (24:25), repetition (3:11), paronomasia and assonance (11:2), alliteration (8:27), puns (6:25), examples (24:30-34), comparison (15:11), and rhyme (11:2; 12:25).

5. *Wisdom and didactic poetry.* In Pss. 49:5 (Eng. 49:4) and 78:2, the author refers to his psalm as a mashal. We have here yet another literary type, that of wisdom poetry or didactic poetry, used by wisdom teachers to express their reflections and exhortations. For the history of the form, comparison with the two poems Job 18:5-21 and 20:4-29, both of which discuss the fate of the wicked, is instructive. The former is a single unified composition, but the latter poem clearly originated through juxtaposition of individual sayings or groups of sayings and does not give an impression of unity. In many cases independent aphorisms have been borrowed but not integrated into their context (Job 20:10, 16, 24-25). In Ps. 37:16, too, is a saying of this sort within the context of a poem; here and in Psalm 112 the alphabetic form facilitates such stringing together of material.

Besides Job 18, there are other wisdom poems that were composed as single units, e.g., Proverbs 8 (wisdom's description of herself as the ideal teacher), Proverbs 9 (Dame Wisdom and Dame Foolishness invite men to dine with them), and Job 28 (a poem on the inaccessibility of wisdom). In all these instances we are dealing with late texts from the postexilic period.

There are also a few psalms that represent wisdom or didactic poetry.[6] Psalms 37, 49, 73, and 91 share a common theme, based on the doctrine of retribution that supports practical wisdom: concern over the prosperity of the godless and the affliction of the devout. The doubt cast on the doctrine of retribution is answered by reference to God's ultimate destruction of the wicked and deliverance of the devout or by a confident "nevertheless" based on fellowship with God, which transcends all distress. In Psalm 78, the poet interprets Israel's

[5] Cf. the tabular survey in Skladny (§ 49), pp. 67-68.
[6] S. Mowinckel, "Psalms and Wisdom," *VTSuppl,* III (1955), 205-24.

history in such a way as to provide a guide by which his readers may conduct their lives (cf. also Psalms 105, 106). In Psalms 1 and 128, the introductory word *'ašrê*, "Happy is . . . , blessed is . . . ," also found in Ps. 127:5, is typical of wisdom literature, the only place this expression is found, where it corresponds to the cultic formula *bārûk*, "blessed. . . ." Poems such as these are an outgrowth of the approbation formula of wisdom instruction (e.g., Job 5:17). The introduction to Psalm 133, "Behold, how good and pleasant . . . ," is likewise typical of wisdom literature. The alphabetic Psalms 34, 111, and 112 are at least influenced by wisdom and may perhaps be counted among the wisdom poems. Psalms devoted to the theme of the law, like 19:8-15 (Eng. 19:7-14) and 119, show the influence of later wisdom theology.

6. *Parable, fable, allegory.* The parable is a prose type, an outgrowth of the metaphors and similes frequently found in aphorisms.[7] The best illustration is the parable of the poor man's lamb told by Nathan to David after David's transgression with Bathsheba (II Samuel 12). It is also not uncommon in the discourses of the prophets (e.g., Isa. 28:4*b*).

The fable is a didactic poem or narrative that takes its material from the world of animals or plants. In place of open controversy, it expresses a topical truth or criticism in veiled terms; it may even inveigh against unpopular persons, classes, and institutions in this fashion.[8] Besides Sumerian and Assyro-Babylonian fables, there are pictorial representations of animals from Egypt and northern Mesopotamia, dating from the second millennium, that presuppose animal fables. The OT preserves the fable told by Jotham (Judg. 9:8-15), which mocks a pointless and even dangerous monarchy. In Judg. 9:16-20 it is given a new function, and serves as a warning against Abimelech. II Kings 14:9 recounts a fable told by King Joash, intended as a warning to the lowly not to exalt themselves; 14:10 applies the fable to King Amaziah. The popularity of the fable is shown by its influence upon other literary types: the parable, in which human beings and other creatures appear together (Isa. 5:1-7; 10:15; 29:16; 45:9; Jer. 18:1-11), the legend (Jonah 2:1 [Eng. 1:17]; 2:11 [Eng. 2:10]; 4:5-11), and allegory (Ezek. 17:1-10; 19:1-9; 31:1-18).

Allegory consists of a series of metaphors, each of which is significant and must be interpreted; inanimate objects or abstract ideas are often personified, e.g., wisdom and folly. A more extended allegory, a description of old age, is found in Eccles. 11:9–12:8. Ezekiel was particularly fond of this rhetorical form, albeit in highly schematic shape; in this respect he exhibits the influence of wisdom instruction (cf. besides the passages mentioned also Ezekiel 15, 16, and 23).

7. *Lists.* Finally, Israel was familiar with the construction of scholarly lists typical of educational wisdom. Only remnants of such lists have been preserved,

[7] C. E. Macartney, *The Parables of the Old Testament*, 2nd ed., 1955.

[8] H. Gressmann, *Israels Spruchweisheit im Zusammenhang der Weltliteratur*, 1925; H. Gunkel, *Das Märchen im Alten Testament*, 1921; K. Meuli, *Herkunft und Wesen der Fabel*, 1954; R. J. Williams, "The Fable in the Ancient Near East," in *Irwin-Festschrift*, 1956, pp. 3-26; A. Wünsche, *Die Pflanzen-Fabel in der Weltliteratur*, 1905.

and these remnants themselves have been used in other compositions. Encyclopedic lists of this type were used in numerical sayings (see 3 above), Genesis 1, and Psalms 104 and 148 in order to discuss natural phenomena, which are of a different sort but nevertheless have a rational order. The book of Job contains many poems dependent upon lists: 24:5-8, 14-16*a;* 28; 30:2-8; 36:27–37:13; 40:15-24; 40:25–41:26 (Eng. 41:1-34); 38:4–39:30.[9] Especially noteworthy is God's answer to Job, which mentions a series of examples drawn from both animate and inanimate nature, quite possibly selected from an onomasticon. The list of natural phenomena does not follow the Egyptian pattern, but depends instead on the cosmology and the geographical, climatic, and zoological conditions of Palestine; this suggests the existence of native Israelite onomastica.

8. *In other books of the OT.* Our survey of the various literary types of wisdom shows that they are not restricted to the wisdom books proper, but are also found in other books of the OT. Wisdom instruction was not a strictly defined specialty. Its representatives worked with ideas from every conceivable intellectual milieu; conversely, those who were trained in the wisdom schools were active in various fields (cf. the association with the temple in Jer. 36:10). Furthermore, we may think in terms of a simple kind of popular wisdom ("family wisdom") having existed since remote antiquity. Thus wisdom instruction pervaded the total life of Israel to a much greater extent than the preserved remnants of wisdom literature suggest.

The narrative books of the OT in particular contain many proverbs, together with significant instances of other literary types (riddle, parable, fable). The Psalter came to include a whole series of didactic wisdom poems; some of the prophetical books, too, contain sayings of wisdom instructors, e.g., Isa. 3:10-11; 32:6-8; 40:18-20 + 41:7; 44:9-20; 46:5-8. Baruch, Jeremiah's scribe and biographer, was at least educated in the wisdom school. Although Isaiah frequently disagrees violently with the "wise" politicians, whose situation is perfectly familiar to him, he and other prophets not uncommonly make use of rhetorical forms borrowed from wisdom, e.g., Isa. 28:23-29; Amos 3:3-6.[10] It is going too far, however, to call wisdom one source of the genuinely prophetical literary types.[11]

Finally, the rhetorical forms of wisdom instruction make up a not inconsiderable portion of apocalyptic literature. It contains what one might call "scientific" sections dealing with astronomical problems arising in the calculation of the time of the eschaton, as well as elements of historiography with the theory of world periods. In addition, it should not be forgotten that apocalyptic is the product of eschatological prophecy.[12]

[9] For details, cf. G. Fohrer, *Das Buch Hiob,* 1963.

[10] For details, cf. J. Lindblom, "Wisdom in the Old Testament Prophets," *VTSuppl,* III (1955), 192-204; S. Terrien, "Amos and Wisdom," in *Essays Muilenburg,* 1962, pp. 108-15; H. W. Wolff, *Amos' geistige Heimat,* 1964.

[11] This is the view espoused by H. W. Wolff, "Der Aufruf zur Volksklage," *ZAW,* LXXVI (1964), 48-56, who finds here the basis for prophetical exhortation.

[12] G. von Rad, *Theologie des Alten Testaments,* II, 1960 (4th ed., 1965), 314-21, considers apocalypticism to be an outgrowth of wisdom rather than prophetism, on the questionable and

§ 48 Compilation and Transmission

1. *Compilation and transmission.* It follows from the very nature of wisdom instruction that its insights and exhortations were collected and handed down. They were not meant for a single day, but for many generations. Even though the Egyptian view that the transmission of wisdom instruction paved the way for the order of the universe clearly did not play an important role in Israel, efforts were nevertheless made to guarantee the preservation of wisdom received from God or from the fathers. Therefore the first task of the wisdom instructors is to collect the familiar aphorisms, teach them to others, and write them down for posterity. Another source of knowledge is personal experience, so that the wisdom teachers also worked creatively, transforming familiar material and coining new aphorisms. Some works of wisdom literature bear the stamp of a significant literary personality (Job, Ecclesiastes, Ecclesiasticus). In the late period of Israel it was even possible to lament that there was no end to the writing of books (Eccles. 12:12).

There was also a practical reason for all this writing: instruction in the wisdom schools.[1] Aphorisms constituted at least a portion of the material used for learning to read and write. Wisdom instruction was therefore very early committed to writing, and many copies represent nothing more than writing drill. Excavations have frequently unearthed schoolroom exercises outside of Israel. In addition, as the formula "Hear, my son" shows, instruction made use of the oral transmission of aphorisms, which the students were required to learn by heart. To make this task easier, study aids were provided by bringing together certain related sayings: besides the numerical sayings, four aphorisms beginning with the letter *bêt* (Prov. 11:9-12),[2] two pairs of aphorisms beginning with the words "heart" and "good" respectively (15:13-14, 16-17), and minor poems like those concerning the dangers of offering surety (6:1-5), laziness (6:6-11), and deception (6:12-15). We also have instances of juxtaposition based on catchwords or similarity of content (Proverbs 16; royal proverbs) or antithesis (Prov. 26:4-5; to answer a fool or not).

2. *Formation of wisdom books.* The collecting of aphorisms was therefore an important way in which documents of wisdom literature came into being. There were also other methods and principles, resulting in several different forms of literature.

a) The simplest method is the growth of a book out of various collections.

---

contestable assumption that prophetism in *Heilsgeschichte* is rooted in certain election traditions not found in apocalypticism.

[1] H. Brunner, *Altägyptische Erziehung,* 1957; L. Dürr, *Das Erziehungswesen im Alten Testament und im Antiken Orient,* 1932; J. Hempel, "Pathos und Humor in der israelitischen Erziehung," in Von *Ugarit nach Qumran, Eissfeldt-Festschrift,* 1958, pp. 63-81; S. N. Kramer, "Die sumerische Schule," *WZ Halle,* V (1955/56), 695-704; E. Otto, "Bildung und Ausbildung im alten Ägypten," *ZÄS,* LXXXI (1956), 41-48.

[2] This corresponds to the arrangement of the Sumerian proverb collections according to the first written sign.

It is easy to see that the book of Proverbs comprises several originally independent collections. They were simply strung together in their primitive form, and still retain their superscriptions. But these collections are not in every case the earliest forms discernible. Some of them in turn represent compilations of smaller collections. Thus the process of addition leads from the smallest collections, conceived as mnemonic aids, to larger and larger units.

b) Following Egyptian prototypes, such collections can constitute an "instruction." In this case, the assembled aphorisms clarify certain specific basic ideas. Examples are Proverbs 1–9 and the book of Ecclesiastes.

c) Yet another form is the literary "instruction," which treats a single coherent theme. Prov. 31:10-31, a poem in praise of the perfect wife, is such a form.

d) The final stage is represented by the carefully thought out literary composition, which, despite occasional use of already extant material, must be understood as the individual creation of its author. The classic example is the book of Job.

3. *Later wisdom books*. Later wisdom books, which did not become part of the OT, include the book of Ecclesiasticus or Jesus ben Sirach (collections of wisdom aphorisms arranged in part according to subject matter, poems concerning wisdom, psalmlike songs, retrospective eulogy on the great figures of Israel's history), the Wisdom of Solomon (poems or treatises), and IV Maccabees (a philosophical tract).

CHAPTER TWO: THE WISDOM BOOKS

§ 49 PROVERBS

ATD: H. RINGGREN, 1962. BOT: J. VAN DER PLOEG, 1952. HAT: B. GEMSER, 2nd ed., 1963. HK: W. FRANKENBERG, 1898. HS: H. WIESMANN, 1923. IB: C. T. FRITSCH, 1955. ICC: C. H. TOY, 1899, reprinted 1948. KeH: W. NOWACK, 2nd ed., 1883. KHC: G. WILDEBOER, 1897. SAT: P. VOLZ, 2nd ed., 1921. SZ: H. L. STRACK, 2nd ed., 1899. Individual commentaries: A. BARUCQ, 1964 ("Sources Bibliques").

E. G. BAUCKMANN, "Die Proverbien und die Sprüche des Jesus Sirach," *ZAW*, LXXII (1960), 33-63; G. BOSTRÖM, *Proverbiastudien*, 1935; M. DAHOOD, *Proverbs and Northwest Semitic Philology*, 1963; A. DRUBBEL, "Le conflit entre la Sagesse profane et la Sagesse religieuse," *Bibl*, XVII (1936), 45-70, 407-28; *idem*, *Les livres sapientiaux d'Israël dans leurs sources préexiliques*, 1936; J. W. GASPAR, *Social Ideas in the Wisdom Literature of the Old Testament*, 1947; H. GESE, *Lehre und Wirklichkeit in der alten Weisheit*, 1958; K. KOCH, "Gibt es ein Vergeltungsdogma im Alten Testament?" *ZThK*, LII (1955), 1-42; G. KUHN, *Beiträge zur Erklärung des salomonischen Spruchbuches*, 1931; A. D. POWER, *The Proverbs of Solomon*, 1949; *idem*, *Side Lights on the Book of Proverbs*, 1950; H. RANSTON, *The Old Testament Wisdom Books and their Teaching*, 1930; H. RINGGREN, *Word and Wisdom*, 1947; G. SAUER, *Die Sprüche Agurs*, 1963; E. SCHMITT, *Leben in den Weisheitsbüchern Job, Sprüche und Jesus Sirach*, 1954; P. W. SKEHAN, "A Single Editor for the Whole Book of Proverbs," *CBQ*, X (1948), 115-30; U. SKLADNY, *Die ältesten Spruchsammlungen in Israel*, 1962; C. I. K. STORY, "The Book of Proverbs and Northwest Semitic Literature," *JBL*, LXIV (1945), 319-37; G. WALLIS, "Zu den Spruchsammlungen Prov 10,1–22,16 und 25–29," *ThLZ*, LXXXV (1960), 147-48.

1. *Terminology and structure*. This book derives its name from the superscription in 1:1: "The proverbs (Greek *paroimíai*) of Solomon, son of David, king of Israel." Although tradition looks upon Solomon as its author, considering him to be the wise man par excellence, it in fact comprises an anthology of Israelite and non-Israelite wisdom instruction dating from several centuries.

It derives neither from Solomon nor from Solomon's period, but came into being gradually through a considerable period of time. This is shown by (*a*) the various superscriptions (1:1; 10:1; 22:17; 24:23; 25:1; 30:1; 31:1), each of which introduces a distinct collection of sayings; (*b*) the divergent locations of the fourth and fifth collections in the LXX (24:23-34 following 30:14; 25–29 following 31:9), which point to relative independence of the collections even in the late period; (*c*) the borrowing of non-Israelite material, indicated by the superscriptions 30:1 and 31:1; and (*d*) differences in form and content between the collections.

Eight collections or sections are individually recognizable, numbering three major collections and five minor collections or sections, which have been appended to the second and third major collections:

A 1–9	The proverbs of Solomon	
B 10–22:16	The proverbs of Solomon	
C	22:17–24:22	The words of the wise
D	24:23-34	These also are sayings of the wise.
E 25–29	These also are the proverbs of Solomon which the men of Hezekiah king of Judah copied.	
F	30	The words of Agur son of Jakeh of Massa[1]
G	31:1-9	The words of Lemuel, king of Massa, which his mother taught him
H	31:10-31	Poem in praise of the perfect wife (no superscription)

2. *Collection A.*[2] Collection A (1–9), apart from a few individual proverbs, e.g., 1:7-9; 3:1-12, contains for the most part wisdom poems, sometimes of brief compass, e.g., 3:13-18, 21-26; 6:1-5, 6-11, more frequently of considerable length, e.g., 2:1-22; 4:1-27; 8; 9. In some of them a father admonishes his son, warning him against intercourse with strange women, against giving surety, against laziness, deceit, and other abominations, and extolling the value and blessing that comes from wisdom and the fear of God. In other poems the speaker is personified wisdom or foolishness. The collection is not all of a piece, but the product of gradual accretion, as can be seen not only from the use of separate poems, but also from the division of the warning against strange women (5:1-23; 6:20-35) by the interpolated poems (6:1-19). As to the date, there is much to suggest the later postexilic period, with considerable Greek and Hellenistic influence, so that 1–9 may be dated toward the end of the fourth century B.C. As the latest section, these chapters were placed at the beginning of the book (cf. Genesis 1, Psalm 1).

The long sentences are striking and contrary to Hebrew idiom; chapter 2 actually constitutes one single sentence. Form-critically, we may note the influence of the prophetical invective and threat and of hymnic style. In 7:16, *ʾēṭûn* is a Greek loanword (*othónē*). The warning against strange and foreign women has replaced a warning against religious apostasy. The concept of wisdom has been influenced by the fervor of prophetical preaching and the myth of the primal man (8:22-31), and above all by a Gnostic myth according to which wisdom seeks a dwelling place with man and union with him.[3] Finally, there is a close connection with Ecclesiasticus.

[1] Instead of "the oracle," read *hammaśśāʾî*.

[2] In addition to Boström, see A. Hulsbosch, "Sagesse créatrice et éducatrice," *Augustinianum*, I (1961), 217-35; 433-51; II (1962), 5-39; III (1963), 5-27; P. Humbert, "La 'femme étrangère' du livre des Proverbes," *RES* 1937, pp. 49-64; A. Robert, "Les attaches littéraires bibliques de Proverbes I–IV," *RB*, XLIII (1934), 42-68, 172-204, 374-384; XLIV (1935), 344-65, 502-25; P. W. Skehan, "The Seven Columns of Wisdom's House in Prov 9,1," *CBQ*, IX (1947), 190-98; W. Staerk, "Die sieben Säulen der Welt und des Hauses der Weisheit," *ZNW*, XXXV (1936), 232-61.

[3] For details, cf. Fohrer in *ThW*, VII, 491-92. W. F. Albright, *From the Stone Age to Christianity*, 1948, pp. 365-66, assumes Canaanite or Phoenician influence, but this suggestion is unlikely. There is then no reason to consider Proverbs 1–9 the earliest portion of the book, going back to Solomon (Fritsch). H. Donner, "Die religionsgeschichtlichen Ursprünge von Prov Sal 8," *ZÄS*, LXXXII (1957), 8-18; W. A. Irwin, "Where Shall Wisdom Be Found?" *JBL*, LXXX

3. *Collection B.* Collection B (10–22:16) consists of 375 individual proverbs joined together without logical sequence or coherent plan (the earliest form of collection). For ease in learning, however, several aphorisms have often been juxtaposed on the basis of assonance and catchwords, e.g., 10:11*b,* 12*b;* 10:14-15, or subject matter, e.g., 10:18-21, which deal with speaking, and 16:10-15, which apply to the king.

This collection comprises two subsidiary collections, 10–15 and 16–22:16, each of which in turn comprises other minor collections that can no longer be distinguished, as doublets consisting of whole and half verses show (10:1 = 15:20; 10:2*b* = 11:4*b*; 10:6*b* = 11:11*b*; 10:8*b* = 10:10*b*; 10:13*b* = 19:29*b*).[4] Both subsidiary collections discuss, with variations and repetitions, the conduct and state of the wise and of the foolish, of the righteous and of the wicked. There are, however, characteristic differences. The first subsidiary collection consists almost entirely of direct statements, the majority of which use antithetical parallelism. The religious tone is less developed than in the second subsidiary collection, in which the number of admonitions is somewhat greater and synthetic parallelism dominates.

The aphorisms bear witness to the high estimation in which the king was held, frequently deal with the administration of justice, and refer to the life of an agricultural nation with a striking contrast between rich and poor. Many of the sayings refer to the relationship between parents and children and show high esteem for women. Apart from its general religious character, the collection is especially noteworthy for the way in which it judges human conduct on the basis of whether it is pleasing or abhorrent to Yahweh. Yahweh alone possesses the true measure, by which he judges men's hearts (16:2; 17:3; 20:27; 21:2), helps the righteous, and punishes evildoers (10:29).[5]

In dating the collection and its aphorisms, one must note both the existence of a monarchy (e.g., 14:28, 35; 16:10, 12-15; 19:12; 20:2, 8, 26, 28; 21:1; 22:11), which may point to the preexilic period—but by no means must necessarily do so, since the book of Ecclesiastes, which is certainly postexilic, frequently mentions the king—and also the appearance of Aramaic words (14:34, *ḥesed,* "reproach"; 17:10, *nḥt,* "go deep"; 18:24, *r* ʿʿ, "break"; 19:20, *qbl,* "accept"), which probably did not penetrate into the language until the exilic period.[6] It follows that a portion of the aphorisms or minor collections, perhaps

(1961), 133-48; H.-J. Kraus, *Die Verkündigung der Weisheit,* 1951; J. de Savignica, "La sagesse en Proverbs VIII,23-31," *VT,* XII (1962), 211-15; R. B. Y. Scott "Wisdom in Creation: The *ʾĀmôn* of Proverbs VIII 30," *ibid.,* X (1950), 213-23; R. Stecher, "Die persönliche Weisheit in den Proverbien Kap. 8," *ZKTh,* LXXV (1953/54), 411-51; R. A. Waser, "A Brief Study of the Relationship between the Eighth Chapter of Proverbs and the Prologue of St. John's Gospel," in *MacDonald Presentation Volume,* 1933, pp. 425-54.

[4] Cf. also Gemser, pp. 55-57.

[5] There is no direct, automatic connection between behavior and fate, between a deed and its consequences (Koch); neither does Yahweh merely guarantee the connection between a deed and its consequences, rather than fashioning it (Skladny).

[6] Eissfeldt*, p. 641, contrary to G. R. Driver, "Hebrew Poetic Diction," *VTSuppl,* I (1953), 26 ff.

even the basic content of both subsidiary collections, may derive from the preexilic period; as a whole, however, Collection B was not completed until the postexilic period.

4. *Collection C.* Collection C (22:17–24:22), which constitutes the first appendix to B, is divided into two completely different sections.

As has long been recognized,[7] the first subsidiary collection (22:17–23:11) is closely related to the Egyptian Instruction of Amen-em-opet, which probably dates between the tenth and sixth centuries B.C.[8] The introductory poem (22:17-21) and the ten themes discussed (22:22–23:11) follow—often word for word—their Egyptian source. Even the division of this source into thirty chapters ("houses") seems to have been borrowed by the Israelite redactor for the entire collection 22:17–24:22 (cf. 22:20, where the RSV correctly reads "thirty sayings" for the Hebrew "day before yesterday" or "adjutants"). The redactor was not, however, a mere translator; he used a third of the Egyptian Instruction to produce an anthology that treats the themes in a different order; in 22:26-27 he has interpolated a saying of his own. The borrowing may have taken place toward the end of the Israelite monarchy (22:29).

Following Oesterley and Kevin, Drioton in particular has championed the view that the Instruction of Amen-em-opet in fact depends on Prov. 22:17 ff., or that its author translated into Egyptian the wisdom book of a Jewish colony in Egypt and that the author of Prov. 22:17 ff. also drew upon this same book, which is no longer preserved.[9] This view, however, has been so thoroughly refuted, most recently by Montet and Couroyer, that it cannot be maintained.[10]

In the second subsidiary collection (23:12–24:22), 23:13-14 has been borrowed from the Instruction of Ahikar vi. 82. The other sayings have no foreign associations; some statements and admonitions have strong religious overtones (23:17; 24:12, 18, 21). It is possible that 24:1, 3, 5 (7, 10) mark the beginning of an alphabetic collection.[11]

5. *Collection D.* Collection D (23:23-34), which constitutes the second appendix to B, contains sayings directed against partiality in judging and against laziness. The universality of its statements makes it impossible to date.

6. *Collection E.* Collection E (25–29), which, according to its superscription,

[7] A. Erman, "Das Weisheitsbuch des Amen-em-ope," *OLZ*, XXVII (1924), 241-52; H. Gressmann, "Die neugefundene Lehre des Amen-em-ope und die vorexilische Spruchdichtung Israels," *ZAW*, XLII (1924), 272-96.

[8] This is the view espoused by H. Brunner in *Handbuch der Orientalistik*, I, 2 (1952), 106 (XXII–XXVI Dynasty). A different date, probably deliberately too early, is suggested by Albright in Gemser, p. 83, and *VTSuppl*, III (1955), 6 (twelfth–eleventh century).

[9] W. O. E. Oesterley, "The 'Teaching of Amen-em-ope' and the Old Testament," *ZAW*, XLV (1927), 9-24; R. O. Kevin, "The Wisdom of Amen-em-apt and its Possible Dependence upon the Hebrew Book of Proverbs," *JSOR*, XIV (1930), 115-57; O. Drioton, "Sur la Sagesse d'Aménémopé," in *Mélanges Robert*, 1957, pp. 254-80; *idem*, "Le Livre des Proverbes et la Sagesse d'Amén-ém-opé," in *BEThL*, XII (1959), 229-41.

[10] Gemser, p. 85; P. Montet, *L'Égypte et la Bible*, 1959, pp. 111-28; B. Couroyer, "L'origine égyptienne de la Sagesse d'Amenemopé," *RB*, LXX (1963), 208-24.

[11] Gemser, pp. 85, 87; G. Boström, *Paronomasi i den äldre Hebreiska Maschalliteraturen*, 1928, p. 197, points out the parallels between Prov. 24:1, 19, 14 and Ps. 37:1, 37*b*.

derives from the men of Hezekiah, contains primarily aphorisms consisting of a single verse, although some longer ones occur (25:4-5; 26:18-19); there are more direct statements than admonitions. This collection, too, is divided into two subsidiary collections (25–27 and 28–29). The first subsidiary collection exhibits mostly synthetic parallelism, numerous sayings in the form of true similes, and clever rules based on practical experience. The second exhibits mostly antithetical parallelism and many sayings ethical or religious in tone.

The themes are in many respects similar to those found in collection B; 16–22:16 and 25–29 share a strikingly large number of similar and identical aphorisms,[12] so that the circles of their collectors were closely related. Although the first subsidiary collection clearly presupposes the situation of an agricultural nation and draws its images from the realm of nature, while in the second subsidiary collection political life comes to the fore, it is not possible to define them as closely as Skladny does, calling the former a code of conduct for farmers and artisans, the latter a code of conduct for rulers.

The superscription states that the collection came into being during the reign of Hezekiah (*ca.* 700 B.C.), a period of national restoration. This is quite likely true. At least the majority of the aphorisms themselves therefore derive from the middle period of the monarchy.[13]

7. *Collection F.* Collection F (30)[14] constitutes the first appendix to E. Vss. 1-6 and 32-33 provide a framework for material consisting mostly of numerical sayings (vss. 7-9, 11-14, 15-16, 18-19, 21-23, [24-28], 29-31; vss. 7 and 11 must be supplemented). Correctly interpreted, the superscription calls the author a resident of Massa, pointing to a North Arabian tribe in the northern region of Transjordan; in addition, there are many points of contact with the Canaanite environment familiar to us from the Ugaritic texts (Sauer). The text was therefore probably borrowed from the border region between Israel and Canaan. There is nothing to suggest a definite date. The verses of the framework, however, are similar in content to the book of Job; here the wise man exhibits from the very outset the attitude Job achieved only at the conclusion of his experiences. The numerical sayings therefore probably represent earlier foreign material, while the verses of the framework seem to have been added after the model of the book of Job.

8. *Collection G.* Collection G (31:1-9), which constitutes the second appendix to E, contains warnings against intercourse with women (vss. 2-3) and the enjoyment of wine (vss. 4-7), as well as an admonition to aid the oppressed (vss. 8-9). This collection derives from the same area as the words of Agur.

9. *"The Perfect Wife."* The "poem in praise of the perfect wife" (31:10-31 [H])[15] provides an antithesis to the warning against women in 31:2-3 and constitutes the third appendix to E. It is an alphabetic song that gives us an in-

[12] Gemser, p. 99.

[13] H. Cazelles, *VTSuppl,* III (1955), 29, finds North Israelite wisdom in the basic stratum of 25–29.

[14] In addition to Sauer, E. F. Sutcliffe, "The Meaning of Proverbs 30,18-20," *Irish ThQ,* XXVII (1960), 125-31; C. C. Torrey, "Proverbs, Chapter 30," *JBL,* LXXIII (1954), 93-96.

[15] M. B. Crook, "The Marriageable Maiden of Prov 31,10-31," *JNES,* XIII (1954), 137-40.

sight into the position, esteem, and recognition enjoyed by the wife of a respected man; it portrays her as a developed personality after the fashion of Gen. 2:18. It most likely dates from the postexilic period.

10. *Redaction.* The redaction of the book took place by the addition of other collections before and after a nucleus collection. This nucleus is represented by chapters 25–29, a collection that came into being in the time of Hezekiah; some of it may in fact date back to the time of Solomon. To it were added the two appendixes 30 and 31:1-9 (the latter and the nucleus of 30 possibly still in the preexilic period); and, in the postexilic period, an additional collection of sayings, likewise attributed to Solomon, with its own appendixes (10–24) was placed before the other. Then 31:10-31 was added as a contrast to 31:2-3, and, last but by no means least, the collection 1–9, which came into being in the fourth century. The date of this last collection provides the *terminus a quo* for the origin of the book as a whole; it cannot have reached its final form before the end of the fourth century.

The priority of place given to the latest collection gives the book a tone that differs from the purpose and goal of the earlier collections—instruction in practical wisdom appropriate to the education of royal officials. As the book now stands, it claims to be the instruction given by a father to his son, which places it in the milieu of what is universally human. In addition, it enters the realm of the all-inclusive system of theological wisdom, in which fear of God is accounted the highest wisdom, while foolishness is equated with rejection of the law.

§ 50 The Book of Job

ATD: A. Weiser, 3rd ed., 1959. BK: F. Horst, 1960-ff. COT: J. H. Kroeze, 1961. EH: N. Peters, 1928. HAT: G. Hölscher, 2nd ed., 1952. HK: K. Budde, 2nd ed., 1913. HS: P. Szczygiel, 1931. IB: S. L. Terrien, 1954. ICC: S. R. Driver and G. B. Gray, 1921, reprinted 1951. KAT²: G. Fohrer, 1963. KeH: A. Dillmann, 4th ed., 1891. KHC: B. Duhm, 1897. SAT: P. Volz, 2nd ed., 1921. SZ: W. Volck, 1889. Individual commentaries : E. J. Kissane, 1939, reprinted 1946; E. König, 1929; F. Stier, 1954; N. H. Torczyner (Tur-Sinai), 1941, reprinted 1957.

F. Baumgärtel, *Der Hiobdialog,* 1933; G.-W. H. Bickell, "Kritische Bearbeitung des Job-Dialogs," *WZKM,* VI (1892), 137-47, 241-57, 327-34; VII (1893), 1-20, 153-68; *idem, Das Buch Job nach Anleitung der Strophik und der Septuaginta,* 1894; F. Buhl, "Zur Vorgeschichte des Buches Hiob," in BZAW, XLI (1925), 52-61; M. Buttenwieser, *The Book of Job,* 1922; M. Dahood, "Some Northwest-Semitic Words in Job," *Bibl,* XXXVIII (1957), 306-20; B. D. Eerdmans, *Studies in Job,* 1939; C. L. Feinberg, "The Poetic Structure of the Book of Job and the Ugaritic Literature," *BS,* CIII (1946), 283-92; G. Fohrer, *Studien zum Buche Hiob,* 1963; K. Fullerton, "The Original Conclusion to the Book of Job," *ZAW,* XLII (1924), 116-35; H. Gese, *Lehre und Wirklichkeit in der alten Weisheit,* 1958; J. Hempel, "Das theologische Problem des Hiob," *ZSTh,* VI (1929), 621-89 (= *Apoxysmata,* 1961, pp. 114-73); J. Herz, "Formgeschichtliche Untersuchungen zum Problem des Hiobbuches," *WZ Leipzig,* III (1953/54), 162-75; W. A. Irwin, "Poetic Structure in the Dialogue of Job," *JNES,* V (1946), 26-39; *idem,* "Job's Redeemer," *JBL,*

LXXXI (1962), 217-29; M. JASTROW, JR., *The Book of Job,* 1920; A. JEPSEN, *Das Buch Hiob und seine Deutung,* 1963; C. G. JUNG, *Antwort auf Hiob,* 1962 (Eng. *Answer to Job,* 1963); E. G. KRAELING, *The Book of the Ways of God,* 1938; C. KUHL, "Neuere Literarkritik des Buches Hiob," *ThR* NF, XXI (1953), 163-205, 257-317; *idem,* "Vom Hiobbuche und seinen Problemen," *ibid.,* XXII (1954), 261-316; J. LINDBLOM, *Boken om Job og hans lidande,* 1940; *idem, La composition du Livre de Job,* 1945; H. MÖLLER, *Sinn und Aufbau des Buches Hiob,* 1955; N. RHODOKANAKIS, "Das Buch Hiob," *WZKM,* XLV (1938), 169-90; H. RICHTER, "Erwägungen zum Hiobproblem," *EvTh,* XVIII (1958), 320-24; *idem,* "Die Naturweisheit des Alten Testaments im Buche Hiob," *ZAW,* LXX (1958), 1-20; *idem, Studien zu Hiob,* 1959; H. H. ROWLEY, "The Book of Job and its Meaning," *BJRL,* XLI (1958/59), 167-207 (= *From Moses to Qumran,* 1963, pp. 141-83); N. M. SARNA, "Epic Substratum in the Prose of Job," *JBL,* LXXVI (1957), 13-25; E. SCHMITT, *Leben in den Weisheitsbüchern Job, Sprüche und Jesus Sirach,* 1954; M. SEKINE, "Schöpfung und Erlösung im Buche Hiob," in *Von Ugarit nach Qumran* (Eissfeldt-Festschrift), 1958, pp. 213-23; P. W. SKEHAN, "Strophic Patterns in the Book of Job," *CBQ,* XXIII (1961), 125-43; S. SPIEGEL, "Noah, Danel and Job," in *Ginzberg Jubilee Volume,* I (1954), 205-55; W. B. STEVENSON, *The Poem of Job,* 2nd ed., 1948; N. H. TORCZYNER (TUR-SINAI), *Das Buch Hiob,* 1920; *idem,* "Hiobdichtung und Hiobsage," *MGWJ,* LXIX (1925), 234-48; A. WEISER, "Das Problem der sittlichen Weltordnung im Buche Hiob," *ThBl,* II (1923), 154-64 (= *Glaube und Geschichte im Alten Testament,* 1961, pp. 9-19); C. WESTERMANN, *Der Aufbau des Buches Hiob,* 1956; E. WÜRTHWEIN, *Gott und Mensch in Dialog und Gottesreden des Buches Hiob,* Habilitationsschrift, Tübingen, 1938.

1. *Structure.* The book of Job is among the most stimulating and gripping books of the Bible; it is at the same time a poetic work of art of the highest order. The book is anonymous, being named not for its author but for its central character, Job, whom the archaic framework narrative and Ezek. 14:14, 20 show to be a legendary figure of antiquity. In its present form, the book exhibits the following structure:

I: 1–2, a prologue with six scenes, describing Job's religious devotion and prosperity (1:1-5), the decision to test his devotion in the course of a first conversation in heaven (1:6-12), Job's testing through the loss of his possessions and children ("Job's messengers") and his successful passing of the test (1:13-22), the decision to put him to the test a second time (2:1-6), Job's testing through sickness (2:7-10), and the visit of his three friends Eliphaz, Bildad, and Zophar (2:11-13).

II: 3–42:6, discourses in poetic form: first, an extensive dialogue between Job and his friends in three cycles of speeches (3–11; 12–20; 21–28), the last of which, after several short songs or poems in 26 and 27, concludes with a song about wisdom (28). Then follow more speeches by Job contrasting his present state with his former state, an oath of purgation, and a challenge to God (29–31). Next come the speeches of Elihu, a friend not previously mentioned (32–37). The conclusion consists of two speeches by God (38–40:2; 40:6–41:26 [Eng. 40:6–41:34]) and Job's two replies (40:3-5; 42:1-6), in which he humbles himself and submits.

III: 42:1-17, an epilogue with two scenes, describing God's judgment upon Job's friends (42:7-9) and Job's restoration (42:10-17).

The style of the book shows its author to be an almost unequaled master of baroque imagination and great learning; he uses images both numerous and varied to express the most diverse moods in one and the same speech, as well as expressions that seldom or never occur elsewhere.

2. *The framework.* The framework is divided into a prologue and an epilogue (1–2; 42:7-17). It is almost universally accepted that this framework was originally an independent narrative, a legend whose point was didactic and parenetic, set in a foreign land outside Israel.[1] The relationship of the legend to the poetic discourses remains disputed—did the poet himself join the two, and in what way, or is the legend a later addition? Also disputed are the original form of the legend and the changes it may have undergone in the course of transmission. Batten, Alt, Kraeling, and Lindblom have assigned separate sections of the legend to various stages; Pfeiffer* assumes an Israelite revision of the totally foreign narrative; Cassuto, Spiegel, and Sarna consider it the prose form of an ancient poetical epic, possibly Canaanite. These and other observations can be stated more precisely: the Job legend (*a*) exhibits features of tradition that suggest at least four different periods and circles, and (*b*) was revised and to a certain extent altered when it was coupled with the poetic discourses.

a) From the earliest, pre-Israelite form of the legend [2] derive the names of Job, the Sabeans and Chaldeans, and probably also Job's friends, the picture of Job as a seminomadic farmer, and—in agreement with Ugaritic parallels—the position of Job's daughters, the arrangement of the servants, the heavenly council, and the divine beings inhabiting heaven. In the earlier preexilic period, the Israelite form of the Job legend was constructed after the model of the narrative technique used in the earlier source strata of the Hexateuch. Here belong primarily the statement of Job's prosperity in terms of cattle and slaves, the sacrifices to appease God's wrath, the description of God's beneficent governance, and the adaptation of the whole to Yahwism, as well as its stylistic structure and execution. The use of the Job legend in the exilic period, suggested by Ezek. 12:12-23, has left only a few traces in the vocabulary. Such traces also derive from the postexilic period (42:16-17 has been influenced by P), during which we may also reasonably date the influence of wisdom instruction (1:1, 21*a*; 2:3, 10) and the revision of the scenes in heaven by the introduction of Satan.

b) The most important alteration undertaken by the author of the poetic

[1] Rowley, p. 184, has recently espoused the old thesis that the poet also composed the framework. Cf. especially A. Alt, "Zur Vorgeschichte des Buches Hiob," *ZAW*, LV (1937), 265-68; L. W. Batten, "The Epilogue of the Book of Job," *AThR*, XV (1933), 125-28; G. Fohrer, "Zur Vorgeschichte und Komposition des Buches Hiob," *VT*, VI (1956), 249-67 (=*Studien zum Buche Hiob*, 1963, pp. 26-43); *idem*, "Überlieferung und Wandlung der Hioblegende," in *Baumgärtel-Festschrift*, 1959, pp. 41-62 (=*Studien zum Buche Hiob*, 1963, pp. 44-67); *idem*, "4QOrNab, 11QTgJob und die Hioblegende," *ZAW*, LXXV (1963), 93-97; K. Kautzsch, *Das sogenannte Volksbuch von Hiob*, 1900.

[2] On the individual stages or phases, see Fohrer in *Baumgärtel-Festschrift*.

discourses was the introduction of the three friends, probably using names that were already part of the tradition. In 2:11-13 and 42:7-9, these friends have replaced Job's relatives and acquaintances, whose sympathy visit is still inappropriately preserved in 42:11.[3] In addition, the poet adapted the legend to his poem formally and stylistically by leaving the narrative text in its prose form but changing the direct speech to verse, and—apart from common idioms—by introducing the divine name "Yahweh" in the narrative prose, while using the expression "Elohim" and the other terms for God in the poetic passages.

3. *The poem*. The poem itself comprises (*a*) the dispute between Job and his three friends, in three cycles of speeches, and (*b*) the exchange between Job and God.

There is no lack of interpretations suggesting large-scale additions to or revision of an original book of Job. The speeches of God and Job's replies, as well as the speeches of Elihu, have frequently been considered secondary, with only the dispute between Job and his friends recognized as genuine. Furthermore, changes have been proposed even for material belonging to these latter speeches. Some have wanted to retain only a portion of them (Fullerton: 3–19; Rhodokanakis: 3–17:1 and 38–40:5); others, by the omission of numerous individual sections, have sought to reduce them to a single cycle and a monologue on the part of Job (Baumgärtel, Kraeling). Torczyner (Tur-Sinai) has even undertaken to analyze the text into minimal fragments and construct a new text out of them (1941); more recently, however, he has rejected his earlier attempt (1957), on the grounds that the supposed loss of great portions of the original poem prevents any reconstruction. In all these views, the final criterion of judgment is restriction to Job's personal situation. Therefore everything is removed from his speeches that does not appear to contribute to the picture of the sufferer enraged at God but nevertheless faithful to him; everything is removed from the speeches of Job's friends that does not appear to serve the purposes of their attack upon Job and its effect upon him. Literary analysis is therefore in large measure determined by a prior interpretation of the book.

a) The cycles of speeches are clearly planned so as to comprise in each case three speeches by Job and a reply by each of his friends. The reader should note that from the moment Job breaks his seven days' silence he takes the initiative and provides each new impetus; he "speaks" and his friends react and "reply." This is the situation in the first cycle. It begins with chapter 3, which must be called the first speech of Job and not placed at the beginning as a monologue. The first and second cycles (3–11; 12–20) have been preserved intact; only the hymns in 9:5-10; 12:12-25 and the instruction in 12:7-11 are later additions.[4]

[3] This is also suggested by 38:1 and 42:7, which presuppose a temptation of Job by his relatives and friends and a brief divine utterance of recognition after his trial.

[4] K. Fullerton, "On Job, Chapters 9 and 10," *JBL*, LIII (1934), 321-49; W. A. Irwin, "The First Speech of Bildad," *ZAW*, LI (1933), 205-16; M. Löhr, "Die drei Bildad-Reden im Buche Hiob," in BZAW, XXXIV (1920), 107-12.

The situation is different in the case of the third cycle (chapters 21 ff.).[5] The eighth speech of Job (23:1-17) and Bildad's reply (25:1-6) are very brief; of the ninth speech of Job we have only the introduction (26:1-4) and perhaps a fragment preserved in a few verses of 27; Zophar's reply is completely missing. Kalt[6] and Peters have sought to explain this circumstance as a deliberate attempt on the part of the poet to express the flagging efforts of Job's friends; but Job's speeches, too, become shorter and weaker. Radical solutions along opposite lines have been suggested: Baumgärtel restricts the original compass of the third cycle to 23:2-17; Buhl and Fullerton consider 24–28 a conglomerate of fragments of diverse origin. Volz and Westermann prefer to break up the cycle from 23 or 24 on and assign the fragments they consider original to other parts of the book.

In contrast to these attempts, the complete speeches in 21 and 22, and the undisputed fragments of speeches in the following chapters, show that attempts to restore the third cycle as much as possible are on the right track. That many improbable juxtapositions have resulted is only to be expected. It is probably safe to say, however, that 23:1-17 contains the incomplete eighth speech of Job and 25:1-6 what remains of Bildad's reply. The ninth speech of Job, introduced by 26:1-4, certainly includes a portion of 27, most likely vss. 1-6, 11-12. No trace is left of Zophar's reply. The cycle has been supplemented by the addition of four songs in 24 (vss. 1-4, 10-12, 22-23; 5-8; 13-17; 18-21), a hymn to God's power and creative will (26:5-14), and a song describing the end of the wicked (27:7-10, 13-23). Finally, there is the wisdom song in chapter 28.

b) The second part of the poem begins with the speeches in 29–31, usually and wrongly termed Job's "final speeches." Their purpose, however, is not to conclude Job's dispute with his friends, but to lead up to God's appearance. Between them, the speeches of God, and Job's replies there is an intimate form-critical, material, and theological connection. They must therefore be called the challenges of Job. The song in 30:2-8 is a later addition.

The speeches of God and Job's replies have been bitterly disputed. Ever since Vernes and Studer first expressed doubts as to their genuineness,[7] many scholars, from Volz and Baumgärtel to, most recently, Kuhl, have denied that the author of the Job poem wrote these speeches; several have taken the mere appearance of God to mark the original conclusion. In the OT, however, it is the words spoken by God that make a theophany significant. In the context of the book as a whole, it is absolutely necessary for God to speak; even the ancient Job legend contained such a speech, which is alluded to in 42:7 and drawn upon in 38:1. If we assume, therefore, that a speech by God is a necessary part of the

[5] G. A. Barton, "The Composition of Job 24–30," *JBL*, XXX (1911), 66-77; P. Dhorme, "Les c. 25–28 du livre de Job," *RB*, XXXIII (1924), 343-56; F. Giesebrecht, *Der Wendepunkt des Buches Hiob: Capitel 27 und 28*, 1879; M. A. Régnier, "La distribution des c. 25-28 du livre de Job," *RB*, XXXIII (1924), 186-200; R.-J. Tournay, "L'ordre primitif des chapitres XXIV–XVIII du Livre de Job," *ibid.*, LXIV (1957), 321-34.

[6] E. Kalt, *Das Buch Job*, 1924.

[7] G. L. Studer, *Das Buch Hiob*, 1881; M. Vernes, "Bulletin critique de la religion juive," *RHR*, I (1880), 206-38.

Job poem, we are confronted with the difficult question of its extent and limits, because the text as preserved contains two speeches by God (38:1–40:2; 40:6–41:26 [Eng. 40:6–41:34]) and two replies by Job (40:3-5; 42:1-6).[8]

Many scholars retain the present double structure, attempting to account for it with more or less artificial explanations (Dillmann, Weiser).[9] The two passages describing the hippopotamus and the crocodile (40:15–41:26 [Eng. 40:15–41:34]), however, are probably later expansions. If so, the second speech by God is at once called into question, because all that remains of it is 40:8-14.[10] Furthermore, in 40:3-5 Job surrenders his position and declares that he will henceforth keep silent. After this statement, an additional speech by God would be mere carping, and a second reply by Job would be an automatic contradiction. In fact, the separation of 40:2 from 40:8-14, to which it belongs, led to the shift of the superscriptions and the introduction (40:1, 6-7), finally giving the impression of two speeches by God.

In view of this, others have assumed that only one of the two speeches is original—Siegfried,[11] Fullerton, and Lindblom defend the authenticity of the first, Eissfeldt* of the second, although Eissfeldt also ponders whether there may not have been different versions of the book of Job, each having a speech by God, which were later interwoven. But just as two so diverse versions of one and the same poem are highly improbable, so also, taken independently, 38–39 and 40:6-14 do not represent finished speeches.

The natural solution to the problems is to assume a single speech by God, consisting of the present material but omitting the superscriptions and introduction added in 40:1, 6-7, followed by a single reply by Job (Bickell, Budde, Duhm, Hölscher, *et al.*). Then the speech by God comprises 38–39; 40:2, 8-14; the introduction in 38:2-3 corresponds to the concluding passage 40:2, 8-14, and we have the same structure exhibited by Job's challenges (introductory wish, concluding challenge). Job's answer is contained in 40:3-5; 42:2-3, 5-6 (42:1 is a secondary superscription; 42:4 repeats 38:3). The songs concerning the hippopotamus (40:15-24) and the crocodile (40:25–41:26 [Eng. 41:1-34])[12] are expansions that have contributed to the present division. These zoological descriptions—for of course we are not dealing with the mythical monsters of primordial time—are on a different plane and employ a different vocabulary from the speech by God, whose interrogative form they seldom employ and whose insistent tone is foreign to them. The animals are quite

[8] G. Fohrer, "Gottes Antwort aus dem Sturmwind, Hi 38–42," *ThZ,* XVIII (1962), 1-24 (=*Studien zum Buche Hiob,* 1963, pp. 108-29); L. J. Kuyper, "The Repentance of Job," *VT,* IX (1959), 91-94; R. A. F. MacKenzie, "The Purpose of the Yahweh Speeches in the Book of Job," *Bibl,* XL (1959), 435-45; G. von Rad, "Hiob XXXVIII und die altägyptische Weisheit," *VTSuppl,* III (1955), 293-301 (=*Gesammelte Studien zum Alten Testament,* 1958, pp. 262-71).

[9] Cf. Kuhl in *ThR,* NF XXI (1953), 268-69, and Fohrer, KAT, 2nd ed., p. 37.

[10] 40:6-7 have been borrowed from 38:1, 3.

[11] C. Siegfried, *The Book of Job,* 1893 ("The Sacred Books of the Old Testament").

[12] G. R. Driver, "Mythical Monsters in the Old Testament," in *Studi Orientali Levi della Vida,* I (1956), 234-49.

vaguely associated with Palestine, while the illustrations used in God's speech agree with the particular circumstances of that land.

Despite many misgivings, the situation is probably different in the case of the passage describing the mother ostrich (39:13-18),[13] which does not differ stylistically from the rest of God's speech and fills out the two sets of four strophes describing the animal world that follow the two sets of four strophes describing inanimate nature. Originally, however, the passage probably described only the speed of the ostrich; vss. 15 and 17, describing its lack of wisdom, are later additions.

4. *Later additions.* The song in chapter 28 telling of wisdom's inaccessibility to man is a large addition to the poem.[14] *Pace* König *et al.*, it must be considered completely impossible from the mouth of Job, to whom it is assigned (Kraeling, Kissane, Hölscher, *et al.*). All the rest of the book is concerned with a kind of wisdom quite unlike the wisdom described in this song. Its inaccessibility to man in fact renders the arguments of God's speech superfluous, just as conversely that latter's ironic tone is incomprehensible after the judicious diffidence of the wise man who sings the song. The meditative approach of the song stands in marked contrast to all the speeches in the poem. Considerations of form and content suggest that the song does not derive from the author of the poem, but from a representative of the theological wisdom system rejected by the poet.

Since the time of Eichhorn* and Stuhlmann,[15] the speeches of Elihu (32–37) have frequently been considered another large-scale interpolation—and rightly so, although not a few scholars have argued for their genuineness (among earlier scholars, Budde, Cornill*, *et al.;* more recently, Ridderbos, Dennefeld, *et al.*).[16] Three groups of arguments support the view that these chapters are a later addition. First, they are not connected in any way with the rest of the book. Elihu is introduced without prior preparation and vanishes again quite as suddenly after his speeches; neither Job nor God takes up his arguments (not even in 42:7). His speeches have even been interpolated at the wrong place, interrupting the continuity between Job's challenges and God's speech.[17] Second, the concept of wisdom in these speeches differs substantially from that in the Job poem proper (and from that of chapter 28); the argumentation proceeds in a different way, developing presupposed theological concepts.

[13] J. Böhmer, "Was ist der Sinn von Hiob 39,13-18 an seiner gegenwärtigen Stelle?" *ZAW*, LIII (1935), 289-91.

[14] M. Löhr, "Job c. 28," in *Haupt-Festschrift*, 1926, pp. 67-70.

[15] M. H. Stuhlmann, *Hiob*, 1804.

[16] L. Dennefeld, "Les discours d'Élihou," *RB*, XLVIII (1939), 163-80; G. Fohrer, "Die Weisheit des Elihu (Hi 32–37)," *AfO*, XIX (1959/60), 83-94 (=*Studien zum Buche Hiob*, 1963, pp. 87-107); W. A. Irwin, "The Elihu Speeches in the Criticism of the Book of Job," *JR*, XVII (1937), 37-47; J. H. Kroeze, "Die Elihureden im Buche Hiob," *OTS*, II (1943), 156-70; H. Nichols, "The Composition of the Elihu Speeches," *AJSL*, XXIX (1910/11), 97-186; W. Posselt, *Der Verfasser der Elihu-Reden (Job Kap. 32–37)*, 1909; N. H. Ridderbos, "De redevoeringen van Elihu," *GThT*, XXXVIII (1937), 353-82; W. E. Staples, *The Speeches of Elihu*, 1924.

[17] In many passages the author of the speeches appears to have been familiar with later additions to the Job poem or to have used a corrupt text; for details, cf. the discussion in Fohrer.

Both observations presuppose a different intellectual and conceptual approach from that of the author of the poem. What contribution the speeches make to the problem of Job has already been rejected as useless by Job's speeches in the dialogue. Finally, the speech differs formally from that of the Job poem. Apart from numerous differences of language and style, the author, despite his repeated invitations to verbal dispute, uses the rhetorical form of the lecture delivered by a wisdom instructor, with polemical overtones.

5. *The original book and its origin.* Taking into account the disturbances in the text and eliminating the large-scale additions, we arrive at the following structure for the original composition of the Job poet:

I: 1–2 Introduction by means of the prologue.
II: 3–27:12 Part one: the direct dispute between Job and his friends and the indirect dispute with God:
3–11 First cycle
12–20 Second cycle
21–23; 25; 26:1-4; 27:1-6, 11-12 Third cycle (fragmentary).
III: 29–31; 38–42:6 Part two: the direct dispute between Job and God:
29–31 Job's challenges
38–39; 40:2, 8-14 God's speech
40:3-5; 42:2-3, 5-6 Job's reply
IV: 42:7-17 Conclusion by means of the epilogue.

The date of the book cannot be determined precisely. The upper limit is fixed by the fact that the poet used the Job legend in a postexilic form and that he drew on Jeremiah and the book of Lamentations.[18] The list of kings, counselors, and officials in 3:14-15 corresponds to the Persian governmental structure (cf. Ezra 7:28; 8:25), and 19:23-24 presupposes a knowledge of the rock inscription of Darius I. The vocabulary points to the same period. If we also take into account the general intellectual milieu, we arrive at the fifth or fourth century B.C. as the date of the book's origin. The additions were added in the third century at the latest.

The place of origin has sometimes been identified as Egypt, Edom, or Arabia.[19] In all probability, however, the poet lived in Palestine, as many details suggest. Above all, he localized the Job legend in a way that makes sense only from the point of view of Palestine ("the people of the east" = the region of Ṣafa, in the northern part of Transjordan) and in God's speech used subject matter appropriate to the situation in Palestine.

6. *Relationship to tradition.* In discussing the possible use of traditional material by the Job poet, we must first study the possibility of extrabiblical

[18] Job 3:3-11 is based on Jer. 20:14-18; Job 6:15-21 on Jer. 15:18; Job 6:23 on Jer. 15:21; and 19:9-12 on Lamentations.

[19] Egypt: P. Humbert, *Recherches sur les sources égyptiennes de la littérature sapientiale d'Israël,* 1929, pp. 75-106; Edom: Pfeiffer*; Arabia: F. H. Foster, "Is the Book of Job a Translation from an Arabic Original?" *AJSL,* XLIX (1932/33), 21-45; D. S. Margolioth, *The Relations Between Arabs and Israelites Prior to the Rise of Islam,* 1924.

prototypes. It must be confessed that there is no demonstrable evidence for the often assumed familiarity of the poet with Greek poetry and philosophy. In reply to the supposed parallels in Greek poetry (Fries[20]) and the traces of Greek thought in Job (Jastrow, Jr.), the interpretation of the book of Job as an imitation of a tragedy by Euripedes (Kallen[21]) or as influenced by Aeschylus' *Prometheus Bound* (Slotki[22]), other scholars have more properly pointed out the differences, many of them fundamental, between Job and Greek poetry. The same holds true for the Indian poem concerning the misfortunes of King Yudishthira (Holstijn[23]).

Within the ancient Near East, any dependence of the Job poet on Canaanite literature is probably out of the question; the similarity to the Ugaritic texts in poetical structure is not very great (Feinberg). The situation is not much different with regard to Egyptian disputation literature, which in times of crisis and doubt produced discussions in dialogue form; these include the Dialogue of the Disconsolate Man with his Soul, the Laments of the Eloquent Peasant, the Prophecy of Nefer-rehu (Neferti), the Admonitions of Ipu-wer, and the Instruction of Amen-em-opet.[24] These works, however, discuss the problems of injustice in this world and the fate that awaits man after death, questions that are peripheral in the book of Job. The formal parallels of the dialogue, which is sometimes set in a framework narrative, and of the lamenting, rhetorical, and at times didactic mode of presentation, do not, however, go beyond the common idioms of wisdom literature.

Above all, scholars have made reference to Sumerian and Babylonian texts:[25] the Dialogue of a Sufferer with his Devout Friend,[26] "I Will Praise the Lord of Wisdom" (*ludlul bēl nēmeqi*),[27] The Righteous Suffer,[28] and The Man and His God,[29] to name the most important.[30] Gese has grouped the majority of these together as a single literary type, the "paradigm of the answered lament"; but they exhibit such striking differences (monologue *vs.* dialogue; thanksgiving prayers with description of prior distress *vs.* lament followed by favorable oracle) that they probably represent different literary types. In addition, form-critically they resemble the psalms more than they do the book of Job; neither are they especially similar to the latter book in content, the more so since they depict precisely the kind of conduct rejected by Job despite his friends' argu-

[20] K. Fries, *Das philosophische Gespräch von Hiob bis Platon,* 1904.

[21] H. M. Kallen, *The Book of Job as a Greek Tragedy Restored,* 1918.

[22] J. J. Slotki, "The Origin of the Book of Job," *ET*, XXXIX (1927/28), 131-34.

[23] W. Holstijn, "Een 'arische' Jobeïde," *NThSt,* XXII (1939), 52-60.

[24] Cf. especially H. Junker, *Pyramidenzeit,* 1949; E. Otto, *Der Vorwurf an Gott,* 1951.

[25] Gese, pp. 51-62; S. N. Kramer, "Sumerian Literature and the Bible," in *Studia Biblica and Orientalia,* III (1959), 185-204; A. Kuschke, "Altbabylonische Texte zum Thema 'Der leidende Gerechte'," *ThLZ,* LXXXI (1956), 69-76; W. G. Lambert, *Babylonian Wisdom Literature,* 1960; J. J. Stamm, *Das Leiden des Unschuldigen in Babylon und Israel,* 1946.

[26] *ANET*, pp. 438-40; Lambert, pp. 63-91.

[27] *AOT*, pp. 273-81; *ANET*, pp. 434-37; Lambert, pp. 21-62.

[28] J. Nougayrol, "Une version ancienne du 'Juste souffrant'," *RB,* LIX (1952), 239-50.

[29] J. J. A. van Dijk, *La Sagesse suméro-accadienne,* 1953, pp. 122-27.

[30] Cf. also Van Dijk, pp. 121-22, 128-33.

ments. And it is certainly going too far to take as a point of departure certain Babylonian psalms in which the king supposedly declares his innocence using a negative confession, interpret the Sumerian and Babylonian texts just mentioned as the transitional form of a "Job-type," trace this development to the book of Job, and then finally retrace one's steps so as to associate the figure of Job with the royal ideology and its passion ritual.[31] The only positive conclusion is that the dialogue form as a kind of debate is found as early as Sumerian wisdom literature, where the disputation, with an added introduction, is followed by the judgment of the deity and the reconciliation of the disputants.

Only in his use of this form does the Job poet base his work on ancient prototypes, which were already traditional at the time he wrote. In other respects, however, his work is not dependent on any literary model; as a whole, it stands unique in the ancient Near East.

7. *History of the material and motifs.* Detailed study of the motifs and subject matter of the poem shows that the Job poet drew upon an extensive body of material. He makes use of the international lore of wisdom instruction, presupposes a knowledge of ancient myths (e.g., 3:8; 15:7-8), and undertakes systematic scientific endeavors (e.g., 10:8-11; 38–39). He is an educated man writing for an educated audience. Above all, he is deeply immersed in the traditions of the OT faith and the other material and motifs found in the literature of the OT. In the entire book there are only a few verses that do not contain echoes of and similarities to other books of the OT. In particular, the poet's presuppositions include practical wisdom, with its two-sided doctrine of retribution based on an order determined and enforced by God. It remains true, however, that the poet is living through a crisis of the theological wisdom system, which founders on the reality of life and on the occasionally experienced irruption of the numinous.

The poet, though familiar with international literature, had to frame his own plan for the book as a whole, without relying on prototypes. In the same way, he employed systematic and scientific endeavors, but to describe situations involving the irruption of the irrational and questions that were concrete rather than abstract. He was likewise immersed in the material and motifs of the OT, but, in the crisis convulsing the traditional faith of his time, had to find his own path to secure foundations. As is so often the case, we find particular examples of these tendencies in a juxtaposition of tradition and new interpretation, in a revision of traditional material and concepts, which become means whereby the poet seeks to express his own ideas.

8. *Form criticism.* Questions of form criticism have recently been given detailed study along two very different lines.

Following Volz and Bentzen*, Westermann considers the book a dramatized lament, which, like all the laments in the OT, is composed of a lament directed to God, a complaint, and an indictment of enemies (in this case, Job's friends). Richter, on the contrary, following Köhler, takes as his sole point of departure

[31] I. Engnell, *Gamla Testamentet,* I (1945), 68.

the literary types associated with the legal system. He interprets the book as a legal action comprising a preliminary attempt at reconciliation (4–14), a formal legal attempt at reconciliation between Job and his friends (15–31), Elihu's appeal of the case, and God's judgment in the form of a secular lawsuit between God and Job, after which Job withdraws his accusation. Despite their important insights, both studies are too one-sided; the actual state of affairs is more complex.

The formal elements of the dispute between Job and his friends derive primarily from three domains.[32] Wisdom instruction provides both isolated individual forms and the "disputations of the wise," found in Egyptian literature and presupposed by I Kings 10:1 ff. The legal system provides both the individual forms associated with a legal action and the "litigants' addresses to the court," since the judges were often trained in wisdom schools. Cultic poetry furnishes mostly the rhetorical and stylistic forms used in laments and hymns.

In Job's dispute with God, Job's challenges are chiefly modeled after the psalms of lament (a "narrative account" of distress and protestation of innocence); the demonstration of innocence conforms to an apodictic series of rules of conduct and behavior together with an oath before the court. The purpose of these speeches is not to obtain a cultic oracle from Yahweh following the lament. Instead, they issue a legal challenge to God, which, however, is not intended to obtain God's judgment in the legal action but to lead up to a personal confrontation with God. God's speech apparently corresponds to the oracle of Yahweh following a lament or God's judgment in a legal case; unlike these, however, it is not unambiguously positive or negative. It is in fact a counterargument, and its function is to confront Job with a decision. In its extended middle section it makes use of scholarly lists typical of educational wisdom. Job's answer corresponds to the thanksgiving or statement of confidence made by the worshiper after the oracle from Yahweh or to the acceptance of judgment in a legal action. In addition to forms drawn from the psalms and the legal realm, it also contains wisdom forms; in content, it describes Job's radical conversion as Job's reply when God confronts him with a decision.

In addition, a duality of form and function should be noted. Not uncommonly the rhetorical forms come to serve new functions in the context in which they are used. These functions differ more or less markedly from the original significance of these forms, and can even represent the precise opposite; this is true particularly for the lament (3; 6–7) and the hymn (3:17-19; 7:17-18; 9:12-13; 10:8-17; 23:13). Detailed study of this phenomenon is the task of exegesis.[33]

The contrast between form and function shows that the form used does not necessarily correspond to the content or provide a clue as to its nature. This must be remembered in any formal analysis of the book of Job as a whole.

[32] We omit the curse in 3, the originally prophetical forms in 22, and the oath in 27.

[33] Cf. also the summary in G. Fohrer, "Form und Funktion in der Hiobdichtung," *ZDMG*, CIX (1959), 31-49 (=*Studien zum Buche Hiob* [1963], 68-86).

It is best described as a poem with a framework narrative, containing both a personal and theoretical disputation on the "problem of Job."

9. *The problem of the book.* The poet does not discuss the problem of theodicy in the form of the undeserved suffering of the righteous or God's justice in contrast to human experience; this approach would run counter to the Israelite preference for concrete and subjective thought. Neither does he simply describe what happens. His concern is instead with a vital problem: the problem of human existence in suffering, the question of how a sufferer should conduct himself. Job conducts himself in the way he finds both possible and proper; his friends seek to instruct him in conduct that, in their view, would be better; God confronts him with a decision in regard to his conduct.

The ancient Near Eastern answers to this problem are mostly in terms of magical or cultic influence upon the demons or gods that cause the suffering. The book of Job provides some other answers, which, to be sure, the poet is unable to accept. The framework narrative thinks of suffering as a test imposed upon man, who must remain firm in his devotion while he suffers. Job's friends trace human misery back to human guilt, and demand that Job purge himself of evil, turn to God in humility, or undergo radical conversion. Elihu only modifies this argument in detail. In contrast to these views stands the Promethean and Titanic defiance of Job, who is convinced of his own innocence. The poet goes through all these views, both orthodox and heretical, even having God condemn Job's orthodox friends and accept the intercession of the formerly heretical Job. He finally arrives at his own solution, which bears witness to the profound influence of the prophetical faith.[34] Proper conduct for the sufferer is humble and devout silence with trust in God—based on the insight that suffering derives from God's mysterious and inscrutable but nevertheless meaningful action, and on assurance of fellowship with God, beside which all else pales into insignificance.

§ 51 Ecclesiastes (Qoheleth)

ATD: W. Zimmerli, 1962. BOT: J. van der Ploeg, 1953. COT: G. C. Aalders, 1948. HAT: K. Galling, 1940. HK: K. Siegfried, 1898. HS: A. Allgeier, 1925. IB: O. S. Rankin, 1956. ICC: G. A. Barton, 1908, reprinted 1948. KAT: H. W. Hertzberg, 1932. KAT²: H. W. Hertzberg, 1962. KeH: F. Hitzig and W. Nowack, 2nd ed., 1883. KHC: G. Wildeboer, 1898. SAT: P. Volz, 2nd ed., 1922. SZ: W. Volck, 1889. Individual commentaries: A. Bea, 1950; R. Gordis, 2nd ed., 1955; R. Kroeber, 1963; G. Kuhn, 1926; E. Podechard, 1912 ("Études Bibliques"); J. Steinmann, 1955; M. Thilo, 1923; V. Zapletal, 2nd ed., 1911.

G.-W. H. Bickell, *Der Prediger über den Wert des Daseins,* 1884; H.-J. Blieffert, *Weltanschauung und Gottesglaube im Buch Kohelet,* Dissertation, Rostock, 1938; M. J. Dahood, "Qoheleth and Recent Discoveries," *Bibl,* XXXIX (1958), 302-18; K. Galling, "Kohelet-Studien," *ZAW,* L (1932), 276-99; *idem,* "Stand und Aufgabe der Kohelet-Forschung," *ThR,* NF VI (1934), 355-73; *idem, Die Krise der*

[34] Cf. also Isa. 51:7-8; Ps. 73:25-28.

Aufklärung in Israel, 1952; *idem*, "Das Rätsel der Zeit im Urteil Kohelets (Koh 3,1-15)," *ZThK*, LVIII (1961), 1-15; H. L. Ginsberg, *Studies in Koheleth*, 1950; *idem*, "Supplementary Studies in Koheleth," *PAAJR*, XXI (1952), 35-62; *idem*, "The Structure and Contents of the Book of Koheleth," *VTSuppl*, III (1955), 138-49; R. Gordis, "Quotations in Wisdom Literature," *JQR*, XXX (1939/40), 123-47; *idem*, "Qoheleth and Qumran—A Study of Style," *Bibl*, XLI (1960), 395-410; H. W. Hertzberg, "Palästinische Bezüge im Buche Kohelet," *ZDPV*, LXXIII (1957), 113-24, also in *Baumgärtel-Festschrift*, 1959, pp. 63-73; P. Kleinert, "Sind im Buche Koheleth ausserhebräische Einflüsse anzuerkennen?" *ThStKr*, LVI (1883), 661-82; *idem*, "Zur religions- und kulturgeschichtlichen Stellung des Buches Koheleth," *ibid*., LXXXII (1909), 493-529; L. Levy, *Das Buch Qoheleth, ein Beitrag zur Geschichte des Sadduzäismus*, 1912; O. Loretz, *Qohelet und der Alte Orient*, 1964; A. H. MacNeile, *An Introduction to Ecclesiastes*, 1904; A. Miller, "Aufbau und Grundprobleme des Predigers," in *Miscellanea Biblica*, II (1934), 104-22; A. Neher, *Notes sur Qohélét*, 1951; J. Pedersen, "Scepticisme israélite," *RHPhR*, X (1930), 317-70; H. Ranston, *Ecclesiastes and the Early Greek Wisdom Literature*, 1925; H. H. Rowley, "The Problems of Ecclesiastes," *JQR*, XLII (1951/52), 87-90; W. E. Staples, "The 'Vanity' of Ecclesiastes," *JNES*, II (1943), 95-104; W. Zimmerli, *Die Weisheit des Predigers Salomo*, 1936.

1. *Canonical status, terminology, authorship*. The book of Ecclesiastes is one of the five Megilloth; it was appointed to be read on the Feast of Booths. It must therefore have acquired not a little authority soon after it came into being, and was among those documents that gradually came to form the third division of the Hebrew canon. The fragments found in Cave 4 at Qumran, dating from about the middle of the second century B.C., show that at that time it possessed a kind of canonical status. The book nevertheless did not go uncontested. Even the epilogue (12:9-14) seems to deal with such challenges; while vss. 9-11 praise the book on account of its pleasing and true words, vs. 12 seems more like a warning against this kind of literary activity, and vss. 13 and 14 seek to salvage Ecclesiastes for practical use by interpreting it in the spirit of law-centered Judaism. At a later date reservations came to be expressed concerning its place in the Canon; these made reference to internal inconsistencies within the book and passages contradictory to the rest of the OT. The most important collection of diverse opinions from the second century C.E. is contained in Mishna Yadayim iii. 5. None of this altered the book's canonical status.

The book derives its title from the superscription in 1:1: "The words of Qoheleth, the son of David, king in Jerusalem." The word *qōhelet* was translated as *ekklēsiástēs, concionator*, "preacher," and has sometimes been further interpreted by the addition of the name "Solomon" in place of "son of David." The word is a feminine participle of *qhl;* in the books of Ezra and Nehemiah, the substantive from this root refers to the great community assemblies. It is not a translation error for an Aramaic masculine participle (Ginsberg). The term must mean something like "assembly," "that which assembles." Its use to designate a man comes about through its use at first to designate an activity or office, from which it was gradually extended to the man holding the office.

Ezra 2:55, 57 contains parallels to this use: terms for official functions—"scribal office" and "office of gazelle-catcher"—first were extended to the people holding the office and finally became personal names. In similar fashion, "Qoheleth" refers first of all to the office of leading and speaking in assembly and then to the person of the leader and speaker. Thus the expression ascribes to the "son of David" in the superscription a special talent for speaking, an attribute of the wise man.

In agreement with the superscription, the author appears several times as a king (1:12, 16; 2:7, 9); reinterpretation in the sense of "head of a school" (Levy) or revocalization to mean "rich man, property owner" (Ginsberg) are improbable. Although 1:16 ("all who were over Jerusalem before me") seems to imply a series of kings,[1] the king referred to is undoubtedly Solomon, since he was the only king besides David who ruled over Israel (1:12). In fact, Solomon was considered the ideal wise man, so that such a book was easily ascribed to him.

Of course actual Solomonic authorship is out of the question. The association with Solomon is a mere literary form, only slightly disguised and not carried out systematically. Apart from all the evidence for a late dating of the book, from chapter three on there are no further references to Solomon, and the later aphorisms concerning the king indicate that their author was a subject. He attaches no importance to playing the role of Solomon throughout. His impersonation of Solomon at the beginning of the book is probably an imitation of the Egyptian custom of tracing wisdom instruction back to an earlier king. Solomon, to whom a portion of the book of Proverbs was already ascribed at the time Ecclesiastes was written, was the appropriate figure on account of his wisdom and fabulous wealth. In reality, the author was an anonymous wisdom teacher, as the epilogue explicitly states (12:9). In style, form, and content his book clearly counts as wisdom literature.

2. *Development and structure*. As is so often the case, the views concerning the development and structure of the book cluster around two extremes.

On the one hand, Thilo and Bea have attempted to demonstrate the existence of systematic arrangement and logical development. This is practically out of the question, since ideas are occasionally repeated, and the outcome of the author's meditations is as clear in 1–2 as it is in 11–12. The difficulties involved in finding a logical order cannot be removed by rearranging the text and omitting parts of it, as Bickell in particular has tried to do on the basis of his assumption that the leaves of the original manuscript were inadvertently confused and their content further distorted by additions and transpositions. The very hypothesis that we are dealing with a codex and not a scroll is dubious. On the other hand, Siegfried has analyzed the book into a whole series of sources and redactions: a basic pessimistic document, an Epicurean Sadducee, a wisdom teacher, an orthodox Jew who emphasizes God's just dominion over the world, not to mention additional glossators, redactors, and epiloguists. Podechard

[1] Talmud Bab. Baba bathra 15*a* says that Hezekiah and his men composed the book.

(together with MacNeile and Barton) represents the same view in less extreme form, finding the work of Qoheleth, two of Qoheleth's students, and a wise man writing in poetic form, as well as a few additional isolated sections. The occasional repetitions, contradictions, and irregularities are not sufficient, however, to justify such extreme conclusions.

Between these two extremes we find a view approaching the former, according to which the book exhibits a complete unity of intellectual structure and definite forward progress (Hertzberg), although most of the sections could be interchanged at random without difficulty. Another view, noting the procedure generally employed in wisdom literature, assumes that the book is a collection of aphorisms and groups of aphorisms; in this view, the aphorisms first took shape individually and were later compiled to form series (Galling).

The book possesses no clear structure and no intellectual development; even a clear train of thought can be constructed only with difficulty. The individual aphorisms represent the original material; it is hardly likely that their composition was a continuous process. The presence of repetitions, contradictions, and irregularities cannot be denied, and suggests that the aphorisms were formulated over a considerable period of time. As usual, the next step was the juxtaposition of aphorisms in groups on the basis of catchwords or similarity of content. The sayings in 1:12–2:16, for instance, examine the roles played by wisdom and folly. In 5:9–6:9 (Eng. 5:10–6:9), Qoheleth discusses the futility of wealth, in 7:1–8:1 true wisdom, in 8:2–9:12 the opacity of injustice, and in 9:13–10:11 the worthlessness of wisdom. As a third element there is also a kind of order to the book as a whole. The aphorisms in 1–3 introduce the basic critical posture of the wise man, followed from 4 on by its application to particular questions of human life; at the conclusion, 11:1-8 and 11:9–12:8 summarize once again Qoheleth's basic ideas and his positive advice.

3. *The aphorisms.* Apart from the epilogue (12:9-14) and some minor additions, all the aphorisms derive from the same author, whom we call Qoheleth, as vocabulary and style particularly show. The individual units cannot always be delimited with assurance, because in many cases there are no introductory and concluding formulas and the form-critical criteria are often insufficient. This explains why the exegetes differ in their enumeration of the aphorisms.

The question of whether we are dealing with prose or poetry is not unimportant in the case of a wisdom book; here again, views differ widely: prose (König,[2] Podechard), prose and poetry alternating (Delitzsch, Renan, Nötscher[3]), poetry with a regular meter (Grimme, Haupt,[4] Bickell), and poetry with irregular meter (Zapletal,[5] Hertzberg). Now the epilogue itself

[2] E. König, "Poesie und Prosa in der althebräischen Literatur abgegrenzt," *ZAW*, XXXVII (1917/18), 152-57.

[3] F. Delitzsch, 1875 ("Biblischer Commentar über das AT," IV:4); F. Nötscher, 1948 ("Echter-Bibel"); E. Renan, 1882.

[4] H. Grimme in *ZDMG*, LI (1897), 689; P. Haupt, *Koheleth oder Weltschmerz in der Bibel*, 1905.

[5] V. Zapletal, קהלת, *Liber Ecclesiasticus, Textum hebr. critice et metrice ed.*, 1906.

presupposes in 12:9*b* that we are dealing with proverbs in metrical form; there is no reason to contradict the epilogue's statement. The rhythm, however, is not even and regular; the difficult and unfamiliar ideas of the author could not be accommodated so easily. But an irregular and frequently changing meter, which is easily mistaken for prose, can be detected everywhere.

Qoheleth writes in a thoroughly individual and peculiar style, which the reader must quickly recognize.[6] His language is likewise characterized by a series of oft-repeated key words, of which we shall mention only "vain," "toil," "gain," and "lot." [7] His language is late, as the studies of Delitzsch, Siegfried, and Podechard amply demonstrate, and permeated with numerous aramaisms. This has even led to the thesis that the book was originally written in Aramaic and then translated into Hebrew (supported particularly by Zimmermann, Torrey,[8] Ginsberg). In this case, however, one would assume that the aramaisms would also have been translated and that the present use of assonance goes back to the translator. Qoheleth's dependence on OT books and the dependence of Ecclesiasticus on Qoheleth, as well as the fiction of Solomonic authorship, presuppose a Hebrew text. A translation as late as the Maccabean period is out of the question if the book already possessed canonical status in the middle of the second century B.C. (Qumran). Gordis has made the most outspoken attack on this thesis.[9]

Dahood assumes instead the strong linguistic influence of Phoenician, even concluding that Qoheleth lived in one of the coastal cities of Phoenicia.[10] His vocabulary, however, which Dahood cites to demonstrate a mercantile environment, is almost half made up of common words, and orthography without *matres lectionis* was certainly still known in Hebrew at the time of Qoheleth. This thesis, too, can be accepted only with hesitation.

4. *Origin*. The book's language, which is later than that of Ezra, Nehemiah, and Malachi, sets the fourth century as the upper limit for dating it. We may observe in addition that 5:3-5 (Eng. 5:4-6) is clearly dependent on Deut. 23:22-24 (Eng. 23:21-23). Furthermore, 5:14 (Eng. 5:15); 6:3*b*-5, 10-11; 8:4 are dependent on the book of Job. The discoveries at Qumran, however, eliminate the possibility, which has occasionally been suggested, of composition

[6] Cf., for example, the detailed discussion in Gordis, pp. 87-111.

[7] Cf. also Hertzberg, pp. 30-32.

[8] C. C. Torrey, "The Question of the Original Language of Kohelet," *JQR*, XXXIV (1948/49), 151-60; F. Zimmermann, "The Aramaic Provenance of Qohelet," *ibid*., pp. 17-45; *idem*, "The Question of Hebrew in Qohelet," *ibid*., XL (1949/50), 79-102.

[9] R. Gordis, "The Original Language of Qohelet," *JQR*, XXXVII (1946/47), 67-84; *idem*, "The Translation Theory of Qohelet Re-Examined," *ibid*., XL (1949/50), 103-16; *idem*, "Koheleth—Hebrew or Aramaic?" *JBL*, LXXI (1952), 93-109; *idem*, "Was Kohelet a Phoenician?" *ibid*., LXXIV (1955), 103-14.

[10] M. J. Dahood, "Canaanite-Phoenician Influence in Qoheleth," *Bibl*, XXXIII (1952), 30-52, 191-221; *idem*, "The Language of Qoheleth," *CBQ*, XIV (1952), 227-232; a similar view is espoused by C. H. Gordon, *Ugaritic Literature*, 1949, p. 133, who elsewhere seeks to demonstrate North Israelite characteristics: "North Israelite Influence on Postexilic Hebrew." *IEJ*, V (1955), 85-88.

around 125 B.C. (Renan), 100 B.C. (Leimdörfer,[11] König, Haupt), or in the period of Herod (Graetz[12]). Furthermore, about 180 B.C., Ecclesiasticus was familiar with the book and made use of it.[13] When one also considers the book's intellectual milieu, one must agree with the frequently proposed dating in the second half of the third century.

It is useless, however, to search the book for historical allusions reflecting this date. The verses frequently mentioned in this connection (4:13-16; 9:13-16; 10:16) deal with historical circumstances more likely typical than unique. The various references to the "king," in which Hertzberg claims to see allusions to Qoheleth's pro-Egyptian attitude in the struggles between Seleucids and Ptolemies, are likewise vague and follow the general trend of wisdom instruction in their ideas and suggestions.

Egypt and Palestine have most frequently been suggested as the book's place of origin.[14] In fact, literature and intellectual life flourished in Egyptian Alexandria during the third century, not least among the Jewish population. There is, however, clear evidence pointing to Palestine, cited primarily by Galling and Hertzberg: boundary walls and quarrying (10:8-9), fountains and cisterns (12:6), the typical Palestinian house (10:18), wind, clouds, and rain (11:4; 12:2). It is therefore best to picture Qoheleth living in Palestine and more specifically in Jerusalem (mention of the sanctuary in 4:17 [Eng. 5:1]; 5:5 [Eng. 5:6]; 8:10).

5. *Form criticism.* The uniqueness of Qoheleth's thought is suggested even by a form-critical study of his aphorisms. Apart from general observations (1:2-11; 3:1-9) and isolated proverbs in the manner of traditional wisdom (10), aphorisms framed in the first or second person singular are typical of Qoheleth (e.g., first person: 1:12-15, 16-18; second person: 4:17–5:6 [Eng. 5:1-7]; 5:7-8 [Eng. 5:8-9]). Both are ancient stylistic forms used in wisdom discourse. In the former, the wise man recites examples of practical experience, not necessarily his own.[15] The latter agrees with the pedagogical purpose of wisdom instruction, though without implying that a particular student is being addressed.

Most important is the transformation of the simple aphorism form, whether short or long, into a progressive structure. In its briefest form, like that exhibited in 1:16-18, the wise man goes through three steps: he takes as his point of departure his own observations or his collection of others' experiences, then states his conclusion, and finally adds a proverb or the like to reinforce it. Within the compass of an aphorism this form can be repeated (2:1-11, 12*b*) or expanded. A related tripartite form is found, for example in 3:1-15: theme, conclusion, and proverb cited as motivation.

[11] D. Leimdörfer, 2nd ed., 1892.

[12] H. Graetz, 1871.

[13] For details, cf. Hertzberg, pp. 46-49.

[14] Dahood, *op. cit.* (note 10), suggests the Phoenician coast; Gordon, *op. cit.* (note 10), the eastern Diaspora.

[15] Cf. O. Loretz, "Zur Darbietungsform der 'Ich-Erzählung' im Buche Qohelet," *CBQ,* XXV (1963), 46-59.

We see here a structural change in wisdom instruction, brought about by a change in the psychological milieu. The individual, the ego, takes on a certain distance from the events or circumstances with which it appears to be linked. The observing subject confronts his observations as an independent personality.[16] In addition, in order to reinforce or justify his views, Qoheleth goes back to earlier proverbs. In criticizing the wisdom of his own time, as remains to be shown, he relies on traditional material rejected on account of its pragmatic observations and rules by wisdom theology, whose goal is an all-inclusive system. Here we have a conservative trait in the makeup of the critical observer and thinker with his unique personality.

6. *The character of Qoheleth.* In defining the nature of Qoheleth's wisdom, many scholars have taken a more or less marked dependence on foreign literatures as their point of departure.[17]

Before comparison between the OT and ancient Near Eastern literature became common, scholars assumed Greek influence almost exclusively (especially Pfleiderer[18]), discovering the ideas of many Greek philosophers in Qoheleth. This theory, somewhat modified, has been represented down to the present day. Dependence upon Theognis, among others, has been suggested (Ranston). At the beginning of the Hellenistic period, when Qoheleth lived, the influence of the Greek spirit seems highly probable. One can even interpret particular expressions like *ʿāśâ ṭôb,* "enjoy oneself" (3:12), and *miqreh,* "fate" (2:14; 3:19; 9:2-3), as Grecisms. At most, however, we should think in terms of occasional contacts and a general influence of the Greek spirit (Eissfeldt*), which could easily have been transmitted by intercourse with Hellenistic circles.

On the other hand, a series of specific phenomena point to Egyptian influence; Humbert[19] and Galling in particular have noted these. The relationship—as yet unexplained—to the Papyrus Insinger may have played some role here. Some passages in Ecclesiastes seem to presuppose literary relationships, for example with the Wisdom of Anii (2:4 ff.), the introduction to the Teaching of Ptahhotep (11:9–12:8), and its conclusion (9:1). Since it is highly unlikely that Qoheleth himself read any Egyptian texts, we should perhaps think in terms of influence mediated by Aramaic translations, whose existence in the fifth century is attested by the Ahikar fragment from Elephantine and six fragments of an Egyptian narrative.

Even more striking, however, are the relationships to the wisdom and disputation literature of Mesopotamia; in many respects one may even speak of dependence. Loretz, who views Qoheleth exclusively in the light of this tradition, has pointed out an astonishingly close structural parallelism between the two, noting in particular striking similarities to the Gilgamesh Epic.

[16] H. Gese, "Die Krisis der Weisheit bei Koheleth," in *Les Sagesses du Proche-Orient ancien,* 1963, pp. 139-51.

[17] With regard to the following discussion, cf. the most recent detailed study by Kroeber, pp. 47-59, and Loretz.

[18] E. Pfleiderer, *Die Philosophie des Heraklit von Ephesus im Lichte der Mysterienidee,* 1886.

[19] P. Humbert, *Recherches sur les sources égyptiennes de la littérature sapientiale d'Israël,* 1929.

The existence of parallels, however, does not always point to literary or intellectual dependence, especially in wisdom instruction, which in similar stages of development can draw similar conclusions from the same practical experience. This holds true, for example, with respect to Qoheleth's statements about the political and social environment and his admonitions to practice restraint in cultic matters.

Taken alone, however, this perspective does not suffice for an understanding of the wisdom of Qoheleth. It must above all be viewed in its relationship to that *ḥokmâ*, "wisdom," with which he takes issue. Like the Job poet, he has lost his faith in the doctrine of retributive justice, the theoretical basis for the wisdom of the theological system. This raises the question whether the failure of this doctrine brings down the whole system of wisdom instruction, so that it can no longer furnish a basis for man's life. This would be all the worse because it is equally impossible to master human existence by complete devotion to the pursuit of pleasure. Qoheleth does assign a position of relative value to wisdom theology (2:3, 14, 16; 4:13; 10:12); ultimately, however, it brings no real "gain" (2:15; 9:11), but is no better than folly (1:16-17; 6:8). In this way Qoheleth attacks the self-confidence with which the system seeks to comprehend the totality of the universe and of life, pointing out the limits that render all security and therefore all "gain" impossible: death and women (2:15-16, 21; 7:26). All in all, man's fate does not depend on his righteous and pious conduct, as the doctrine of retribution asserts, but lies impenetrable and inscrutable in the hand of God (8:17; 9:1).

If the system of wisdom theology falls, what then? All that is left, in place of extensive "gain," is to enjoy actively the "portion" in life that has been granted one. The first part of Qoheleth's advice to enjoy life has close parallels in the Egyptian Harper's Song and in the counsel given by the gods' cupbearer in the Gilgamesh Epic, which likewise mentions the negative limit (death). The second part of Qoheleth's advice—the active life—finds its counterpart in the comfort Gilgamesh receives from his great project, the city wall of Uruk, except that for Gilgamesh the work is the result of his activity, while Qoheleth has in mind the activity itself. It is unlikely that these parallels are accidental, even if similar ideas have been expressed elsewhere. They are associated with the conservative side of Qoheleth, which can be seen even in the realm of form criticism. Qoheleth appropriated an ancient viewpoint and opposed it to the system of wisdom theology, which he was criticizing. For this system is like Gilgamesh's striving for immortality, because its purpose is to create something unique, enduring, and definitive. In its stead, Qoheleth points out man's limited possibilities and seeks to recall the earlier pragmatic stage of wisdom instruction. Therefore he is not universally skeptical and resigned, as is usually assumed, but only with respect to the possibilities of a theological system that claims to be a panacea, and of course also with respect to folly. There still remains the possibility suggested already in the Gilgamesh Epic—but reinterpreted as a possibility granted by God, which man receives from his hand as the "portion" allotted him (2:24-25; 3:13; 5:17-18 [Eng. 5:18-19]).

PART FOUR

The Formation of the Prophetical Books and the Apocalyptic Book

CHAPTER ONE: GENERAL

§ 52 Prophecy in the Ancient Near East and in Israel

E. Balla, *Die Botschaft der Propheten*, 1958; W. Baumgartner, "Die Auffassungen des 19. Jh. vom israelitischen Prophetismus," *AfK*, XV (1922), 21-35 (= *Zum Alten Testament und seiner Umwelt*, 1959, pp. 27-41); T. Chary, *Les prophètes et le culte à partir de l'exil*, 1955; C. H. Cornill, *Der israelitische Prophetismus*, 13th ed., 1920 (Eng. *The Prophets of Israel*, 1917); B. Duhm, *Israels Propheten*, 2nd ed., 1922; O. Eissfeldt, "The Prophetic Literature," in *The Old Testament and Modern Study*, 1951, pp. 115-61; G. Fohrer, "Neuere Literatur zur alttestamentlichen Prophetie," *ThR*, NF XIX (1951), 277-346; XX (1952), 193-271, 295-361; *idem*, "Die Propheten des Alten Testaments im Blickfeld neuer Forschung," *Das Wort im evangelischen Religionsunterricht* (Wien), 1954/55, No. 6, pp. 15-24; *idem*, "Die Struktur der alttestamentlichen Eschatologie," *ThLZ*, LXXXV (1960), 401-20; *idem*, "Remarks on Modern Interpretation of the Prophets," *JBL*, LXXX (1961), 309-19; *idem*, "Zehn Jahre Literatur zur alttestamentlichen Prophetie (1951-1960)," *ThR*, NF XXVIII (1962), 1-75, 235-97, 301-74; A. Guillaume, *Prophecy and Divination among the Hebrews and other Semites*, 1938; H. Gunkel, *Die Propheten*, 1917; A. Haldar, *Associations of Cult Prophets among the Ancient Semites*, 1945; F. Heiler, *Erscheinungsformen und Wesen der Religion*, 1961; J. Hempel, *Worte der Profeten*, 1949; R. Hentschke, *Die Stellung der vorexilischen Propheten zum Kultus*, 1957; A. J. Heschel, *Die Propheten*, 1936; *idem*, *The Prophets*, 1962; J. Hessen, *Platonismus und Prophetismus*, 1939; G. Hölscher, *Die Profeten*, 1914; E. Jacob, "Le prophétisme israélite d'après les recherches récents," *RHPhR*, XXXII (1952), 59-69; E. Jenni, *Die alttestamentliche Prophetie*, 1962; A. R. Johnson, *The Cultic Prophet in Ancient Israel*, 2nd ed., 1962; J. Lindblom, *Profetismen i Israel*, 1934 (Eng. *Prophecy in Ancient Israel*, 1962); *idem*, "Gibt es eine Eschatologie bei den alttestamentlichen Propheten?" *StTh*, VI (1953), 79-114; *idem*, "Zur Frage des kanaanäischen Ursprungs des altisraelitischen Prophetismus," in *Von Ugarit nach Qumran* (Eissfeldt-Festschrift), 1958, pp. 89-104; *idem*, *Prophecy in Ancient Israel*, 1962; S. Mowinckel, *Psalmenstudien III: Kultprophetie und prophetische Psalmen*, 1923; R. Rendtorff, "Erwägungen zur Frühgeschichte des Prophetentums in Israel," *ZThK*, LIX (1962), 145-67; H. Graf Reventlow, "Prophetenamt und Mittleramt," *ibid.*, LVIII (1961), 269-84; N. H. Ridderbos, *Israels Profetie en "Profetie" buiten Israel*, 1955; T. H. Robinson, "Neuere Propheten-Forschung," *ThR*, NF III (1931), 75-103; H. H. Rowley, "The Nature of Prophecy in the Light of Recent Study," *HThR*, XXXVIII (1945), 1-38 (= *The Servant of the Lord*, 1952, pp. 89-128); *idem*, *Prophecy and Religion in Ancient China and Israel*, 1956; *idem*, "Ritual and the Hebrew Prophets," *JSS*, I (1956), 338-60; B. Vawter, *The Conscience of Israel*, 1961; A. C. Welch, *Kings and Prophets of Israel*, 1952; *idem*, *Prophet and Priest in Old Israel*, 2nd ed.,

1953; C. F. Whitley, *The Prophetic Achievement*, 1963; H. W. Wolff, "Hauptprobleme alttestamentlicher Prophetie," *EvTh*, XV (1955), 446-68 (= *Gesammelte Studien zum Alten Testament*, 1964, pp. 206-31).

1. *The ancient Near East*. The history of religions and what ancient Near Eastern material has been discovered show that prophetism as such was no more unique to Israel and the OT than, say, the priesthood. A considerable body of evidence gathered by Lindblom and Heiler shows that it is neither limited to specific periods or regions nor associated with particular nations, races, or religions. Male and female prophets, or figures like prophets, can appear in more or less highly developed form wherever human beings live. What they share in common lies in the realms of general structure and psychology; in the content of the revelations they proclaim, the differences are enormous. A prophet or prophetess is accordingly a person with charismatic gifts, consciously aware of having been singled out and called, who feels constrained to proclaim messages and perform actions suggested in the form of divine revelations during a state of spiritual inspiration, possibly accompanied by mild or intense ecstasy.

Within the ancient Near East the existence of this phenomenon has so far not been unambiguously demonstrated for Egypt. Attempts to do so[1] have met with doubt or outright rejection.[2] Nevertheless, apart from study of the texts so far known, which is by no means finished, Pliny's description (*Historia naturalis* viii. 185) of youths who were seized by frenzy during a cultic ceremony about the bull of Apis and predicted things to come demonstrates the appearance of prophets.

There is considerable evidence for prophets in the settled areas of western Asia, especially in Syria-Palestine and Mesopotamia, and occasionally for the Hittites.[3] The OT itself mentions the prophets of the Canaanite god Baal (I Kings 18:19-20; II Kings 10:19) and presupposes prophecy as an international phenomenon (Jer. 27:9). Until recently the classic extrabiblical evidence was the report of the Egyptian Un-Amun of his voyage along the coast of Syria from the city of Byblos (about 1100 B.C.), where one of the attendants of the local king went into ecstasy and pronounced a divine oracle.[4] As early as the Sumerian period, however, there was a term for an ecstatic of this sort, which probably means "the man who enters the heavens." [5] For the eighteenth century a letter of the ambassador of King Zimri-Lim of Mari to Aleppo speaks of an *āpilum*, "answerer," with a female counterpart, whose normal sphere of activity

[1] F. Daumas, "Littérature prophétique et exégétique égyptienne et commentaires esséniens," in *Mémorial Gelin*, 1961, pp. 203-22; A. Erman and H. Ranke, *Ägypten*, 1923, pp. 325-26; G. Lanczkowski, "Ägyptischer Prophetismus im Lichte des alttestamentlichen," *ZAW*, LXX (1958), 31-38; *idem*, *Altägyptischer Prophetismus*, 1960.

[2] H. Bonnet, *Reallexikon der ägyptischen Religionsgeschichte*, 1952, pp. 608-609; S. Herrmann, "Prophetie in Israel und Ägypten," *VTSuppl*, IX (1963), 47-65.

[3] A. Goetze, *Kleinasien*, 1933, p. 139; Eissfeldt*, p. 103.

[4] *AOT*, pp. 71-77; *ANET*, pp. 25-29.

[5] V. Christian, "Sum. lú-an-ná-ba-tu = akkad. maḫḫû 'Ekstatiker'," *WZKM*, LIV (1957), 9-10.

was the sanctuary.[6] For the period about 1700 five letters from Mari, on the middle Euphrates, bear witness to the appearance of a messenger of God, called a *muḫḫûm;*[7] another letter mentions the appearance of a prophetess, called a *muḫḫûtum.*[8] They belong to a class of men and women associated with the temple of a deity, from whom they received messages through omens, dreams, and ecstatic experiences; they pronounced these messages as oracles. In the following period,[9] too, there were priests and priestesses in Babylonia that supported the king by means of "spoken dreams." For Assyria there is evidence for another kind of ecstatic prophecy through individual priestesses known by name, especially in the Ishtar temple of Arbela. In the fifteenth century a letter from Rewašša of Taanach mentions an *ummânu* of Astarte, learned in magic and prediction.[10] Finally, the inscription of King Zakir of Hamath (*ca.* 800 B.C.) probably mentions seers.[11]

Even though it is impossible to sketch a continuous history, we may conclude from this evidence that ecstatic prophecy is a very ancient phenomenon in ancient Near Eastern civilization, and that priest and prophet were accepted as belonging together. This kind of prophetical activity was known to the early Israelite, who came from northern Mesopotamia; the Israelite groups and tribes who settled in Palestine encountered it in its Canaanite form.

Since before the occupation of Canaan the Israelites led a nomadic or semi-nomadic life, it is important to note that a second kind of prophetism seems indigenous to this way of life: that of the seer. Pedersen in particular has discussed this form.[12] Admittedly, we can study it only in the more recent form of the Arabic *kāhin;* but the stability of life in the Near East suggests strongly that it was the nomadic form of prophetism. As the word itself suggests, the seer's contact with the divine world was primarily through vision and secondarily through hearing, so that he proclaimed his oracles mostly on the basis of prescient visions and dreams. We may still see in Balaam how the seer generally derives his oracles from the first thing he sees.

2. *Ancient Israel.* In ancient Israel we find both sociologically conditioned forms of prophetism: the nabi (*nābî',* "called one"), encountered in the form

[6] A. Malamat, "History and Prophetic Vision in a Mari Letter," *Eretz-Israel,* V (1958), 67-73.

[7] A. Lods, "Une tablette inédite de Mari, intéressante pour l'histoire ancienne du prophétisme sémitique," in *T. H. Robinson-Festschrift,* 1950, pp. 103-10; A. Malamat, "'Prophecy' in the Mari Documents," *Eretz-Israel,* IV (1956), 74-84; W. von Soden, "Verkündigung des Gotteswillens durch prophetisches Wort in den altbabylonischen Briefen aus Mâri," *WdO* I (1947-52), 397-403; C. Westermann, "Die Mari-Briefe und die Prophetie in Israel," in *Forschung am Alten Testament,* 1964, pp. 171-88.

[8] *ARM,* VI, Letter 45, ed. J. R. Kupper; M. Noth, "Remarks on the Sixth Volume of Mari Texts," *JSS,* I (1956), 322-33.

[9] *AOT,* pp. 281-84.

[10] W. F. Albright, "A Prince of Taanach in the Fifteenth Century B.C.," *BASOR,* XCIV (1944), 12-27.

[11] *AOT,* pp. 443-44; *ANET,* 2nd ed., 1955, pp. 501-502.

[12] J. Pedersen, "The Role Played by Inspired Persons among the Israelites and the Arabs," in *T. H. Robinson-Festschrift,* 1950, pp. 127-42.

of the ecstatic prophet associated with the exciting fertility cults of settled areas; and the seer (*rō'eh, ḥōzeh*), encountered among nomadic cultures. The seer, like all Israel's nomadic heritage, soon became insignificant; one of the last great representatives of this type was Nathan. Even in later prophetism, however, the appearance of prophets as lone individuals, their mysterious knowledge of the unknown, and the frequently minimal role of ecstasy derive from this source. More and more emphasis came to be placed on ecstatic prophetism. Ecstasy could be extraordinarily intense and have a prolonged effect, affecting whole multitudes of men, so that the early nebiim usually appear in groups and are more intimately associated with sanctuary and cult than are the seers (I Sam. 10:5 ff.). The extent to which this phenomenon determined the subsequent development of prophetism is shown by the juxtaposition in Jer. 29:26 of "madman" and "who prophesies."

Under the influence of Yahwism, seers and nebiim together gave rise to Israelite prophetism proper, as I Sam. 9:9 suggests. The immediate result was various transitional forms. Besides the bands of prophets, who are mentioned repeatedly, we have individual figures like Ahijah of Shilo (I Kings 11:29 ff.; 12:15; 14:1 ff.; 15:29); Zedekiah (I Kings 22:11); and Micaiah the son of Imlah (I Kings 22:13 ff.). The first figures of whom we can recover a relatively clear picture, however, are Elijah (I Kings 17–19) and Elisha (II Kings 2–13).

3. *The period of so-called literary prophecy.* In the period of so-called literary prophecy the earlier forms gradually gave rise to a comprehensive class of prophets which, though having its own complex structure, can be referred to as a whole by the term "professional cultic prophecy." Besides the unorganized prophets who wandered through the countryside, this class included cult prophets and court prophets. The cult prophets functioned alongside the priests at the sanctuaries; some of their oracles and discourses can be found in various psalms, in isolated sections of the prophetical books, or in entire books. The court prophets were associated with the royal sanctuaries and employed as advisers by the rulers. Professional cultic prophecy existed well into the postexilic period, although the charismatic nature of this prophecy means that we cannot speak of a permanent institution, a prophetical "office." At the shrines, to which they were not as closely linked as the priests, these prophets pronounced divine oracles or interceded before God. Without exception they represent the official cultic and nationalistic form of Yahwism, characterized essentially by its belief that Israel's intimate relationship with Yahweh guarantees *eo ipso* Israel's righteous status in his eyes. This status can be destroyed by isolated transgressions but can always be restored by appropriate acts of atonement. Individuals can also transgress this status and are then called to account. Therefore the professional prophets proclaim that every enemy of Israel and of Yahweh will be destroyed, while the people of Yahweh is assured of salvation (Jer. 14:13).

Beside these professional prophets stand the great individual prophets of the preexilic period, a group small in number: Amos and Hosea, Isaiah and Micah, Zephaniah, Jeremiah, and Ezekiel. In them OT prophecy reaches its apex. They do not exercise their ministry as professionals, but on the basis of a special call that has uprooted them from their chosen profession. Within the life of their nation they do not function as members of a guild or of a class, nor as representatives of a clan or of a tribe, nor as officials of a sanctuary or of a king; they think of themselves exclusively as representatives and messengers of their God, beyond all ties of family and society, nation and cult. In contrast to the professional prophets, they see man as being essentially unrighteous before God. He has fallen to this state through his refusal to trust in God and submit to him, through rebellion against God and apostasy from him. This, the basic attitude of mankind as a whole toward God, appears behind all the individual transgressions censured by the prophets. They therefore expect that the warning reverses that have already been suffered will be followed by an annihilating judgment, although this is not in fact God's will. Since this fate is not inescapable, any more than man's perverse attitude is invincible, the prophets mention the possibility of forgiveness and new salvation. Their central theme is therefore the either/or of man's destruction or deliverance, though this does not make them simply preachers of repentance. The call to conversion points to a possibility of deliverance; this is the sum and substance of the preaching of Amos, Isaiah, and Micah. In the case of Hosea, Jeremiah, and Ezekiel, however, at a later stage in their ministry a second possibility is offered: conversion is replaced by deliverance through God. In both instances we are dealing with a basic inward and outward transformation resulting in a new man, who lives in fellowship with God and does his will, so that God rules in the world. These prophets, at least, do not base their preaching on a dead ideology but on a personal life of faith.

During this period, when prophets were mentioned in Israel the professional prophets were usually meant. They were the dominant class, beside whom the others appeared only as isolated figures. The great individual prophets were exceptional phenomena. This view did not begin to change until the Exile, under the influence of Deuteronomistic theology, when people realized that these few had been right and the professional prophets wrong. In the postexilic period, therefore, professional prophecy became more and more insignificant; the professional prophets were absorbed finally in the guilds of Temple singers, while the words of the great individual prophets were increasingly collected and considered sacred.

4. *Eschatological prophecy.* With Deutero-Isaiah, toward the end of the Exile, begins eschatological prophecy, which draws upon the traditions of both the great individual prophets and the optimistic professional prophets. Apart from Deutero-Isaiah and a few anonymous prophets, who still preached a profound and daring message, we are dealing in this period for the most part with epigones who lacked the directness and austerity of the earlier prophets, as Isaiah 24–27, 33, 34–35, 56–66, Joel, Haggai, Zechariah, and Malachi show, as well as individual passages scattered through other books. It is therefore easy to see why they decreased in numbers and esteem and why Rabbinic theology was concerned to restrict the appearance of legitimate prophets to an idealized early period. Eschatological prophecy reinterprets the either/or of the great

individual prophets as a temporal before/after. Here we see the influence of the optimistic preaching of the professional cultic prophets, on the basis of which God's saving will is emphasized one-sidedly. At the same time, the downfall of Judah and the Exile are thought of as the judgment that had been proclaimed. Since this judgment is no longer viewed as an always imminent possibility but as a unique historical event, it can only be followed by a new and final period of deliverance. The eschatological prophets therefore distinguish between two ages between which they see themselves standing and depict with great variety and often in glowing colors the transition from the one age to the other, as well as the age to come, in which God himself or his representative the "Messiah" will rule over all. Nevertheless, besides these expectations, often quite materialistic, other echoes are heard: the conversion of all men to the one God and eternal peace under his dominion.

5. *Apocalyptic.* After the eschatological expectations of the late exilic and postexilic period were shattered, because despite the promises of the prophets all remained as it had always been and extensive circles in the community had turned their backs on eschatology, eschatology underwent a transformation. Drawing on wisdom theology and foreign ideas, especially dualistic Iranian cosmology, it turned into apocalyptic. Of the writings produced by this movement only the book of Daniel became a part of the OT. This book inaugurates a series of apocalyptic writings that seek to unveil the mysteries of the end time and provide revelations concerning the coming and passing of the ages of the world, in order both to determine the time when all history will end and to fix the place of the present age. A sharp contrast is drawn between the whole of world history and the kingdom of God, which will begin after a last judgment yet to come. Apocalyptic thus combines a dualistic view of God and the world with the idea of the abolition of the present world through a new creation and the inauguration of a theocracy, to which those who live in apocalyptic expectation will belong either immediately or after their resurrection. At this point earlier prophecy has been completely replaced by a new way of thought and a new faith.

§ 53 Prophetical Preaching: Its Literary Types and Their Traditions

L. Alonso Schökel, *Estudios de Poética Hebrea,* 1963; R. Bach, *Die Aufforderungen zur Flucht und zum Kampf im alttestamentlichen Prophetenspruch,* 1962; F. Baumgärtel, "Die Formel ne'um jahwe," *ZAW,* LXXIII (1961), 277-90; K. Beyer, *Spruch und Predigt bei den vorexilischen Schriftpropheten,* Dissertation, Erlangen, 1933; H. J. Boecker, *Redeformen des Rechtslebens im Alten Testament,* 1964; H. A. Brongers, *De scheppingtradities bij de profeten,* 1945; I. Engnell, "Profetia och tradition," *SEÅ,* XII (1947), 110-39; G. Fohrer, "Die Gattung der Berichte über symbolische Handlungen der Propheten," *ZAW,* LXIV (1952), 101-20; *idem, Die symbolischen Handlungen der Propheten,* 1953; *idem,* "Prophetie und Geschichte," *ThLZ,* LXXXIX (1964), 481-500; B. Gemser, "The rîb- or Controversy-Pattern in Hebrew Mentality," *VTSuppl,* III (1955), 120-37; E. Gerstenberger, "The Woe-

Oracles of the Prophets," *JBL*, LXXXI (1962), 249-63; H. GRESSMANN, *Der Messias*, 1929, pp. 65-148; K. HARMS, *Die falschen Propheten*, 1947; J. HARVEY, "Le 'Rîb-Pattern', réquisitoire prophétique sur la rupture de l'alliance," *Bibl*, XLIII (1962), 172-96; J. HEMPEL, "Jahwegleichnisse der israelitischen Propheten," *ZAW*, XLII (1924), 74-104 (= *Apoxysmata*, 1961, pp. 1-29); *idem*, "Prophet and Poet," *JThSt*, XL (1939), 113-32; H. W. HERTZBERG, "Die prophetische Kritik am Kult," *ThLZ*, LXXV (1950), 219-26 (= *Beiträge zur Traditionsgeschichte und Theologie des Alten Testaments*, 1962, pp. 81-90); F. HESSE, "Wurzelt die prophetische Gerichtsrede im israelitischen Kult?" *ZAW*, LXV (1953), 45-53; G. HÖLSCHER, *Die Profeten*, 1914; F. HORST, "Die Visionsschilderungen der alttestamentlichen Propheten," *EvTh*, XX (1960), 193-205; E. JENNI, *Die politischen Voraussagen der Propheten*, 1956; A. S. KAPELRUD, "Cult and Prophetic Words," *StTh*, IV (1950), 5-12; L. KÖHLER, *Deuterojesaja (Jesaja 40–55) stilkritisch untersucht*, 1923; H.-J. KRAUS, *Die prophetische Verkündigung des Rechts in Israel*, 1957; J. LINDBLOM, *Die literarische Gattung der prophetischen Literatur*, 1924; *idem*, "Einige Grundfragen der alttestamentlichen Wissenschaft," in *Bertholet-Festschrift*, 1950, pp. 325-37; W. F. LOFTHOUSE, " 'Thus Hath Jahveh Said'," *AJSL*, XL (1923/24), 231-51; F. MAASS, "Zur psychologischen Sonderung der Ekstase," *WZ Leipzig*, III (1953/54), 297-301; S. MOWINCKEL, " 'The Spirit' and the 'Word' in the Pre-Exilic Reforming Prophets," *JBL*, LIII (1934), 199-227; *idem*, "Ecstatic Experience and Rational Elaboration in the Old Testament Prophecy," *AcOr* (Leiden), X (1935), 264-91; *idem*, "La connaissance de Dieu chez les prophètes de l'Ancien Testament," *RHPhR*, XXII (1942), 69-105; *idem*, "Ekstatiske innslag i profetens oplevelser," *NTT*, XLIX (1948), 129-43, 193-221; E. OSSWALD, *Falsche Prophetie im Alten Testament*, 1962; G. QUELL, *Wahre und falsche Propheten*, 1952; G. VON RAD, *Theologie des Alten Testaments*, II, 4th ed., 1965 (Eng. *Old Testament Theology*, II, 1965); R. RENDTORFF, "Priesterliche Kulttheologie und prophetische Kultpolemik," *ThLZ*, LXXXI (1956), 339-42; *idem*, "Tradition und Prophetie," *Theologia Viatorum*, VIII (1962), 216-26; *idem*, "Botenformel und Botenspruch," *ZAW*, LXXIV (1962), 165-77; E. ROHLAND, *Die Bedeutung der Erwählungstraditionen Israels für die Eschatologie der alttestamentlichen Propheten*, Dissertation, Heidelberg, 1956 (1957); J. F. ROSS, "The Prophet as Yahweh's Messenger," in *Essays Muilenburg*, 1962, pp. 98-107; I. P. SEIERSTAD, *Die Offenbarungserlebnisse der Propheten Amos, Jesaja und Jeremia*, 1946; D. VETTER, *Untersuchungen zum Seherspruch im Alten Testament*, Dissertation, Heidelberg, 1963; E. VON WALDOW, *Der traditionsgeschichtliche Hintergrund der prophetischen Gerichtsreden*, 1963; C. WESTERMANN, *Grundformen prophetischer Rede*, 2nd ed., 1964 (Eng. *Basic Forms of Prophetic Speech*, 1967); H. W. WOLFF, "Die Begründungen der prophetischen Heils- und Unheilssprüche," *ZAW*, LII (1934), 1-22 (= *Gesammelte Studien zum Alten Testament*, 1964, pp. 9-35); *idem*, *Das Zitat im Prophetenspruch*, 1937 (= *Gesammelte Studien zum Alten Testament*, pp. 36-129); *idem*, "Das Thema 'Umkehr' in der alttestamentlichen Prophetie," *ZThK*, XLVIII (1951), 129-48 (= *Gesammelte Studien zum Alten Testament*, pp. 130-50); *idem*, "Das Geschichtsverständnis der alttestamentlichen Propheten," *EvTh*, XX (1960), 218-35 (= *Gesammelte Studien zum Alten Testament*, pp. 289-307); *idem*, "Der Aufruf zur Volksklage," *ZAW*, LXXVI (1964), 48-56; E. WÜRTHWEIN, "Der Ursprung der prophetischen Gerichtsrede," *ZThK*, XLIX (1952), 1-16; *idem*, "Kultpolemik oder Kultbescheid?" in *Weiser-Festschrift*, 1963, pp. 115-31; cf. also the bibliography to § 52, especially the articles by FOHRER in *ThR*, NF XIX, XX, and XXVIII, which cite additional bibliography.

1. *The function of the prophets.* The prophets begin their work after the experience of a call. This work may go on continuously despite rejection (Hos. 9:7*b*) or denials on the part of the people (Ezek. 12:21-28); it can be interrupted by external coercion (Amos 7:10-13) or discontinued temporarily by the prophet on account of its failure (Isa. 8:16-18) or on account of his inward conversion to a new message (Ezek. 3:22-27; 24:25-27; 33:21-22). It is of the nature of prophetism that the message is preached directly to those that are to receive it. Therefore for the most part the prophets proclaim their short or long discourses directly and orally. To this extent the expression "literary prophecy" is, strictly speaking, erroneous, and should only be applied with reservations to those prophets whose discourses, unlike those of other prophets, were written down at a specific stage in their transmission. In addition, the prophets often performed symbolic actions, which constitute a second type of proclamation through actions rather than words. More than the spoken word, these actions emphasize that the message of the prophets strives to be efficacious. They go back originally to magical actions, whose performance was thought to effect what they represented. For the prophets, of course, the assurance that the event proclaimed will come to pass rests not on the magical efficacy of the action but on the will and power of God, whereby he realizes what the symbolic action proclaims (Fohrer).

2. *Development of the prophetic oracle.* The development of the prophetic oracle—like the actions or experiences described in the biographical accounts of the prophets—normally consists of an extended process involving at least four stages (Hempel*). The first stage is a moment of personal experience of God, in which God's "spirit" or "word" comes to the prophet—the "spirit" being most important in the case of the nabi and cult prophet, the "word" in the case of the great individual prophets—or in which he is transported to another sphere. In this moment he has a "secret experience" (Gunkel); instances include visions like Isaiah 6, auditions like Jer. 4:5 ff., sudden inspirations like Isa. 7:13-17, and miraculous knowledge like that in Jeremiah 4–6 concerning the foe from the north. The secret experience takes place in the full light of spiritual and intellectual consciousness but can be accompanied by an ecstatic experience. Contrary to an exaggerated assessment that traces all experiences to ecstasy, which is viewed as the source of prophetical knowledge (Hölscher), ecstasy can only be termed a possible concomitant of secret experiences, though it can of course become so intense as to be an experience of being entranced or transported, as in the case of Ezekiel. It must also be distinguished from the ecstatic union of mysticism because the prophet remains conscious of himself as a person vis-à-vis God. It is therefore more accurate to follow Lindblom in calling it an ecstasy of concentration, in which the psyche concentrates on a specific emotion or a specific idea or constellation of ideas, while the normal influence of consciousness is abolished and the external senses more or less cease to function. In short, the prophet is gripped by a power that he cannot escape. What he experiences or perceives he is constrained to put into words and to

proclaim (Jer. 20:9; Amos 3:8). Therefore, immediately after his secret experience the prophet begins to ponder over it.

In the second stage come the prophet's interpretation and exposition of his unique experience according to the faith by which he lives. The new experience is interpreted in such a way that the individual experience is incorporated into the prophet's previous total picture of God's nature and will, enlarging it and vitalizing it. This interpretation usually distinguishes between true and false prophecy.

Next follows, as the third stage, the process of intellectual revision. Since what has been experienced must be proclaimed, it cannot remain at the babbling level of glossolalia, but must be translated into comprehensible and rational words. This takes place so naturally that the prophet sometimes adds an appropriate motivation or appends an obvious conclusion to the word of Yahweh. At the same time, this stage produces words spoken by the prophet in his own right, which he forms without any preceding secret experience on the basis of his certainty that he can speak as Yahweh's messenger. This much can generally be said: the less meditation and rational revision a prophetical oracle betrays, the more tersely and unconditionally it proclaims God's will, the more clearly it preserves as its nucleus a primitive complex of sounds (e.g., Isa. 8:1), the closer we are to its origin (Hempel*).

The third stage is paralleled by a fourth, that of artistic development, to which belong the adaptation of the message to a specific, sometimes very ancient, rhetorical form and its clothing in metrical poetry. This development can draw upon an image or an idea and elaborate it artistically, e.g., the fire that goes forth from Yahweh (Amos 1:3 ff.) or his hand (Isa. 9:7 ff. [Eng. 9:8 ff.]).

3. *Style of the prophetic oracle.* In the style of the prophetic oracle,[1] one can frequently still note the influence of the prophet's experience, so that the images follow hard upon each other, the language seems unrefined, and abrupt transitions occur. A good example of this agitated poetic style is the description in Jer. 4:5-8, 13-22, filled with dramatic vitality. In addition, we frequently encounter a kind of secretive mode of expression, as in the names of Isaiah's children (Isa. 7:3; 8:1-4). A further characteristic is the use of poetic periphrase, like Jeremiah's "foe from the north," whom he later states to be the Babylonians, and the "bloody city" (Nah. 3:1). Finally, we may mention the use of concrete images and superlatives, which surpasses even the usual Israelite idiom. Characteristic of prophetical style, furthermore, are the introductory and concluding formulas that characterize a prophetical discourse as Yahweh's word: "Thus says Yahweh . . ." introduces the discourse by employing the ordinary messenger formula, and ". . . oracle of Yahweh" concludes it in most cases. These formulas are subject to various poetic transformations. In addition, we frequently find introductory formulas belonging to the prophet personally; these state the identity of the divine "I" that sends the prophet and of the recipient of the message, or who else is called upon to give ear (Isa. 1:2). Likewise the state of

[1] On the following discussion, cf. H. Gunkel, *Die Propheten,* 1917.

the prophet during his secret experience can be described (Isa. 8:11). To a large extent the introductory formulas, like the accounts of the prophets' calls and visions, serve to legitimate the prophet and support his authority. Finally, the prophet can expand the beginning of a discourse by adding a motivation to explain the following declaration of God's will (Amos 4:1).

Syntactic and grammatical characteristics include the numerous questions and imperatives, as well as the so-called prophetic perfect to express future events that appear as real and certain to the prophet as though they had already come to pass.

4. *Literary types*. The literary types used by the prophets in their preaching can be classified into three great groups: prophetical sayings, prophetical reports, and imitations of rhetorical forms from other spheres of life. Scholarship in this area has not progressed continuously but exhibits a variety of new and different approaches, usually restricted to one part of the total complex: the prophetical sayings that accuse men of sin and on the basis of this accusation proclaim God's judgment as punishment. The sayings containing promises, the prophetical reports, and the imitative forms have usually been ignored and have only recently been elucidated in numerous monographs.

Once Baudissin* had recognized that the prophetical books are composed of numerous individual sayings and reports, Steuernagel* worked out the principal forms taken by the sayings: the indictment of the people on account of their sins, which he equated with the call to repentance; and the declaration of judgment, intended to convert the people. While Hölscher established the similarity of these sayings to magical incantations and discovered their rhythmic structure, Gunkel[2] worked out the multitude of rhetorical forms used by the prophets, borrowed in large part from other areas of life, and found what he considered the basic original prophetical form in the sayings describing the future of different nations and peoples. Gressmann, on the other hand, considered the basic prophetical form to be a combination of disaster and salvation declaration (in which the threat is usually associated with an invective), which remained a unit until prophecy of disaster became dissociated from prophecy of salvation. Studies of individual prophetical documents—Balla on Amos, Scott on Isaiah, Wildberger on Jeremiah[3]—are based essentially on the insights of Gunkel, which Hempel*, drawing upon newly discovered material, summarized and modified.

Lindblom and Köhler took a different approach, starting with the so-called messenger formula, "Thus says Yahweh," and emphasizing the message character of the prophetical saying. Wolff utilizes this approach to an even greater extent, understanding the prophet as a messenger to proclaim Yahweh's judgment and deliverance, whose sole function as a "mediator" is to substantiate Yahweh's message. This approach surrenders the possibility of understanding a prophet's

[2] H. Gunkel, "Propheten II seit Amos," *RGG*, 1st ed., 1866-86.

[3] E. Balla, *Die Droh- und Scheltworte des Amos*, 1926; R. B. Y. Scott, "The Literary Structure of Isaiah's Oracles," in *T. H. Robinson-Festschrift*, 1950, pp. 175-86; H. Wildberger, *Jahwewort und prophetische Rede bei Jeremia*, 1942.

message on the basis of an experience he has had in order to gain an apparently more objective basis for the prophetical saying as God's word. Westermann, too, in his detailed study of the prophetical sayings that proclaim disaster, interprets them uniformly as the words of a messenger. As the basic form of prophetical discourse he arrives at a prophetical word of judgment that agrees in structure with ordinary legal proceedings: it contains two elements, a motivation and a declaration (instead of invective and threat), conveyed by the prophet. This, however, is probably not the final word. The apparent objectification of God's word has been purchased too dearly, at the expense of those personal factors that are undoubtedly present and distinguish a saying of Isaiah from a saying of Hosea or Jeremiah. If one prefers not to revert to an all-inclusive theory of inspiration, one must admit that the prophet has a part as a human individual in the formal and material construction of what he says. Since, as a human individual, he has a psyche, it is impossible to avoid psychological study that takes the prophetical experience into account. In addition, it is form-critically inaccurate to term the prophetical saying the speech of a messenger simply because it frequently employs the messenger formula, as Rendtorff has shown. If the prophet himself has at least contributed largely to the form of the word of Yahweh that he proclaims, and if his personal opinion is found in the motivation for the threatened disaster and in numerous other sayings that are not called Yahweh's word, it is a dubious course to fly from the one extreme of the experience theory to the other of the messenger theory. In fact, we are only dealing with two among many aspects arising from our study of a most complex phenomenon.

A. The purpose of the prophetical saying is to convey the will of Yahweh as it affects the future course of history in consequence of man's present way of life. It is inaccurate, if not misleading, to call the prophetical saying "prophecy" in the sense of "prediction"; Luther, for instance, limited this expression mostly to the false prophets of Israel and the pagan prophets. The essential point is not the miraculous prediction of events soon to come; in fact, the prophets frequently erred in this matter. What is crucial is that what is announced is already on the point of coming to pass; the prophet has just enough time to point out what is happening and summon men to draw the proper conclusions for the present. The prophet speaks of the future in order to determine and structure the present in which he lives, which it is his task and goal to influence.

a) The primitive form of the prophetical saying is the oracle. Originally, a person would obtain such an oracle from a cult prophet at a sanctuary, in response to an inquiry addressed by the prophet to the deity or addressed to the prophet directly. It was a counterpart to the priestly oracle (§ 10.1), and can still be found in a series of psalms, e.g., 20:7-9 (Eng. 20:6-8); 60:8-10 (Eng. 60:6-8); 85:9-10 (Eng. 85:8-9); 95:7-11, where it was also pronounced in response to a lament (§ 39.3). It also occurs in a series of prophetical sayings, e.g., I Kings 14:5 ff.; II Kings 20:1; Jer. 37:17. An oracle is usually marked by the introduction *kô 'āmār yhwh* (*ṣ*e*bā'ôt*), a cultic liturgical formula.[4] An oracle always declares the immediate future to be favorable or unfavorable on the basis of the present situation, thereby granting the person concerned the chance so to act in the present moment as to secure the good or avoid the evil through his conduct. In II Kings 20:2 ff., for example, Hezekiah successfully proceeds in this manner. In addition, the prophet could intercede with Yahweh. The oracle proper is on its way to becoming a prophetical saying, either positive or negative, when it is offered without being asked, as in II Kings 20:1.

b) The negative prophetical saying is a threat, with or without motivation, announcing imminent disaster on account of human sin. This form predominates in the great individual prophets. Jer. 28:8-9 practically makes it the criterion of a true prophet's message, while in the case of a prophet who prophesies salvation only the realization of his prophecy demonstrates that Yahweh has sent him.

Westermann has subjected this form of saying to a thorough investigation, with many pertinent observations. He prefers to call it a "word of judgment" and seeks to show that it comprises two elements, the motivation (indictment) and declaration (sentence), instead of the usual two distinct literary types, invective and threat. He distinguishes the word of judgment directed to individuals, the earliest type, from the declaration of judgment addressed to the people or nation in literary prophecy; from this second form he derives all the other important prophetical literary types. Now it is probably not of crucial importance whether the prophetical saying in question is called "threat," "word of judgment," "declaration of disaster," or some similar expression. The second term, however, does tend once more toward objectification, while "threat" refers to a verbal statement that certainly does not have to be associated with an appropriate gesture. "Threat" leaves open the matter of whether what is threatened actually comes to pass; this is not at all a disadvantage but fits the situation exactly, since many threats are retracted, e.g., Amos 7:1-6, or, more frequently, were never realized, e.g., Isa. 22:14. The expression may therefore be retained. Further misgivings are engendered by the one-sided legal definition of this type of prophetical saying, the derivation of many other rhetorical forms from it, and, last but not least, the view that the so-called invective is not an independent literary type but rather the motivation for the declaration of disaster, an absolutely necessary component of this literary type. One must rather distinguish carefully between the motivation belonging to a threat and the independent invective.

The threat may appear in three forms: as pure threat without motivation,[5] as threat with motivation,[6] and as a combination of invective and threat.[7] It

[4] Cf. F. Baumgärtel, "Zu den Gottesnamen in den Büchern Jeremia und Ezechiel," in *Rudolph-Festschrift*, 1961, pp. 1-29.

[5] Limiting ourselves to two prophets: Isa. 3:25–4:1; 7:18-19, 20, 21-22; 10:24-27; 17:1-2, 3, 4, 5*a*, 5*b*, 6; 18; 29:9-11; 30:27-33; 32:9-14; Amos 3:12*b*-15; 4:16-17; 8:9-10, 11-14.

[6] Isa. 3:1-9, 16-24; 8:5-8; 28:1-4, 14-22; 29:13-14; 30:6-7, 8-14, 15-17; Amos 1:3 ff.; 4:1-3.

[7] Isa. 5:8-10, 11-13; 22:1-14, 15-19; 30:1-4; 31:1-3; Amos 3:9-11; 4:7-11; 6:1-7, 13-14; 8:4-7.

can be subdivided into three types: the threat addressed to individuals, to the prophet's own nation, and to foreign nations.

The threat addressed to individuals,[8] e.g., Amos 7:16-17 (in incomplete form, e.g., I Kings 21:17-19; II Kings 1:3-4), comprises the following sequence: summons to listen; motivation; declaration of disaster, introduced by the messenger formula. It presupposes at the outset God's favor toward the group as a whole, from which an individual is excluded on account of his transgression, but without further consequences for the group. Among the great individual prophets Amos, Isaiah, and Jeremiah continue to employ it to supplement their threats.

The threat addressed to the prophet's own nation begins with Amos. It is based on a complete reversal of the situation in the eyes of the great individual prophets, who no longer see their nation in God's favor but in God's disfavor. Frequently, but not always, it contains a motivation, which may exhibit an expanded form or be replaced by an invective; then follows, introduced by the messenger formula or merely by *therefore,* the declaration of disaster, which will come to pass through the intervention of Yahweh; a description of the results of this intervention concludes the threat.

The threat addressed to foreign nations is usually constructed like the threat against Israel. Originally it was probably similar to the threat addressed to individuals because it originated in the optimistic message of the professional cultic prophets, who announced disaster for the enemy and therefore salvation for their own nation (Nahum, Habakkuk). It may also be associated with the taunt song (Isa. 37:22-35) or follow the pattern of the Egyptian execration texts, as the series in Amos 1:3 ff. still shows. The great individual prophets associated it with the threat of disaster to Israel, so that it acquired a new meaning, bearing witness to the surpassing majesty of God.

c) The positive prophetical saying is a declaration of salvation or a promise which, in a present state of distress, announces a favorable turn of fortune. Indirectly, the threats of the professional prophets against foreign nations were at the same time declarations of salvation for Israel. Here we may also mention prophetical intercession, whose goal may be a positive oracle. Once again, there were positive sayings addressed to individuals (to which the exhortation in Isa. 7:1-9 conforms), to the prophet's own nation, and to foreign nations. While the first two types are already found in optimistic professional prophecy, the latter first appears in eschatological prophecy. In the great individual prophets, however, positive sayings are rare; they are found only in Hosea, Jeremiah, and Ezekiel.

The fully developed form of the positive saying, which Begrich terms *priesterliches Heilsorakel* ("priestly oracle of deliverance"),[9] is found in the sayings of Deutero-Isaiah. It comprises a promise of divine intervention on behalf of the person or persons seeking aid, a statement of the consequences of

[8] Cf. also the list in Westermann, p. 98.

[9] J. Begrich, "Das priesterliche Heilsorakel," *ZAW*, LII (1934), 81-92 (= *Gesammelte Studien zum Alten Testament,* 1964, pp. 217-31).

this intervention, and a statement of Yahweh's purpose in granting the petition.

d) The invective is in part a secondary literary type. It derives its great importance from the relevance of the prophet's message to his own time. In it the prophet reproaches an individual or the nation for its sin and guilt. This form has two roots. First, it may develop as a form-critically autonomous element from the motivation for a threat; it may then stand by itself (Isa. 1:4-9; Amos 5:12; 6:12) or be combined once more with a threat. Second, the invectives introduced by the word *hôy*, "woe," constitute an independent group, e.g., Isa. 5:8 ff.; 10:5-15; 29:15. They are likewise formulated by the prophet, and may have their roots in the curses employed by magic and wisdom, the more so because the introductory "woe" itself suggests a threatened disaster.[10]

e) Exhortations and warnings are found among the prophetical sayings from early times, as the Mari letters show. They may also have had a place in optimistic cultic prophecy. In any event, the great individual prophets give them a new function. They are among the primitive forms of prophetical discourse that can be derived from the oracle. Their purpose is to require the petitioner to follow a course of conduct that will have favorable consequences for the future. In the case of the great individual prophets, who almost always themselves composed their metrically structured exhortations, these forms invariably call upon the hearer to turn from the path of sin and commit himself to a new way of life based on obedience and submission to God. Jeremiah can even summarize his entire ministry from this point of view (25:3-7). The mention of conversion is by no means limited to words of invective and promise (the latter not until eschatological prophecy, cf. Isa. 44:21-22); it also occurs in warnings of imminent disaster and as a condition for deliverance from it, e.g., Isa. 1:18-20; Amos 5:14. Despite the proclamation of apparently unconditional judgment, reference is made to possible deliverance.

B. The different types of prophetical report go back in part to very ancient forms that later became less important.

a) The seer saying is the precursor of the prophetical vision and audition report. I Kings 22:17 is typical: the seer tells the listener what he has seen and its interpretation as spoken by Yahweh. In the same way Balaam must see before he can speak (Num. 22:41); then Yahweh puts a word in his mouth (Num. 23:5). When it is recorded, it is clearly introduced by the word *nāʾūm*, "utterance," which appears in the prophetical saying as a transitional or concluding formula (Num. 24:3 [there translated "oracle" by the RSV]) (Baumgärtel).

The objectivizing view of the prophetical saying is equally inaccurate when applied to the seer-saying. Vetter's study shows that it is neither a literally reported nor a modified word of God, but always the personal discourse of the seer, who is expressly designated as the subject by the introductory and transi-

[10] For this reason, *pace* Westermann, pp. 48-49, we must retain the word "invective," because there is at least a root in the magical interpretation of existence. It is scarcely possible, however, to follow Gerstenberger in deriving the invective entirely from popular ethics, and certainly not in his conclusion that the remonstrances of the prophets do not permit us to draw conclusions concerning the situation they addressed.

tional formulas of his own speech, although he does not speak on the basis of his own personal authority but rather on the basis of Yahweh's authorization.

b) In the report of a vision the prophet describes his perceptions during a secret experience. Probably through the influence of the seer tradition, such a vision can be based on everyday things: a basket of ripe fruit (Amos 8:1-3), a boiling pot (Jer. 1:13), or an almond rod (Jer. 1:11). It can also involve the vision of exalted or mysterious events and circumstances, so that in any case an interpretation is needed, which the prophet can clothe in the guise of a word of Yahweh. Just in these instances the individuality of imagination, thought, and speech of the individual prophets makes itself felt (cf. Isaiah 6; Jer. 1:4-10; Ezek. 1:1–3:15). We may follow Horst in distinguishing three types of vision: presence visions (the presence of Yahweh), word-symbol or word-assonance visions, and event visions.

c) The report of an audition can be distinguished from the prophetical saying by the express statement that the prophet has heard the voice of Yahweh speaking to him, e.g., Isa. 5:9. He may also perceive other voices, which he records, e.g., commands given in the land threatened with disaster (Jer. 4:5*b* ff.) or the lamentation of the people doomed to destruction (Jer. 4:31).

d) Quite frequently vision and audition are linked with each other, as in the reports concerning them, not least in the first experience of this sort, which should be mentioned as a special case: the call experience, which summons the prophet to the service of Yahweh. These reports share a common root with the report of the call of Moses in the Yahwist's account and with the patriarchal narratives of Genesis that report a theophany and positive oracle followed by a cultic act: they represent the experience of the call, endowment, and commissioning of a charismatic.

e) The report of a symbolic action, such as the prophets frequently performed, is linked to an earlier form: the report of magical actions. The Yahwist's account of the Egyptian plagues clearly shows this connection.[11] When complete, it exhibits three main elements: Yahweh's command to perform the action, the account of the action itself (often lacking because the performance of the action was taken for granted) and the interpretation of the action; cf. Ezek. 12:1-11; 24:15-24. Three subsidiary elements may also be present: data concerning witnesses, statements expressing Yahweh's promise to realize what is symbolized, and statements relating the action to the symbolized event.

C. To a surprisingly great extent the prophets borrowed rhetorical forms from other realms of life, imitated them, and used them in new functions. The traditional prophetical literary types were far from being sufficient for the great individual prophets and the eschatological prophets; they needed other forms for their message. In the process, they extended the use of many literary types (taunt song and dirge); other types are familiar only from their prophetical imitations. In many cases, of course, it is proper to ask whether we are really dealing with true literary types or merely with analogous stylistic forms.

Everyday life furnishes the following types, which were borrowed or imitated:

[11] Cf. G. Fohrer, *Überlieferung und Geschichte des Exodus*, 1964, pp. 60-79.

drinking song, love song, taunt song, and dirge (the latter two extended by the prophets; § 40). From this realm comes also the discussion,[12] which usually begins with a question addressed to the other speaker and goes on in the form of a statement so framed as to obtain agreement, arriving finally at the crucial statement; it may also progress from an indisputable general statement to the contested statement, or cite an objection and answer it in the same breath (Amos 3:2). Finally, also from the realm of everyday life, the prophets make use of summonses to battle or to flight.

From the cultic realm the prophets borrowed and imitated the following: hymnic style and hymns, laments (§ 39), the summons to lamentation ceremonies, priestly torah (§ 10.3), and cultic instruction, as well as liturgies used by the cult or cult prophets and the "cantata," a combination of various parts without shift of speaker.[13]

From the realm of wisdom instruction derive the corresponding rhetorical forms (§ 47); from the realm of historical narrative derives the prophetical interpretation of history (e.g., Amos 4:6-12; Isa. 9:7-20 [Eng. 9:8-21] + 5:25-29); and from the legal realm derives the prophetical judgment discourse,[14] comprising in particular the indictment, the summons to trial and naming of witnesses, the inauguration of the proceedings by the divine judge with his accusation (Isa. 1:2-3; 3:12-15), as well as the dispute between two parties found in Deutero-Isaiah and, on occasion, the sentence.

Precisely because of this variety it is crucially important not only to determine the rhetorical form but also to determine the function for which the prophet intends to use it. The duality of form and function, of original "*Sitz im Leben*" and modified "use in discourse" is nowhere so evident as in the words of the prophets.

5. *Relationship to tradition.* The relationship of the prophets, particularly the great individual prophets, to tradition has recently been the subject of intensive study. Of course, the prophets were never thought to be totally independent of tradition; but earlier their opposition to Israel's traditions and the completely new element of their message was most emphasized, while now the situation is at times almost reversed: the prophets are seen almost without exception in relationship to the ancient traditions that they actualize, not least in their relationship to the law, which has gained new esteem. " 'Moses,' i.e., the proclaimer of the old law, becomes an evangelist, while the prophets become the Pauline Moses, the proclaimer of the law." [15]

[12] Cf. J. Begrich, *Studien zu Deuterojesaja*, 1938 (reprinted 1963), pp. 42-47.

[13] J. Lindblom, *Die Jesaja-Apokalypse, Jes 24–27*, 1938.

[14] Deriving this form from everyday legal procedure, as Boecker and Hesse do. Würthwein, on the other hand, derives it from the cult and Harvey from international treaty law. Von Waldow takes a mediating position.

[15] W. Zimmerli, *Das Gesetz und die Propheten*, 1963, p. 77. The modern picture of the prophets thus agrees in many points with the doubtlessly inaccurate picture provided by the Chronicler, summarized ironically by J. Wellhausen, *Geschichte Israels*, I, 1878, p. 111: "They proclaim nothing new, nothing independent; like Jahve himself, they merely administer

We are left with a complex and diverse picture. One view includes all the OT prophets under the heading of ancient Near Eastern cult prophecy and the cultic form characteristic of the entire ancient Near East, with its royal ideology. Others look upon them as representatives of ancient Israelite traditions, historical, legal, or cultic, which they actualize, radicalize, or interpret eschatologically, so that ultimately they can even be considered cultic officials with practically nothing of their own to say, who merely recite the hallowed liturgy. In addition, we must mention their association with wisdom instruction and even magic, from which derives the idea of the efficacy of the prophets' preaching. Undoubtedly—apart from the cult prophets, who in any case lived in the realm of cultic religion—the great individual prophets made use of ancient Near Eastern ideas and tradition, especially those of Israel and the OT, just as they drew upon the traditional form of prophetical preaching. Obviously they grew up in this milieu, were familiar with it, and availed themselves of it. With good reason, therefore, albeit at times too one-sidedly and misleadingly, all kinds of material have been brought together from various realms to illustrate their traditional background and depict it in all its complexity.[16]

Certainly the prophets are not revolutionaries who would like to discard the whole existing order and begin afresh; neither are they the end product of a long development leading to an ethical monotheism exemplified in them. By the same token, however, they do not seek the reform or reformation of ancient traditions. Their relationship to the traditions is of a different order. The crucial point for their message is not their connection with these traditions, the general cultural traditions of their people and, through them, the more extensive traditions of the ancient Near East. What matters is their own experience of the terrible and gracious presence of God, based on the impulses of primitive Mosaic Yahwism, which come to life in them in a purified and more advanced form. At this very point the great individual prophets constitute a unique phenomenon. They give up the religious forms deriving in many cases from compromise with other ideas and practices and speak on the basis of a truth they experience existentially. In so doing they do not eliminate tradition, although it is not basic to their faith, but avail themselves of it for the proclamation of their message. In the process they revised this tradition and reinterpreted it, as the reinterpretation of the Day of Yahweh (Amos 5:18-20; Isa. 2:12-17), among other examples, shows, so as to be able with its help to express what they had to say.

§ 54 Compilation and Transmission

H. Birkeland, *Zum hebräischen Traditionswesen*, 1938; K. Budde, "Eine folgenschwere Redaktion des Zwölfprophetenbuchs," *ZAW*, XXXIX (1921), 218-29; A. H. J. Gunneweg, *Mündliche und schriftliche Tradition der vorexilischen Prophetenbücher*

---

the Tora of Moses, mechanically predicting good or ill fortune, depending on whether the law has been faithfully kept or neglected."

[16] A summary bibliography is given in G. Fohrer, "Tradition und Interpretation im Alten Testament," *ZAW*, LXXIII (1961), p. 25 n. 59.

als Problem der neueren Prophetenforschung, 1959; S. MOWINCKEL, *Jesaja-disiplene*, 1926; *idem*, *Prophecy and Tradition*, 1946; T. H. ROBINSON, "Die prophetischen Bücher im Lichte neuer Entdeckungen," *ZAW*, XLV (1927), 3-9.

1. *The development of the tradition.* In an earlier day the prophetical books were naturally assumed to be single units and esteemed as the unchanged word of God. Beginning in the eighteenth century, study of the prophets began increasingly to distinguish between the word of God and the words of the prophets and devoted its interest primarily to the human words preserved in the prophetical books, though without discussing the question of their preservation and transmission. More recent studies have taken a third step, examining the process by which the prophets' words were transmitted. At the same time, they ascribe an important share in the development of the tradition contained in the prophetical writings to the men who preserved and transmitted (and, according to some, even added to) the words of the prophets.

Following our basic observations in § 3, we may assume that the prophetical sayings and reports were soon recorded and transmitted in writing. Most of them were written down while the prophets were still alive, following their oral proclamation or the performance of the symbolic acts. In later times they may even have been written down beforehand. Of course, we have little concrete data about these written records, but we can nevertheless venture a few conclusions.

In Isa. 8:16, which describes the end of the prophet's activity in terms of binding up the testimony and sealing the teaching, the divergent readings of the versions cast doubt upon the phrase "among my disciples"; it interrupts the otherwise regular meter and must be considered a later addition.[1] Isa. 30:8 does not describe the writing down of prophetical sayings, but rather the incising of an inscription, whose text is given in vs. 9.[2] This disproves the assumption that the sayings were written down for future ages in order to provide subsequent legitimation for the prophets that violently attacked their contemporaries.

That the prophetical preaching was rapidly set down in writing is shown by the influence the words spoken by Jeremiah before his deportation had on Ezekiel[3] and by the influence of Amos upon Isaiah.[4] In the former instance, it is possible to assume a personal association in Jerusalem; this is out of the question for Amos, who came from Tekoa and made his appearance in the Northern Kingdom of Israel, and Isaiah, who resided in Jerusalem. Since, however, Isaiah was influenced by Amos, the latter's words must have been extant in Jerusalem about fifteen years after they were spoken. Furthermore, Jeremiah has his words written down so that Baruch can recite them in the Temple, which he is not allowed to enter (Jeremiah 36). We are dealing here with an expedient necessitated by the situation; the purpose of course is that the weight of the

[1] For details, cf. G. Fohrer, "The Origin, Composition and Tradition of Isaiah I–XXXIX," *Annual of Leeds University Oriental Society*, III (1961/62), 29-32.

[2] *Ibid.*, pp. 32-33.

[3] G. Fohrer, *Die Hauptprobleme des Buches Ezechiel*, 1952, pp. 135-40.

[4] R. Fey, *Amos und Jesaja*, 1963.

collected sayings will make an impression that the individual saying could not achieve (vs. 3). The motivation changes, however, when King Jehoiakim burns the scroll and Jeremiah has another written, although it could no longer be read publicly and the first scroll had fulfilled its purpose. Jer. 36:29*b* gives us the proper context: the king seeks to render the threats of disaster ineffectual by destroying the scroll and trying to seize its authors, Jeremiah and Baruch, while the new scroll is intended to secure the validity of Jeremiah's pronouncements; their threat continues unabated.

The major reason why the prophetical sayings and reports were written down, collected, and transmitted (besides which, of course, there could be other, personal, reasons) was therefore to preserve the efficacy of a word once it had been spoken, and perhaps even increase it, by preserving the word in writing. Each time the words were read or recited, their power was released once more and made efficacious.[5] This implies that the prophetical sayings were written down very soon after they were proclaimed orally. The spoken word had to be recorded quickly so as to preserve its effectiveness. Even the collection of individual texts, which took place at a later date, and their gradual assembly into books may largely have come about for reasons of efficacy. Gradually, of course, theological and cultic reasons for the continued preservation and transmission of the prophetical writings became increasingly dominant as these writings came to be considered holy scripture. Even under these circumstances, however, we have an echo of the conception that the prophetical word comes to life when it is read in the context of worship.

2. *The development of the prophetical writings.* In most cases, the development of the prophetical writings followed the same lines observed in the case of the songs and the wisdom books. Minor collections of sayings and reports in written form grew into larger collections, and these grew into books. This holds true too for most of the prophetical books; only a few of them are essentially unified compositions. The basic principle can be clearly seen in the case of the book of Isaiah, which consists of three independent groups of writings, and the Book of the Twelve, which consists of twelve separate books. Here, however, we are dealing with the final product.

Often, though not invariably, the original minor collections can still be recognized. These represent the first stage in the growth of the book. In some cases they have their own superscriptions, like Jer. 23:9, "Concerning the prophets"; 30:1-4, with the command to write down certain words and the introduction "These are the words"; 46:1, "The word of Yahweh which came to Jeremiah the prophet concerning the nations"; and 50:1, "The word which Yahweh spoke concerning Babylon." Sometimes catchwords furnish the organizing principle, like "idols" (Ezekiel 6) and "sword" (Ezekiel 21); sometimes identity or similarity of subject matter, like Ezek. 12:21–13:23 concerning prophets and persons in authority and 34 concerning shepherds and sheep; sometimes similar events, as in the collections of reports concerning symbolic actions

[5] Cf. also Fohrer, *op. cit.* (note 1), pp. 33-37.

(4–5; 12:1 ff.; 24); and sometimes the compilation of words deriving from the same period, as in Isaiah 7–8.

Since the time of T. H. Robinson, a different classification has been common, which recognizes three types of text: poetic sayings, either first-person speech of Yahweh or words of the prophet; first-person prose reports of the prophet; and third-person prose reports concerning the prophet. The "simple" prophetical books comprise usually a collection of the same type; the "composite" books comprise several types. Quite apart from the fact that the second type consists not of prose but of poetry written in short verses, the third type simply does not exist in many cases, because in the ancient Near East an autobiographical report could be composed in the third person, and also because it can contain collections of prophetical sayings in short verses. We must therefore be content with distinguishing the minor collections.

In the case of the more extensive writings, the second stage in the growth of a book is the assembling of several minor collections to form larger collections, like Isaiah 1–12 and Ezekiel 1–24. The linking of these larger collections can then be termed the third stage. In individual cases, of course, we find variations in this process, which has merely been outlined schematically.

3. *Structure of the collections and books.* Various principles determined the structure of the collections and books. The earliest and most important was clearly the chronological principle, by which sayings or collections were juxtaposed or linked in the order in which they were produced. We see this principle at work in the priority of place given to call narratives such as Jer. 1:4-10; Ezek. 1:1–3:15; and the corresponding section Isa. 40:1-8, as well as in the order of the Isaiah collections in Isaiah 5–10 (§ 56.5), the words of Jeremiah contained in Jer. 1:1–25:14, which derive from different periods (§ 59.6), and the order in which the dated words of Ezekiel were included in his book. The order of Hosea 1–3 also, with the two reports of his marriage, is probably intended to be chronological; the way in which the passages dealing with the Servant of Yahweh are inserted in Isaiah 40–55 may suggest the same principle for Deutero-Isaiah.

Occasionally one may also note a qualitative principle at work, which has led to a passage considered particularly important being placed at the beginning of a prophetical book. This is especially true of Isaiah 1, which provides a cross-section of the prophet's message, for the collection Hosea 1–3, which should be interpreted similarly, and for the self-contained complex Amos 1:3–2:16.

In the course of time, arrangement according to an eschatological schema became the most important principle. Such a schema, made up of the two parts "disaster–deliverance," is found in the minor collections of Isaiah 1–35, where almost invariably the major portion of the collection has appended to it an eschatological promise, which transforms the either/or proclaimed by Isaiah (judgment and punishment or deliverance through conversion) into a before/after of transitory disaster and eternal deliverance. The same schema accounts for the order of Isaiah 1–39 followed by 44–66, Amos 1:2–9:7 followed by 9:8-15, as well as Micah 1–3 followed by 4–5 and 6:1–7:7 followed by 7:8-20.

The collection Hosea 1–3, by contrast, is pre-eschatological, while the book as a whole concludes with the promise 14:2-9.

The composition of the first part of the book of Isaiah, comprising the two sections 1–12 and 13–23, still follows the two-part schema; but the addition of the collections in 24–35 marks the first step toward a three-part schema. The latter provides the basis for the books of Ezekiel and Zephaniah, as well as the earlier form of the book of Jeremiah preserved in the LXX. Here threats against foreign nations are interpolated between the threats against Israel and the promises to Israel (and perhaps to foreign nations) because judgment upon the foreign nations is considered a transitional stage leading up to the deliverance of Israel: Ezekiel 1–24; 25–32; 33–48; Zephaniah 1–2:3; 2:4–3:8; 3:9-20; Jeremiah 1–25:14; 25:15 ff. and 46–51; 26–35*. This method of composition imposes upon the prophets' preaching the two- or three-part eschatological schema, transforming it from the literary point of view into eschatological writings, although this contradicts the message of the preexilic prophets.

4. *Later prophetic-apocalyptic books.* Later prophetic-apocalyptic books, which did not become a part of the OT, include Ethiopic and Slavonic Enoch (collections of several apocalypses), the Assumption of Moses (an apocalypse with framework sections), IV Esdras (accounts of seven visions), the Syriac and Greek Baruch apocalypse (accounts of visions), in part the Sibylline Oracles (fictitious pagan, Jewish, and Christian prophecies), and finally fragments of many apocalyptic writings from Qumran.

CHAPTER TWO: THE PROPHETICAL BOOKS (THE LATTER PROPHETS)

§ 55 Survey

The prophetical books are traditionally classified as the "major" and "minor" prophets. To the major prophets belong the extensive books of Isaiah, Jeremiah, and Ezekiel, the first of which in fact comprises three prophetical writings that must be studied separately. The term "minor prophets" has been applied (the first recorded instance being Augustine *City of God* xviii. 29) to the series of shorter books from Hosea to Malachi, of which the book of Zechariah once again comprises more than one writing. Ecclus. 49:12 calls these books the "Twelve Prophets" on account of their number and agrees with the Jewish canon in assuming that they have been brought together in one comprehensive book, the Dodekapropheton or Book of the Twelve Prophets. The Hebrew canon arranged these writings according to their actual or supposed chronological order; this order will be followed in our presentation. The LXX, on the other hand, arranges five of the first six books according to their length (Hosea, Amos, Micah, Joel, Obadiah) and places the story of the prophet Jonah in sixth position.

It would be possible to study the prophetical books in the historical sequence of the prophets, so as to produce at the same time a historical survey of literary prophecy. Insurmountable external difficulties arise, however, because many of the books contain both individual sayings and more extensive sections deriving from a period far removed from the century of the prophet with whom the book in question is concerned. One must either treat these sections in anticipation of their historical milieu or divide up the books in the course of the presentation. In order to escape these disadvantages, we shall take up the books in the sequence of the Hebrew canon.

§ 56 Isaiah I (Isaiah 1–39)

ATD: O. Kaiser, 2nd ed., 1963 (chap. 1–12). EH: F. Feldmann, 1925-26. HK: B. Duhm, 4th ed., 1922. HS: J. Fischer, 1937-39. IB: R. B. Y. Scott, 1956. ICC: G. B. Gray, 1912, reprinted 1947 (chap. 1-27). KAT: O. Procksch, 1930. KeH: A. Dillman and R. Kittel, 2nd ed., 1898. KHC: K. Marti, 1900. SAT: H. Schmidt, 2nd ed., 1923. SZ: C. von Orelli, 3rd ed., 1904 (Eng. *The Prophecies of Isaiah*, 1895). Individual commentaries: A. Bentzen, 1943; G. Fohrer, 2nd ed., 1966-67 ("Zürcher Bibelkommentare"); E. J. Kissane, 1941-43, revised ed. 1960; E. König, 1926.

S. H. Blank, *Prophetic Faith in Isaiah*, 1958; K. Budde, "Über die Schranken, die Jesajas prophetischer Botschaft zu setzen sind," *ZAW*, XLI (1923), 154-203; T. K. Cheyne, *Introduction to the Book of Isaiah*, 1895; C. H. Cornill, "Die Komposition des Buches Jesaja," *ZAW*, IV (1884), 83-105; H. DONNER, *Israel unter den Völkern*, 1964; H. J. EATON, "The Origin of the Book of Isaiah," *VT*, IX (1959), 138-57; I. EITAN, "A Contribution to Isaiah Exegesis," *HUCA*, XII/XIII (1937/38), 55-88; G. FOHRER, "The Origin, Composition and Tradition of Isaiah I–XXXIX," *Annual of Leeds University Oriental Society*, III (1961/62), 3-38; K. FULLERTON, "Viewpoints in the Discussion of Isaiah's Hopes for the Future," *JBL*, XLI (1922), 1-101; F. GIESEBRECHT, *Beiträge zur Jesajakritik*, 1890; G. HÖLSCHER, "Jesaja," *ThLZ*, LXXVII (1952), 683-94; F. C. JENNINGS, *Studies in Isaiah*, 1935; D. JONES, "The Traditio of the Oracles of Isaiah of Jerusalem," *ZAW*, LXVII (1955), 226-46; L. J. LIEBREICH, "The Compilation of the Book of Isaiah," *JQR*, XLVI (1955/56), 259-77; XLVII (1956/57), 114-38; O. LORETZ, "Der Glaube des Propheten Isaias an das Gottesreich," *ZKTh*, LXXXII (1960), 40-73, 159-81; S. MOWINCKEL, *Profeten Jesaja*, 1925; *idem*, "Die Komposition des Jesajabuches Kap. 1–39," *AcOr* (Leiden), XI (1933), 267-92; *idem*, "Komposisjonen av Jesajaboken kap. 1–39," *NTT*, XLIV (1943), 159-71; *idem*, *Jesaja*, 1949; R. B. Y. SCOTT, "The Literary Structure of Isaiah's Oracles," in *T. H. Robinson-Festschrift*, 1950, pp. 175-86; J. STEINMANN, *Le prophète Isaïe*, 2nd ed., 1955; O. S. VIRGULIN, *La 'Fede' nella Profezia d'Isaia*, 1961; T. C. VRIEZEN, "Essentials of the Theology of Isaiah," in *Essays Muilenburg*, 1962, pp. 128-46; *idem*, *Jahwe en zijn stad*, 1962; J. ZIEGLER, "Zum literarischen Aufbau verschiedener Stücke im Buche des Propheten Isaiah," *BZ*, XI (1933), 131-49, 237-54; cf. also the bibliography in FOHRER, *ThR*, NF XIX, XX, and XXVIII (§ 52).

1. *Isaiah*. Isaiah was the son of a certain Amoz, who is otherwise unknown. He was probably of aristocratic origin (7:3; 8:2) and grew up in Jerusalem (7:3; 22:15-16). That he began his career as a wisdom teacher[1] does not necessarily follow from his use of wisdom forms and vocabulary and his polemic against the "wise" politicians; probably, however, he received such an education. He was married to a woman specifically called a "prophetess" (8:3);[2] his sons Shear-jashub ("the remnant that returns") and Maher-shalal-hashbaz ("the spoil speeds, the prey hastes") (7:3; 8:3) are used in his prophetical ministry by virtue of their symbolic names.

According to 6:1, Isaiah was called to be a prophet in the year King Uzziah (Azariah) died, 746 or 740.[3] He carried out his ministry during the reigns of Jotham, Ahaz, and Hezekiah, a politically troubled period during which four Assyrian kings, Tiglath-pileser III (745–727), Shalmaneser V (726–722), Sargon II (721–705), and Sennacherib (704–681), sought to conquer the Syro-Palestinian states and advance toward Egypt. His last words date from the year 701; according to an apocryphal legend, he is said to have died a martyr's death under King Manasseh.

2. *Isaiah's ministry*. Isaiah's ministry can be divided into four periods. During the first period, from his call to just before the Syro-Ephraimite War (746/40–

[1] R. T. Anderson, "Was Isaiah a Scribe?" *JBL*, LXXIX (1960), 57-58; J. Fichtner, "Jesaja unter den Weisen," *ThLZ*, LXXIV (1949), 75-80.

[2] A. Jepsen, "Die Nebiah in Jes 8,3," *ZAW*, LXXII (1960), 267-68.

[3] The year of Uzziah's death cannot be determined precisely. There can be no doubt, however, that Isaiah 6 describes the call of the prophet and not a continuation and transformation of his message, as J. Milgrom assumes ("Did Isaiah Prophesy during the Reign of Uzziah?" *VT*, XIV [1964], 164-82), dating Isa. 1:10–6:13 in the reign of Uzziah.

736), he is concerned mostly with the internal situation in Judah following a period of considerable political and economic prosperity. His words from this period are found for the most part in 1–3 and 5. The second period includes the Syro-Ephraimite War, in which Damascus and Northern Israel undertook to force Judah to join their anti-Assyrian league (736–735). Isaiah opposes not only this alliance, but also King Ahaz's policy of declaring himself a vassal of the Assyrian king and calling upon him for help in meeting the attack. When he met with no response, he remained inactive for many years (8:16-18). His words from this period are found in 7–8; 9:7-20 (Eng. 9:8-21) + 5:25-29; 17:1-6; 28:1-4. Not until after the defeat of both aggressors, on the occasion of King Hezekiah's first attempt, in league with other states, to free himself from the status of a vassal (716–711) does Isaiah come forward again in a third period of activity. After the collapse of the revolt brought about by the Assyrians' capture of Ashdod, he falls silent once again. His words from this period are found in 14:28-32; 18; 20; 28:7-22; 29:1-14; 30:8-17. The fourth period falls in the years of Hezekiah's second attempt to achieve independence by means of a general Palestinian revolt supported by Egypt. This attempt led to the devastation of Judah, the loss of extensive regions, the threatened capture of Jerusalem, and the complete submission of Hezekiah. Isaiah's words from this period, during which he began to change his mind about Assyria, are found in 1:4-9; 10:5-15, 27*b*-32; 14:24-27, and in the portion of 28–32 that does not belong to earlier periods.

3. *Sayings and reports.* The sayings and reports that constitute Isaiah's preaching are contained in seven minor collections which, together with other collections of sayings, individual sayings, and narratives, gradually came to constitute the entire prophetical writing. Externally, this is shown by the superscriptions in 1:1 and 2:1, which can derive at the earliest from the period of the Exile, as is demonstrated by the sequence Judah–Jerusalem, which came into use at that time, and 13:1, which is modeled on 2:1. The collection consists for the most part of three elements: the body of the collection, one or more fragments of Isaiah's words, and a concluding promise. As an appendix to the fragments, the promises may at once be set apart as later additions.

Body	Fragments	Promises
A. 1:2-26 (27-28)	1:29-31	2:2-4 (5)
B. 2:6–4:1	(3:25–4:1?)	4:2-6
C. 5:1-23*; 10:1-3 (4)	5:14-17, 24	——
D. 6:1–8:18	8:19, 21-22	(8:23*b* [Eng. 9:1*b*]) 9:1-6 (Eng. 9:2-7)
E. 9:7-20 (Eng. 9:8-21); 5:25-29 (30); 10:5-15	10:27*b*-32 (33-34)	11:1-9 (10, 11-16)
F. 13–23*; 28:1-4	——	28:5-6 (23:17-18)
G. 28:7–32:14	——	32:15-20

The later passages interpolated into the collections are discussed in 4 N.

It is frequently assumed that there were several independent collections of sayings. Duhm finds these to be: 1–12; 13–23; 24–27; and 28–33, with the conclusion 34–35. Procksch considers 1; 2–6; 9:7–10:4 (Eng. 9:8–10:4); 28–31 (32) to be collections of Isaiah and 7:1–9:6 (Eng. 7:1–9:7); 11; 10:5 ff. and 14:24 ff.; 15–23 to be collections of his pupils. Budde and Mowinckel, on the contrary, assume that there was an early book of Isaiah that was later revised, expanded, and rearranged. The latter scholar comes close to the first assumption through his view that the book comprises three collections of Isaiah's sayings and three alien collections. More recently, scholars have been more inclined to think in terms of smaller collections of sayings, which, according to Liebreich, were arranged with great art by a redactor, and in terms of strong influence exerted by the prophet's disciples on the growth of the tradition, so that, according to Jones, they reinterpreted the tradition after the fall of Jerusalem, while Deutero-Isaiah, the greatest of Isaiah's disciples, constitutes the final stage. According to Eaton, these disciples expanded the tradition and adapted it to suit each new situation, though even 40–66 are still related to the thought of Isaiah. In this view the entire book of Isaiah is not an anthology of the sayings of several or many prophets, but instead exhibits an intellectual unity that reflects the development of Isaiah's ideas in his disciples.

A. The body of the first collection[4] comprises the five sayings 1:2-3, 4-9, 10-17, 18-20, 21-26. The situation depicted in 4-9 places it in the year 701; vss. 2-3 cannot be dated with assurance; the rest fit best with the end of the first period of Isaiah's ministry. They constitute a planned composition; the train of thought passes through the themes of sin, the judgment that follows upon sin, possible deliverance from the judgment, and a possible realization of this deliverance. The collection has the nature of a compendium of Isaiah's message or a cross-section of it and has therefore been placed at the beginning of the book.

B. The body of the second collection[5] comprises the sayings 2:6-22; 3:1-9, 12-15, 16-24, together with 3:25–4:1, if the last-mentioned passage is not in fact composed of two fragments. The whole collection is organized around the idea that pride and arrogance of the ruling class of Judah, rebuked in 3:1-24, will be humbled and shattered on the Day of Yahweh.

C. The so-called Song of the Vineyard (5:1-7) constitutes the nucleus of the third collection.[6] The following sayings, brought together because they all begin with the word *hôy,* "woe," are intended to spell out the details of the indictment that leads Isaiah to speak of bloodshed and a cry of lament (5:7). Perhaps at the outset only two such sayings (5:8-13) were appended, concluding with the fragments 5:14-17. Later the sayings 5:18-23 and the fragment 5:24 were added. Here belongs also the isolated saying 10:1-3.

[4] G. Fohrer, "Jesaja 1 als Zusammenfassung der Verkündigung Jesajas," *ZAW,* LXXIV (1962), 251-68 (cf. P. R. Ackroyd, *ibid.,* LXXV [1963], 320-21); L. G. Rignell, "Isaiah Chapter I," *StTh,* XI (1957), 140-58; E. Robertson, "Isaiah Chapter I," *ZAW,* LII (1934), 231-36.

[5] K. Budde, "Zu Jesaja 1–5," *ZAW,* XLIX (1931), 16-40, 182-221; L (1932), 38-72; H. L. Ginsberg, "Gleanings in First Isaiah," in *Kaplan Jubilee Vol.,* 1953, pp. 245-59; H.-M. Weil, "Exégèse d'Isaïe 3,1-15," *RB,* XLIX (1940), 76-85.

[6] A. Bentzen, "Zur Erläuterung von Jes 5,1-7," *AfO,* IV (1927), 209-10; H. Junker, "Die literarische Art von Is 5,1-7," *Bibl,* XL (1959), 259-66.

D. The body of the fourth collection[7] comprises first of all the sayings and reports from the period of the Syro-Ephraimite War; these are in strict chronological order: 7:1-9,[8] 10-17,[9] 18-22; 8:1-4,[10] 5-8, 11-15. To this series were added two framework sections: the report of Isaiah's call in chapter 6,[11] which interprets the prophet's failure on the basis of vss. 9-10; and his decision to halt his prophetical activity and await the realization of his pronouncements (8:16-18).

E. Isa. 9:7-20 (Eng. 9:8-21) + 5:25-29, which deals with the Northern Kingdom of Israel in the form of a historical interpretation and a threat, together with 10:5-15, dealing with the arrogant Assyrian king, once constituted an independent fifth collection of sayings directed against foreign nations and rulers. The incomplete text 10:27*b*-32, of which the beginning is missing, also refers to the Assyrians. The interpolation of collection D has split the first unit and isolated a portion of it (like 10:1-3, which belongs to C).[12]

F. The sixth collection has been absorbed into 13–23 along with many sayings of other prophets.[13] It contains almost exclusively oracles against foreign nations and persons. Their sequence can be explained on the basis of the Egyptian execration texts, in which the nations and persons being cursed are listed in a fixed geographical order (south, north, west), with Egypt, as the center, mentioned last. In Isaiah's different geographical situation, we have the order east, west, north, south, center:

[7] K. Budde, *Jesajas Erleben*, 1928; J. Lindblom, *A Study of the Immanuel Section in Isaiah Isa VII,1–IX,6*, 1958.

[8] S. H. Blank, "The Current Misinterpretation of Isaiah's *She'ar Yashub*," *JBL*, LXVII (1948), 211-15; L. Köhler," שאר ישוב und der nackte Relativsatz," *VT*, III (1953), 84-85; N. Müller, *Die Vorstellung vom Rest im Alten Testament*, Dissertation, Leipzig, 1939; E. Würthwein, "Jesaja 7,1-9," in *Heim-Festschrift*, 1954, pp. 47-63.

[9] S. H. Blank, "Immanuel and which Isaiah?" *JNES*, XIII (1954), 83-86; K. Budde, "Das Immanuelzeichen und die Ahaz-Begegnung Jesaja 7," *JBL*, LII (1933), 22-54; J. Coppens, "La Prophétie de la ʿAlmah," *EThL*, XXVIII (1952),648-78; G. Fohrer "Zu Jes 7,14 im Zusammenhang von Jes 7,10-22," *ZAW*, LXVIII (1956), 54-56; C. H. Gordon, " ʿAlmah in Isaiah 7,14," *JBR*, XXI (1953), 106; N. K. Gottwald, "Immanuel as the Prophet's Son," *VT*, VIII (1958), 36-47; E. Hammershaimb, "Immanuelstegnet," *DTT*, VIII (1945), 223-44; L. Köhler, "Zum Verständnis von Jes 7,14," *ZAW*, LXVII (1955), 48-50; E. G. H. Kraeling, "The Immanuel Prophecy," *JBL*, L (1931), 277-97; S. Mowinckel, "Immanuelprofetien Jes 7," *NTT*, XLII (1941), 129-57; L. G. Rignell, "Das Immanuelzeichen," *StTh*, XI (1957), 99-119; J. J. Stamm, "Die Immanuel-Weissagung," *VT*, IV (1954), 20-33; *idem*, "Neuere Arbeiten zum Immanuel-Problem," *ZAW*, LXVIII (1956), 46-53; H. W. Wolff, *Frieden ohne Ende*, 1962.

[10] S. Morenz, " 'Eilebeute'," *ThLZ*, LXXIV (1949), 697-99; L. G. Rignell, "Das Orakel 'Maher-salal Has-bas'," *StTh*, X (1956), 40-52.

[11] I. Engnell, *The Call of Isaiah*, 1949; E. Jenni, "Jesajas Berufung in der neueren Forschung," *ThZ*, XV (1959), 321-39; L. J. Liebreich, "The Position of Chapter Six in the Book of Isaiah," *HUCA*, XXV (1954), 37-40; C. F. Whitley, "The Call and Mission of Isaiah," *JNES*, XVIII (1959), 38-48.

[12] J. Schelhaas, "Het verband in Is 10,5–12,6," *GThT*, L (1950), 105-20.

[13] C. C. Torrey, "Some Important Editorial Operations in the Book of Isaiah," *JBL*, LVII (1938), 109-39.

14:24-27	against Assyrian	= the east
14:28-32	against the Philistine cities	= the west [14]
17:1-6	against Damascus and Northern Israel	= the north
18; 20	to and against Egypt	= the south
22:1-14, 15-19	against Jerusalem and a local official	= the center

Perhaps the saying in 28:1-4, directed against Samaria, also belonged originally to this collection.

G. The seventh collection comprises fifteen sayings of Isaiah,[15] which can be easily distinguished, deriving from the third and fourth periods of his ministry in the time of Hezekiah. It was clearly assembled according to the chronological principle. Isa. 32:9-14 constitutes the conclusion, probably intentionally; as the similarity in form and content to 22:1-14 shows, it is the last recorded word of Isaiah.

4. *Later passages.* Isaiah 1–39 contains numerous passages that undoubtedly or probably do not derive from Isaiah, although his authorship of them has been assumed or thought possible by a series of careful exegetes (e.g., Sellin* and Procksch). These later words include four additional collections or complexes of traditions (H—L), the promises appended to the Isaiah collections (M), and several sayings interpolated in the collections (N).

H. One large collection of anonymous sayings concerning foreign nations, which has been fused with Isaiah collection F, is to be found, with minor additions, in 13:1–14:23; 15–16; 19; 21; 23. It was characterized by the title *maśśā'*, "oracle," borne by its units. The most important sections are 13:2-22, against Babylon (sixth century);[16] 14:4*b*-21, a mocking poem of Canaanite origin against a mighty ruler,[17] likewise made to refer to Babylon by the framework 14:1-4*a*, 22-23; 15:1-9+16:2; 16:1, 3-5; and 16:6-12, concerning Moab (probably postexilic);[18] 19:1-15, against Egypt (postexilic); 21:1-10, against Babylon (an exilic vision and audition experience);[19] 21:11-12, concerning

[14] J. Begrich, "Jesaja 14,28-32," *ZDMG,* LXXXVI (1933), 66-79; W. A. Irwin, "The Exposition of Isaiah 14,28-32," *AJSL,* XLIV (1928), 73-87.

[15] A. Guillaume, "Isaiah's Oracle Against Assyria (Isaiah 30,27-33) in the Light of Archaeology," *BSOAS,* XVII (1955), 413-15; W. W. Hallo, "Isaiah 28,9-13 and the Ugaritic Abecedaries," *JBL,* LXXVII (1958), 324-38; L. Köhler, "Zwei Fachwörter der Bausprache in Jes 28,16," *ThZ,* III (1947), 390-93; A. Kuschke, "Zu Jes 30,1-5," *ZAW,* LXIV (1952), 194-95; L. J. Liebreich, "The Parable taken from the Farmer's Labors in Isaiah 28,23-29," *Tarbiz,* XXIV (1954/55), 126-28; J. Lindblom, "Der Eckstein in Jes 28,16," *NTT,* LVI (1955), 123-32; L. Rost, "Zu Jesaja 28,1 ff.," *ZAW,* LIII (1935), 292; S. C. Thexton, "A Note on Isaiah XXVIII 25 and 28," *VT,* II (1952), 81-83.

[16] K. Budde, "Jesaja 13," in BZAW, XXXIII (1918), 55-70.

[17] G. Quell, "Jesaja 14,1-23," in *Baumgärtel-Festschrift,* 1959, pp. 131-57.

[18] For a different view, cf. E. Power, "The Prophecy of Isaias against Moab (Is 15,1–16,5)," *Bibl,* XIII (1932), 435-51; W. Rudolph, "Jesaja XV–XVI," in *Driver-Festschrift,* 1963, pp. 130-43; Hitzig, Sellin, and Procksch consider this section earlier than Isaiah.

[19] K. Galling, "Jesaia 21 im Lichte der neuen Nabonidtexte," in *Weiser-Festschrift,* 1963, pp. 49-62; J. Obermann, "Yahweh's Victory over the Babylonian Pantheon, the Archetype of Is 21,1-10," *JBL,* XLVIII (1929), 307-28; R. B. Y. Scott, "Isaiah 21,1-10; the Inside of a Prophet's Mind," *VT,* II (1952), 278-82.

Edom, and 21:13-15, concerning Dedan (probably postexilic); 23:1-14, concerning Phoenicia (probably fourth century).[20]

I. A second complex of traditions, the so-called Isaiah Apocalypse (24–27), was placed before Isaiah collection G.[21] In it prophetical pronouncements and songs are juxtaposed and often closely related. Several of them taken together seem at one time to have constituted independent sections, which were later assembled by addition and expansion to form new sections. In this way a unified composition arose (Lindblom calls it a cantata), which at first glance practically appears to be a single literary unit but is in fact composed of three prophetical liturgies and several individual pieces. As to the date of this complex, the period of Isaiah (most recently supported by Beek, van Zyl, *et al.*) is out of the question, as is the second century, when the book of Isaiah in its complete form was extant at Qumran (Duhm, Marti, Procksch, Ludwig). Most of the texts probably came into being during the fifth century (Lindblom, Anderson).

24:1-20	First prophetical liturgy: eschatological judgment of the world, with the dissolution of city life (vss. 1-3 pronouncement, 4-16aα song, 16aβ-20 pronouncement)
24:21–25:12	Second prophetical liturgy: disarming of Yahweh's enemies through the destruction of their major cities and universal covenant feast marking the beginning of God's reign (24:21-23 proclamation, 25:10*b*-11, 12 are additions. 25:1-5 thanksgiving, 25:6-8 proclamation, 25:9-10*a* thanksgiving).
26:1-6, 7-21	Transitional texts: thanksgiving and prayer of an individual on behalf of the community.
27:1-6, 12-13	Third prophetical liturgy: final battle of Yahweh, preservation of Israel, and reunion of all Israelites (vs. 1 proclamation, 2-6 song, 12-13 proclamation)
27:7-11	Theological meditation on the possibility of bringing the pre-eschatological period of distress to an end and the necessary conditions.

Many different interpretations, however, have found their supporters. Some interpret the chapters as a literary unit. Lindblom, for instance, thinks of them as a cantata comprising four eschatological songs and four thanksgiving songs following the conquest of Babylon by Xerxes I, and Mulder has them refer to the Moabite city of Dibon about 270 B.C. Others think in terms of composite

[20] For a different view, cf. W. Rudolph, "Jesaja 23,1-14," in *Baumgärtel-Festschrift*, 1959, pp. 166-74.

[21] B. W. Anderson, "Isaiah XXIV–XXVII Reconsidered," *VTSuppl*, IX (1963), 118-26; M. A. Beek, "Ein Erdbeben wird zum prophetischen Erleben (Jesaja 24–27)," *ArOr*, XVII (1949), 31-40; G. Fohrer, "Der Aufbau der Apokalypse des Jesajabuchs (Is 24–27)," *CBQ*, XXV (1953), 34-45; G. Hylmö, *De s. k. profetiska liturgiernas rytm, stil och komposition*, 1929; W. Kessler, *Gott geht es um das Ganze*, 1960; J. Lindblom, *Die Jesaja-Apokalypse, Jes 24–27*, 1938; P. Lohmann, "Die selbstständigen lyrischen Abschnitte in Jes 24–27," ZAW, XXXVII (1917/18), 1-58; O. Ludwig, *Die Stadt in der Jesaja-Apokalypse*, Dissertation, Bonn, 1961; E. S. Mulder, *Die Teologie van die Jesaja-Apokalipse, Jesaja 24–27*, 1954; O. Plöger, *Theokratie und Eschatologie*, 2nd ed., 1962; W. Rudolph, *Jesaja 24–27*, 1933; A. H. van Zyl, "Isaiah 24–27: Their Date of Origin," *OuTWP*, 1962, pp. 44-57.

structure and a gradual process of growth. Duhm, for instance, finds here a compilation of apocalyptic prophecies and songs dealing with the destruction of Samaria by John Hyrcanus in the year 110; Eissfeldt* finds a similar compilation of earlier songs and prophecies after a disaster that befell Moab in the third century. Yet others think in terms of a basic nucleus that has been expanded in several stages. Steuernagel* considers the nucleus to be 24:1-23; Plöger, however, finds in 24 several thematically related units (vss. 1-6, 7-13, 14-20). Still others, finally, think in terms of a collection of independent utterances. Rudolph has counted ten of these, seven of which derive from a single author after the capture of Babylon by Alexander the Great; Kessler, on the other hand, finds a larger unit in 27, which refers as a whole to several cities (Babylon, Samaria, a Moabite city). Each of these hypotheses merely isolates one element from the complex process of growth; they must all be rejected in favor of a more inclusive approach.

K. To the Isaiah collection G has been appended a third complex of traditions from the postexilic period, which comprises two prophetical liturgies (33:1-6, 7-24)[22] and the eschatological discourses in 34–35, which are dependent on Deutero-Isaiah.[23]

L. As the last component, the Isaiah legends in 36–39 were borrowed from II Kings 18:13; 18:17–20:19 and appended to the whole.[24] Comparison with their source indicates minor textual alterations in the book of Isaiah; 38 in particular differs from II Kings 20, and the so-called Psalm of Hezekiah has been added (38:9-20).[25]

M. The promises include 2:2-4, describing the eschatological pilgrimage of all nations to Mount Zion. This passage is also preserved in Mic. 4:1-3 (4), where the text even seems to be closer to its original form. Despite the recent ascription of this passage to Isaiah by Wildberger and Junker,[26] it must be termed an anonymous eschatological prophecy.[27] The subject matter and mode of expression demonstrate quite conclusively that the promise in 4:2-6 does not derive

[22] H. Gunkel, "Jesaia 33, eine prophetische Liturgie," *ZAW*, XLII (1924), 177-208.

[23] W. Caspari, "Jesaja 34 und 35," *ZAW*, XLIX (1931), 67-86; A. Mailland, *La "petite apocalypse" d'Isaïe*, Dissertation, Lyon, 1956; J. Muilenburg, "The Literary Character of Isaiah 34," *JBL*, LIX (1940), 339-65; A. T. E. Olmstead, "II Isaiah and Isaiah, Chapter 35," *AJSL*, LIII (1937/37), 251-53; M. H. Pope, "Isaiah 34 in Relation to Isaiah 35, 40–66," *JBL*, LXXI (1952), 235-43; R. B. Y. Scott, "The Relation of Isaiah, Chapter 35, to Deutero-Isaiah," *AJSL*, LII (1935/36), 178-91; C. C. Torrey, "Some Important Editorial Operations in the Book of Isaiah," *JBL*, LVII (1938), 109-39.

[24] J. Meinhold, *Die Jesajaerzählungen Jesaja 36–39*, 1898; H. M. Orlinsky, "The Kings-Isaiah Recensions of the Hezekiah Story," *JQR*, XXX (1939/40), 33-49.

[25] J. Begrich, *Der Psalm des Hiskia*, 1926; P. A. H. de Boer, "Notes on Text and Meaning of Isaiah XXXVIII, 9-20," *OTS*, IX (1951), 170-86.

[26] H. Junker, "Sancta Civitas, Jerusalem Nova," *Trierer ThZ*, XV (1962), 17-33; G. von Rad, "Die Stadt auf dem Berge," *EvTh*, VIII (1948/49), 439-47 (= *Gesammelte Studien zum Alten Testament*, 1958, pp. 214-24); H. Wildberger, "Die Völkerwallfahrt zum Zion," *VT*, VII (1957), 62-81.

[27] S. H. Blank, *Prophetic Faith in Isaiah*, 1958; E. Cannawurf, "The Authenticity of Micah IV 1-4," *VT*, XIII (1963), 26-33; B. Renaud, *Structure et attaches littéraires de Michée IV–V*, 1964; cf. also the commentaries of Fohrer and Kaiser.

from Isaiah. Despite many opinions to the contrary,[28] 9:1-6 (Eng. 9:2-7) also derives from the late period. Attempts have been made to preserve the tradition of Isaiah's authorship through nonmessianic interpretation; Alt in particular gives an impressive interpretation of this passage as a promise directed toward those territories of Israel that the Assyrians conquered in 732. It is, however, a product of postexilic eschatological and messianic prophecy. Despite the fullness and profundity of its ideas, 11:1-9, with its announcement of the Messiah and his reign of peace, also bears the stamp of postexilic prophecy; this is shown by such evidence as the late concept of permanent possession of the spirit (vs. 2) and the dependence of vs. 9 on Isa. 65:25 and Hab. 2:14. The promises in 23:17-18 and 28:5-6, which have been appended to the sixth collection, are definitely of late origin, as is the promise in 32:15-20, appended to the seventh collection, which in subject matter and even language is closely related to 32:9-14,[29] and also begins with a half verse, so that what has been stated in vss. 9-14 shall remain in effect "until the Spirit is poured out upon us from on high."

N. We shall merely list the later passages that have been interpolated into the Isaiah collections. These include threatening sayings of anonymous prophets (7:23-25; 10:20-23; 17:9-11), direct promises for Israel (8:23*b* [Eng. 9:1*b*]; 11:10, 11-16; 17:7-8; 29:17-24; 30:18-26; 32:1-5), indirect promises for Israel (8:9-10;[30] 10:16-19, 24-27*a*, 33-34; 17:12-14), wisdom sayings (3:10-11; 32:6-8), a thanksgiving and hymn (12), and an oracle concerning Eliakim (22:20-23, 24-25).

5. *Growth of the book*. The assembly of the individual collections to form a single book did not begin until late. Isaiah collections C and E were first combined; their original order was then disturbed by the interpolation of collection D (5:25-29 separated, with several verses lost; 10:1-3 also separated). This interpolation is connected with the chronological arrangement of the collections because C contains sayings from the first period of Isaiah's ministry, D from the second period, and E from the second and fourth periods. These collections were probably brought together in the exilic period (sixth century), when the creation of such books became more common. In the same period collection B with its exilic superscription was placed at the beginning; this type of addition took place with some frequency (Genesis 1, Psalm 1, Proverbs 1–9). Somewhat later, collection A with its superscription (1:1) was added. The book existed in this form for a considerable period and was given a liturgical conclusion by the addition of chapter 12.

Probably during the course of the fifth century the last collections were added in three stages, taking into account the two- or three-part eschatological

[28] A. Alt, "Jesaja 8,23–9,6," in *Bertholet-Festschrift*, 1950, pp. 29-49 (= *Kleine Schriften*, II [1953], 206-25); J. Coppens, "Le roi idéal d'Is, IX,5-6 et XI,1-5, est-il une figure messianique?" in *Mémorial Gelin*, 1961, pp. 85-108; M. B. Crook, "A Suggested Occasion for Isaiah 9,2-7 and 11,1-9," *JBL*, LXVIII (1940), 213-24; H.-P. Müller, "Uns ist ein Kind geboren," *EvTh*, XXI (1961), 408-19.

[29] Cf. Fohrer *ad loc.*

[30] M. Saebø, "Zur Traditionsgeschichte von Jesaia 8,9-10," *ZAW*, LXXVI (1964), 132-44.

schema. The date can be arrived at by observing that collection F was not incorporated until after it was fused with the *maśśā'* collection directed against foreign nations; this latter collection, however, contains oracles from the sixth or fifth century—apart from the passage 23:1-14, which may have been added even later. This addition produced a two-part eschatological schema. The subsequent addition of collection G, already provided with its own eschatological framework in 24–27 and 33–35, led to the three-part schema. The Isaiah legends from the book of Kings were probably borrowed soon afterward. This means that Isaiah 1–39 achieved its present form in the fifth or, at the latest, fourth century:

1–12 primarily threats against Judah and Jerusalem;
13–23 threats against foreign nations;
24–35 promises as a framework surrounding threats against Judah and Jerusalem;
36–39 historical appendix.

6. *Message.* Isaiah's message reflects the encroachments of the Assyrians upon the Syro-Palestinian political system during the eighth century and the defensive efforts of the states involved. His sayings therefore constantly reiterate the themes of God's action in the world of men and nations and—after Isaiah's attack on the internal situation in Judah during the first period of his ministry—the relationship between faith and politics. We may summarize these themes by stating that man must neither practice authoritarian power politics nor look upon God's action as a mere spectator;[31] he must endure tension and uncertainty, trusting in God's omnipotence. At first, Isaiah looks upon the Assyrian king as God's authorized servant and instrument; ultimately, however, he announces the downfall of the Assyrian king, when he sees, after the Assyrian attack upon Palestine, that the Assyrian by no means considers himself God's instrument, but rather seeks to put his own plans for political power into effect. Nevertheless, this assessment of enormous political and military power is a new and striking feature in Isaiah's preaching.

Naturally Isaiah is familiar with the traditions of his nation—probably with the prophetical traditions, especially since in some respects he is influenced by Amos and follows him,[32] and certainly the cultic traditions, although he rejects the cult as a means of salvation (1:10-17) and uses the expressions and idioms borrowed from it ironically or else transforms them into their opposite (Yahweh, the rock, becomes a rock of stumbling [8:14]; he "who dwells on Mount Zion" is a guarantor of Israel's destruction [8:18]). Above all, he shows himself to be familiar with the historical tradition,[33] unfolding the history of the Northern Kingdom of Israel from the wars with the Philistines and Arameans to the great earthquake, perhaps the one used to date the appearance of Amos,

[31] C. A. Keller, "Das quietistische Element in der Botschaft des Jesaja," *ThZ,* XI (1955), 81-97.

[32] R. Fey, *Amos und Jesaja,* 1963.

[33] G. Fohrer, "Prophetie und Geschichte," *ThLZ,* LXXXIX (1964), 481-500; H. Wildberger, "Jesajas Verständnis der Geschichte," *VTSuppl,* IX (1963), 83-117.

and frequently mentioning the time of David and Solomon, when Yahweh intervened in battle on behalf of David (28:21), when David encamped in Jerusalem (29:1), when Yahweh there laid the cornerstone and foundation for the new government quarter on Mount Zion (14:32; 28:16), and when the city was faithful and honorable (1:21).[34]

The ideal relationship existing between Yahweh and Israel in the time of David is not based on a legal treaty—Isaiah never speaks of a "covenant"—but on a living personal relationship, in which Yahweh is the lover and bridegroom (5:1 ff.), Israel his family or clan (*'am*), and the Israelites his sons (1:2-3, 4; 30:9). Now, however, they are corrupt, mendacious, worse than the father's cattle (1:2-4; 5:2; 30:9), and Israel is merely "this nation," which—as the history of the Northern Kingdom shows—has not heeded the calamities sent by Yahweh as warnings and has not returned to him. Therefore, God will bring into being his monumental "conspiracy" against Judah and carry out his judgment, destroying the sinful way of life that rebels against the divine will. The announcement of the end of this guilt-stained way of life echoes through Isaiah's message with sublime and awful monotony, from his call to his last words (22:1-14; 32:9-14).

In this situation deliverance can come only through man's complete transformation and his doing God's will in his daily life (1:16-17), through obedience (1:18-20) and the penitent return offered by the name of the prophet's son (7:3). Yahweh will help those who dwell in Jerusalem if they "believe" in him and rely on him (7:9), wait for him in quietness and trust (30:15), and whisper humbly and softly from the dust, with a voice like that of a ghost (29:4). Then even all Judah could be the "remnant" that survives the terrible onslaughts of war. Throughout his ministry Isaiah remains a prophet of repentance.[35]

§ 57 Isaiah II (Isaiah 40–55)

Cf. the commentaries in § 56. IB: J. Muilenburg, 1956. KAT: P. Volz, 1932. SAT: M. Haller, 2nd ed., 1925. Individual commentaries: G. Fohrer, 1964 ("Zürcher Bibelkommentare"); C. R. North, 1964.

[34] Isaiah does not, however, espouse any so-called election tradition; these can be found only by including the utterances of the later eschatological prophets that have been interspersed throughout Isaiah's material. It would be more correct to say that the election tradition of standard Yahwism was destroyed for Isaiah at his call: his question "How long?" presupposes that Yahweh will vex but not destroy; in answer, however, he receives an announcement of utter desolation. This turns the confident assumption that Israel automatically enjoys Yahweh's favor into the certainty that Israel stands condemned.

[35] No unconditional promise of salvation can be found in Isaiah (Blank, Vriezen, Whitley); such a promise can only be put together out of the optimistic utterances inserted later into the book. The "remnant" in Isaiah is no saving quantity but rather the survivors of the catastrophe; cf. E. W. Heaton, *The Old Testament Prophets*, 1958, pp. 191-95; G. von Rad, *Theologie des Alten Testaments*, II, 1960 (4th ed. 1965), 175-76. Isaiah knows of no eternal "plan" of Yahweh for judgment and salvation (J. Fichtner, "Jahves Plan in der Botschaft des Jesaja,"

B. W. ANDERSON, "Exodus Typology in Second Isaiah," in *Essays Muilenburg*, 1962, pp. 177-95; J. BEGRICH, *Studien zu Deuterojesaja*, 1938, reprinted 1963; J. W. BEHR, *The Writings of Deutero-Isaiah and the Neo-Babylonian Royal Inscriptions*, 1937; S. H. BLANK, "Studies in Deutero-Isaiah," *HUCA*, XV (1940), 1-46; P. A. H. DE BOER, *Second-Isaiah's Message*, 1956; W. CASPARI, *Lieder und Gottessprüche der Rückwanderer*, 1934; F. M. CROSS, JR., "The Council of Yahweh in Second Isaiah," *JNES*, XII (1953), 274-77; O. EISSFELDT, "The Promises of Grace to David in Isaiah 55,1-5," in *Essays Muilenburg*, 1962, pp. 196-207; K. ELLIGER, *Deuterojesaja in seinem Verhältnis zu Tritojesaja*, 1933; G. FOHRER, "Zum Text von Jes XLI 8-13," *VT*, V (1955), 239-49; *idem*, "Die Struktur der alttestamentlichen Eschatologie," *ThLZ*, LXXXV (1960), 401-20; L. GLAHN and L. KÖHLER, *Der Prophet der Heimkehr (Jesaja 40–66)*, 1934; H. GRESSMANN, "Die literarische Analyse Deuterojesajas," *ZAW*, XXXIV (1914), 254-97; M. HARAN, "The Literary Structure and Chronological Framework of the Prophecies in Is XL–XLVIII," *VTSuppl*, IX (1963), 127-55; *idem*, *Between Ri'shonôt (Former Prophecies) and Ḥadashôt (New Prophecies)*, 1963; E. HESSLER, *Gott der Schöpfer. Ein Beitrag zur Komposition und Theologie Deuterojesajas*, Dissertation, Greifswald, 1961; A. S. KAPELRUD, "Levde Deuterojesaja i Judea?" *NTT*, LXI (1960), 23-27; L. KÖHLER, *Deuterojesaja (Jesaja 40–55) stilkritisch untersucht*, 1923; T. J. MEEK, "Some Passages Bearing on the Date of Second Isaiah," *HUCA*, XXIII (1950/51), 173-84; B. J. VAN DER MERWE, *Pentateuchtradisies in die prediking van Deuterojesaja*, 1955; J. MORGENSTERN, "Two Prophecies from 520–516 B.C., *HUCA*, XXII (1949), 365-431; *idem*, "Jerusalem—485 B.C.," *ibid.*, XXVII (1956), 101-79; XXVIII (1957), 15-47; XXXI (1960), 1-29; *idem*, "The Message of Deutero-Isaiah in its Sequential Unfolding," *ibid.*, XXIX (1958), 1-67; XXX (1959), 1-102; 1961; S. MOWINCKEL, "Die Komposition des deuterojesajanischen Buches," *ZAW*, XLIX (1931), 87-112, 242-60; L. M. PÁKOZDY, *Deuterojesajanische Studien*, I–II, 1940-42; Š. PORÚBČAN, *Il Patto Nuovo in Is 40–66*, 1959; R. RENDTORFF, "Die theologische Stellung des Schöpfungsglaubens bei Deuterojesaja," *ZThK*, LI (1954), 3-13; L. G. RIGNELL, *A Study of Isaiah Ch. 40–55*, 1956; U. SIMON, *A Theology of Salvation*, 1953; S. SMITH, *Isaiah Chapters XL–LV*, 1944; W. B. STEVENSON, "Successive Phases in the Career of the Babylonian Isaiah," in *BZAW*, LXVI (1936), 89-96; C. STUHLMUELLER, "The Theology of Creation in Second Isaias," *CBQ*, XXI (1959), 429-67; W. TANNERT, *Jeremia und Deuterojesaja*, Dissertation, Leipzig, 1956; C. C. TORREY, "Isaiah 41," *HThR*, XLIV (1951), 121-37; F. TREU, "Anklänge iranischer Motive bei Deuterojesaja," *StTh* (Riga), II (1940), 79-95; E. VON WALDOW, *Anlass und Hintergrund der Verkündigung des Deuterojesaja*, Dissertation, Bonn, 1953; *idem*, *". . . denn ich erlöse dich", eine Auslegung von Jesaja 43*, 1960; C. WESTERMANN, "Das Heilswort bei Deuterojesaja," *EvTh*, XXIV (1964), 355-73; *idem*, "Sprache und Struktur der Prophetie Deuterojesajas," in *Forschung am Alten Testament*, 1964, pp. 92-170; cf. also the bibliography in FOHRER, *ThR*, *NF* XIX, XX, and XXVIII (§ 52).

1. *Deutero-Isaiah.* In 1783 Eichhorn* and in 1789 Döderlein[1] stated their view that Isaiah 40–66 derives from an exilic prophet. In 1892 Duhm espoused this theory vigorously, though restricting it to 40–55 and ascribing 56–66 to

---

ZAW, LXIII [1951], 16-33), the more so because the expressions in question do not occur in the promises at all, and the supposed plan is so unstable and variable that we are dealing instead with decisions reached in each particular case, subject always to change.

[1] J. C. Döderlein, *Esaias*, 3rd ed., 1789, pp. xii-xv.

a later period. Duhm's view has largely won the day and may be considered almost universal. Of course, the conservatives, as always, support the unity of the book of Isaiah (Allis, Young);[2] but to do so flies in the face of statements actually made in 40–55, according to which Jerusalem and the Temple are destroyed (44:26-28; 51:3; 52:9), the people languish in exile in Babylonia (42:22, 24; 43:14; and *passim*), Babylon (and not Assyria) is threatened with destruction (47; 48:14), and Cyrus has already embarked on his victorious campaign (41:2-3, 25; 44:28; 45:1-3). In addition, the different vocabulary, the exuberant style, and the unique theological milieu—all completely different from Isaiah—must be taken into account.

Since the prophet whose sayings are preserved in 40–55 is anonymous, he is referred to as Deutero-Isaiah (Second Isaiah). He may have had the same name as his predecessor Isaiah, which would account for the association of his book with the earlier one; there is no evidence to support this suggestion, however. The juxtaposition has sometimes been explained on the basis that the prophets speaking in 40–55 and 56–66 were "disciples" of Isaiah, members of his "school." The existence of such a school, however, for more than two centuries is in itself unlikely; the assumption collapses completely when one observes that it is based entirely on the late addition to Isa. 8:16 and that Deutero-Isaiah nowhere appears to have been particularly influenced by Isaiah. We must instead start from the observation that, to a greater extent than in the other prophetical books, all kinds of sayings of later prophets have been interpolated into Isaiah 1–39. Deutero-Isaiah agrees with their basic eschatological approach, so that the addition of his writings seemed appropriate. Furthermore, in the later period Isaiah was often considered the prophet par excellence, so that association with his book amounted to official recognition of Deutero-Isaiah's preaching, which was frequently disputed.

2. *Place and date.* Deutero-Isaiah's ministry fell in the latter part of the Babylonian Exile (597/587–538), when the Babylonian Empire was threatened with destruction and Cyrus, the Persian king, was awaited as the deliverer of the oppressed peoples.[3] From him the prophet expects liberation of the deported Judeans, return to Jerusalem, and reconstruction of the Temple. For Yahweh has called Cyrus, declared him his "anointed" (45:1), and will make use of him to help Israel. Beyond this, it is hardly possible to date the sayings of Deutero-Isaiah more precisely. His highly poetic sayings are too ambiguous and scintillating, often transcend space and time, and place over everything a veil that conceals reality (Eissfeldt*). We can define their date only by saying that they came into being between the beginning of Cyrus' victorious career (550) and the capture of Babylon (538); 52:13–53:12 may suggest in addition that the prophet died before 538.

[2] O. T. Allis, *The Unity of Isaiah,* 1951; R. Margalioth, *The Indivisible Isaiah,* 1964; E. J. Young, *Studies in Isaiah,* 1954.

[3] M. Haller, "Die Kyros-Lieder Deuterojesajas," in *Gunkel-Festschrift,* I (1923), 261-77; E. Jenni, "Die Rolle des Kyros bei Deuterojesaja," *ThZ,* X (1954), 241-56; C. E. Simcox, "The Rôle of Cyros in Deutero-Isaja," *JAOS,* LVII (1937), 158-71; U. Simon, "König Cyrus und die Typologie," *Judaica,* XI (1955), 83-89.

Stevenson and Smith think they have discovered clear historical references. The former distinguishes five periods in Deutero-Isaiah's ministry between 547 and 538. The latter considers him the leader of an anti-Babylonian underground movement for five years, until he was executed by his people. Closer examination shows, however, that these theories are based on insufficient evidence. Neither can we go as far as Morgenstern, who ascribes only 40–48 to Deutero-Isaiah (in reverse chronological order, making 48 the earliest and 40 the latest chapter), while connecting 49–55 with the authors of 56–66 and associating these words with a terrible catastrophe that he claims befell the Jews in 485 B.C., or as Caspari, who denies that a single author wrote the chapters and interprets them instead as a collection of prophetical utterances and songs of those who returned to Palestine, with the most important place given to their marching song.

More numerous have been the attempts to distinguish two periods in Deutero-Isaiah's ministry, marked by a division between 40–48 and 49–55. Kuenen* and Kittel, for example, derive the first section from the years prior to the conquest of Babylon or Cyrus' edict of liberation, and the second from the time after the Israelites' return to Jerusalem. Baudissin* and Volz date the second section in the period between the conquest and the edict. In fact, the passages referring to Cyrus and the conquest of Babylon are found in 40–48; in 46:1-2; 47, expectations are expressed that did not come to pass as described, so that they must have been written before 538. But this fact is due to the structure of the composition, not a change in the historical situation, the more so because the unity of style and thought in 40–55 cannot be disregarded. In somewhat different fashion Begrich distinguishes between the prophet's eschatological preaching after the revolt of Cyrus against Astyages of Media in 553/552, and the transfer of this hope to Cyrus as a deliverer sent by God after the Lydian War (547/546), involving a basic transformation in the preaching of Deutero-Isaiah. The evidence for such a division, however, is much too scant and precarious; there is no reference to specific events; and the passages referring to Cyrus are quite as eschatological as the rest. A later dating is proposed by Haran, who claims that (apart from chapter 40, which may be earlier) 40–46 and 48 were written in the period between the liberation edict (538) and the return of the first group, which Deuero-Isaiah is said to have joined, while 49–66 derive from his subsequent ministry in Palestine.

Deutero-Isaiah's words were therefore preached in the course of a period that cannot be precisely defined; it is likewise impossible to distinguish several periods in his ministry. It remains, however, to answer the question of where the prophet exercised his ministry. The most likely suggestion is Babylonia (Volz). Deutero-Isaiah is familiar with the situation there; his style is influenced by the first-person hymns of Ishtar and the Babylonian royal inscriptions (Behr); in 45:7 he is already engaged in controversy with Iranian dualism. Most of his utterances, which are marked by the characteristics of oral proclamation, are directed to the exiles; some of them reply to their objections, which must have been presented to him directly.

Others have located his ministry in Phoenicia (Duhm, on account of 45:14;

49:12), Egypt (Ewald, Marti, Hölscher), or Palestine (Mowinckel, following Seinecke). These suggestions are as unlikely as that of a ministry divided between Babylonia and Palestine, based on the division into 40–48 and 49–55 (Kuenen*, Kittel, Procksch, *et al.*).

3. *Literary forms.* Engnell has attempted to explain the character of Deutero-Isaiah's writings as a prophetical imitation of a liturgy belonging to the annual festivals of the royal ritual, drawing at the same time upon OT passion psalms of the king and Babylonian Tammuz liturgies. In contrast to this approach, we shall essentially follow Begrich's careful determination of the literary types of the 65 or so individual sayings of the prophet, although Westermann's recent differentiation must be taken into account. It is soon noted that the typical rhetorical forms of the preexilic literary prophets—invective, threat, and exhortation—have become quite rare. In their place four other forms predominate: the fully developed oracle of deliverance, which goes back to the promises of the nationalistic cultic prophets; the hymn praising the imminent act of deliverance (particularly the first-person divine hymn, previously not customary in Israel); the prophetical forensic discourse to demonstrate that Yahweh alone is God; and the discussion to turn back doubts and objections to the prophet's message. The last of these in particular points to oral proclamation and eliminates the assumption that the prophet worked only as a writer (Begrich, Eissfeldt*). Oral delivery is further supported by stylistic features: direct address, challenges, rhetorical questions, and sermon-like exposition. At the same time, Deutero-Isaiah's at times violent arguments show that he cannot have appeared at cultic observances as an official spokesman or cultic prophet (von Waldow). This conclusion is also not supported by the occurrence of hymnic forms, because the use or imitation of forms proper to another sphere does not mean that the prophet was employed in it. We may assume, however, that for practical reasons Deutero-Isaiah used cultic observances as an opportunity for proclaiming his message to the numerous participants.

4. *Oracles concerning the Servant of Yahweh.* The passages dealing with the Servant of Yahweh (Ebed-Yahweh songs) occupy a special place in the history of interpretation. Ever since Duhm isolated the poems 42:1-4 (5-7); 49:1-6; 50:4-9; 52:13–53:12 as a group of texts of a particular type, violent discussion has raged; the literature has grown almost beyond bounds. North gives a comprehensive survey of the development of the problem and the various attempts at its solution.[4]

Even the number of these passages and their extent are disputed. Following Duhm, many consider 42:5-7 a later addition; others include it with the preceding verse, interpreting 42:1-7 (or even 42:1-9) as a single unit. The

[4] C. R. North, *The Suffering Servant in Deutero-Isaiah*, 2nd ed., 1956; also O. Eissfeldt, *Der Gottesknecht bei Deuterojesaja (Jes 40–55) im Lichte der israelitischen Anschauung von Gemeinschaft und Individuum*, 1933; *idem*, "Neue Forschungen zum 'Ebed-Jahwe-Problem," *ThLZ* LXVIII (1943), 273-80; H. A. Fischel, "Die Deuterojesaianischen Gottesknechtslieder in der jüdischen Auslegung," *HUCA*, XVIII (1943/44), 53-76; G. Fohrer in *ThR*, NF XIX, XX, and XXVIII (§ 52); H. Haag, "Ebed-Jahwe-Forschung 1948-1958," *BZ*, NF III (1959), 174-204; C. Lindhagen, "The Servant of the Lord," *ET*, LXVII (1955/56), 279-88, 300-302.

introductory formula, however, shows 42:5-7 to be an independent saying, to be numbered with the Servant of Yahweh passages. Isa. 42:8-9 does not derive from Deutero-Isaiah. In addition, 50:4-11 is sometimes taken as a single unit, although vss. 10-11 differ so greatly from 4-9 that they must comprise an independent utterance. We are therefore dealing with six passages, the first four of which are spoken by the Servant of Yahweh (42:1-4, 5-7; 49:1-6;[5] 50:4-9 [6]), while the last two of them are about him (50:10-11; 52:13–53:12).[7]

The Ebed-Yahweh songs do not constitute an independent corpus of material, whose components have been scattered through the writings of Deutero-Isaiah; neither, however, are they connected organically with their surroundings. Only in theme do they represent a coherent group. For reasons that are no longer quite clear they were placed, like the Confessions of Jeremiah (§ 59.3 B), at various places in the book between other sayings. This was justified to the extent that they were composed at different times: 42:1-4, 5-7 are undoubtedly the earliest; 49:1-6 and 50:4-9 address themselves to a later period, when failure has been recognized and there is an apparent threat; in 50:10-11 and 52:13–53:12 this threat has been intensified to the utmost limit.

Comparison with the other utterances of Deutero-Isaiah shows that he is the author of at least the first four. They are his in both language and style, as well as in basic theological content, with universalistic monotheism, eschatological expectation, and the idea of mission. Depending on how they are interpreted, they can of course be set apart from the rest of Deutero-Isaiah's message through their personal, almost autobiographical character and their application of the term "servant" to an individual person. This distinction in content, however, would not exclude Deutero-Isaiah's authorship.

Morgenstern,[8] on the contrary, ascribes these texts together with a few other verses to an unknown author in the vicinity of the coastal city Dor or in Galilee about 450 B.C. and finds in them, after all sorts of rearrangement, a Hebrew drama on the Greek model, representing a sectarian Jewish document. The Servant is a king of the Davidic line; his prototype might be the Menahem whom Morgenstern claims to have been executed after Persian conquest of Jerusalem in 485 B.C.

The crucial question concerns the figure and significance of the Servant. A glossator has answered this question in the collective sense by the addition of "Israel" in 49:3; the prophet that speaks in 61:1 answers it in the individual sense by describing his own activity in terms of the Ebed-Yahweh songs. These

[5] J. A. Brewer, "Two Notes on Isaiah 49,1-6," in *Kohut Memorial Volume,* 1935, pp. 86-90; C. H. Giblin, "A Note on the Composition of Isaias 49,1-6 (9a)," *CBQ,* XXI (1959), 207-12.

[6] L. G. Rignell, "Jesaja kap. 50." *STKv,* XXIX (1953), 108-19.

[7] H. L. Ginsberg, "The Arm of YHWH in Isaiah 51–63 and the Text of Isa 53,10-11," *JBL,* LXXVII (1958), 152-56; H. W. Hertzberg, "Die 'Abtrünnigen' und die 'Vielen'," in *Rudolph-Festschrift,* 1961, pp. 97-134; R. Kittel, *Jes 53 und der leidende Messias im Alten Testament,* 1899; H. S. Nyberg, "Smärtonas man," *SEÅ,* VII (1942), 5-82; L. G. Rignell, "Isa 52,13–53,12," *VT,* III (1953), 87-92; H. W. Wolff, "Wer ist der Gottesknecht in Jes 53?" *EvTh,* XXII (1962), 338-42; E. J. Young, *Isaiah 53,* 1952.

[8] J. Morgenstern, "The Suffering Servant—A New Solution," *VT,* XI (1961), 292-320, 406-31.

two major interpretations have found their supporters to the present day. Recently there have been added two others: a mediating, fluid, or integral interpretation and the interpretation of the Servant as an idea.

a) The collective interpretation, supported, for example, by Baudissin*, Budde, Smend, Wellhausen, and more recently by Steuernagel*, Hölscher, König, Eissfeldt, and Lods,[9] makes no distinction between the Servant of the Ebed-Yahweh songs and the Servant mentioned elsewhere in Deutero-Isaiah's preaching and understands him to be historical or ideal Israel or a part of Israel, viz., those who suffer (de Boer) or those who live in the Exile (Kaiser). In support of this view one can cite the common OT practice of using individuals to represent peoples or nations and Deutero-Isaiah's utterances that refer to Israel as an individual (41:8 ff., 13; 42:19; 44:1-2). It can be objected that personal traits are quantitatively more apparent in the Ebed-Yahweh songs and are at least in part biographical, as befits an individual. In addition, according to this interpretation Israel instructs itself, educates itself, and suffers vicariously on behalf of itself, which appears improbable.

b) The individual interpretation sees in the Servant a particular person. In the history of interpretation this view has suffered from the wide divergence of opinions as to what individual is represented.[10] Sellin alone identified the servant as Zerubbabel (1898), Jehoiachin (1901), and Moses (1922), until he finally came to support a fourth interpretation. Others have suggested a torah instructor of the postexilic period (Duhm) or an unknown martyr of the Exile, represented at the same time as an eschatological figure (Kittel, similarly Rudolph), who is set up in contrast to Cyrus as a divine savior (Hempel) or to whom Deutero-Isaiah's disciples attached their hope (Mowinckel 1931). Others have thought in terms of a universal messianic figure awaited in the future (Gressmann, Engnell) or the Messiah himself (Delitzsch, Fischer, van der Ploeg, Cazelles, *et al.*). In contrast to these suggestions, most of which are quite vague, the most important individual interpretation is the reference to Deutero-Isaiah himself, on which Isa. 61:1 is already based.[11] It was originally espoused by Mowinckel (1921), who later gave it up, and accepted by many others (Gunkel, Haller, Begrich, Weiser*, *et al.*), sometimes in modified form (Volz excludes 52:13–53:12). In particular one must mention the view ex-

[9] K. Budde, *Die sogenannten Ebed-Jahwe-Lieder*, 1900; O. Eissfeldt, *op. cit.* (note 4); G. Hölscher, *Geschichte der israelitischen und jüdischen Religion*, 1922, pp. 122-24; O. Kaiser, *Der Königliche Knecht*, 1959; R. Smend, *Lehrbuch der alttestamentlichen Religionsgeschichte*, 2nd ed., 1899, pp. 352-60; J. Wellhausen, *Israelitische und jüdische Geschichte*, 5th ed., 1904, pp. 161-62.

[10] H. Cazelles, "Les Poèmes du Serviteur," *RSR*, XLIII (1955), 5-55; I. Engnell, "The 'Ebed Yahweh Songs and the Suffering Messiah in 'Deutero-Isaiah'," *BJRL*, XXXI (1948), 54-93; J. Fischer, *Isaias 40–55 und die Perikopen vom Gottesknecht*, 1916; H. Gressmann, *Der Messias*, 1929, pp. 285-323; J. van der Ploeg, *Les Chants du Serviteur de Jahvé dans la seconde partie du Livre d'Isaïe*, 1936; W. Rudolph, "Der exilische Messias," *ZAW*, XLIII (1925), 90-114; E. Sellin, *Serubbabel*, 1898; *idem*, *Der Knecht Gottes bei Deuterojesaja*, 1901; *idem*, *Mose*, 1922.

[11] S. Mowinckel, *Der Knecht Jahwäs*, 1921; H. Gunkel, *Ein Vorläufer Jesu*, 1921; E. Sellin, "Tritojesaja, Deuterojesaja und das Gottesknechtsproblem," *NkZ*, XLI (1930), 73-93, 145-73.

pressed by Sellin (1930) and supported by Elliger, according to which only the first songs were composed by Deutero-Isaiah with himself as their subject, whereas 52:13–53:12 was composed by Trito-Isaiah, his disciple, as a dirge for the departed master. This view is able to explain many problems.

c) The fluid or integral interpretation seeks to combine the collective and individual interpretations.[12] According to Nyberg, the Servant belongs to past, present, and future, combining reminiscences of historical persons (patriarchs, Moses, David, prophets) and mythical figures (Tammuz, Baal), individual and collective traits, so that as an individual figure he represents the entire nation. North and Rowley assume a development in Deutero-Isaiah's understanding of the Servant: first Israel, followed by a transfer to the vicarious suffering and death of an individual. Eissfeldt*, while essentially retaining the collective interpretation, has recently also seen in the Servant the father and representative of the nation, conceived of as a prophet, who must shape the people and suffer on their behalf, so that the Servant is identical with Israel and yet also not identical. All this raises the question whether such complex ideas may be considered probable.

d) For Lindblom,[13] finally, the Servant embodies the idea of Israel's worldwide mission and is no more to be interpreted as a person or a group than is the prodigal son (Luke 15:11 ff.).

With respect to the content of the Ebed-Yahweh songs,[14] the interpretation of the Servant as Deutero-Isaiah himself appears most apposite. It explains the divergences from the rest of the prophet's preaching. In 42:1-4, 5-7 he gave himself and perhaps others an account of his mission and work and worked out his understanding of his prophetical calling. Later, in the first-person songs 49:1-6; 50:4-9, in a fashion similar to that of Jeremiah, he spoke of his inner doubts and struggles, which were occasioned by his lack of success and the hostility he aroused, leading even to threats and persecution. He may have been threatened also by intervention of the Babylonian authorities, as was to be expected from his anti-Babylonian message. In this situation his life's work and his faith were at stake, so that in both utterances, as in a kind of prophetical testament, he sought to lay down the meaning of his mission and of his life. On the other hand, 50:10-11 and 52:13–53:12 cannot derive from Deutero-

[12] H. S. Nyberg, "Smärtonas man" (note 7); H. H. Rowley, "The Suffering Servant and the Davidic Messiah," *OTS*, VIII (1950), 100-36.

[13] J. Lindblom, *The Servant Songs in Deutero-Isaiah*, 1951.

[14] J. Coppens, Nieuw licht over de Ebed-Jahweh-Liederen, 1950; *idem*, "Les origines littéraires des Poèmes du Serviteur de Yahvé," *Bibl*, XL (1959), 248-58; *idem*, "Le Serviteur de Yahvé," *BEThL*, XII (1959), 434-54; V. de Leeuw, *De Ebed Jahweh-profetieën*, 1956; W. F. Lofthouse, "Some Reflections on the 'Servant Songs'," *JThSt*, XLVIII (1947), 169-76; H. G. May, "The Righteous Servant in Second Isaiah's Songs," *ZAW*, LXVI (1954), 236-44; R. Press, "Der Gottesknecht im Alten Testament," *ibid.*, LXVII (1955), 67-99; J. Scharbert, "Stellvertretendes Sühneleiden in den Ebed-Yahwe-Liedern und in altorientalischen Ritualtexten," *BZ*, NF II (1958), 190-213; *idem*, *Heilsmittler im Alten Testament und im Alten Orient*, 1964; N. H. Snaith, "The Servant of the Lord in Deutero-Isaiah," in *T. H. Robinson-Festschrift*, 1950, pp. 187-200; W. Staerk, *Die Ebed-Jahwe-Lieder in Jes 40 ff.*, 1913; R.-J. Tournay, "Les Chants du Serviteur dans la Seconde Partie d'Isaïe," *RB*, LIX (1952), 355-84.

Isaiah. They look back upon the life and work, already finished, of the prophet as the Servant of Yahweh and presuppose his execution following a legal process. These two passages therefore probably derive from the circle of his disciples, who, particularly in the last song, arrived at a new interpretation of the life, suffering, and ignominious death of the prophet.

Finally, recent study is typified by a penetrating search for the roots of the conception associated with the Servant of Yahweh. In particular, scholars have pointed out mythological or cult-mythological features and royal features in the Ebed-Yahweh songs and suggested a corresponding influence.

Gressmann was the first to point out the presence of cult-mythological conceptions of a dying and rising vegetation god; others followed his lead. Engnell in addition pointed out the connection with the ideology of sacral kingship and its cult. Lindhagen,[15] too, attempts to demonstrate in detail the cultic basis of the Servant concept and the way in which it has been colored by the royal ideology. Böhl [16] makes reference to the royal substitute in Babylonia and Assyria, while Kaiser finds royal features transferred to the nation as a whole through a bold reinterpretation. Hyatt,[17] on the contrary, assumes the existence of four different roots: the concept of "corporate personality," according to which the entire community can benefit from the righteousness of an individual; the Israelite views concerning the ideal prophet; the theory of the sacrificial system, according to which the person and work of the Servant constitute a single unity; the vegetation cults, which provided the images and concepts. One could also point out that the prophets, through their intercession and performance of symbolic actions, already perform a kind of vicarious office.

For the last song two general conceptions are more important: the idea, intimately connected with traditional thought and religion, that suffering is a punishment decreed by God to repay sin, so that the prophet, too, has suffered because of sin; and the idea of exchange and substitution, according to which the Servant took upon himself the guilt, suffering, and diseases of others, while they share his innocence and immunity, his deliverance.

5. *Composition and structure.* The composition and structure of Deutero-Isaiah's work, made up of the individual sayings, is not completely clear. Two opposite views are espoused: Budde,[18] Hessler, and Muilenburg believe that the work follows a conscious plan with a coherent train of thought. Volz, too, thinks that Deutero-Isaiah arranged the sayings according to their subject matter and chronology. Mowinckel, on the contrary, finds merely a disconnected series of sayings arranged by a disciple of the prophet by means of catchwords, without any particular order. Neither view, in its extreme form, is probably accurate.

Mowinckel is right in saying that a clear organization of the entire work

[15] C. Lindhagen, *The Servant Motif in the Old Testament,* 1950.

[16] F. M. T. de Liagre Böhl, "Prophetentum und stellvertretendes Leiden in Assyrien und Israel," in *Opera Minora,* 1953, pp. 63-80.

[17] J. P. Hyatt, "The Sources of the Suffering Servant Idea," *JNES,* III (1944), 79-86.

[18] K. Budde, in E. Kautzsch, *Die Heilige Schrift des Alten Testaments,* I, 4th ed., 1922.

and a truly coherent train of thought are out of the question unless the exegete resorts to artificial interpretations, and that juxtaposition on the basis of catchwords can frequently be noted. We are nevertheless not dealing with a chaotic mass. Apart from 41:1-6, the passages mentioning Cyrus and announcing the fall of Babylon are found in 44:24–48:22; the programmatic passages describing the reconstruction in Palestine occur primarily in 49–55. Finally, 55:8-13 refers back to the beginning (40:3-5), so that the entire composition has a kind of framework. We are therefore confronted with a kind of order (Eissfeldt*). Apparently, though, the work did not come into being through the combination of several minor collections, each bearing its own particular stamp; it was assembled all at once, partially on the basis of the principles just mentioned, partially on the basis of catchwords. Finally, it is not impossible that a chronological principle was also at work. The work is introduced by 40:1-8, a substitute for a call narrative; the Ebed-Yahweh songs were obviously interpolated at various points in the order in which they were composed. This principle may also have determined the order of other sayings even though we cannot recognize it at work.

Elliger thinks that Trito-Isaiah, a disciple of Deutero-Isaiah, acted as collector and redactor, putting the work together on the basis of content, at times revising and supplementing the sayings he had before him, and producing the finished document even before Cyrus conquered Babylon. This hypothesis presupposes that Isaiah 56–66 derives from a single author who was a disciple of Deutero-Isaiah. If, as seems likely (§ 58), this is not true, the theory collapses. Furthermore, there is such a great difference between the two works that it is impossible to assume Trito-Isaiah's influence on the work of Deutero-Isaiah (Weiser*).

Probably, however, some secondary additions have found their way into 40–55. These include six sayings that deal in various ways with the theme of eschatological expectation: 42:8-9; 45:8, 18-19; 48:1-11; 51:11-16; 52:1-6. Three additional texts, which most likely derive from a wisdom teacher, deal with the theme of rejection of idolatry: 40:18-20 + 41:7; 44:9-20; 46:5-8.

6. *Message*. Deutero-Isaiah's message cannot be apportioned to various periods of his ministry. In the case of this prophet, such periods are identifiable, if at all, only in his understanding of his own mission. His preaching can, however, be organized according to theme and content, so as to provide insight into his message.

a) Introduction in place of call narrative: 40:1-2, 3-5, 6-8

b) Uniqueness of God: 40:12-17; 21-26; 41:21-29; 43:8-13; 44:6-8

c) Eschatological deliverance:
Hymns: 40:27-31; 42:10-17; 44:23; 48:17-19; 49:13; 51:9-10
Exhortations: 42:18-25; 44:21-22; 55:6-7, 8-9

d) Salvation for Israel:
Deliverance: 41:8-13; 43:1-7, 22-28; 46:3-4, 12-13; 49:7, 24-26; 50:1-3; 51:17-23; 54:4-6; 55:1-5
Cyrus, the deliverer: 41:1-6; 44:24-28; 45:1-3, 4-7, 9-10, 11-13; 46:9-11; 48:12-16

Destruction of Babylon and new exodus: 41:14-16; 43:14-15; 46:1-2; 47; 48:20-22; 52:11-12
Return (through the desert): 41:17-20; 43:16-21; 44:1-5; 49:8-12; 55:12-13
Arrival and reconstruction: 40:9-11; 49:14-21; 52:7-10; 54:1-3, 11-17
Concluding promises: 54:7-8, 9-10; 55:10-11

e) Salvation and the gentiles: 45:14-17, 20-25; 49:22-23; 51:1-8

f) The Servant of Yahweh:
Discourses of the Servant: 42:1-4, 5-7; 49:1-6; 50:4-9
Discourses concerning the Servant: 50:10-11; 52:13–53:12.

This survey shows that Deutero-Isaiah's message is dominated by a faith in eschatological deliverance; the novelty lies in the word "eschatological." While some of the earlier prophets preach faith in Yahweh's deliverance, Deutero-Isaiah, following minor earlier beginnings, is the first eschatological prophet, the first to distinguish two ages, and—standing on the border line between them—to see about him the imminent change of circumstances. He therefore distinguishes between the "former things" or "things of old" and the "new" things, the "time of favor" and the "day of salvation" (43:18-19; 49:8).[19] Influenced by preexilic professional cultic and nationalistic prophecy with its promise of salvation for Israel, he thinks once more in terms of a basic situation of God's favor, merely interrupted, and places one-sided emphasis on God's saving will. The Exile is the judgment that had been threatened; it will be followed by a time of salvation outside history, in which everything will be eternal (45:17; 51:6, 8; 54:8, 9-10). Longing for this time implies a desire to be delivered from history and from the necessities of everyday life.

Deutero-Isaiah's expectations for the time of salvation, exaggerated and in part quite materialistic, are based on the relationship between Yahweh and Israel, which he sometimes describes as a personal relationship: Jerusalem as a wife and mother (49:14 ff.; 54:1-3, 4-6), the Israelites as Yahweh's sons (45:11), whom, as members of his family and clan, he "redeems" (*gā'al* used to express the notion of deliverance). From Deuteronomistic theology Deutero-Isaiah borrows the concept of election; he does not associate it with the idea of the covenant, however, but rather bases election upon creation (43:1, 15; 44:2; 45:11; 46:3; 54:5) and concludes that Israel's election makes it Yahweh's servant (43:10; 44:2, 21; 45:4; 48:20). The idea of the covenant scarcely appears at all (42:6; 54:9-10; 55:3).

In Deutero-Isaiah eschatological thought is linked with the outlines of a comprehensive theology, which is based on the uniqueness of God. Up to the time of Deutero-Isaiah, one can speak only of a practical monotheism, which binds Israel to Yahweh alone without regard for the existence of other gods. Deutero-Isaiah, following the beginnings made by Jeremiah, represents a theoretical monotheism, which expressly denies the existence of other gods. As a result,

[19] A. Bentzen, "On the Ideas of 'the Old' and 'the New' in Deutero-Isaiah," *StTh*, I (1948/49), 183-87; K. Elliger, "Der Begriff 'Geschichte' bei Deuterojesaja," in *Schmitz-Festschrift*, 1953, pp. 26-53; C. R. North, "The 'Former Things' and the 'New Things' in Deutero-Isaiah," in *T. H. Robinson-Festschrift*, 1950, pp. 111-26.

all events and all phenomena from the creation of the world through eternity are associated with the one God. Thus with a single stroke Deutero-Isaiah links prehistory, history, and eschatology with each other and with God. In all this God is at work: therein lies the guarantee for the future. Because he created the world and mankind and has determined their fate since the beginning, he will continue to do so at the dawn of the final age. Despite all this, Deutero-Isaiah's preaching, because of its connection with the optimistic message of the earlier professional prophets, contains questionable nationalistic and materialistic traits. It therefore does not constitute the apex of OT prophecy, but rather marks the beginning of its decline.

§ 58 Isaiah III (Isaiah 56–66)

Cf. the commentaries in §§ 56–57; W. Kessler, *Gott geht es um das Ganze. Jesaja 56–66 und 24–27,* 1960.

R. Abramowski, "Zum literarischen Problem des Tritojesaja," *ThStKr,* XCVI/XCVII (1925), 90-143; K. Cramer, *Der geschichtliche Hintergrund der Kap. 56–66 im Buch Jesaja,* 1905; K. Elliger, *Die Einheit des Tritojesaja,* 1928; *idem,* "Der Prophet Tritojesaja," *ZAW,* XLIX (1931), 112-41; H. Gressmann, *Über die Jes 56–66 vorausgesetzten zeitgeschichtlichen Verhältnisse,* 1898; W. Kessler, "Zur Auslegung von Jesaja 56–66," *ThLZ,* LXXXI (1956), 335-38; *idem,* "Studien zur religiösen Situation im ersten nachexilischen Jahrhundert und zur Auslegung von Jesaja 56–66," *WZ Halle,* VI (1956/57), 41-73; E. Littmann, *Über die Abfassungszeit des Tritojesaja,* 1899; W. S. McCullough, "A Re-Examination of Isaiah 56–66," *JBL,* LXVII (1948), 27-36; H. Odeberg, *Trito-Isaiah (Isaiah 56–66),* 1931; A. Zillessen, " 'Tritojesaja' und Deuterojesaja," *ZAW,* XXVI (1906), 231-76; W. Zimmerli, "Zur Sprache Tritojesajas," *Schweiz. Theol. Umschau,* XX (1950), 110-22; cf. also the bibliographies in Fohrer, *ThR,* NF XIX, XX, and XXVIII (§ 52).

1. *Trito-Isaiah.* The separation of Isaiah 56-66 as an independent prophetical work was accomplished by Duhm in his commentary on Isaiah (1892), in which he ascribed these chapters to a prophet active in Jerusalem shortly before the time of Nehemiah, calling him Trito-Isaiah (Third Isaiah). With few exceptions (König, Torrey, Glahn), this view has carried the day. In fact, the differences between 40–55 and 56–66 are considerable. Apart from its general Palestinian point of view, the latter chapters presuppose throughout the existence of the new Temple, which was dedicated in 515. The prophet takes issue with religious and politico-economic dissension in the life of the Temple community and with the doubts arising, after decades of waiting in vain, concerning the eschatological hope. Deutero-Isaiah's comprehensive theology is given up; the worldly and materialistic character of eschatological expectations is considerably advanced. Despite the dependence of a few sections on Deutero-Isaiah, there is a deep gulf between the two works.

2. *Authorship and origin.* Duhm's hypothesis provided the two points around which discussion has centered: unity of authorship and date of origin. More precisely, we may ask whether the sections brought together in 56–66 derive

from a single author or from several authors and in what period or periods the author or authors are to be dated.

Duhm's hypothesis of a single author dating from the fifth century has been supported primarily by Littmann and Zillessen, and, in the broader sense, by Hölscher, Pfeiffer*, *et al.* Elliger, too, assumes that there was a single author, but dates him around 520 and seeks on the basis of language and style to show that this author was a disciple of Deutero-Isaiah, who edited and assembled the work of his master and whose own words are found in 55–66. Against this view, it has correctly been pointed out that critical examination reveals only a few similarities between the two writings; the differences turn out to be much greater. The demonstration is therefore unsuccessful (Weiser*). Above all, there are in many cases such major differences or even contradictions between the individual sections of 55–66 that they can scarcely be derived from a single author. This objection applies to the views of McCullough, who ascribes the work to a Palestinian prophet of the Isaianic school to be dated about 587–562, and to those of Kessler, who also assumes a single author, dating him in the period between the return of the deportees and Malachi and finding him concerned with pastoral questions and the message of Deutero-Isaiah. Scholars therefore are usually inclined to assume the existence of several authors (Budde, Volz, Eissfeldt*, Weiser*, *et al.*), dating from various periods, although the period from the eighth to the third century, which has sometimes been suggested, is too long.

All the evidence points to multiple authorship. The chapters do not have any internal unity of content or intellectual similarity such as we find in Deutero-Isaiah and other prophets. In addition, some sections exhibit what at first seems to be a striking similarity to Deutero-Isaiah; they express similar optimistic expectations, depicted in the same colors (especially in 60–62). But the meaning of the expressions and idioms employed is more or less radically altered, so that the most likely assumption is literary dependence on Deutero-Isaiah and deliberate borrowing from him. Other sections, however, lack his influence, if they do not in fact diverge completely. This suggests an entirely different basic attitude on the part of the authors. Only 60–62 can be ascribed to a single hand. For the rest, the above-mentioned relationship to Deutero-Isaiah probably is responsible for the fact that 56–66 were linked to his work.

3. *The sayings or sections.* The work of "Trito-Isaiah" comprises fourteen independent sayings or sections. Isaiah 56:1-8 is a prophetical torah, in which a prophet imparts divine instruction to the effect that eunuchs and foreigners may belong to the community; this was a burning question after the restoration of the Temple, which is mentioned in the passage, so that this utterance can probably be dated in the early part of the fifth century. This section was placed at the beginning because 56:5*b* echoes 55:13, providing a connection with Deutero-Isaiah. Despite some similarities, however, the prophet in question differs from Deutero-Isaiah in the stress he places on cult, sabbath, and law, and in the expressions he uses. The difference is so great that he cannot possibly be termed a disciple of Deutero-Isaiah.

In 56:9–57:13 we have a prophetical liturgy comprising a threat and invective (56:9-12), a short lament (57:1-2), and a prophetical judgment discourse with summons, indictment, and sentence (57:3-13). It is directed against the leaders of the community, who are accused of neglecting their duties, seeking profit and pleasure, and turning from Yahweh to sexual cults. The prophet clearly dissociates himself from the prophets of the cult mentioned in 56:1-8. He is largely dependent on Jeremiah and Ezekiel (cf. particularly 56:9 and Jer. 12:9*b*), but also exhibits points of contact with Deutero-Isaiah, suggesting that he lived in the postexilic period, perhaps the beginning of the fifth century.

The saying 57:14-21, in which the tone is predominantly one of promise, does not base the eschatological salvation it proclaims on election or covenant, but on man's status as God's creature. This saying imitates Deutero-Isaiah, as the echo of 40:3 in vs. 14 shows; otherwise, however, its point of view is unambiguously postexilic.

Isaiah 58:1-12[1] is a combination of exhortation and promise that borrows from earlier prophets (vs. 1*a* echoes Hos. 8:1; vs. 1*b*, Mic. 3:8; vs. 8*b*, Isa. 52:12), so that a certain derivative aura cannot be overlooked. We may note this also in the passage's estimation of fasting, which is criticized as an outward ritual practice for which love of one's neighbor should be substituted, but which at the same time counts as a good work in God's eyes.

Isaiah 58:13-14 is a saying concerning the sanctity of the sabbath; one hesitates to call its author a prophet. It resembles the preceding saying in its tone of pastoral exhortation and promise and in its dependence on recognized earlier statements (vs. 14*a* depends on Deut. 32:13; vs. 14*b* depends on Isa. 50:5*b*). Its author, however, is more closely connected with the cult; he does not reject the cultic institution, but seeks to purge it of abuses.

Chapter 59 is a prophetical liturgy, comprising two consecutive invectives (59:1-4, 5-8), a communal lament (59:9-15*a*), and an oracle of deliverance (59:15*b*-20 [vs. 21 is a later addition]). In the opening verses the prophet borrows from 50:1-3, and elsewhere, too, uses expressions or ideas belonging to Deutero-Isaiah (cf. vs. 19*a*). His theme, however, belongs to the fifth century: the problem of the delay of eschatological salvation, both after the Exile and after the completion of the new Temple; the prophet attempts to solve this problem by pointing to sin as the reason for the delay. We may think of the beginning of the fifth century as its time of origin.

The three oracles of salvation in 60,[2] 61, and 62 derive from a prophet of the early postexilic period who borrows extensively from Deutero-Isaiah, sometimes using whole sentences more or less literally (e.g., 60:4*a* from 49:18*a*; 60:9*b* from 55:5*b*; 60:13*a* from 41:19*b*), sometimes using particular turns of

[1] J. Morgenstern, "Two Prophecies from the Fourth Century B.C. and the Evolution of Yom Kippur," *HUCA*, XXIV (1952/53), 1-74.

[2] A. Causse, "La vision de la nouvelle Jérusalem (Esaïe LX) et la signification sociologique des assemblées de fête et des pèlerinages dans l'orient sémitique," in *Mélanges Syriens Dussaud*, II (1939), 739-50; P. Grelot, "Un parallèle babylonien d'Isaïe LX et du Psaume LXXII," *VT*, VII (1957), 319-21.

phrase (e.g., 60:9*a* from 51:5*b*) and sometimes using similar expressions to clothe identical ideas (e.g., 60:10*b* drawing on 54:7-8). In many cases, however, he gives the words a different meaning; in 62:10-11, for instance, a description that had referred to God now refers to Jerusalem and its inhabitants. Above all, he lacks the universal outlook and theocentric approach of Deutero-Isaiah, while the eschatological promise emphasizes complete happiness on earth for Jerusalem. The prophet focuses on this city, not on God; salvation is restricted to it, while the other nations function only as servants of the saved community. Here the prophet shows himself to be a descendant of earlier optimistic and nationalistic prophecy.

This tendency is even more marked in 63:1-6, which begins as a dialogue welcoming the hero returning from battle, followed by the hero's self-glorification. In this fashion the prophet depicts the return of Yahweh as a blood-stained warrior, victorious over his enemies, and his deliverance of his people through eschatological vengeance upon the nations.

In 63:7–64:11 we have a communal lament beginning with an interpretation of history. The lament comprises four sections: the hymnic-narrative historical study (63:7-14[3]), two impassioned laments and petitions (63:15-19*a*; 63:19*b*–64:6), and an additional petition (64:7-11). Since this passage borrows its content from Deuteronomistic theology, exhibits no points of contact with Deutero-Isaiah, presupposes the situation after the downfall of Judah and the destruction of Jerusalem, and prays for a change, it probably came into being in the early or middle decades of the Babylonian Exile. It is therefore the earliest text in Isaiah 40–66. Its author may have been a cult prophet.

Chapter 65 [4] consists of three loosely connected prophetical utterances intended to constitute a larger unity. These are an invective and threat against members of the community that have apostatized from Yahweh (65:1-7); two units each comprising a promise for the devout and a threat against the apostate (65:8-12, 13-25). The whole is constructed about the twin foci of eschatological salvation and perdition. Vs. 11 mentions two deities: Gad, "Fortune," here probably not an epithet but a specific god, as among the Nabateans; and Meni, a goddess personifying "Fate" or "Destiny." The presence of these deities makes it doubtful whether this passage can be dated, like others, in the beginning of the fifth century. The Israelites in and around Jerusalem seem first to have become familiar with these cults when the Nabateans penetrated into Palestine around the fourth century, when this section was probably composed.

The daring prophetical utterance in 66:1-4 rejects the building of a temple, not specifically defined, in a rationalistic fashion reminiscent of wisdom instruction, and also rejects the entire sacrificial cult as idolatry. Historically, it can only be directed against the efforts to rebuild the Jerusalem Temple after the Exile, in particular against the exertions of the circle around the prophets Haggai and Zechariah about the year 520.

[3] J. Morgenstern, "Isaiah 63,7-14," *HUCA*, XXIII (1950/51), 185-203.

[4] H. G. Jefferson, "Notes on the Authorship of Isaiah 65 and 66," *JBL*, LXVIII (1949), 225-30.

Like 65, 66:5-24 is a unit comprising three prophetical utterances, which announce the imminent eschatological crisis and its consequences. Their dominant note is promise, but they also contain threats. The first threatening saying is directed against the apostate (66:5, 17); the second deals mostly with the happiness of the devout community (66:6-16); the third, also a promise, ends with a prospect of the consequences of the last judgment (66:18-24). Since this section appears to have been influenced by 65 and the phrase "all nations and tongues" in vs. 18 belongs to a very late date, it can perhaps be ascribed to the third century.

In dating the sections of 56–66, we arrive at the following sequence:

a) 63:7–64:11	Middle of the sixth century
b) 66:1-4	About 520
60, 61, 62	Early postexilic period
c) 56:1-8	
56:9–57:13	Beginning of the fifth century
59	
d) 57:14-21	
58:1-12	Postexilic, not precisely datable
58:13-14	
63:1-6	
e) 65	Fourth century
f) 66:5-24	Third century

4. *Thematic groups*. The various sayings and sections all focus on two groups of themes characteristic of the postexilic cultic community in and around Jerusalem. First, they deal with all kinds of disputed points in the regulation of community life, with troubles caused by the wretched living conditions, and with the attack upon poor leadership, syncretistic tendencies, and polytheism. Second, and most important, imminent eschatological expectations are called into question. The Exile, the judgment that had earlier been threatened, had long been over; the day of salvation should have arrived or at least been on its way. Since this was far from being the case, there was a difficult and serious problem, which the prophets of this period had to deal with again and again. For the rest, we may note the further decline of eschatological prophecy into completely worldly and materialistic expectations for the time of salvation.

§ 59 Jeremiah

ATD: A. Weiser, 4th ed., 1961. BOT: B. N. Wambacq, 1957. HAT: W. Rudolph, 2nd ed., 1958. HK: F. Giesebrecht, 2nd ed., 1907. HS: F. Nötscher, 1934. IB: J. P. Hyatt, 1956. KAT: P. Volz, 2nd ed., 1928. KeH: F. Hitzig, 2nd ed., 1866. KHC: B. Duhm, 1901. SAT: H. Schmidt, 2nd ed., 1923. SZ: C. von Orelli, 3rd ed., 1905 (Eng. *The Prophecies of Jeremiah*, 1889). Individual commentaries: C. H. Cornill, 1905 (Eng. 1895); E. A. Leslie, 1954.

F. Augustin, "Baruch und das Buch Jeremia," *ZAW*, LXVII (1955), 50-56; F.

BAUMGÄRTEL, "Zu den Gottesnamen in den Büchern Jeremia und Ezechiel," in *Rudolph-Festschrift*, 1961, pp. 1-29; W. BAUMGARTNER, *Die Klagegedichte des Jeremia*, 1917; A. BENTZEN, *Helgen eller Højeforraeder? Jeremias og hans folk*, 1943; H. BIRKELAND, *Jeremia, profet og dikter*, 1950; S. H. BLANK, *Jeremiah, Man and Prophet*, 1961; W. ERBT, *Jeremia und seine Zeit*, 1902; A. GELIN, *Jérémie*, 1952; H. W. HERTZBERG, *Prophet und Gott*, 1923; W. L. HOLLADAY, "Prototype and Copies: A New Approach to the Poetry–Prose Problem in the Book of Jeremiah," *JBL*, LXXIX (1960), 351-67; *idem*, ""The Background of Jeremiah's Self-Understanding," *ibid.*, LXXXIII (1964), 153-64; F. HORST, "Die Anfänge des Propheten Jeremia," *ZAW*, XLI (1923), 94-153; J. P. HYATT, "The Deuteronomic Edition of Jeremiah," *Vanderbilt Studies in the Humanities*, I (1951), 71-95; *idem*, *Jeremiah, Prophet of Courage and Hope*, 1958; H. G. MAY, "Towards an Objective Approach to the Book of Jeremiah: The Biographer," *JBL*, LXI (1942), 139-55; *idem*, "The Chronology of Jeremiah's Oracles," *JNES*, IV (1945), 217-27; J. W. MILLER, *Das Verhältnis Jeremias und Hesekiels sprachlich und theologisch untersucht*, 1955; G. C. MORGANS, *Studies in the Prophecy of Jeremiah*, 1956; S. MOWINCKEL, *Zur Komposition des Buches Jeremia*, 1914; A. NEHER, *Jérémie*, 1960; R. RENDTORFF, "Zum Gebrauch der Formel n^{e}'um jahwe im Jeremiabuch," *ZAW*, LXVI (1954), 27-37; H. GRAF REVENTLOW, *Liturgie und prophetisches Ich bei Jeremia*, 1963; T. H. ROBINSON, "Baruch's Roll," *ZAW*, XLII (1924), 209-21; F. SCHWALLY, "Die Reden des Buches Jeremia gegen die Heiden. XXV. XLVI–LI," *ibid.*, VIII (1888), 177-217; J. SKINNER, *Prophecy and Religion, Studies in the Life of Jeremiah*, 3rd ed., 1930, reprinted 1936; G. A. SMITH, Jeremiah, 4th ed., 1929; B. STADE, "Bemerkungen zum Buche Jeremia," *ZAW*, XII (1892), 276-308; H.-J. STOEBE, "Jeremia, Prophet und Seelsorger," *ThZ*, XX (1964), 385-406; W. TANNERT, *Jeremia und Deuterojesaja*, Dissertation, Leipzig, 1956; D. W. THOMAS, *The "Prophet" in the Lachish Ostraca*, 1946; *idem*, "Again 'the Prophet' in the Lachish Ostraca," in *Von Ugarit nach Qumran* (Eissfeldt-Festschrift), 1958, pp. 244-49; C. C. TORREY, "The Background of Jeremiah 1–10," *JBL*, LVI (1937), 193-216; E. VOGT, "Jeremias-Literatur," *Bibl*, XXXV (1954), 357-65; P. VOLZ, *Studien zum Text des Jeremia*, 1920; *idem*, *Der Prophet Jeremia*, 3rd ed., 1930; A. C. WELCH, *Jeremiah: His Time and his Work*, 2nd ed., 1951; C. F. WHITLEY, "The Date of Jeremiah's Call," *VT*, XIV (1964), 467-83; H. WILDBERGER, *Jahwewort und prophetische Rede bei Jeremia*, 1942; cf. also the bibliographies in FOHRER, *ThR*, NF XIX, XX, and XXVIII (§ 52).

1. *Jeremiah.* Jeremiah comes from a family of priests at Anathoth (Ras el-Kharrubeh, near Anata), northeast of Jerusalem. The location does not imply that he was a descendant of Abiathar, who was banished to Anathoth (I Kings 2:26).[1] Since Jeremiah refers to himself as a young man at the time of his call, he was probably born around 650. We may conclude from 16:1-2 that he never married.[2] In the thirteenth year of Josiah (626 B.C.), he experienced his call to be a prophet (1:2; 25:3); his ministry lasted, with interruptions, more than four decades, extending through the downfall of the state of Judah. The course of his life from the second period of his ministry on is recounted in extensive narrative sections; his personality, his spiritual growth and struggles

[1] Thus the conclusions drawn by Neher from this supposed relationship turn out to be untenable.

[2] M. D. Goldman, "Was Jeremiah Married?" *ABR*, II (1952), 42-47.

can be discerned, apart from the features that shine through his sayings, above all in his laments or confessions (3 B). This evidence tells us more about him than we can learn about the other prophets.

Horst assumes that Jeremiah did not appear until after the death of Josiah, during the reign of Jehoiakim, because he says nothing about Josiah's reform of the cult; Hyatt, May, and Whitley support similar hypotheses. These theories founder on the explicit dating of Jeremiah's call, the derivation of 3:6-13 from the period of Josiah, and the existence of the Assyrian Empire, presupposed in 2:18, which no longer existed in the period of Jehoiakim.[3] In addition, Reventlow interprets Jeremiah's call (1:4-10) as a formal ordination following a liturgical ritual, with symbolic actions performed by cultic functionaries; this theory is completely at variance with the description of the call as a vision and audition. Finally, the identification of Jeremiah with the prophet mentioned in the Lachish Letters (iii. 20), proposed by Chapira and Dussaud,[4] has been refuted by Tur-Sinai (who thinks in terms of Uriah, mentioned in Jer. 26:20-23) and above all by Thomas.

2. *Jeremiah's activity*. Jeremiah's ministry can be divided into four periods, whose messages reflect both the internal circumstances of Judah and the crucial events of those decades in the realm of world politics, which also determined the personal fortunes of the prophet:[5] the situation in Judah before and after the reformation of Josiah, his death in battle in 609 B.C., the appointment of King Jehoahaz by the Judeans and Jehoiakim by the Egyptians, the latter's harsh rule and final rebellion against renewed Babylonian hegemony, the first deportation (597), imposed upon his successor Jehoiachin as a punishment, the reign of Zedekiah, the last king, with the siege and capture of Jerusalem, and the flight to Egypt of a Judean group following the murder of Gedaliah.

The first period of Jeremiah's ministry, in which the sayings and report in chapters 1–6 fall,[6] lasts from his call to some time before the conclusion of Josiah's reformation (622 B.C.). Apparently he made his first appearance at Anathoth, announcing the judgment to come (Duhm); he soon moved to Jerusalem, only to discover that the situation there was even worse. And so he accuses his people of apostasy from Yahweh, excoriates their sins in the cultic, moral, and political realm, and announces the judgment that will therefore come. Beside this message stands the call to deliverance through repentance. When, however, Jeremiah perceives the fruitlessness of his preaching, he considers

[3] H. H. Rowley, "The Early Prophecies of Jeremiah in Their Setting," *BJRL*, XLV (1962/63), 198-234.

[4] R. Dussaud, "Le prophète Jérémie et les lettres de Lakish," *Syria*, XIX (1938), 256-71.

[5] F. M. Cross, Jr., and D. N. Freedman, "Josiah's Revolt against Assyria," *JNES*, XII (1953), 56-58; H. L. Ginsberg, "Judah and the Transjordan States from 734 to 582 B.C.E.," in *Marx Jubilee Volume*, I (1950), 347-68; A. Malamat, "The Last Wars of the Kingdom of Judah," *JNES*, IX (1950), 218-27; M. B. Rowton, "Jeremiah and the Death of Josiah," *ibid.*, X (1951), 128-30.

[6] Torrey's assumption that Jeremiah 1–10 is a unified pseudepigraphic work from the third century is unlikely.

his mission ended and leaves matters in Yahweh's hands (6:10-11, 27-29), withdraws into silence, and says nothing for many years.

To carry out the judgment, Jeremiah expects the mysterious "foe from the north" (4:6, 15-16; 6:22).[7] Despite the fundamental objections of Wilke, this foe is usually thought of as the Scythians (Duhm, *et al.*), less frequently as the Medes (Gunkel, Gressmann) or the Chaldeans; others find here the influence of mythological conceptions. It is probably more accurate to assume that at first Jeremiah was not thinking in terms of a particular people (Lauha, Wambacq, Rudolph), although his description of the foe may have incorporated individual reports concerning the Scythians. Only much later did the Babylonians come to be viewed as the instrument of Yahweh's punishment.

It is sometimes assumed that Jeremiah interrupted his activity after Josiah's reformation,[8] remaining silent because he supported the reformation and its effects (Nötscher; a similar view is espoused by Weiser*), or that he welcomed the reformation and lent it his active support (Robert, Bewer), or at least agreed with the basic ideas of Deuteronomy and rejected only those circles that were using the law for their own purposes (Granild). Contrary to these views, some hold that, after an initial period of support, Jeremiah soon rejected the reformation (Eissfeldt*, Rudolph, Rowley) or that he rejected it from the very outset (Hyatt, May). It is out of the question that Jeremiah supported Josiah's reformation and ceased his activity on account of its successes; such a view would render incomprehensible the final negative evaluation of Judah (6:27-29). This judgment shows that he did not interrupt his activity on account of the reformation and its successes, but before the reformation took place. He may quite well have sided with the reformation's attack on paganism and its support of social action. But did he not see from the very beginning those questionable aspects of the reformation that eventually led him to reject it: emphasis on the cultic laws and the Jerusalem Temple? If so, then he did not change his attitude, which from the very outset was ambivalent toward Deuteronomy and the reformation.

After a long period of silence Jeremiah resumed his prophetical activity during the reign of Jehoiakim. The second period falls in the years 608–597; the utterances and reports deriving from it are scattered throughout 7–20; 22; 25:1-14, to which may be added the oracles against the nations (25:15 ff.;

[7] B. S. Childs, "The Enemy from the North and the Chaos Tradition," *JBL*, LXXVIII (1959), 187-98; H. Gressmann (and H. Gunkel) in *ZAW*, XLII (1924), 157-58; J. P. Hyatt, "The Peril from the North in Jeremiah," *JBL*, LIX (1940), 499-513; A. Lauha, *Zaphon*, 1943; F. Wilke, "Das Skythenproblem im Jeremiabuch," in *Kittel-Festschrift*, 1913, pp. 222-54.

[8] J. A. Bewer, *The Book of Jeremiah*, I, 1951; H. Cazelles, "Jérémie et le Deutéronome," *RSR*, XXXIX (1951), 5-36; S. Granild, "Jeremia und das Deuteronomium," *StTh*, XVI (1962), 135-54; J. P. Hyatt, "Jeremiah and Deuteronomy," *JNES*, I (1942), 156-73; A. F. Puukko, "Jeremias Stellung zum Deuteronomium," in *BWAT*, XIII (1913), 126-53; H. H. Rowley, "The Prophet Jeremiah and the Book of Deuteronomy," in *T. H. Robinson-Festschrift*, 1950, pp. 157-74 (= *From Moses to Qumran*, 1963, pp. 187-208); J. N. Schofield, "The Significance of the Prophets for Dating Deuteronomy," in *Studies in History and Religion*, ed. E. A. Payne, 1942, pp. 44-60 (suggests that Deuteronomy came into being under Jeremiah's influence).

46:3 ff.) and the narratives describing Jeremiah's life. In the first years of this period Jeremiah attacks primarily the Temple and the cult, exhorting the people to turn and repent because judgment is imminent. Now, however, he gains bitter enemies: King Jehoiakim and the priests whom he has exasperated by his criticism. He just manages to escape being condemned to death for blasphemy (26). Informers, insidious attacks, and assassination attempts, apparently stemming in part from his own family, threaten him. Finally, he is scourged, placed in the stocks, and forbidden to visit the Temple (20:1 ff.). From this period come his moving laments or confessions, in which he struggles with himself and with God (3 B). As a last warning the prophet, prevented from visiting the Temple, has Baruch write down his earlier sayings and recite them in the Temple. Jehoiakim thereupon orders their arrest, and both must hide until his death. It is in this period that Jeremiah probably performed the symbolic action reported in 13:1-11. Only when the Babylonian advance came near does he appear to have taken up residence once more in Jerusalem (35).

The third period lasts from the accession of Zedekiah to the period following the downfall of Judah and Jerusalem (597–586). Since Jeremiah had apparently been right in his threats, Zedekiah seeks to follow his advice, but is unable to carry the day against the nationalistic anti-Babylonian faction. Neither does Jeremiah have any luck with the nationalistic professional prophets during the revolutionary movement of 594 or among the deportees in Babylon (27–29). In 588 the Babylonians besiege Jerusalem, and Jeremiah is once more threatened and persecuted; at the last moment he escapes death, as 37–38 describe in detail. Despite respectful treatment on the part of the Babylonians after the fall of Jerusalem and despite their offers, he remains in Palestine with the remnant of the people, in order to assist with the reconstruction attempts of Gedaliah, which end with the latter's death. Jeremiah is forced to emigrate to Egypt with a group of refugees (42–43).

There we may place the fourth period of his ministry, which is briefly recounted in 43:8-13 and 44. In Egypt he passes into oblivion; legend says he died a martyr's death.

3. *Written transmission.* Basic to Jeremiah's prophetical activity are the oral proclamation of his sayings and the performance of symbolic actions. He employs the usual rhetorical forms used and imitated by the prophets, infusing them with fresh poetic ability and expressiveness. He may have written down the sayings belonging to his first period as soon as it was ended. In any case, however, written transmission begins in the year 605. At that time Jeremiah dictated his words from 626–605 to Baruch to be recited in public. After Jehoiakim destroyed this scroll, seeking to render the threats of judgment ineffectual, Jeremiah had a copy made in order to preserve the efficacy of his words. This second scroll probably had the same scope and content as the first, so that there is no need to distinguish between a so-called original scroll and an expanded scroll. The passive phrase in 36:32, "many similar words were added," most probably refers to expansion of the scroll at a significantly later date. This

raises the question of the scroll's nature and content and also of whether there are other complexes of tradition.

A. With regard to the scroll, the data contained in the book of Jeremiah allow us to say that it contained only sayings and no reports, that the sayings in question came from the period prior to 605, that they were exclusively or primarily of threatening character, that they were directed against Judah, Jerusalem, and the foreign nations, and that the scroll, having been read aloud three times in one day, cannot have been too extensive. With regard to its detailed content, however, opinions differ.

Eissfeldt* considers it a record rather like a diary, with the various sections in the first person, couched in a parenetic prose style similar to the diction of Deuteronomy. Apart from the accounts of visions and auditions in chapter 1,[9] he thinks the so-called original scroll comprised 3:6-13; 7:1–8:3; 11:6-14; 13:1-14; 16:1-13; 17:19-27; 18:1-12; 19:1-2, 10-11; 22:1-5; 25*. In what he assumes was the second scroll were added 24; 27; 32; 35. This corresponds in large measure to what Rudolph assumes to be speeches of Jeremiah in a later Deuteronomistic redaction, which, therefore, could not in his opinion have constituted the original scroll. He thinks instead primarily of sayings directed against Judah and Jerusalem from the major part of 1:4-6, 30; 8:4-9, 13-17; 9:1-7 (Eng. 9:2-8); 13:1-11, 20-22, 25-27; 14:1–15:3; 23:9-12 and against the nations in 25:15-38; 46:1–49:33 (insofar as these are from Jeremiah); and possibly 9:9-10, 16-21, 24-25 (Eng. 9:10-11, 17-22, 2526); 11:1516; 13:23-24; 16:16-17; 17:1-4; 18:13-17. The latter passages belonged in any case to the second scroll, to which are also ascribed 10:17-22; 12:7-14; 13:12-19; 15:5-9; 23:33; 24; 27; 49:34 ff. Apart from the exegetical problem of whether many of these texts really go back to Jeremiah and do not, as seems more likely, represent later additions to the book, one must ask whether the original scroll of Rudolph's theory is not too comprehensive and Eissfeldt's* definition of its content on formal grounds, following the model of chapter 25, too one-sided. It is easy to see why Sellin-Rost* and Weiser* express reservations, maintaining that it is impossible to bring together with any assurance the fragments contained in the scrolls.

It is probably hopeless to try to reconstruct an original scroll. The sayings of Jeremiah from the years 626–605 cannot be divided into a first group, which constituted an original scroll, and a second group, "similar words." The wording of chapter 36 does not allow us to assign the threats, for example, to an original scroll and the invectives and exhortations in addition to a second scroll. If,

[9] K. Budde, "Über das erste Kapitel des Buches Jeremia," *JBL*, XL (1921), 23-37; J. Lindblom, "Der Kessel in Jer 1,13 f.," *ZAW*, LXVIII (1956), 225-27; H. Michaud, "La vocation du 'prophète des Nations'," in *Hommage Vischer*, 1960, pp. 157-64; B. Stade, "Der 'Völkerprophet' Jeremia und der jetztige Text von Jer Kap. 1," *ZAW*, XXVI (1906), 97-123; W. G. Williams, "Jeremiah's Vision of the Almond Rod," in *Papers Irwin*, 1956, pp. 90-99; P. S. Wood, "Jeremiah's Figure of the Almond Rod," *JBL*, LXI (1942), 99-103.

however, we are dealing only with two copies of a single scroll, having identical content, we can probably define it. To it belonged:[10]

a) The sayings from the first period of Jeremiah's ministry, particularly 2:1-3 + 7-11, 5-6, 12-13, 18, 23-25, 26-28, 31-32; 3:1, 6-13, 19-20; 3:21–4:2; 4:3-4, 5-8 + 13-22, 29-31; 5:1-3 + 6, 4-5, 7-9, 30-31; 6:4-5, 13-15, 20-21, 22-26.
b) Part of the sayings from the second period: 7:1-15, 16-20, 21-23; 8:4-7, 21-23; 9:1-2, 3-5, 9, 14-15, 16-17, 19-21 (Eng. 9:2-3, 4-6, 10, 15-16, 17-18, 20-22); 11:1-14; 13:15-16; 14:2–15:2; 18:1-11; 25:1-14.
c) The oracles against the nations: 25:15 ff.*; 46:3-6, 7-10, 11-12.

The reports of symbolic actions that also derive from the second period (13:1-11;[11] 16:1-9), the lamentations of Jeremiah, and the sayings concerning the king (most of which are later) do not enter into consideration. Most of the scroll, therefore, interrupted only by interpolations, is still to be found in 2–9 and 11; it is by and large continuous and generally in chronological order.[12] Only a comparatively few sayings were later displaced to chapters 13–14, 18, 25, and 46.

The sayings contained in the scroll look back in part to the desert period with its state of untroubled confidence between Yahweh and Israel, in contrast to the present apostasy from Yahweh in the religious and political realms; other sayings attack the Temple and the cult. Some announce the invasion of the foe from the north as agents of God's judgment; others, in the form of lamentations and dirges, depict the terrors of the judgment.

In conclusion, we must say a word about the first-person prose passages, which Eissfeldt* includes in the scrolls.[13] Duhm denied Jeremiah's authorship of them on stylistic grounds; he has been followed by other scholars, including Mowinckel, who derive them from a Deuteronomistic author living in the time of Ezra who used expressions taken from Jeremiah. Mowinckel considers these passages a third source of the book of Jeremiah (in addition to the sayings of Jeremiah and narratives). Eissfeldt* and Weiser* disagree, ascribing these passages once more to Jeremiah; Weiser* (like Miller) assumes that he used a cultic rhetorical form antedating Deuteronomy. There is no evidence of such a form, however, either in direct use or in prophetical imitation. Rudolph takes a mediating position. According to him, we are dealing with prose texts that,

[10] W. Eichrodt, "The Right Interpretation of the Old Testament: A Study of Jeremiah 7,1-15," *Theology Today*, VII (1950), 15-25; G. Fohrer, "Jeremias Tempelwort 7,1-15," *ThZ*, V (1949), 401-17; E. Gerstenberger, "Jeremiah's Complaints," *JBL*, LXXXII (1963), 393-408; J. Milgrom, "The Date of Jeremiah, Chapter 2," *JNES*, XIV (1955), 65-69; L. M. Pákozdy, "Der Tempelspruch des Jeremia," *Zeichen der Zeit*, XII (1958), 372-81; P. F. Stone, "The Temple Sermons of Jeremiah," *AJSL*, L (1933/34), 73-92; A. Strobel, "Jeremias, Priester ohne Gottesdienst?" *BZ*, NF I (1957), 214-24.

[11] E. Balla, "Jeremia 13,1-11," in *Heiler-Festschrift*, 1942, pp. 83-110; E. Baumann, "Der linnene Schurz Jer 13,1-11," *ZAW*, LXV (1953), 77-81; A. de Bondt, "De linnen gordel uit Jer 13,1-11," *GThT*, L (1950), 17-39.

[12] Chapter 10 contains nothing by Jeremiah, so that 11:1-14 originally followed directly after chapter 9.

[13] J. Bright, "The Date of the Prose Sermons of Jeremiah," *JBL*, LXX (1951), 15-35.

as their vocabulary shows, have undergone Deuteronomistic revision: 7:1–8:3; 11:1-14; 16:1-13; 17:19-27; 18:1-12; 21:1-10; 22:1-5; 25:1-14; 34:8-22; 35. The following observations may be made: (1) As a whole, these passages cannot possibly all derive from Jeremiah. To this extent Duhm was not completely wrong. The later additions include at least 7:24-28; 7:29–8:3; 16:10-13; 17:19-27. (2) That the remaining sections are influenced by the style and ideas of Deuteronomy is not surprising, but only to be expected; we find this phenomenon elsewhere, e.g., in 14:2–15:2. From the second period of his ministry on, Jeremiah was dependent on the theological language of his time, which was influenced by Deuteronomy, just as in his first period he borrowed form and content from the preaching of earlier prophets. (3) Finally, the utterances of Jeremiah with which we are here concerned (7:1-15, 16-20, 21-23; 11:1-14; 16:1-9; 18:1-11; 21:1-7, 8-10; 22:15; 25:1-14; 34:8-22; 35) are by no means prose; they consist of short verses. We are therefore not dealing with a third source of the book of Jeremiah, but with Jeremiah's original words, some of which belonged to the scroll we have been discussing.

B. The sayings not included in the scroll include above all the lamentations or confessions of Jeremiah (11:18-23; 12:1-6; 15:10; 17:14-18; 18:18-23; 20:7-13, 14-18; and, last in terms of subject matter, 15:15-20 [15:21 is a later addition]).[14] At one time they constituted an independent collection, the more so because Jeremiah did not intend them for immediate publication and because they are still to be found within 11–20, distributed according to principles that cannot be determined. They can be termed dialogues[15] or disputes with God,[16] but their most immediate parallels are individual laments like those contained in the Psalter (Baumgartner). In them is revealed a crisis brought about by the prophet's abandoning himself to God. For this surrender means that he must remain in a state of uncertainty and tension vis-à-vis himself and those about him; in this state of tension he is caught between surrender to God and surrender to the world. This very tension conjures up the crisis for Jeremiah, in which surrender to God turns into criticism that reaches the point where Jeremiah abandons his understanding of his prophetical mission and therefore demands Jeremiah's own conversion, his surrender of his own distress and anxiety before the divine imperative (15:15-20).

Reventlow espouses the view that the "I" of these passages is to be understood according to the principle of "corporate personality," having merely exemplary significance as a member of the people, so that any search for personal biographical features and the destiny of an individual is illegitimate. In view of the autobiographical details, this interpretation is unlikely.

[14] G. M. Behler, *Les confessions de Jérémie,* 1959; S. H. Blank, "The Confessions of Jeremiah and the Meaning of Prayer," *HUCA,* XXI (1948), 331-54; J. L. Mihelic, "Dialogue with God," *Interpr,* XIV (1960), 43-50; G. von Rad, "Die Konfessionen Jeremias," *EvTh,* III (1936), 265-76.

[15] N. P. Bratsiotis, *Εισαγωγὴ εἰς τοὺς Μονολόγους τοῦ 'Ιερεμίου,* 1959, includes them among the monologues.

[16] Blank (note 14), with strong emphasis on the legal contest; W. L. Holladay, "Jeremiah's Lawsuit with God," *Interpr,* XVII (1963), 280-87, turns them into a judgment upon Yahweh.

C. Under the title "concerning the royal house of Judah," 21:11–23:8 contains a series of sayings concerning the dynasty and especially individual kings. Apart from the more general sayings in 21:13-14 and 23:1-2, the following derive from Jeremiah: the sayings concerning Jehoahaz (22:10), Jehoiakim (22:1-5, 6-7, 13-19), and Jehoiachin (22:24-27, 28, 29-30). An additional royal saying is found in 13:18-19. This collection, to which was prefixed 21:1-7, 8-10 during the composition of the book on account of the words there addressed to King Zedekiah, came into being no earlier than the time of Zedekiah and probably even later because, like the minor collections in the book of Isaiah, it follows the two-part eschatological schema, concluding with a late prophecy of messianic character (23:3-8).

D. Another minor collection with the title "concerning the prophets" is found in 23:9-40.[17] The sayings that derive from Jeremiah (23:9-12, 13-15, 16-17, 21-22, 25-32) should probably be assigned to his third period, in which he was in violent conflict with the cult prophets.

E. Chapters 30–31 represent a minor collection of optimistic utterances. Besides the earlier superscription in 30:4, "These are the words which Yahweh spoke concerning Israel [and Judah]," there is a later and more detailed one in 30:1-3, which even tells how the words were written on a scroll.[18]

There is a wide divergence of opinions concerning these two chapters. While Volz and Rudolph consider the bulk of the material to be a single unified poem, most scholars find here a collection of independent sayings. Stade and Smend deny Jeremianic authorship completely. Cornill and Giesebrecht recognize a genuine nucleus in chapter 31, as do Eissfeldt*, Pfeiffer*, and Sellin-Rost* in 30–31. Volz and Rudolph derive the chapters almost entirely from Jeremiah. Eissfeldt* and Weiser* date the chapters in Jeremiah's early period; Sellin-Rost* and Rudolph, however, date them from Josiah's annexation of North Israelite territory prior to 609.

When a prophet like Jeremiah launches a violent attack against optimistic prophecy, the occurrence of optimistic sayings is surprising, though not impossible. Chapters 24 and 32 also have the character of promises. Closer examination reveals 30–31 to be a collection of individual sayings, of which Jeremiah probably composed 30:5-7, 12-15; 31:2-6, 15-17, 18-20, 21-22, 31-34, 35-37. The passage dealing with the new covenant probably also derives from him. The faith in deliverance that Jeremiah expresses in these and other oracles of salvation, together with reasons of form and content, suggests the third period of the

[17] H.-J. Kraus, *Prophetie in der Krisis*, 1964.

[18] A. Gelin, "Le sens du mot 'Israël' en Jérémie XXX-XXXI," in *Mémorial Chaine*, 1950, pp. 161-68; M. D. Goldman, "The Authorship of Jeremiah Chapter XXXI," *ABR*, II (1952), 109-10; H. W. Hertzberg, "Jeremia und das Nordreich Israel," *ThLZ*, LXXVII (1952), 595-602 (= *Beiträge zur Traditionsgeschichte und Theologie des Alten Testaments*, 1962, pp. 91-100); J. P. Hyatt, "Torah in the Book of Jeremiah," *JBL*, LX (1941), 381-96; W. Lempp, "Bund und Bundeserneuerung bei Jeremia," *ThLZ*, LXXX (1955), 238-39; R. Martin-Achard, "La nouvelle alliance, selon Jérémie," *RThPh*, XII (1962), 81-92; H. Ortmann, *Der Alte und der Neue Bund bei Jeremia*, Dissertation, Berlin, 1940; M. Sekine, "Davidsbund und Sinaibund bei Jeremia," *VT*, IX (1959), 40-57.

prophet's ministry as their date (a similar dating is maintained by Pfeiffer*). It is hardly likely that they go back to political events under Josiah.

F. The oracles against foreign nations in 46–51[19] constitute an extensive collection. Originally, they were probably introduced by the passages concerning Yahweh's cup of staggering (25:15-16, 27-29) and Yahweh's judgment upon the nations (25:30-31, 34-38); like the oracles against Egypt, they were taken from Jeremiah's scroll (cf. 3 A). The oracles against Egypt (46), the Philistines (47), Moab, Ammon, and Edom (48:1-47; 49:1-6, 7-22), and Damascus (49:23-27) exhibit a kind of geographical order, with Jerusalem as the hypothetical center (south—west—east—north), into which the following oracles against Arab tribes (49:28-33) and Elam (49:34-39) do not fit. The conclusion is provided by the oracles against Babylon (50:1–51:58), to which is appended the report of a symbolic action (51:59-64) out of the Baruch document.

Here again, opinions differ greatly. Following Schwally and Stade, Volz in particular denied the Jeremianic authorship of these chapters, finding in them a single collection of ten national poems from the middle of the sixth century. Pfeiffer* and Sellin-Rost* arrive at a similar conclusion on stylistic grounds. At least the oracles against Babylon are frequently derived from the late exilic period, e.g., by Wambacq. Eissfeldt*, Weiser*, and Bentzen, on the other hand, assume a small nucleus of Jeremiah's words; Rudolph finds a somewhat larger one. Most recently Eissfeldt* finds Jeremianic material in 50–51 as well as 46. Bardtke, too, assumes Jeremianic authorship for a nucleus of the revised and expanded sayings, as well as an original book of oracles against foreign nations, comprising 1:2, 4-10; 25:15-17, the nucleus of 46–49, and 25:27-29. He derives this book from the early period of Jeremiah, who, he thinks, belonged at first to an order of nebiim and appeared as a prophet against the nations. But 1:10 does not provide sufficient support for such a far-reaching thesis, the more so because there is no trace of a later revolution in Jeremiah's preaching.

To Jeremiah himself can be ascribed only the oracles against Egypt (46:3-6, 7-10, 11-12) and the general oracles (25:15-16, 27-29; 25:30-31, 34-38), deriving from the second period. Reasons of style and content suggest other, later authors for all the other texts, the more so because parts of chapter 48 were borrowed from Isaiah 15–16, parts of 49 from Obadiah 1-10, and parts of 50–51 from other portions of the book of Jeremiah.

G. A series of sayings and reports have been transmitted individually rather than in the context of collections; these include particularly sayings from the third period. From the first period we have the call report (1:4-10), the reports concerning the visions and auditions that took place soon after the call (1:11-12,

[19] H. Bardtke, "Jeremia der Fremdvölkerprophet," *ZAW*, LIII (1935), 209-39; LIV (1936), 240-62; K. Budde, "Über die Capitel 50 und 51 des Buches Jeremia," *JDTh*, XXIII (1878), 428-70, 529-62; O. Eissfeldt, "Jeremias Drohorakel gegen Ägypten und gegen Babel," in *Rudolph-Festschrift*, 1961, pp. 31-37; A. Kuschke, "Jeremia 48,1-8," *ibid.*, pp. 181-96; A. Malamat, "The Historical Setting of Two Biblical Prophecies on the Nations," *IEJ*, I (1950), 149-59; F. North, "The Oracle against the Ammonites in Jeremiah 49,1-6," *JBL*, LXV (1946), 37-43.

13-19), and the sayings dealing with the interruption of Jeremiah's work (6:10-11, 27-29). From the second period we have reports of symbolic actions (13:1-11; 16:1-9) and Jeremiah's word to the Rechabites (35:1-19). From the third period we have 8:18-20; 13:12-14; 23; 15:5-9; 16:16-18; 17:1-4; 21:1-7, 8-10, 13-14; 22:20-23; 24; 32:1-15. From the fourth period, finally, we have 2:14-17.

4. *The Baruch document.* The Baruch ben Neriah mentioned in 36 as Jeremiah's amanuensis appears several times (32:12; 43:3; 45). It turns out that at least from 605 on he dwelt continually in the presence of Jeremiah, shared his lot, and finally accompanied him to Egypt. Despite the objections of Mowinckel, who thinks that Baruch was involved only in the writing of the scroll in 605, it is reasonable to assume that he took part in preserving the traditions about Jeremiah. To him have therefore been ascribed, probably correctly, a series of narratives that presuppose special familiarity with the prophet and his fate but cannot derive from Jeremiah himself. This Baruch document[20] includes the following narratives, which can be divided into three groups by the dates given or other criteria:

I From the beginning to the fourth year of Jehoiakim's reign:

26	Circumstances of the Temple sermon 7:1-15
19:1, 2*a**, 10-11*a*, 14-15; 20:1-6	Breaking of the flask and maltreatment by Pashhur[21]
36 (37:1-2)	Jeremiah's scroll
45	Oracle for Baruch

II From the fourth year of Zedekiah's reign:

27:1-3, 12*b*; 28	Jeremiah's yoke and conflict with Hananiah.[22]
29	Jeremiah's letter to the deportees
51:59-64	Arrangements for a symbolic action in Babylonia

III From the siege of Jerusalem to Jeremiah's stay in Egypt:

34:1-7, 8-22;[23] 37:3–44:30.

Groups I and II constitute preludes to group III, which is emphasized by virtue of its very extent. Jeremiah's threats, contained in the scroll (whose necessity the preceding narratives are intended to explain), were not realized in 594, thanks to Jeremiah's intervention and Zedekiah's appeasement of Babylonia. They were, however, realized a few years later in the downfall of Judah and Jerusalem and in the flight of those who had been left behind in Palestine to Egypt, so that the future now lies solely with those who had been deported to Babylonia, if they will take Jeremiah's letter to heart. In this fashion Baruch

[20] L. Rost, "Zur Problematik der Jeremiabiographie Baruchs," in *Meiser-Festschrift,* 1951, pp. 241-45.

[21] The so-called Tophet Speech does not form a part of the Baruch document (Eissfeldt*), since it is only an expansion of the report of the symbolic action and never existed independently.

[22] Kraus, *op. cit.* (note 17); H. Schmidt, "Das Datum der Ereignisse von Jer 27 und 28," *ZAW,* XXXIX (1921), 138-44.

[23] M. David, "The Manumission of Slaves under Zedekiah," *OTS,* V (1948), 63-79.

seeks to demonstrate the final realization of the prophet's predictions, on account of which he has suffered so much. This is what the Baruch document is intended to represent, not a passion story (Kremers, Weiser)[24] or a biography of Jeremiah, and certainly not a supplement to the scroll (Sellin*).

The manner in which Baruch composed his account can be seen from a comparison of Jeremiah's Temple sermon (7:1-15) with Baruch's account (26). Baruch has depicted the circumstances surrounding Jeremiah's preaching as accurately as possible, but reproduced merely the basic ideas of the prophet's sermon in abbreviated form, at the same time changing the emphasis slightly. He probably treated all Jeremiah's utterances in similar fashion. There is nevertheless a difference between the account of events and the record of the utterances because the former is in prose and the latter in short verses.

The original order of the Baruch document has been disturbed. The transfer of chapter 45 to its present position can be explained as an attempt to except Baruch, now dwelling in Egypt, from the threats against the Egyptian Jews. The transfer of 51:59-64 was made so as to associate these verses with the oracles against Babylonia (50–51). Chapter 36 may owe its present position to an attempt to ascribe all the words of Jeremiah in 1–35, including the promises, to the scroll, thereby legitimizing them.

5. *Later passages*. The dominant view tends to minimize the number of later passages that have been added to Jeremiah's scroll, the other minor collections, and the Baruch decument. In opposition to this tendency, it must be emphatically stated that, as in Isaiah 1–39, the number of additions is considerable. Of course, in the case of one saying or another it is possible to ask whether we are not in fact dealing with a Jeremianic saying, possibly revised. Only rarely, however, can we answer affirmatively.

In any case, the historical appendix in 52 is clearly an addition. It largely corresponds with II Kings 24:18–35:30. In addition 52:28-30 provides information from another source concerning the Judeans deported in the years 597, 587, and 582. Unlike Isaiah 36–39, these chapters were not added for the purpose of assembling all information concerning the prophet, because Jeremiah is not even mentioned. Instead, the account of the downfall of Jerusalem and the amnesty granted to Jehoiachin, the captured king, is intended to show how Jeremiah's threats came to be realized and how the subsequent change of fortune was according to his promises.

Apart from minor additions and glosses, the following utterances of other authors have been incorporated into the book of Jeremiah:

a) Invectives: 2:19-22, 29-30; 3:2-5; 7:24-28; 9:6-7 (Eng. 9:7-8)
b) Threats: 2:33-37; 4:9-12, 27-28; 5:10-11, 12-17, 26-29; 6:1-3, 6-9, 12, 16-19; 7:29–8:3; 8:8-17; 9:24-25 (Eng. 9:25-26); 11:15-17; 13:20-22, 24, 25-27; 15:3-4, 11-14; 18:13-17; 22:11-12; 23:19-20

[24] H. Kremers, "Leidensgemeinschaft mit Gott im Alten Testament," *EvTh*, XIII (1953), 122-40; A. Weiser, "Das Gotteswort für Baruch Jer 45 und die sogenannte Baruchbiographie," in *Heim-Festschrift*, 1954, pp. 35-46 (= *Glaube und Geschichte im Alten Testament*, 1961, pp. 321-29).

c) Laments: 9:18 (Eng. 9:19); 10:17-20; 12:7-13; 13:17
d) Exhortations: 5:18-25; 21:11-12
e) Promises: 3:14-18; 12:14-17; 16:14-15, 19-21; 23:3-8; 30:8-11, 16-24; 31:7-14, 23-30, 38-40; 32:16-44; 33:1-13, 14-26
f) Apocalyptic: 4:23-26
g) Didactic material and commentary: 9:10-13 (Eng. 9:11-14); 16:10-13; 17:19-27; 22:8-9; 23:23-24, 33-40
h) Wisdom: 9:22-23 (Eng. 9:23-24); 10:1-16; 17:5-13; 23:18
i) Oracles against foreign nations: 46:13–51:58

6. *Growth of the book.* The growth of the book was a long and complex process which cannot be analyzed in all details. It appears to have begun in the exilic period. That the work of several redactors over a long period was involved and that the text was still not settled in the third century are shown by the frequent repetition of verses or groups of verses elsewhere in the book [25] and by the text of the LXX, shorter by about an eighth; some sections have been abbreviated, but others did not even exist in the Hebrew prototype, e.g., 33:14-26. The Jeremiah fragments from Qumran, some of which represent the Masoretic text or a preliminary stage of it, while others represent the shorter text of the Hebrew prototype of the LXX, show that both types of text existed side by side.

We are therefore not dealing with a single redactor, whom Volz identified with Baruch and Rudolph with the author of the "utterances of Jeremiah in Deuteronomistic recension." Neither are we dealing with parallel work of Jeremiah (1–25) and Baruch (26–36 and 37–45), as Saydon asserts,[26] or with large-scale alterations on the part of Baruch, such as Augustin assumes.

The basis of the book is furnished by the records of the sayings and reports of Jeremiah, especially the early scroll, which provides the basic material for 2–9 (utterances from the first period in 2–6; utterances from the second period, down to 605, in 7–9 and scattered throughout some of the following chapters). In addition, there are the other minor collections discussed above, as well as individual reports and sayings, belonging especially to the third and fourth periods, which Baruch either copied down directly or summarized within the narrative framework of his document. From 11 on, these have all been brought together, though there are not always clear reasons to explain their order. Then the Baruch document, with the transpositions noted above, was interpolated at the appropriate places. Finally, the numerous later sayings were gradually added.

At the outset chronological principles presumably were followed in the use of the scroll and the incorporation of the Baruch document. Ultimately, however, the three-part eschatological schema controlled the composition of the book. It lies behind the order found in the LXX:

[25] Thus, for example, Jer. 8:10*a*-12 derives from 6:12-15; 8:15 from 14:9; 9:8 (Eng. 9:9) from 5:9; 10:12-16 from 51:15-19; 15:13-14 from 17:3-4; 20:12 from 11:20; 25:4 from 7:25-26; 30:23-24 from 23:19-20; 38:2 from 21:9; 46:27-28 from 30:10-11; 49:17 from 19:8; 49:19-21 from 50:44-46; 49:22 from 48:40-41; 49:26 from 50:30.

[26] P. P. Saydon, "Il libro di Geremia. Struttura e composizione," *RivBibl*, V (1957), 141-62.

1:1–25:14	Threats against Judah and Jerusalem
25:15-38; 46–51	Threats against foreign nations (LXX = 25:14–32:38)
26–35	Promises for Israel and Judah (LXX = 33–42), to which were added, because of the nature of the sources:
36–45	Major portion of the Baruch document (LXX = 43–51)
52	Appendix

In the textual tradition in which the Masoretic text is based, this order has been altered by the transposition of most of the oracles against foreign nations (46–51); only the introduction (25:15-38) remained in its original place:

1–25	Threats against Judah and Jerusalem (including 25:15-38)
26–35	Promises for Israel and Judah
36–45	Major portion of the Baruch document
46–51	Threats against foreign nations
52	Appendix

7. *Message*. Jeremiah's message is not determined by a cultic setting; neither does it bear to any marked degree the stamp of any preexisting tradition. There is no evidence that at the beginning of his ministry he appeared as a nabi prophesying against foreign nations (Bardtke); that he later appeared on occasion as a cultic prophet, acting as an intercessor and prayer leader (Eissfeldt*, Weiser*); or that he functioned throughout his ministry as the ordained holder of a liturgical office (Reventlow). The few oracles against foreign nations spoken by Jeremiah suggest quite the opposite conclusion. The occasional imitation of a cultic literary type (such as the prophetical liturgy in 14:2–15:2) precludes cultic recitation more than suggesting it, although for practical reasons Jeremiah may now and then have preached his message to people participating in a Temple ceremony.

Naturally Jeremiah was familiar with the traditions of Mosaic Yahwism and its development in Palestine, the more so because, like the other great individual prophets, he leads the ancient faith into new territory. Much more markedly than the effect of tradition, however, do we notice his human personality; herein he differs from his predecessors (Hertzberg, Wildberger). In him the line between the utterance of Yahweh and the words of the individual prophet is blurred; intensely personal and lyric tones make themselves heard in his preaching. From the moment of his call he resists the divine imperative, feels his solidarity with his people, and intercedes with God on their behalf as long as possible, at the same time imploring them to turn back from the coming destruction. His ambivalence finally brings him to the crisis expressed in his laments or confessions, a crisis that ends, not in darkness and despair, but in his own conversion and free obedience toward God.

In line with this personal stamp his prophecy bears, Jeremiah uses the covenant idea and association formula (11:1 ff.; 24:7) developed and legitimized by Deuteronomic theology,[27] thus availing himself of the theological language

[27] Cf. R. Smend, *Die Bundesformel*, 1963.

of his age; at the same time, however, he retains the earlier prophetical description of the relationship between Yahweh and Israel as a personal relationship, described in terms of a family, characterizing it, like Hosea, as a marriage relationship (2:2; 3:6 ff.) or speaking of the Israelites as Yahweh's sons (3:19, 22; 4:22). Like Hosea, whose powerful influence he shows, particularly in his first period,[28] he begins the story of the relationship with the deliverance from Egypt (2:6); unlike the theology of Deuteronomy, however, he traces this deliverance back, not to Israel's election, but to God's love. Like Hosea, he limits the period of a pure relationship between Israel and Yahweh to the time of Moses and the desert wandering (2:2), when there was as yet no sacrifice (7:22). Entrance into the settled land of Canaan marked the beginning of apostasy from Yahweh (2:7), which Jeremiah prefers to describe in terms drawn from nature rather than from history (8:4-7) and which he depicts in almost classic fashion in 3:19-20. Because this apostasy has continued to the present day, God's destroying judgment is imminent—Yahweh would no longer heed even the intercession of a Moses or a Samuel (15:1). Contrary to popular opinion, Judah and Jerusalem no longer live in a state of favor with God, a state that can be easily restored if necessary; their situation is essentially one of imminent disaster, as 6:14 makes completely clear. Like his predecessors, Jeremiah sees the only chance for deliverance in repentance and conversion, which he urgently demands; in the year 605 he can even summarize his entire message as a demand for repentance (25:1 ff.). But once repentance and conversion have proved to be impossible and the judgment upon Judah has begun with the first deportation (15:5-9; 22:20-23), he comes to the expectation of Yahweh's intervention to aid and deliver those deported from Judah and, earlier, from Israel, whom disaster had already struck, as 24 and the Jeremianic sayings in 30–31 show. His hope for the future is sober and far removed from the descriptions of the eschatological prophets (31:6; 32:15; 35:18-19). The central fact is that Yahweh will give the people a heart to know him and that, after the breaking of the Sinai covenant, he will not renew it, but replace it with a new covenant, in which God's will is placed within man and written on his heart, so that man will know God and obey him by nature (31:31-34).

All in all, Jeremiah develops the theology of his predecessors in his own fashion: the tension between God and man producing a completely personal relationship with God, a mutual fellowship with God that finds its expression above all in prayer, a profound resignation of the whole man to God, a resignation refined and purified through crisis; a fundamental interpretation of sin, not as individual transgressions, but as a basic perversion of human life; all the more urgent, therefore, the call to repentance, followed, since God is not only righteousness but also and above all love, by the turn to faith in redemption, a hope for true fellowship with God in a new covenant, in which God's dominion, too, will be achieved.

[28] K. Gross, *Die literarische Verwandschaft Jeremias mit Hosea,* Dissertation, Berlin, 1930; *idem,* "Hoseas Einfluss auf Jeremias Anschauungen," *NkZ,* XLII (1931), 241-65, 327-43.

§ 60 Ezekiel

ATD: W. Eichrodt, 1959-66. BK: W. Zimmerli, 1956-ff. BOT: A. van den Born, 1954. COT: G. C. Aalders, 1955-57. HAT: A. Bertholet and K. Galling, 1936. G. Fohrer and K. Galling, 1955. HK: R. Kraetzschmar, 1900. HS: P. Heinisch, 1923. IB: H. G. May, 1956. ICC: G. A. Cooke, 1936, reprinted 1951. KAT: J. Herrmann, 1924. KeH: R. Smend, 2nd ed., 1880. KHC: A. Bertholet, 1897. SAT: H. Schmidt, 2nd ed., 1923. SZ: C. von Orelli, 2nd ed., 1896. Individual commentaries: C. H. Cornill, 1886; I. G. Matthews, 1939.

P. Auvray, "Le problème historique du livre d'Ézechiel," *RB*, LV (1948), 503-19; *idem*, "Remarques sur la langue d'Ézechiel," *BEThL*, XII (1959), 461-70; F. Baumgärtel (§ 59); G. R. Berry, "Was Ezekiel in the Exile?" *JBL*, XLIX (1930), 83-93; *idem*, "The Composition of the Book of Ezekiel," *ibid.*, LVIII (1939), 163-75; A. van den Born, *De historische situatië van Ezechiels prophetie*, 1947; *idem*, "Ezechiel-Pseudo-Epigraaf?" *StC*, XXVIII (1953), 94-104; L. E. Browne, *Ezekiel and Alexander*, 1952; W. H. Brownlee, *The Book of Ezekiel, the Original Prophecy and the Editor*, Dissertation, Duke University, 1947; M. Burrows, *The Literary Relations of Ezekiel*, Dissertation, Philadelphia, 1925; M. Buttenwieser, "The Date and Character of Ezekiel's Prophecies," *HUCA*, VII (1930), 1-18; G. Dahl, "Crisis in Ezekiel Research," in *Quantulacumque Lake*, 1937, pp. 265-84; L. Dürr, *Die Stellung des Propheten Ezechiel in der israelitisch-jüdischen Apokalyptik*, 1923; W. Eichrodt, *Krisis der Gemeinschaft in Israel*, 1953; J. Finegan, "The Chronology of Ezekiel," *JBL*, LXIX (1950), 61-66; O. R. Fischer, *The Unity of the Book of Ezekiel*, Dissertation, Boston, 1939; G. Fohrer, "Die Glossen im Buche Ezechiel," *ZAW*, LXIII (1951), 33-63; *idem*, *Die Hauptprobleme des Buches Ezechiel*, 1952; *idem*, "Das Symptomatische der Ezechielforschung," *ThLZ*, LXXXIII (1958), 241-50; H. Haag, *Was lehrt die literarische Untersuchung des Ezechiel-Textes?* 1943; J. B. Harford, *Studies in the Book of Ezekiel*, 1935; V. Herntrich, *Ezechielprobleme*, 1932; J. Herrmann, *Ezechiel-Studien*, 1908; G. Hölscher, *Hesekiel, der Dichter und das Buch*, 1924; L. Horst, *Leviticus 17–26 und Hesekiel*, 1881; C. G. Howie, *The Date and Composition of Ezekiel*, 1950; W. A. Irwin, *The Problem of Ezekiel*, 1943; *idem*, *Ezekiel Research since 1943*, *VT*, III (1953), 54-66; C. Kuhl, *Die literarische Einheit des Buches Ezechiel*, 1917; *idem*, "Zur Geschichte der Hesekiel-Forschung," *ThR*, NF V (1933), 92-118; *idem*, *Ältere Materialien im Buche Hesekiel*, Habilitationsschrift, Berlin, 1939; *idem*, "Neuere Hesekiel-Literatur," *ThR*, NF XX (1952), 1-26; *idem*, "Der Schauplatz der Wirksamkeit Hesekiels," *ThZ*, VIII (1952), 401-18; M. Lubliner, *Der Mensch in der Verkündigung Ezechiels*, Dissertation, Marburg, 1946; N. Messel, *Ezechielfragen*, 1945; J. W. Miller (§ 59); W. O. E. Oesterley, "The Book of Ezekiel: A Survey of Recent Literature," *ChQR*, CVI (1933), 187-200; K. von Rabenau, "Die Entstehung des Buches Ezechiel in formgeschichtlicher Sicht," *WZ Halle*, V (1955/56), 659-94; *idem*, "Die Form des Rätsels im Buche Hesekiel," *ibid.*, VII (1957/58), 1055-57; *idem*, "Das prophetische Zukunftswort im Buch Hesekiel," in *von Rad-Festschrift*, 1961, pp. 61-80; H. Graf Reventlow, "Die Völker als Jahwes Zeugen bei Ezechiel," *ZAW*, LXXI (1959), 33-43; *idem*, *Wächter über Israel. Ezechiel und seine Tradition*, 1962; H. H. Rowley, "The Book of Ezekiel in Modern Study," *BJRL*, XXXVI (1953/54), 146-90; M. A. Schmidt, "Zur Komposition des Buches Hesekiel," *ThZ*, VI (1950), 81-98; J. Smith, *The Book of the Prophet Ezekiel*, 1931; S. Spiegel, "Ezekiel or Pseudo-Ezekiel?" *HThR*, XXIV (1931), 245-321; *idem*, "Toward Certainty in Ezekiel," *JBL*, LIV (1935), 145-71; J. Steinmann,

Le Prophète Ézéchiel et les débuts de l'exil, 1953; C. C. TORREY, *Pseudo-Ezekiel and the Original Prophecy*, 1930; *idem*, "Ezekiel and the Exile," *JBL*, LI (1932), 179-81; *idem*, "Certainly Pseudo-Ezekiel," *ibid.*, LIII (1934), 291-320; *idem*, "Notes on Ezekiel," *ibid.*, LVIII (1939), 69-86; C. H. TOY, "The Babylonian Element in Ezekiel," *JBL*, I (1881), 59-66; M. TSEVAT, "The Neo-Assyrian and Neo-Babylonian Vassal Oaths and the Prophet Ezekiel," *ibid.*, LXXVIII (1959), 199-204; C. J. M. WEIR, "Aspects of the Book of Ezekiel," *VT*, II (1952), 97-112; W. ZIMMERLI, "Das Gotteswort des Ezechiel," *ZThK*, XLVIII (1951), 249-62; *idem*, *Erkenntnis Gottes nach dem Buche Ezechiel*, 1954; *idem*, "Das Wort des göttlichen Selbsterweises (Erweiswort), eine prophetische Gattung," in *Mélanges Robert*, 1957, pp. 154-64; *idem*, "Israel im Buche Ezechiel," *VT*, VIII (1958), 74-90; cf. also the bibliographies in FOHRER, *ThR*, NF XIX, XX, and XXVIII (§ 52).

1. *The data of the book.* According to the book named after him, Ezekiel, the son of a certain Buzi, began as a priest. During the first deportation to Babylonia, in 597, he was brought with others to Tel-abib on the river Chebar, a canal running from Babylon through Nippur to Uruk, probably the modern *shaṭṭ en-nīl*[1] (1:1; 3:15). He was married; his wife died about 587, before or during the siege of Jerusalem (24:18). In the fifth year of the deportation (593/2) he was called to be a prophet; according to the last date given in his book (29:17), his ministry lasted until 571. He prophesied therefore for something more than twenty years, during which he exhorted, warned, and comforted his fellow sufferers in the Exile, though he concerned himself mostly with the fate of far-off Judah and Jerusalem, to which he addressed first his threat (1–24) and later his promise (33–48). He visited Jerusalem several times in visionary trances (8–11; 40 ff.).

Modern study of the book has so frequently cast doubt on these statements and developed such diverse theories concerning the date and place of Ezekiel's ministry, his person and the content of his preaching, the growth of the book and the history of its text, that neither a brief introduction into the history of the book's interpretation nor the presentation of a particular theory will suffice. More than in the case of the other prophetical books, a historical survey of the problems is necessary.

2. *The historical problems.* The historical problems have arisen from the doubts cast on the traditional view, according to which Ezekiel either limits himself to addressing Judah and Jerusalem, directly affecting their fate in almost magical fashion, or else contrasts his message of disaster to the hopes the deportees still had for Jerusalem, while always remaining there in spirit. He always appears primarily as a prophet to Judah and Jerusalem, although he lives among the deportees in Babylonia. Since it is almost impossible to imagine such a prophet, it was natural that this view should arouse doubts. The violent attacks made on it during recent decades have shaken it to its very foundations and produced completely different theories concerning the place and date of Ezekiel's ministry. Not infrequently, Ezekiel's appearance as a prophet of the

[1] According to E. Vogt, "Der Nehar Kebar: Ez 1," *Bibl*, XXXIX (1958), 211-16, we are dealing with a small canal in the immediate vicinity of Nippur.

early sixth century in Babylonia has been ascribed to a redaction of the book that is responsible for the present historical or Babylonian background, while the actual ministry of the prophet and the origin of his book have been assigned to a different time or place. Little thought, however, has been given to how difficult it is to conceive of such large-scale redactional activity in ancient Israel, to how many new difficulties are connected with the suggested theories, and to the extent to which they render an understanding of the person and message of Ezekiel more difficult. The traditional view of the prophet of the Exile, with his mind fixed on Judah and Jerusalem, has certainly proved untenable. On the other hand, there is no real reason to assume another date or another place for Ezekiel's ministry. He was active in the period defined by the dates given in his utterances[2] and lived among the Judean deportees in Babylonia. The problem of his relationship to them and to Jerusalem, however, which gave rise to the attacks on the traditional view, can be solved very simply.

a) The most radical theories are those that assign the ministry of Ezekiel or the origin of the book of Ezekiel to a period different from that indicated in the book and usually also to a different location.

After occasional attempts to date Ezekiel earlier, Smith placed his activity in the territory of Northern Israel in the time of King Manasseh, the early seventh century. Only in 4:4-5 and 37:16, however, does *Israel* definitely refer to the Northern Kingdom; it usually refers to the Southern Kingdom and its deportees. According to Torrey, the core of the book is a pseudepigraphic work written about 230 B.C., purporting to be a prophecy written in 666 predicting the abominations and punishment of King Manasseh; a redactor later ascribed this work to the exilic prophet Ezekiel. This theory presupposes, however, that the book represents a literary unity, which is not true. Torrey's deeper reason, his attempt to demonstrate the fictitious nature of the Exile tradition, has been made untenable by archaeological evidence. According to Messel, the prophet was active around 400 among the deportees that had returned to Palestine, and his book goes back to the work of a redactor around 350. Messel is unable to explain, however, why both employ the fiction of the Exile; in the Persian Empire, it was unnecessary to employ such a disguise in order to attack an idolatrous party in Jerusalem.[3] According to Browne, the book is a pseudepigraphon from the time of Alexander the Great, dealing with his appearance in the East. To arrive at this interpretation, however, he must, among other things, assume the presence in the book of two distinct systems of cryptic dating and an allegorical significance of the sins censured by Ezekiel. The end result is only a self-contradictory criticism of the Samaritans and their temple.[4] Finally, van den Born interprets the book as the pseudepigraphic autobiography of a well-read author in the time of Ezra and Nehemiah, with a theology like that of the

[2] R. Dussaud, "Les dates des prophéties d'Ézéchiel," *RHR*, LXXVI (1917), 145-64.

[3] Cf. also the criticism of J. J. Stamm, *ThZ*, III (1947), 304-9.

[4] That a date in the period of Alexander is not in accord with the material presented in Ezekiel has been shown in detail by M. Vogelstein, *HUCA*, XXIII (1950/51), 197-220.

Priestly Document; the unity found in the book's language, ideas, and structure is due to revision by a school. Apart from this unlikelihood, van den Born's most important reason, the dependence of the book on postexilic texts (which Burrows once sought to demonstrate), has long been shown to be invalid. There is no evidence in favor of a date different from that suggested in the book of Ezekiel.

b) In addition, theories have been expressed concerning merely the location of Ezekiel's activity that diverge from the data of the book.

Herntrich, for instance, wanted to limit the prophet's activity exclusively to Palestine. Like others, he found a contradiction in the statement that Ezekiel was addressing the Jerusalemites and announcing the end of the city while living among the deportees, to whom he apparently gave no thought. He must therefore have exercised his ministry in Jerusalem, and a redactor must be responsible for the transfer to Babylonia. Harford and Berry espoused a similar view; Matthews, Irwin, and Frost [5] also distinguish between the prophet in Jerusalem and the Babylonian redactor. In like fashion, May, according to whom Ezekiel returned to Jerusalem from Babylonia in 591, thinks in terms of a ministry exclusively in Jerusalem, beginning in that year. As the parallel addresses to foreign nations in prophetical sayings show, however, Ezekiel's addressing the Judeans and Jerusalemites does not necessarily mean that he was in Jerusalem. In addition, he soon addressed some of his utterances to the deportees (11:14-21; 14:12-23). Their worries and anxieties centered on the continued existence of Jerusalem with its Temple and their return to it. In reply, Ezekiel spoke his oracles of disaster, announcing the capture of Jerusalem, the deportation of its inhabitants, and a long exile. Apart from these considerations, a transfer of Ezekiel's activity to Palestine requires far-reaching textual alterations and the assumption of an uncommonly thorough revision of the book by the redactor.

c) Yet another theory has sought to avoid these difficulties by locating Ezekiel's activity in two places, both in Palestine and in Babylonia.

Bertholet in particular has espoused the view that Ezekiel was in Jerusalem when he was called to be a prophet in the "scroll vision" (2:3–3:9) (593 B.C.). He remained there until the beginning of the siege and then, after a brief interval at another spot in Palestine, went to Babylonia, where he was called to be a prophet for the deportees through the "chariot throne vision" (1:4–2:2) (585 B.C.). Similar opinions, with some modifications, are held by Spiegel, Kuhl, Steinmann, Augé, and Jozaki.[6] According to Fischer, Ezekiel was deported in 597, but returned to Jerusalem on account of his call. Only after the destruction of the city did he join the deportees as a prophet. The views of Pfeiffer* are similar, except that he thinks Ezekiel returned to Babylonia at the beginning of or in the course of the siege. These assumptions, too, require textual emendations and transpositions of large sections of the book for which there is no convincing evidence. The point of departure is always an isolated passage, which must

[5] S. B. Frost, *Old Testament Apocalyptic*, 1952, p. 84.

[6] R. Augé, *Ezequiel*, 1955; S. Jozaki, "A Study on Ezekiel 11,14-21," *Kwansei Gakuin University Annual Studies*, VI (1958), 29-41.

be interpreted one-sidedly or on the basis of certain presuppositions, or else yields the desired meaning only through emendation. Therefore, the assumption of a double ministry of Ezekiel is also unconvincing. For this reason Cooke, M. Schmidt, Howie, Zimmerli, Eichrodt, Rowley, and others, with minor variations in detail, have maintained the view that Ezekiel prophesied among the deported exiles and that the book contains the written deposit of his preaching.

d) According to the text of the book, Ezekiel was deported in 597 and called to be a prophet in 593/2; these dates may be considered a secure foundation. Furthermore, the dates given in the individual sections are genuine and original; they are based on the year of the deportation of King Jehoiachin, who often was still considered the legal ruler vis-à-vis Zedekiah, who was looked upon merely as regent.[7] Since Ezekiel accompanied Jehoiachin into exile, at the great turning point of his ministry he can speak of "our exile" (33:21; 40:1). In addition, the linguistic usage is that of the period around 600 B.C. The literary affinities with other OT books, together with the past and contemporary historical events presupposed, point to the early exilic period.[8] Nothing suggests Jerusalem as one or the only location of Ezekiel's ministry; on the contrary, everything points to Babylonia. Ezekiel's familiarity with circumstances in Jerusalem does not go beyond what he could know from the period before the exile and learn from later information. Of the utterances of Jeremiah, he is familiar essentially with those from the period before 597. There is nothing to suggest that he spent the crucial years under Zedekiah in Jerusalem and experienced there the misery of the city's siege and capture. The details of the city's fall he learned only quite a bit later, from a refugee.

If Ezekiel lived in Babylonia and exercised his prophetical ministry there, it is no longer possible to state that he was entrusted with a message for Jerusalem, to which he spoke from Babylonia, although he continually dwelt on its fate. He understood his mission as being exclusively to the Judean exiles; he was to dash their hopes for Jerusalem's deliverance and alleviate their dread of its destruction. His preaching was meant for their ears, and he worked among them as their prophet. This can be seen above all in the phrase "rebellious house," which refers exclusively to the exiles, in the entire sections dealing with the Babylonian situation and in direct references to it, in the above-mentioned statement of those to whom his words were addressed,[9] and in the references to Mesopotamian traditions. Of course, he did not proclaim his message without any reference to Jerusalem. By announcing God's judgment upon Jerusalem through words and symbolic actions, he contributes indirectly to the realization of this judgment, because such announcement, according to the theory then

[7] Even after his deportation, Jehoiachin appears to have possessed land in Palestine, on the basis of seal impressions from Tell Beit Mirsim and Er-Rumele, dating after 597, with the inscription "Eliakim, steward of Yaukîn"; cf. W. F. Albright, "The Seal of Eliakim and the Latest Pre-Exilic History of Judah, with some Observations on Ezekiel," *JBL*, LI (1932), 77-106.

[8] Fohrer, *Hauptprobleme*, pp. 105-202.

[9] *Ibid.*, pp. 203-59.

prevalent, is efficacious. For those around him this may well have been the source of his lasting significance.

3. *Ezekiel's activity.* Ezekiel's ministry can be divided into three periods. In the first period, which lasts from his call to the fall of Jerusalem (593/2–587), he seeks by means of unconditional announcement of disaster to free the exiles from their dependence on the existence of Jerusalem and the Temple, by destroying their confidence in their inviolability and a speedy turn of fortune. This is the purpose served by the sayings and symbolic actions in 4–12, 16–17, 19, and 21–24. Ezekiel severs the union of Yahweh and Jerusalem, demands assent to this separation and a decision in favor of Yahweh. For the exiles, to have faith means to free themselves from their dependence on the Temple city, understand the judgment upon it, and accept it. When the fall of Jerusalem was imminent or known by rumor, Ezekiel fell silent until the report of an eyewitness loosed his tongue (3:22-27; 24:25-27; 33:21-22).

Now Ezekiel's ministry changes. He seeks to comfort those who have lost hope and to guide the people's wish to return to Yahweh into the proper channels. This second transitional period (586–585) is a period of conditional optimism: salvation for the faithful, death for the wicked. Ezekiel therefore settles accounts with the former ruling class of Judah (34) and with the nationalist prophets (13:3, 6, 9), exhorting the exiles to repent and return to Yahweh and to live a life according to his will (3:16*b*-21; 33:1-20). The coming of salvation is also served by the judgment announced against other nations, which have looked upon Jerusalem's destruction with satisfaction and capitalized upon it, or are to be considered typical examples of wicked conduct (25 ff.).

To be sure, Ezekiel was bound to realize that what he required of the exiles surpassed human ability and that the future could not consist merely in the survival of a few faithful people. He saw a new period of salvation in the unconditional prophecies of salvation he uttered in the third period of his ministry (after 585);[10] only the deliberately apostate and the external enemies threatening Israel are excluded. He looks forward to a reunited Israelite kingdom in a flourishing Palestine (36–37) and to Yahweh's return to the rebuilt Temple, from which streams of blessing proceed (40–48), while catastrophe overtakes those who still threaten Jerusalem with attack (38–39). Especially significant is the promise of a new heart of flesh and the gift of God's spirit, so that the Israelites will do God's will as of their own accord and live in fellowship with him (36:26 ff.). This parallel to the new covenant spoken of by Jeremiah shows that Ezekiel, too, followed the path from demand for repentance to promise of deliverance.

4. *The manner of Ezekiel's preaching.* The development of Ezekiel's prophetical preaching and the way in which he carried out his ministry exhibit several peculiarities. For him, as for his great predecessors, the "word" of Yahweh that comes to him stands in the foreground. In addition, he lays claim to the "spirit"

[10] J. Böhmer, "Die prophetische Heilspredigt Ezechiels," *ThStKr*, LXXIV (1901), 173-228; J. Delorme, "Conversion et pardon selon le prophète Ézéchiel," in *Mémorial Chaine*, 1950, pp. 115-44.

of Yahweh, the vivifying and impelling power of the early nebiim and cult prophets; he thereby denies them their source of inspiration. Furthermore, ecstasy, a phenomenon that accompanies the visions,[11] plays a more important role than in the case of the other prophets and occurs more frequently. As one of its elements, frequently mentioned in Ezekiel, it can involve apparent transport to Jerusalem or a plain. Finally, Ezekiel performed more symbolic actions than the other prophets; the accounts of these will be found in 4–5; 12; 21; 24; 37; and 3:22-27; 24:25-27; 33:21-22, which belong together.

The most frequent rhetorical types, apart from the reports of visionary and ecstatic experiences and symbolic actions, are the threatening forms: sixteen threats, nineteen threats with motivation, ten combinations of invective and threat, eight prophetical laments and dirges, and three threats associated with other literary types. Besides a few invectives and exhortations, we find a whole series of historical, argumentative, didactic, and allegorical utterances, which bear witness to a rationalistic and meditative element in Ezekiel's thought. Finally, we must not overlook the promises, which occupy a considerable portion of the book. We may note also that we are often dealing with lengthy poems and discussions as well as briefer sayings.

Von Rabenau has made many useful contributions to the form-critical problems of the book in his various studies, although his attempt to answer in this fashion the literary question of the book's origin runs up against the limitations of form-critical analysis. Special mention should be made of his classification of "future-utterances" (i.e., sayings depicting future deliverance or disaster, including promises of salvation and threats) into various motifs: the root, the deed, its execution, the outward and inward consequences of God's intervention. Zimmerli isolates the sayings that conclude with such formulas as "they shall know that I am Yahweh," calling them "utterances of God's self-demonstration"; he attempts to derive this form, which occurs frequently in Ezekiel, from I Kings 20:13, 28. But the occurrence of this formula twice in anecdotal prophetical utterances does not provide a broad enough basis for the assumption that centuries later Ezekiel made use of an early literary type. Furthermore, I Kings 20:28 turns out not to be an early utterance but a secondary interpolation, which interrupts the continuity. The situation in I Kings 20:13-14 is more complex, but essentially no different. It therefore seems more likely that these prophetical sayings were not Ezekiel's prototype, but were instead given their present form by the last Deuteronomistic redactor of the books of Kings on the basis of Ezekiel's words. In addition, we are not dealing here with a new literary type, but with an interpretive formula that has been appended to other literary types. Its purpose is to provide a proper understanding of the event reported or announced, because every event needs interpretation. This is precisely the function of its first occurrences in the Yahwist's material: Exod. 7:17; 8:6, 18 (Eng. 8:10, 22); 9:29; 11:7. It is intended to summon the listener to judge

[11] E. Baumann, "Die Hauptvisionen Ezechiels in ihrem zeitlichen und sachlichen Zusammenhang untersucht," *ZAW*, LXVII (1955), 56-67; R. Dussaud, "Les visions d'Ézéchiel," *RHR*, XXXVII (1898), 301-13; H. Pope, "Ezekiel and his Vision," *JThSt*, XXIV (1935), 275-88.

that it is Yahweh who has intervened or is about to intervene, with his wrath or with his aid.

5. *Later passages.* Large portions of the utterances and accounts preserved in the book have often been ascribed to later hands. Of the 1,273 verses in the book, Hölscher's analysis ascribes only 170 to Ezekiel; Irwin's, 251. Both take the distinction between poetry and prose as the criterion of genuineness and deny Ezekiel's authorship of everything that cannot be fitted into the schema of long verses with parallel members.[12] Irwin also distinguishes between the brief images or parables that derive from Ezekiel and the appended interpretation, which comes from another hand. In fact, if one applies the usual criterion of Israelite poetry, very few passages will be found that consist of long verses (mostly in 17; 19; 26–28). The situation changes as soon as the theory of short verses is applied. Although the text is more corrupt than in any other prophetical book, it turns out that all the utterances and reports of Ezekiel can be analyzed metrically as long or short verses.

Other reasons, too, for denying Ezekiel's authorship of many individual passages are not persuasive. These include the assumption of copious additions to Ezekiel's prophecy through oral tradition (Hempel*) or through an editor, to whom May ascribes some five hundred verses, as well as the more or less arbitrary judgments favoring a particular theory of the place and date of Ezekiel's ministry or exegetical considerations. Nevertheless, the material preserved under the name of Ezekiel contains a series of later passages deriving from various authors and various periods. Their subject matter is diverse, and they may be in either poetry or prose. These passages include particularly 6:8-10; 16:30-34, 44-63; 17:22-24; 21:33-37 (Eng. 21:28-32); 22:6-13, 15-16, 23-31; 23:36-49; 27:9*b*, 11-24; 28:20-26; 30:13-19; 32:9-16; 33:7-9; and a large number of sections in the last portion of the book: 40:38-43; 41:15*b*-26; 43:10-27; 45:18-20; 45:21–46:15; 46:16-24; 48.

6. *Transmission of the sayings and reports.* Earlier, the predominant view concerning the transmission of Ezekiel's sayings and reports held that the words of the prophet represented entirely or for the most part literary compositions with very little if any oral proclamation and that the book was a unified work composed according to a conscious plan. The dates distributed throughout the book seemed to argue for this view. Smend, for example, praised the carefully considered structure of the book, from which not a single piece could be removed without endangering the whole. This view, however, has turned out to be erroneous.

First, we must assume an intimate association of oral proclamation and written preservation. Oral proclamation is suggested by 2:4-7; 3:4-7, 16*b*-21; 8:1; 11:25; 14:1; 20:1; 21:5 (Eng. 20:49); 24:19-24; 33:30-33. Unlike the other prophets, however, Ezekiel probably wrote down his sayings and reports himself

[12] A. van Selms, "Literary Criticism of Ezekiel as a Theological Problem," *OuTWP,* 1961, pp. 24-37, suggests that the poetical texts were divinely inspired, while the prose represents only Ezekiel's exhortations, meditations, commentaries, and glosses on the poetry. This was in any case not the view of Ezekiel, who derives his utterances from Yahweh without distinction.

rather than relying on oral tradition. This is suggested by the occasionally complex metrical structure, the additions or alterations made by Ezekiel, and the additions of later readers, both usually at the end of the various sections. Usually oral proclamation or the performance of symbolic actions seems to have preceded written preservation, which took place later. Sometimes, however, Ezekiel seems to have written down his inspirations at once and proclaimed them later or even kept them to himself, so that they became known only much later (e.g., 3:16*b*-21).

Second, the unity of the book was called into question by the observation that the dates apply only to the sections they introduce, not to all sections intervening between them and the next date given. All sorts of tensions, repetitions, and contradictions showed up, including the chronologically erroneous placement of many sections, such as 3:16*b*-21, 22-27, and the interweaving of originally independent sections, especially in 8–11 and 40–48. For quite a while scholars followed Kraetzschmar in seeking to evade the consequences of these observations by assuming several recensions or versions of the Ezekiel tradition, combined by a redactor. Herrmann, however, proved conclusively that the book is a collection of individual sections and collections, though produced by Ezekiel himself in the course of his long ministry. Thus at one stroke all those theories collapsed that found in the book a unified pseudepigraphic work dating from a later period.

The last step was the recognition that the prophet himself did not assemble the collections and words he had written down, but that this had been undertaken at a later date by one or more editors. Some think in terms of a long process involving many hands (Freedman[13]); others ascribe the process to an "editor" (May) or a particular circle of disciples (van den Born, Zimmerli), whose expansions, enrichments, and exegetical contributions have more or less overgrown the words of Ezekiel. Some take as their point of departure a kind of proto-scroll composed by Ezekiel, into which sayings and passages were interpolated from his other extant writings or from the memory of his disciples and hearers; the whole was later consciously supplemented (von Rabenau).

Accepting this general view, Eissfeldt* and Weiser* take as their point of departure original collections of a special kind. According to them, Ezekiel himself composed two first-person reports rather like journals, with dates referring to certain significant events. One deals with Jerusalem and Israel, the other with Tyre and Egypt. When they were combined, the latter was interpolated between the threats and promises of the former. In addition, Ezekiel left other discourses and poems in the first person, with more general subject matter, either as collections or in isolation. Either before or after the two sets of memoirs were linked together these were added, more likely by someone else than by Ezekiel himself. This hypothesis, which takes the dates as its point of departure, is open to the objection that we find undated sections referring to specific significant events, e.g., 21:23-29 (Eng. 21:18-24), 24:15-24; 29:6*b*-9, and

[13] D. N. Freedman, "The Book of Ezekiel," *Interpr*, VIII (1954), 446-72.

that when different sections deal with the same question the one is dated, the other not, e.g., 14:1-11 and 20:1-32; 30:20-21 and 30:22-26.[14]

Several stages can be distinguished in the process of collection and transmission. Contrary to the assumption of a unified literary work or of a purely oral tradition, Ezekiel at least wrote down his words and reports before or after his oral preaching or performance of symbolic actions and left them in this form, as his own supplements and the later additions at the end of many sections show. For the arrangement and assembling of the utterances and reports and for the organization of the material as a whole he was not responsible.

In the next stage the individual records were brought together to form minor collections. Some of these comprise reports of visionary and ecstatic experiences or symbolic actions. Others were put together on the basis of catchwords; most were assembled on the basis of identical or similar subject matter. In accordance with the two-part eschatological schema, words of comfort and deliverance were often appended to collections of utterances threatening disaster.

The following collections can be distinguished (later additions within them have been listed in section 5 above):

1:1–3:15	Call report[15]
3:16*a*; 4–5	Reports of symbolic actions
6	Sayings with the catchword "idol"
7	Sayings concerning imminent judgment[16]
8:1–11:13	Reports of visionary and ecstatic experiences[17]
	Appendix: 11:14-21 Promise for the exiles
12:1-20	Reports of symbolic actions
12:21–13:21	Sayings concerning the reliability of prophetical utterances and other prophets
	14 Two isolated utterances[18]
15–20	Sayings concerning sin, judgment, and responsibility:
	15–16 Sin and judgment of Israel[19]

[14] For details, cf. Fohrer, *Hauptprobleme,* pp. 42-44.

[15] L. Dürr, *Ezechiels Vision von der Erscheinung Gottes (Ez C. 1 u. 3) im Lichte der vorderasiatischen Altertumskunde,* Dissertation, Würzburg, 1917; E. Höhne, *Die Thronwagenvision Hezekiels,* Dissertation, Erlangen, 1953; O. Procksch, "Die Berufungsvision Hesekiels," in BZAW, XXXIV (1920), 141-49.

[16] J. Göttsberger, "Ez 7,1-16 textkritisch und exegetisch untersucht," *BZ,* XXII (1934), 195-223.

[17] E. Balla, "Ezechiel 8,1–9,11; 11,24-25," in *Bultmann-Festschrift,* 1949, pp. 1-11; T. H. Gaster, "Ezekiel and the Mysteries," *JBL,* LX (1941), 289-310; F. Horst, "Exilsgemeinde und Jerusalem in Ez 8–11," *VT,* III (1953), 337-60; H. G. May, "The Departure of the Glory of Yahweh," *JBL,* LVI (1937), 309-21; H. W. F. Saggs, "The Branch to the Nose," *JThSt* NS, XI (1960), 318-29.

[18] S. Daiches, "Ezekiel and the Babylonian Account of the Deluge, Notes on Ez 14,12-20," *JQR,* XVII (1905), 441-55; M. Noth, "Noah, Daniel und Hiob in Ezechiel 14," *VT,* I (1951), 251-60; W. Zimmerli, "Die Eigenart der prophetischen Rede des Ezechiel," *ZAW,* LXVI (1955), 1-26.

[19] E. Baumann, "Die Weinranke im Walde," *ThLZ,* LXXX (1955), 119-20; O. Eissfeldt, "Ezechiel als Zeuge für Sanheribs Eingriff in Palästina," *PJB,* XXVII (1931), 58-66

	17	Sin and judgment of the monarchy[20]
	18	Responsibility and retribution[21]
	19	Sin and judgment of the monarchy
	20	Sin and judgment of Israel
21	Sayings with the catchword "sword" [22]	
22	Sayings concerning blood guiltiness and individual sins	
	23	Isolated utterance concerning the sisters Oholah and Oholibah
24	Reports of symbolic actions[23]	
25	Sayings concerning the lands around Judah, arranged after the pattern of the execration texts with Judah as the hypothetical center: Ammon = North (east) Moab = East Edom = South (east) Philistines = West	
26–28	Sayings concerning Tyre (28:20-26 concerning Sidon)[24]	
29–32	Sayings concerning Egypt[25]	
33	Sayings from the second period of Ezekiel's ministry[26]	
34	Sayings concerning shepherds and sheep[27]	
35	Sayings concerning Edom	

(= *Kleine Schriften,* I [1962], 239-46); *idem,* "Hesekiel Kap. 16 als Geschichtsquelle," *JPOS,* XVI (1936), 286-92 (= *Kleine Schriften,* II [1963], 101-6).

[20] R. S. Foster, "A Note on Ezekiel XVII 1-10 and 22-24," *VT,* VIII (1958), 374-79; M. Greenberg, "Ezekiel 17 and the Policy of Psammetichus II," *JBL,* LXXVI (1957), 304-309; L. P. Smith, "The Eagle(s) of Ezekiel 17," *ibid.,* LVIII (1939), 43-50.

[21] H. Junker, "Ein Kernstück der Predigt Ezechiels," *BZ* NF, VII (1963), 173-85; K. Koch, "Tempeleinlassliturgien und Dekaloge," in *von Rad-Festschrift,* 1961, pp. 45-60.

[22] J. A. Bewer, "Beiträge zur Exegese des Buches Ezechiel, 5. Hes 21,14-22," *ZAW,* LXIII (1951), 197-200; F. Delitzsch, "Das Schwertlied Ez 21,15-22," *Zeitschrift für Keilschriftforschung,* 1885, pp. 385-98; H. H. Guthrie, Jr., "Ezekiel 21," *ZAW,* LXXIV (1962), 268-81.

[23] J. Hempel, "Eine Vermutung zu Hes 24,15 ff.," *ZAW,* LI (1933), 312-13; J. L. Kelso, "Ezekiel's Parable of the Corroded Copper Caldron," *JBL,* LXIV (1945), 391-93.

[24] W. E. Barnes, "Ezekiel's Denunciation of Tyre," *JThSt,* XXXV (1934), 50-54; J. Dus, "Melek Ṣōr Melqart?" *ArOr,* XXVI (1958), 179-85; I. Engnell, "Die Urmenschvorstellung und das Alte Testament," *SEÅ,* XXII/XXIII (1957/58), 265-89; J. Garrett, "A Geographical Commentary on Ezekiel XXVII," *Geography,* XXIV (1939), 240-49; J. H. Kroeze, "The Tyre-Passages in the Book of Ezekiel," *OuTWP,* 1961, pp. 10-23; C. Mackay, "The King of Tyre," *ChQR,* CXVII (1934), 239-58; H. G. May, "The King in the Garden of Eden: A Study of Ezekiel 28,12-14," in *Essays Muilenburg,* 1962, pp. 166-76; H. P. Rüger, *Das Tyrusorakel Ez 27,* Dissertation, Tübingen, 1961; W. H. Schoff, *The Ship "Tyre,"* 1920; S. Smith, "The Ship Tyre," *PEQ,* LXXXV (1953), 97-110.

[25] W. G. Ballantine, *Ezekiel* 32, 1892; O. Eissfeldt, "Schwerterschlagene bei Hesekiel," in *T. H. Robinson-Festschrift,* 1950, pp. 73-81; J. Plessis, *Les prophéties d'Ézéchiel contre l'Égypte,* 1912.

[26] W. Eichrodt, "Das prophetische Wächteramt," in *Weiser-Festschrift,* 1963, pp. 31-41; P. Auvray, "Le Prophéte comme guetteur (Ez XXXIII,1-20)," *RB,* LXXI (1964), 191-205.

[27] W. H. Brownlee, "Ezekiel's Poetic Indictment of the Shepherds," *HThR,* LI (1958), 191-203; J. G. Remboy, "Le thème du berger dans l'oeuvre d'Ézéchiel," *Studii Biblici Franciscani Liber Annuus,* XI (1960/61), 113-44.

36–39 Sayings and reports concerning the creation of the new Israel[28]
40–48 Sayings and reports concerning the outward rebuilding of Israel[29]

A further stage was the use of the collections with dates as the basis and skeleton for a chronologically structured book, so that following the report of the call seven collections determined the guiding principle: 3:16*a* + 4–5; 8–11: 13; 15–20; 24:1-24; 40–48; 26–28:19; 29–32. The other collections and individual sections without dates seem to have been incorporated on the basis of the date suggested by their subject matter or the appropriateness of their material, so that the perspective fluctuates between chronology and subject matter. This was followed by a series of alternations belonging to the redactional revision of the growing book. Only one of these, however, changes the historical picture of the prophet: the transposition of 3:16*b*-21, 22-27; 4:4-8; 24:25-27 to their present place, producing the impression that Ezekiel was called from the very outset to be a "pastor," that for most of his ministry, except for the proclamation of his prophecies, he remained dumb, and that he symbolically announced the duration of the Exile at the outset by lying on his side, suggesting that its length was predetermined.

Finally, the complex of oracles against foreign nations was inserted after the threats against Judah and Jerusalem, thus giving the book three major portions corresponding to the three-part eschatological schema:

1–24 Threats against Judah and Jerusalem
25–32 Threats against foreign nations
33–48 Promises for Ezekiel's nation

The fragments that could be detached from the Ezekiel scroll found in Cave 11 at Qumran show that the Hebrew text was fixed in a form very similar to the Masoretic text by the middle of the first century B.C. at the latest.[30]

7. *Ezekiel's personality.* Ever since the suggestions of Klostermann,[31] there has been a problem of Ezekiel's personality. Various phenomena in the life of the prophet, usually associated with ecstatic experiences and transportation, together

[28] J. G. Aalders, *Gog en Magog in Ezechiël,* 1951; W. E. Barnes, "Two Trees Become One: Ezek XXXVII 16-17," *JThSt,* XXXIX (1938), 391-93; J. A. Bewer, "Das Tal der Wanderer in Hesekiel 39,11," *ZAW,* LVI (1938), 123-25; G. Gerleman, "Hesekielbokens Gog," *SEÅ,* XII (1947), 148-62; J. L. Myres, "Gog and the Danger from the North in Ezekiel," *PEFQSt,* LXIV (1932), 213-19; E. Riesenfeld, *The Resurrection in Ezekiel XXXVII and in the Dura-Europos Paintings,* 1948.

[29] A. Bertholet, *Hesekiels Verfassungsentwurf,* 1896; G. A. Cooke, "Some Considerations on the Text and Teaching of Ezekiel 40–48," *ZAW,* XLII (1924), 105-15; K. Elliger, "Die grossen Tempelsakristeien im Verfassungsentwurf des Ezechiel (42,1 ff.)," in *Alt-Festschrift,* 1953, pp. 79-103; W. R. Farmer, "The Geography of Ezekiel's River of Life," *BA,* XIX (1956), 17-22; H. Gese, *Der Verfassungsentwurf des Ezechiel (Kap. 40–48),* 1957; J. Jeremias, "Hesekieltempel und Serubbabeltempel," *ZAW,* LII (1934), 109-12.

[30] W. H. Brownlee, "The Scroll of Ezekiel from the Eleventh Qumran Cave," *RdQ,* IV (1963/64), 11-28.

[31] A. Klostermann, "Ezechiel," *ThStKr,* L (1877), 391-431.

with his dumbness (3:22 ff.) and his symbolic lying on his side (4:4-8), have been interpreted as symptoms of a more or less profound mental disturbance or illness in Ezekiel, with pathological features approaching those of schizophrenia.[32] That this suggestion is in error has been demonstrated several times with convincing arguments (Herrmann, Cooke, *et al.*). The striking phenomena are associated with symbolic actions and are symptoms of ecstasy.

Despite all the peculiarities of his style, Ezekiel's ideas are completely comprehensible. His thought processes do not differ from those of a healthy man. He does not invent incomprehensible neologisms; his sentences follow the rules of grammar, his ideas are connected logically with each other, their sequence yields a meaningful continuity. Probably, however, an extreme polarity can be observed in his nature. He is a sensitive ecstatic and yet thinks logically and systematically. He combines burning passion with pedantic casuistry, bold hopes for the future with a sober sense of reality. He speaks coldly and bluntly and yet feels full sympathy for the devout and the wicked, lamenting the judgment to come. In contrast to his creative intellectual power and his effortless rhetorical fluency stand his adherence to traditional concepts and formulas and the piling up of synonymous expressions, which give his style a dry, long-winded, and ponderous effect. In this polarity the internal unity of his personality is grounded in his experience and consciousness of being sent as a prophet.

8. *Ezekiel's message and its problems.* The problems posed by Ezekiel's preaching have long been suggested by the epithets often attached to him: the "father of Judaism" and the "father of apocalyptic." These titles identify him with the stream of priestly tradition and make him a harbinger of apocalyptic writing. The latter epithet is based on a misunderstanding of the Gog oracle in 38–39; Ezekiel exhibits nothing of apocalypticism. Observations of many kinds, however, seem to support the former title.

He has, for instance, been called both priest and prophet (Cooke); in many passages the interests of the man of priestly origin are uppermost (Herrmann) or the priest completely obscures the prophet (Procksch[33]). His theology has been called that of the Priestly Document (Haag) or of the priestly lawgiver in the Pentateuch (van den Born), and his preaching described as the prophetical radicalization and intensification of sacral law, with a massive irruption of legal structures into prophetical discourse (Zimmerli). Although above all else a prophet, he is rooted in the sacral traditions of the priesthood (von Rad [34]). In contrast to this view stands the opinion of Balla,[35] who considers Ezekiel to be dependent for the most part on the theology of Deuteronomy, whose mode of expression has left its stamp on his vocabulary.

A unique theory in extreme form is espoused by Reventlow, who takes as his

[32] B. Baentsch, "Pathologische Züge in Israels Prophetentum," *ZWTh,* L (1907), 52-81; Bertholet; F. Giesebrecht, *Die Berufsbegabung der alttestamentlichen Propheten,* 1897; K. Jaspers, "Der Prophet Ezechiel," in *Kurt Schneider-Festschrift,* 1947, pp. 77-85; Kraetzschmar; Pfeiffer*; Steuernagel*.

[33] O. Procksch, *Theologie des Alten Testaments,* 1950, pp. 305 ff.

[34] G. von Rad, *Theologie des Alten Testaments,* II, 1960 (4th ed., 1965), 237-38.

[35] E. Balla, *Die Botschaft der Propheten,* 1958, pp. 284-85.

point of departure the Holiness Code (§ 20.3), interpreted as the ritual for a cultic ceremony, with which the text of the book of Ezekiel has many points of contact. By means of an exclusively form-critical analysis, Reventlow seeks to demonstrate that Ezekiel's various rhetorical forms reflect the various aspects of an hypothetical "office" of prophet held by Ezekiel. This office is the direct continuation of the office of the functionary who pronounced blessings and curses at the Covenant Festival; the situation has changed, but the form remains the same. The man who holds this office, the prophet, is celebrating the sacred liturgy. The subject matter and form of his entire message are determined by the traditions of the Covenant Festival. The foundation for this hypothesis is not exactly secure. The Holiness Code can hardly be understood as a ritual for cultic recitation, and the almost universally recognized priestly glossing or revision of much of the text of Ezekiel can hardly be considered an original part of the prophet's words. Reventlow not only absolutizes the "covenant tradition" of Israel as the core of the OT, although it represents merely a single late component of a more comprehensive complex, but is also forced to slight the historical element and deny the contemporary significance of the prophets' words.

In contrast to the views described here, it is our task to comprehend the manifold and various relationships of Ezekiel to tradition and to the theology of his period.

Ezekiel is the first prophet to draw extensively on non-Israelite traditions, including not a few that were originally mythological. This tendency can frequently be observed after his time, so that the use of such traditions may be considered practically a mark of late origin. It is plainly based on a changed set of convictions, influenced if not actually brought about by the deportation and life in the diaspora. In addition to Canaanite and Phoenician material (16; 23; 28; 29:1 ff.), Ezekiel makes use particularly of Mesopotamian subject matter, images, cultic practices, and so forth (1–3:9; 9:1 ff.; 14:21; 16:23-24; 17:3-4; 21:26-27 [Eng. 21:21-22]; 28; 29; 31; 32; 34; 44:1-3; 47). In addition, he frequently draws upon ancient popular material for concepts, narratives, songs, and poems (14:12 ff.; 16; 17; 19; 21:13 ff. [Eng. 21:8 ff.]; 23; 26:19-21; 28; 31; 32:17-32) (Kuhl).

A second characteristic of Ezekiel is his increased emphasis on historical judgment, like that suggested in his reinterpretation of the image of Israel as a vine (15) and of the marriage between Yahweh and Israel (16). Above all he reinterprets the whole sweep of Israel's history (20:1-32), selecting, omitting, or adding certain motifs in order to show that even in Egypt the Israelites practiced idolatry, i.e., that they were sinful from the very beginning and remained disobedient and rebellious to the present day, despite the increasingly severe threats made by Yahweh and the measures taken by him. The influence of Israel's narrative traditions, however, is less than that of the mythological or popular traditions. From Israel's history Ezekiel borrowed primarily legendary motifs (14:12 ff.; 21:13 ff. [Eng. 21:8 ff.]; 26:19-21; 28:13; 31:9; 32:27) and the

Blessing of Jacob (Genesis 49; cf. Ezek. 15; 17:1-10; 19:1-9, 10-14; 21:32). In addition, he refers frequently to Amos, Hosea, Isaiah, and Micah.

Ezekiel's roots in the theology of his time are illustrated by his frequent points of contact with Jeremiah, on whom he may even be literarily dependent (Miller); with the theology of Deuteronomy in his interpretation of history, appreciation for the law, address to the individual, demand for cultic centralization, and criticism of the monarchy; with the priestly theology of the Holiness Code, despite the evident differences in style and content, so that both may derive from a preexilic Jerusalemite law code (§ 20.3); and with cultic concepts and practices, with which Ezekiel, who had been a priest, was doubtless familiar.

The crucial point of departure for Ezekiel, however, is his call experience, in which, despite the traditional view that God and his land belong together and that the former can be served only in the latter, he learns that God's presence is not restricted to a single place, that the believer may experience it wherever he may happen to live. This represents a fundamental break with tradition. It is no longer true that in one's native land encounter with God and real life are possible, while dwelling in a foreign land is like death; now life and death together lie in man's inward and outward conduct, wherever he may dwell and in whatever circumstances he lives.

Ezekiel is therefore not concerned with objective testimony to God's acts, but with proper conduct on the part of man and God's correlative reaction. Here every man is responsible for himself and must decide personally for his salvation or destruction (18:1-20; 33:1 ff.). The criterion is a man's conduct in the crucial moment in which God tests the individual, so that in actual practice the actions of every moment can determine God's judgment; man must therefore always be alert to exhortation and ready to repent (3:16*b*-21). Therefore the sins of the present, which correspond to the sins of history as a whole, weigh so heavy: they are abomination, i.e., the institutions and practices of idolatry, and bloodguilt and blasphemy, i.e., ethical and social offenses. They must of their own necessity lead to the threatened judgment of destruction, which Ezekiel sees carried out against Jerusalem in the fall of the city.

In the face of sin and judgment Ezekiel takes up the old prophetical exhortation to repent and return to Yahweh (18:30-31) and occasionally credits to human efforts the transformation he demands; he also, however, and more frequently, expects it as a consequence of God's redemptive action: as the forgiveness of the sin that man cannot blot out (36:25), as the renewal of the very core of life through a new heart that is no longer cold, unfeeling, and incapable of change (11:19-20; 36:26), and as the gift of God's spirit, which leads man to do God's will (11:19; 36:27). When he is redeemed and renewed, each man will be able as of his own accord to will and do what is right, in harmony with the divine commandments, so that God's will may be done on earth. All men together will constitute a community living in intimate fellowship not only with one another but also and above all with God (11:20; 36:28).

§ 61 Hosea

ATD: A. Weiser, 3rd ed., 1959; K. Elliger, 4th ed., 1959. BK: H. W. Wolff, 1961. BOT: D. Deden, 1953-56. COT: C. van Gelderen and W. H. Gispen, 1953; G. C. Aalders, 1958. HAT: T. H. Robinson and F. Horst, 2nd ed., 1954. HK: W. Nowack, 3rd ed., 1922. HS: J. Lippl and J. Theis, 1937; H. Junker, 1938. IB: J. Mauchline, J. A. Thompson, H. E. W. Fosbroke, J. D. Smart, R. E. Wolfe, C. L. Taylor, Jr., D. W. Thomas, R. C. Dentan, 1956. ICC: W. R. Harper, G. A. Smith, W. H. Ward, J. A. Bewer, H. G. Mitchell, 1905-12, reprinted 1948-53. KAT: E. Sellin, 2nd and 3rd ed., 1929-30. KeH: F. Hitzig and H. Steiner, 4th ed., 1881. KHC: K. Marti, 1904. SAT: H. Gressmann, 2nd ed., 1921; H. Schmidt, 2nd ed., 1923. M. Haller, 2nd ed., 1925. SZ: C. von Orelli, 3rd ed., 1908. Individual commentaries: B. Duhm, 1910 and in *ZAW*, XXXI (1911), 1-43, 81-110, 161-204; T. Laetsch, 1956; B. M. Vellas, 1949-50; J. Wellhausen, 4th ed., 1963.

A. Allwohn, *Die Ehe des Propheten Hosea in psychoanalytischer Beleuchtung*, 1926; R. Bach, *Die Erwählung Israels in der Wüste*, Dissertation, Bonn, 1952; L. W. Batten, "Hosea's Message and Marriage," *JBL*, XLVIII (1929), 257-73; E. Baumann, " 'Wissen um Gott' bei Hosea als Urform von Theologie?" *EvTh*, XV (1955), 416-25; W. Baumgartner, *Kennen Amos und Hosea eine Heilseschatologie?* 1913; F. Buck, *Die Liebe Gottes beim Propheten Osee*, 1953; K. Budde, "Der Abschnitt Hosea 1–3," *ThStKr*, XCVI/XCVII (1925), 1-89; *idem*, "Zu Text und Auslegung des Buches Hosea," *JBL*, XLV (1926), 280-97; *JPOS*, XIV (1934), 1-41; *JBL*, LIII (1934), 118-33; *idem*, "Hosea 1 und 3," *ThBl*, XIII (1934), 337-42; M. J. Buss, *A Form-Critical Study in the Book of Hosea with Special Attention to Method*, Dissertation, Yale University, 1958; G. Farr, "The Concept of Grace in the Book of Hosea," *ZAW*, LXX (1958), 98-107; G. Fohrer, "Umkehr und Erlösung beim Propheten Hosea," *ThZ*, XI (1955), 161-85; H. Frey, "Der Aufbau der Gedichte Hoseas," *WuD*, V (1957), 9-103; H. L. Ginsberg, "Studies in Hosea 1–3," in *Kaufmann Jubilee Volume*, 1960, pp. 50-69; R. Gordis, "Hosea's Marriage and Message: A New Approach," *HUCA*, XXV (1954), 9-35; A. Heermann, "Ehe und Kinder des Propheten Hosea," *ZAW*, XL (1922), 287-312; P. Humbert, "Les trois premiers chapitres d'Osée," *RHR*, LXXVII (1918), 157-71; *idem*, "Osée le prophète bedouin," *RHPhR*, I (1921), 97-118; E. Jacob, "L'héritage cananéen dans le livre du prophète Osée," *ibid.*, XLIII (1963), 250-59; J. Lindblom, *Hosea, literarisch untersucht*, 1927; J. L. McKenzie, "Knowledge of God in Hosea," *JBL*, LXXIV (1955), 22-27; H. S. Nyberg, "Das textkritische Problem des Alten Testaments am Hoseabuch demonstriert," *ZAW*, LII (1934), 241-54; *idem*, *Studien zum Hoseabuch*, 1935; *idem*, *Hoseaboken*, 1941; G. Östborn, *Yahwe and Baal*, 1956; J. Rieger, *Die Bedeutung der Geschichte für die Verkündigung des Amos und Hosea*, 1929; T. H. Robinson, "Die Ehe des Hosea," *ThStKr*, CVI (1934/35), 301-13; H. H. Rowley, "The Marriage of Hosea," *BJRL*, XXXIX (1956/57), 200-33; H. Schmidt, "Die Ehe des Hosea," *ZAW*, XLII (1924), 245-72; E. Sellin, "Die geschichtliche Orientierung der Prophetie des Hosea," *NkZ*, XXXVI (1925), 607-58, 807; N. H. Snaith, *Mercy and Sacrifice*, 1953; W. F. Stinespring, "Hosea, The Prophet of Doom," *Crozer Quarterly*, XXVII (1950), 200-207; D. A. Tushingham, "A Reconsideration of Hosea, Chapters 1–3," *JNES*, XII (1953), 150-59; R. Vuilleumier, *La tradition cultuelle d'Israël dans la prophétie d'Amos et d'Osée*, 1960; L. Waterman, "Hosea, Chapters 1–3, in Retrospect and Prospect," *JNES*, XIV (1955), 100-109; H. W. Wolff, " 'Wissen um Gott' bei Hosea als Urform von Theologie," *EvTh*, XII (1952/53),

533-54; *idem*, "Erkenntnis Gottes im Alten Testament," *ibid.*, XV (1955), 426-31; *idem*, "Hoseas geistige Heimat," *ThLZ*, LXXXI (1956), 83-94; cf. also the bibliographies in FOHRER, *ThR*, NF XIX, XX, and XXVIII (§ 52).

1. *Hosea's personal situation.* Concerning Hosea's personal situation, we learn only the name of his father Beeri and what chapters 1 and 3 tell us of his marital life and his children. This is not so much because the message he was commissioned to deliver relegates the biographical element to the background as because the later Judean transmission of his words was not interested in the details of his life. He was active in Northern Israel and probably dwelt there. There is no reason to assume from the images of nature and animals he employs that he was a farmer and cattle breeder (Sellin), from his knowledge of the priestly milieu (4:1 ff.; 5:1 ff.) that he was a priest (Duhm), or from the taunt in 9:7 that he belonged to a guild of nebiim (Eissfeldt*; Sellin-Rost*). He was, however, a member of the intelligentsia, as his knowledge of the past, his judgment upon history and the present, and his mode of expression all show (T. H. Robinson). When we also note the way wisdom has influenced his language, we may conclude that he was educated in a wisdom school, which served primarily for the training of royal officials.

Hosea was very early aware of his call to be a prophet, since his marriage (1:2-3) probably took place, as was customary, when he was a young man, and his activity as a prophet lasts more than three decades. It began while the dynasty of Jehu was still on the throne, as is shown by the threat in 1:4 as well as by the superscription (1:1), with its reference to Jeroboam II (786/82–753/46), followed by his son Zechariah, who was soon murdered. The additional mention of the four kings of Judah, which is a later addition, is intended to make Hosea a contemporary of Isaiah. His activity continued long after the end of the dynasty of Jehu. He experienced the period of internal strife and royal assassinations (7:7; 8:4), the Syro-Ephraimite War (5:8 ff.), and the foreign ambitions of Hoshea, the last king (7:11-12; 12:2 [Eng. 12:1]), but obviously not the fall of Samaria and the dissolution of the Northern Kingdom. We may therefore date the period of his activity roughly between 755/750 and 725. He probably carried out his ministry mostly in Samaria, and on occasion at a sanctuary like Bethel or Gilgal.

2. *Hosea's wife and children.* The most discussed and disputed problem is that of Hosea's marriage and children, as reported in chapters 1 and 3. According to the third-person report in 1, Hosea is to marry an *'ēšet zᵉnûnîm* ("unchaste woman") named Gomer bat Diblaim and have children by her, who are to receive the symbolic names "Jezreel," "Not pitied," and "Not my people." According to the first-person report in 3, the prophet is to marry *again*—an adulteress, whom he is to keep shut up for a long time, not even visiting her himself. The very impropriety of this description has led to various interpretations; the prophet could not possibly have married an unchaste woman, as Jerome explains, *quia si fiat turpissimum est.* The different theories can be classified into several basic types.

a) The report in chapter 1 is understood in the following ways: (1) It is to be interpreted allegorically (Gressmann, Young,[1] *et al.*), so that it does not report a real marriage, but is instead the literary form given to a threat. (2) It reports a real event, but deletions are made from the text so as to free Gomer from all reproach (Hosea married a woman who bore him children: Hölscher[2]) or the text is not taken literally, so that the prophet married a blameless woman who later became unfaithful to him (Wellhausen). (3) It reports a real marriage with an unchaste woman entered into by Hosea deliberately and with full awareness (Heermann, van den Born,[3] *et al.*); the account has occasionally been romantically elaborated in remarkable fashion (Gunkel[4]) or explained psychoanalytically (Allwohn, Sellers[5]).

b) The report in chapter 3 is understood in the following ways: (1) It is to be interpreted allegorically, perhaps as an allegorical parallel to chapter 1 (Humbert, Gressmann, May,[6] *et al.*). (2) It is a parallel account to chapter 1, to be understood literally, in which Hosea himself depicts what someone else describes in chapter 1 (Lindblom, Mowinckel,[7] Gordis: a second revelation). (3) It is considered a later addition because its message is that of promise (Hölscher, Batten, Stinespring).

c) Most frequently 1 and 3 are taken together and, along with 2, viewed as a continuous narrative (particularly by Budde and H. Schmidt), or else 1 and 3 are considered reports of two stages in a lengthy series of events (Eissfeldt*). In this view the "marriage story" of Hosea, as it has occasionally been called, deals with one and the same woman, Gomer, who became unfaithful to the prophet some time after their marriage, came into someone else's possession either by running away or through divorce, but is finally bought back by Hosea so that she may reform. On the basis of the assumption that Canaanite rites of initiation were practiced at the sanctuaries of Yahweh and that Hosea's wife submitted to them, while the prophet himself only gradually came to recognize the impiousness of this practice (Sellin-Rost*), Wolff has extended the rites so as to have them apply to all marriageable Israelite girls and turned the narrative into a kind of theological marriage story with a symbolic and allegorical meaning. Rudolph has attacked this theory.[8]

Arguments against the allegorical interpretation of chapter 1 include the impossibility of understanding the name "Gomer" allegorically and the use of symbolic names in Isa. 7:3; 8:1-4. The clear and unambiguous wording of the text argues against the various qualifications that have been suggested, as does the damage to the meter brought about by arbitrary deletions. Arguments

[1] Young*, pp. 245-46.

[2] G. Hölscher, *Geschichte der israelitischen und jüdischen Religion,* 1922, p. 106.

[3] A. van den Born, *De symbolische handelingen der Oud-Testamentische profeten,* 1935, pp. 52-53.

[4] H. Gunkel, "Hosea," *RGG,* 2nd ed., 1928, II, pp. 20-21 ff.

[5] O. Sellers, "Hosea's Motives," *AJSL,* XLI (1924/25), 243-47.

[6] H. G. May, "An Interpretation of the Names of Hosea's Children," *JBL,* LV (1936), 285-91.

[7] S. Mowinckel in *Det Gamle Testamentet,* III, 1944, pp. 576-77.

[8] W. Rudolph, "Präparierte Jungfrauen?" *ZAW,* LXXV (1963), 65-73.

against the allegorical interpretation of chapter 3 include its autobiographical style and the impossibility of understanding the price stated in verse 2 allegorically. The view that chapter 3 is intended as a concrete parallel to chapter 1 founders on the necessity for arbitrary emendations and the absolute contradiction between 1:3, which speaks of begetting children, and 3:3, which speaks of the woman's complete seclusion. The occurrence of optimistic utterances elsewhere in Hosea indicates that chapter 3 should not be omitted as a later addition. The juxtaposition of both reports to form a more or less detailed story of Hosea's marriage founders on the clear statement in 1:2 that the woman was already unchaste, the lack of any evidence for a terrible experience in the course of Hosea's marriage or for Gomer's having run away or been divorced, the differing style of the reports, and the clear introduction of a second woman in 3:1.

d) We may therefore assume that chapters 1 and 3 recount two marriages of Hosea to two different women.[9] In actual fact, he first married a prostitute, probably a temple prostitute (H. Schmidt, T. H. Robinson, *et al.*), and had children by her, to whom he gave symbolic names in order to announce the future destiny of Israel; in effect, he performed a large-scale symbolic action. At a later date he entered into a second marriage with another woman (Duhm, Heermann, van den Born, Vriezen[10])—once again a symbolic action, announcing this time not Yahweh's destroying judgment but a different course of action. While the first marriage and the naming of the children inaugurate Hosea's activity (as can be seen both from their significance and from the introduction in 1:2), the second marriage took place toward the end of his activity, in the setting of his incipient message of salvation. The contrast between the two shows how a prophet of judgment can turn into a prophet of hope and deliverance. This does not enable us to distinguish well-defined periods in Hosea's ministry, but does suggest a gradual change in his message.

3. *Sayings*. In addition to the two reports in chapters 1 and 3, numerous sayings from Hosea's preaching are preserved, more frequently in the first person, with Yahweh speaking, than as the prophet's words with Yahweh referred to in the third person. In the occasional use of legal forms and motifs and in the influence of educational wisdom, with its abundance of images and metaphors applied to Yahweh and Israel, we can trace Hosea's antecedents. The limits of the individual sayings are difficult to determine, however, because there are often no introductory or concluding formulas. Scholarly opinion has therefore vacillated between the assumption of numerous very short sayings (T. H. Robinson) and that of larger units (Eissfeldt*, Frey).

Recently Wolff has assumed the presence of "kerygmatic units," i.e., series of sayings all originating on the same occasion when Hosea was preaching and immediately assembled as "scenes." Between the sayings we are to imagine either objections on the part of listeners or a turning of the prophet's attention

[9] We are not, however, dealing with two simultaneous marriages (J. M. P. Smith, *The Prophets and their Times*, 2nd ed., 1941, pp. 70-76) or with the rehabilitation of a prostitute in addition to marriage (Pfeiffer*).

[10] Vriezen* (1948).

to another group among those present. The meaning of these "kerygmatic units," however, is not really clear: while 4:4-19[11] and 5:1-7[12] are termed scenes, 2:4-17 (Eng. 2:2-15), despite the unity of the situation, is said to be a loose structure of various sayings and 2:18-25 (Eng. 2:16-23) a free series of sayings and fragments, but at the same time a real unit. At a more basic level the question remains whether we should assume "scenes" in which the prophet appears at all, or whether we are not instead dealing with collections of individual sayings from various periods and situations, assembled on the basis of catchwords or subject matter. The example of other prophetical books suggests that the latter view is more likely.

The hypothesis that denies Hosea's authorship of all or most of the optimistic oracles (Marti, Stinespring) cannot be sustained in this form; while 2:1-3 (Eng. 1:10–2:1) surely does not derive from Hosea,[13] most of these oracles are shown by their style and content to be Hoseanic. Neither is it possible to deny Hosea all the references to Judah (Nowack, Marti); the book of Hosea did undergo a Judahite redaction that added the word "Judah" quite frequently, but in 5:8-14 the reference to the Syro-Ephraimite War suggests that Judah was mentioned from the beginning.

The sayings of Hosea, many of which have a very corrupt text, may be classified into literary types as follows. The units are in most cases quite small.

Threat: 5:8-9; 9:7*a*, 11-13, 14; 11:10; 13:9-11; 13:14, 15; 14:1 (Eng. 13:16)
Threat with motivation: 2:10-11, 13 + 15 (Eng. 2:8-9, 11 + 13); 4:4-6; 5:10; 7:1-2, 13*a*; 8:1-3, 7-10; 10:6*b*-8, 9-10, 13*b*-15; 12:11-12
Invective and threat: 4:7-10, 16-19; 5:1-2, 12-14; 7:11-12; 8:4*b*-6, 11-13; 9:1-6, 9, 15-17; 10:1-2; 11:1-7; 13:1-3, 5-8
Invective: 4:12-14; 5:3-4, 6-7; 6:7-11; 7:3-6, 7, 8-9, 15-16; 8:4*a*; 9:8, 10; 10:5-6*a*; 12:2, 8-9; 13:12-13
Exhortation: 10:12-13*a*; 13:4; (with conditional threat) 2:4-5 (Eng. 2:2-3)
Prophetical judgment discourse: 4:1-2
Historical sayings: 5:11; 10:11; 12:3-7, 13-15
Prophetical liturgy: 5:15–6:6; 14:2-9
Disputation: 9:7*b*; 10:3-4
Promise: 2:16-17, 18-19 + 21-22, 20, 23-25 (Eng. 2:14-15, 16-17 + 19-20, 18, 21-23); 11:8-9; 12:10
Later additions, apart from minor glosses, include: 2:1-3, 6-7, 8-9, 12, 14 (Eng. 1:10–2:1; 2:4-5, 6-7, 10, 12); 4:15; 5:5; 7:13*b*-14; 11:11; 12:1; 14:10 (Eng. 14:9).

4. *Transmission.* As the first-person report in chapter 3 shows, Hosea himself had a hand in the writing down of his sayings and reports. We may assume that

[11] H. Junker, "Textkritische, formkritische und traditionskritische Untersuchungen zu Os 4,1-10," *BZ*, NF IV (196), 165-85; N. Lohfink, "Zu Text und Form von Os 4,4-5," *Bibl*, XLII (1961), 303-32; L. Rost, "Erwägungen zu Hosea 4,13 f.," in *Bertholet-Festschrift*, 1950, pp. 451-60; I. Zolli, "Hosea 4,17-18," *ZAW*, LVI (1938), 175.

[12] K. Elliger, "Eine verkannte Kunstform bei Hosea," *ZAW*, LXIX (1957), 151-60.

[13] For a different view, see H. W. Wolff, "Der grosse Jesreeltag," *EvTh*, XII (1952/53), 78-104 (= *Gesammelte Studien zum Alten Testament*, 1964, pp. 151-81).

they were all put in written form soon after their oral proclamation and were rescued after the fall of the Northern Kingdom by being brought to Judah. This means that Hosea is the only North Israelite prophet whose own traditional material was preserved.

Chapters 1–3 constitute a minor collection of sayings and reports of symbolic actions and are therefore not a single literary unit (Budde) or a collection of memoirs (Wolff). The third-person account (1:2-9) of the first marriage and the naming of the children, which may go back to Hosea himself despite its style, is placed at the beginning, as is chronologically correct. It corresponds to the report of the second marriage (3), which derives from the end of Hosea's ministry. In chapter 2[14] appropriate utterances have been inserted, first of a threatening (2:4-15* [Eng. 2:2-13*]), then of a promising, nature (2:16-25 [Eng. 2:14-23]), so that the collection contrasts the two stages of the prophet's message: threat of disaster at the beginning, promise of salvation at the end.

Chapters 4–14 now constitute a large collection of sayings, most involving invective and threat, which focus on the two major themes of Hosea's polemic: criticism of the cult, especially the Canaanite cult or its influence; and criticism of the monarchy, with its policies based on human power. The whole corpus appears to be made up of several smaller collections arranged according to catchwords or similarity of subject matter. Thus sayings from the period of the Syro-Ephraimite War are brought together (5:8-14),[15] as are sayings that refer to the early history of Israel (12).[16] As a result of the complete fusion of the sections, however, such details are more suggestive than clearly observable. In any case, this collection does not go back to Hosea.

Eissfeldt* finds brought together in 4–9:9 sayings directed against the cult and political injustice and in 9:10–14:10 (Eng. 14:9) sayings that through historical retrospect derive Israel's sinfulness from its past. Wolff, on the other hand, distinguishes two complexes of traditions, 4–11 and 12–14, each consisting of several "scenes." The second of these complexes, according to Wolff, comes from the last days of the Northern Kingdom under Shalmaneser V.

After the fall of the Northern Kingdom, adherents or friends of the prophet—there is no reason to speak of students or disciples—were able to see to it that the traditional material, probably still in the form of individual collections, was brought to Judah. There this material was brought together, probably in the preexilic period, as the interpolation "and David their king" in 3:5 suggests, and

[14] C. H. Gordon, "Hos 2,4-5 in the Light of New Semitic Inscriptions," *ZAW*, LIV (1936), 277-80; P. Humbert, "La logique de la perspective nomade chez Osée et l'unité d'Osée 2,4-22," in BZAW, XLI (1925), 158-66; C. Kuhl, "Neue Dokumente zum Verständnis von Hosea 2,4-15," *ZAW*, LII (1934), 102-9.

[15] A. Alt, "Hosea 5,8–6,6, ein Krieg und seine Folgen in prophetischer Beleuchtung," *NkZ*, XXX (1919), 537-68 (= *Kleine Schriften*, II [1953], 163-87).

[16] P. R. Ackroyd, "Hosea and Jacob," *VT*, XIII (1963), 245-59; M. Gertner, "An Attempt at an Interpretation of Hosea XII," *ibid.*, X (1960), 272-84; H. L. Ginsberg, "Hosea's Ephraim, more Fool than Knave," *JBL*, LXXX (1961), 339-47; E. Jacob, "La femme et le prophète," in *Hommage Vischer*, 1960, pp. 83-87; T. C. Vriezen, "Hosea 12," *NThSt*, XXIV (1941), 144-49; *idem*, "La tradition de Jacob dans Osée 12," *OTS*, I (1942), 64-78.

subjected to a Judahite recension (cf. 1:7; 4:15; 5:5). This most likely took place in the Deuteronomic period, with its delight in written records, during which Jeremiah's scroll also came into being; this explains the occasional Deuteronomistic tone as a result of the redaction. The final editing took place in the exilic or early postexilic period. From this last redaction comes the concluding utterance (14:10 [Eng. 14:9]), a wisdom aphorism, which shows that the book was preserved, despite the disappearance of interest in the former Northern Kingdom of Israel, as an instructive document of Yahweh's governance in the fate of the devout and the apostate.

5. *Message*. In many respects Snaith has accurately characterized the prophet and his message: Hosea's personal experience of God as the ultimate basis of life gives rise on the one hand to his view of religion as a personal relationship to God and fellowship with him, and on the other to his severe condemnation of sin and threat of judgment. He is nevertheless aware of a hope for salvation, whose content can be described best in terms of righteousness and justice, steadfast love and mercy (2:21 [Eng. 2:19]).

For Hosea's spiritual and traditional roots, however, we find a motley array of suggestions. On the one hand, his criticism of his milieu has been derived from a nomadic ideal (Humbert, *et al.*), although he does not look upon the desert period as an ideal in itself, but as the time of the first love between Yahweh and Israel. He has been seen as taking a severely anti-Canaanite stance (Östborn), as engaged in "homeopathic" borrowing of Canaanite elements to transform them in the service of Yahwism (Jacob), or as being closely related to Levitical and early Deuteronomic circles (Wolff). Hosea the prophet has been looked upon as a politician, first demanding the subordination of Israel to the house of David and finally expecting the unification of the entire nation under a single ruler (Caquot), as a whole-hearted adherent of the cult, who seeks only to do away with cultic deviations and abuses (Vuilleumier), or as a preacher basing his concept of Yahweh's love, for example, on an ancient covenant tradition (Moran, Lohfink).[17] Bach claims to have found in Hosea an otherwise unknown tradition of how Yahweh found Israel in the desert.

Like the other prophets of the period before Jeremiah, Hosea is unfamiliar with any covenant theology. The few occasions when the word "covenant" appears do not refer to any relationship between Yahweh and Israel.[18] Hos. 1:9 contains only a vague anticipation of the later association formula.[19] To describe the relationship between Yahweh and Israel, Hosea, like the young Jeremiah after him, uses instead images and metaphors drawn from family life and from the world of plants and animals. The Israelites are Yahweh's sons, whom he as a father called out of Egypt (11:1 ff.); the relationship between Yahweh and Israel is a marriage relationship (1:2 ff.; 2:18 [Eng. 2:16]; 3). In 1:2 the

[17] N. Lohfink, "Hate and Love in Osee 9,15," *CBQ*, XXV (1963), 417; W. L. Moran, "The Ancient Near Eastern Background of the Love of God in Deuteronomy," *ibid.*, pp. 77-87.

[18] Hos. 2:20 refers to the establishment of a relationship with the animals; 6:7 and 10:4, to a covenant between the king and his people; 12:2, to a foreign treaty; 8:1 is secondary.

[19] R. Smend, *Die Bundesformel*, 1963.

nature imagery is so strong that the land itself and not the people in it is described as Yahweh's wife. Hosea derives this relationship, which begins with the deliverance from Egypt (12:10; 13:4), not from the concept of election, but, in agreement with the personal relationship he presupposes, from God's love (11:1). The pure relationship of the desert and Mosaic period (9:10) ceased upon acquaintance with the Baal cult and civilized prosperity (9:10; 11:1-2; 13:5-8). Despite the warnings of the prophets and the word of Yahweh (6:5), the nation has rebelled against Yahweh throughout its entire history down to the present day (1:4; 9:9; 10:9)—worthy offspring of Jacob, depicted as their malicious prototype (12:3-7). Thus at first Hosea sees only sin yielding to judgment: destruction like that of Admah and Zeboiim (11:8) or annulment of the exodus and a new period of captivity (9:1-6; 11:1-7).

At first Hosea sees a possibility of deliverance in repentance and return to Yahweh (5:15–6:6),[20] which will result in God's grace and mercy (10:12-13*a*; 14:2-9 [Eng. 14:1-8]). But he comes to see that man cannot deliver himself from the disaster he has brought upon himself (5:3-4; 13:12-13); his sin and guilt represent a barrier even to God (6:11*b*–7:2). At this point Hosea ventures a crucial step toward belief in redemption (Fohrer). God's gracious mercy does not become effective only after the repentance and return that man must accomplish; it is instead the active principle, which human decision and action must follow and respond to. This belief in redemption makes its appearance in 12:10 and 3; in the return to the pre-Palestinian situation Israel will return quite concretely to the sources of its faith, in order to make a new beginning. Yahweh will woo Israel so that Israel will allow itself to be helped, and then lead Israel back to Palestine so that, as in the days of its youth, it may live in intimate and lasting fellowship with God[21] (2:16-25 [Eng. 2:14-23]). At the beginning of Hosea's preaching the curse is upon the apostate nation, threatened with destruction on account of its sin (1:2-9); at the end the curse is transformed into a blessing (2:23-25 [Eng. 2:21-23]), based on the redemptive grace of God, who has made it possible for Israel to be totally transformed.

§ 62 Joel

Cf. commentaries in § 61; individual commentaries: M. Bič, 1960; B. Kutal, 1932; G. M. Rinaldi, 1938.

G. Amon, *Die Abfassungszeit des Buches Joel,* Dissertation, Würzburg, 1942; J. Bourke, "Le jour de Yahvé dans Joël," *RB,* LVI (1959), 5-31, 191-212; W. Cannon, " 'The Day of the Lord' in Joel," *ChQR,* CIII (1927), 32-63; L. Dennefeld,

[20] F. König, "Die Auferstehungshoffnung bei Osee 6,1-3," *ZKTh,* LXX (1948), 94-100; H. Schmidt, "Hosea 6,1-6," in *Sellin-Festschrift,* 1927, pp. 111-26; J. J. Stamm, "Eine Erwägung zu Hos 6,1-2," *ZAW,* LVII (1939), 266-68.

[21] For this concept Hosea uses the phrase *daʿat 'ĕlōhîm;* cf. E. Baumann, " 'Wissen um Gott' bei Hosea als Urform der Theologie?" *EvTh,* XV (1955), 416-25; W. Eichrodt, " 'The Holy One in Your Midst'," *Interpr,* XV (1961), 259-73; for a different view, cf. H. W. Wolff, " 'Wissen um Gott' bei Hosea als Urform der Theologie," *EvTh,* XII (1952/53), 533-54; cf. also XV (1955), 426-31.

Les problèmes du livre de Joël, 1926; H. Holzinger, "Sprachcharakter und Abfassungszeit des Buches Joel," *ZAW*, IX (1889), 89-131; K. Jensen, "Inledningsspörgmaal i Joels bog," *DTT*, IV (1941), 98-112; A. Jepsen, "Kleine Beiträge zum Zwölfprophetenbuch I," *ZAW*, LVI (1938), 85-96; A. S. Kapelrud, *Joel Studies*, 1948; H. J. Kritzinger, *Die profesie van Joël*, 1935; E. O. A. Merx, *Die Prophetie des Joel und ihre Ausleger von den ältesten Zeiten bis zu den Reformatoren*, 1879; J. M. Myers, "Some Considerations Bearing on the Date of Joel," *ZAW*, LXXIV (1962), 177-95; O. Plöger, *Theokratie und Eschatologies*, 2nd ed., 1962; M. Treves, "The Date of Joel," *VT*, VII (1957), 149-56; cf. also the bibliographies in Fohrer, *ThR*, NF XIX, XX, and XXVIII (§ 52).

1. *Joel.* The superscription (1:1) gives us only the prophet's name: Joel, the son of Pethuel. The manner, place, and date of his activity, as well as the origin of the book, must be deduced from the book itself. The Masoretic text divides it appropriately into four chapters; the LXX and Vulgate, followed by the English translations, group chapters 2 and 3 of the Hebrew together as chapter 2, while Luther groups 3 and 4 together as chapter 3.[1] The subject matter of the book deals with three themes: chapters 1 and 2 describe a plague of locusts and a drought, both interpreted as signs of the imminent Day of Yahweh. Joel twice summons the community to a general day of penance to put an end to the catastrophes; oracles from Yahweh promise future deliverance to the people. Chapter 3 (Eng. 2:28-32) promises the pouring out of Yahweh's spirit upon the entire population of Judah, including the slaves. Chapter 4 (Eng. 3) announces the final judgment upon all nations, who are summoned to the valley of Jehoshaphat, but protection and fecundity for Judah and Jerusalem.

2. *Interpretation of chapters 1–2.* The first problem raised by the material preserved in the book of Joel is that of the significance of chapters 1 and 2 (Eng. 1–2:27).[2] Are we dealing here with apocalyptic imagery and the announcement of future events or with the description of a past or present situation?

Earlier the former view was dominant (Merx, *et al.*); the latter, however, has more and more come to be accepted (Wellhausen, Nowack, Marti, Sellin, Robinson, Eissfeldt*, Weiser*, *et al.*). Since the utterances concerning the Day of Yahweh (1:15; 2:1-2, 11), which certainly announce a future event, appear to contradict this latter theory, Duhm, Robinson, *et al.* have eliminated these verses or partial verses as later additions based on 3–4 (Eng. 2:28–3:21). Wolff has recently suggested a middle course between the two basic views, making 1:4-20 refer to an economic catastrophe that has already taken place and 2:1-17 refer to a coming, final catastrophe that will befall Jerusalem.

It is clear that chapter 1 is not speaking of the future but of an event that has just taken place and whose effects are still felt. This holds true for chapter 2

[1] E. Nestle, "Miscellen I. Zur Kapiteleinteilung in Joel," *ZAW*, XXIV (1904), 122-27.

[2] W. Baumgärtner, "Joel 1 und 2," in BZAW, XXXIV (1920), 10-19; K. Budde, " 'Der von Norden' in Joel 2,20," *OLZ*, XXII (1919), 1-5; E. Kutsch, "Heuschreckenplage und Tag Jahwes in Joel 1 und 2," *ThZ*, VIII (1962), 81-94; M. Plath, "Joel 1,15-20," *ZAW*, XLVII (1929), 159-60.

as well; 2:1-17 cannot be viewed in isolation, and its Hebrew imperfects have present meaning. The whole section clearly bears the marks of an exciting experience, as language, imagery, and tone show (Weiser*). The liturgical framework and style form a striking contrast. In particular, two peculiarities may be noted:

The present distress is depicted in 1:5-20 as a plague of locusts[3] coupled with a drought, but in 2, where the imagery of the Day of Yahweh is used, as a plague of locusts alone. This suggests a certain difference between 1 and 2, which seem to refer to separate events. This impression is reinforced by the repeated summons to proclaim a day of penance.

A second difference exists with respect to the references made to the Day of Yahweh and the resulting eschatological interpretation of the events. While 1:15, the only mention of the Day of Yahweh in chapter 1, turns out to be a later addition, the verses in chapter 2 mentioning the Day of Yahweh are firmly linked to their context and cannot be eliminated. This reinforces the impression that 1 and 2 refer to two different events, the second of which, a plague of locusts, was interpreted from the very outset as the harbinger or beginning of the Day of Yahweh.

3. *Unity of the book.* The second problem of the Joel tradition is that of the book's unity, more concretely, of the relationship between chapters 1–2 (Eng. 1:1–2:27) and 3–4 (Eng. 2:28–3:21). Earlier interpreters, without giving the matter much thought, considered the book a unity on the assumption that the whole was a prophecy concerning the future. This view has in part been replaced by a division into two sections, in part accepted in a modified form on a different basis. In addition, as a middle course, we find the assumption of unity of authorship.

a) Duhm[4] especially questioned the unity of the book, seeing in 1–2 (Eng. 1–2:27) a poet's description of a swarm of attacking locusts and in 3–4 (Eng. 2:28–3:21) an eschatological exposition by a synagogue preacher of the Maccabean period, who also interpolated the references to the Day of Yahweh in 1–2. With several variations, many scholars adopted this assumption of a two-stage composition of the book: Oesterley-Robinson*, 1–2 from the postexilic period, 3–4 about 200; Robinson, several independent utterances in 1–2 from the period following the fourth century, 3–4 in part later, not brought together before the third century; Jepsen, a basic stratum of three sections in 1–4, dating from the exilic period, supplemented and expanded by an apocalypticist; Sellin-Rost*, 1–2 dating from the fifth century, 3–4 from about 380 in its present form. Plöger assumes three stages in the growth of the book: a later record, somewhat exaggerated, of Joel's oral preaching (1–2), a section to guarantee the eschatological interpretation of the Day of Yahweh (4), and a further section (3) in support of the eschatological faith (originating in a sectarian group).

b) Apart from a more or less casual retention of the unity of the book like

[3] O. R. Sellers, "Stages of Locust in Joel," *AJSL* LII (1935/36), 81-85; J. A. Thompson, "Joel's Locusts in the Light of Near Eastern Parallels," *JNES*, XIV (1955), 52-55.

[4] B. Duhm, "Anmerkungen zu den Zwölf Propheten, X. Buch Joel," *ZAW*, XXXI (1911), 184-88.

that of Bič and the reservations frequently expressed concerning its division, we may single out for special mention two attempts to provide a new basis for the book's unity. Kapelrud considers the book the liturgy of a cult prophet at the Jerusalem Temple on the occasion of a plague of locusts, structured after the ritual of the New Year's Enthronement Festival and drawing freely upon the ideas and language of the fertility cult. Wolff considers it an artfully and symmetrically structured literary work, in which lament (1:4-20) corresponds to promise (2:21-27), announcement of catastrophe (2:1-11) to promise of better days (4:1-3, 9-17 [Eng. 3:1-3, 9-17]), and summons to repentance (2:12-17) to promise of an outpouring of the Spirit (3 [Eng. 2:28-32]).

c) Weiser* maintains unity of authorship; according to him, Joel wrote down his words after the plagues and added the apocalyptic prophecy in 3–4 (Eng. 3). Bourke proposes a similar theory, according to which the first section, cultic and liturgical, was linked to the second by Joel by means of 2:18-27, so that in 1–2 Joel used the concept of the Day of Yahweh historically and in 3–4 eschatologically.

In fact, both style and language, as well as a similar dependence on other prophets in 1–2 and 4, suggest a single author. To this extent we may agree with the reservations concerning a division of the book. But just as 1 and 2 seem to refer to different events, so 3 and 4 seem to treat yet other themes, all held together by the catchword "Day of Yahweh" in 2–4, since 1:15 should be eliminated as a later addition. This argues against the assumption of a literary or cultic unity to be found in the book. Finally, chapter 3 (Eng. 2:28-32) does not constitute an independent section, but itself consists of three fragments (3:1-2, 3-4, 5 [Eng. 2:28-29, 30-31, 32]) that represent a later addition to the prophecy of Joel (a similar view is held by Robinson[5]). There is general agreement that the invective and threat in 4:4-8 (Eng. 3:4-8) is a later interpolation.

In short, the material of the Joel tradition comprises three originally independent sections that preserve words spoken by the prophet in Jerusalem on different occasions, quite likely in chronological order. The first unit, chapter 1, comprises Joel's sayings on the occasion of a plague of locusts and a drought:

1:2-4 Unprecedented plague
1:5-14 Summons to proclaim a day of penance
1:16-20 Lament and prayer preceding the day of penance or spoken by the prophet in the course of it

The second unit, chapter 2, comprises sayings on the occasion of another plague of locusts, which is now interpreted as a sign of the Day of Yahweh:

2:1-11 Description of the plague
2:12-14 Summons to repentance
2:15-18 Summons to proclaim a day of penance
2:19-20 Favorable oracle of Yahweh

[5] Robinson finds two fragments: vss. 1-2, 3-5.

2:21-24 Thanksgiving
2:25-27 Oracle of promise

The first three sections therefore precede the day of penance; the last three were spoken on it in response of the people's lament.

At a later date Joel expatiated on the eschatological ideas hinted at in chapter 2. This third unit can be termed a prophetical liturgy (Eng. chapter 3):

4:1-3 Announcement of judgment upon the nations (threat with motivation)
4:9-12 Summons to the nations to assemble (messenger saying)
4:13-17 Announcement of the Day of Yahweh
4:18-20 Promise for Judah and Jerusalem

4. *Date of Joel's activity.* The date of Joel's activity can first of all be determined by his dependence on a series of other prophets, particularly Isaiah 13; Jeremiah 4–6; 46; 49–51; Ezekiel 29–32; 35; 38–39; Obadiah 17*a;* Zephaniah 1–2; Malachi 3. Second, his language belongs to the latest literary stratum of the OT. These observations are further supported by the presupposed internal situation of Jerusalem: leadership consisting of elders and priests; priests referred to as "ministers of Yahweh" and "ministers of the altar" (1:9, 13; 2:17); the tamid offering as a cultic institution of the postexilic community (1:9, 13; 2:14). All this is in harmony with the situation in the period after Ezra and Nehemiah. This conclusion is supported, finally, by the few historical allusions: the catastrophe of Judah and Jerusalem in the distant past (4:1-3 [Eng. 3:1-3]); the rebuilt Temple (1:9, 14, 16; 2:17; 4:18 [Eng. 3:18]) and city wall (2:7, 9). The supplement (4:4-8 [Eng. 3:4-8]) probably derives from the period prior to 343 (the destruction of Sidon by Artaxerxes III Ochus) (Wolff). All the evidence points to the first half of the fourth century B.C. as the date of Joel.

Completely different dates have also been suggested: as far back as the ninth century (Amon, Bič, Laetsch) or eighth century (Kutal, *et al.*). Such a dating must be considered completely out of the question. Others think of the time around 600 (Kapelrud), the Exile (Jepsen), or the early postexilic period (Augé,[6] Myers: *ca.* 520). A date around 300 (Treves) or in the Maccabean period (Jensen) is too late.

The location of this later book between Hosea and Amos was probably occasioned by certain similarities in content to Amos, particularly the identity of 4:16*aa* (Eng. 3:16*aa*) with Amos 1:2*a* and of 4:18*a* (Eng. 3:18*a*) with Amos 9:13*b*. In both cases Joel depends on Amos. At the same time, it was probably intended that Amos, contrary to his own message, should be understood from the viewpoint of Joel's markedly eschatological preaching.

5. *Message.* Joel is a cult prophet attached to the Temple at Jerusalem with an eschatological message. With this single difference he continues in a later period the preaching of the preexilic cult prophets, with its propensity for pro-

[6] R. Augé, *Profetes Menors,* 1957.

claiming salvation for Israel and destruction for Israel's enemies. He conforms to earlier prophecy in order to legitimate himself in an age that no longer paid much heed to new prophets. The content of his message induces him to select particularly the traditions concerning the Day of Yahweh and the oracles against foreign nations.

The concept of the Day of Yahweh has a long history, so that we must not think in terms of an almost uninterrupted homogeneous use of the earliest form of this concept well into the late period, ignoring its historical transformations. Originally Yahweh was expected to intervene militarily in Israel's campaign against its enemies. This expectation gradually became an article of faith, an all-inclusive hope for salvation associated with the theophany concept. Amos 5:18-20 and Isa. 2:12-17 took up the expectation of salvation and reinterpreted it: the Day of Yahweh will bring Israel not salvation but destruction. Zephaniah 1–2 follows this conception. This in turn leads to the later eschatological prophecies, which, like Isaiah 13 and Joel, undertake an eschatological reinterpretation. Having seen the threatened judgment upon Israel carried out in the fall of Jerusalem and the Exile, they look forward to an eschaton bringing new salvation for Israel and destruction for the impious great power or for the nations; to depict this they use the imagery of the Day of Yahweh.

Joel's prophecy is marked by a combination of cultic prophecy with eschatology that distinguishes him from the great preexilic prophets. He takes as his point of departure the economic tribulations of everyday life brought about by natural disasters, but all the while his eye is on the day of the eschatological peripeteia. He carries out his mandate, seeking to avert economic disaster and calling upon the nation to turn to God in its distress. He demands that the leaders summon a cultic penitential assembly, with fasting and lamentation, but at the same time emphasizes the necessity for the people to turn to God with all their heart, albeit without presupposing any particular sin. He speaks of the universal compass of the Day of Yahweh, but only in judgment upon the nations in contrast to his particularistic restriction of salvation to his own people.

§ 63 Amos

Cf. Commentaries in § 61; individual commentaries: R. S. Cripps, 2nd ed., 1955; E. Hammershaimb, 2nd ed., 1958; B. Kutal, 1933.

E. Balla, *Die Droh- und Scheltworte des Amos,* 1926; E. Baumann, *Der Aufbau der Amosreden,* 1903; W. Baumgartner (§ 61); G. J. Botterweck, "Zur Authentizität des Buches Amos," *BZ,* NF II (1958), 161-76; K. Cramer, *Amos,* 1930; H. Gese, "Kleine Beiträge zum Verständnis des Amosbuches," *VT,* XII (1962), 417-38; R. Gordis, "The Composition and Structure of Amos," *HThR,* XXXIII (1940), 239-51; S. Jozaki, "The Secondary Passages of the Book of Amos," *Kwansei Gakuin University Annual Studies,* IV (1956), 25-100; A. S. Kapelrud, "God as Destroyer in the Preaching of Amos and in the Ancient Near East," *JBL,* LXXI (1952), 33-38; *idem, Central Ideas in Amos,* 1956, reprinted 1961; L. Köhler, *Amos,* 1917; *idem,* "Amos-Forschungen von 1917–1932," *ThR,* NF IV (1932), 195-213; S. Lehming, "Erwägungen zu Amos," *ZThK,* LV (1958), 145-69; V. Maag, *Text, Wortschatz und*

Begriffswelt des Buches Amos, 1951; W. S. McCullough, "Some Suggestions about Amos," *JBL,* LXXII (1953), 247-54; J. Morgenstern, "Amos Studies," *HUCA,* XI (1936), 19-140; XII/XIII (1937/38), 1-53; XV (1940), 59-305; XXXII (1961), 295-350; A. Neher, *Amos,* 1950; E. Osswald, *Urform und Auslegung im masoretischen Amostext,* Dissertation, Jena, 1951; H. Graf Reventlow, *Das Amt des Propheten bei Amos,* 1962; J. Rieger (§ 62); W Schmidt, "Die deuteronomistische Redaktion des Amosbuches," *ZAW,* LXXVII (1965), 168-92; I. P. Seierstad, "Erlebnis und Gehorsam beim Propheten Amos," *ibid.,* LII (1934), 22-41; S. Speier, "Bemerkungen zu Amos," *VT,* III (1953), 305-10; *idem,* "Bemerkungen zu Amos, II," in *Homenaje a Millás-Vallicrosa,* II (1956), 365-72; S. L. Terrien, "Amos and Wisdom," in *Essays Muilenburg,* 1962, pp. 108-15; R. Vuilleumier (§ 61); J. D. W. Watts, "The Origin of the Book of Amos," *ET,* LXVI (1954/55), 109-12; *idem, Vision and Prophecy in Amos,* 1958; A. Weiser, *Die Profetie des Amos,* 1929; H. W. Wolff, *Amos' geistige Heimat,* 1964; E. Würthwein, "Amos-Studien," *ZAW,* LXII (1950), 10-52; cf. also the bibliographies in Fohrer, *ThR,* NF XIX, XX, and XXVIII (§ 52).

1. *Amos and his profession.* Amos comes from Tekoa (modern Khirbet Taquʿa), a village located about ten miles south of Jerusalem, on the boundary between the settled area and the steppe.[1] He dwelt there as a *nōqēd,* "shepherd" (1:1), or a *bōqēr,* "herdsman" (7:14), more likely an independent owner of cattle than a hired shepherd (Eissfeldt*). In addition, 7:14 states that he was engaged in the care of sycamore figs, so that he may have owned property in the hill country between the mountains and the coastal plain or by the Dead Sea. In other words, his occupation was thoroughly "middle-class" (Stoebe[2]). On the one hand, therefore, he can declare that he does not have to earn his living as a nabi or as a member of a company of nebiim, engaging in the corresponding activities; on the other, he can stress the personal call of Yahweh, which took him from his regular occupation (7:15).

Although the statements of the Amos tradition sound unambiguous, attempts have recently been made to assign Amos to a different milieu. Bič,[3] for example, on the basis of the Ugaritic title *nqd* applied to cultic assistants and the hypothesis that *bqr* originally meant haruspicy, attempts to find in Amos a cultic functionary engaged in hepatoscopy and haruspicy; Murtonen, however, has disproved this suggestion.[4] Most scholars take 7:14*a* as their point of departure: *lōʾ-nābîʾ ʾānōkî wᵉlōʾ ben-nābîʾ ʾānōkî.*[5] Since there is no verb, the sentence is

[1] We are not dealing with an unknown place of the same name in the Northern Kingdom, as has been suggested by H. Schmidt, "Die Herkunft des Propheten Amos," in BZAW, XXXIV (1920), 158-71.

[2] H. J. Stoebe, "Der Prophet Amos und sein bürgerlicher Beruf," *WuD,* V (1957), 160-81.

[3] M. Bič, "Der Prophet Amos—ein Haepatoskopos," *VT,* I (1951), 293-96.

[4] A. Murtonen, "The Prophet Amos—a Hepatoscoper?" *VT,* II (1952), 170-71.

[5] P. R. Ackroyed, "Amos VII,14," *ET,* LXVIII (1956/57), 94; G. A. Danell, "Var Amos verkligen en nabi?" *SEÅ,* XVI (1951), 7-20; G. R. Driver, "Amos VII,14," *ET,* LXVII (1955/56), 91-92; A. H. J. Gunneweg, "Erwägungen zu Amos 7,14," *ZThK,* LVII (1960), 1-16; A. S. Kapelrud, "Amos og hans yrke," *NTT,* LIX (1958), 76-79; J. MacCormack, "Amos VII,14," *ET,* LXVII (1955/56), 318; H. H. Rowley, "Was Amos a Nabi?" in *Eissfeldt-Festschrift,* 1947, pp. 191-98; E. Vogt, "Waw explicative in Amos VII,14," *ET,* LXVIII (1956/57), 301-2.

ambiguous on the purely syntactic level. Rowley interprets it merely as saying that Amos was not a nabi before his call, with which his prophetical activity began, finding no rejection of Yahweh's call to be a prophet. Watts sees the sentence as a statement of Amos' authority ("not I, but Yahweh sent me!"). Vogt understands Amos to be declaring that he is not a professional prophet but rather a prophet chosen by Yahweh. Others seek to demonstrate with the help of 7:14 that Amos worked as a cult prophet.

Würthwein interprets the verse as meaning "I was not a prophet, but now I am"; MacCormack shares a similar view. On the basis of this and other assumptions he concludes that Amos was first of all a nabi prophesying salvation, who pronounced the threats against the foreign nations in 1:3–2:3 and interceded on behalf of Israel (7:1-6), and later became a prophet of doom. Several arguments disprove this contention: the unity of 1:3–2:16, with its concluding threat against Israel, must not be discarded; the crime of one foreign nation against another (2:1-3) must not be slighted; the four visions in 7:1-9; 8:1-3 must not be assigned to completely different periods; and intercession must not be restricted to the optimistic cult prophets. Gunneweg goes even further, ascribing to Amos as nabi not only the prophecies of salvation for Israel and the intercession, but also the cultic judgment discourse with its prophecy of disaster. Driver and Ackroyd look upon the verse as an irritated question expressing Amos' confidence: "Am I not considered a prophet because I am a herdsman?" In this view, too, Amos was calling himself a nabi, although in 7:10 ff. Amaziah does not question Amos' status as a prophet. Danell comes to a more limited conclusion, suggesting that Amos was a nabi *extra ordinem,* who did not belong to any guild but did earn his living in Israel through his appearance as a prophet. According to Kapelrud, on the contrary, Amos was neither a herdsman and farmer nor a cultic prophet, but an official in charge of large flocks and their shepherds, e.g., those belonging to the sanctuaries, and was therefore a well-educated man belonging to a high social class. Any attempt to interpret *nqd* in this sense, however, raises the question of how, according to 1:1, there could be several such overseers in the little village of Tekoa.

Reventlow goes beyond the theories just mentioned, attempting to demonstrate that Amos' activity is to be understood within the framework of a clearly defined "office," and that this is the ancient office of the nabi, maintained by the "covenant proclamation," i.e., the ritual blessings and curses of the so-called Covenant Festival. He bases his conclusion on 7:10-17, translating vs. 14 in the past tense, and on 3:3-8, within which vs. 8 represents a refusal to abide by an order not to practice his calling. The reports of visions in 7–8 are interpreted as a ritual corresponding to certain functions of the prophetical office. In addition, 1:3–2:16 is a political ritual, 4:6-11 a cursing ritual, and 9:13-15 a supplementary blessing ritual. Form-critical study is thereby made to yield far-reaching conclusions, to which one must take exception if only on account of the one-sidedness of the method. First of all, the original *Sitz im Leben* is not equivalent to an institution, nor is an institution equivalent to an office. The *Sitz im Leben* is rather a specific occasion, e.g., a dirge upon a person's death. Second, *Sitz im Leben* must be distinguished from *Sitz in der Rede* ("setting in discourse"), as when Amos employs the prophetical dirge as a threat against Israel (5:1-3), so that free use of a fixed form for other purposes is quite common. The hypothesis of a prophetical office does not help us understand Amos; Smend's opposition[6] to this view is justified.

It appears instead to be more accurate to follow Baumann, Lehming, Stoebe, *et al.*,[7] in interpreting 7:14*a* as Amos' denial that he was one of the professional prophets and his statement of the contrast between them and the prophet called by Yahweh. In fact, the whole discussion, sometimes quite agitated, is dealing with a pseudo problem, because the verse is removed from its context in 7:10-17 and considered in isolation. Amaziah orders Amos to go to Judah to earn his living, and Amos merely declares that his previous occupation, from which Yahweh has called him and sent him to Israel, provides him with sufficient resources, and that he is by no means dependent on his prophetical activity for income.

2. *Date of Amos' activity.* Amos 1:1; 7:9, 10-11 indicate as the date of Amos' prophetical activity the reign of Jeroboam II in Northern Israel (786/82–753/46), which parallels the rule of Uzziah in Judah. The earthquake mentioned in 1:1 does not help us determine the date more precisely, but the content of the prophet's words shows that Israel was then in a period of political, economic, and cultural prosperity and could point to noteworthy successes (6:1, 13). This suggests the middle or late years of Jeroboam's reign (II Kings 14:23-29), so that we may date Amos' ministry between 760 and 750.[8]

His mandate at the time of his call had sent him, a Judean, into the Northern Kingdom of Israel. There he probably first appeared at Samaria, the capital (3:9 ff.; 4:1 ff.; 6:1 ff.), then at the state sanctuary in Bethel, to address the multitude assembled for a festival. Just because his words hit home, this activity lasted but a short time. The high priest accused him of making an insurrection before the king and banished him (7:10-13). Amos obviously returned to his homeland. There is little likelihood of his further activity in Judah (Weiser*: 9:1-4).[9]

3. *Sayings and reports; minor collections.* Amos' sayings and reports have for the most part the character of invective and threat. This holds true also for the visions in which Yahweh, upon the intercession of the prophet, declares himself willing at first to withhold his judgment. In the series 1:3–2:16 and in the 27 shorter sayings we find almost exclusively threats, threats with motivation, together with combinations of invective and threat, some of which arise in the course of discussion (3:1-2, 12*a;* 5:18-20). In the threats with motivation the

[6] R. Smend, "Das Nein des Amos," *EvTh,* XXIII (1963), 404-23.

[7] E. Baumann, "Eine Einzelheit," *ZAW,* LXIV (1952), 62; S. Lehming, "Erwägungen zu Amos," *ZThK,* LV (1958), 145-69; Stoebe (note 2); S. Cohen, "Amos *Was* a Navi," *HUCA,* XXXII (1962), 175-78.

[8] Cripps suggests 742/41 or, at the earliest, 744/43.

[9] In 6:1 "Zion" is a general term for the site of a capital, parallel to "mountain of Samaria."

motivation can precede the threat (1:3-5; 5:18-20, 26-27; 6:8-10), be contained in the threat (3:1-2, 12*b*-15), or follow the threat (3:12*a;* 8:11-14). Other literary types occur less frequently: combination of dirge and threat (5:1-3); combination of exhortation and threat (5:4-6); invective (5:12; 6:12); historical interpretation (4:6-11); prophetical torah (5:21-25); exhortation (5:14-15); ironic exhortation (4:4-5); discussion (3:3-6, 8; 9:7).

The only larger unit of oral proclamation is the part of 1:3–2:16 that goes back to Amos. Morgenstern's assumption that Amos delivered a long coherent address during a New Year festival at Bethel, isolated fragments of which are preserved in the book of Amos, is unlikely. Apart from 1:3–2:16 and the report of Amos' banishment from Bethel (7:10-17), we are dealing, as in the case of most of the other prophets, with individual sayings and reports of visions spoken in isolation. They show Amos to be a master of language and form, who knows how to depict scenes and formulate sentences concisely and vividly as well as pregnantly and acutely (Eissfeldt*), and had probably learned much from the wisdom instruction of his seminomadic environment.

The first-person style of the vision reports and 5:1 clearly shows that Amos was responsible for the writing down of the sayings and reports during his lifetime. It is unlikely, however, that this took place at Jerusalem during his return from Bethel to Tekoa (Caspari[10]); Tekoa itself seems more probable. Amos probably dictated the material there; the first-person style does not indicate an autograph. In addition, we have a report from another source in 7:10-17, which was apparently composed by a different hand on the basis of the prophet's narrative.

The individual sayings and reports were later assembled into minor collections, likewise by another hand. Some of these can be recognized by the hymnic passages appended to them. Following Eissfeldt*, we can distinguish nine groups:

A. The series of sayings in 1:3–2:16 constitutes a large-scale composition that was planned and executed as such from the beginning. In it Amos first attacks the surrounding nations, whom he threatens with disaster on account of their transgressions, only to turn suddenly upon Israel herself. As Bentzen[11] correctly recognized in principle, the sequence of nations threatened is determined by the model of the Egyptian execration texts, although the elimination of later additions modifies the scheme somewhat; in addition, it is hardly likely that Amos imitated the Egyptian ritual.

1:3-5	against Aram	= North
1:6-8	against the Philistines	= West
1:13-15	against Ammon	= East
2:1-3	against Moab	
2:6-16	against Israel	= Center

[10] W. Caspari, "Wer hat die Aussprüche des Propheten Amos gesammelt?" *NkZ,* XXV (1914), 701-15.

[11] A. Bentzen, "The Ritual Background of Amos 1,2–2,16," *OTS,* VIII (1950), 85-99; cf. also M. A. Beek, "The Religious Background of Amos 2,6-8," *OTS,* V (1948), 132-41; B. K. Soper, "For Three Transgressions and for Four," *ET,* LXXI (1959/60), 86-87.

B. There follow three small collections of sayings, in each of which the first unit begins with "Hear this word. . . ." The first collection (3:1-15) contains six sayings: 3:1-2, against faith in election; 3:3-6, a demonstration that Yahweh is responsible for all calamities, citing other examples of the connection between cause and effect;[12] 3:8, concerning the prophetical obligation to speak; 3:9-11, against the wickedness of Samaria; 3:12*a*, concerning complete destruction, illustrated by an example from shepherd life; 3:12*b*-15, concerning the destruction of the sanctuary and dwelling places.

C. A second collection beginning with "Hear this word . . ." (4:1-13) contains three sayings: 4:1-3, a threat of disaster against the women of Samaria; 4:4-5, an ironic exhortation to join in cultic worship; and 4:6-12, an invective in the form of historical interpretation, with the refrain-like statement that the Israelites have always refused to return to Yahweh, while all that remains of the threat is the introduction (vs. 12*a*). The collection closes with a hymnic fragment (4:13).

D. The third collection beginning with "Hear this word . . ." (5:1-6, 8-9) contains a dirge threatening Israel (5:1-3) and an exhortation to seek Yahweh rather than the sanctuaries (5:4-6).[13] The conclusion is again provided by a hymnic fragment (5:8-9).

E. The three following collections of sayings are so arranged that in each case the first saying begins with "Woe . . . ." The first of these collections (5:7, 10-17) comprises four sayings: 5:7, 10-11 (emending the beginning of 7) and 5:12, concerning legal injustice; 5:14-15, an exhortation to do what is good; and 5:16-17, concerning the lamentations to be heard when disaster comes.

F. The second collection beginning with "Woe . . ." (5:18-27)[14] comprises a prophetical reinterpretation of the Day of Yahweh (5:18-20), Yahweh's rejection of the cult and reference to the time of Moses, when there was no sacrifice (5:21-25), and a condemnation of idolatry (5:26-27). The latter two sayings must be carefully distinguished.

G. The third collection beginning with "Woe . . ." (6:1-14) comprises five sayings: 6:1-7, against the upper class of Samaria; 6:8-10, concerning the complete destruction of the city; 6:11, concerning the destruction of the houses; 6:12, concerning the perversion of justice; and 6:13-14, concerning political arrogance.

H. A collection made up of several sections, beginning with "Hear this . . . ," is found in 8:4–9:6. It contains first of all a saying against the merchants (8:4-7), which was transmitted independently for a considerable period; to it has been added a hymnic fragment (8:8). It was then combined with 8:9–9:6, which had independently brought together threats of darkness (8:9-10) and

[12] B. Holwerda, *De exegese van Amos 3,3-8,* 1948; H. Junker, "Leo rugiit etc. Eine textkritische und exegetische Untersuchung über Amos 3,3-8," *Trierer ThZ,* LIX (1950), 4-13.

[13] F. Hesse, "Amos 5,4-6, 14 ff.," *ZAW,* LXVIII (1956), 1-17.

[14] J. P. Hyatt, "The Translation and Meaning of Amos 5,23-24," *ZAW,* LXVIII (1956), 17-24; H. Junker, "Amos und die 'opferlose Mosezeit'," *ThGl,* XXVII (1935), 686-95; E. Würthwein, "Amos 5,21-27," *ThLZ,* LXXII (1947), 143-52.

of famine (8:11-14), the account of a vision concerning Yahweh's pursuit of the Israelites (9:1-4), and a concluding hymnic fragment (9:5-6). To the whole an isolated saying of Amos was later appended (9:7).

I. The accounts of the four visions in 7:1-9;[15] 8:1-3 constitute an independent collection. Since in the first two Amos intercedes successfully on Israel's behalf, while in the latter two he does not intercede, and since none of Amos' other sayings contain any suggestion of intercession with Yahweh on Israel's behalf, these visions belong at the beginning of the prophet's ministry, after his call. They surely do not antedate the call (Weiser), represent it (Wellhausen, Budde), or constitute the conclusion of Amos' ministry (Sellin). The collector or a redactor has interpolated the outside account of Amos' banishment from Bethel (7:10-17)[16] after the report of the third vision, because he equated the sword with which Jeroboam is threatened in the vision (7:9) with the one mentioned in the threat contained in the narrative (7:10-11).

4. *Later passages*. To the sayings and reports of Amos have been added some later passages. These include, first of all, the hymnic sections already mentioned (4:13; 5:8-9; 8:8; 9:5-6),[17] which neither derive from Amos (Botterweck) nor were added by him (Watts). They do not serve to conclude liturgical pericopes (Weiser*), but to conclude the minor collections, like the promises at the end of the Isaiah collections.

The following passages also surely do not derive from Amos: the saying placed as an epigraph at the beginning of the book (1:2), which derives from the redactor and, like Joel 4:16 (Eng. 3:16), reinterprets Yahweh's roaring from heaven (Jer. 25:30) as a roaring from Jerusalem;[18] the oracles against Tyre (1:9-10), Edom (1:11-12), and Judah (2:4-5), which differ from the other oracles against the nations, with the oracle against Edom referring probably to its conduct at the fall of Jerusalem in 587 and the oracle against Judah couched in Deuteronomistic style, so that these two were not formulated until the Exile; the saying concerning Yahweh's revelation of his intentions to the prophets (3:7), which represents a postexilic retrospect of prophetical preaching.

Finally, the conclusion of the book (9:8-15) is also secondary,[19] despite many attempts to ascribe it to Amos[20] or assume Amos' authorship at least of vss. 8-10, restricting the addition to vss. 11-15 (Eissfeldt*, Weiser*, Kapelrud). The

[15] H. Junker, "Text und Bedeutung der Vision Amos 7,7-9," *Bibl,* XVII (1936), 359-64; H. S. Mackenzie, "The Plumb-Line (Amos 7,8)," *ET,* LX (1949), 159.

[16] L. Rost, "Zu Amos 7,10-17," in *Zahn-Festgabe,* 1928, pp. 229-36.

[17] T. H. Gaster, "An Ancient Hymn in the Prophecies of Amos," *Journal of the Manchester Egyptian and Oriental Society,* XIX (1935), 23-26; F. Horst, "Die Doxologien im Amosbuch," *ZAW,* XLVII (1929), 45-54 (= *Gottes Recht,* 1961, pp. 155-66); J. D. W. Watts, "An Old Hymn Preserved in the Book of Amos," *JNES,* XV (1956), 33-39.

[18] For a different view, cf. A. Bertholet, "Zu Amos 1,2," in *Bonwetsch-Festschrift,* 1918, pp. 1-12 (the echo of a call experience); Sellin-Rost*, p. 125 (genuine in form and content).

[19] As Wellhausen, p. 96, rightly observes: "Roses and lavender instead of blood and iron. . . . After he [Amos] has just far surpassed all his earlier threats, he cannot suddenly blunt their effect, cannot finally cause Yahweh's cup of wrath to flow milk and honey."

[20] E.g., Botterweck, Gordis, Maag, Neher, and Sellin. Weiser*, on the other hand (p. 216), finds here an offensive expression of malicious deceit.

anemic and feeble threat against "the sinful kingdom" is at once reduced to a judgment of purification (9:8-10); we are dealing here with a promise dating from the Exile.[21] The promise made to the "fallen booth of David" (9:11-12) presupposes the fall of the dynasty and of Jerusalem, and is probably to be interpreted eschatologically. The sayings in 9:13, 14-15, with their promises of miraculous fertility and the restoration of Israel at the end, are clearly eschatological, and were probably formulated in the postexilic period. Cripps has spelled out in detail the essential reasons for denying Amos' authorship of 9:8-15.

5. *Growth of the book.* The growth of the book took place as follows: First the series of sayings in A and the minor collections B–G were combined to form a larger collection. A, an impressive survey of Amos' preaching, was placed at the beginning; B–D and E–G were brought together in two groups using identical introductory phrases. To this larger collection was appended collection I, already expanded by the addition of the outside report in 7:10-17, because it contained reports of the beginning and end of Amos' ministry. Collection H was apparently placed at the conclusion deliberately because its sayings and above all the vision in 9:1-4 threaten unconditional destruction. This compilation may well have taken place in the late preexilic period.

Others assume only two large collections brought together to form the book. Weiser*, for example, assumes a vision document with five reports of visions and a collection of sayings concluding with 7:10-17. Gordis assumes a collection 1–7:9 containing material antedating Amos' banishment from Bethel and a supplement 7:10-17, together with a collection 8:1–9:15 containing material from the period after his banishment. Watts assumes a book of oracles written down in Northern Israel (1–6) and another book containing the visions and the outside report (7–9). These views, however, overlook the composite character of 1–6, get into difficulties with the order of the sayings in 8:4 ff., or are forced to ascribe the vision reports 7:7-9 and 8:1-3, identical in form, to two different periods.

During the exilic period the book underwent a redaction in the Deuteronomistic spirit (Schmidt), which, among other things, added the epigraph in 1:2. Afterward, in the postexilic period, possibly even toward the end of the sixth century, the optimistic ending (9:8-15) was added, giving the book the form of the two-part eschatological schema.

6. *Message.* Amos' message is not determined by his devotion to the traditions of the cult [22] or to so-called apodictic law;[23] neither did he limit himself to

[21] Robinson (p. 107) suggests that vss. 9-10 are a fragmentary exilic promise, connected with the preceding material by means of verse 8*d*.

[22] Kapelrud; C. Sant, "Religious Worship in the Book of Amos," *Melita Theologica,* III (1950), 75-93; IV (1951), 34-48; Vuilleumier.

[23] R. Bach, "Gottesrecht und weltliches Recht in der Verkündigung des Propheten Amos," in *Dehn-Festschrift,* 1957, pp. 23-34. The proof, however, is insufficient; cf. Smend (note 6), pp. 405-9. Ancient Near Eastern law is also cited by L. Dürr, "Altorientalisches Recht bei den Propheten Amos und Hosea," *BZ,* XXIII (1935/36), 150-57, for Amos 2:7.

activity in the political and social realm.[24] The foundation of his message is rather the No he said to Israel's social conduct, to its understanding of history, to the cult, and to its way of life in general. Of course, there is an intimate relationship between Yahweh and the people (7:8; 8:2), described in 3:2 by the verb *yāda'* as an intimate bond like that of marriage. But Amos ironically rejects all dependence on a faith in election (3:2) and treats with equal irony Israel's claim to be the "first of the nations" (6:1-7). He does not even find any preference for Israel in the deliverance from Egypt, because Yahweh has guided other nations in the same fashion.[25] Contrary to its obligation to obey, because, for instance, Yahweh has raised up Nazirites and prophets (2:11), Israel has deserted its God, as Amos shows above all by pointing to social and cultic sins, which constitute his major point of attack. He condemns as perverse (4:4-5; 5:4-5, 21-25) the observance of festival and sacrificial regulations, whose origin in the Mosaic period he denies (5:25); at the same time, he observes that the people are filled with pride and self-confidence, eating and drinking well, and, like David, babble their songs (6:1-6), a sign of their generally sinful attitude. Even in the field of international relations he presupposes God-given rules whose transgression Yahweh will punish, even if Israel is not affected (2:1-3). Here he lays the groundwork for a universal theology without nationalistic restrictions.

The existing situation gives Yahweh the right to hold Israel responsible with special rigor (3:2). He has therefore again and again sent plagues—all calamities in fact derive from him (3:3-6)—as easily understood exhortations to the people to repent and return to him (4:6-11). All this, however, has been in vain, and therefore all that is left is the destruction to come on the Day of Yahweh, whose traditional optimistic interpretation Amos transforms into its opposite (5:18-20). Israel will perish completely unless the repentance it has so long refused—which Amos interprets as the seeking of Yahweh (5:4) and doing what is good (5:14)—does not take place at the last moment. Even in this case, however, God remains completely free; Israel's repentance and return do not obligate him to forgive. All that Amos can bring himself to declare is a "perhaps" of deliverance (5:15). The tension between God's wrath and God's grace remains.

§ 64 Obadiah

Cf. commentaries in § 61; individual commentaries: B. Kutal, 1933.

H. Bekel, "Ein vorexilisches Orakel über Edom," *ThStKr*, LXXX (1907), 315-43; M. Bič, "Ein verkanntes Thronbesteigungsfestorakel im Alten Testament," *ArOr*, XIX (1951), 569-78; *idem*, "Zur Problematik des Buches Obadjah," *VTSuppl*, I (1953), pp. 11-25; A. H. Edelkoort, "De profetie van Obadja," *NedThT*, I (1946/47), 276-93; O. Olávarri, "Cronología y estructura literaria del oráculo escatológico de Abdías," *EstBíbl*, XXII (1963), 303-13; T. H. Robinson, "The

[24] F. Dijkema, "Le fond des prophéties d'Amos," *OTS*, II (1943), 18-34; Morgenstern.
[25] The reference to the Exodus in 2:10 is secondary.

Structure of the Book of Obadiah," *JThSt,* XVII (1916), 402-8; W. RUDOLPH, "Obadja," *ZAW,* XLIX (1931), 222-31; J. THEIS, *Die Weissagung des Abdias,* 1917; H. VELDCAMP, *Het gezicht van Obadja,* 1957; cf. also the bibliographies in FOHRER, *ThR,* NF XIX, XX, and XXVIII (§ 52).

1. *The individual sayings.* Concerning the prophet of this, the shortest prophetical writing of the OT, we know only that his name was Obadiah (1)—unless this name, which means "servant of Yahweh," was later added to a perhaps anonymous document, after the model of I Kings 18:3 ff. According to the superscription, the prophet's message, which is called a *ḥāzôn,* "vision," the general term from the exilic period on, is directed against Edom on account of its hostile attitude toward Judah. The question of defining the individual sayings has been answered in many different ways, while the question of whether 2-9 in particular is to be understood as a historical retrospect (Wellhausen, Nowack, *et al.*) or as the announcement of future events (Orelli, Sellin, *et al.*) has since been decided in the latter sense (Eissfeldt*, Weiser*, *et al.*).

Some exegetes maintain the unity of the entire book, refusing to divide it into several sayings (Aalders, Edelkoort, Bič); Bič understands it as a liturgically expanded oracle for the Enthronement Festival and derives it from cultic drama. Most exegetes, however, assume the presence of two sayings; Rudolph, for instance, divides it into 1-14, 15*b*; and 15*a*, 16-18, with 19-21 forming a conclusion. Weiser* clearly joins 19-21 to the preceding saying. Eissfeldt* likewise finds one saying in 1-14, 15*b* (2-9 a threat, 10-14, 15*b* a motivation), to which have been added 15*a*, 16-18 and 19-21, supplements composed by two different authors. Sellin-Rost* divide as follows: 1-10 the original oracle, 11-14 a later addition, 15*a*, 16-18 and 19-21 two supplements. Robinson analyzes the entire book into eight sayings or fragments of sayings.

Consideration of the subject matter and the idioms or formulas suggests a division into five sayings with a supplement of a different kind:

1*b*-4 Threat against Edom, with concluding formula *n^{e}'ūm yahweh*

5-7 Threat against Edom, in which vs. 7 (rearranged in the order $7a\gamma + a$, $7a\beta + b$) belongs before vs. 6, which forms a clear conclusion

8-11 Threat with motivation against Edom, with the formula *n^{e}'ūm yahweh* absorbed into the introductory question and a single half verse forming the conclusion

12-14, 15*b* Threat against Edom, motivated with an appended warning

15*a*, 16-18 Threat against Edom at the time of the Day of Yahweh, when all nations shall be destroyed. Vs. 15*a* clearly marks a new beginning, and we have *kî yahweh dibbēr* as a concluding formula

19-21 Promise for Israel.[1]

2. *Date.* Suggested dates for the book's origin range from the ninth to the middle of the fourth century. Most scholars, however, assume that the prophet appeared in the period after the fall of Jerusalem in 587 (Deden, Edelkoort,

[1] J. Gray, "The Diaspora of Israel and Judah in Obadiah v. 20," *ZAW,* LXV (1953), 53-59; W. Kornfeldt, "Die jüdische Diaspora in Ab,20," in *Mélanges Robert,* 1957, pp. 180-86.

Eissfeldt*, *et al.*). This event alone provides a reasonable occasion for the threats against Edom in 1*b*-18, the more so since all other such threats, including Amos 1:11-12, are likewise based on the fact that at that time Edom was ranged with the enemy and gloated over Judah's misfortune. Obadiah's precise details, which surpass other descriptions, show also that he was an eyewitness to the events and preached his message soon afterward. The borrowing in Jer. 49:7 ff. does not affect these conclusions, because the saying in question does not derive from Jeremiah, not to mention the fact that the verses identical with Obadiah are a later addition to the basic stratum of the passage.

The saying in 19-21, which must be considered a supplement, announces the occupation of the Palestinian territory west of the Jordan, with the exception of Judah, by the Israelite and Judean diaspora, together with a military campaign against Edom on the part of those returning. This passage can derive only from the postexilic period.

Sellin, on the contrary, sought to derive 1-10 from the period after the defection of Edom from Judah (II Kings 8:20-21), about 850 B.C., 11-14 from the period after 586, and 15*b*, 16-21 from the fifth century. His primary evidence for 1-10 was the use of the Obadiah verses in Jeremiah 49. Others have suggested the eighth century (Kutal, Bič). Wellhausen, interpreting 2-9 as a description of Arab tribes invading Edom, thought of the fifth century. Robinson distributes the sayings and fragments throughout the period from the end of the sixth century to the beginning of the fourth.

3. *Message.* Obadiah's message shows him to be a representative of the optimistic prophecy attacked by Jeremiah. He may have been a cult prophet among the population remaining in Palestine after the Babylonian deportation. Central to his message, however, is not religious nationalism, but the ethical seriousness of his faith and his hope for God's compensatory justice. The expectation of just retribution, clearly stated in 15*b*, runs through all his sayings. It is connected with the concept of the Day of Yahweh as a day of judgment against the nations, on which Edom above all will receive its just desert. The appended promise, according to which Judah-Israel, a nation of brothers overthrown with the help of Edom, will rise again, places the book within an eschatological framework (threats of disaster against a foreign nation —promise for the prophet's own nation).

§ 65 Jonah

Cf. commentaries in § 61.

G. C. Aalders, *The Problem of the Book of Jonah*, 1948; T. E. Bird, *The Book of Jona*, 1938; W. Böhme, "Die Composition des Buches Jona," *ZAW*, VII (1887), 224-84; T. Boman, "Jahve og Elohim i Jonaboken," *NTT*, XXXVII (1936), 159-64; B. S. Childs, "Jonah," *SJTh*, XI (1958), 53-61; A. Feuillet, "Les sources du livre de Jonas," *RB*, LIV (1947), 161-86; *idem*, "Le sens du livre de Jonas," *ibid.*, pp. 340-61; S. D. Goitein, "Some Observations on Jonah," *JPOS*, XVII (1937), 63-77; E. Haller, *Die Erzählung von dem Propheten Jona*, 1958; O. Komlós, "Jonah Legends," in *Études Orientales Hirschler*, 1950, pp. 41-61; O. Loretz, "Herkunft und Sinn der

Jona-Erzählung," *BZ*, NF V (1961), 18-29; H. SCHMIDT, *Jona*, 1907; L. STOLLBERG, *Jona*, Dissertation, Halle, 1927; cf. also the bibliographies in FOHRER, *ThR*, NF XIX, XX, and XXVIII (§ 52).

1. *Narrative.* The book of Jonah is a narrative concerning a prophet; it does not contain his words, as the other prophetical books do entirely or for the most part. It therefore occupies a special place among the prophetical books, where it was placed on account of its subject matter, although it does not even claim to have been written by a prophet. Most closely related to it are the prophetical legends in the books of Kings. Its antihero, Jonah the son of Amittai, it probably meant to be identical with the prophet of the same name from Gath-hepher (Khirbet ez-Zurraʿ, northeast of Nazareth), in the territory of Zebulun, who gave a promise to Jeroboam II (II Kings 14:25). Since the authors of the books of Kings did not use the narrative, it was clearly not extant around 600 B.C. in either oral or written tradition. Solely its incorporation among the books of the Dodekapropheton actually or purportedly deriving from the eighth century expresses the redactors' view that it was composed then or at least refers to the prophet mentioned in II Kings 14:25.

The book tells how Jonah seeks to evade Yahweh's command to summon the Assyrian capital Nineveh to repentance by fleeing on a ship, has himself cast overboard during a storm unleashed by God (1), is swallowed by a great fish, and is vomited out upon dry land after three days (2). He then obeys Yahweh's renewed command and achieves the repentance and conversion of Nineveh, so that Yahweh relents from his planned judgment (3). The prophet is enraged, but Yahweh proves that his rage is unjustified by the example of a castor-oil plant (4).

2. *Historicity and origin of the narrative material.* Questions concerning the historicity and origin of the narrative material have been debated time and again.[1] From the time of Augustine on, the early Christian typological interpretation gave way increasingly to an emphasis on the literal sense of the words.[2] Even today, readers here and there consider the narrative historical, even to the rescue from the fish, or relate it to an earlier account of the eighth-century Jonah and his threat against Nineveh, no longer preserved. Even some critical scholars consider the possibility that the early Jonah was given a message for Nineveh just as Elisha was given a message for Damascus, and that our narrative therefore has a historical nucleus (Sellin-Rost*). But this makes the silence of the authors of the books of Kings, who were vitally interested in prophecy, even more inexplicable.

We are in fact dealing with a legend, first current in oral tradition, related to a historical figure merely through the use of his name, interwoven with many other themes, some mythological and reminiscent of fairy tales. They have been

[1] Cf. A. Vaccari, "Il genere letterario del libro di Giona in recenti pubblicazioni," *Divinitas*, V (1961), 1-28.

[2] E. Biser, "Zum frühchristlichen Verständnis des Buches Jonas," *Bibel und Kirche*, XVII (1962), 19-21.

brought together by the author to form a unified work, and it is not always possible to distinguish in detail between what he found ready to hand and what he himself added. Some motifs, such as Jonah's prophetical appearance at Nineveh, are typically Israelite. The sudden change to disgust with life is also characteristic of Israelite thought. The mythological and fairy-tale motifs, including especially the experience with the fish, which occurs in the Greek saga of Heracles and Perseus, are quite widespread. Komlós has recorded myths from Assyria, Babylonia, India, and elsewhere, features of which can be found in the Jonah narrative. They may have influenced the narrative by way of northern Palestine and Phoenicia. In fact, since the nautical motif was always present, a story originating in this area may have been associated in Israel with the name "Jonah."

Israelite revision of an originally foreign narrative would explain the alternation between the divine names "Yahweh" and "Elohim," the second of which is found in 3:(3), 4-10; 4:(6), 7-9. Previous scholars have suggested that the two terms indicate different sources (Böhme, H. Schmidt) or express a particular theology by referring to the gracious and familiar God Yahweh and the *deus absconditus* Elohim (Boman), but these suggestions are unsatisfactory.

3. *Literary type.* In literary type, therefore, the book is not a historico-biographical prophetical narrative, for which none of the evidence is present, but rather a midrashic and didactic tract in schematic and repetitive style, influenced by wisdom literature. The midrashic and didactic element has recently been pointed out by several scholars.[3]

4. *Date.* For dating the book, whose existence in the second century B.C. is presupposed by Ecclus. 49:10 and Tob. 14:4, 8, the preexilic period is out of the question. The late Hebrew style and vocabulary and the aramaisms (1:4-6, 12; 2:1; 3:7; 4:6, 8) point to a much later date. In addition, the Assyrian Empire and its capital, which fell in 612, appear as entities from a distant past (3:3). This, together with the book's purpose (to be discussed below), means that the book was not composed before the fifth century (Deden, Weiser*), and more likely even in the fourth century (Sellin-Rost*).[4]

5. *Thanksgiving psalm.* The thanksgiving sung by Jonah during his three-day stay in the fish's belly (2:3-10)[5] does not belong to the original book of Jonah but is a later interpolation. It is similar to the thanksgivings in the Psalter. It is shown to be an addition by the fact that vss. 6-7 do not deal with the stay in the fish's belly and that a thanksgiving for a deliverance already experienced is completely out of place in Jonah's situation, since he should in fact be praying for help. There is nothing to suggest the date or origin of the song; it may be earlier or later than the book.

[3] Midrash is suggested by Loretz; J. Schildenberger, "Der Sinn des Buches Jonas," *Erbe und Auftrag*, XXXVIII (1962), 93-102; J. Schreiner, "Eigenart, Aufbau, Inhalt und Botschaft des Buches Jonas," *Bibel und Kirche*, XVII (1962), 8-14; a didactic work is suggested by R. Augé, *Profetes Menors*, 1957; Weiser*; a parable is suggested by Feuillet.

[4] Augé's dating (note 3) about 250 is probably too late.

[5] A. R. Johnson, "Jonah 2,3-10," in *T. H. Robinson-Festschrift*, 1950, pp. 82-102.

6. *Purpose.* The book is neither an act of expiation, in which the prophet criticizes his behavior (Goitein), nor a prophetical treatment of God's mercy. Neither is the influence of Deutero-Isaiah's universalistic concept of salvation clearly and uniquely in evidence (Childs, Weiser*). Instead, we are here dealing with a development of the universalistic ideas of postexilic wisdom theology, in association with the prophetical ideas that first come to light in Amos. In any event, the book's purpose is universalistic: it states that God's mercy is not meant for Israel exclusively, but can be granted to the people and even the animals of a hated foreign city if they truly repent and turn to Yahweh. The book opposes the kind of particularism, incarnate in Jonah, that restricts salvation to Israel and finds the threats to apply unconditionally to other nations. To this extent it may be called a tract against particularistic intolerance and arrogance (Weiser*) and, on account of the divine mercy that transcends all boundaries, an expansion of Ezek. 18:23 influenced by the idea of mission. Of course, it does not contain any statement making this point directly, so that it can equally well be an exemplary expression of the universalistic and humanistic theology of its author, a man associated with both prophetism and wisdom.

§ 66 Micah

Cf. commentaries in § 61.

W. Beyerlin, *Die Kulttraditionen Israels in der Verkündigung des Propheten Micha,* 1959; A. Bruno, *Micha und der Herrscher aus der Vorzeit,* 1923; B. A. Copass and E. L. Carlson, *A Study of the Prophet Micah,* 1950; K. Elliger, "Die Heimat des Propheten Micha," *ZDPV,* LVII (1934), 81-152; E. Hammershaimb, "Einige Hauptgedanken in der Schrift des Propheten Micha," *StTh,* XV (1961), 11-34; A. Jepsen, "Moreseth-Gath, die Heimat des Propheten Micha," *PJB,* XXIX (1933), 42-53; A. S. Kapelrud, "Eschatology in the Book of Micah," *VT,* XI (1961), 392-405; J. Lindblom, *Micha, literarisch untersucht,* 1929; B. Renaud, *Structure et attaches littéraires de Michée IV–V,* 1964; L. P. Smith, "The Book of Micah," *Interpr,* VI (1952), 210-27; B. Stade, "Bemerkungen über das Buch Micha," *ZAW,* I (1881), 161-72; cf. also the bibliographies in Fohrer, *ThR,* NF XIX, XX, and XXVIII (§ 52).

1. *Micah.* Micah, who is not identical with the Micaiah ben Imlah of I Kings 22, is said by the superscription of his book (1:1) to have come from Moresheth-gath (modern Tell ej-Judeideh), a small village in the hill country of Judah southwest of Jerusalem. It lies in the territory taken from Judah by Sennacherib in 701, though Micah does not seem to have experienced this. He was probably a free farmer, thoroughly familiar with the grievances that originated in the capital, perhaps even suffering from them himself.

It is questionable whether he appeared as a prophet as early as the time of kings Jotham and Ahaz, as 1:1 states. He was undoubtedly active in the time of Hezekiah, as we learn from Jer. 26:18. Since 1:2-9 is directed against Samaria, which is still standing, Micah's activity must have begun before the fall of Samaria in 722, while he is unacquainted with the Assyrian campaign of 711, not to mention the later campaign of 701. His ministry, therefore, lasts from around 725 to some time before 711. This makes him a younger contemporary of Isaiah, whose ministry follows chronologically that of Hosea in Israel. It is therefore not surprising that he was familiar with Isaiah's utterances, just as Isaiah was familiar with those of Amos, who had preceded him. At least two of Micah's sayings are influenced by Isaiah: 1:10-15 by Isa. 10:27*b*-32, and 2:1-3 by Isa. 5:8-10.

It is not impossible that Micah first appeared as a prophet in his hometown. Moresheth-gath is at least the imaginary scene of 1:10-15. Jerusalem is a more likely site for his other sayings.

The question of what sayings of Micah have been preserved cannot be answered simply by reference to the book named after him, because the proportion of the material in it due to him is disputed. The four sections into which it falls must therefore be examined independently:

1–3	Invectives and threats against Israel and Judah
4–5	Promises
6:1–7:7	Exhortations, invectives, and threats
7:8-20	Promises

Lippl and Copass-Carlson ascribe almost the entire book to Micah; the former denies his authorship only of 7:8-20, finding in 4:1-5 an earlier saying used by both Isaiah and Micah; the latter vacillate between Isaiah and Micah as author of 4:1-5. Robinson, on the contrary, though dating some sayings in 4–7 in the preexilic period, finds nothing by Micah in these chapters. The general conclusion of critical scholarship is that 1–3 and 6–7:7 derive almost *in toto* from Micah, while 4–5 and 7:8-20 represent later promises, although one saying or another from 4–5 is occasionally also ascribed to Micah.

2. *First collection.* The situation is clear in the case of the collection of sayings found in 1–3.[1] There can be no doubt that everything here is an original utterance of Micah, expanded only by a few later additions and the promise in 2:12-13, which dates from the exilic or postexilic period. The collection is organized according to subject matter. It begins in 1 with two general sayings directed against Israel and Judah, followed in 2:1–3:8 by sayings directed against the ruling classes and cult prophets in Jerusalem; it concludes with an all-inclusive threat (3:9-12).

In 1:2-9 we have a prophetical judgment discourse against Israel and Judah, consisting of three parts: announcement of the trial, indictment and Yahweh's judgment, lament of the prophet. This unit should not be limited to vss. 2-7 (Eissfeldt*, Weiser*) or analyzed into several smaller units (Robinson *et al.*).

The next section, 1:10-15, is a threat in which the names of villages in the hill country of Judah are made to reveal in a punning sense what will befall

[1] K. Budde, "Das Rätsel von Micha 1," *ZAW*, XXXVII (1917/18), 77-108; *idem* "Micha 2 und 3," *ibid.*, XXXVIII (1919/20), 2-22; H.-M. Weil, "Le chapitre 2 de Michée expliqué par Le Premier Livre des Rois, chapitres 20–22," *RHR*, CXXI (1940), 146-61.

them when the land is devastated. It definitely does not depict the advance of an attacking army; neither, however, is it a true dirge in which Micah laments the separation of this land from Judah by Sennacherib in 701 (Elliger). The observation that the apparently random northern boundary of the places mentioned corresponds to the boundary of the land cut off by Sennacherib is contradicted by the observation that the southern boundary, beyond which additional territory was also cut off, is itself made to run at random. Micah's gaze clearly moves from east to west; north and south play no role at all. Vs. 1:16 is a later addition.

The next section, 2:1-3 (the taunt and its explanation in vss. 4-5 are a later addition[2]), is an invective and threat, as is 3:1-4. The passage 2:6-9 (with vs. 10 as a later addition) is an invective, growing out of discussion, against the ruling classes. In 2:11 we have an invective and in 3:5-8 an invective and threat against the cult prophets, against whom Micah asserts his own authority.

The conclusion, 3:9-12, is a threat with motivation announcing the complete devastation of Jerusalem; according to Jer. 26:18, this threat was still a living memory after more than a century.

3. *Second collection.* Later Micah was known only for his threat. This in itself argues against his authorship of the promises contained in the second collection of sayings (4–5).[3] Some scholars have preferred to ascribe at least 4:1–5:8 (Eng. 4:1–5:9) to him (H. Schmidt, Sellin, *et al.*) or have suggested the possibility for 4:9, 10, 14 (Eng. 5:1) (Wellhausen, Nowack, Sellin-Rost*, *et al.*); 5:1-4 (Eng. 5:2-5) (Weiser*, Sellin-Rost*, *et al.*); or the nucleus of 5:9-14 (Eng. 5:10-15) (Wellhausen, Nowack, Eissfeldt*, Weiser*, *et al.*). Some have seen in 4:14; 5:1-5 (Eng. 5:1-6) earlier sayings from the period before Micah (Crook); others have seen in 4–5 exilic and postexilic sayings from the circle of Micah's hypothetical disciples (Marsh). There is, however, no convincing proof for any of this. The assumption that messianic prophecies must derive from the preexilic period of the monarchy is erroneous; Haggai and Zechariah themselves contradict it. The similarities of these ideas to those in the book of Isaiah proves nothing, because the passages in Isaiah are disputed, to say the least.

In reality, scarcely a single sentence of the sayings in 4–5 is conceivable in the preexilic period. Most of the ideas and phrases occur elsewhere for the most part or exclusively in utterances that definitely date from a later period. Renaud especially has given detailed study to these relationships and instances of dependence; he finds in the chapters an anthology of midrashic exegesis, which he ascribes to a postexilic priestly school of the fifth century. Though this view probably goes too far in the other direction, the postexilic origin of these

[2] For a different view, see A. Alt, "Micha 2,1-5," *NTT,* LVI (1955), 13-23 (= *Kleine Schriften,* III [1959], 373-81).

[3] M. B. Crook, "The Promise in Micah 5," *JBL,* LXX (1951), pp. 313-20; J. Marsh, *Amos and Micah,* "Torch Bible Commentaries," 1959; B. Stade, "Bemerkungen über das Buch Micha," ZAW, I (1881), 161-72; *idem,* "Weitere Bemerkungen zu Micha 4. 5," *ibid.,* III (1883), 1-16.

chapters is clearly established. They presuppose the fall of Jerusalem (4:8), the Exile, and the dispersion (4:6-7); the Davidic dynasty is a thing of the past (5:1-3 [Eng. 5:2-4]).

We are therefore dealing here with a collection of individual sayings of unknown eschatological prophets of the postexilic period. They promise that Jerusalem will be appointed the focal point of God's peaceful kingdom (4:1-5, borrowed in Isa. 2:2-4),[4] that the city will be rebuilt and its scattered people assembled (4:6-7, 8), that the hostile nations will be destroyed (4:9-12, 13-14; 5:4-5 [Eng. 4:9-12; 4:13–5:1; 5:5-6]), that a descendant of David will reign as Messiah (5:1-3 [Eng. 5:2-4]), that Israel will rule its adversaries (5:6-8 [Eng. 5:7-9]), and that instruments of human power and paganism will be abolished (5:9-14 [Eng. 5:10-15]). Thus 4:1-5 and 5:9-14 (Eng. 5:10-15) constitute a homogeneous framework for the entire section.

4. *Third collection.* The third collection, 6:1–7:7, begins with a lengthy judgment discourse (6:1-8) which comprises the announcement of the trial, Yahweh's indictment, the offer of sacrifice by an individual, and God's demand, summarized by the prophet, for justice, love, and devout conduct (a statement drawn from wisdom tradition).[5] This is followed by an invective and threat against the wicked city (6:9-16) and, in what sounds like an elaboration of Isa. 57:1-2, a lament over the perversity of the people and a brief threat (7:1-6[7]). Scholars have attempted to ascribe these utterances to Micah (Eissfeldt*, Weiser*, Sellin-Rost*, *et al.*). This view is contradicted by our previous observations concerning the growth of the prophetical books in accordance with the two-part (or, with expansion, three-part) eschatological schema (§ 54.3). These observations mean that we must be dealing here with a collection of later sayings appended as such to the preceding double collection. There is no concrete evidence for Micah's authorship; excoriation of wicked conduct and demands for righteousness are appropriate in any period. The wisdom theology, with its emphasis on the role of the individual (6:1-8), and the description of social disintegration (7:1-6) suggest a date in the fifth century before the appearance of Nehemiah (Pfeiffer*).[6]

5. *Fourth section.* The fourth section (7:8-20) was recognized as a prophetical liturgy by Gunkel.[7] It comprises a song of confidence (vss. 8-10), an oracle of deliverance (11-13), a prayer similar to a community lament (14-17), and a statement of assurance that the prayer will be heard (18-20); the whole

[4] This view is also supported by E. Cannawurf, "The Authenticity of Micah IV 1-4," *VT,* XIII (1963), 26-33.

[5] Prov. 11:2; Ecclus. 16:25; G. W. Anderson, "A Study of Micah 6,1-8," *SJTh,* IV (1951), 191-97; A. Deissler, "Micha 6,1-8," *Trierer ThZ,* LXVIII (1959), 229-34; J. P. Hyatt, "On the Meaning and Origin of Micah 6,8," *AThR,* XXXIV (1952), 232-39; H. J. Stoebe, "Und demütig sein vor deinem Gott," *WuD,* VI (1959), 180-94.

[6] For 6:1-8 Hyatt even thinks in terms of a Hasidic group of the fourth or third century B.C.

[7] H. Gunkel, "Der Micha-Schluss," *ZS,* II (1924), 145-78; O. Eissfeldt, "Ein Psalm aus Nord-Israel (Micha 7,7-20)," *ZDMG,* CXII (1963), 259-68; B. Reicke, "Mik. 7 såsom 'Messiansk' text," *SEÅ,* XII (1947), 279-302; B. Stade, "Micha 1,2-4 und 7,7-20, ein Psalm," *ZAW,* XXIII (1903), 163-71.

section is built around a personification of Zion. This unit cannot be combined with 7:1-7 to form a liturgical text dealing with the suffering and restoration of the king (Reicke), since 7:1-7 is an independent text. Neither should 14*a* (Hebrew ". . . who dwells alone in a forest in the midst of Carmel") suggest a North Israelite psalm from the catastrophic year 732 or 722 B.C. (Eissfeldt), since the translation in the singular is based only on the Masoretic pointing; the context demands a plural form, which would remove any reference to Yahweh's dwelling on Carmel.[8] As scholars generally assume, the liturgy, which is reminiscent of Trito-Isaiah, with its eschatological promise of Jerusalem's exaltation, derives from the postexilic period.

6. *Structure of the book*. Structurally, the book follows the two-part eschatological schema, twice repeated. First the eschatological promises in 4–5 were appended to Micah's invectives and threats in 1–3, producing the sequence disaster–deliverance. The same "before and after" is repeated in the sections 6:1–7:7 and 7:8-20, which were appended later.

7. *Message*. The small number of sayings in the collection 1–3 that can safely be ascribed to Micah[9] suggests that, even if we assume a brief ministry for this prophet, only a portion of his preaching has been preserved. He nevertheless turns out to be a powerful and markedly individual figure. He had firsthand experience with the social evils he attacks, especially the Jerusalem-based dissolution of ancient agrarian law in favor of large property owners. The violence of his attacks and the bitterness of his threats, which go beyond what is usually found in prophecy, are explained by his sympathy with the sufferings of the peasants and his contempt for the professional cult prophets, who say what the rich want them to say for financial gain. He gives a more basic reason in his description of his mission (3:8): with power, justice, and might he is to confront Israel with its sin. Knowing the righteousness that God wills, he attacks the false security of those who think they stand in God's favor and are therefore protected against any disaster. To the claim to be God's people he replies (2:6-8) tersely and caustically, "You are anything but 'my people!' " His only message, therefore, can be inescapable destruction.

§ 67 Nahum

Cf. commentaries in § 61; individual commentaries: O. Happel, 1902; W. A. Maier, 1959.

J. S. Cochrane, *Literary Features of Nahum*, Dissertation, Dallas Theological Seminary, 1954; A. Haldar, *Studies in the Book of Nahum*, 1947; P. Humbert, "Le

[8] Even if one prefers to retain the singular, "Carmel" could be a site on the eastern slope of the mountains of Judah, as has been shown by A. Jepsen, "Karmel, eine vergessene Landschaft?" *ZDPV*, LXXV (1959), 74-75, for I Samuel 25; II Chron. 26:10; cf. Josh. 15:55.

[9] This casts doubt upon the interesting but hypothetical study of Beyerlin because it derives its amphictyonic interpretation of Judah, under the name of Israel, from 4:14; 5:1-5; 6:2; it also finds Micah's supposed use of the Exodus, occupation, and Davidic covenant traditions basically only in chapters 4–7. The same holds true for the studies of Hammershaimb and Kapelrud, who consider Micah a prophet of both disaster and deliverance.

problème du livre de Nahoum," *RHPhR*, XII (1932), 1-15; P. KLEINERT, "Nahum und der Fall Ninives," *ThStKr*, LXXXIII (1910), 501-34; A. LODS, "Trois études sur la littérature prophétique," *RHPhR*, XI (1931), 211-19; J. L. MIHELIC, "The Concept of God in the Book of Nahum," *Interpr*, II (1948), 199-208; G. SMIT, *Het boek van den profet Nahum*, 1934; cf. also the bibliographies in FOHRER, *ThR*, NF XIX, XX, and XXVIII (§ 52.

1. *Nahum*. The superscription of the book of Nahum tells us only that he comes from Elkosh, but the location of this town, which tradition places near Nineveh as well as in Judea and Galilee, is completely unknown. The opening verse terms Nahum's message an "oracle concerning Nineveh," using the word *maśśāʾ*, frequently applied to oracles against foreign nations. It also describes what follows as the "book of Nahum's vision," using the word *ḥāzôn*, whose use in this sense is late.

2. *Date*. The date of Nahum's activity can be derived in general terms from the superscription and from the content of his sayings, which announce disaster for the Assyrian capital Nineveh, still standing at the time of the oracles. On the one hand, 3:8 ff. presupposes a knowledge of the Assyrians' capture of the Egyptian city Thebes in 663, though it is unclear how far in the past this event lies. On the other hand, Nineveh, which was conquered in 612, is still standing, since Nahum quite clearly is threatening its destruction (Elliger, Robinson). The book cannot possibly be understood as a retrospect after the fall of the city (Humbert, Lods, Sellin), the more so because the textual emendation suggested in 1:9 to support this interpretation is without foundation. The lack of any indictment against Judah by no means presupposes the reformation of Josiah. We may therefore think generally of the time between 663 and 612.

With respect to a more definite dating, opinions differ. Maier thinks in terms of the years prior to 654, and Ungern-Sternberg[1] assigns the sayings of Nahum to the years 630–587. Usually, however, scholars think in terms of the period shortly before 612, when the Assyrian Empire was clearly drawing to an end (H. Schmidt, Horst, Pfeiffer*, Haldar, *et al.*). Elliger and Weiser* also date the majority of the sayings in this period; the former, however, considers some of the sayings more than a decade earlier (the victory song 2:1, 3 [Eng. 1:15, 2:2]), while the latter considers 1:2-9, 1:12-13 + 2:1-3 (Eng. 1:15–2:2), and 3:18-19 supplements to the prophecy of Nahum after the fall of Nineveh. Bentzen*, however, considers an origin soon after 626 probable.

Two pieces of evidence in the book may take us somewhat further. The context suggests that "the wicked" mentioned in 2:1 (Eng. 1:15) is the Assyrian king Ashurbanipal; the verse would then presuppose his death in 626. In addition, the announcement in 2:3 (Eng. 2:2) suggests that Josiah's success in regaining large portions of what had been the Northern Kingdom of Israel still lies in the future; the verse expresses a hope for "all Israel" that remains to be realized. This means that at least the saying containing 2:1, 3 (Eng. 1:15; 2:2)

[1] R. von Ungern-Sternberg and H. Lamparter, *Der Tag des Gerichtes Gottes*, 1960.

dates from the period shortly after 626 and before the political successes of Josiah.

3. *The hymn.* Nahum's sayings are introduced by a hymn in alphabetic form,[2] which, with the omission of the glosses 1:2*b*, 3*a*, comprises 1:2-9. With a transposition in vs. 9, the hymn goes as far as the letter *mêm*. It depicts Yahweh's appearance for judgment (1:2-5), in which he will destroy his adversaries forever but deliver his followers from trouble (6-9). The hypothetical third section, depicting Yahweh's carrying out of his judgment in detail, has been omitted because the following sayings of Nahum are devoted to this theme.

Humbert, however, restricts the psalm to vss. 2-8, while Horst includes vs. 10 and Oesterley-Robinson* think the psalm may extend as far as 2:4 (Eng. 2:3). Gunkel and Bickell in particular have tried to reconstruct it all the way to *tāw*; vss. 10 ff., however, are completely different in both style and content.

With respect to the relationship of the psalm to Nahum and his book, Junker derives the psalm from Nahum, and Weiser* considers this a serious possibility. Horst, on the contrary, assumes that Nahum took the psalm, which was already extant, and placed it before his own writings. Pfeiffer* considers it a later addition.

Now the psalm does not reflect any particular historical situation, but rather speaks in general terms of Yahweh's vengeance upon his adversaries, as is appropriate in a hymn. This fact and the alphabetic form do not argue against Nahum's authorship, but the psalm does differ from Nahum in both style and content. Stylistically it exhibits no idiosyncracies and no refinements beyond what is usual; it is, however, informed with genuine religious vitality. The reverse is true of Nahum's sayings: there we find marked poetic creativeness placed in the service of ideas that are more political and nationalistic than religious. Although this means we must deny Nahum's authorship of the psalm, it remains possible that he himself placed it at the beginning of his utterances, the more so because the hymn breaks off at precisely the point where the prophetical sayings thematically begin.

4. *The sayings.* The beginnings of the first two sayings of Nahum have been telescoped in the course of their transmission; but, with the exception of 1:14, which can be assigned to either the first or the second saying, the original structure can easily be recovered.[3] The first utterance (1:12-13; 2:1, 3 [Eng. 1:12-13, 15; 2:2]) turns out to be a prophetical liturgy, comprising a promise for Judah (1:12-13); the proclamation of a festival with a motivation (2:1 [Eng. 1:15]), which functions as a promise; and a concluding motivation (2:3 [Eng. 2:2]), which possibly should be considered the response of the assembly.

[2] W. R. Arnold, "The Composition of Nahum 1–2,3," *ZAW*, XXI (1901), 225-65; H. Gunkel, "Nahum I," *ibid.*, XIII (1893), 223-44; O. Happel, *Der Psalm Nahum* (*Nahum* 1), 1900; P. Humbert, "Essai d'analyse de Nahoum 1,2–2,3," *ZAW*, XLIV (1926), 266-80; W. C. Graham, "The Interpretation of Nah 1,9–2,3," *AJSL*, XLIV (1927/28), 27-48; P. Humbert, "La vision de Nahoum 2,4-11," *AfO*, V (1928/29), 14-19.

[3] It is best to follow Weiser* against Nowack, Schmidt, and Sellin, taking 1:14 with 1:10-11; 2:2, 4-14 (Elliger finds in 1:12-14 three fragments; Horst finds in 1:11, 14 two fragments).

This is followed in 1:10-11, 14; 2:2, 4-14 (Eng. 2:1, 3-13) by a second prophetical liturgy, with Yahweh and the prophet as speakers. It comprises a threat with motivation against Nineveh (1:10-11, 14), a report of a vision and audition (2:2, 4-11 [Eng. 2:1, 3-10]), a mocking dirge (2:12-13 [Eng. 2:11-12]), and a threat (2:14 [Eng. 2:13]).

A third prophetical liturgy is found in 3:1-7, which comprises a report of a vision and audition together with a double motivation of the threat against Nineveh contained in this section (3:1-4), a threat placed in Yahweh's mouth (3:5-6), and a mocking dirge (3:7).

We come finally to the last sayings, a mocking threat (3:8-17) and a mocking dirge (3:18-19), both once more directed against Nineveh.

5. *The book as a whole.* It is usually assumed that the book of Nahum as a whole, like most of the prophetical books, represents a collection of originally independent sayings, between which there is no outward connection apart from the subject matter. Other views, however, have also been expressed.

Humbert, followed especially by Sellin, considers the book a single unified liturgy for a thanksgiving celebration on the occasion of the fall of Nineveh, which was recited in the Jerusalem Temple on the following New Year festival; the psalm (1:2 ff.) and the concluding lament over Nineveh were recited by the congregation. Weiser*, too, believes that the entire book (put together in two stages out of genuine threats and supplementary material) was recited during the festal cult in 612. Sellin-Rost* likewise think in terms of a festival liturgy made up of the prophecy in 2:2 ff. (Eng. 2:1 ff.) and the preceding psalm together with an utterance of Yahweh (1:12–2:1 [Eng. 1:12-15]). Finally, Bentzen* assumes a liturgy modeled after the ritual preparatory to a military campaign. In contrast to the others, he dates the liturgy in the period after 626.

Haldar, on the contrary, assumes that the book is a religio-political work produced by a cultic circle in Jerusalem which, for its political propaganda against Nineveh, equated the political enemy with cultic and mythological enemies, as well as actualizing motifs found throughout the ancient Near East. On this hypothesis he maintains the unity of the book.

In fact, the individual sayings do not appear to stand in isolation; they presuppose and continue the thought of each other, thereby constituting a whole with an objective unity. In addition, there are liturgical elements: the psalm functions as an introductory hymn, which a choir or the congregation could have sung; 2:3 (Eng. 2:2) is a kind of response to 2:1 (Eng. 1:15). Furthermore, we find the form of the prophetical liturgy (an imitation of the cult) thrice repeated. Of course, this very fact and the lack of any dialogue between God and man mean that we are not dealing with a liturgy intended for cultic recitation. What we probably have in the book is an artfully assembled series of utterances belonging to various literary types, what might be termed a "cantata" to be recited in the cult by prophets.[4] Another real possibility is the interpretation of the hymn and its following section (1:12-13; 2:1, 3 [Eng.

[4] Lindblom applies this term to Isaiah 24–27.

1:15; 2:2]) as a real liturgy, concluding with a response of the people (2:3 [Eng. 2:2]). In this case the other sections should be considered independent sayings.

6. *Message.* Nahum's message does exhibit some genuinely prophetical insights: it acknowledges Yahweh as lord of all nations, speaks of Assyria's commission to punish Judah, and excoriates Assyria's policies as being against God's will, for which reason the announced upheavals will take place. Primarily, however, Nahum is a representative of optimistic prophecy with a strong feeling of nationalism that dominates the cultic element. In his view Yahweh acts—even when using foreign nations—exclusively with Judah in mind and for Judah's benefit, in order to realize the hope of all Israel. Striking features are the gloating mockery in 3:8-17—a saying that does not even mention God—and the idea of vengeance that even threatens the destruction of the enemies' children (3:10). When first heard, the accounts of the visions must have aroused people in the same way. This attitude even affects the rhetorical forms that are used: the mocking dirges, one of which (3:7) follows immediately upon an utterance of Yahweh. To this extent we may follow Haldar in speaking of the almost propagandistic character of the book, even though rejecting as remote his derivation of the book's ideas and expressions from ancient Near Eastern myths and cults. Nahum's cantata may have served to promote Judah's dissociation from Assyria, begun by King Josiah after the death of Ashurbanipal. He nevertheless belongs among the cult prophets, with whom Jeremiah had to struggle a few years later and who came dangerously close to the boundary between true and false prophecy.[5]

§ 68 Habakkuk

Cf. commentaries in § 61.

W. H. Brownlee, *The Text of Habakkuk in the Ancient Commentary from Qumran,* 1959; K. Budde, "Habakuk," *ZDMG,* LXXXIV (1930), 139-47; *idem,* "Zum Text von Habakuk Kap. 1 und 2," XXXIV (1931), 409-11; W. W. Cannon, "The Integrity of Habakkuk cc. 1.2.," *ZAW,* XLIII (1925), 62-90; M. Delcor, "La geste de Yahvé au temps de l'Exode et l'espérance du psalmiste en Habacuc III," in *Miscellanea Biblica Ubach,* 1954, pp. 287-302; B. Duhm, *Das Buch Habakuk,* 1906; P. Humbert, *Problèmes du livre d'Habacuc,* 1944; L. Lachmann, *Das Buch Habbakuk,* 1932; E. Nielsen, "The Righteous and the Wicked in Habaqquq," *StTh, VI* (1953), 54-78; J. W. Rothstein, "Über Habakkuk, Kap. 1 und 2," *ThStKr,* LXVII (1894), 51-85; H. Schmidt, "Ein Psalm im Buche Habakkuk," *ZAW,* LXII (1950), 52-63; B. Stade, "Habakuk," *ibid.,* IV (1884), 154-59; W. Staerk, "Zu Habakuk 1,5-11. Geschichte oder Mythos?" *ibid.,* LI (1933), 1-28; C. C. Torrey, "The Prophecy of Habakkuk," in *Kohut Memorial Volume,* 1935, pp. 565-82; H. H. Walker and N. W. Lund, "The Literary Structure of the Book of Habakkuk," *JBL,* LIII (1934), 355-70; cf. also the bibliographies in Fohrer, *ThR,* NF XIX, XX, and XXVIII (§ 52).

[5] The relatively high estimation of Nahum by Horst and Mihelic minimizes this prophet's optimistic nationalism.

1. *Habakkuk*. Habakkuk, whose name is not firmly attested (the LXX reads *ambakoum*), is referred to in the superscription (1:1) as a professional prophet (nabi) with a message against foreign nations (*maśśā'*). He was probably associated with the Jerusalem Temple, where he actively sought to receive a vision (2:1), proclaimed the instruction that he received (2:4), and wrote it upon a tablet (2:2; cf. Isa. 8:1). Apart from his own book he is mentioned in the late, unhistorical legend of Bel and the Dragon, an addition to the book of Daniel.

2. *Transmission and individual problems*. Habakkuk's material begins (1:2-4) with an individual lament over a violent and wicked man, which nevertheless, like lamentation of a prayer leader, refers to the distress of the people as a whole. This is answered by a favorable oracle of Yahweh (1:5-11), which announces a change of fortune that Yahweh is summoning the Chaldeans to bring about. In place of a thanksgiving or statement of confidence there follows (1:12-17) a second lament with questions and statements; it bemoans the fact that the wicked man is still allowed to swallow up the righteous and to slay nations. In what follows the prophet strives to receive a vision, is ordered by Yahweh to write down the favorable oracle that he receives, and is exhorted to await its realization confidently (2:1-4). The next section comprises five "woes" (2:5-17,[1] expanded by the addition of 2:18-19, 20), which confront the rapacious and brutal man with his transgressions and announce the corresponding punishments.

The announcement of the Chaldeans' coming (1:5-11) has occasionally been considered out of place, interrupting the single lament 1:2-4, 12-17; the verses in question have either been removed (Wellhausen *et al.*) or, interpreted as Yahweh's first reply, placed after 2:4 (Budde) or 2:5*a* (Rothstein). We are, however, dealing with two independent laments in different meter, the second of which presupposes the oracle of Yahweh in 1:5-11 and inquires why the judgment announced therein against the wicked has not long since come to pass. Furthermore, a series of two laments and two oracles is not unusual. In addition, 2:5(*a*) is often appended to the second oracle of Yahweh, 2:1-4 (Weiser*, Brownlee,[2] *et al.*). To do so, however, is to deny the parallel structure of the woes, each of which contains four long verses. The saying beginning with 2:6*b* must be preceded by another in 2:5-6*a*. This means that 2:4 itself must constitute Yahweh's second oracle (Stenzel *et al.*).[3]

Chapter 3 has its own superscription, "a prayer of the nabi Habakkuk," together with liturgico-musical notes.[4] Apart from the later addition in vss. 17-19, the chapter comprises a central section, vss. 3-15, which depicts in hymnic fashion the appearance of Yahweh, his battle reflected in the tumult of nature, and his victory over the ungodly on behalf of his people, together with

[1] The first "Woe . . ." should be restored at the beginning of 2:5, and 2:17 placed directly after 2:13; M. Stenzel, "Habakkuk II 15-16," *VT*, III (1953), 97-99.

[2] W. H. Brownlee, "The Placarded Revelation of Habakkuk," *JBL*, LXXXII (1963), 319-25.

[3] M. Stenzel, "Habakuk 2,1–4,5a," *Bibl*, XXXIII (1952), 506-10.

[4] J. H. Eaton, "The Origin and Meaning of Habakkuk 3," *ZAW*, LXXVI (1964), 144-71; W. A. Irwin, "The Psalm of Habakkuk," *JNES*, I (1942), 10-40.

a framework, vss. 2 and 16, which describes the prophet's reception of the vision. Ever since Stade, many scholars have denied Habakkuk's authorship of 3, explaining it as a supplement dating from the postexilic period (Irwin denies Habakkuk's authorship but maintains the preexilic dating). H. Schmidt considers not only the processional hymn 3:1-17 but also 1:2-4, 12-13; 3:18-19 (which he thinks constitute an individual lament) to be later additions. The Habakkuk Commentary from Qumran (1QpHab) discusses only chapters 1–2 and takes no account of chapter 3. This cannot be cited as evidence against Habakkuk's authorship of 3, however, because many reasons can be adduced for the failure to mention chapter 3. There is no reason to conclude that chapter 3 was not a part of the book of Habakkuk at the time. That chapter 3 was written by the author of 1–2 is shown by the identity of subject matter, the similarity of language, and the reference of 3:2 to 2:1-4. The ecstatic visionary experience of the prophet presupposed in 2:1-4 is depicted in 3:2 in terms of its effect upon him.

3. *The prophecy as a whole*. The prophecy of Habakkuk as a whole does not constitute a literary unity (Walker-Lund); neither, however, is it merely a collection of sayings (Eissfeldt*, Weiser*). Balla,[5] despite his erroneous dating, and Sellin, Humbert, and Nielsen, despite their erroneous identification of the wicked man, are essentially right in identifying the book as a prophetical liturgy. More precisely, we may say that 1–2 constitutes a prophetical imitation of a cultic liturgy, in which Habakkuk is the sole speaker. In lament and prayer he uses the vocabulary of cultic poetry; he also employs cultic literary types (lament and hymn), appears in the Jerusalem Temple leading the community in prayer, undergoes an ecstatic visionary experience there, and writes his oracle down. Above all, 1–2 exhibit the twice-repeated sequence lament–oracle; in its own fashion, Jer. 14:2–15:2 exhibits the same structure.[6] The woes are closely associated with this pattern: they both presuppose the two oracles of Yahweh and, within the framework of the whole, occupy the position following lament and positive oracle usually occupied by statement of assurance or thanksgiving:

1:2-4 First lament
1:5-11 First oracle of Yahweh
1:12-17 Second lament
2:1-4 Reception and proclamation of the second oracle of Yahweh
2:5-17 Woes, functioning as assurance of a favorable response

Assuming that Habakkuk recited this liturgy in the cult and wrote down the saying in 2:4 which constitutes its nucleus, it still remains to define the role of

[5] E. Balla in *RGG*, 2nd ed., II [1928], 1556-57.

[6] The double development from lament to petition is found in Ps. 22:1-12, 13-22 (Eng. 22:1-11, 12-21); 59:2-6, 7-15 (Eng. 59:1-5, 6-14); 69:1-7, 8-13 (Eng. 69:1-6, 7-12); 88:2-10, 11-13, 14-19 (Eng. 88:1-9, 10-12, 13-18); 102:2-23, 24-29 (Eng. 102:1-22, 23-28); 109:1-20, 21-31; 140:2-6, 7-2 (Eng. 140:1-5, 6-11). The double development from invocation and lament to assurance of a favorable reply or to an oath is found in Ps. 35:1-10, 11-27; 86:1-13, 14-17; a triple structure is found in Psalm 71.

chapter 3, which several scholars prefer to trace back to Egyptian (Zolli[7]), Babylonian (Irwin[8]), or Ugaritic traditions (Cassuto, Gaster, Albright[9]), overlooking the much more marked influence of the OT theophanies. Chapter 3 can also hardly be interpreted as a psalm of lament drawing its ideas from the conceptual world of the autumnal New Year festival (Mowinckel[10]). The verses of the framework (3:2, 16) characterize it as a vision report and connect it with 2:1-4. Weiser* has therefore gone so far as to suggest that it is the vision to be written upon the tablets in the Temple and that it originally followed 2:1-3. The liturgical structure of 1–2, however, requires that the woes follow directly upon the favorable oracle, which by its very nature is brief. Chapter 3 is far too extensive to be such an oracle. In 3:2-16 we definitely have a description of the vision that was granted to Habakkuk (2:1 ff.). It was recorded independently of the prophetical liturgy, to which it was appended as a supplementary and corroborating conclusion. At the same time, it shows why the prophet was content with Yahweh's second oracle although it represents no advance beyond the first, and why he was able to pronounce the woes as an "assurance of a favorable response": his vision had convinced him completely.

4. *The central problem: the wicked man and the Chaldeans.* The central problem of Habakkuk's prophecy is the identification of the "wicked man" who is indicted and threatened and the determination of the role of the Chaldeans (1:6). First of all, the two must probably be distinguished rather than equated, whether or not 1:5-11 is omitted. Habakkuk therefore was not bewailing the cruel treatment of various nations, especially Judah, at the hands of the Chaldeans (Wellhausen, Sellin, Nötscher, *et al.*). Yahweh is just arousing the Chaldeans (1:6), while the oppression at the hands of the wicked man has lasted a considerable period. These Chaldeans are the founders of the Neo-Babylonian Empire, just making their appearance on the stage of ancient Near Eastern history. This interpretation must be adhered to, even though it has clearly at times appeared too simple and been denied, even when the wicked man is not identified with the Chaldeans.

a) Various scholars have interpreted the Chaldeans to be the Persians (Lauterburg[11]), the Seleucids about 170 B.C. (Happel[12]), a mythological demonic power sent as a punishment by Yahweh (Staerk), or an unidentified conquering nation (Horst). These suggestions fly in the face of the completely unambiguous text of 1:6, as does the assumption that Habakkuk interpolated the Chaldeans as a secondary addition (Elliger). Above all, starting with Duhm several schol-

[7] I. Zolli, "Una teofania biblica e la riforma religiosa di Amenofi IV Echenaton," in *Actes du XXe Congrès International des Orientalistes*, 1940, pp. 278-85.

[8] W. A. Irwin, "The Mythological Background of Habakkuk Chapter 3," *JNES*, XV (1956), 47-50.

[9] W. F. Albright, "The Psalm of Habakkuk," in *T. H. Robinson-Festschrift*, 1950, pp. 1-18; U. Cassuto, "Il capitolo 3 di Habaquq e i testi di Ras Shamra," *Annuario Studi Ebraici*, 1935-37, pp. 7-22; T. H. Gaster, "On Habakkuk 3,4," *JBL*, LXII (1943), 345-46.

[10] S. Mowinckel, "Zum Psalm des Habakuk," *ThZ*, IX (1953), 1-23.

[11] Lauterburg, *ThZ a. d. Schweiz*, XIII (1896), 74-102.

[12] O. Happel, *Das Buch des Propheten Habakkuk*, 1900.

ars, emending *Chaldeans* to *Kittim*, have suggested the Greeks under Alexander the Great, a suggestion to which Budde has objected strenuously. There is no evidence for such an emendation, which is quite arbitrary. The Habakkuk Commentary of Qumran, it is true, interprets 1:6 as referring to the Kittim, i.e., the Seleucids or Romans of the second or first century B.C.; despite this historical updating, however, the text as quoted actually speaks of the Chaldeans, so that this early evidence actually argues against any emendation.

b) The wicked man against whom the Babylonians will take the field has occasionally been identified as the Judean king Jehoiakim, possibly as the representative of the godless elements in Judah (Rothstein, Oesterley-Robinson*, Humbert, Nielsen). Although the idea that Yahweh is sending a foreign nation to carry out his judgment against Israel is quite in line with prophetical thought, this interpretation is out of the question because in several passages Habakkuk clearly refers to a foreign power (1:17; 2:5, 8) and announces that Yahweh will help his "anointed," i.e., the king of Judah (3:13). The term *maśśā'* applied to Habakkuk's prophecy likewise indicates that he is speaking against a foreign nation. The only possible candidate in the period where the Babylonians are first making their appearance is the Assyrians, who are also suggested by the connection between 2:17 and Isa. 37:24, as well as the echoes of Nahum (1:11; 2:13; 3:1). Thus Habakkuk is announcing that Assyrian rule, under which Judah suffered along with other nations, is about to be destroyed by the Babylonians, acting as Yahweh's instrument. This is the meaning of the saying that Habakkuk clearly wrote down as the nucleus of his vision (2:4): " 'He who is puffed up' [or: 'The wicked man'] 'has' no life in him, but the righteous will remain alive because of his faithfulness."

5. *Date*. This argument allows us to fix the date of Habakkuk's prophecy. It must have been composed after 626, when the Chaldeans appeared on the brink of history following the successful revolt of Nabopolassar, and before the fall of the Assyrian Empire in 612. Since Assyrian rule was still felt to be oppressive, which was impossible after the measures taken during Josiah's reformation, in which Judah declared its independence from Assyria and experienced a rebirth of nationalism, Habakkuk must have appeared before 622. Humbert's study of the book's vocabulary points to the same period. He should perhaps be dated a little later than Nahum, who plainly knows nothing of the Chaldeans. That they will bring about the fall of Assyria is the new message that Habakkuk pronounces.

6. *The character of Habakkuk*. Like Nahum, Habakkuk is a cult prophet. To him Judah is the "righteous" (2:4), to whom he promises aid rather than demanding humility and repentance. He sees God's righteousness not as a demand placed upon his people but as a contrast to the wicked empire. Especially in comparison with the contemporaneous utterances of Jeremiah (1–6), his prophecy exhibits a degree of nationalistic optimism that cannot be overlooked. In contrast to Nahum, however, the nationalistic element is not central, but rather his dismay at the moral injustice of the Assyrian empire and the question of God's righteous governance in history. Although, after the first oracle of Yah-

weh, Habakkuk is still without the confidence that comes of faith, he shares the true prophetical awareness of the majesty of God, who intervenes on behalf of those who are unjustly treated, possesses power over all the nations, raises them up or brings them low, and uses them as instruments of his will. These insights bring him finally to demand the confident endurance of the faithful, contrary to all appearances.

§ 69 Zephaniah

Cf. commentaries in § 61.

C. H. Cornill, "Die Prophetie Zephanjas," *ThStKr*, LXXXIX (1916), 297-332; G. Gerleman, *Zephanja*, 1942; J. P. Hyatt, "The Date and Background of Zephaniah," *JNES*, VII (1948), 25-29; F. Schwally, "Das Buch Ssefanjâ," *ZAW*, X (1890), 165-240; L. P. Smith and E. L. Lacheman, "The Authorship of the Book of Zephaniah," *JNES*, IX (1950), 137-42; D. L. Williams, "The Date of Zephaniah," *JBL*, LXXXII (1963), 77-88; cf. also the bibliographies in Fohrer, *ThR*, NF XIX, XX, and XXVIII (§ 52).

1. *Genealogy and date.* In quite unusual fashion the superscription (1:1) gives for Zephaniah a genealogy that goes back four generations; the last person named bears the name Hezekiah. It has been suggested that this refers to the king of Judah who bore this name, so that Zephaniah was of royal blood; if such were the case, however, Hezekiah's royal status would have been mentioned, the more so because the name itself was common in Judah. More likely, the ancestors of the father were named so as to avoid the embarrassing misconception that Zephaniah's father, Cushi, was an Ethiopian and not a Judean.

The superscription also correctly dates Zephaniah during the reign of Josiah (639–609). The content of the book reveals more precisely that the Deuteronomic reformation had not yet taken place: alien gods are still worshiped in Jerusalem (1:4-5). Since 1:8 mentions only the royal princes and not the king himself, at least a portion of Zephaniah's sayings can derive from the period of the king's minority. His ministry can therefore be dated around 630 B.C.

It is therefore inadvisable to follow Hyatt and Williams in rejecting the statement of the superscription and placing Zephaniah's ministry at least two decades later, under Jehoiakim, or to follow Smith and Lacheman in interpreting the book as a pseudepigraphic work composed around 200 B.C.

2. *Sayings.* Zephaniah seems to have left his sayings, as usual, in the form of individual utterances. For the most part we are dealing with small units (Elliger, Horst). Five sayings against Judah and Jerusalem can definitely be ascribed to Zephaniah: 1:4-5, 7-9, 12-13, 14-16; 2:1-3. In them he attacks idolatry, the imitation of practices deriving from alien religions, and the self-confident who doubt Yahweh's wrath. Using the concept of the Day of Yahweh as transformed by Amos and Isaiah, he threatens the judgment that will come on this day so impressively that its echoes are still heard in the Latin poem modeled on 1:14-16, "*Dies irae, dies illa.*" Like Amos, he sees a possibility of deliverance if the people

repent in time and turn to righteousness and humility (2:3). Of the appended threats aganst foreign nations, only the sayings against the Philistine cities (2:4) and against Assyria (2:13-14), together with the comprehensive threat (3:6-8), can be traced to Zephaniah. The only passage in the last section that derives from him is 3:11-13, announcing a purifying judgment that will leave a humble and lowly remnant of Israel, which will then seek its modest happiness by taking refuge in Yahweh. Some scholars (Oesterley-Robinson* *et al.*) have suggested that the Scythian invasion, which, according to Herodotus' account, swept over Palestine between 630 and 625, occasioned Zephaniah's threats, especially his announcement of the Day of Yahweh. This, however, is unlikely; apart from the fact that the assumption of a Scythian attack is itself problematical, Zephaniah makes no reference to it.

To the sayings of Zephaniah just discussed were added first three not particularly profound threats (1:2-3, 10-11, 17-18), the last of which, after the fashion of a later period, announces the last judgment for all the inhabitants of the earth. Several oracles against foreign nations also derive from a later period: 2:5-7, against the Philistine coast; 2:8-11, against Moab and Ammon; 2:12, against the Cushites; 2:15, an addition to the saying against Assyria; and 3:1-5, against Jerusalem. Later eschatological promises are to be found in 3:9-10, which discusses the transformation of the nations, and 3:14-15, 16-18*aα*, 18*aβ*, sayings influenced by Deutero-Isaiah.

3. *Redaction.* Whether the nine sayings of Zephaniah were first brought together in minor collections is dubious in view of their small number, the more so because the later sayings have been interpolated between them. The material now found in 1:2–3:13 was probably assembled in one large redaction and later expanded by the addition of the sayings in 3:14-20. In particular, the addition of these latter sayings, which added unmixed expectations of salvation to Zephaniah's modest outlook for the future, gave the book a structure that follows the three-part eschatological schema:

1:2–2:3 Threats against the prophet's own nation
2:4–3:8 Threats against foreign nations
3:9-20 Promises

4. *Message.* According to Gerleman, Zephaniah, a disciple of Isaiah, directs his preaching against the circles of the cult prophets at Jerusalem, from whom Deuteronomy derives. He is nevertheless influenced by their ideas, so that in him the strain of pessimistic prophecy represented by Isaiah comes near to the school of religious nationalism, with the concept of the remnant providing the basis for synthesis. We may say more generally that Zephaniah followed in the footsteps of Isaiah, Amos, and Micah, in particular developing and elaborating the interpretation of the Day of Yahweh put forward by the first two. Yahweh's terrible judgment will overwhelm the sinful ruling class of Judah and Jerusalem along with other nations. If, however, the people make use of the time remaining to recall the commandments of Yahweh, if they repent and turn to righteous-

ness and humility, a portion of Israel will be spared, like the remnant of an army that escapes after a bloody defeat; as in the days of their fathers, they will dwell humble and lowly, but faithful, upon Mount Zion, will act righteously, and live in peace.

§ 70 Haggai

Cf. commentaries in § 61.

P. R. Ackroyd, "Studies in the Book of Haggai," *JJS*, II (1951), 163-76; III (1952), 1-13; *idem*, "The Book of Haggai and Zechariah 1–8," *ibid.*, pp. 151-56; *idem*, "Some Interpretative Glosses in the Book of Haggai," *ibid.*, VII (1956), 163-67; *idem*, "Two Old Testament Historical Problems of the Early Persian Period," *JNES*, XVII (1958), 13-27; A. Bentzen, "Quelques remarques sur le mouvement messianique parmi les Juifs aux environs de l'an 520 avant Jésus-Christ," *RHPhR*, X (1930), 493-503; P. F. Bloomhardt, "The Poems of Haggai," *HUCA*, V (1928), 153-95; K. Galling, "Serubbabel und der Hohepriester beim Wiederaufbau des Tempels in Jerusalem," in *Studien zur Geschichte Israels im persischen Zeitalter*, 1964, pp. 127-58, later version, "Serubbabel und der Wiederaufbau des Tempels in Jerusalem" in *Rudolph-Festschrift*, 1961, pp. 67-96; F. Hesse, "Haggai," *ibid.*, pp. 109-34; F James, "Thoughts on Haggai and Zechariah," *JBL*, LIII (1934), 229-35; F. S. North, "Critical Analysis of the Book of Haggai," *ZAW*, LXVIII (1956), 25-46; J. W. Rothstein, *Juden und Samaritaner*, 1908; L. Waterman, "The Camouflaged Purge of Three Messianic Conspirators," *JNES*, XIII (1954), 73-78; H. W. Wolff, *Haggai*, 1951; cf. also the bibliographies in Fohrer, *ThR*, NF XIX, XX, and XXVIII (§ 52).

1. *Haggai.* The prophet Haggai, who is also mentioned in Ezra 5:1; 6:14, seems to have been among those who returned from the Babylonian Exile, since he supports their endeavors wholeheartedly. He is called a nabi (1:1), and was probably a cult prophet at Jerusalem. The suggestion that he was already very old and was of priestly ancestry does not follow from 2:3-4, 10-19. The period of his prophetical ministry is fixed by the dates mentioned for his utterances. They extend from the first day of the sixth month (August 29) to the twenty-fourth day of the ninth month (December 18/19) of the second regnal year of the Persian King Darius (520 B.C.). His words are supplemented by Zechariah 1–8 and Ezra 3–6.

2. *Sayings.* Haggai's sayings are not in prose; they are preserved in the metrical form of short verses. The question must remain open whether Haggai proclaimed them in this form or adapted them to it later as the proper meter for a report.

In 1:1-11 he calls upon the people to rebuild the Temple, which the Babylonians had destroyed; he interprets the prevailing misery as Yahweh's punishment, inflicted because the people think only of their own houses and not of the Temple. In this saying vss. 7-8 belong after vs. 11; when they were displaced, vs. 6 came to be included once more in *9a*, in order to preserve the transition to the following sentences. The appended report (1:12-14) tells of the success of Haggai's demand and the beginning of the construction work. As Rothstein has shown,[1] the fragmentary date in 1:15*a* goes with the second saying, 2:15-19 (expanded by the addition of vss. 17, 18*b*). A few weeks after the beginning of construction, probably on the day the new cornerstone was laid, it promises an end to the drought that has produced all the misery and, for the future, rich blessings. The third saying comprises 1:15*b;* 2:1-9. In the face of complaints over the wretchedness of the new building in comparison with the Temple of Solomon, which are the product of clearheaded observation, not of reactionary conservatism,[2] Haggai promises that the new Temple will in fact surpass the former in glory because, as a consequence of the world convulsion of the eschaton, the treasures of all nations will flow to it. The next section, 2:10-14, reports how Haggai seeks a priestly torah, according to which what is unclean has a contagious effect, but not what is holy. Haggai concludes, as Rothstein has shown by referring to Ezra 4:1-5, that the people must refuse to let the ruling class of Samaria or those Judeans who remained in the land in 587 participate in the building of the Temple and in its worship; otherwise the Temple and its cult would become unclean. The last saying, 2:20-23, is a promise for Zerubbabel, the commissar of Davidic ancestry appointed by the Persians, that, after the imminent destruction of the other kingdoms, Yahweh will make him like his "signet ring," the messianic king of the eschaton. Here and in Zechariah we encounter the messianic hope for the first time, at the outset applied to a specific person, later applied generally to a descendant of the Davidic dynasty.

3. *The book.* The book came into being as a collection and revision of Haggai's sayings. The collector added redactional introductions to them, in which he refers to Haggai as "the prophet" and says that the word of Yahweh came to (*'el*) him or through his mediation (*b^{e}yad*). He also is probably responsible for the interpolation of the report in 1:12-14. The whole is structured chronologically: the sayings follow one another in the sequence in which they were pronounced. This sequence is interrupted only by the transposition of the saying at the laying of the cornerstone from its proper place after 1:15*a* to its present position (2:15-19). Whether this is due to a confusion of the dates or to a desire to conceal the laying of the cornerstone, which Sheshbazzar had already undertaken in 537, cannot be determined.

Rothstein and Sellin assume instead that the book constitutes a section taken from a comprehensive account of the building of the Temple, to which the report of Zechariah's activity also belonged; this is unlikely. Although everything in the book is associated with the building, it does not exhibit the style of a historical report. Eissfeldt* assumes that the book was put together out of two different collections, Haggai's memoirs and a collection of his sayings; this, too, is hardly likely. The brief report in 1:12-14 is too scant a foundation to support the assumption of memoirs; the seeking of the torah (2:10-14), which could not be presented in any other way, and the redactional introductions to the sayings cannot be cited as further evidence. Neither can we

[1] For a different view, see K. Galling in *Rudolph-Festschrift,* 1961, p. 79 n. 52.

[2] According to Galling, *op. cit.,* p. 80, Haggai is not referring to the new construction, but to the chaotic ruins of the destroyed Temple.

assume, with North, that a short basic narrative containing three extremely brief oracles has been expanded by the addition of considerable secondary material.

4. *Message.* Haggai's preaching is outwardly influenced by the fact that he appeared at a time of crisis for the new Persian Empire. This must have aroused hope in Judah that Yahweh would finally bring about the long-awaited transformation of all things and inaugurate the age of eschatological salvation, exercising dominion over the world through his Davidic representative. In view of the Persian crisis, the major question of the postexilic period demanded an answer: When would the eschatological eon begin? Haggai associates it with the building of the Temple, hearing Yahweh himself exhort the people to this work in terms of the doctrine of retribution (drought—blessing): the Temple must be built without further excuses! Haggai looks upon the day of the cornerstone-laying as the beginning of the peripateia—the future holds only blessing!—and expects, upon completion of the building, a convulsion that will shake all nature and all nations, as the transition is completed and the time of salvation truly begins.

Haggai does still exhibit prophetical traits, emphatically defending God's honor. In at least equal degree we find traits associated with the cult prophets and the law, connected with eschatological and messianic ideas and a materialistic picture of the age of salvation. Haggai is no more than an epigone of the prophets; his real significance lies in his having started the construction of the Temple, but also in his having rejected willing but cultically suspect helpers, thereby inaugurating the sequestration that was to be typical of later Judaism. The twenty-fourth day of the ninth month, 520 B.C., when this took place, may be called the birthday of Judaism.

§ 71 ZECHARIAH (ZECHARIAH 1–8)

Cf. commentaries in § 61; individual commentaries: M. BIČ, 1962; M. F. UNGER, 1963.

C. L. FEINBERG, "Exegetical Studies in Zechariah," *BS*, XCVII (1940)—CIII (1946); K. GALLING, "Die Exilswende in der Sicht des Propheten Sacharja," *VT*, II (1952), 18-36 (= *Studien zur Geschichte Israels im persischen Zeitalter*, 1964, pp. 109-26); A. JEPSEN, "Kleine Beiträge zum Zwölfprophetenbuch, III," *ZAW*, LXI (1945-48), 95-104; K. MARTI, *Der Prophet Sacharia, der Zeitgenosse Serubbabels*, 1892; *idem*, "Zwei Studien zu Sacharja," *ThStKr*, LXV (1892), 207-45, 716-34; *idem*, "Die Zweifel an der prophetischen Sendung Sacharjas," in *Wellhausen-Festschrift*, 1914, pp. 279-97; H. G. May, "A Key to the Interpretation of Zechariah's Vision," *JBL*, LVII (1938), 173-84; L. G. RIGNELL, *Die Nachtgesichte des Sacharja*, 1950; J. W. ROTHSTEIN, *Die Nachtgesichte des Sacharja*, 1910; cf. also the bibliographies in FOHRER, *ThR*, NF XIX, XX, and XXVIII (§ 52).

1. *Zechariah and his date.* According to redactional statements in 1:1, *7b*, Zechariah was the son of Berechiah and the grandson of Iddo. Ezra 5:1; 6:14, however, correctly call him the son of Iddo. There has been confusion with

another Zechariah, perhaps the son of Jeberechiah mentioned in Isa. 8:2. Neh. 12:16 calls him the head of the priestly house of Iddo, so that he, like Jeremiah and Ezekiel, was of priestly descent, although this does not necessarily mean that he functioned as both prophet and priest. It does, however, explain the priestly interests in his prophecy and certain points of contact with Ezekiel.

The date of his prophetical activity is fixed at least to some extent by the three dates in 1:1, *7a*; 7:1, which cover the period from the eighth month of the second year of Darius (520) to the ninth month of his fourth year (518 B.C.). It is likely, however, that his appearances extended beyond the latter date, as the saying in 3:8-9 suggests; it may have been pronounced at or following the dedication of the new Temple in 515. In any event, he is a younger contemporary of Haggai, who probably returned from the Exile with Zerubbabel. He began his prophetical preaching somewhat later than Haggai, continued it alongside him for a time, and extended his ministry after the close of Haggai's. He also backed the building of the Temple, but devoted most of his preaching to the themes of the irruption of the eschatological age and the organization of the eschatological community, together with the practical problems of his period.

2. *Sayings and reports.* It has long been recognized (albeit with various explanations) that the traditional material associated with Zechariah is found only in chapters 1–8 of the book that bears his name. Considered in detail, this material comprises both sayings and two kinds of report.

A. The most striking are the "night visions," i.e., visions during the night, found in 1:7–6:8. They are all interrelated and are devoted to the theme of the eschatological time of salvation, which is about to arrive, or rather is already arriving.

1. 1:7-15	Vision of "riders": God's jealous love is unshakable, despite appearances to the contrary.[1]
2. 2:1-4 (Eng. 1:18-21)	Vision of "horns": God convulses the nations and calls them to account.
3. 2:5-9 (Eng. 2:1-5)	Vision of a "measuring line": Jerusalem is set up as capital of God's kingdom, protected by God without obstructive and unnecessary city walls.
4. 3:1-7	Vision of a "heavenly court": Despite all accusations, Joshua is appointed high priest and the Temple precincts are withdrawn from secular control.[2]
5. 4:1-*6aα*, *10b*-14	Vision of a "lampstand": The messianic rule is divided between a political and a cultic representative (Zerubbabel and Joshua).[3]

[1] H. W. Hertzberg, " 'Grüne' Pferde," *ZDPV*, LXIX (1953), 177-80; R. Press, "Das erste Nachtgesicht des Propheten Sacharja," *ZAW*, LIV (1936), 43-48.

[2] K. Galling, "Das vierte Nachtgesicht des Propheten Sacharja," *ZMR*, XLVI (1931), 193-208; H. Schmidt, "Das vierte Nachtgesicht des Propheten Sacharja," *ZAW*, LIV (1936), 48-60.

[3] J. Böhmer, "Was bedeutet der goldene Leuchter Sach 4,2?" *BZ*, XXIV (1938/39), 360-64; H. Frey, "Der siebenarmige Leuchter und die Ölsöhne," in *von Bulmerincq-Gedenkschrift*, 1938, pp. 20-63; K. Möhlenbrink, "Der Leuchter im fünften Nachtgesicht des Sacharja," *ZDPV*, LII (1929), 257-86; L. Rost, "Bemerkungen zu Sacharja 4," *ZAW*, LXIII (1952), 216-21 (= *Das kleine Credo*, 1965, pp. 64-70).

6. 5:1-4	Vision of a "scroll": The question of false ownership in Judah is decided in favor of the ancient rights of the returning exiles.
7. 5:5-11	Vision of an "ephah": The people's sins are absolved in the time of salvation.[4]
8. 6:1-8	Vision of "chariots": The people will be reinforced by the return of the diaspora, brought about by the spirit of God.

With the exception of the fourth vision, the reports follow a kind of formal pattern with individual variations: the content of the vision is described, the prophet inquires about its meaning, and the accompanying angel replies. The images and ideas derive primarily from three realms: Israelite conceptions (the heavenly court session), myth and fairy tale (entrance to heaven, heavenly heralds and messengers on horses of different colors, smiths and horns, a flying scroll, an ephah in which someone is concealed in the dark, winged creatures bearing the ephah), and foreign cults (a lampstand with an olive tree on either side).

Exegetical studies have been devoted to several of the vision reports. Here we need only discuss the different views concerning the fourth report. H. Schmidt divides 3:1-10 into two reports, one concerning the appointment of Joshua as high priest, the other concerning the coming of the Messiah. Jepsen, Elliger, and Horst eliminate 3:1-7 from the cycle and consider it an originally independent report. In fact, the divergence from the formal pattern and the lack of a symbolic image are striking. The content of the vision is nevertheless indispensable within the context of the whole; the vision itself forms a counterpart to the vision immediately following, just as the first corresponds to the eighth, the second to the seventh, and the third to the sixth.

The date in 1:7*a*, which is followed immediately by "I saw in the night . . ." (1:8), refers directly to the first vision. It can no longer be determined whether the other visions came to Zechariah in the same night, as the text now suggests, or whether the reports of visions occurring over the course of several nights have simply been linked together without further dates. In any case, the date in 1:7*a* is correct; the visions should not be dated a few months earlier, in the time of Haggai (Jepsen). The date is intimately connected with the report. What has been said holds true also with respect to the theory of Galling, who connects the date with the report in 6:9 ff., and also places the night visions together with additional sayings in a different chronological sequence, corresponding to their supposed historical background—the return of the most important group of exiles under Zerubbabel around the turn of the year 521/520 (while Bič denies all connection between the texts and any historical situation, on the grounds that they are to be understood purely eschatologically): the visions of "riders," "horns," "measuring line," and "chariots" are located in Babylonia at the time of departure (along with 2:10-11 [Eng. 2:6-7]); the visions of "lampstand," "scroll," and "ephah" are dated

[4] L. Rost, "Erwägungen zu Sacharjas 7. Nachtgesicht," *ZAW*, LXVIII (1940/41), 223-28 (= *Das kleine Credo*, 1965, pp. 70-76).

about the time construction began on the Temple (together with 2:14-16 [Eng. 2:10-12]; 4:*6aβ*-10*a*, and perhaps 3:1 ff.; 1:16-17 and perhaps 6:15*a* are dated earlier).

B. Two additional reports concerning concrete events are found in 6:9-15 and 7:1-3 + 8:18-19. The text 6:9-15,[5] which has been revised several times, tells of Yahweh's command to perform a symbolic action, whereby Zechariah is to crown Zerubbabel the political messianic ruler of the eschaton. Later the coronation was made to refer to the high priest Joshua and the text was expanded by several additions (vss. 10*a*, 11*bβ*, 12*b*, 14, 15*aβ*, 15*b*). In the second report[6] Zechariah replies to an inquiry whether the fast in memory of the destruction of the Temple should continue to be observed; he answers that all four fast days that recall the fall of Jerusalem should cease and become joyous festivals.

C. We come finally to the sayings of Zechariah. The first, 1:1-6, an exhortation to return to Yahweh with a prophetical interpretation of history as its motivation, precedes the vision reports. In addition, 1:16, 17; 2:12-13, 14, 15-16 (Eng. 2:8-9, 10, 11-12);[7] 3:8-9;[8] 4:7*aβ*-10*a* have been appended to the vision reports on the basis of appropriate catchwords (2:10-11, 17 [Eng. 2:6-7, 13]; 3:10 are later additions), probably in order to emphasize, clarify, or particularize their ideas. We may follow Rignell in distinguishing on the one hand announcements, on the other interpretations and explanations. Additional sayings have been collected in 7–8 and interpolated into the report of the inquiry concerning fasting, which serves as a framework: 7:4-6, concerning the perversity of fasting; 7:7-14, a historical interpretation dealing with Jerusalem's deserved misfortune; 8:1-2, 3, 4-5, 6, 7-8, 9-13, 14-15, concerning the imminent eschatological salvation; and 8:16-17, a concluding exhortation to speak the truth and do what is right, but to eschew lying and wickedness. The last verses (8:20-22, 23) are a late addition, dealing with the conversion of the nations.

3. *Growth of the book.* Any discussion of the growth of Zechariah's book must take as its point of departure the observation that the major portion of 1–6 exhibits a well-planned internal structure. Literarily, too, it gives the impression of being a single unified whole. The vision reports form the nucleus within the framework of an introductory saying (1:1-6) and the report of a symbolic action (6:9-15) We are not dealing with a mere collection, but with a consciously fashioned composition, a small book that Zechariah may well have

[5] J. Ley, "Zu Sacharja 6,9-15," *ThStKr*, LXVI (1893), 771-82; L. Waterman, "The Camouflage Purge of Three Messianic Conspirators," *JNES*, XIII (1954), 83-87.

[6] F. S. North, "Aaron's Rise in Prestige," *ZAW*, LXVI (1954), 191-99; Waterman, *op. cit.* (note 5).

[7] S. Feigin, "Some Notes on Zach 2,4-17," *JBL*, XLIV (1925), 203-13.

[8] E. E. Le Bas, "Zechariah's Enigmatical Contribution to the Corner-Stone," *PEQ*, LXXXII (1950), 102-22; *idem*, "Zechariah's Climax to the Career of the Corner-Stone," *ibid.*, LXXXIII (1951), 139-55; A. E. Rüthy, "'Sieben Augen auf einem Stein'," *ThZ*, XIII (1957), 523-29; E. Sellin, "Der Stein des Sacharja," *JBL*, L (1931), 242-49; *idem*, "Noch einmal der Stein des Sacharja," *ZAW*, LXIX (1942/43), 59-77.

written at a single sitting. The individual sayings were interpolated into this work at a later date. Whether this interpolation goes back to Zechariah can no longer be determined; at least in the case of 4:6*aβ*-10*a*, which interrupts a vision report, it is unlikely.

The second portion of the book (7:1–8:19) comprises a collection of sayings within the framework of an inquiry concerning fasting. The division of the report and its use as a framework point to a deliberate process of compilation that can hardly go back to Zechariah himself. The first saying, 7:4-6, is associated with the inquiry through the catchword "fasting"; the reference to the perversity of fasting leads to a censorious interpretation of history, contrasted at once with the promises of salvation, which are fittingly concluded with an exhortation to proper conduct.

4. *Message*. Zechariah is the type of a visionary prophet. He consciously bases his message—and thereby indicates his derivative character—on earlier prophetical tradition, to which he refers (1:1-6; 7:7-14). He does strive to maintain the seriousness of their demand for righteousness and truth and for return to God. The important thing is therefore not the observance of fasts, but obedience to the ethical commandments of God, on account of whose transgression judgment has come upon Judah. But all this is over; the new age of eschatological salvation is at hand, in which the former fast days will be seasons of joy. In all this Zechariah's message resembles that of Haggai. Unlike Haggai, however, he looks not only to the rebuilding of the Temple, but also to the absolution and inward renewal of the nation before the time of salvation begins, and provides an ethical foundation for the expectation of material prosperity.[9] He emphasizes the transcendence of God, to whom only the mediating angel has access. This angel bears the events and prayers of the world before God's throne and then brings the prophet the utterance of revelation that he is to proclaim. Finally, Zechariah apportions the messianic dignity to two representatives, taking into account the high priest; as the Qumran texts show, the circles in early Judaism that produced these texts borrowed this conception. Here we may see priestly influence upon Zechariah.

§ 72 Zechariah 9–14

Cf. commentaries in § 61.

P. R. Ackroyd, "Criteria for the Maccabean Dating of Old Testament Literature," *VT*, III (1953), 113-32; C. Brouwer, *Wachter en Herder*, 1949; W. W. Cannon, "Some Notes on Zechariah c. 11," *AfO*, IV (1927), 139-46; B. Heller, "Die letzten Kapitel des Buches Sacharja im Lichte des späteren Judentums," *ZAW*, XLV (1927), 151-55; T. Jansma, "Inquiry into the Hebrew Text and the Ancient Versions of Zechariah IX–XIV," *OTS*, VII (1950), 1-142; A. Jepsen, "Kleine Beiträge zum Zwölfprophetenbuch, II," *ZAW*, LVII (1939), 242-55; D. Jones, "A Fresh Interpretation of Zechariah IX–XI," *VT*, XII (1962), 241-59; P. Lamarche, *Zacharie IX–XIV*, 1961; B. Otzen, *Studien über Deuterosacharja*, 1964; O. Plöger, *Theokratie und*

[9] F. James, "Thoughts on Haggai and Zechariah," *JBL*, LIII (1934), 229-35.

Eschatologie, 2nd ed., 1962; B. Stade, "Deuterozacharja," *ZAW*, I (1881), 1-96; II (1882), 151-72, 275-309; W. Staerk, *Untersuchungen über die Komposition und Abfassungszeit von Zach 9–14*, 1891; cf. also the bibliographies in Fohrer, *ThR*, NF XIX, XX, and XXVIII (§ 52).

1. *Major problems*. Zechariah 9–14 and the book of Malachi exhibit three essentially identical superscriptions: 9:1, "An oracle. The word of Yahweh . . ."; 12:1, "An oracle. The word of Yahweh concerning Israel . . ."; and Mal. 1:1, "An oracle. The word of Yahweh to Israel. . . ." We may therefore assume from the outset that we are dealing with three small prophetical works, the first two of which, at least, are anonymous:

Deutero-Zechariah Zechariah 9–11
Trito-Zechariah Zechariah 12–14
Malachi.

A redactor of the Book of the Twelve appended these writings to those of the last prophet mentioned by name, just as similar sizable blocks of material were appended to Isaiah (Isaiah 40–66) and Micah (Micah 4–7). The third document, however, was later restored to independent status under the name "Malachi," probably so as to yield twelve books.

Deutero- and Trito-Zechariah pose three interrelated problems: the boundaries of the units, single or multiple authorship, and date. These problems must be dealt with at the same time, as has been the universal practice. They are, however, extremely difficult to solve because the texts exhibit both archaic—either preexilic or archaizing—features and late features. Furthermore, they refer in some cases to historical events or situations, but these references either are too ambiguous or transcend our knowledge of Israelite and Judean history. Finally, the actual text is often uncertain or corrupt, so that divergent interpretations are possible. Previous analyses of Zechariah 9–14 therefore exhibit a bewildering variety of interpretations.

The simplest solution is to trace these chapters back to Zechariah himself, as some do even today (Brouwer, Feinberg, Ridderbos).[1] The first divergent view to be suggested was based on the observation that Matt. 27:9-10 quotes 11:12-13 as an utterance of Jeremiah, to whom 9–11 or 9–14 were therefore ascribed. Stade and Marti maintained unity of authorship, the former dating 9–14 in the early period of the Diadochi (300–280 B.C.), the latter in the Maccabean period (*ca.* 160 B.C.). Lamarche, seeking to demonstrate that the entire complex possesses an extremely artful and well-thought-out structure, likewise assumes a single author, whom he dates around 500–480 B.C. Since the close of the eighteenth century, however, scholars have suggested the period prior to 722 for 9–11, which apparently discusses Ephraim and its enemies Assyria and Egypt, and the period prior to 587 for 12–14, which mentions only Judah. According

[1] Feinberg (§ 71); J. Ridderbos, *De kleine profeten*, III, 1935.

to Bertholet,[2] the author of 9–11 was the Zechariah son of Jeberechiah mentioned in Isa. 8:2. This view does away with unity of date and authorship, and, with the few exceptions already mentioned, it has been generally accepted, although opinions differ widely with regard to the authorship and date of the individual sections.

Frequently, for instance, 9–11 has been thought to contain a basic preexilic stratum, which was revised in the Hellenistic period (Kuenen*, Baudissin*, Steuernagel*), or this has been suggested for a portion of these chapters (Horst, Tadmor,[3] Jepsen). For the most part, however, and essentially correctly, scholars have limited their suggestions to the postexilic period. Bič considers 9–14 as two collections of oracles dating roughly from the time of Zechariah; Jones considers 9–11 a literary unit from the fifth century dealing with the work of a prophet in or near Damascus; Tsevat [4] considers 12 a description of the insurrection led by the ruling class in Jerusalem in 486/5 B.C., in an attempt to restore the Davidic monarchy. Elliger, Delcor,[5] *et al.* suggest instead the early Hellenistic period; Eissfeldt* ascribes 9–11 to one author, 12–14 to another, while Oesterley-Robinson* assume collections of sayings by several authors. Sellin, finally, considers 9–13 (with 14 as a later supplement) a pseudepigraphic apocalypse, which he dates in the Maccabean period. Lassalle and Treves also date 9–14 in this period;[6] the latter ascribes these chapters at least in part to Judas Maccabeus. Recently Otzen has introduced further distinctions, assuming four complexes of traditions: 9–10, deriving from Judean circles in the time of King Josiah; 11, from the period immediately before the fall of the Judean state; 12–13, deriving from Judean circles in the early exilic period; and 14, from the late postexilic period.

2. *Deutero-Zechariah.* In the writings of Deutero-Zechariah (Zechariah 9–11), following Elliger, we may distinguish two series of sayings. The first series consists of lengthy sayings based on a concrete historical situation: 9:1-8, 11-17; 10:3-12; 11:4-16. The second series consists of shorter sayings, whose text is better preserved. These sayings, which are of a general nature, alternate regularly with the sayings of the first series: 9:9-10; 10:1-2; 11:1-3, 17. The first series can be ascribed to an author who dealt prophetically with historical events from the siege of Tyre by Alexander the Great in 332 B.C. to the first decades of the conflict among the Diadochi. The second series probably contains individual sayings of various authors from the same or a later period.

a) The first saying, 9:1-8, appears to have been pronounced after the begin-

[2] L. Berthold, *Historisch-kritische Einleitung in sämmtliche kanonische und apokryphische Schriften des Alten und Neuen Testaments,* IV, 1814, pp. 1697-1728.

[3] H. Tadmor, "Azriyau of Yaudi," *Scripta Hierosolymitana,* VIII (1961), 232-271 (266-271).

[4] M. Tsevat, "Sociological and Historical Observations on Zechariah XII," *Tarbiz,* XXV (1955/56), 111-17.

[5] M. Delcor, "Hinweise auf das samaritanische Schisma im Alten Testament," *ZAW,* LXXIV (1962), 281-91.

[6] S. Lassalle, "Le Deutéro-Zacharie date du temps des Maccabées," *Bulletin Renan,* LXXXVII (1962), 1-4; M. Treves, "Conjectures Concerning the Date and Authorship of Zechariah IX–XIV," *VT,* XIII (1963), 196-207.

ning of the siege of Tyre; with threats against Hadrach, Damascus, Hamath, Tyre, Sidon, and the Philistine cities, it announces the collapse of the Persian Empire in the west, together with divine assistance for Judah.[7] The next saying in this series, 9:11-17, is a promise of victorious power for Judah and Ephraim; it reflects the change of a wait-and-see attitude toward Alexander into hostility (as the gloss in vs. 13, ". . . over your sons, O Greece," correctly states). The next saying, 10:3-12, promises Judah and Joseph a return to their own land, while Assyria and Egypt will perish; it reflects the situation in the first decades of the conflict between the Diadochi. The next passage, 11:4-16, is an imitation of a report of a symbolic action:[8] the good shepherd loses patience with the sheep and they with him, he resigns his office, breaks the staffs named "grace" and "union," and throws his wages, thirty shekels of silver, to the Temple caster to be melted down. The brotherhood between Judah and Israel is broken—probably with the final schism between Jerusalem and the Samaritans. In any case, this approach is more likely than the interpretation of the three shepherds said to have been destroyed in a month (vs. 8, quite possibly a late addition) as the Israelite kings Zechariah, Shallum, and Menahem (Ewald), the Tobiads Simon, Menelaus, and Lysimachus (Sellin), the rebellious high priests Lysimachus, Jason, and Menelaus (Marti), or even Galba, Otho, and Vitellius (Calmet). All the sayings exhibit archaizing elements, possibly as a deliberate eschatological stylistic form (Weiser*), but possibly also as a legitimation of the author.

b) Between these sayings stand: 9:9-10, the announcement of the humble Messiah who will bring peace, possibly influenced by the "godliness of the poor," encountered particularly in the psalms; 10:1-2, an exhortation to ask rain from Yahweh rather than resorting to teraphim and diviners, which can hardly refer to anything but natural precipitation; 11:1-3, a threat against a world power, which consists of an entrance song, a prophetical taunt song, and a collective dirge; and 11:17, an invective and threat against the wicked shepherd.

3. *Trito-Zechariah.* The work of Trito-Zechariah (Zechariah 12–14) comprises five sections. With the exception of 12:9-14, their point is purely eschatological and makes no reference to concrete historical facts. Except for the secondary part of the superscription, no mention is made of Israel, but only of Jerusalem and Judah. Above all, the fate and internal development of Jerusalem are emphasized. Taken as a whole, the sections follow Deutero-Zechariah; they are more likely supplements by one or several authors than a single composition.

[7] M. Delcor, "Les allusions à Alexandre le Grand dans Zach 9,1-8," *VT,* I (1951), 110-24; K. Elliger, "Ein Zeugnis aus der jüdischen Gemeinde im Alexanderjahr 332 v. Chr.," *ZAW,* LXII (1949/50), 63-115; E. G. H. Kraeling, "The Historical Situation in Zech 9,1-10," *AJSL,* XLI (1924/25), 24-33; A. Malamat, "The Historical Setting of Two Biblical Prophecies on the Nations," *IEJ,* I (1950), 149-59.

[8] F. F. Bruce, "The Book of Zechariah and the Passion Narrative," *BJRL,* XLIII (1960/61), 336-53; S. Feigin, "Some Notes on Zechariah 11,4-17," *JBL,* XLIV (1925), 203-13; J. Kremer, *Die Hirtenallegorie im Buche Zacharias auf ihre Messianität hin untersucht,* 1930; M. Rehm, "Die Hirtenallegorie Zach 11,4-14," *BZ,* NF IV (1960), 186-208.

The first section, 12:1-8, describes the miraculous deliverance of Jerusalem from the mortal danger threatened by the attack of the nations, which inaugurates the eschaton. The text has apparently been secondarily expanded so as to refer to Judah. The second section, 12:9-14, clearly refers to a judicial murder; it describes the change of attitude on the part of the Jerusalemites toward the victim and a concomitant remission of sins. Though some identify them with the well-known victim, Onias III (Sellin) and Simon (Duhm) are out of the question, since their death dates are too late (170 and 134 B.C., respectively); neither, however, is the interpretation of the victim as a martyr-Messiah (Elliger) very likely, because this idea was probably foreign to early Judaism. A closer identification is impossible, although Plöger thinks merely in terms of mourning ritual according to the common forms employed ever since the high priest Johanan murdered his brother Jesus (between 411–408).

The third section, 13:1-6, announces the removal of uncleanness in the form of idols and prophets; in particular, visionary prophecy is rejected on the basis of the words found in sacred traditions and documents. A different hand is probably responsible for 13:7-9. Ewald [9] assigned this section to Deutero-Zechariah; but one can hardly follow him in this theory, since, like 12:1-8, it describes in its own way the final threat to the nation and its ultimate salvation, between which, however, lies a harsh judgment to which two thirds of the people will fall victim. Chapter 14 has been revised several times; its development is now almost impossible to trace. It describes first the terrible eschatological distress of Jerusalem and its removal through the appearance of Yahweh (vss. 1-5), then the natural phenomena accompanying Yahweh's entrance into Jerusalem (vss. 6-12), and the effects of Yahweh's appearance on the enemies of Jerusalem and the entire Gentile world, which will share in the salvation of the eschaton (vss. 12-21).

4. *Summary.* In summary we may say that the author of the historically related sections in 9–11 should be dated in the last decades of the fourth century. From the same period, or a bit later, derive the individual interpolated sayings. The work of Deutero-Zechariah, therefore, as a collection of sayings of several unknown prophets, probably came into being about 300. Even later is the work of Trito-Zechariah (12–14), which may generally be dated in the first half of the third century. It also comprises utterances of several authors. To the extent that we are dealing in 9–14 with prophets and not merely with imitators of the prophetical styles, we are dealing with epigones of the late period who hope for God's dominion in the form of a Jewish Israelite empire, with Jerusalem and its cult, aspiring to ritual holiness, at the center. They consider a decisive battle with the Gentile world, felt to be hostile, to be inescapable; its outcome, however, will be victory for Israel. They associate all this with the beginning of the eschatological time of salvation. Not by chance does the author of 13:1-6 reject the prophecy of his period.

[9] H. G. A. Ewald, *Die Propheten des Alten Bundes,* I (1840), 308-24.

§ 73 Malachi

Cf. commentaries in § 61; individual commentaries: A. von Bulmerincq, 1926-32.
D. Cameron, "A Study of Malachi," *Transactions of the Glasgow University Oriental Society*, VIII (1938), 9-12; O. Holtzmann, "Der Prophet Maleachi und der Ursprung des Pharisäerbundes," *ARW*, XXIX (1931), 1-21; E. Pfeiffer, "Die Disputationsworte im Buche Maleachi," *EvTh*, XIX (1959), 546-68; C. C. Torrey, "The Prophecy of 'Malachi'," *JBL*, XVII (1898), 1-15; cf. also the bibliographies in Fohrer, *ThR*, NF XIX, XX, and XXVIII (§ 52).

1. *Malachi.* The book of Malachi is the third short prophetical work, following Zechariah 9–11 and 12–14, appended by a redactor to Zechariah 1–8. It was later given independent status once more in order to yield twelve books in the Dodekapropheton. Although the superscription (1:1) "An oracle. The word of Yahweh to Israel . . ." goes on to say, ". . . by *mal'ākî*," now transliterated as "Malachi," the work is in fact anonymous. The word is not a proper name (Laetsch), but the "my messenger" from 3:1, since the messenger of Yahweh who is to prepare his way has been equated with the author of the work. We find this stage of development in the LXX ("through my messenger"); later, the word was interpreted as a proper name.

2. *Sayings.* In contrast to Zechariah 9–14, which contains utterances of several authors, the sayings of the book of Malachi derive from a single author. We are dealing with six clearly defined units, which Pfeiffer, by comparison with Isa. 40:27-31 and Amos 5:18-20, has shown to be in the form of discussions. These take place in three stages: (*a*) an initial statement is made; (*b*) the partner in the discussion objects; (*c*) the statement is substantiated in detail and the necessary conclusion is drawn.

Section 1:2-5 discusses the demonstration of Yahweh's love for Israel (Jacob), which has been preserved, while the related nation of Edom (Esau) must perish.

Section 1:6–2:9 accuses the priests of offering inferior sacrifices and threatens them with a curse if they persist.

Section 2:10-16 reproves the men who wantonly commit adultery and divorce their wives.

Section 2:17–3:5 addresses itself to doubts concerning God's righteous retaliation, pointing to the imminent day of judgment.

Section 3:6-12 blames the current calamity, a bad harvest due to drought and locusts, on a withholding of tithes from the Temple and promises rich blessings if the people will return to Yahweh.

Section 3:13-21 (Eng. 3:13–4:3) once more attacks those who doubt, explaining that on the day of judgment those who fear Yahweh will receive God's reward, while the wicked will be destroyed.

The book as a whole presents no particular literary problems. The sayings contain three accusations against the people (1:2-5; 2:10-16; 3:6-12), one accusation against the priests (1:6–2:9), and two against those who doubt (2:17–3:5; 3:13-21 [Eng. 3:13–4:3]). This does not, however, justify Sellin's attempt to link 3:6-12 with 1:2-5 (or the attempt of Weiser* to do the same for 2:1-16 as well), yielding a long sermon exhorting the people to repent. These sections are in fact three independent sayings.

The conclusion, 3:22, 23-24 (Eng. 4:4, 5-6), certainly does not derive from the author of the sayings, but consists of two later additions. The first equates the message of the prophet with the law of Moses; the second improves on the announcement of the messenger who precedes the judgment (3:1) by declaring this messenger to be Elijah and removes the onset of the Day of Yahweh into the future. Another later addition is 2:11*b*-13*a*; some exegetes assume still other additions, especially 1:11-14.

3. *Date.* The prophet is almost universally dated in the first half of the fifth century—most likely about 465—after Haggai and Zechariah because he presupposes the Temple and its cult (1:10; 3:1, 10) and before Nehemiah and Ezra because the very abuses are rampant that they put an end to (careless fulfillment of cultic obligations, easy divorce). This agrees with the stylistic and intellectual influence of Deuteronomy, while there is no trace of influence of the Priestly Code.

Bulmerincq, too, in his commentary, which is still unexcelled for thoroughness, assumes the decades 485–445, although he considers Malachi an assistant of Ezra, who, when speaking of the "messenger" (3:1), is referring to his master, about to depart from Babylon. The utterance in 3:6 ff. contains the last words spoken by this figure; they accompany Ezra's reformation. Probably, however, Ezra should be dated in a somewhat different period (§ 35.6). Holtzmann is certainly incorrect in assuming that "those who feared Yahweh" (3:16) are identical with the "synagogue" of the Hasideans mentioned in I Macc. 2:42 and that the book was composed in the first half of the third century.

4. *Message.* The book addresses its message to a community whose imminent eschatological expectations, aroused by Haggai and Zechariah, have not been fulfilled, and whose deep disappointment finds expression in indifference and neglect of the cult. In this situation the prophet assures those who doubt that the coming final judgment is inescapable. Unlike Haggai and Zechariah, he is vague about the date of the onset of the eschaton, proclaiming God's judgment as a possibility that can any day become reality. The important thing is for men to prepare for it by fulfilling their cultic and moral obligations and for the community to remain pure. In view of the disappointment of eschatological hopes, he thereby embarks upon the course of legalistic religion later prescribed by Ezra; but he also exhibits true prophetical insights. He demands humble veneration of God, who is a great king, feared by the nations (1:14), whose name is great throughout the world, and to whom pure offerings are made (1:11). Man's duty is to return uprightly to Yahweh (3:7) and accept with all his heart the obligation to obey Yahweh's will.

CHAPTER THREE: THE APOCALYPTIC BOOK

§ 74 Daniel

ATD: N. W. Porteous, 1963. BOT: J. T. Nelis, 1954. COT: G. C. Aalders. HAT: A. Bentzen, 2nd ed., 1952. HK: G. Behrmann, 1894. HS: J. Goettsberger, 1928. IB: A. Jeffery, 1956. ICC: J. A. Montgomery, 2nd ed., 1949. KAT[2]: O. Plöger, 1965. KeH: F. Hitzig, 1850. KHC: K. Marti, 1901. SAT: M. Haller, 2nd ed., 1925. SZ: J. Meinhold, 1889. Individual commentaries: A. A. Bevan, 1892; R. H. Charles, 1929; J. Linder, 1939; E. J. Young, 1949.

W. Baumgartner, *Das Buch Daniel*, 1926; *idem*, "Neues keilschriftliches Material zum Buche Daniel?" *ZAW*, XLIV (1926), 38-56; *idem*, "Das Aramäische im Buche Daniel," *ZAW*, XLV (1927), 81-133 (= *Zum Alten Testament und seiner Umwelt*, 1959, pp. 68-123); *idem*, "Ein Vierteljahrhundert Danielforschung," *ThR*, NF XI (1939), 59-83, 125-44, 201-28; M. A. Beek, *Das Daniel-Buch*, 1935; O. Eissfeldt, "Daniels und seiner drei Gefährten Laufbahn im babylonischen, medischen und persischen Dienst," *ZAW*, LXXII (1960), 134-48; C. J. Gadd, "The Harran Inscriptions of Nabonidus," *AnSt*, VIII (1958), 35-92; A. von Gall, *Die Einheitlichkeit des Buches Daniel*, 1895; H. L. Ginsberg, *Studies in Daniel*, 1948; *idem*, "The Composition of the Book of Daniel," *VT*, IV (1954), 246-75; M. J. Gruenthaner, "The Four Empires of Daniel," *CBQ*, VIII (1946), 72-82, 201-12; G. Hölscher, "Die Entstehung des Buches Daniel," *ThStKr*, XCII (1919), 113-38; A. van Hoonacker, "L'historiographie du livre de Daniel," *Muséon* XLIV (1931), 169-76; A. Jepsen, "Bemerkungen zum Danielbuch," *VT*, XI (1961), 386-91; H. Junker, *Untersuchungen über literarische und exegetische Probleme des Buches Daniel*, 1932; K. Koch, "Die Weltreiche im Danielbuch," *ThLZ*, LXXXV (1960), 829-32; *idem*, "Spätisraelitisches Geschichtsdenken am Beispiel des Buches Daniel," *HZ*, CLXIII (1961), 1-32; H. Kruse, "Compositio libri Danielis et idea Filii Hominis," *VD*, XXXVII (1959), 147-61, 193-211; J. Meinhold, *Die Composition des Buches Daniel*, 1888; W. Möller, *Der Prophet Daniel*, 1934; M. Noth, "Zur Komposition des Buches Daniel," *ThStKr*, XCVIII/XCIX (1926), 143-63; *idem*, *Das Geschichtsverständnis der alttestamentlichen Apokalyptik*, 1954 (= *Gesammelte Studien zum Alten Testament*, 2nd ed., 1960, pp. 248-73); O. Plöger, *Theokratie und Eschatologie*, 2nd ed., 1962; H. H. Rowley, "The Biblingual Problem of Daniel," *ZAW*, L (1932), 256-68; *idem*, "Early Aramaic Dialects and the Book of Daniel," *JRAS* (1933), 777-805; *idem*, *Darius the Mede and the Four World Empires in the Book of Daniel*, 2nd ed., 1959; *idem*, "The Unity of the Book of Daniel," *HUCA*, XXIII (1950/51), 233-73; *idem*, "The Composition of the Book of Daniel," *VT*, V (1955), 272-76; W. B. Stevenson, "The Identification of the Four Kingdoms of the Book of Daniel," *Transactions of the Glasgow University Oriental Society*, VII (1934/35), 4-8; M. Thilo, *Die Chronologie des Danielbuches*, 1926; C. C. Torrey, "Notes on the Aramaic Part of Daniel," *Transactions of the Connecticut Academy*, XV (1909), 241-82; E. J. Young, *The Messianic Prophecies of Daniel*, 1954; F. Zimmermann, "The Aramaic Origin of Daniel 8–12," *JBL*, LVII (1938), 255-72; *idem*, "Some Verses in Daniel in the Light of a Translation Hypothesis," *ibid.*, LVIII (1939), 349-54; *idem*, "Hebrew Translation in Daniel," *JQR*, LI (1960/61), 198-208.

1. *The claim of the book; Daniel.* The book of Daniel comprises (*a*) six narratives or legends dealing with the experiences of Daniel and his friends under Nebuchadnezzar, Belshazzar, Darius, and Cyrus at Babylon (1–6) and (*b*) four reports from Daniel concerning a dream and three visions under Belshazzar, Darius, and Cyrus, dealing with events from the end of the Babylonian Exile to the inauguration of God's eschatological rule (7–12). The second portion of the book, which is written in the first person (though not the first, which is written in the third person), therefore, claims to have been written by the Daniel who was deported to Babylon in 605 B.C. In both synagogue and church, tradition has generally accepted this claim and considered Daniel the author. Down to the present day, repeated efforts have been made to demonstrate the accuracy of the claim (Möller, Linder, Young). This is in contrast to the statement of the Neoplatonist Porphyry (d. *ca.* A.D. 304),[1] preserved in Jerome's commentary on Daniel (*ca.* A.D. 400); in the course of his attack on other "apocalypses," Porphyry dates the book in the second century B.C. and terms most of its "prophecies" *vaticinia ex eventu.* The Antioch school (Theodoret, Polychronius of Apamea), too, represented a view similar to that generally accepted today.

It is dubious whether the Daniel of the book was actually a historical figure. His name and the names of his friends were certainly common in the fifth century (Ezra 8:2; Neh. 8:4; 10:3, 7, 24 [Eng. 10:2, 6, 23]), though they are found in other periods, too. Ezek. 14:14, 20 mentions a certain Daniel together with Noah and Job as a righteous man of early days, and Ezek. 28:3 compares him as a wise man with the king of Tyre. The book of Jubilees (4:20) mentions a Danel as the uncle and father-in-law of Enoch, which, by the biblical genealogy, would make him the great-great-grandfather of Noah. Significantly, this form of the name corresponds to that found in the Ugaritic epic of Aqhat, from the middle of the second millennium, which tells of a King Danel who protected the rights of widows and orphans. Thus the figure of the wise and upright Daniel seems ultimately to be of Canaanite provenience. This is not out of harmony with the fact that the book named for him ascribes him to the sixth century; just as he is transferred to the time of Ezekiel, who mentions him, so likewise the ancient figure of Job in the OT book is transferred to a later time, albeit not precisely defined. In the case of Daniel, this is also in line with the general practice of the apocalypticists, who employ for their writings names and figures from prehistory and early history without any intention of deceiving the readers as to their age. In most cases (though not in the case of Daniel, who is placed in the sixth century) this device is probably due to the assumption of a correspondence between events of the first and the last days: the representatives of the beginning, on account of their familiarity with that period, are called upon to announce the corresponding events of the end. In any case, the book of Daniel is pseudonymous.

Furthermore, the book cannot possibly have been written during or shortly after the Babylonian Exile, in the sixth century: (*a*) It is mentioned only in

[1] A. von Harnack, *Porphyrius, "Gegen die Christen,"* 1916, pp. 67-74.

late works: Or. Sib. 3:338 ff. (*ca.* 140) and I Macc. 2:59-60 (*ca.* 100), but not in the "praise of the fathers" (Ecclesiasticus 44–49, *ca.* 200). (*b*) As the fragments of the book from Qumran, which are not in canonical style, show, it was not yet considered canonical in the first century B.C. Although it was later occasionally reckoned among the Prophets (Matt. 24:15; Josephus *Contra Ap.* i. 40; *Ant.* x. 267 ff.), in the Hebrew canon it finally took its place not with the Prophets, but with the Writings. (*c*) The language of 2:4*b*–7:28 is Imperial Aramaic; that of 1:1–2:4*a*; 8–12 is late Hebrew. Both sections have Persian and Greek loanwords. (*d*) The author's knowledge of the history of the exilic period is inaccurate: there was no deportation in 605 B.C.; Belshazzar was the son of the last Babylonian king, Nabonidus, not of Nebuchadnezzar, and he himself never became king; Darius (wrongly called "the Mede") was one of Cyrus' successors, not his predecessor. (*e*) The religious ideas—avoidance of the name of Yahweh, angelology, belief in resurrection—are not those of the sixth century, but of a much later period.

2. *Literary problems.* Instead of accepting the book's own claim, modern scholarship almost unanimously agrees with the statement of Porphyry that the book of Daniel came into being in the second century B.C. Opinions differ only as to whether it should be ascribed to an author living in that period and—disregarding the author's use of earlier material—considered a literary unit, or whether this author used a document about a century older for the first half of the book and composed only the second half himself. Occasionally an earlier source has also been proposed for the second half of the book or parts of it.

a) Most recently Rowley, following von Gall, Marti, and Charles, has espoused the assumption of the book's unity. This view, in somewhat mitigated form, is also represented by Bentzen, according to whom the author used an orally transmitted cycle of legends for 1–6, and by Eissfeldt*, according to whom the author used earlier narratives for 1–6 and mythological elements together with historical observations for 7–12.

b) More frequently an earlier nucleus or basis is assumed for 2:4*b*–6:29 (Eng. 2:4*b*–6:28) and in part also for 1:1–2:4*a* and 7. Meinhold, for instance, derives 2:4*b*–6:29 (Eng. 2:4*b*–6:28) from the period around 300, with 7 as a somewhat later appendix; Hölscher takes a similar position, as does Montgomery, deriving 1–6 from the third century. Sellin-Rost* assume an earlier book of Daniel, consisting of 2-6 with the Hebrew introduction in 1 and perhaps already the Aramaic apocalypse in 7. Sellin* considers 1–7 a Daniel biography from the third century. Haller and Noth also assume 1–7 to be pre-Maccabean. Haller takes 7, Noth 2 and 7, to be the earliest parts of the nucleus, dating them as early as the fourth century. By contrast, Ginsberg suggests 4 authors: for 1–6 (between 292 and 261 B.C.); 7 (between 175 and 167); 8 and 10–12 (166 or 165); and 9 (somewhat later).

c) More in line with the traditional view are Junker, who assumes earlier sources from the exilic period for 8–12; Eerdmans,[2] who derives 2 and 7 from

[2] B. D. Eerdmans, *De Godsdienst van Israël*, II (1930), 49-55; *idem*, *The Religion of Israel*, 1947, pp. 222-27.

the exilic period; Löwinger, who considers the narrative of Nebuchadnezzar's dream historical (2); and Kruse, who postulates a basic stratum deriving from the exilic period, revised about 300 and 164 B.C.

3. *Narratives.* In chapter 1, the first of the narratives or legends in the third person, we find an account of the deportation to Babylon in the third year of Jehoiakim (605 B.C.), the education of Daniel and his friends at the Babylonian court, and their faithful adherence to the dietary laws. In chapter 2[3] Daniel divines and interprets a dream of Nebuchadnezzar, demonstrating thereby his surpassing wisdom and gaining honor from the king. The martyr legend in 3:1-30[4] tells how Daniel's three friends, upon refusing to worship an idol set up by the king, are thrown into a furnace, but are delivered by an angel. Nebuchadnezzar's letter to his subjects (3:31–4:34 [Eng. 4:1-37]) tells how the dream interpreted by Daniel for the king was fulfilled and the king was afflicted with madness for seven years. The next section, 5:1–6:1 (Eng. 5:1-31),[5] tells of Belshazzar's feast and the mysterious inscription on the wall, which Daniel interprets as referring to the fall of the Babylonian Empire, brought about at once by Darius. Finally, 6:2-29 (Eng. 6:1-28)[6] tells how Daniel disobeys an interdict against prayer promulgated by Darius and is thereupon cast into a den of lions, from which he is delivered.

In literary type these narratives are in part martyr legends (albeit with a happy ending), in part oriental "court tales" (Baumgartner). They were originally independent narratives, as can be seen from the fact that Daniel does not appear in 3, that 2 and 4, as well as 3 and 6, are variations on identical themes, and that the presentation is not always coherent (cf. the date in 2:1 with 1:3, 5, 18). They do not contain any "historical" nucleus. While their knowledge of the period treated is vague, the apparently precise recording of personal and geographical names, official titles and political structures, legal procedures and chronological details, is an example of the "listing style," [7] intended to make the narratives vivid and lend credibility to their author. The narratives contain only vague reminiscences of the Babylonian and Persian court, and obviously came into being in the eastern Jewish Diaspora during the Hellenistic period, as is generally

[3] W. Baumgartner, "Zum Traumerraten in Daniel 2," *AfO*, IV (1927), 17-19; *idem*, "Zu den vier Reichen von Daniel 2," *ThZ*, I (1945), 17-22; L. Dequeker, *Wereldrijk en Godsrijk in Dan 2 en 7*, Dissertation, Louvain, 1959; S. Löwinger, "Nebuchadnezzar's Dream in the Book of Daniel," in *Goldziher Memorial Volume*, I (1948), 336-452.

[4] J. B. Alexander, "New Light on the Fiery Furnace," *JBL*, LXIX (1950), 375-76; G. B. Sanders, "The Burning Fiery Furnace," *Theology*, LVIII (1955), 340-45.

[5] A. Alt, "Zur Menetekel-Inschrift," *VT*, IV (1954), 303-5; O. Eissfeldt, "Die Menetekel-Inschrift und ihre Deutung," *ZAW*, LXIII (1951), 105-14; E. G. H. Kraeling, "The Handwriting on the Wall," *JBL*, LXIII (1944), 11-18; J. Melkman, "Daniël 5," *NThT*, XXVIII (1939), 143-50; H. H. Rowley, "The Historicity of the Fifth Chapter of Daniel," *JThSt*, XXXII (1930/31), 12-31.

[6] A. Bentzen, "Daniel 6," in *Bertholet-Festschrift*, 1950, pp. 58-64; E. Casin, "Daniel dans la 'fosse' aux lions," *RHR*, CXXXIX (1951), 129-61.

[7] Cf. A. S. Kapelrud, *The Question of Authorship in the Ezra-Narrative*, 1944, p. 26.

assumed.[8] Without any basic enmity toward the pagan state and its ruler, they paint a picture of the religious man who, confronted with temptation and danger, proves true and is therefore delivered and rewarded.

Soon after they came into being, these narratives were linked together to form a legend cycle and harmonized with each other. Thus chapter 2, in which Daniel alone is the protagonist, mentions his friends in passing; chapter 5 looks back to chapter 4. The Aramaic used in 2:4*b*–6:29 (Eng. 2:4*b*–6:28) also serves to link the narratives together, while chapter 1 represents the Hebrew introduction to the legend cycle, presupposing 2–6. Until the formation of the legend cycle, the most likely assumption is oral tradition (Bentzen), not—as is often claimed—a pre-Maccabean book of Daniel.

4. *Reports.* The first-person reports contain the following material: Chapter 7[9] tells of a dream concerning the destruction of the four world empires symbolized by animals and the rule of the "son of man"; chapter 8[10] recounts the vision of a battle between a ram and a he-goat, interpreted as referring to the kings of Media and Persia and Alexander, whose place is taken by four other horns (kings), from one of which in turn a little horn (an evil king) comes forth. In the next vision, chapter 9,[11] the angel Gabriel instructs Daniel concerning the meaning of the seventy years of exile announced in Jer. 25:11; 29:10, which actually represent weeks of years, i.e., 490 years in all, and concerning the events of this period, particularly the suspension of the Yahweh cult in Jerusalem. In the extended vision 10–12,[12] another angel reveals the course of history from Cyrus through the other Persian kings, Alexander the Great, the four states into which the empire broke up and the struggle between those in the south and those in the north, down to the last king of the north, who desecrates God's sanctuary. Then follows the announcement of this king's death, the deliverance of the faithful, and their resurrection to eternal life while the wicked are doomed to eternal disgrace. Finally, in two additions, the waiting period is set at 1290 (12:11) or 1335 (12:12) days.

The author was certainly familiar with ecstatic visions. There can be no

[8] On the relationship to the "Prayer of Nabonidus," 4QOrNab, cf. W. Dommershausen, *Nabonid im Buche Daniel,* 1964; R. Meyer, *Das Gebet des Nabonid,* 1962; J. T. Milik, " 'Prière de Nabonide'," *RB,* LXIII (1956), 407-15; for earlier studies, see especially W. von Soden, "Eine babylonische Volksüberlieferung von Nabonid in den Danielerzählugen," *ZAW,* LIII (1935), 81-89.

[9] J. Coppens and L. Dequeker, *Le Fils d'homme et les Saints du Très-Haut en Dan 7,* 2nd ed., 1961; M. Haller, "Das Alter von Daniel 7," *ThStKr,* XCIII (1920/21), 83-87; M. Noth, "Die Heiligen des Höchsten," *NTT,* LVI (1955), 146-61 (= *Gesammelte Studien zum Alten Testament,* 2nd ed., 1960, pp. 274-90); A. B. Rhodes, "The Kingdom of Men and the Kingdom of God," *Interpr,* XV (1961), 411-30.

[10] S. Krauss, "Some Remarks on Daniel 8,5 ff.," *HUCA,* XV (1940), 305-11.

[11] A. Lagrange, "Le Prophéties messianiques de Daniel," *RB,* XXXIX (1930), 179-98; G. Lambert, "Une exégèse arithmétique du chapitre IX de Daniel," *NRTh,* LXXIV (1952), 409-17.

[12] B. J. Alfrink, "L'idée de Résurrection d'après Dan, XII,1-2," *Bibl,* XL (1959), 355-71; H. B. Kossen, "De oorsprong van de voorstelling der opstanding uit de doden in Dan 12,2," *NedThT,* X (1956), 296-301.

doubt, however, that we are not dealing here with real visions; they contain too many traditional features and too much historical analysis. They are literary productions similar to reports of visions in Hellenistic Roman literature.[13] The bulk of the material is historical retrospect from an apocalyptic perspective, i.e., *vaticinia ex eventu*.[14] These are followed by prophetic glimpses of the future, whose failure to correpond to later events proves them to be true prophecies. All these reports, however, like chapter 2, look forward to one and the same goal of history: alleviation of the oppression brought about by the last wicked king and the coming of God's final kingdom. The fate of Palestinian Judaism is always in view, which means that the reports were composed in Palestine—as we shall see, in the first half of the second century B.C. We may think in terms of a gradual development, as the difference in approach and language suggests: 7 is a dream report in Aramaic; 8–12 are vision reports in Hebrew. Chapter 7 was apparently composed first, as a continuation of 1–6, and the whole was gradually expanded by the addition of 8–12.

The author drew upon various kinds of earlier material and motifs. The fourth animal in 7 derives from a mythological figure, either the chaos monster (Gunkel),[15] or, more likely, a Syrian Typhon figure (Eissfeldt*)[16] or one of the monsters with which Baal must fight.[17] It is also more likely that the "ancient of days" in 7:9 corresponds to the Canaanite god El[18] than that he derives from the Irano-Babylonian religion,[19] although subsequent Iranian influence on this conception and on the figure of the "son of man" is possible. The latter is interpreted in 7:27 as referring to Israel, but derives from the expectation of a transcendent and heavenly Messiah.[20] The use of a ram as a symbol for Persia and of an ibex or he-goat as a symbol for Greece and Syria can

[13] A. J. Festugière, *La Révelation d'Hermès Trismégiste*, I (1944), esp. pp. 52 ff.

[14] E. Osswald, "Zum Problem der vaticinia ex eventu," *ZAW*, LXXV (1963), 27-44.

[15] H. Gunkel, *Schöpfung und Chaos*, 2nd ed., 1921, pp. 323-35.

[16] O. Eissfeldt, *Baal Zaphon*, 1932, pp. 25-27.

[17] A. S. Kapelrud, *Baal in the Ras Shamra Texts*, 1952, pp. 98-109; J. Obermann, *Ugaritic Mythology*, 1948, pp. 56-71.

[18] O. Eissfeldt, *El im ugaritischen Pantheon*, 1951; M. H. Pope, *El in the Ugaritic Texts*, 1955.

[19] H. Gressmann, *Der Messias*, 1929, pp. 343-73.

[20] J. A. Emerton, "The Origin of the Son of Man Imagery," *JThSt* NS, IX (1958), 225-42; A. Feuillet, "Le Fils de l'homme de Daniel et la tradition biblique," *RB*, LX (1953), 170-202, 321-46; E. G. M. Kraeling, "Some Babylonian and Iranian Mythology in the Seventh Chapter of Daniel," in *Or. Stud. Pavry*, 1933, pp. 228-31; T. W. Manson, "The Son of Man in Daniel, Enoch, and the Gospels," *BJRL*, XXXII (1949/50), 171-93; O. Moe, "Der Menschensohn und der Urmensch," *StTh*, XIV (1960), 119-29; *idem*, "Menneskesønnen og Urmennesket," *TTKi*, XXXII (1961), 65-73; J. Morgenstern, "The 'Son of Man' of Daniel 7,13 ff.," *JBL*, LXXX (1961), 65-77; S. Mowinckel, *He that Cometh*, 1956, pp. 346-450; J. Muilenburg, "The Son of Man in Daniel and the Ethiopic Apocalypse of Enoch," *JBL*, LXXIX (1960), 197-209; P. Parker, "The Meaning of 'Son of Man'," *ibid.*, LX (1941), 151-57; L. Rost, "Zur Deutung des Menschensohnes in Daniel 7," in *Fascher-Festschrift*, 1958, pp. 41-43; E. Sjöberg, "Människosonen och Israel i Dan 7," *Religion och Bibel*, VII (1948), 1-16; S. H. P. Thompson, "The Son of Man—Some Further Considerations," *JThSt*, NS XII (1961), 203-209; E. J. Young, *Daniel's Vision of the Son of Man*, 1958.

be explained by the assignment of different lands to the signs of the zodiac according to astronomical geography (Cumont).[21] We may probably assume Iranian influence in the concept of the tutelary angels of the nations (10:13-14, 20-21).[22] In addition, the author probably made use of written historical descriptions, especially for chapter 11.[23]

5. *Growth of the book.* The growth of the book took place as follows: The author—an anonymous Jew from Jerusalem—took over the legend cycle 1–6, which had been transmitted orally and furnished with an introduction, made it topical, and provided it with a systematic unity. He himself composed the dream and vision accounts in 7; 8–12, making use of mythological motifs and historical data; he may also have been stimulated by the legends themselves. He joined these reports to 1–6, forming one continuous book. The two sections almost parallel each other chronologically: 1–6 tells of the experiences of Daniel and his friends under Nebuchadnezzar, Belshazzar, Darius, and Cyrus (6:29 [Eng. 6:28]); 7–12 tells of Daniel's dream and visions under Belshazzar, Darius, and Cyrus. Furthermore, the dream report in 7 seems to be linked with both 2 and 12, and to constitute the fulcrum of the book (Plöger). Despite the reservations of Porteous, it is probably correct to call the book as a whole an apocalypse, albeit in an early and undeveloped form, the more so because the borrowings from prophetical writings, the psalms, and wisdom literature have not really been fully assimilated.

The prayer of Daniel (9:4-20) in particular is a later expansion; it uses the divine name "Yahweh," which is avoided elsewhere in the book.[24] Furthermore, 12:11-12 is probably a later addition; it twice corrects the period remaining before the eschaton. The LXX contains still more "additions" to Daniel (some of which occur at different points in Theodotion): after 3:23, the prayer of Azariah and the song of the three men in the furnace, linked by a short prose section; after the canonical book, the narrative of Susanna and the double narrative of Bel and the Dragon.

The text of the LXX, which differs markedly from the Hebrew text, was soon supplanted by the translation of Theodotion; all that remains is one manuscript and the recently discovered fragments of the text in the Chester Beatty papyri.

6. *Date.* The date of the book can be determined quite exactly. The visions all point to the same historical situation: the persecution of the Jews by Antiochus IV Epiphanes (175–164 B.C.),[25] the king of the Seleucid Empire that emerged from the wars of the Diadochi after the death of Alexander the Great. On the one hand, the author is familiar with the return of Antiochus from his second campaign against Egypt (169 B.C.) and the "abomination that makes desolate"

[21] F. Cumont, "La plus ancienne géographie astrologique," *Klio,* IX (1909), 263-73.

[22] A. Bertholet, "Der Schutzengel Persiens," in *Or. Stud. Pavry,* 1933, pp. 34-40.

[23] G. A. Barton, "The Composition of the Book of Daniel," *JBL,* XVII (1898), 62-86.

[24] B. N. Wambacq, "Les prières de Baruch (1,15–2,19) et de Daniel (9,5-19)," *Bibl,* XL (1959), 463-75.

[25] Dates according to R. Hanhart, "Zur Zeitrechnung des I und II Makkabäerbuches," in BZAW, LXXXVIII (1964), 49-96.

(11:31), the desecration of the Jerusalem Temple by an altar of Zeus (167 B.C.).[26] On the other hand, he shows no knowledge of Antiochus' death in Persia (December 164), since the announcement of the future that begins in 11:40 does not agree with the actual course of events. The book was therefore completed before mid-December 164 B.C. at the latest, the more so because it is not certain that 8:14 refers to the rededication of the Temple on 14 December 164. In any case, however, the author worked on his book for a considerable period, so that it must be dated generally in the period 167–164 B.C.

This shows at once that the interpretation of the four empires in 2 and 7 as the Babylonian, Persian, Greek, and Roman (proposed on the basis of the NT historical conception in Mark 13 and II Thess. 2:4) is incorrect. The book of Daniel refers instead to the Babylonian, Median, and Persian Empires, followed by the Greco-Hellenistic Empire of Alexander the Great and the Diadochi, at whose end the reign of God will begin.

7. *The two languages*. The book is peculiar in using two languages: 1:1–2:4*a* is in Hebrew, 2:4*b*–7:28 in Aramaic, and 8–12 once more in Hebrew. No generally acceptable explanation has been given. We may perhaps suppose that the author took the legend cycle, transmitted orally in Aramaic, revised it, and reduced it to writing in this language; he then composed the dream report in 7 in the same language but, for reasons unknown, changed languages for 8–12. In addition, he probably translated the introduction (1:1–2:4*a*) into Hebrew.

Other attempted explanations can be grouped into four classes, following Eissfeldt*: (*a*) a mechanical explanation, according to which part of the Hebrew original was lost and replaced with an Aramaic translation (Bevan, Goettsberger); (*b*) the assumption of an Aramaic original, some sections of which were translated into Hebrew (Zimmermann, Ginsberg); (*c*) the use of both languages by the author himself, who in the course of time came to consider Hebrew more appropriate than Aramaic (Rowley) or, following the example of such books as Ezra and Nehemiah, wanted to record certain sections in Aramaic, the language of the "documents" (Eissfeldt*); (*d*) the use of an earlier book, 1–6, and perhaps even the report in 7, written in Aramaic (with the introduction translated), and the composition of the author's own sections in Hebrew (Sellin, Hölscher, Montgomery).

8. *Apocalypse*. The conquests of Alexander the Great and the rule of the Ptolemies evoked only minor reactions in Jerusalem. Under Seleucid rule, however, the efforts of Antiochus to unify his empire produced a situation of conflict out of which the book of Daniel grew. There was dissension among the Jews in Judea and Jerusalem: some favored hellenization, while others, continuing the attitude represented by Nehemiah and Ezra, opposed hellenization with all the means at their disposal. In the period of growing religious persecution and at least at the beginning of the military conflict, various groups that were ready or

[26] G. C. Aalders, "De 'Gruwel der Verwoesting'," *GThT*, LX (1960), 1-5; M. A. Beek, "'De Gruwel der Verwoesting'," *NThT*, XXIX (1940), 237-52; G. Cotter, "The Abomination of Desolation," *Canadian JTh*, IV (1957), 159-64; H. H. Rowley, "Menelaus and the Abomination of Desolation," in *Studia Orientalia Pedersen*, 1953, pp. 303-15.

felt themselves obligated to resist joined together; they differed so strongly in their theological views, however, that the movement soon disintegrated. Daniel represents the incipient apocalyptic tendency whose heyday was shortly to follow.

The book is the only apocalypse in the OT. It seeks to reveal the coming and passing of the ages and to lay bare the secrets of the end. From this perspective it strives to determine when history will end and the status of the present. In 8:26 the end seems to lie in the distant future, but this is based on the retrospective presentation of history as "prophecy" down to the time of the author. What seemed far off to the "Daniel" of the Exile has meanwhile come quite near.

The apocalyptic view of history is a further development of eschatology; it sets up a contrast between all of world history and the reign of God. It looks upon the course of history as a homogeneous unit that finds its end in a goal fixed by God: the last judgment, which will be followed, for the devout, by a new timeless age. Until this time, history comprises the epochs of successive empires. The statue made of various metals brought down by a stone (2) is an image of world history, viewed as a unit and at the same time divided into epochs. Until the eschaton this is where man must live, burdened with the heritage of the past, facing critical decisions in the present, responsible toward the future.

Uniting these points of view, the book seeks to strengthen the patience and courage of the devout who are suffering persecution, to give them new hope, and to exhort them, like Daniel, to remain loyal to their faith to the point of martryrdom. It seeks to assure them that the period of suffering will soon be past because the day is near when God will bring the powers of the world to an end and inaugurate his eternal reign. In this connection the book answers the questions whether those who have fallen in the struggle on behalf of their faith can share in the eschatological salvation and whether at the last judgment all must answer before God's judgment seat: it announces the resurrection—the faithful to eternal life, the rest to eternal shame and contempt (12:2). The faithful are apparently those who adhere to the views of the book. Thus we see in the background a sectarian community that considers itself the true Israel and awaits the resurrection, at which they will reign with God and his angels (Plöger).

This sectarian atmosphere may be the reason why the book of Daniel not only exerted a marked influence on the later apocalyptic writings of Judaism and Christianity, but has been looked upon again and again by apocalyptic and chiliastic sects as the focus of the Bible. This view is due, of course, to inadequate study of this very Bible, and is quite unjustifiable. The book's permanent significance lies in its exhortation to unshakable religious loyalty and in its idea of history, which calls men to decision and responsibility, coupled with the desire for life under the rule of God.

PART FIVE

The Compilation and Transmission of the Old Testament

CHAPTER ONE: ORIGIN AND HISTORY OF THE CANON

§ 75 TERMINOLOGY AND TRADITIONAL THEORY

K. BUDDE, *Der Kanon des Alten Testaments,* 1900; F. BUHL, *Kanon und Text des Alten Testaments,* 1891 (Eng. *Canon and Text of the Old Testament,* 1892); A. EBERHARTER, *Der Kanon des Alten Testaments zur Zeit des Ben Sira,* 1911; F. V. FILSON, *Which Books Belong in the Bible? A Study of the Canon,* 1957; F. HESSE, "Das Alte Testament als Kanon," *NZSTh,* III (1961), 315-27; G. HÖLSCHER, *Kanonisch und Apokryph,* 1905; F. HORST, "Das Alte Testament als Heilige Schrift und als Kanon," *ThBl,* XI (1932), 161-73; A. JEPSEN, "Kanon und Text des Alten Testaments," *ThLZ,* LXXIV (1949), 65-74; *idem,* "Zur Kanongeschichte des Alten Testaments," *ZAW,* LXXI (1959), 114-36; P. KATZ, "The Old Testament Canon in Palestine and Alexandria," *ZNW,* XLVII (1956), 191-217; XLIX (1958), 223; E. KÖNIG, *Kanon und Apokryphen,* 1917; J. LEIPOLDT and S. MORENZ, *Heilige Schriften,* 1953; A. LODS, "Tradition et canon des Écritures," *EThR,* XXXVI (1961), 47-59; G. MENSCHING, *Das heilige Wort,* 1937; F. MICHAÉLI, "A propos du Canon de l'Ancien Testament," *EThR,* XXXVI (1961), 61-68; G. ÖSTBORN, *Cult and Canon,* 1950; H. W. ROBINSON, "Canonicity and Inspiration," *ET,* XLVII (1935/36), 119-23; L. ROST, "Zur Geschichte des Kanons bei den Nestorianern," *ZNW,* XXVII (1928), 103-6; W. STAERK, "Der Schrift- und Kanonbegriff der jüdischen Bibel," *ZSTh,* VI (1929), 101-19; A. C. SUNDBERG, *The Old Testament of the Early Church,* 1964; S. ZEITLIN, *A Historical Study of the Canonization of the Hebrew Scriptures,* 1933.

1. *The canon; deuterocanonical and noncanonical books.* The OT is more than a superficial assemblage of the individual books whose development has been discussed above. As a whole, it is set apart by the concept of a "canon." It is therefore necessary to trace the growth of this unified whole and inquire into the origin of the canon of the OT as sacred scripture, determining the essential steps and motives in the process.

The word "canon" is connected with the Semitic word *qāneh,* "reed," taken over into Greek by analogy to refer to a "straight staff." Greek philosophy used it in the transferred sense "plumb line," "rule," "norm." The word retained this sense in Philo, in the NT (Gal. 6:16; II Cor. 10:13 ff.), and in the third-century church. Not until the fourth century was it made to refer to the Bible by the Council of Laodicea (360) and by Athanasius (*De decretis Nicaenae synodi* 18. 3), where it refers to the true faith in the proclamation of the church. The identification of the canon with the Bible was undertaken by the Latin church. The term therefore refers to the Bible or the OT alone as a book based on divine revelation, which furnishes the rule and norm for faith and conduct; formally, it means the list or catalog of documents that are reckoned to the Bible. Of course, before the concept "canon" was borrowed, there were other expressions with essentially the same broad meaning: "Holy Scripture(s)" or "Scripture(s)" as terms for the OT in the NT, the Mishna, Philo, and Josephus; and "making the hands unclean" in Mishna Yadayim 3. 5, describing the effect of the sacred material of the canonical books upon people who touched them. Strictly speaking, the concept of a canon automatically excludes all possibility of changing the text of the Bible. In practice, however, it was always applied quite loosely, as was true of its substantial and formal meanings. It is wise, therefore, not to press the concept too far.

The canon of the Hebrew OT, which gained general but not universal acceptance, is divided into three parts: the Law, the Prophets, and the Writings. From the eighth century of our era on, the second part has been subdivided into the "Former Prophets" (Joshua–II Kings) and the "Latter Prophets" (the prophetical books); it cannot be determined whether these expressions refer chronologically to the sequence in which the books came into being or physically to their position in the canon. The earlier religious books that were not accounted canonical are traditionally referred to as the Apocrypha and Pseudepigrapha. These expressions are ambiguous, however, and are out of date since the discovery of the Qumran documents, most of which cannot be assigned to either group. It is more accurate to call the books in question deuterocanonical and noncanonical.

The term "Apocrypha," usually applied to the deuterocanonical books since the time of Karlstadt (1520), calls them "secret" or "hidden," in the sense that they were not written by the authors traditionally assigned to them or that, on account of their difficulty, they should be made accessible only to the initiated. In the case of the OT Apocrypha the expression originally meant that they were to be excluded from public use, as was the case in Hellenistic Judaism, without necessarily excluding them at the same time from the canon. In the Greek and Latin Bibles they are in fact considered a part of the OT in the broader sense. This group comprises the following writings: I Esdras, I–III Maccabees, Tobit, Judith, the Prayer of Manasseh, additions to Daniel, additions to Esther, Baruch, the Letter of Jeremiah, Ecclesiastics or Jesus Sirach, and the Wisdom of Solomon. Apart from IV Maccabees (Codex Alexandrinus) and II Esdras (Vulgate), eastern portions of the church assigned this status to additional writings; it is better, however, to restrict the term "deuterocanonical" to the first group listed. The churches took them over in whole or in part from the Greek OT as works of edification or a kind of supplement to the canon. According to Luther's definition, they are not to be given equal status with the canonical books, but are good and useful to read.

The term "Pseudepigrapha," which is applied to the noncanonical religious books, is also not quite accurate, because it means that the books are current under the (false) name of an assumed author, i.e., are pseudonymous. This is not true of all the Pseudepigrapha, however, some of which are anonymous; it is true, furthermore, of some of the canonical and deuterocanonical books (e.g., Song of Solomon, Daniel; Baruch, Letter of Jeremiah). It is impossible to give a complete survey of the noncanonical books, the more so because some are extant only in fragments and others are known only by their titles. The usual list comprises the Letter of Aristeas, the book of Jubilees, the Martyrdom and Ascension of Isaiah, the Psalms of Solomon, the Odes of Solomon, IV Maccabees, the Sibylline Oracles, Ethiopic and Slavonic Enoch, the Ascension of Moses, II Esdras, the Syriac and Greek Apocalypse of Baruch, the Testaments of the Twelve Patriarchs, and the Life of Adam and Eve. In addition, there are the Qumran documents: the Manual of Discipline, the Damascus Document, the War Scroll, the Thanksgiving Scroll, and others.

2. *Traditional theory.* The traditional theory concerning the origin of the canon, which was generally accepted until well into the eighteenth century, is first found in Josephus. In *Contra Apionem* i. 8 (*ca.* A.D. 95) he states that the Jews possess 22 authentic books in their original condition (counting Ruth with Judges and Lamentations with Jeremiah), which exhibit the following characteristics: (*a*) they were written by inspired men in the period from Moses to Artaxerxes I (465–424); (*b*) their material holiness distinguishes them from profane literature; (*c*) they are limited in number; and (*d*) their wording is sacrosanct. According to II Esdras 14:18-48 (*ca.* A.D. 100), the canon was formed by Ezra, who is dated in the exilic period. When Jerusalem was destroyed, he dictated the documents that had perished to his five assistants in forty days, numbering 24 canonical works[1] and 70 others intended for the wise (apocalypses). This view, which was taken over by Christianity in the second century, was given a new form in 1538 by Elias Levita. This form was henceforth considered authoritative: the 24 books of the OT were already extant in the time of Ezra, but he and the men of the "great synagogue" brought them together, divided them into the three sections of the Hebrew canon, and fixed their order.

In fact, these and similar theories are inaccurate and untenable. Some books of the OT are later than the time of Ezra and cannot have been known to him (Chronicles, Ecclesiastes, Daniel, *et al.*). The placing of Chronicles, Ezra, and Nehemiah in the third portion of the canon instead of the first, and of Daniel in the third instead of in the second, is incomprehensible by this theory. The divergent forms of the canon preserved by the Samaritans and by the LXX also speak against the tradition. Finally, there never was a "great synagogue" in the sense meant by the Talmud. The canon in fact came into being through a long historical process, in which three stages can be distinguished: the preservation and transmission of the words deriving from divine revelation (basis), the collection of sacred writings (prehistory), and the development of the canon proper.

[1] The number 24 instead of the usual 39 comes from counting Samuel, Kings, the Book of the Twelve, and the Chronicler's History each as one book.

§76 The Formation of the Hebrew Canon

1. *Basis*. The basis for a canon of Holy Scriptures is the ancient belief that God's revelation is expressed in human words and that certain human utterances therefore represent the word of God and can claim divine authority and possess normative value. This is true of the *instruction* given by priests (*tôrâ*), the *word* of advice or caution given in rules of conduct (*dābār*), the *judgment* rendered by a judge or lawgiver (*mišpāṭ*), the *saying* of a prophet (*dābār*), the *song* of a singer (*šîr*), and the *proverb* spoken by a wise man (*māšāl*). They are all traced back to divine inspiration, although this inspiration is not found so actively at work in the song and proverb. These utterances were at first proclaimed orally; they were addressed to their own time and often forgotten afterward. Many, however, were deemed to have lasting significance. These were preserved and handed on either orally or in writing, combined with others to form collections and books, and looked upon as scriptures sacred in nature, providing norms for the conduct of life.

In this way the first three types of utterance—instruction, word, and judgment—gradually came to constitute the *law* (*tôrâ*) in the narrower sense. Its elements were marked as being worthy of careful attention and transmission by means of statements concerning their origin and therefore their holiness: the decalogues were written at Yahweh's dictation or by him personally (Exod. 24:12; 31:18; 32:15-16; 34:28); Moses is to set the judgments in Exod. 21:2–22:16 (Eng. 21:2–22:17) before the people for their acceptance (Exod. 21:1); the Deuteronomic law must have nothing added to it or taken from it and must be preserved at a holy place (Deut. 4:2; 13:1 [Eng. 12:32]; 31:26). This does not yet imply a collection of sacred scriptures, and certainly not a process of canonization, because new law codes came into force down to the time of the Holiness Code and P. Not until Ezra's reformation, which stabilized the law, did the period end when a new law with divine authority could come into being.

The prophetical sayings, which are so often transmitted with express reference to their divine authority, were certainly first intended for the ears of the prophets' contemporaries. Since, however, what a prophet had announced came to pass only rarely during his lifetime, they were written down so that they might remain in force—quite apart from the fact that they contain much material that can be considered divine utterances regulating conduct without being restricted to the time they were spoken. The eschatological prophets themselves presuppose this general validity when, conscious of being epigones, they refer back to the earlier prophets (Isa. 48:3; Zech. 1:4; 7:7). Finally, after contemporary prophecy had become a dubious quantity in the postexilic period (Zech. 13:1-6), learned apocalypticism utilized the earlier prophetical sayings as the authoritative criterion for their calculations of the future.

Song and proverb could also be looked upon frequently as effectual utterances, as the study of the literary types in particular shows. Furthermore, cultic songs were often handed down and used for centuries, so that they received the halo of age. Finally, however, these were limited to traditions dating back to a specific period, and later utterances failed to gain the same acceptance, probably through analogy to the situation obtaining with respect to laws and prophetical sayings.

The motives for preserving and collecting the human utterances that were looked upon as the word of God varied in detail and changed from time to time. The reason is often connected with the ancient conception of the magical power inherent in the written word (Num. 5:11 ff.). The prophetical sayings especially were transmitted in this way in order to preserve and perhaps enhance the power of the spoken word of Yahweh, so that God's will expressed in these sayings might come to pass in the future. From this root springs ultimately the conception of the material holiness of such scriptures. There is also a personal idea at work when the words dictated or written by Yahweh are handed on and obeyed. In addition, the prophets themselves may at times have had the further purpose, when what they had announced actually came to pass, of receiving from posterity that recognition denied them during their lifetime. The ancient narratives from the patriarchal period to the conquest were first of all preserved because they provided a religious and legal claim to the settled area. Cultic considerations also played a certain role—primarily in the case of the cultic songs—although the cult is far from being the *Sitz im Leben* of the OT as holy scripture (Weiser*). In the preexilic period and, to a large extent, in the postexilic period as well, the Israelite cult was primarily sacrificial and did not focus on the spoken or written word. A cult of the latter type only came into being alongside the sacrificial cult with the beginning of synagogue worship during the Exile. The real motive for the preservation and transmission of God's utterances and the gradual development of the OT as a collection of holy scriptures and as a canon was the effort to bring about and guarantee a comprehensive regulation of life and conduct on the basis of God's will.

2. *Prehistory.* The collection of sacred documents represents the prehistory of the canon in the narrower sense. In the case of the Pentateuch this began with the composition of the earlier source strata, which also contained the ancient collections of laws and rules of conduct. More important was the impetus given by Josiah's reformation, with the introduction of the Deuteronomic law as an obligatory norm according to which all of life should be shaped, so that, in the period immediately following, Deuteronomy practically became the first holy scripture. The subsequent development of narrative and legal complexes down to the origin of P reached its culmination in the introduction of the Pentateuch, supplemented by the addition of P, by Ezra as the foundation and norm for the Jerusalem community. Once again, cultic considerations were not dominant, but rather the desire to regulate all of life. From that time forward the entire Pentateuch—the *tôrâ,* the Law—was holy scripture, which the Samaritans therefore retained when they and Jerusalem went their separate ways. Hellenistic Judaism first translated the Pentateuch alone into Greek, and John 10:34; 15:25 even uses the term "law" to refer to the entire OT. Of course, this did not immediately mean that the Pentateuch had canonical character, since its scope and text

had not yet been finally determined; additions and alterations were still possible, as a comparison of the Masoretic text with the LXX shows.

The collections of the "Former" and "Latter" Prophets came into being at the same time as the "Law," and ultimately for the same reason. The books Joshua–II Kings, of which Joshua originally even went with the Pentateuch to form a single unit, presuppose the earlier narrative of Israel's history and continue the story of Israel's relationship to Yahweh; the prophets interpret all this through their utterances. Taken as a whole, the books furnish direct or indirect instructions on how to live a life according to God's will. Of course only the collection of the "Former" Prophets derives from the same circles as compiled the "Law." The organization of the prophetical collections and books, as well as the comparatively important position given to eschatological prophecy, suggests that the "Latter" Prophets were brought together by eschatological circles in order to set up a body of sacred scripture in contrast to the noneschatological religion of the law. This made it possible to associate the keeping of the law with expectation of the eschaton. Since the Chronicler's History and above all Daniel were not absorbed into these groups, they must have been considered closed collections essentially complete by the end of the fourth century. This is in agreement with the fact that about 190 B.C. Jesus Sirach mentions the prophets Isaiah, Jeremiah, and Ezekiel, together with the Twelve Prophets (Ecclus. 48:22 ff.). Of course, the collection did not have canonical character. This can be seen from the textual differences, often considerable, between the Masoretic text and the LXX in the books of Samuel and Kings, from the different view of history furnished by the books of Chronicles, and from the acceptance of new texts into the prophetical books already extant (e.g., Zechariah 12–14).

The compilation of the third group of books, the "Writings"—in the sense of "remaining writings" or "things merely written" and not meant to be read aloud at public worship—did not begin until the two other collections were closed; it extended over a long period of time. In addition to the Law and the Prophets, Sirach's grandson about 117 B.C. mentions only the "other books handed down by the fathers"; Philo, about the middle of the first century after Christ, speaks of "psalms and the other writings" (*De vita contemplativa* xxv); Luke 24:44 simply speaks of the psalms. According to II Macc. 2:13-14 (first century after Christ), Nehemiah is said to have brought together not only historical books and prophets, but also a psalter and the correspondence with the Persian kings; Judas is said to have undertaken a more comprehensive collection of writings of the fathers, probably with reference to the "Writings." That this group did not play an important role is seen from use of the term "the Law and the Prophets" for the OT (Matt. 5:17; Acts 28:23). Only gradually did the third group gain recognition; to it were assigned, rather haphazardly at the outset, those books that were thought worthy to belong in it. Of these, the Psalter seems to have been the first to be considered holy scripture, as is understandable for this collection of songs. The situation is similar in the case of Lamentations, since they were used at ceremonies memorializing the destruction of Jerusalem and were ascribed to Jeremiah. The same was true of the book of Esther, which was the festival scroll for the Feast of Purim. Wisdom literature could claim divine inspiration; in addition, Proverbs and Ecclesiastes were traced back to Solomon, together with the Song of Songs, while Ruth, in its final form, tells of David's ancestry and takes place in the period of the Judges. In the case of Daniel, too, a date of origin (the Exile) within the period of revelation was probably decisive. Of the Chronicler's History, Ezra and Nehemiah were accepted first because of their association with the Law and the cult; later the books of Chronicles, which had continued to lead a separate existence, were included. Matt. 23:35 does not, however, permit us to conclude that this was already true in the NT period. The final selection and above all the sequence of the books in the third group were determined after the time of Christ.

3. *The formation of the Hebrew canon.* The formation of the Hebrew canon in the strict sense did not take place until the time of Sirach and his grandson, about 190 and 117 B.C. respectively. About 117 there was a series of sacred writings, some of which were brought together in two collections but were still subject to possible alteration. A third collection was just coming into being; its scope and name were not yet determined. By the time of Josephus and II Esdras, however, about A.D. 100, the Jewish canon was a fully developed concept; the number of canonical writings was also fixed. The canon was therefore completed between 100 B.C. and A.D. 100, and the so-called synod held at Jamnia, about twelve miles south of Jaffa, apparently made some contribution to the process. Later disputes about individual books made no change in the canon.

The formation of the canon was a dogmatic decision that defined the collection of holy scriptures and marked it off by postulating a specific period of revelation (from Moses to Artaxerxes I). The reasons for this decision derived from the historical situation. In the first place, apocalypticism was flourishing. It appeared claiming inspiration, and with the aid of this inspiration began once more to fuse alien religious ideas with those of Israel, introducing again the danger of syncretism. The writings of the apocalypticists even claimed superiority to the Law, since they were traced back to pre-Mosaic figures so as to appear to antedate the Law of Moses (Adam, Enoch, Noah, the patriarchs). The writings of other groups and factions, like the Qumran community, must have appeared equally dangerous. The latter group made use of deuterocanonical and noncanonical literature and did not limit themselves to a defined canon. Above all, however, the missionary drive of early Christianity presented a threat, the more so because it took over the Greek translation of the LXX and attacked the Hebrew documents. From these sides the danger threatened that legalistic Judaism would be undermined from within and broken up from without. In defense, the Pharisaic party defined the canon and gained acceptance for it against the opposition of the Sadducees, who recognized the Torah alone as a normative book. Pharisaism distinguished sharply between sacred and profane literature, including among the former the 24 writings that seemed to possess the four characteristics mentioned by Josephus (§ 75.2). The formation of the canon may be considered complete around A.D. 100.

4. *Structure.* For the grandson of Jesus Sirach the structure of the Hebrew canon was already fixed with respect to the first two sections and outlined with respect to the third. The final result is as follows:

a) The *Law* comprises the Pentateuch, with the names and order of the individual books fixed from the beginning.

b) The *Prophets,* not divided into two main divisions until the eighth century of our era, comprise first of all the historical books, whose sequence is chronologically determined: Joshua, Judges, Samuel, and Kings. Ruth was occasionally linked with Judges. Among the prophetical books the sequence differs. The Masoretic text contains Isaiah, Jeremiah, Ezekiel, and the Twelve, in that order; Talmud Bab. Baba bathra 14b gives the first three in the order Jeremiah, Ezekiel, Isaiah for the eastern Diaspora. Occasionally Lamentations has been connected with Jeremiah.

c) For a considerable period the *Writings* appeared in various orders. At the beginning we often find Psalms, Job, Proverbs; or Psalms, Proverbs, Job; and at the end the Chronicler's History. In addition, from the sixth century on the five *m^egillôt,* the Festival Scrolls for the major feasts of the year, were brought together, in the following order from the twelfth century:

Song of Songs	for Passover
Ruth	for the Feast of Weeks
Lamentations	for the fast in memory of Jerusalem's destruction
Ecclesiastes	for the Feast of Booths
Esther	for Purim.

§ 77 Other Forms of the Canon

1. *Samaritans.* In the early Hellenistic period, when the center of gravity of Palestinian Judaism was in Judea and particularly in Jerusalem, the adherents of Yahwism in the heart of the former Northern Kingdom of Israel, called Samaria ever since it had become an Assyrian province, separated from Judea and formed their own community, that of the Samaritans, with its cultic center on Mount Gerizim near Shechem. Their canon comprises only the five books of the Torah. The *sēper hayyāmîm,* a presentation of their history from Joshua through the Roman Empire down to the Middle Ages, has noncanonical status. For the biblical period it contains considerable passages from the historical books of the OT in a unique recension. On this presentation, which is now being published for the first time, is based the so-called book of Joshua. Another important noncanonical book is the Samaritan version of the story of Moses in the Teaching of Marqah (Memar Marqā), which came into being in the first centuries of the Christian era.[1]

2. *Hellenistic Judaism.* The canon of Hellenistic Judaism, the Alexandrian Canon of the LXX, was formed on a similar basis to that of the Samaritans. At

[1] J. Macdonald, *Memar Marqah,* 1963.

the same time, it is essentially identical to the Sadducean view, so that it certainly embodies an earlier Jewish tradition. Canonical status belongs only to the Torah, which holds a position superior to all other writings. These latter were not given canonical status but were prized and read as edifying books. As a consequence, they were ordered according to different principles from those of the Hebrew canon, and other writings, which had been excluded from the Hebrew canon, could be accepted on a par with the rest. This resulted in the following structure:

a) Torah (Pentateuch)

b) Historical books: Joshua through Kings, including Ruth, together with Chronicles, Ezra, Nehemiah, and Esther

c) Poetic and didactic books: Psalms, Proverbs, Ecclesiastes, Song of Songs, Job

d) Prophetical books: Hosea, Amos, Micah, Joel, Obadiah, Jonah, and the following six books of the Masoretic text, together with Isaiah, Jeremiah, Lamentations, Ezekiel, and Daniel.

In groups *b–d* additional deuterocanonical and noncanonical books were interpolated. Here the practice of the manuscripts and editions of the LXX varies.

3. *Christianity*. At the very outset Christianity did not borrow the nascent Pharisaic theory of the canon and bind itself to a formally defined canon. This can be seen from the way in which passages from noncanonical books are introduced with the same formula of quotation used for canonical writings (I Cor. 2:9; also Luke 11:49; John 7:38; Eph. 5:14; James 4:5-6; Jude 14-15). Opposition to Judaism and the spread of Christianity throughout the Mediterranean world resulted in the use of the Greek translation of the OT and less dependence on the Hebrew canon than on the Alexandrian collection, which was therefore given up by Judaism and taken over by the church. Of course, the Pharisaic theory of the canon also exerted its influence, so that the final outcome was a mixture of the two theories.

The Greek church theoretically distinguished the canonical scriptures from what were merely "books for reading," but this distinction was not very important in practice. The Hebrew canon was expanded at the Synod of Jerusalem (1672) to include the Wisdom of Solomon, Ecclesiasticus, Tobit, and Judith.

The Latin and Catholic church, on the contrary, in practice followed the LXX. The efforts of Jerome and later scholars to gain recognition for the Hebrew canon were unsuccessful. Instead, the Council of Trent (1546) recognized the Vulgate as being canonical, thereby finally accepting the collection of the LXX.

The evangelical churches adhere more closely to the Hebrew canon and hold the deuterocanonical books in lower estimation. Luther evaluated them less by formal criteria than by their content, with Ecclesiasticus and the Wisdom of Solomon coming off best; conversely, he included the canonical books in his criticism. Though essentially recognizing the Hebrew canon, he altered the sequence of the books to correspond more closely to the Vulgate. The Jewish theory of the canon was not accepted until the days of early Protestant Orthodoxy. The Reformed Church shows a growing tendency to reject the deuterocanonical books.

CHAPTER TWO: TEXTUAL HISTORY OF THE OLD TESTAMENT

§ 78 THE MASORETIC TEXT

W. F. ALBRIGHT, "New Light on Early Recensions of the Hebrew Bible," *BASOR*, CXL (1955), 27-33; V. APTOWITZER, *Das Schriftwort in der rabbinischen Literatur*, 1906-15; M. BAILLET, J. T. MILIK, and R. DE VAUX, *Les "Petites Grottes" de Qumran*, 1962; H. BARDTKE, "Der Traktat der Schreiber (Sopherim)," *WZ Leipzig*, III (1953/54), 13-31; D. BARTHÉLEMY and J. T. MILIK, *Qumran Cave I*, 1955; H. BAUER, *Der Ursprung des Alphabets*, 1937; P. BENOIT, J. T. MILIK, and R. DE VAUX, *Les Grottes de Murabbaʿat*, 1960; Z. BEN-ḤAYYIM, *Studies in the Traditions of the Hebrew Language*, 1954; S. A. BIRNBAUM, *The Qumrân (Dead Sea) Scrolls and Palaeography*, 1952; L. BLAU, *Studien zum althebräischen Buchwesen*, 1952; F. F. BRUCE, *The Books and the Parchments*, 1950; M. BURROWS, *The Isaiah Manuscript and the Habakkuk Commentary*, 1950; F. M. CROSS, JR., "The Evolution of the Proto-Canaanite Alphabet," *BASOR*, CXXXIV (1954), 15-24; *idem*, *The Ancient Library of Qumrân*, 1958; *idem*, "A Ugaritic Abecedary and the Origins of the Proto-Canaanite Alphabet," *BASOR*, CLX (1960), 21-26; *idem*, "The Development of the Jewish Scripts," in *Essays Albright*, 1961, pp. 133-202; *idem* and D. N. FREEDMAN, *Early Hebrew Orthography*, 1952; D. DIRINGER, "The Palestinian Inscriptions and the Origin of the Alphabet," *JAOS*, LXIII (1943), 24-30, 176-78; *idem*, *The Alphabet*, 3rd ed., 1952; *idem*, *The Story of the Aleph Beth*, 1958; *idem*, *Writing*, 1962; H. DONNER and W. RÖLLIG, *Kanaanäische und aramäische Inschriften*, 1962-65; E. EHRENTREU, *Untersuchungen über die Massora*, 1925; I. J. GELB, *Von der Keilschrift zum Alphabet*, 1958 (Eng. *The Story of Writing*, 1962); M. GERTNER, "The Masorah and the Levites," *VT*, X (1960), 241-84; C. D. GINSBURG, *The Massorah Compiled from Manuscripts*, 1880-1905; *idem*, *Introduction to the Massoretico-Critical Edition of the Hebrew Bible*, 1897, reprinted 1966; M. H. GOSHEN-GOTTSTEIN, *Text and Language in Bible and Qumran*, 1960; H. IBSCHER, "Der Kodex," *Jahrbuch der Einbandkunst*, IV (1937), 3-15; P. KAHLE, *Der masoretische Text des Alten Testaments nach der Überlieferung der babylonischen Juden*, 1902; *idem*, *Masoreten des Ostens*, 1913, reprinted 1966; *idem*, "Die überlieferte Aussprache des Hebräischen und die Punktation der Masoreten," *ZAW*, XXXIX (1921), 230-39 (= *Opera Minora*, 1956, pp. 38-47); *idem*, "Die Punktation der Masoreten," in BZAW, XLI (1925), 167-72 (= *Opera Minora*, pp. 48-53); *idem*, *Masoreten des Westens*, 1927-30, reprinted 1966; *idem*, "Die hebräischen Bibelhandschriften aus Babylonien," *ZAW*, XLVI (1928), 113-37; *idem*, "The Hebrew Ben Asher Bible Manuscript," *VT*, I (1951), 161-67; *idem*, "The Massoretic Text of the Bible and the Pronunciation of Hebrew," *JJS*, VII (1956), 133-53; *idem*, *The Cairo Geniza*, 2nd ed., 1959; *idem*, "Die Aussprache des Hebräischen in Palästina vor der Zeit der tiberischen Masoreten," *VT*, X (1960), 375-85; *idem*, *Der hebräische Bibeltext seit Franz Delitzsch*, 1961; *idem*, *Die Kairoer Genisa*, 1962; P. KATZ, "The Early Christians' Use of Codices instead of Rolls," *JThSt*, XLVI (1945), 63-65; B. KENNICOTT, *Vetus Testamentum Hebraice cum variis lectionibus*, 1776-80; F. G. KENYON, *Our Bible and the Ancient Manuscripts*, 5th ed., 1958; P. DE LAGARDE, *Materialien zur Kritik und Geschichte des Pentateuchs*, I, 1867; M. MANSOOR, "The Massoretic Text in the Light of Qumran," *VTSuppl*, IX (1963),

305-21; M. MARTIN, *The Scribal Character of the Dead Sea Scrolls*, 1958; R. MEYER, "Die Bedeutung der linearen Vokalisation für die hebräische Sprachgeschichte," *WZ Leipzig*, III (1953/54), 85-94; *idem*, "Bemerkungen zu den hebräischen Aussprache-traditionen von Chirbet Qumrān," *ZAW*, LXX (1958), 39-48; O. PARET, *Die Überlieferung der Bibel*, 3rd ed., 1963; C. RABIN, "The Dead Sea Scrolls and the History of the Old Testament Text," *JThSt* NS, VI (1955), 174-82; B. J. ROBERTS, "The Divergencies in the Pre-Tiberian Massoretic Text," *JSS*, I (1949), 147-55; *idem*, *The Old Testament Text and Versions*, 1951; G. B. DE ROSSI, *Variae lectiones Veteris Testamenti*, 1784-88; C. ROTHMÜLLER, *Masoretische Eigentümlichkeiten in der Schrift*, 1927; I. L. SEELIGMANN, "Indications of Editional Alterations in the Massoretic Text and the Septuagint," *VT*, XI (1961), 201-21; P. W. SKEHAN, "The Qumran Manuscripts and Textual Criticism," *VTSuppl*, IV (1957), 148-60; *idem*, "Qumran and the Present State of Old Testament Studies: The Masoretic Text," *JBL*, LXXVII (1959), 21-25; A. SPERBER, "Problems of the Masora," *HUCA*, XVII (1942/43), 293-394; E. L. SUKENIK, *The Dead Sea Scrolls*, 1955; J. L. TEICHER, "The Ben Asher Bible Manuscripts," *JJS*, II (1950/51), 17-25; G. E. WEIL, "Propositions pour une étude de la tradition massorétique Babylonienne," *Textus*, II (1962), 103-19; *idem*, "La nouvelle édition de la Massorah (BHK IV) et l'histoire de la Massorah," *VTSuppl*, IX (1963), 266-84; E. WÜRTHWEIN, *Der Text des Alten Testaments*, 2nd ed., 1963 (Eng. *The Text of the Old Testament*, 1957).

1. *The text has a history.* The growth of the books and the formation of the canon of the OT by no means concludes the story of its development. The text, too, has its own history, both in the present form of the Hebrew OT and in the ancient versions. On the one hand, despite written transmission and even after the beginning of its final definition, the consonantal text was subject to alteration. In addition, the fixation of the pronunciation, which at first was transmitted orally, was a process extending for many centuries after the formation of the canon. On the other hand, in most cases a period of time—often quite long—separates the first reduction of the OT books to writing from the earliest preserved manuscripts. Except for the latest writings, this represents a period of at least several centuries, within which the books were copied again and again and the text more or less markedly altered, whether deliberately or by error. Therefore a certain degree of familiarity with the textual history is indispensable for an understanding of the growth of the OT. Here we are dealing primarily with problems of textual transmission, the development and consolidation of various textual recensions, the efforts of scribes to make accurate copies, the fixation of a universally accepted consonantal text, the addition of the vocalization to fix the pronunciation, and, finally, the origin of the *textus receptus*.

2. *Traditional theory.* According to the traditional theory, the present Hebrew text was fixed at a very early date and thereafter was handed down through the centuries with unique fidelity. In part this theory applied not only to the consonantal text, but also to its vocalization. Judaism, it is true, was divided over the question of whether the vocalization was an innovation, as Simḥa asserted in his *Maḥzor Vitry* (twelfth century of our era), or derived from Sinai, as the Karaites declared, e.g., Judah Hadassi (*ca.* 1100). Predominantly, however, it accepted the latter view, which also became the orthodox

teaching of the church. In 1538 Elias Levita[1] established once again the late origin of the vocalization, which he ascribed to the Middle Ages. Protestantism at first followed his lead; but then, under the influence of the Jewish exegetes who were consulted concerning the OT and the dogma of inspiration, it adopted the traditional view (e.g., M. Flacius Illyricus, both Buxtorfs). The opposition is represented primarily by Ludwig Cappellus and, on the Catholic side, Richard Simon. Today the theory they attacked no longer needs to be refuted.

Until very recent times, however, a variation of it has been accepted. Toward the end of the eighteenth century Kennicott and de Rossi published their collections of variants from numerous Hebrew manuscripts and editions in order to show that the variations in the consonants and vocalization were fortuitous, insignificant, and did not represent variant readings, and that the manuscripts and editions presuppose a generally recognized and authoritative archetype. They and their successors, e.g., Rosenmüller, Olshausen, and de Lagarde, dated this authoritative manuscript early, some in the first half of the fifth century, some as early as the second century of our era. This theory, however, founders on the fact that the manuscripts on which it is based date from the twelfth century at the earliest, and that they exhibit more variants than Kennicott and de Rossi assumed. Furthermore, Aquila, the most literal of the ancient versions, is based on a Hebrew text that is not identical with the Masoretic text and therefore also not with any archetype. The Talmud contains OT quotations that diverge from the Masoretic text or have been secondarily assimilated to it (Aptowitzer, Strack); and as late as the twelfth century quite divergent forms of the Hebrew text were current in rabbinic circles.

It is no longer possible to maintain the old theory. The study of the OT now confronts a completely changed situation, which has produced basic new insights into the history of the text. The manuscripts discovered at Qumran provide information concerning the state of the text in the period immediately before Christ and the beginning of the Christian era. The material from the genizah of the synagogue in Old Cairo, which has been known and worked on since the beginning of this century, provides information about the text between the sixth and ninth centuries of our era, if it does not in fact date from a somewhat later period. Kahle's studies based on this material, which have also drawn on numerous other manuscripts, have laid the foundations for a new evaluation of the history of the text. We may safely assume that the transmission of the OT text goes back to a single original document; but this document has subsequently gone through many recensions. This multiplicity stands at the beginning of that part of the text's history that can still be traced, in the course of which Judaism strove to reduce the multiplicity to an authoritative textual unity—a goal that was reached only after centuries of effort, in the Middle Ages.

3. *Scroll and writing system.* The text was primarily transmitted in writing. Certainly passages were also learned by heart, but on the basis of a written document. The scribe probably did not use tablets such as were used for short docu-

[1] G. E. Weil, *Élie Lévita,* 1963.

ments, but rather the scroll mentioned in Jer. 36:2; Ezek. 2:9-10; Zech. 5:2; Isa. 34:4, which was divided into columns and written upon with ink. Such scrolls were made out of papyrus imported from Egypt or out of animal skin, which was more durable; later the Torah scrolls had to consist of leather or parchment. Since a papyrus scroll can only attain a certain length, this fixed the maximum compass of the books or the collection of several originally independent writings on a single scroll. From the second century of our era on, manuscripts of the OT and its books for private use were also produced in book form (codices). Manuscripts that were no longer used were stored in the genizoth of the synagogues and periodically given solemn burial in order to prevent their desecration. For this reason almost all ancient manuscripts have perished. The contents of the walled-up and forgotten genizah of Old Cairo constitute an exception, as do the Qumran manuscripts, which were obviously hidden during an emergency, and the other discoveries in the Desert of Judah, which were left there after the violent death of their owners.

For many centuries the writing system used the ancient Hebrew script which developed from the Canaanite-Phoenician alphabetic script in Palestine after the Israelite occupation. Paleography can largely determine the forms of the letters in various epochs from documents that have been discovered in increasing number: the so-called Gezer Calendar (usually dated between 1100 and 900 B.C.),[2] the Samaria Ostraca (first or second half of the eighth century),[3] Papyrus Murabbaʿat 17 (possibly eighth century),[4] inscriptions stamped on jars and seals (from the eighth and seventh centuries on),[5] the inscription from the Siloam tunnel in Jerusalem (*ca.* 700),[6] the petition on the ostracon of Meṣad Ḥašabyahu (end of the seventh century),[7] and the ostraca with reports addressed to the commandant at Lachish (588).[8] This script was used until

[2] *AOT*, p. 444; H. Donner and W. Röllig, *Kanaanäische und aramäische Inschriften*, I (1962), 34; II (1964), 181-82.

[3] A. Jirku, "Das Inschriften-Material der amerikanischen Ausgrabungen in Samarien," *OLZ*, XXVIII (1925), 273-81; G. A. Reisner, C. S. Fisher, and D. G. Lyon, *Harvard Excavations at Samaria*, I (1924), 227-46; II, 1924, plate 55; Y. Yadin, "Recipients or Owners. A Note on the Samaria Ostraca," *IEJ*, IX (1959), 184-87; *idem*, "A Further Note on the Samaria Ostraca," *ibid.*, XII (1962), 64-66.

[4] F. M. Cross, Jr., "Epigraphic Notes on Hebrew Documents of the Eighth–Sixth Centuries B.C., II," *BASOR*, CLXV (1962), 34-46.

[5] Y. Aharoni, "Excavations at Ramat Raḥel," *BA*, XXIV (1961), 98-118; K. Galling, *Biblisches Reallexikon*, 1937, pp. 337-40, 481-90; P. W. Lapp, "The Royal Seals from Judah," *BASOR*, CLVIII (1960), 11-22; J. B. Pritchard, *Hebrew Inscriptions and Stamps from Gibeon*, 1959; *idem*, "More Inscribed Jar Handles from el-Jib," *BASOR*, CLX (1960), 2-6.

[6] *AOT*, p. 445; H. Donner and W. Röllig, *Kanaanäische und aramäische Inschriften*, I (1962), 34; II (1964), 186-88.

[7] J. Naveh, "A Hebrew Letter from the Seventh Century B.C.," *IEJ*, X (1960), 129-39; S. Yeivin, "The Judicial Petition from Meẓad Ḥashavyahu," *BiOr*, XIX (1962), 3-10; additional ostraca have been found at Tell ʿArad; cf. *PEQ*, XCIV (1962), 99; also Y. Aharoni and R. Amiran, "Tell Arad," *IEJ*, XII (1962), 144-45.

[8] *ANET*, pp. 321-22; U. Cassuto, "Die Ostraka von Lakisch," *MGWJ*, LXXXIII (1939/1963), 81-92; D. Diringer, "Ostraca," in *Lachish*, III (1953), 331-39; H. Donner and

well into the postexilic period. The Samaritans adopted the Pentateuch in this form when they split with Jerusalem, preserving and developing it in their own way. The Qumran texts contain fragments of the books of the Pentateuch and of the book of Job written in the ancient Hebrew script.[9] In like fashion, it is used as an archaism on coins of the Maccabean period (second century B.C.) and the Bar Kochba revolt (A.D. 132-5).[10]

During the postexilic period another type of script came into being, developed from the Aramaic script under the simultaneous influence of the old Hebrew script. This is called "square script" from the form of the letters, or "Assyrian script," from its origin in the Syro-Aramaic linguistic region. Up to now the earliest example is a short inscription from ʿAraq el-Emir in Transjordan, which more likely dates from *ca.* 300 B.C. than from the fifth or even sixth century.[11] When the books of the OT were put into this script cannot be determined precisely; the rabbinic tradition that attributes it to Ezra can hardly be correct. Since Papyrus Nash, containing the Decalogue and Deut. 6:4, witnesses to its use in the second century[12] and most of the Qumran texts witness to its use in the second and first centuries, it appears most likely to assume that the transition to square script was made in the early Hellenistic period at the earliest and was completed about 200 B.C. at the latest.

4. *Efforts to guarantee accurate transmission.* Already in the pre-Christian period there was concern for as accurate a transmission of the text as possible. This is shown by the Letter of Aristeas, dating from the second century, and by the many measures taken to secure the accuracy of the text that may be seen in the Qumran material. This effort was limited, however, to individual schools or parties, so that a series of parallel recensions came into being. The later Masoretic text itself betrays the presence of several recensions; in itself it is one of several early recensions, whose existence can be demonstrated from the Samaritan Pentateuch, the Hebrew *Vorlagen* behind the Peshitta and LXX, as well as from the OT texts from Qumran and other sites in the Desert of Judah. The Qumran texts are of particular importance for determining the

---

W. Röllig, *Kanaanäische und aramäische Inschriften,* I (1962), 35-36; II (1964), 189-99; N. H. Torczyner, *The Lachish Letters* (*Lachish I*), 1938.

[9] M. Baillet in *RB,* LXIII (1956), 55; J.-D. Barthélemy and J. T. Milik, *Qumran Cave I,* 1955, pp. 51-54; P. W. Skehan, "Exodus in the Samaritan Recension from Qumran," *JBL,* LXXIV (1955), 182-87.

[10] L. Kadman, *Corpus Nummorum Palaestinensium,* I, 1956; II, 1957; III, 1960; L. Y. Rahmani, "The Coins from Naḥal Seelim and Naḥal Hardof," *IEJ,* XI (1961), 63-64; A. Reifenberg, *Ancient Jewish Coins,* 2nd ed., 1947; W. Wirgin and S. Mandel, *The History of Coins and Symbols in Ancient Israel,* 1958.

[11] F. M. Cross, Jr., "The Development of the Jewish Scripts," in *Essays Albright,* 1961, p. 191; B. Mazar, "The Tobiads," *IEJ,* VII (1957), 141-42, 229; C. C. McCown, "The ʿAraq el-Emir and the Tobiads," *BA,* XX (1957), 63-76; O. Plöger, "Hyrkan im Ostjordanland," *ZDPV,* LXXI (1955), 70-81.

[12] W. F. Albright, "A Biblical Fragment from the Maccabaean Age: The Nash Papyrus," *JBL,* LVI (1937), 145-76; S. S. Cook, "A Pre-Massoretic Biblical Papyrus," *PSBA,* XXV (1903), 34-56.

early recensions.[13] Many manuscripts are similar to the Samaritan, while a fragment containing a major portion of the text of I Sam. 1:22–2:25, dating from the first century B.C., appears to resemble the Hebrew *Vorlage* of the LXX more than the Masoretic text; the fragments of the book of Jeremiah contain both the Masoretic text and the shorter text of the LXX. Thus from the second and first centuries B.C. we have witnesses to three major recensions of the Hebrew text, of which the first is an early stage in the development of the Masoretic text, the second resembles the *Vorlage* of the LXX, and the third resembles the Samaritan text form. In addition, there are various popular recensions represented in the manuscripts which differ from the three major forms. Despite this multiplicity, which existed until the early Christian period, during the first century B.C. at the latest efforts were underway aimed at replacing the various textual forms with a single uniform text, as the incomplete Isaiah scroll from Qumran makes clear, existing side by side with the complete scroll, which differs much more extensively from the Masoretic text.

A survey of the published or announced finds of OT texts in Hebrew from the caves at Qumran and other sites in the Desert of Judah exhibits both their variety and their fragmentary state of preservation (abbreviations: 1Q= Qumran Cave 1, etc.; Mur=Wadi Murabbaʿat; Ḥev=Naḥal Ḥever):

MurGen-Num	Fragments of Genesis 32–35; Exodus 4–6; Numbers 34; 36
1QGen	Genesis 1; 3; 22–24 (portions)
2QGen	Genesis 19; 36 (portions)
4QGen	several manuscripts
4QpaleoGen^{l}	Genesis 26 (portions; old Hebrew script)
6QGen	Genesis 6 (portions; old Hebrew script)
8QGen	Genesis 17–18 (portions)
1QEx	Exodus 16; 19–21 (portions)
2QEx^{a}	Exodus 1; 7; 9; 11; 12; 21; 26; 30; 32 (portions)
2QEx^{b}	Exodus 4; 12; 18; 21–22; 27; 31; 19; 34 (portions)
2QEx^{c}	Exodus 5 (portions)?
4QEx	several manuscripts
4QEx^{a}	Exodus 1 and other passages (portions)
4QEx^{b}	
4QEx^{f}	
4QpaleoEx^{l}	Exodus 1–27 (portions; old Hebrew script)
4QpaleoEx^{m}	Exodus 6–37 (portions; old Hebrew script)
1QLev	fragments of several scrolls, old Hebrew script
2QLev	Leviticus 11 (portions; old Hebrew script)
4QLev	several manuscripts
6QLev	Leviticus 8 (portions; old Hebrew script)
11QLev	fragment of a scroll; old Hebrew script
2QNum^{a}	Numbers 3–4 (portions)

[13] The enormous literature devoted to the Qumran texts and similar discoveries in the Desert of Judah cannot be listed even selectively. For a survey, see C. Burchard, *Bibliographie zu den Handschriften vom Toten Meer*, 1957 (1959); II, 1965; also the continuing bibliography in *RdQ*.

2QNum^{b}	Numbers 33 (portions)
2QNum^{c}	Numbers 7? (portions)
2QNum^{d}	Numbers 18? (portions)
4QNum	several manuscripts
4QNum^{b}	mixed text with Samaritan traits
perg5/6ḤevNum	Numbers 20:7-8
1QDtn^{a}	Deuteronomy 1; 4; 8; 9; 11; 13; 14; 16 (portions)
1QDtn^{b}	Deuteronomy 1; 8; 9; 11; 15; 17; 21; 24; 25; 28–33 (portions)
2QDtn^{a}	Deuteronomy 1 (portions)
2QDtn^{b}	Deuteronomy 17 (portions)
2QDtn^{c}	Deuteronomy 10 (portions)
4QDtn	several manuscripts
4QDtn^{a,c,j}	
4QDtn^{n}(?)	Deuteronomy 32 (portions)
4QDtn^{q}	Deuteronomy 32 (portions)
4QDtn^{x}	Deuteronomy 32 (portions)
4QpaleoDtn^{r}	Deuteronomy 7–34 (portions; old Hebrew script)
4QpaleoDtn^{s}	Deuteronomy 26 (portions; old Hebrew script)
5QDtn	Deuteronomy 7–9 (portions)
pap6QDtn	Deuteronomy 26:19?
11QDtn	fragments
MurDtn	Deuteronomy 10–12; 14–15 (portions)
4QJos	several manuscripts
1QJdg	Judges 6; 9 (portions)
4QJdg	several manuscripts
1QSam	I Samuel 18; II Samuel 20; 21; 23 (portions)
4QSam	several manuscripts
4QSam^{a}	I Samuel 1–2; II Samuel 4; 24 (LXX text form)
4QSam^{b}	I Samuel 16; 19; 21; 23 (LXX text form)
4QKings	
5QKings	I Kings 1 (portions)
pap6QKings	I Kings 3; 12; 22; II Kings 5–10 (portions)
1QIsa^{a}	complete scroll
1QIsa^{b}	incomplete scroll
4QIsa	12-15 manuscripts
4QIsa^{a}	Isaiah 1–26 (portions)
4QIsa^{c}	Isaiah 11 and other passages (portions)
4QIsa^{h}	Isaiah 42 (portions)
5QIsa	Isaiah 40 (portions)
MurIsa	Isaiah 1 (portions)
2QJer	Jeremiah 42–44; 46–49 (portions)
4QJer	several manuscripts
4QJer^{a}	
4QJer^{b}	Jeremiah 9–10 and other passages (portions; LXX text form)
1QEzek	Ezekiel 4–5 (portions)
3QEzek	Ezekiel 16 (portions)
4QEzek	several manuscripts
11QEzek	Ezekiel 4–5; 7; 10; 13 (portions; rest of scroll incapable of being unrolled)

4QXII	several manuscripts
4QXII[a]	
4QXII[c]	Hosea, Joel, Amos, Zephaniah, Malachi (portions)
4QXII[d]	Hosea (portions)
4QXII[e]	Zechariah (portions)
4QXII[f]	Jonah (portions)
4QXII[g]	Hosea–Nahum and other passages (portions)
MurXII	Joel, Amos, Obadiah, Jonah, Micah, Nahum, Habakkuk, Zephaniah, Haggai, Zechariah (portions)
5QAm	Amos 1 (portions)
1QPs[a]	Psalms 86; 92; 94; 95; 96; 119 (portions)
1QPs[b]	Psalms 126–128 (portions)
1QPs[c]	Psalm 44 (portions)
2QPs	Psalms 103; 104 (portions)
3QPs	Psalm 2 (portions)
4QPs[a]	Psalms 5; 6; 25; 31; 33; 35; 36; 38; 71; 47; 53; 54; 56; 63; 66; 67; 69 (portions)
4QPs[b]	Psalms 91–94; 98–100; 102; 103; 112–116; 118 (portions)
4QPs[c]	Psalms 18; 16; 27; 28; 35; 37; 45; 49–53 (portions)
4QPs[d]	Psalms 147; 104 (portions)
4QPs[e]	Psalms 76–78; 81; 86; 88; 89; 104; 105; 109; 115; 116; 120; 125; 126; 129; 130 (portions)
4QPs[f]	Psalms 22; 107; 109 (portions)
4QPs[g,h]	Psalm 119
4QPs[j]	Psalms 48; 49; (portions)
4QPs[k]	Psalms 26; 27; 30; 135 (portions)
4QPs[l]	Psalm 104 (portions)
4QPs[m]	Psalms 93; 95; 97; 98 (portions)
4QPs[n]	Psalms 135; 136 (portions)
4QPs[o]	Psalms 114–116 (portions)
4QPs[p]	Psalm 143 (portions)
4QPs[q]	Psalms 31; 33; 35 (portions)
5QPs	Psalm 119 (portions)
pap6QPs	Psalm 78 (portions)
8QPs	Psalms 17; 18 (portions)
11QPs[a]	Psalms 101–103; 105; 109; 146; 148; 121–132; 119; 135; 136; 118; 145; 139; 137; 138; 93; 141; 133; 144; 142; 143; 149; 150; 140; 134; also II Samuel 23:7; Ecclesiasticus 51:13 ff.; and seven noncanonical songs (portions)
11QPs[b]	Psalms 2; 9; 12–14; 17; 18; 43; 59; 77; 78 (portions)
11QPs[c]	Psalms 35–40; 68; 78; 81 (portions)
5/6ḤevPs	Psalms 15; 16 (portions)
2QJob	Job 33 (portions)
4QJob[a,b]	primarily Job 36
4QpaleoJob[c]	Job 13–14 (portions; old Hebrew script)
4QProv[a,b]	Proverbs 1–2; 14–15 (portions)
2QRuth[a]	Ruth 2–4 (portions)
2QRuth[b]	Ruth 3 (portions)
4QRuth	several manuscripts

4QSong	several manuscripts
4QSong^{b}	
6QSong	Song of Songs 1 (portions)
3QLam	Lamentations 1; 3 (portions)
4QLam	one manuscript
5QLam^{a}	Lamentations 4–5 (portions)
5QLam^{b}	Lamentations 4 (portions)
4QEccles	several manuscripts
4QEccles^{a}	Ecclesiastes 5–7 (portions)
1QDan^{a}	Daniel 1–2 (portions)
1QDan^{b}	Daniel 3 (portions)
4QDan	several manuscripts
4QDan^{a}	Daniel 2; 7–8 (portions)
4QDan^{b}	Daniel 7–8 and other passages (portions)
4QDan^{c}	
pap6QDan	Daniel 8?; 10–11 (portions)
4QChron	
4QEzra	Ezra 4–5 (portions)

In addition, the commentaries (*p*^{e}*sārîm*) of the Qumran community quote the text under discussion:

3QpIsa	Isaiah 1:1
4QpIsa^{a}	Isaiah 10–11 (portions)
4QpIsa^{b}	Isaiah 5 and several later chapters (portions)
pap4QpIsa^{c}	Isaiah 30 and other chapters (portions)
4QpIsa^{d}	Isaiah 54 and other passages (portions)
4QpHos^{a}	Hosea 5:14-15?
4QpHos^{b}	Hosea 2 (portions)
1QpMic	Micah 1; 6 (portions)
4QpNah	Nahum 1–3 (portions)
1QpHab	Habakkuk 1–2
1QpZeph	Zephaniah 1–2 (portions)
1QpPs	Psalms 57; 68 (portions)
4QpPs37	
4QpPs45	

We may finally mention the quotation collections:

4Q Eschatological Midrashim
4Q Patriarchal Blessings
4Q Testimonia
4Q Tanhumim

5. *Basic form of the Masoretic text.* The decisive step toward alleviating the difficulties brought about by a multiplicity of recensions by fixing a uniform text (and thereby at least the basic form of the Masoretic text) was taken at the same time the canon was completed, after the fall of Jerusalem in A.D. 70, and in the context of necessary defense against incipient Christian anti-Jewish polemic. The rabbis' dissatisfaction with the condition of the Hebrew text was combined with a renewed conviction of the inspiration and sanctity of the words of the Bible. On the one hand, therefore, efforts were made to produce a

"semiofficial" text, on whose basis the rabbis could answer the Christian attacks; on the other, an attempt was made to fix every detail of the text revealing God's truth as precisely and unambiguously as possible. This took place first of all in Palestine, where above all the excavated remains of the synagogues in Galilee bear witness to the religious and cultural activity of Judaism, which flourished in the second century and even had the patronage of the Roman Emperor. Later, especially after Christianity had been adopted as the state religion, many Jewish scholars fled to Babylonia where they forged new centers, such as those in Sura and Nehardea, and, after the destruction of the latter (A.D. 259), in Pumbedita.

The basic form of the consonantal text of what was later to be the Masoretic text (though not the supposed archetype) was probably essentially fixed by the time of Rabbi Aqiba in the early second century of this era, and provided the basis for subsequent development. The progress made in this direction can be seen from the translations made by Aquila, Theodotion, and Symmachus in the second and third centuries, which, in contrast to the multiplicity of textual forms at Qumran, take as their point of departure a Hebrew *Vorlage* with roughly the form of the Masoretic text. Even at this time and afterward there remained a series of differences, consisting mostly of orthographic and dialectal variants. The various schools sought to preserve as many of their favorite readings as possible, so that the final unified text reflects their contention and represents a kind of compromise between the various opposing views.

6. *The work of the "scribes."* The next period in the history of the text is marked by the activity of the "scribes," who copied new scrolls from the ancient ones. On the one hand, they took extreme care to copy every word and every letter from one manuscript into the next; a copy with more than three scribal errors was usually confiscated by the official correctors. On the other hand, they had a share in the gradual growth of what was to be the uniform text, since they compared the copy with its *Vorlage* and with other manuscripts. In their work they could also draw upon oral traditions concerning the forms of the text and the pronunciation of the words. In addition, they strove for a proper understanding of the text. They began to place short notes in the margins of the manuscripts, to mark words needing elucidation, and, by means of various signs, to indicate passages whose text appeared dubious to them.

These signs include (1) the *puncta extraordinaria* occurring in ten passages in the Pentateuch and five in other books, which probably indicate a dubious text; (2) *paseq,* whose date and meaning is disputed; (3) the inverted *nun* found in nine passages, which may be intended to indicate a transposition in the text; (4) the "corrections of the scribes," primarily to correct dogmatically objectionable passages, e.g., Gen. 18:22; (5) the "omissions of the scribes"; (6) *sebirin* to indicate unusual forms or meanings of words. There may be added (7) the abbreviations of words in the text, which are not indicated.

7. *The Masoretes.* The work of the Masoretes, beginning in the late fifth

and early sixth centuries, marks a new period in the history of the text. The term, which applies both to the Masoretic text and its fixed and definitive form, probably derives from the Late Hebrew verb *māsar,* "hand down." The pronunciation of the substantive is not definitely known (either *māsōrâ* or *massōrâ*); it refers to the formal "transmission" of the text. The men who saw to this transmission were called the Masoretes ("transmitters") or, after the eleventh century, Nakdanim ("pointers"). They do not constitute a single coherent group, nor is the Masora a single complete work resulting from a uniform development. Two great groups of Masoretes may be distinguished, whose character has been studied in particular by Kahle: (*a*) the Masoretes of the West, in Palestine, whose studies flourished in the period of Arab rule in the eighth and ninth centuries and whose major center was Tiberias; and (*b*) the Masoretes of the East, in Babylonia, from the third to the ninth centuries, with centers in Sura, Nehardea, and Pumbedita. Both groups are themselves divided into several schools or "families."

a) After the early notes and primarily oral tradition of the scribes, work on the consonantal text began with a general written codification of the textual notes. This gave rise to (1) the *masora marginalis,* including the *masora parva* with short notes (between the lines in Babylonia and at the side of the text in Palestine) and the *masora magna* with longer notes in the margins (beside and beneath the text in Babylonia, in the top and bottom margins in Palestine); and (2) the *masora finalis,* which at the end of a book or of the entire OT brought together all the material in alphabetic sequence. Although all the notes were accepted only at the home of the school that produced them, the result was a degree of uniformity in principles and procedures. In this way the text, which now acquired the authority of a standard text, was protected against all tampering and alteration. One primary result was to preserve irregularities in the form of the text. The rules are contained in two tractates, Sepher Torah and Sopherim.

b) For many centuries the text was unvocalized and the pronunciation only suggested to a slight extent by the addition of *matres lectionis,* so that it is dificult to determine how early Hebrew was pronounced. Not a few wanted to leave it at that; they opposed the introduction of signs to indicate the vowels. These make their first appearance in private manuscripts in the form of points and lines. Vocalization began gradually and unofficially in the sixth or seventh century and then gained universal acceptance. The eastern and western schools went separate ways.

The Babylonian vocalization, which Kahle has determined from the fragments found in the genizah at Old Cairo and other manuscripts, was developed between the seventh and tenth centuries; the extant texts exhibit considerable differences. On the basis of this evidence a two-stage development can be traced: a simple vocalization, which has many signs in common with Nestorian Syriac; and, from the eighth century on, a complex vocalization, which was developed under the influence of the strictly biblicistic Karaites. Western influence later gave rise to mixed forms.

The Palestinian vocalization also began with a simple system, which Simḥa in *Maḥzor Vitry* calls the "pointing of the land of Israel." It is related to both the vocalization of the Samaritan Pentateuch and the simple Babylonian form, so that either the Palestinian and Samaritan forms are based on the simple Babylonian, or all possess a common origin. Later the simple Palestinian system developed more and more along the lines of the Tiberian system that superseded it, whose predecessor it may be considered. The Tiberian vocalization, too, arose under the influence of the Karaites toward the end of the eighth century; it reached its full development about 900 and, under the two famous Tiberian families of Masoretes Ben Asher and Ben Naphtali, carried the day so completely against all other systems that these latter have only been rediscovered in recent decades. From this time on, the Tiberian system alone was used for vocalized Hebrew text. Scholars generally hold that most of the *qere-ketib* readings came into being in this period; these do not represent textual emendations, but are either alternative readings from earlier tradition or differences in pointing between the Ben Asher and Ben Naphtali recensions, i.e., from the later development of the Tiberian vocalization.

8. *Development of the textus receptus.* The Tiberian vocalization does not bring the history of the text to an end. There still remained a long process leading up to the *textus receptus* (Masoretic text). First the other systems had to be driven out, and then the internal struggle between the two Tiberian schools or "families" had to be resolved.

The work of the Ben Asher family can be traced through five generations. The most important were Moses ben Asher, from whom the codex of the Prophets belonging to the Karaite synagogue at Cairo (completed in 895) derives, and his son Aaron ben Asher, who provided a codex of the entire OT with vocalization and Masora, three-quarters of which was saved and brought to Israel from the synagogue at Aleppo.[14] These two manuscripts do not agree completely with the later official text, which shows that the process of development was not yet concluded, although the authority of Maimonides in the twelfth century gained the descision for this form of the text. Since the Aleppo Codex was not available, the third edition of the *Biblia Hebraica* used the copy contained in Leningrad Codex B 19a (1008), thus going back beyond the *textus receptus,* which had previously been used everywhere.

The vocalization of the Ben Naphtali family exhibits minor divergences from that of the Ben Asher family; there may also be differences in the consonantal text.[15] This is the form of the text on which Codex Reuchlinianus at Karlsruhe (1105) is based. Mishael ben Uzziel compiled a list of the differences in

[14] I. Ben-Zvi, "The Codex of Ben Asher," *Textus,* I (1960), 1-16; M. Goshen-Gottstein, "The Authenticity of the Aleppo Codex," *ibid.,* pp. 17-58; D. S. Löwinger, "The Aleppo Codex and the Ben Asher Tradition," *ibid.,* pp. 59-111; for a different evaluation, see A. Dotan, "Was the Aleppo Codex Actually Vocalized by Aharon ben Asher?" *Tarbiz,* XXXIV (1964/65), 136-55.

[15] S. H. Blank, "A Hebrew Bible Manuscript in the Hebrew Union College Library," *HUCA,* VIII/IX (1931/32), 229-55.

vocalization shortly after the decision of Maimonides;[16] according to this list, the Ben Naphtali text goes into more detail in the pronunciation and placing of the metheg.

In actual fact each form of the text influenced the other, so that finally, in the fourteenth century, a neutral mixed text, the *textus receptus,* came into being. It furnishes the basis for editions of the Bible down to the second edition of the *Biblia Hebraica,* with the exception of the unsuccessful attempt of Baer-Delitzsch, which, on the basis of an arbitrary application of an inadequate knowledge of the Masora, sought to produce what would be a trustworthy text. Editions of portions of the OT begin in 1477 (a psalter printed at Bologna); the first complete editions appeared in 1488 at Soncino, in 1491–93 at Naples, and in 1494 at Brescia (used by Luther). The first rabbinic Bible, containing the Masoretic text with targum and rabbinic commentary in the margin, edited by Felix Pratensis, was published in 1516–17 by Daniel Bomberg at Venice;[17] the revised second edition, edited by Jacob ben Ḥayyim, appeared there in 1524-25. For a long time it furnished the standard text for all subsequent editions. For the rest, the polyglot Bibles of the sixteenth and seventeenth centuries also contain the *textus receptus.*

9. *Division of the text.* The practice of dividing the books of the OT began very early. Even the Qumran texts exhibit a division into sections, which does not, however, coincide with the later division. For the Torah, the Mishna (*ca.* A.D. 200) presupposes the final division of the text into units according to subject matter; these units are called *pārāšôt.* The *pārāšôt* include larger (*pᵉtû-ḥôt,* "open") and smaller (*sᵉtûmôt,* "closed") units; at first the former were distinguished by the omission of the remainder of the line begun or of an entire line; the latter were distinguished by the insertion of a space within the line. Later a space was left in both cases and a *peh* or *sāmek,* as appropriate, was inserted before the new section.

In addition, there was a new division for liturgical purposes. In Palestine the Torah was read in a three-year cycle; for this purpose it was divided into 154 *sᵉdārîm.* In Babylonia the cycle was annual and the text was divided into 53 or 54 *pārāšôt.*

Stephen Langton of Canterbury introduced the division into chapters about 1205 for the Vulgate; Rabbi Solomon ben Ishmael borrowed it for a Hebrew manuscript. The division into verses, however, was already known to the Talmud, and may go back to the "scribes." It differed greatly in Palestine and Babylonia, however. Enumeration of the verses begins in 1563 with an edition of the Psalter, and in 1571 for the entire OT.

[16] L. Lipschütz, *Ben-Ascher-Ben-Naphtali, der Bibeltext der tiberiensischen Masoreten,* 1937; *idem,* "Mishael ben Uzziel's Treatise on the Differences between Ben Asher and Ben Naphtali," *Textus,* II (1962), Hebrew pp. 1-58.

[17] P. Kahle, "Felix Pratensis—à Prato, Felix. Der Herausgeber der ersten Rabbinerbibel, Venedig, 1516/17," *WdO,* I (1947-52), 32-36.

§ 79 Non-Masoretic Text Forms

M. Baillet, "Un nouveau fragment du Pentateuque samaritain," *RB* LXVII (1960), 49-57; A. von Gall, *Der hebräische Pentateuch der Samaritaner*, 1914-18; J. Hempel, "Innermasoretische Bestätigungen des Samaritanus," *ZAW*, LII (1934), 254-74; P. Kahle, "The Abisha' Scroll of the Samaritans," in *Studia Orientalia Pedersen*, 1953, pp. 188-92; F. Pèrez Castro, *Séfer Abiša'*, 1959; *idem*, "Das Kryptogramm des Sefer Abischa'," *VTSuppl*, VII (1960), 52-60; S. Talmon, "The Samaritan Pentateuch," *JJS*, II (1950/51), 144-50; *idem*, *Selections from the Pentateuch in the Samaritan Version*, 1956-57.

H. Barnstein, *The Targum of Onkelos to Genesis*, 1896; A. Berliner, *Targum Onkelos*, 1884; K.-H. Bernhardt, "Zu Eigenart und Alter der messianisch-eschatologischen Zusätze im Targum Jeruschalmi I," in *Fascher-Festschrift*, 1959, pp. 68-83; W. H. Brownlee, "The Habakkuk Midrash and the Targum of Jonathan," *JJS*, VII (1956), 169-86; P. Churgin, *Targum Jonathan to the Prophets*, 1928; L. Delekat, "Ein Septuagintatargum," *VT*, VIII (1958), 225-52; A. Díez Macho, "Un importante manuscrito targúmico en la Biblioteca Vaticana," in *Homenaje a Millás-Vallicrosa*, I (1954), 375-463; *idem*, "Nuevos fragmentos del Targum palestinense," *Sefarad*, XV (1955), 31-39; *idem*, "Un nuovo Targum a los profetas," *EstBibl*, XV (1956), 287-95; *idem*, "Una copia de todo al Targum jerosolimitano en la Vaticana," *ibid.*, pp. 446-47; *idem*, "Una copia completa del Targum palestinense al Pentateuco en la Biblioteca Vaticana," *Sefarad*, XVII (1957), 119-21; *idem*, "Un segundo fragmento del Targum Palestinense a los Profetas," *Bibl*, XXXIX (1958), 198-205; *idem*, " 'Onqelos Manuscript with Babylonian Transliterated Vocalization in the Vatican Library," *VT*, VIII (1958), 113-33; *idem*, "The Recently Discovered Palestinian Targum," *VTSuppl*, VII (1960), 222-45; M. Ginsburger, *Das Fragmententhargum*, 1899; *idem*, *Pseudo-Jonathan*, 1903; P. Grelot, "Les Targums du Pentateuque," *Semitica*, IX (1959), 59-88; P. Kahle, "Das palästinische Pentateuchtargum und das zur Zeit Jesu gesprochene Aramäisch," *ZNW*, XLIX (1958), 100-16; P. de Lagarde, *Prophetae chaldaice*, 1872; *idem*, *Hagiographa chaldaice*, 1873; A. Marmorstein, *Studien zum Pseudo-Jonathan-Targum*, I, 1905; *idem*, "Einige vorläufige Bemerkungen zu den neuentdeckten Fragmenten des jerusalemischen (palästinensischen) Targums," *ZAW*, XLIX (1931), 231-42; A. E. Silverstone, *Aquila and Onkelos*, 1931; A. Sperber, "Zur Textgestalt des Prophetentargums," *ZAW*, XLIV (1926), 175-76; *idem*, "Zur Sprache des Prophetentargums," *ibid.*, XLV (1927), 267-88; *idem*, "The Targum Onkelos in its Relation to the Masoretic Hebrew Text," *PAAJR*, VI (1935), 309-51; *idem*, *The Bible in Aramaic*, 1959-ff.; J. F. Stenning, *The Targum of Isaiah*, 2nd ed., 1953; S. Wohl, *Das Palästinische Pentateuch-Targum*, 1935.

A. Baumstark, "Pešiṭtā und palästinensisches Targum" *BZ*, XIX (1931), 257-70; J. Bloch, "The Printed Text of the Peshiṭta Old Testament," *AJSL*, XXXVI (1920/21), 136-44; L. Delekat, "Die syrolukianische Übersetzung des Buches Jesaja und das Postulat einer alttestamentlichen Vetus Syra," *ZAW*, LXIX (1957), 21-54; *idem*, "Die Peschitta zu Jesaja zwischen Targum und Septuaginta," *Bibl*, XXXVIII (1957), 185-99, 321-35; *idem*, "Die syropalästinische Jesaja-Übersetzung," *ZAW*, LXXI (1959), 165-201; G. Diettrich, *Ein Apparatus criticus zur Pešitto zum Propheten Jesaja*, 1905; D. M. C. Englert, *The Peshitto of Second Samuel*, 1949; M. H. Goshen-Gottstein, "Prolegomena to a Critical Edition of the Peshitta," *Scripta Hierosolymitana*, VIII (1960), 26-67; L. Haefeli, *Die Peschitta des Alten Testaments mit Rücksicht auf ihre textkritische Bearbeitung und Herausgabe*, 1927; J. Hänel, *Die aussermasoreti-*

schen Übereinstimmungen zwischen der Septuaginta und der Peschittha in der Genesis, 1911; C. HELLER, *Untersuchungen über die Peschîttâ zur gesamten hebräischen Bibel*, I, 1911; C. PETERS, "Peschittha und Targumim des Pentateuchs," *Muséon*, XLVIII (1935), 1-54; A. RAHLFS, "Beiträge zur Textkritik der Peschita," *ZAW*, IX (1889), 161-210; A. VÖÖBUS, "The Oldest Extant Traces of the Syriac Peshitta," *Muséon*, LXIII (1950), 191-204; *idem*, "Das Alter der Peschitta," *OrChr*, XXXVIII (1954), 1-10; *idem*, "Der Einfluss des altpälästinischen Targums in der Textgeschichte der Peschitta des Alten Testaments," *Muséon*, LXVIII (1955), 215-18; *idem*, *Peschitta und Targumim des Pentateuchs*, 1958; M. WILCOX, "Some Recent Contributions to the Problem of Peshitta Origins," *Abr-Nahrain*, I (1961), 63-67.

G. BERTRAM, "Zur Septuaginta-Forschung," *ThR*, NF III (1931), 283-96; V (1933), 173-86; X (1938), 69-80, 133-59; G. GERLEMAN, *Synoptic Studies in the Old Testament*, 1948; R. HANHART, "Fragen um die Entstehung der LXX," *VT*, XII (1962), 139-63; S. JELLICOE, "Aristeas, Philo and the Septuagint Vorlage," *JThSt*, NS XII (1961), 261-71; P. KAHLE, "Die Septuaginta," in *Eissfeldt-Festschrift*, 1947, pp. 161-80; *idem*, "Problems of the Septuagint," *Studia Patristica*, I (1957), 328-38; *idem*, "The Greek Bible Manuscripts used by Origen," *JBL*, LXXIX (1960), 11-18; P. KATZ, "Notes on the Septuagint," *JThST*, XLVII (1946), 30-33, 166-69; XLVIII (1947), 194-96; *idem*, "Das Problem des Urtextes der Septuaginta," *ThZ*, V (1949), 1-24; *idem*, "Septuagintal Studies in the Mid-Century," in *Essays Dodd*, 1956, pp. 176-208; F. G. KENYON, *Recent Developments in the Textual Criticism of the Greek Bible*, 1933; *idem*, *The Text of the Greek Bible*, 2nd ed., 1949; G. MERCATI, "D'un palimpsesto Ambrosiano contenente i salmi esapli," *Atti Acad. Scienze Torino*, XXXI (1895), 655-76; *idem*, *Psalterii Hexapli Reliquiae*, I, 1958; G. F. MOORE, "The Antiochian Recension of the LXX," *AJSL*, XXIX (1912/13), 37-62; E. NESTLE, *Septuagintastudien*, 1886-1911; H. M. ORLINSKY, "On the Present State of Proto-Septuagint Studies," *JAOS*, LXI (1941), 81-91; *idem*, "The Septuagint—Its Use in Textual Criticism," *BA*, IX (1946), 21-34; *idem*, *The Septuagint*, 1949; *idem*, "Qumran and the Present State of Old Testament Studies: The Septuagint Text," *JBL*, LXXVIII (1959), 26-33; J. PRIJS, *Jüdische Tradition in der Septuaginta*, 1948; O. PROCKSCH, *Studien zur Geschichte der Septuaginta*, 1910, A. RAHLFS, *Lucians Rezension der Königsbücher*, 1911; H. H. ROWLEY, "The Proto-Septuagint Question," *JQR*, XXXIII (1942/43), 497-99; I. SOISALON-SOININEN, *Der Charakter der asterisierten Zusätze in der Septuaginta*, 1959; A. SPERBER, "The Problem of the Septuagint Recensions," *JBL*, LIV (1935), 73-92; H. B. SWETE, *Introduction to the Old Testament in Greek*, 2nd ed., 1914; H. ST. J. THACKERAY, *Some Aspects of the Greek Old Testament*, 1927; J. W. WEVERS, "Septuaginta-Forschungen," *ThR*, NF XXII (1954), 85-138, 171-90; F. WUTZ, *Die Transkriptionen von der Septuaginta bis Hieronymus*, 1933; *idem*, *Systematische Wege von der Septuaginta zum hebräischen Urtext*, 1937; J. ZIEGLER, *Die Septuaginta*, 1962.

A. ALLGEIER, *Die altlateinischen Psalterien*, 1928; J. BACHMANN, *Dodekapropheton Aethiopum*, 1892; *idem*, *Die Klagelieder Jeremiae in der äthiopischen Bibelübersetzung*, 1893; A. V. BILLEN, *The Old Latin Texts of the Heptateuch*, 1927; A. BÖHLIG, *Untersuchungen über die koptischen Proverbientexte*, 1936; *idem*, *Der achmimische Proverbientext nach Ms. Berol. Orient. Oct. 987*, I, 1958; J. O. BOYD, *The Text of the Ethiopic Version of the Octateuch*, 1905; F. C. BURKITT, *The Old Latin and the Itala*, 1896; L. DIEU, "Le texte coptesahidique des Livres de Samuël," *Muséon*, LIX (1946), 445-52; A. DILLMANN, *Octateuchus Aethiopicus*, 1853-55; A. DOLD, *Konstanzer altlateinische Propheten- und Evangelienbruchstücke mit Glossen*, 1923;

idem, Neue St. Galler vorhieronymianische Propheten-Fragmente, 1940; R. ECKER, *Die arabische Job-Übersetzung des Gaon Saadja ben Josef al-Fajjûmi,* 1962; H. C. GLEAVE, *The Ethiopic Version of the Song of Songs,* 1951; G. GRAF, *Geschichte der christlichen arabischen Literatur,* I (1944), reprinted 1953; W. K. M. GROSSOUW, *The Coptic Versions of the Minor Prophets,* 1938; F. L. HALLOCK, "The Coptic Old Testament," *AJSL,* XLIX (1932/33), 325-35; R. KASSER, *Papyrus Bodmer III,* 1958; *VI,* 1960; *XVI,* 1961; *XVIII,* 1962; *XXI,* 1963; *XXII,* 1964; O. LÖFGREN, *Die äthiopische Übersetzung des Propheten Daniel,* 1927; S. A. B. MERCER, *The Ethiopic Text of the Book of Ecclesiastes,* 1931; J. B. PAYNE, "The Sahidic Coptic Text of I Samuel," *JBL,* LXXII (1953), 51-62; A. RAHLFS, *Die Berliner Handschrift des Sahidischen Psalters,* 1901; K. T. SCHÄFER, *Die altlateinische Bibel,* 1957; J. SCHÄFERS, *Die äthiopische Übersetzung des Propheten Jeremia,* 1912; *J. Schildenberger, Die altlateinischen Texte des Proverbien-Buches,* I, 1941; *idem,* "Die Itala des hl. Augustinus," in *Dold-Festschrift,* 1952, pp. 84-102; H. SPIEGEL, *Arabische Danielversion,* 1906; M. STENZEL, "Zur Frühgeschichte der lateinischen Bibel," *ThRev,* XLIX (1953), 97-103; *idem,* "Die Konstanzer und St. Galler Fragmente zum altlateinischen Dodekapropheton," *Sacris Erudiri,* V (1953), 27-85; *idem,* "Das Zwölfprophetenbuch im Würzburger Palimpsest-codex (cod. membr. No. 64) und seine Textgestalt in Väterzitaten," *ibid.,* VII (1955), 5-34; H. TATTAM, *Prophetae majores, in dialecto linguae aegyptiacae memphitica seu coptica,* I, 1852; J. ZIEGLER, "Beiträge zur koptischen Dodekapropheton-Übersetzung," *Bibl,* XXV (1944), 105-42; *idem,* "Altlateinische Psalterien," *BZ* NF, V (1961), 94-115.

M. ABRAHAMS, *Aquila's Greek Version of the Hebrew Bible,* 1919; D. BARTHÉLEMY, *Les devanciers d'Aquila,* 1963; F. C. BURKITT, *Fragments of the Books of Kings According to the Translation of Aquila,* 1897; F. FIELD, *Origenis Hexaplorum quae supersunt sive Veterum Interpretum Graecorum in totum Vetus Testamentum Fragmenta,* 1875-76; S. KRAUSS, "Two Hitherto Unknown Bible Versions in Greek," *BJRL,* XXVII (1942/43), 97-105; L. J. LIEBREICH, "Notes on the Greek Version of Symmachus," *JBL,* LXIII (1944), 397-403; A. MÖHLE, "Ein neuer Fund zahlreicher Stücke aus den Jesajaübersetzungen des Akylas, Symmachos und Theodotion," *ZAW,* LII (1934), 176-83; C. TAYLOR, *Hebrew-Greek Cairo Genizah Palimpsests,* 1900.

A. ALLGEIER, *Die Psalmen der Vulgata,* 1940; F. AMANN, *Die Vulgata Sixtina von 1590,* 1912; A. BEA, *Die neue lateinische Psalmenübersetzung,* 1949; J. H. MARKS, *Der textkritische Wert des Psalterium Hieronymi juxta Hebraeos,* 1956; G. SCARPAT, *Il liber Psalmorum e il Psalterium Gallicanum,* 1950; F. STUMMER, *Einführung in die lateinische Bibel,* 1928; *idem,* "Einige Beobachtungen über die Arbeitsweise des Hieronymus bei der Übersetzung des Alten Testaments aus der Hebraica Veritas," *Bibl,* X (1929), 3-30; *idem,* "Hauptprobleme der Erforschung der alttestamentlichen Vulgata," in BZAW, LXVI (1936), 233-39; *idem,* "Zur Stilgeschichte der alten Bibelübersetzungen," *ZAW,* LXI (1945-48), 195-231; E. F. SUTCLIFFE, "St. Jerome's Hebrew Manuscripts," *Bibl,* XXIX (1948), 195-204; R. WEBER, *Sancti Hieronymi Psalterium iuxta Hebraeos,* 1954; J. ZIEGLER, "Das neue lateinische Psalterium," *ZAW,* LXIII (1952), 1-15; F. ZORELL, *Psalterium ex hebraeo Latinum,* 2nd ed., 1939.

1. *Survey.* The following forms of the text must be distinguished:

a) The Samaritan recension of the Pentateuch
b) Semitic translations of the OT
1. The Targums

2. The Peshitta

c) The Septuagint (LXX) and its daughter translations
1. The Septuagint
2. The Vetus Latina
3. The Coptic translations
4. The Ethiopic translation
5. Other translations

d) The translations independent of the LXX
1. Aquila
2. Theodotion
3. Symmachus
4. References to other translations

e) The Vulgate

2. *The Samaritan Pentateuch.* The Samaritan Pentateuch is not a version, but more exactly an ancient recension of the Hebrew text. In script and language it corresponds to the state of the Hebrew Pentateuch at the time of the split between Jerusalem and the Samaritans. Apart from minor alterations made for dogmatic reasons, it has remained essentially in that condition. The Samaritan Pentateuch therefore bears witness to a pre-Masoretic text form of the fourth century B.C. In the aids for pronunciation, however, it exhibits several features peculiar to the period of the Tiberian Masoretes. It is not definitely known whether these are based on a secondary assimilation to the Masoretic text (Kahle) or reflect the dialect of northern Israel in the postexilic period (Sperber).[1] There are some 6000 divergences from the Masoretic text, most of which, however, are orthographic. About 1600 agree with the LXX against the Masoretic text; these indicate that we are dealing with a recension or recensions distinct from the recension that developed into the Masoretic text. The Samareitikon quoted in Origen's *Hexapla* is a Greek version whose translator took the Samaritan text as his point of departure and also made use of the LXX.[2] In addition, there is the translation of the Targum into the Aramaic dialect of the Samaritans.[3] The manuscripts of this translation differ considerably among themselves. There are also translations into Arabic from the eleventh and twelfth centuries.[4]

3. *The Targums.* The targums became necessary in the later postexilic

[1] P. Kahle, "Untersuchungen zur Geschichte des Pentateuchtextes," *ThStKr,* LXXXVIII (1915), 402; *idem, The Cairo Geniza,* 2nd ed., 1959, pp. 49-50; A. Sperber, "Hebrew Based upon Greek and Latin Transliteration," *HUCA,* XII/XIII (1937/38), 151 ff.

[2] P. Glaue and A. Rahlfs, *Fragmente einer griechischen Übersetzung des samaritanischen Pentateuchs,* 1911.

[3] L. Goldberg, *Das samaritanische Pentateuchtargum,* Dissertation, Bonn, 1935; P. Kahle, *Textkritische und lexikalische Bemerkungen zum samaritanischen Pentateuchtargum,* Dissertation, Halle, 1898.

[4] A. E. Cowley, *The Samaritan Liturgy,* I–II, 1909; P. Kahle, *Die arabischen Bibelübersetzungen,* 1904, pp. x-xiii; *idem, The Cairo Geniza,* 2nd ed., 1959, pp. 53-55; E. Robertson, "The Relationship of the Arabic Translation of the Samaritan Pentateuch to that of Saadya," in *Saadya Studies,* 1943, pp. 166-76.

period, when Hebrew gave place to Aramaic as the common language and survived only as a liturgical language. As a consequence, the Hebrew text was translated into Aramaic as it was read in the course of worship. This translation (*targûm*) was at first made orally without a written *Vorlage* by a specially appointed translator (*mᵉturgᵉmān*). As early as the pre-Christian period, however, there were written versions of this nature in Aramaic. The existence of early targums is suggested by the quotation from Ps. 22:2 (Eng. 22:1) in Mark 15:34; Matt. 27:46 and of Ps. 68:19 (Eng. 68:18) in Eph. 4:8. In addition, remnants of a targum on Leviticus 16 have been discovered in 4Q and a targum on Job in 11Q; the text of the latter probably goes back to the second half of the second century B.C. and may be identical with the targum condemned by Gamaliel.[5]

None of the targums furnishes a standard version; they were not the work of a single translator, nor do they date from a sharply defined period. Furthermore, they are neither exact translations nor versions of the Hebrew text, but free renderings and paraphrases, often with interpolated narratives and explanatory material, so that they are midrashic in nature. They must therefore be utilized with caution for text-critical study.

a) Targums on the Pentateuch: (1) the Palestinian Targum, reconstructed from fragments in the Old Cairo genizah and other witnesses (Vatican Library ms. Neofiti 1), which is related to the Peshitta in many respects and was still used in the ninth century; (2) the Jerusalem Targum I, from the seventh century, containing almost the entire Pentateuch, mistakenly identified as Targum Jonathan from the Aramaic abbreviation of its name and therefore usually called Targum Pseudo-Jonathan; (3) the Jerusalem Targum II(–III), also called the Fragmentary Targum on account of its state of preservation, usually considered earlier than I; (4) the Targum Onqelos, an official Aramaic rendering of the final Masoretic consonantal text. Targum Onqelos may represent the revision of an earlier targum on the basis of the final text; it was produced in Palestine but edited in Babylonia. Sperber has published a new edition. Whether the name is identical with that of the translator Aquila must remain undecided.

b) Targums on the Prophets: (1) fragments like those appended to Codex Reuchlinianus indicate that there were several early and unofficial renderings in Aramaic; (2) the Targum Jonathan, a rendering similar to that of Onqelos, newly edited by Sperber. The nominal author is often identified with the translator Theodotion, while the Talmud sees in him a pupil of Hillel from the first century of our era.

c) There are targums on the Writings from various periods and of various origin; they differ considerably among themselves. They range from close dependence on the Hebrew text to expanded midrashim; all of them combine early and late material.

4. *The Peshitta.* The Peshitta, the "simple" translation in contrast to the

[5] Cf. the data in G. Fohrer, "4QOrNab, 11QTgJob und die Hioblegende," *ZAW*, LXXV (1963), 93-97.

Hexapla, is the Syriac version of the OT. Many questions concerning its history and status must temporarily remain open, the more so because a general critical edition is only now in preparation. In any case, it is the work of many hands and periods, clearly based on targumic renderings adapted to the Syriac language and later to the needs of the Syriac Christians. The Pentateuch seems to have been translated first. This East Aramaic version exhibits linguistic features of the West Aramaic Palestinian Targum; there are also points of contact between it and readings in the Qumran scrolls. For the time being, it is impossible to define its background precisely.

It is sometimes assumed that the Pentateuch was translated into Syriac (and also revised) about the middle of the first century of our era for the Jewish royal family of Adiabene, east of the Tigris, and that the translation was based on a Palestinian targum (Kahle), if in fact there was not already a Syriac targum that was later transformed into a literal translation. Others assume a Christian origin for the Pentateuch translation, which (according to this theory) was created to satisfy the needs of the Syriac church after A.D. 150 (Pfeiffer *et al.*).

Similar questions arise concerning the translation of the other books of the OT. Opinions differ as to whether it is of Jewish or Christian origin, and a clear decision is impossible. The individual books may even be of different origins, the more so because each seems to have been translated independently. They vary in style and in their dependence on the targums and LXX. Job and the Song of Songs are literal translations; Isaiah, the Minor Prophets, and Psalms are free translations; Ezekiel and Proverbs are more like targums; and Chronicles, which was added later, is a paraphrase. If the Peshitta should turn out to be of Jewish origin in whole or in part, it was nevertheless adopted by the Syriac church and revised, mostly on the basis of the LXX. After the division of the Syriac church in the fifth century, four major recensions of the Christian Peshitta gradually arose: (1) the East Syriac text form of the Nestorians (editions of Urmia and Mosul); (2) the West Syriac text form of the Jacobites (Codex Ambrosianus and an edition by Lee); (3) that of the Melkites; and (4) that of the Maronites, which also represents the West Syriac form.

During the fifth through seventh centuries, other translations into Syriac were made: a Syro-Palestinian or Jerusalemite translation of the Syriac Palestinian Melkites, to the few extant fragments of which have been recently added those found at Khirbet el-Mird; the translation made about 500 by Polycarp for Bishop Philoxenus of Mabbug; and the Syro-Hexapla, the translation by Bishop Paul of Tella (616/17) found in the fifth column of Origen's *Hexapla.* All these represent mixtures of Peshitta and LXX texts.

5. *The Septuagint.* According to the Letter of Aristeas, which dates from the second half of the second century B.C., the Septuagint (LXX) came into being when King Ptolemy II Philadelphus (285–246), at the request of his librarian, had a translation of the Torah into Greek prepared by 72 scholars appointed by the high priest at Jerusalem, who in 72 days created a text that

met with unanimous approval.[6] From the round number comes the name "Translation of the Seventy" or simply "Seventy (Septuagint)." In reality, the letter is a piece of Jewish apologetics of the late Ptolemaic period, written to gain respect for the LXX; it was certainly produced not by Aramaic-speaking but by Greek-speaking Jews. It is true, however, that about the middle of the third century B.C. the translation of the Torah came into being at Alexandria through the work of several translators, and that the translations of the other books of the OT followed over a long period. The reason was the desire of the Greek-speaking Jews to be able to read and understand the OT without having to restrict themselves to the makeshift of using merely Greek transcriptions, i.e., copies of the Hebrew text written in the Greek alphabet. Apart from this, opinions differ concerning the origin and early history of the LXX. At least four theories deserve mention.

The theory first proposed by de Lagarde and Rahlfs, which is still accepted by many scholars (Margolis, Montgomery, Orlinsky, Ziegler, Roberts), assumes a Proto-Septuagint and thinks in terms of an original Greek translation of each individual book or group of books in the OT, followed by a gradual corruption of the text and correction through revisions. Kahle, by contrast, represents the theory that the history of the LXX does not begin with a prototext, but with various targumic renderings of vulgar Hebrew text, and that the Letter of Aristeas was written as propaganda on behalf of a revised translation of the Torah introduced at the same time. This translation, being a standard text, supplanted the previous translations; for the other books there was no standard text, but rather several translations, represented by the various recensions of the LXX, which continued in use. According to the third theory, that of Thackeray, the LXX translations, with the exception of the Torah, took place in two stages: first the sections needed for public recitation in synagogue worship, then, gradually, the other parts. Finally, Wutz proposed the theory—now generally rejected—that the LXX was translated from Greek transcriptions.

Cogent reasons can be advanced in support of the two most important theories (those of de Lagarde and Kahle), namely, the assumption of a Proto-Septuagint and the idea of a Greek targum. In the present state of our knowledge it is impossible to reach a final decision in favor of either theory. We must first have a collection and thorough study of the enormous mass of textual variants from which alone the history of the development of the LXX may someday be reconstructed. We can only say with some assurance that the translation of the Pentateuch—whether in the form of a prototext or of a targum—appeared around the middle of the third century B.C., that of the "Prophets" of the Hebrew collection about 200 B.C., and that of most of the other books in the first century B.C. As a whole, the LXX is a collection of translations of the OT books that came into being in the Egyptian Diaspora and reflect the spirit of Hellenistic Judaism.

When the LXX was adopted by the early church in the first century of this

[6] Later legend extended this to mean that they translated the entire OT, each independent of the rest.

era, it immediately lost authority within Judaism. The aversion to it was strengthened by the recognition of the Hebrew OT in the Diaspora and the realization that there were numerous and considerable differences between the two forms of the text. Judaism finally rejected the LXX completely, and tractate Sopherim i. 8 declared that the day the Torah was translated was as cruel a day for Israel as the day on which the golden calf was made. To the Christian church, however, the many variants within the text of the LXX—whether they should be interpreted as sign of corruption of a prototext or as parallel targums—brought increasing embarrassment.

Origen sought to improve this situation by means of his Hexapla, which he produced in Caesarea between 240 and 245. In it, despite the recognition due the LXX as the official text of the church, he did not use the LXX text as the basis for the OT, but rather the new Hebrew standard text (§78.5). In six parallel columns Origen juxtaposed (1) the Hebrew text in square script; (2) the Hebrew text in Greek transcription; (3) the translation of Aquila; (4) the translation of Symmachus; (5) the LXX; (6) the translation of Theodotion. He also added in part three other anonymous Greek versions, known as Quinta, Sexta, and Septima. The fifth column was the most important, since his purpose was to elucidate the relationship between the LXX and the Hebrew text. This was done primarily by means of three critical marks: the obelus (÷) to mark an addition in the LXX, the asterisk (⁜) to mark an omission, and the metobelus (⅄) to mark the end of each passage in question. The so-called Mercati fragments, however, the remnants of a copy of the second through sixth columns in a palimpsest containing 110 psalm verses, do not contain these signs, so that the question arises whether the *Hexapla* represents only the basis for a future critical edition of the LXX. A second work by Origen is the *Tetrapla,* which lacks the first two columns of the *Hexapla* and, despite the contrary opinion which is frequently expressed, is most likely an abridged edition of the Hexapla.

The new recension produced by Origen was unable, however, to supplant the other forms of the text; instead, the fifth column continued to be published by itself along with the rest and added to the variety. Thanks to Eusebius of Caesarea and Pamphilus, it gained general acceptance at least in Palestine. Two further important forms of the text were (1) the recension of Hesychius, which is traced back to the bishop of this name mentioned by Eusebius and came into being in Egypt in the third century; and (2) the recension of Lucian (according to Jerome, the martyr who died in 312), which was widespread in Syria and Asia Minor. Scholars hold quite diverse theories concerning the Lucianic recension: some think it is a non-Hexaplaric revision of the LXX, others a revision utilizing the Hexaplaric recension, and still others a new translation from the Hebrew.

For a long time, textual witnesses to the LXX were to be found only in quotations from Philo, Josephus, the NT, and the Apostolic Fathers, as well as such Hellenistic Jewish writers as Aristeas and Eupolemus[7]—all dating from the Christian era—and in the Jewish curses from the island of Rheneia near Delos, dating from around 100 B.C.[8]

In the meantime, a considerable number of fragments of the LXX translation itself have turned up:[9] probably from the middle of the second century B.C., a fragment of Papyrus Fuad 266, containing Deut. 31:36–32:7, and Papyrus Greek 458 of the John Rylands Library at Manchester, containing portions of Deuteronomy 23–28; from the first century B.C., the fragments of several manuscripts from Qumran: 4QLXXLev[a], Lev[b], and Num, as well as 7QLXXEx, and, probably from the end of the century, the fragments of a scroll of the Book of the Twelve from Naḥal Ḥever in the Desert of Judah; from the second century of our era, Antinoopolis Papyrus 7, containing portions of Psalms 82–83, and a papyrus fragment from the Bodleian containing portions of Psalms 49–50; from the third century, Antinoopolis Papyri 8 and 9, in particular containing portions of Proverbs, fragments of a Book of Genesis (Berliner Genesis, containing Gen. 1:16–35:8), a manuscript of the Book of the Twelve (Freer Greek ms. V, at Washington, containing Amos 1:10–Malachi), and a Bodmer papyrus containing Psalms 33–34; from the fourth century, Antinoopolis Papyrus 10, containing portions of Ezekiel; from the second through fourth centuries, the remnants of eleven codices published as Chester Beatty Papyri and John H. Scheide Papyri, containing portions of Genesis, Numbers, Deuteronomy, Isaiah, Jeremiah, Ezekiel, Esther, Daniel, Ecclesiasticus, and Enoch. Remnants of the fifth column of the *Hexapla* are preserved directly primarily in Greek manuscripts of the OT, early Christian commentaries, the palimpsest discovered by Mercati at the Bibliotheca Ambrosiana at Milan, and indirectly in the Syriac translation by Paul of Tella in the Codex Ambrosianus.

From the period after 300 we have complete or almost complete manuscripts of the LXX: Codex Vaticanus[10] and Sinaiticus[11] from the fourth century,

[7] E. Schürer, *Geschichte des Jüdischen Volkes im Zeitalter Jesu Christi*, 4th ed., III (1909), 427, 469, 480.

[8] A. Deissmann, *Licht vom Osten*, 4th ed., 1923, pp. 351-62; Schürer, *op. cit.* (note 7), pp. 57, 142, 427.

[9] J. Barns and G. D. Kilpatrick, "A New Psalms Fragment," *PBA*, XLIII (1957), 229-32; J. Barns and H. Zilliacus, *The Antinoopolis Papyri*, Part II, 1960; A. C. Johnson, H. S. Gehman, and E. H. Kase, *The John H. Scheide Biblical Papyri: Ezekiel*, 1938; F. G. Kenyon, *The Chester Beatty Biblical Papyri*, I-VIII, 1933-41; C. H. Roberts, "Two Biblical Papyri in the John Rylands Library," *BJRL*, XX (1936), 219-44; *idem*, *The Antinoopolis Papyri*, Part I, 1950; H. A. Sanders and C. Schmidt, *The Minor Prophets in the Freer Collection and the Berliner Fragment of Genesis*, 1927; M. Testuz, *Papyrus Bodmer VII-IX*, 1959; W. G. Waddell, "The Tetragrammaton in the LXX," *JThSt*, XLV (1944), 158-61.

[10] *Codices e Vaticanis selecti phototypice expressi IV* (*Bibliorum SS. Graecorum Codex Vaticanus gr. 1209*), 1904-07; A. Sperber, "The Codex Vaticanus B," in *Miscellanea Mercati*, I (1946), 1-18.

[11] H. and K. Lake, *Codex Sinaiticus . . . Reproduced in Facsimile from Photographs*, 1911-22; H. J. M. Milne and T. C. Skeat, *The Codex Sinaiticus and the Codex Alexandrinus*, 2nd ed., 1955.

and Alexandrinus[12] and Ephraemi Syri rescriptus[13] from the fifth century.

Recent editions worth mentioning are those of Swete (3 vols., 1887-94, I[4] 1904, II-III[3] 1905, 1907), Brooke-McLean-Thackeray-Manson (4 vols., 1906-), the Göttinger Akademie der Wissenschaften (16 vols., 1931-), and Rahlfs (1 vol., 6th ed. 1959).

The value of the LXX for textual criticism varies greatly. Apart from internal peculiarities and textual corruption, which are present in all the books, the translation, deriving as it does from many hands and many periods, is not of uniform value everywhere. In general, it becomes poorer with increasing distance from the Pentateuch.

6. *The translations dependent on the LXX.* The first of the translations dependent on the LXX is the Old Latin version, the Vetus Latina. From the second and third centuries on, Latin translations of OT books were in use in North Africa, southern Gaul, and Italy. Augustine clearly used the latter, calling it the Itala. It is not clear, however, whether we are dealing here with three different translations or collections of translations, i.e., with separate versions, or with different recensions of a single translation or collection of translations. The only portions fully preserved are the texts of some deuterocanonical books absorbed into the Vulgate, the "Psalterium Romanum" (perhaps revised by Jerome), and a few other translations of the Psalter. For the rest of the text, apart from mixed types there are numerous quotations and other fragments, which are being published by the Abbey of Beuron. They are significant in that they often are based on a pre-Hexaplaric Greek text.

Translations dependent on the Hesychian recension of the LXX include the Coptic translation of the Egyptian Christians. In the third century the Coptic language, a form of Egyptian, developed in several dialects. During the fourth century, and perhaps in part as early as the third, the LXX was translated into these dialects, in which form it was considered an official text. The following versions came into being: (1) the Sahidic, in the vicinity of Thebes, in Upper Egypt; (2) the Bohairic, in Lower Egypt (Alexandria and the Nile delta); (3) the Achmimic, in the vicinity of Panopolis, in Upper Egypt; (4) the Fayyumic, in Middle Egypt; and (5) the related Memphite translation.

The Ethiopic translation was begun in the fourth century, perhaps by Syriac missionaries, and was finished gradually. It is apparently based on the Lucianic recension. Questions of detail cannot be answered, because the manuscripts, the earliest of which dates from the thirteenth century, exhibit many signs of secondary revision, and there is no critical edition.

In the fifth century an Armenian translation was begun. To judge by the preserved fragments, it follows the text of the *Hexapla*. The Georgian translation is later, at least in part. In the ninth century a Slavonic translation was made following the Lucianic recension, on which the Gothic translation of Bishop Ulfila (*ca.* 350) is also based. There are also Arabic translations.

[12] *The Codex Alexandrinus (Royal MS 1 D V–VIII) in Reduced Photographic Facsimile,* I–III, 1909-36.

[13] C. von Tischendorf, *Codex Ephraimi Syri rescriptus,* 1843-45.

7. *The independent Greek translations*. The independent Greek translations came into being when Judaism rejected the LXX and had to replace it with new renderings of the uniform Hebrew consonantal text. We are here concerned primarily with the works of Aquila, Theodotion, and Symmachus.

The translation of Aquila (*ca*. A.D. 130) strives to be as precisely literal as possible, reflecting the spirit of Orthodox Judaism and its theory of inspiration in the attempt to reproduce every detail of the Hebrew text. Of the extant fragments, those from the genizah at Old Cairo are most important.

Also from the second century we have the work of Theodotion, who was more concerned with writing comprehensible Greek. His translation probably represents a corrected version of the LXX assimilated to the Hebrew text. It gained considerable popularity in Christian circles also.

At the beginning of the third century Symmachus made his own new translation, attempting to combine the two previous guidelines—literal rendering of the Hebrew text and good Greek. This text was used by Lucian and Jerome.

There were also other translations of this sort, of which fragments are extant, or which are mentioned in other works. Origen, for example, referred to the so-called Quinta, Sexta, and Septima.

8. *The Vulgate*. The Vulgate was produced by Jerome after he had worked from 382 on at revising the Vetus Latina, of which only the so-called Gallican Psalter and Job are still extant. In 386 he moved to Bethlehem, where between 390 and 405 he translated the OT from Hebrew into Latin, drawing not only on the Vetus Latina but also on Greek translations, and seeking advice from the rabbis. After an initial period of rejection the new translation was universally adopted by the church from the seventh century on (with the exception of the Psalter, which was replaced with the Gallican Psalter), so that it later became known as the "Vulgate" cr "universally popular." The editions of 1590 (Sixtine) and 1592 (Clementine) exhibit many errors, however, which were corrected in 1593 and 1598. A revised text making use of the manuscript material is presently being published in the edition of the Pontifical Vulgate Commission. A new Latin translation of the Psalms and of the canticles used, like the Psalms, in public worship, taking into account both the original text and all the translations, was introduced by Pius XII.

9. *Polyglots*. Some of the non-Masoretic text forms were published along with the *textus receptus* of the Masoretic text in the polyglots of the sixteenth and seventeenth centuries. In many cases these represent the best if not the only editions of these texts, which indicates the need for new critical editions. The following polyglots deserve mention:

a) The Complutensian Polyglot was printed at Alcalà (1514-17). It contains the Masoretic text, Targum Onqelos, the LXX, and the Vulgate.

b) The Antwerp Polyglot (1569-72) contains in addition a targum on almost all the other books.

c) The Paris Polyglot (1629-45) also furnishes the Samaritan Pentateuch together with its targum, the Peshitta, and an Arabic translation.
d) The London Polyglot (1653-57) added fragments of the Vetus Latina, Jerusalem Targums I and II, Ethiopic and Persian translations of parts of the OT, and collections of variants. It was concluded in 1669 with the *Lexicon heptaglottum*.
e) The first parts of a new Madrid Polyglot have been appearing since 1957.

§ 80 Textual Corruption and Textual Criticism

D. R. Ap-Thomas, *A Primer of Old Testament Text Criticism*, 2nd ed., 1965; J. Begrich, "Zur Frage der alttestamentlichen Textkritik," *OLZ*, XLII (1939), 473-83; J. Coppens, *La critique du texte hébreu de l'Ancien Testament*, 2nd ed., 1950; M. J. Dahood, "The Value of Ugaritic for Textual Criticism," *Bibl*, XL (1959), 160-70; *idem*, "Ugaritic Studies and the Bible," *Gregorianum*, XLIII (1962), 55-79; F. Delitzsch, *Die Lese- und Schreibfehler im Alten Testament*, 1920; G. R. Driver, "Glosses in the Hebrew Text of the Old Testament," *OrBiblLov*, I (1957), 123-61; *idem*, "Abbreviations in the Masoretic Text," *Textus*, I (1960), 112-31; G. Fohrer, "Die Glossen im Buche Ezechiel," *ZAW*, LXIII (1951), 33-53; A. Jepsen, "Von den Aufgaben der alttestamentlichen Textkritik," *VTSuppl*, IX (1963), 332-41; H. Junker, "Konsonantenumstellung als Fehlerquelle und textkritisches Hilfsmittel im MT," in BZAW LXVI (1936), 162-74; J. Kennedy, *An Aid to the Textual Criticism of the Old Testament*, 1928; F. S. North, "Textual Variants in the Hebrew Bible Significant for Critical Analysis," *JQR*, XLVII (1956/57), pp. 77-80; J. Reider, "The Present State of Textual Criticism of the Old Testament," *HUCA*, VII (1930), 285-315; E. Robertson, *The Text of the Old Testament and the Methods of Textual Criticism*, 1939; J. Schildenberger, "Textumstellungen und ihre Begründung," in *Mélanges Robert*, 1957, pp. 241-53; S. Talmon, "Double Readings in the Massoretic Text," *Textus*, I (1960), 144-84; *idem*, "Synonymous Readings in the Textual Traditions of the Old Testament," *Scripta Hierosolymitana*, VIII (1961), 335-83; D. W. Thomas, "The Textual Criticism of the Old Testament," in *The Old Testament and Modern Study*, 1951, pp. 238-63; P. Volz, "Ein Arbeitsplan für die Textkritik des Alten Testaments," *ZAW*, LIV (1936), 110-13; L. Waterman, "The Authentication of Conjectural Glosses," *JBL*, LVI (1937), 253-59.

Despite all efforts to fix the Hebrew text of the OT as carefully and precisely as possible, it is by no means free of errors and in many details does not preserve the words that were first written down. Before the text was fixed by the "scribes" and Masoretes, errors crept in and deliberate alterations were made, which were then included in the text and handed down as a part of it.

The scripts and the materials used for writing themselves provided possibilities for error. The form of the scroll made it possible for the text to be damaged or become illegible. Pieces could be torn from the thin papyrus; leather and parchment could be eaten by vermin. The ink could fade, be effaced, or be obliterated, especially when a scroll was used frequently. The first and last columns were especially vulnerable; this probably explains the numerous textual errors in Nahum 1:2 ff. Scrolls containing the entire OT had to be written in very small letters, introducing the possibility of copying errors.

In the Old Hebrew and square scripts several of the letters are so similar in form that they could be easily confused or miscopied, thereby producing errors. Other errors arose—perhaps during dictation—through the confusion of consonants with similar sounds. As a consequence of the script, which at the outset was purely consonantal, many words could be read in two or more ways and were wrongly analyzed with the increasing use of *matres lectionis*. Frequently we also find erroneous division of words, which apparently—as in the Aramaic Sefire treaties (eighth century B.C.)—were not always written separately from the outset. Another source of error lay in the change from the Old Hebrew script to square script.

Other errors include haplography ("single writing"), the omission of similar or identical letters or words occurring in sequence; dittography ("double writing"), the repetition of letters or words; homoioteleuton, omission caused by the eye's jumping from the end of a word to the end of the same word or a similar one elsewhere in the text; homoioarcton, the same phenomenon at the beginning of a word; failure to recognize abbreviations (e.g., *yōd* or *hē'* standing for "*yahweh*"); and, later, erroneous vocalization by the Masoretes.

Furthermore, at an earlier time deliberate alterations were made in the text. These include changes in the divine name, e.g., in the Elohistic Psalter, the introduction of additional divine epithets, the insertion of small common words, the replacement or glossing of rare words or words used in an unusual sense, the removal of objectionable expressions, and the introduction of numerous repetitive, explanatory, supplementary, rectifying, and redactional glosses.

All these textual errors and others create the need for textual criticism. Certainly many doubtful forms will turn out not to be errors, but rather evidence for divergent vulgar texts or dialectal differences; study of Hebrew vocabulary with the aid of other Semitic languages or new archaeological discoveries will show us how to understand an unintelligible or seemingly corrupt word. Even so, however, there will remain a wealth of genuine textual errors or alterations, which demand that we attempt to arrive, whenever possible, at a more reliable or uncorrupt text. The materials available for this work include on the one hand the Hebrew textual traditions, especially the pre-Masoretic, and on the other hand the Samaritan and the various translations. If they are to be used with care, it is of course indispensable to do more than merely collect variants; these texts themselves must be studied with constant reference to their idiosyncrasies and with attention to the particular context. In many cases the only result will be to disclose an already corrupt pre-Masoretic text no more intelligible than the Masoretic text itself. In these cases, in which textual corruption began at a very early date, the only recourse is conjectural emendation appropriate to the context. For the goal of all our work is not the maximum possible retention of the given text, but the understanding of it with the aid of all the means at our disposal.

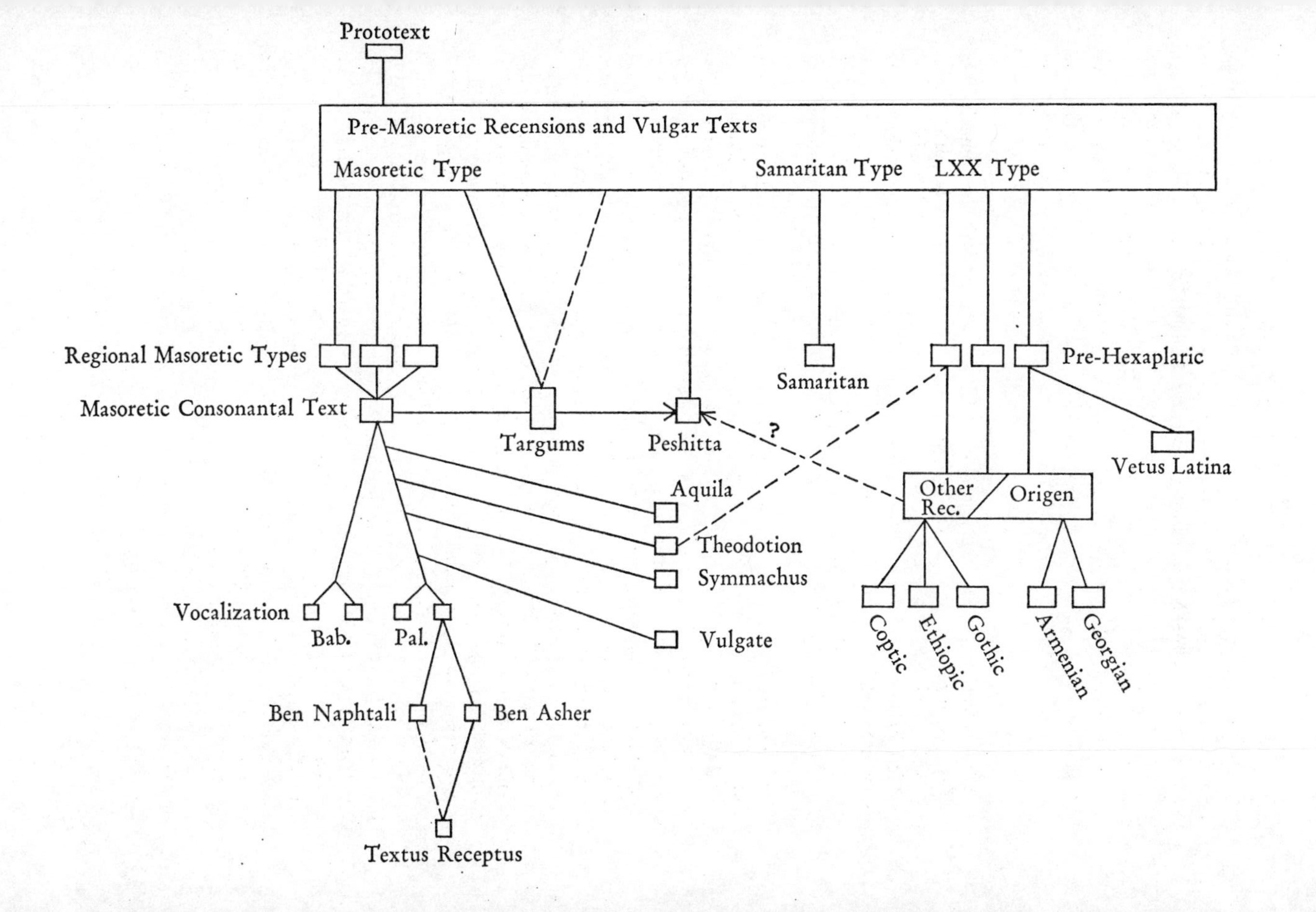
Prototext
Pre-Masoretic Recensions and Vulgar Texts
Masoretic Type
Samaritan Type
LXX Type
Regional Masoretic Types
Masoretic Consonantal Text
Targums
Peshitta
?
Samaritan
Pre-Hexaplaric
Vetus Latina
Other Rec.
Origen
Aquila
Theodotion
Symmachus
Vulgate
Coptic
Ethiopic
Gothic
Armenian
Georgian
Vocalization
Bab.
Pal.
Ben Naphtali
Ben Asher
Textus Receptus

BIBLIOGRAPHICAL SUPPLEMENT

§1 D. R. Ap-Thomas, "An Appreciation of Sigmund Mowinckel's Contribution to Biblical Studies," *JBL*, LXXXV (1966), 315-25; H. Ringgren, "Literaturkritik, Formgeschichte und Überlieferungsgeschichte," *ThLZ*, XCI (1966), 641-50; J. M. Schmidt, "Karl Friedrich Stäudlin—ein Wegbereiter der formgeschichtlichen Erforschung des Alten Testaments," *EvTh*, XXVII (1967), 200-18; K. Scholder, *Ursprünge und Probleme der Bibelkritik im 17. Jahrhundert*, 1966; R. Smend, "Nachkritische Schriftauslegung," in *Parresia* (Festschrift Karl Barth), 1966, pp. 215-37; W. von Soden, "Alter Orient und Altes Testament," *VT*, XVII (1967), 38-47; J. J. Stamm, "Das Einleitungswerk von Otto Eissfeldt," *ThZ*, XXI (1965), 386-99; T. C. Vriezen, "Twenty-five Years of Old Testamentic Study in the Netherlands," *OTS*, XIV (1965), 397-416; D. Zaharopoulos, *Theodore of Mopsuestia's Critical Methods in OT Study*, Dissertation, Boston, 1965.

§2 Y. Aharoni, *The Land of the Bible*, 1966; F. E. Eakin, Jr., "Yahwism and Baalism Before the Exile," *JBL*, LXXXIV (1965), 407-14; O. Eissfeldt, "Die israelitisch-jüdische Religion," in *Saeculum Weltgeschichte*, II (1966), 217-60; *idem*, "Israels Religion und die Religionen seiner Umwelt," *NZSTh*, IX (1967), 8-27; D. N. Freedman, "The Biblical Languages," in *The Bible and Modern Scholarship*, 1965, pp. 294-312; J. Gray, *The Legacy of Canaan; the Ras Shamra Texts and Their Relevance to the Old Testament*, 2nd ed., 1965; A. S. Kapelrud, *Israel, from the Earliest Times to the Birth of Christ*, 1966; W. L. Reed, "The Bible and North Arabia," *Encounter*, XXVI (1965), 143-53; C. Westermann, "Sinn und Grenze religionsgeschichtlicher Parallelen," *TLZ*, XC (1965), 489-96; D. Winston, "The Iranian Component in the Bible, Apocrypha, and Qumran: a Review of the Evidence," *History of Religions*, V (1965/66), 183-216.

§3 G. W. Ahlström, "Oral and Written Transmission," *HThR*, LIX (1966), 69-81; R. Rendtorff, "Literarkritik und Traditionsgeschichte," *EvTh*, XXVII (1967), 138-53; H. Ringgren, "Literaturkritik, Formgeschichte und Überlieferungsgeschichte," *TLZ*, XCI (1966), 641-50.

§4 H. A. Brongers, "Merismus, Synekdoche und Hendiadys in der bibel-hebräischen Sprache," *OTS*, XIV (1965), 100-14; G. Gerleman, "Bemerkungen zum alttestamentlichen Sprachstil," in *Studia biblica et semitica Vriezen*, 1966, pp. 108-14; M. Weiss, "Weiteres über die Bauform des Erzählens in der Bibel," *Bibl*, XLVI (1965), 181-206.

§5 D. Broadribb, *An Attempt to Delineate the Characteristic Structure of Classical Hebrew Poetry*, Dissertation, Melbourne, 1964; *idem*, "Poezio Hebrea: Historia Rigardo," *Biblia Revuo*, III (1965), 19-59; *idem*, "Poezio Hebrea: Kelkaj Pensoj," *Biblia Revuo*, II (1965), 75-88; G. Gerleman, "Bemerkungen zum alttestamentlichen Sprachstil," in *Studia biblica et semitica Vriezen*, 1966, pp. 108-14; W. L. Holladay, "The Recovery of Poetic Passages of Jeremiah," *JBL*, LXXXV (1966), 401-35; H.

Kosmala, "Form and Structure in Ancient Hebrew Poetry," *VT*, XIV (1964), 423-45; XVI (1966), 153-80; E. Z. Melamed, "The Break-up of Stereotype Phrases as an Artistic Device in Biblical Poetry," in *Sefer Segal*, 1964, pp. 188-219; J. Stampfer, "On Translating Biblical Poetry," *Judaism*, XIV (1965), 501-10.

§7 E. Atir, "Zur Frage der Beziehung zwischen der biblischen Josepherzählung und der ägyptischen Brüdererzählung," *Bet Miqra'*, XI (1965/66), 3-8; R. Borger, *Handbuch der Keilschriftliteratur*, 1967- ; A. van den Branden, "Lévitique 1–7 et le tarif de Marseille, CIS I, 165," *RSO*, XL (1965), 107-30; P. J. Calderone, *Dynastic Oracle and Suzerainty Treaty; 2 Sam 7:8-16*, 1966; R. Hentschke, "Erwägungen zur israelitischen Rechtsgeschichte," *Theologia viatorum*, X (1965/66), 108-33; F. Imparati, *Le leggi ittite*, 1964; J. Jeremias, *Theophanie; die Geschichte einer alttestamentlichen Gattung*, 1965; A. Jirku, *Der Mythus der Kanaanäer*, 1966; R. A. F. MacKenzie, "The Formal Aspect of Ancient Near Eastern Law," in *The Seed of Wisdom* (Festschrift T. J. Meek), 1964, pp. 31-44; L. Matouš, "Zur neueren epischen Literatur im Alten Mesopotamien," *ArOr*, XXXV (1967), 1-25; G. Morawe, "Studien zum Aufbau der neubabylonischen Chroniken in ihrer Beziehung zu den chronologischen Notizen der Königsbücher," *EvTh*, XXVI (1966), 308-20; C. Murray, "The Origin of the World and Genesis 1–3," *ABR*, XIII (1965), 1-18; H. Petschow, "Zur Systematik und Gesetzestechnik im Codex Hammurabi," *ZA*, NF XXIII (1965), 146-72; E. Testa, "Il genere letterario della disputa e il racconto di Caino ed Abele," *Bibbia e Oriente*, VIII (1966), 157-66; R. J. Williams, "Literature as a Medium of Political Propaganda in Ancient Egypt," in *The Seed of Wisdom* (Festschrift T. J. Meek), 1964, pp. 14-30.

§8 E. Auerbach, "Das Zehngebot—allgemeine Gesetzesform in der Bibel," *VT*, XVI (1966), 255-76; G. J. Botterweck, "Form und überlieferungsgeschichtliche Studien zum Dekalog," *Concilium*, I (1965), 392-401; P. Buis, "Les formulaires d'alliance," *VT*, XVI (1966), 396-411; R. Criado, " 'Hasta que venge Silo' (Gén. 49,10)," *Cultura Bíblica*, XXIII (1966), 195-219; R. Frankena, "The Vassal-Treaties of Esarhaddon and the Dating of Deuteronomy," *OTS*, XIV (1965), 122-54; E. Gerstenberger, *Wesen und Herkunft des "apodiktischen Rechts,"* 1965; H. Gese, "Der Dekalog als Ganzheit betrachtet," *ZThK*, LXIV (1967), 121-38; A. González Núñez, "El rito de la Alianza," *EstBíbl*, XXIV (1965), 217-38; H. Haag, "Il decalogo nella transmissione oracle," *Bibbia e Oriente*, IX (1967), 3-12; R. Hentschke, "Erwägungen zur israelitischen Rechtsgeschichte," *Theologia viatorum*, X (1965/66,), 108-33; A. R. Hulst, "Bemerkungen zum Sabbatgebot," in *Studia biblica et semitica Vriezen*, 1966, pp. 152-64; H. B. Huffmon, "The Treaty Background of Hebrew *Yāda'*," *BASOR*, CLXXXI (1966), 31-37; J. P. Hyatt, "Moses and the Ethical Decalogue," *Encounter*, XXVI (1965), 199-206; A. Jepsen, "Beiträge zur Auslegung und Geschichte des Dekalogs," *ZAW*, LXXIX (1967), 277-304; J. Klíma, "Au sujet de nouveaux textes législatifs de la Babylonie Ancienne," *ArOr*, XXXV (1967), 121-27; E. Kutsch, "Gesetz und Gnade," *ZAW*, LXXIX (1967), 18-35; J. L'Hour, *La morale de l'alliance*, 1966; D. J. McCarthy, "Covenant in the Old Testament: the Present State of the Inquiry," *CBQ*, XXVII (1965), 217-40; *idem, Der Gottesbund im Alten Testament*, 1966; E. Nielsen, *Die zehn Gebote; eine traditionsgeschichtliche Skizze*, 1965; F. Nötscher, "Bundesformular und 'Amtsschimmel'; ein kritischer Überblick," *BZ*, NF IX (1965), 181-214; A. I. Patrick, *La formation littéraire et l'origine historique du Décalogue*, 1964; J. Priest, "The Covenant of Brothers," *JBL*, LXXXIV (1965), 200-206; W. Richter, *Recht und Ethos; Versuch einer Ortung des weisheitlichen Mahnspruches*,

1966; L. A. Sinclair, "The Courtroom Motif in the Book of Amos," *JBL*, LXXXV (1966), 351-53; J. J. Stamm and M. E. Andrew, *The Ten Commandments in Recent Research*, 1967; M. Treves, "Shiloh (Genesis 49:10)," *JBL*, LXXXV (1966), 353-56; G. M. Tucker, *Contracts in the OT: a Form Critical Investigation*, Dissertation, Yale, 1963; *idem*, "Covenant Forms and Contract Forms," *VT*, XV (1965), 487-503; M. Weinfeld, "Traces of Assyrian Treaty Formulas in Deuteronomy," *Bibl*, XLVI (1965), 417-27; H.-J. Zobel, *Stammesspruch und Geschichte*, 1965; *idem*, "Die Stammessprüche des Mose-Segens (Dtn 33:6-25)," *Klio*, XLVI (1965), 83-92.

§9 H.-J. Kraus, "Der lebendige Gott," *EvTh*, XXVII (1967), 169-200; E. Kutsch, "Gesetz und Gnade," *ZAW*, LXXIX (1967), 18-35; W. Richter, "Das Gelübde als theologische Rahmung der Jakobsüberlieferungen," *BZ*, NF XI (1967), 21-52; A. Schächter, "Bundesformular und prophetischer Unheilsanspruch," *Bibl*, XLVIII (1967), 128-31.

§10 H. M. Dion, "The Patriarchal Traditions and the Literary Form of the 'Oracle of Salvation,'" *CBQ*, XXIX (1967), 198-206; B. de Pinto, "The Torah and the Psalms," *JBL*, LXXXVI (1967), 154-74.

§11 F. A. Ali, "Two Collections of Sumerian Letters," *ArOr*, XXXV (1965), 529-40.

§12 F. Dexinger, *Sturtz der Göttersöhne oder Engel vor der Sintflut?* 1966; F. Festorazzi, *La bibbia e il problema delle origine*, 1966; G. Fohrer, "Die Sage in der Bibel," in *Sagen und ihre Dichtung*, 1965; D. Hermant, "Analyse littéraire du premier récit de la création," *VT*, XV (1965), 437-51; H. Heyde, *Kain, der erste Jahwe-Verehrer*, 1965; W. G. Lambert, "A New Look at the Babylonian Background of Genesis," *JThSt*, NS XVI (1965), 287-300; H. Lubsczik, "Wortschöpfung und Tatschöpfung," *Bibel und Leben*, VI (1965), 191-208; L. Nielsen, "Syndflod og kaos," *DTT*, XXVIII (1965), 206-46; W. H. Schmidt, "Mythos im Alten Testament," *EvTh*, XXVII (1967), 237-54; E. Testa, "Il genere letterario della disputa e il racconto di Caino ed Abele," *Bibbia e Oriente*, VIII (1966), 157-66.

§13 J. R. Bartlett, "The Edomite King-list of Genesis xxxvi. 31-39 and I Chron. i. 43-50," *JThSt*, NS XVI (1965), 301-14; A. F. Johns, "Did David Use Assyrian-type Annals?" *Andrews University Seminary Studies*, III (1965), 97-109; J. L. McKenzie, "Reflections on Wisdom," *JBL*, LXXXVI (1967), 1-9; G. Morawe, "Studien zum Aufbau der neubabylonischen Chroniken in ihrer Beziehung zu den chronologischen Notizen der Königsbücher," *EvTh*, XXVI (1966), 308-20.

§16 AB: Genesis, E. A. Speiser, 1964. ATD: Numbers, M. Noth, 1966. BK: Genesis, C. Westermann, 1966- . BOT: Exodus, G. te Stroete, 1966. Century Bible: Leviticus and Numbers, N. H. Snaith, 1967. HAT: Leviticus, K. Elliger, 1966. *De prediking van het Oude Testament:* Genesis, A. van Selms, 1967.
Individual commentaries: U. Cassuto, 1961-64.

§17 R. J. Coggin, "A Century of Pentateuchal Criticism," *ChQR* (1965), 149-61, 413-25; O. Eissfeldt, "Erwägungen zur Pentateuchquellenfrage," *OLZ*, LXI (1966), 213-18; H. W. Hoffmann, "Kritische Anmerkungen zu einer neuen mathematischen Methode der Textscheidung," *ZAW*, LXXVIII (1966), 219-24.

§18 R. J. Coggin, "A Century of Pentateuchal Criticism," *ChQR* (1965), 149-61, 413-25; O. Eissfeldt, "Erwägungen zur Pentateuchquellenfrage," *OLZ*, LXI (1966), 213-18.

§19 C. Barth, "Zur Bedeutung der Wüstentradition," *VTSuppl*, XV (1966), 14-23; W. Beltz, *Die Kaleb-Traditionen oder ein Beitrag zur theoretischen Diskussion in der Religionswissenschaft*, 1966; S. J. De Vries, "The Origin of the Murmuring Tradition," *JBL*, LXXXVII (1968), 51-58; O. Eissfeldt, " 'Äh^{e}yäh '^{a}šer 'äh^{e}yäh und 'Ēl 'ôlām," *FF*, XXXIX (1965), 298-300; O. Eissfeldt, "Das Gesetz ist dazwischengekommen. Ein Beitrag zur Analyse der Sinai-Erzählung Ex 19–24," *ThLZ*, XXI (1966), 1-6; *idem, Die Komposition der Sinai-Erzählung Exodus 19–34*, 1966; H. Gese, "Bemerkungen zur Sinaitradition," *ZAW*, LXXIX (1967), 137-54; M. Haran, "The Religion of the Patriarchs," *ASTI*, IV (1965), 30-55; H. Hirsch, "Gott der Väter," *AfO*, XXI (1966), 56-58; H. B. Huffmon, *Amorite Personal Names in the Mari Texts*, 1965; A. R. Hulst, "Der Jordan in den alttestamentlichen Überlieferungen," *OTS*, XIV (1965), 162-88; R. Kilian, *Die vorpriesterlichen Abrahamsüberlieferungen, literarkritisch und traditionsgeschichtlich untersucht*, 1966; D. J. McCarthy, "Moses' Dealings with Pharaoh: Ex 7:8–10:27," *CBQ*, XXVII (1965), 336-47; *idem*, "Plagues and the Sea of Reeds," *JBL*, LXXXV (1966), 137-58; D. Neiman, "The Date and Circumstances of the Cursing of Canaan," in A. Altman, ed., *Biblical Motifs*, 1966, pp. 113-34; W. Richter, "Das Gelübde als theologische Rahmung der Jakobsüberlieferungen," *BZ*, NF XI (1967), 21-52; H. Schmid, "Der Stand der Moseforschung," *Judaica*, XXI (1965), 194-221; R. Schmid, "Meerwunder- und Landnahmetraditionen," *ThZ*, XXI (1965), 260-68; H. Seebass, *Der Erzvater Israel und die Einführung der Jahweverehrung in Kanaan*, 1966; E. Testa, "De foedere patriarcharum," *Studii biblici franciscani liber annuus*, XV (1964/65), 5-73; R. de Vaux, "Les patriarches hébreux et l'histoire," *RB*, LXXII (1965), 5-28; M. Weippert, *Die Landnahme der israelitischen Stämme in der neueren wissenschaftlichen Diskussion*, 1967; E. J. Young, "The Call of Moses," *Westminster Theological Journal*, XXIX (1966/67), 117-35.

§20 O. Eissfeldt, "Das Gesetz ist dazwischengekommen. Ein Beitrag zur Analyse der Sinai-Erzählung Ex 19–24," *ThLZ*, XXI (1966), 1-6; *idem, Die Komposition der Sinai-Erzählung Exodus 19–34*, 1966; H. Gese, "Der Dekalog als Ganzheit betrachtet," *ZThK*, LXIV (1967), 121-38; J. P. Hyatt, "Moses and the Ethical Decalogue," *Encounter*, XXVI (1965), 199-206; H.-J. Kraus, "Das Heilige Volk," in *Freude am Evangelium* (Festschrift de Quervain), 1966, pp. 50-61; D. J. McCarthy, *Der Gottesbund im Alten Testament*, 1966; W. L. Moran, "The Literary Connection Between Lv 11:13-19 and Dt 14:12-18," *CBQ*, XXVIII (1966), 271-77; K. H. Walkenhorst, "Sinai in liturgica traditione deuteronomistica et sacerdotali," *VD*, XLIV (1966), 89-96.

§22 J. Blenkinsopp, "Theme and Motif in the Succession Story (2 Sam. xi. 2 ff.) and the Yahwist Corpus," *VTSuppl*, XV (1966), 44-57; G. J. Botterweck, "Israels Errettung im Wunder am Meer," *Bibel und Leben*, VIII (1967), 8-33; R. Criado, " 'Hasta que venge Silo' (Gén. 49,10)," *Cultura Bíblica*, XXIII (1966), 195-219; H. M. Dion, "The Patriarchal Traditions and the Literary Form of the 'Oracle of Salvation,' " *CBQ*, XXIX (1967), 198-206; W. H. Gispen, *Schepping en paradijs*, 1966; H. Haag, "Die Komposition der Sündenfall-Erzählung (Gn 2,4*b*–3,24)," *Tübinger Theologische Quartalschrift*, CXLVI (1966), 1-7; E. Lipinski, "Nimrod et

Assur," *RB*, LXXIII (1966), 77-93; J. L. McKenzie, "Reflections on Wisdom," *JBL*, LXXXVI (1967), 1-9; J. Muilenburg, "Abraham and the Nations; Blessing and World History," *Interpr*, XIX (1965), 387-98; W. Richter, "Urgeschichte und Hoftheologie," *BZ*, NF X (1966), 96-105; E. J. Young, "The Call of Moses," *Westminster Theological Journal*, XXIX (1966/67), 117-35.

§23 G. J. Botterweck, "Israels Errettung im Wunder am Meer," *Bibel und Leben*, VIII (1967), 8-33; H. M. Dion, "The Patriarchal Traditions and the Literary Form of the 'Oracle of Salvation,'" *CBQ*, XXIX (1967), 198-206; A. W. Jenks, *The Elohist and North Israelite Tradition*, Dissertation, Harvard, 1965; R. Kilian, "Der heilsgeschichtliche Aspekt in der elohistischen Geschichtstradition," *ThGl*, LVI (1966), 369-84.

§24 G. J. Botterweck, "Israels Errettung im Wunder am Meer," *Bibel und Leben*, VIII (1967), 8-33; W. H. Gispen, *Schepping en paradijs*, 1966; J. Scharbert, "Traditions- und Redaktionsgeschichte von Gn 6,1-4," *BZ*, NF XI (1967), 66-78; H. Schmid, "Mose, der Blutbräutigam; Erwägungen zu Ex 4,24-26," *Judaica*, XXII (1966), 113-18.

§25 C. Barth, "Mose, Knecht Gottes," in *Parresia* (Festschrift Karl Barth), 1966, pp. 66-81; J. Blenkinsopp, "Are There Traces of the Gibeonite Covenant in Deuteronomy?" *CBQ*, XXVIII (1966), 207-19; C. Brekelmans, "Die sogenannten deuteronomischen Elemente in Gen. bis Num.; ein Beitrag zur Vorgeschichte des Deuteronomiums," *VTSuppl*, XV (1966), 90-96; H. Cazelles, "Passages in the Singular Within Discourses in the Plural of Dtn 1–4," *CBQ*, XXIX (1967), 207-19; J. Dus, "Ein Versuch zur deuteronomischen Kultformel," *VTSuppl*, XV (1966), 113-21; O. Eissfeldt, "Deuteronomium und Hexateuch," *MIOF*, XII (1966), 17-39; R. Frankena, "The Vassal-Treaties of Esarhaddon and the Dating of Deuteronomy," *OTS*, XIV (1965), 122-54; H. Gese, "Bemerkungen zur Sinaitradition," *ZAW*, LXXIX (1967), 137-54; J. M. Grintz, "Die Erzählung von der 'Reform' des Josia und das Deuteronomium," *Bet Miqra'*, XI (1955/56), Heft 4, pp. 3-16; H. Haag, "Il decalogo nella transmissione orale," *Bibbia e Oriente*, IX (1967), 3-12; A. M. La Bonnardière, *Le Deutéronome*, 1967; S. Loersch, *Das Deuteronomium und seine Deutungen*, 1967; E. W. Nicholson, *Deuteronomy and Tradition*, 1967; *idem*, "Josiah's Reformation and Deuteronomy," *Glasgow University Oriental Society Transactions*, XX (1963/64), 77-84; J. G. Plöger, *Literarkritische, formgeschichtliche und stilkritische Untersuchungen zum Deuteronomium*, 1967; A. Schächter, "Bundesformular und prophetischer Unheilsanspruch," *Bibl*, XLVIII (1967), 128-31; J. Schreiner, "Das seelsorgerliche Anliegen des Deuteronomiums," *Anima*, XX (1965), 144-59; M. Weinfeld, *The Provenance of Deuteronomy and the Deuteronomic School*, Dissertation, Jerusalem, 1964; *idem*, "Traces of Assyrian Treaty Formulae in Deuteronomy," *Bibl*, XLVI (1965), 417-27.

§26 A. van den Branden, "Lévitique 1–7 et le tarif de Marseille, CIS I, 165," *RSO*, XL (1965), 107-30; W. H. Gispen, *Schepping en paradijs*, 1966; M. Haran, "The Priestly Image of the Tabernacle," *HUCA*, XXXVI (1965), 191-226; A. Hurvitz, "The use of שש and בוץ in the Bible and Its Implications for the Date of P," *HThR*, LIX (1966), 117-21; R. Kilian, "Hoffnung auf Heimkehr in der Priesterschrift," *Bibel und Leben*, VII (1966), 39-51; B. A. Levine, "The Descriptive Tabernacle Texts of the Pentateuch," *JAOS*, LXXXV (1965), 307-18; H. Schmid, "Die 'Mutter Erde' in der Schöpfungsgeschichte der Priesterschrift," *Judaica*, XXII (1966), 237-43; J. A. Scott, *The Pattern of the Tabernacle*, 1965.

§27 M. C. Astour, "Political and Cosmic Symbolism in Genesis 14 and in its Babylonian Sources," in A. Altmann, ed., *Biblical Motifs*, 1966, pp. 65-112; R. Meyer, "Melchisedek von Jerusalem und Moresedek von Qumran," *VTSuppl*, XV (1966), 228-39; J. Muilenburg, "A Liturgy on the Triumphs of Yahweh," in *Studia biblica et semitica Vriezen*, 1966, pp. 233-51.

§30 O. Eissfeldt, "Deuteronomium und Hexateuch," *MIOF*, XII (1966), 17-39; C. H. J. de Geuz, "Richteren 1,1–2,5," *Vox theologica*, XXXVI (1966), 32-53; J. M. Grintz, "The Treaty of Joshua with the Gibeonites," *JAOS*, LXXXVI (1966), 113-26; Z. Kallai, *The Tribes of Israel* (Hebrew), 1967; J. A. Soggin, "Gilgal, Passah und Landnahme; eine neue Untersuchung des kultischen Zusammenhangs der Kap. iii–vi des Josuabuches," *VTSuppl*, XV (1966), 263-77; E. Vogt, "Die Erzählung vom Jordanübergang Josue 3–4," *Bibl*, XLVI (1965), 125-48; M. Weippert, *Die Landnahme der israelitischen Stämme in der neueren wissenschaftlichen Diskussion*, 1967.

§31 A. Besters, *Le sanctuaire centrale dans Jud. XIX–XXI*, 1965; A. G. van Daalen, *Simson*, 1966; G. R. Driver, "Problems of Judges Newly Discussed," *Annual of Leeds University Oriental Society*, IV (1962/63), 6-25; M. T. Fortuna, "La storia di Ashdod e dei Filistei alla luce dei più recenti scavi," *Bibbia e Oriente*, VIII (1966), 80-75; N. H. Frostig-Adler, "La storia di Jefte," *Annuario di studi ebraici*, II (1964/65), 9-30; C. H. J. de Geus, "De richteren van Israel," *NedThT*, XX (1965/66), 81-100; H. Haag, "Gideon—Jerubbaal—Abimelek," *ZAW*, LXXIX (1967), 305-14; B. Lindars, "Gideon and Kingship," *JThSt*, NS XVI (1965), 315-26; D. A. McKenzie, "The Judge of Israel," *VT*, XVII (1967), 118-21; H. P. Müller, "Der Aufbau des Deboraliedes," *VT*, XVI (1966), 446-59; W. Richter, "Die Überlieferung um Jephtah Ri 10,17–12,6," *Bibl*, XLVII (1966), 485-556; A. Rofe, "The Composition of the Introduction of the Book of Judges (Judges II. 6–III. 6)," *Tarbiz*, XXXV (1965/66), 201-13; K.-D. Schunck, "Die Richter Israels und ihr Amt," *VTSuppl*, XV (1966), 252-62; N. Stemmer, "The Introduction to Judges, 2:1–3:4," *JQR*, LVII (1966/67), 239-41; G. E. Wright, "Fresh Evidence for the Philistine Story," *BA*, XXIX (1966), 70-86.

§32 J. Blenkinsopp, "Theme and Motif in the Succession Story (2 Sam. xi. 2 ff.) and the Yahwist Corpus," *VTSuppl*, XV (1966), 44-57; P. J. Calderone, *Dynastic Oracle and Suzerainty Treaty; 2 Sam 7:8-16;* 1966; K. Galling, "Goliath und seine Rüstung," *VTSuppl*, XV (1966), 150-69: H. Gottlieb, "Traditionen om David som hyrde," *DTT*, XXIX (1966), 11-21; J. H. Grønbæk, "David og Goliat," *DTT*, XXVIII (1965), 65-79; D. A. McKenzie, "The Judge of Israel," *VT*, XVII (1967), 118-21; G. Rinaldi, "Golia e David (I Sam. 17,1–18,8)," *Bibbia e Oriente*, VIII (1966), 11-29; H. Seebass, "I Sam 15 als Schlüssel für das Verständnis der sogenannten königsfreundlichen Reihe I Sam 9,1–10,16, 11,1-15 und 13,2–14,52," *ZAW*, LXXVIII (1966), 148-79; *idem*, "Die Vorgeschichte der Königserhebung Sauls," *ZAW*, LXXIX (1967), 155-71; M. H. Segal, "The Composition of the Books of Samuel," *JQR*, LV (1965), 318-39; LVI (1966), 30-50; J. A. Soggin, "Il regno di 'Ešbaʿal, figlio di Saul," *RSO*, XL (1965), 89-106; H. J. Stoebe, "Zur Topographie und Überlieferung der Schlacht von Mikmas, I Sam 13 und 14," *ThZ*, XXI (1965), 269-80; H. Timm, "Die Ladeerzählung

(1. Sam. 4–6; 2. Sam. 6) und das Kerygma des deuteronomistischen Geschichtswerks," *EvTh*, XXVI (1966), 509-26; M. Tsevat, "The Biblical Narrative of the Foundation of Kingship in Israel," *Tarbiz*, XXXVI (1966/67), 99-109; *idem*, "Studies in the Book of Samuel," *HUCA*, XXXVI (1965), 49-58; A. Weiser, "Die Legitimation des Königs David," *VT*, XVI (1966), 325-54; G. E. Wright, "Fresh Evidence for the Philistine Story," *BA*, XXIX (1966), 70-86.

§33 C. Alcaina Canosa, "Panorama critico del ciclo de Eliseo," *EstBíbl*, XXIII (1964), 217-34; F. I. Andersen, "The Socio-juridical Background of the Naboth Incident," *JBL*, LXXXV (1966), 46-57; C. A. Benito, "Elias en el Monte Carmelo (1 Reyes cap. 18)," *Cuadernos Teologicos*, XIV (1965), 38-51; J. Debus, *Die Sünde Jerobeams*, 1967; F. C. Fensham, "A Possible Explanation of the Name Baal-Zebub of Ekron," *ZAW*, LXXIX (1967), 361-64; D. W. Gooding, "An Impossible Shrine," *VT*, XV (1965), 405-20; *idem*, "The Septuagint's Rival Version of Jeroboam's Rise to Power," *VT*, XVII (1967), 173-89; S. H. Horn, "Did Sennacherib Campaign Once or Twice Against Hezekiah?" *Andrews University Seminary Studies*, IV (1966), 1-28; A. F. Johns, "Did David Use Assyrian-type Annals?" *ibid.*, III (1965), 97-109; R. Kilian, "Die Totenerweckungen Elias und Elisas—eine Motivwanderung?" *BZ*, NF X (1966), 44-56; M. A. Klopfenstein, "1. Könige 13," in *Parresia* (Festschrift Karl Barth), 1966, pp. 639-72; C. van Leeuwen, "Sanchérib devant Jérusalem," *OTS*, XIV (1965), 245-72; J. M. Miller, "The Elisha Cycle and the Accounts of the Omride Wars," *JBL*, LXXXVI (1966), 441-54; G. Morawe, "Studien zum Aufbau der neubabylonischen Chroniken in ihrer Beziehung zu den chronologischen Notizen der Königsbücher," *EvTh*, XXVI (1966), 308-20; M. Noth, *Könige* (Biblischer Kommentar, 9), 1965- ; I. Plein, "Erwägungen zur Überlieferung von I Reg 11,26–14,20," *ZAW*, LXXVIII (1966), 8-24; J. J. Stamm, "Elia am Horeb," *Studia biblica et semitica Vriezen*, 1966, pp. 350-55; E. R. Thiele, "The Azariah and Hezekiah Synchronisms," *VT*, XVI (1966), 103-107; E. Vogt, "Sennacherib und die letzte Tätigkeit Jesajas," *Bibl*, XLVII (1966), 427-37; M. Weitemeyer, "Nabots vingård," *DTT*, XXIX (1966), 129-43; J. G. Williams, "The Prophetic 'Father,'" *JBL*, LXXXV (1966), 344-48.

§34 J. A. Emerton, "Did Ezra Go to Jerusalem in 428 BC?" *JThST*, NS XVII (1966), 1-19; U. Kellermann, *Nehemia; Quellen, Überlieferung und Geschichte*, 1967; F. Michaeli, *Les livres des Chroniques, d'Esdras et de Néhémie*, 1967.

§35 U. Kellermann, "Die Listen in Nehemia 11; eine Dokumentation aus den letzten Jahren des Reiches Juda?" *ZDPV*, LXXXII (1966), 209-27; *idem*, *Nehemia; Quellen, Überlieferung und Geschichte*, 1967; R. W. Klein, "New Evidence for an Old Recension of Reigns," *HThR*, LIX (1966), 93-105; W. E. Lemke, "The Synoptic Problem in the Chronicler's History," *HThR*, LVIII (1965), 349-63; J. Liver, "The Sequence of Persian Kings in Ezra and Nehemiah," in *Sefer Segal*, 1964, pp. 127-38; F. L. Moriarty, "The Chronicler's Account of Hezekiah's Reform," *CBQ*, XXVII (1965), 399-406; J. M. Myers, *I–II Chronicles; Ezra; Nehemiah* (Anchor Bible), 1965; *idem*, "The Kerygma of the Chronicler," *Interpr*, XX (1966), 259-73; H. C. M. Vogt, *Studien zur nachexilischen Gemeinde in Esra-Nehemia*, 1966.

§36 H. Bruppacher, "Die Bedeutung des Namens Ruth," *ThZ*, XXII (1966), 12-18.

§37 H. Bardtke, "Neuere Arbeiten am Estherbuch," *JEOL*, VI:19 (1965/66), 519-

49; W. H. Brownlee, "Le livre grec d'Esther et la royauté divine," *RB*, LXXIII (1966), 161-85; G. Gerleman, *Studien zu Esther*, 1966; C. A. Moore, "A Greek Witness to a Different Hebrew Text of Esther," *ZAW*, LXXIX (1967), 351-58.

§38 R. Borger, *Handbuch der Keilschriftliteratur*, 1967- . G. Sauer, "Erwägungen zum Alter der Psalmendichtung," *ThZ*, XXII (1966), 81-95.

§39 G. W. Anderson, "Enemies and Evil-doers in the Book of Psalms," *BJRL*, XLVIII (1965), 18-29; J. Becker, *Israel deutet seine Psalmen*, 1966; W. Beyerlin, "Die *tōdâ* der Heilsvergegenwärtigung in den Klageliedern des Einzelnen," *ZAW*, LXXIX (1967), 208-24; R. J. Clifford, "The Use of *Hôy* in the Prophets," *CBQ*, XXVIII (1966), 458-64; H. H. Guthrie, *Israel's Sacred Songs*, 1966; J. Jeremias, *Theophanie; die Geschichte einer alttestamentlichen Gattung*, 1965; A. S. Kapelrud, "Die skandinavische Einleitungswissenschaft zu den Psalmen," *Verkündigung und Forschung*, XI (1966), 62-93; C. J. Labuschagne, *The Incomparability of Yahweh in the Old Testament*, 1966; E. Lipinski, *La royauté de Yahwé dans la poésie et le culte de l'ancien Israël*, 1965; F. Luke, "The Songs of Zion as a Literary Category of the Psalter," *Indian Journal of Theology*, XIV (1965), 72-90; B. de Pinto, "The Torah and the Psalms," *JBL*, LXXXVI (1967), 154-74; J. van der Ploeg, "Réflexions sur les genres littéraires des Psaumes," in *Studia biblica et semitica Vriezen*, 1966, pp. 265-77; J. D. W. Watts, "Yahweh Mālak Psalms," *ThZ*, XXI (1965), 241-48; C. Westermann, *Der Psalter*, 1967.

§43 J. S. Ackerman, *An Exegetical Study of Psalm 82*, Dissertation, Harvard, 1966; P. R. Ackroyd and M. A. Knibb, "Translating the Psalms," *Bible Translator*, XVII (1966), 1-11; D. R. Ap-Thomas, "An Appreciation of Sigmund Mowinckel's Contribution to Biblical Studies," *JBL*, LXXXV (1966), 315-25; J. Becker, *Israel deutet seine Psalmen*, 1966; W. Beyerlin, "Die *tôdā* der Heilsvergegenwärtigung in den Klageliedern des Einzelnen," *ZAW*, LXXIX (1967), 208-24; J. W. Bowker, "Psalm CX," *VT*, XVII (1967), 31-41; S. Bullough, "The Question of Metre in Psalm I," *VT*, XVII (1967), 42-49; A. Caquot, "Purification et expiation selon le psaume LI," *RHR*, CLXIX (1966), 133-54; M. J. Dahood, *Psalms* (Anchor Bible), 1965- ; H. Donner, "Ugaritismen in der Psalmenforschung," *ZAW*, LXXIX (1967), 322-50; G. R. Driver, "Psalm CX: Its Form, Meaning and Purpose," in *Sefer Segal*, 1964; G. Giavini, "La struttura letteraria del Salmo 86 (85)," *RivBibl*, XIV (1966), 455-58; A. González Núñez, " 'Cual torrentes del Neguev,' " *EstBíbl*, XXIV (1965), 349-60; J. Hofbauer, "Psalm 77/78, ein 'politisches Lied,' " *ZKTh*, LXXXIX (1967), 41-50; F. N. Jasper, "Early Israelite Traditions and the Psalter," *VT*, XVII (1967), 50-59; A. R. Johnson, *Sacral Kingship in Ancient Israel*, 2nd ed., 1967; A. S. Kapelrud, "Die skandinavische Einleitungswissenschaft zu den Psalmen," *Verkündigung und Forschung*, XI (1966), 62-93; J. L. Koole, "Quelques remarques sur Psaume 139," in *Studia biblica et semitica Vriezen*, 1966, pp. 176-80; J. Leveen, "The Textual Problems of Psalm VII," *VT*, XVI (1966), 439-45; B. Lindars, "Is Psalm II an Acrostic Poem?" *VT*, XVII (1967), 60-67; B. Maggioni, "Osservazioni sul Salmo 29 (28): 'Afferte Domino,' " *Bibbia e Oriente*, VII (1965), 245-51; Z. Malachi, "Zur Erklärung des Wortes 'Selah' in der Bibel," *Bet Miqra'*, XI (1965/66), 104-10; M. Mannati and E. de Solms, *Les Psaumes*, 1966- ; M. Palmer, "The Cardinal Points in Psalm 48," *Bibl*, XLVI (1965), 357-58; B. de Pinto, "The Torah and the Psalms," *JBL*, LXXXVI (1967), 154-74; J. van der Ploeg, "Le Psaume XVII et ses problèmes," *OTS*, XIV

(1965), 273-95; *idem*, "Le Psaume XCI dans une recension de Qumran," *RB*, LXXII (1965), 210-17; N. H. Ridderbos, "The Structure of Psalm XL," *OTS*, XIV (1965), 296-304; G. Rinaldi, "Al termine delle due vie (Salmo 1)," *Bibbia e Oriente*, IX (1967), 69-75; M. Sæbø, "Salme 139 og visdomsdiktningen," *TTKi*, XXXVII (1966), 167-84; J. A. Sanders, *The Psalms Scroll of Qumrân Cave 11 (11 QPsa)*, 1965; E. San Pedro, "Problemata philologica psalmi XIV," *Verbum Dei*, XLV (1967), 65-78; G. Sauer, "Erwägungen zum Alter der Psalmendichtung," *ThZ*, XXII (1966), 81-95; L. Schmidt, *Die Psalmen*, 1967- ; W. H. Schmidt, "Gott und Mensch in Ps. 130; formgeschichtliche Erwägungen," *ThZ*, XXII (1966), 241-53; J. A. Soggin, "Zum ersten Psalm," *ThZ*, XXIII (1967), 81-96; J. J. Stamm, "Erwägungen zu Ps 23," in *Freude am Evangelium* (Festschrift de Quervain), 1966, pp. 120-28; P. Veugelers, *Le Psaume LXXII poème messianique?* 1965; E. Vogt, "Gratiarum actio Psalmi 40," *VD*, XLIII (1965), 181-90; G. Wanke, *Die Zionstheologie der Korachiten in ihrem traditionsgeschichtlichen Zusammenhang*, 1966; C. Westermann, *Der Psalter*, 1967.

§44 S. T. Lachs, "The Date of Lamentations V," *JQR*, LVII (1966/67), 46-56.

§45 J. Angenieux, *Structure du Cantique des Cantiques en chants encadrés par des refrains alternants*, 1965; E. F. F. Bishop, "Palestina in Canticulis," *CBQ*, XXIX (1967), 20-30; O. Loretz, "Die theologische Bedeutung des Hohenliedes," *BZ*, NF X (1966), 29-43; G. Rust, "Dek du Teorioj pri la Alta Kanto de Salomon," *Biblia Revuo*, II (1965), 7-31; J. C. Rylaarsdam, "The Song of Songs and Biblical Faith," *Biblical Research*, X (1965), 7-18; R. N. Soulen, "The *Waṣfs* of the Song and Hermeneutic," *JBL*, LXXXVI (1967), 183-90; P. M. Tragan, *Càntic dels Càntics* (La Bíblia), 1966.

§46 R. Borger, *Handbuch der Keilschriftliteratur*, 1967- ; B. Colless, "Edukado en la Antikva Proksima Oriento," *Biblia Revuo*, V (1966), 49-72; J. Dupont, " 'Béatitudes' égyptiennes," *Bibl*, XLVII (1966), 185-222; D. A. Hubbard, "The Wisdom Movement and Israel's Covenant Faith," *Tyndale Bulletin*, XVII (1966), 3-33; J. L. McKenzie, "Reflections on Wisdom," *JBL*, LXXXVI (1967), 1-9; A. Marzai, *La enseñanza de Amenemope*, 1965; R. E. Murphy, *Introduction to the Wisdom Literature of the Old Testament*, 1965; *idem*, "Die Weisheitsliteratur des Alten Testaments," *Concilium*, I (1965), 855-62; H. H. Schmid, *Wesen und Geschichte der Weisheit; eine Untersuchung zur altorientalischen und israelitischen Weisheitsliteratur*, 1966.

§47 J. L. Crenshaw, "The Influence of the Wise Upon Amos," *ZAW*, LXXIX (1967), 42-52; J. L. McKenzie, "Reflections on Wisdom," *JBL*, LXXXVI (1967), 1-9; A. Marzai, *La enseñanza de Amenemope*, 1965; W. Richter, *Recht und Ethos; Versuch einer Ortung des weisheitlichen Mahnspruches*, 1966; W. M. W. Roth, *Numerical Sayings in the Old Testament*, 1965.

§49 R. Augé, *Proverbis* (La Bíblia), 1966; J. Conrad, "Die innere Gliederung der Proverbien," *ZAW*, LXXIX (1967), 67-76; C. Kayatz, *Studien zu Proverbien 1–9*, 1966; A. Marzai, *La enseñanza de Amenemope*, 1965; R. E. Murphy, "The Kerygma of the Book of Proverbs," *Interpr*, XX (1966), 3-14; F. Vattioni, "Sagezza e creazione in Prov. 3,19-20," *Augustinianum*, VI (1966), 102-105; R. N. Whybray, "Proverbs VIII 23-31 and Its Supposed Prototypes," *VT*, XV (1965), 504-14; *idem*, "Some

Literary Problems in Proverbs I–IX," *VT*, XVI (1966), 483-96; *idem*, *Wisdom in Proverbs*, 1965.

§50 M. Bič, "Le juste et l'impie dans le livre de Job," *VTSuppl*, XV (1966), 33-43; C. Brandwein, "The Legend of Job According to Its Various Stages," *Tarbiz*, XXXV (1965/66), 1-17; H. L. Ginsberg, "Job the Patient and Job the Impatient," *Conservative Judaism*, XXI (1966/67), 12-28; R. Gordis, *The Book of God and Man*, 1965; A. Guillaume, "The Unity of the Book of Job," *Annual of Leeds University Oriental Society*, IV (1962/63), 26-46; J. Prado, "La perspectiva escatológica de Job 19,25-27," *EstBibl*, XXV (1966) 5-39; W. von Soden, "Das Fragen nach der Gerechtigkeit Gottes im Alten Orient," *MDOG*, XCVI (1965), 41-59; S. Terrien, "Quelques remarques sur les affinités de Job avec le Deutéro-Esaïe," *VTSuppl*, XV (1966), 295-310; M. Tsevat, "The Meaning of the Book of Job," *HUCA*, XXXVII (1966), 73-106.

§51 M. J. Dahood, "The Phoenician Background of Qoheleth," *Bibl*, XLVII (1966), 264-82; F. Ellermeier, *Qohelet*, 1967- ; A. M. Figueras, *Eclesiastès* (La Bíblia), 1966.

§52 P. L. Berger, "The Social Location of Israelite Prophecy," *American Sociological Review*, XXVIII (1963), 940-50; R. Borger, *Handbuch der Keilschriftliteratur*, 1967- ; G. Fohrer, "Prophetie und Magie," *ZAW*, LXXVIII (1966), 25-47; *idem*, *Studien zur alttestamentlichen Prophetie*, 1967; M. Gilula, "An Egyptian Parallel to Jeremia I 4-5," *VT*, XVII (1967), 114; N. K. Gottwald, *All the Kingdoms of the Earth*, 1964; H. Gross, *Gab es in Israel ein "prophetisches Amt"?* 1965; W. W. Hallo, "Akkadian Apocalypses," *IEJ*, XVI (1966), 231-42; E. Hammershaimb, *Some Aspects of OT Prophecy from Isaiah to Malachi*, 1966; S. Herrmann, *Die prophetischen Heilserwartungen im Alten Testament*, 1965; A. S. Kapelrud, *Profetene i det gamle Israel og Juda*, 1966; A. Malamat, "Prophetic Revelations in New Documents from Mari and the Bible," *VTSuppl*, XV (1966), 207-27; *idem*, *Prophecy in the Mari Documents and the Bible* (Hebrew), 1967; F. L. Moriarty, "Prophet and Covenant," *Gregorianum*, XLVI (1965), 817-33; J. Muilenburg, "The 'Office' of the Prophet in Ancient Israel," in *The Bible and Modern Scholarship*, 1965, 74-97; L. M. Muntingh, "Profetisme in die Mari-tekste en in die Ou Testament," *Nederlandse Gereformeerd Teologiese Tydskrif*, VII (1966), 48-60; F. Nötscher, "Prophetie im Umkreis des alten Israel," *BZ*, NF X (1966), 161-97; H. M. Orlinsky, "The Seer in Ancient Israel," *Oriens antiquus*, IV (1965), 153-74; A. E. Rüthy, "Wächter und Späher im Alten Testament," *ThZ*, XXI (1965), 300-309; J. Scharbert, *Die Propheten Israels bis 700 v. Chr.*, 1965; H. Schult, "Vier weitere Mari-Briefe 'prophetischen' Inhalts," *ZDPV*, LXXXII (1966), 228-32; G. E. Wright, "The Nations in Hebrew Prophecy," *Encounter*, XXVI (1965), 225-37; A. H. van Zyl, "Die Boodskapper van die Here," *Nederlandse Gereformeerd Teologiese Tydskrif*, VIII (1967), 66-81.

§53 R. J. Clifford, "The Use of *Hôy* in the Prophets," *CBQ*, XXVIII (1966), 458-64; G. Fohrer, *Studien zur alttestamentlichen Prophetie*, 1967; N. K. Gottwald, *All the Kingdoms of the Earth*, 1964; E. Hammershaimb, *Some Aspects of OT Prophecy from Isaiah to Malachi*, 1966; J. H. Hayes, "The Usage of Oracles Against Foreign Nations in Israel," *JBL*, LXXXVII (1968), 81-92; J. Jeremias, *Theophanie; die Geschichte einer alttestamentlichen Gattung*, 1965; A. S. Kapelrud, *Profetene i det gamle Israel og Juda*, 1966; B. O. Long, "The Divine Funeral Lament," *JBL*, LXXXV (1966), 85-86; F. L. Moriarty, "Prophet and Covenant," *Gregorianum*, XLVI (1965), 817-33; J. Muilenburg, "The 'Office' of the Prophet in Ancient Israel," in *The Bible in Modern Scholarship*, 1965, pp. 74-97; E. Scherer, *Unpersönlich formulierte prophetische Orakel; drei Formen prophetischer Rede*, Dissertation, Kirchliche Hochschule Berlin, 1964.

§54 G. Fohrer, *Studien zur alttestamentlichen Prophetie*, 1967; E. Hammershaimb, *Some Aspects of OT Prophecy from Isaiah to Malachi*, 1966; A. S. Kapelrud, *Profetene i det gamle Israel og Juda*, 1966; A. Penna, "Le parti narrative in Isaia e Geremia," *RivBibl*, XIII (1965), 321-36; J. Scharbert, "Das Entstehen der prophetischen Bücher," in K. Schubert, ed., *Bibel und zeitgemässer Glaube*, 1965, pp. 193-237.

§56 M.-L. Henry, *Glaubenskrise und Glaubensbewährung in den Dichtungen der Jesajaapokalypse*, 1967; T. Lescow, "Das Geburtsmotiv in den messianischen Weissagungen bei Jesaja und Micha," *ZAW*, LXXIX (1967), 172-207; J. Lindblom, "Der Ausspruch über Tyrus in Jes. 23," *ASTI*, IV (1965), 56-73; W. McKane, "The Interpretation of Isaiah VII 14-25," *VT*, XVII (1967), 208-19; A. Mattioli, "Due schemi letterari negli Oracoli d'introduzione al Libro d'Isaia: Is 1:1-31," *RivBibl*, XIV (1966), 345-64; J. Mejía, "Isaías 7,14-16: contribución a la exegesis de un texto difícil," *EstBíbl*, XXIII (1964), 107-21; J. A. Miller, "Emmanuel," *Bibbia e Oriente*, VIII (1966), 51-59; J. Morgenstern, "Further Light from the Book of Isaiah Upon the Catastrophe of 485 B.C.," *HUCA*, XXXVII (1966), 1-28; B. D. Napier, Isaiah and the Isaian," *VTSuppl*, XV (1966), 240-51; A. Penna, "Le parti narrative in Isaia e Geremia," *RivBibl*, XIII (1965), 321-46; E. Vogt, "Sennacherib und die letzte Tätigkeit Jesajas," *Bibl*, XLVII (1966), 427-37; H. Wildberger, *Jesaja* (Biblischer Kommentar), 1965- .

§57 S. Herrmann, *Prophetie und Wirklichkeit in der Epoche des babylonischen Exils*, 1967; E. Hessler, "Die Struktur der Bilder bei Deuterojesaja," *EvTh*, XXV (1965), 349-69; G. Kehnscherper, "Der 'Sklave Gottes' bei Deuterojesaja," *FF*, XL (1966), 279-82; E. Kutsch, *Sein Leiden und Tod—unser Heil*, 1967; J. Morgenstern, "Further Light from the Book of Isaiah Upon the Catastrophe of 485 B.C.," *HUCA*, XXXVII (1966), 1-28; *idem*, "Isaiah 49–65," *HUCA*, XXXVI (1965), 1-35; H. M. Orlinsky, "The So-called 'Servant of the Lord' and Suffering Servant in Second Isaiah," *VTSuppl*, XIV (1967), 1-133; J. B. Payne, "Eighth Century Israelitish Background of Isaiah 40–66," *Westminster Theological Journal*, XXIX (1966/67), 179-90; R. A. Rosenberg, "Yahweh Becomes King," *JBL*, LXXXV (1966), 297-307; J. D. Smart, *History and Theology in Second Isaiah*, 1965; C. Westermann, *Das Buch Jesaja; Kapitel 40–66* (Das Alte Testament Deutsch), 1966; *idem*, "Jesaja 48 und die 'Bezeugung gegen Israel,'" in *Studia biblica et semitica Vriezen*, 1966, pp. 356-66.

§58 H.-J. Kraus, "Die ausgebliebene Endtheophanie," *ZAW*, LXXVIII (1966), 317-32; D. Michel, "Zur Eigenart Tritojesajas," *Theologia viatorum*, X (1965/66), 213-30; J. Morgenstern, "Further Light from the Book of Isaiah Upon the Catastrophe of 485 B.C.," *HUCA*, XXXVII (1966), 1-28; J. B. Payne, "Eighth Century Israelitish Background of Isaiah 40–66," *Westminster Theological Journal*, XXIX (1966/67), 179-90; C. Westermann, *Das Buch Jesaja; Kapitel 40–66* (Das Alte Testament Deutsch), 1966.

§59 J. Bright, *Jeremiah* (Anchor Bible), 1965; M. Gilula, "An Egyptian Parallel to Jeremia I 4-5," *VT*, XVII (1967), 114; W. L. Holladay, "Jeremiah and Moses: Further Observations," *JBL*, LXXXV (1966), 17-27; *idem*, "The Recovery of Poetic Passages of Jeremiah," *JBL*, LXXXV (1966), 401-35; J. P. Hyatt, "The Beginning of Jeremiah's Prophecy," *ZAW*, LXXVIII (1966), 204-14; J. G. Janzen, *Studies in the Text of Jeremiah*, Dissertation, Harvard, 1966; M. Kessler, "Form-critical Suggestions on Jer 36," *CBQ*, XXVIII (1966), 389-410; W. McKane, "The Interpretation of Jeremiah XII. 1-5," *Glasgow University Oriental Society Transactions*, XX (1963/64), 38-48; A. Penna, "Le parti narrative in Isaia e Geremia," *RivBibl*, XIII (1965), 321-46; C. Rietschel, *Das Problem der Urrolle*, 1966; G. Sauer, "Mandelzweig und Kessel in Jer 1,11 ff.," *ZAW*, LXXVIII (1966), 56-61; J. Schreiner, "Ein neuer Bund unverbrüchlichen Heils," *Bibel und Leben*, VII (1966), 242-55; *idem*, "Prophetsein im Untergang; aus der Verkündigung des Propheten Jeremias: Jer 1,4-19," *Bibel und Leben*, VII (1966), 15-28; *idem*, "Sicherheit oder Umkehr? Aus der Verkündigung des Propheten Jeremias," *Bibel und Leben*, VII (1966), 98-111.

§60 R. Frankena, *Kanttekeningen van een Assyrioloog bij Ezechiël*, 1965; S. Herrmann, *Prophetie und Wirklichkeit in der Epoche des babylonischen Exils*, 1967; W. Zimmerli, "The Special Form- and Traditio-historical Character of Ezekiel's Prophecy," *VT*, XV (1965), 515-27.

§61 E. M. Good, "The Composition of Hosea," *SEÅ*, XXXI (1966), 21-63; *idem*, *Hosea* (Kommentar zum Alten Testament), 1966; *Studies in the Books of Hosea and* "Hosea and the Jacob Tradition," *VT*, XVI (1966), 137-51; *idem*, "Hosea 5:8–6:6: an alternative to Alt," *JBL*, LXXXV (1966), 273-86; W. Rudolph, "Eigentümlichkeiten der Sprache Hosea," in *Studia biblica et semitica Vriezen*, 1966, 313-17; *idem*, *Hosea* (Kommentar zum Alten Testament), 1966; W. E. Staples, *Studies in the Books of Hosea and Amos*, 1966; J. Wijngaards, "Death and Resurrection in Covenantal Context," *VT*, XVII (1967), 226-39.

§62 H.-P. Müller, "Prophetie und Apokalyptik bei Joel," *Theologia viatorum*, X (1965/66), 231-52; M. Weiss, "On the Traces of a Biblical Metaphor," *Tarbiz*, XXXIV (1964/65), 303-18.

§63 A. Carlson, "Profeten Amos och Davidsriket," *Religion och Bibel*, XXV (1966), 57-78; S. Cohen, "The Political Background of the Words of Amos," *HUCA*, XXXVI (1965), 153-60; J. L. Crenshaw, "The Influence of the Wise Upon Amos," *ZAW*, LXXIX (1967), 42-52; H. Gottlieb, "Amos og kulten," *DTT*, XXX (1967), 65-101; A. S. Kapelrud, "New Ideas in Amos," *VTSuppl*, XV (1966), 193-206; K. W. Neubauer, "Erwägungen zu Amos 5,4-15," *ZAW*, LXXVIII (1966), 292-316; H. Schmidt, " 'Nicht Prophet bin ich, noch bin ich Prophetensohn'; zur Erklärung von Amos 7,14a," *Judaica*, XXIII (1967), 68-75; L. A. Sinclair, "The Courtroom Motif in the Book of Amos," *JBL*, LXXXV (1966), 351-53; W. E. Staples, "Epic Motifs in Amos," *JNES*, XXV (1966), 106-12; *idem*, *Studies in the Books of Hosea and Amos*, 1966; L. L. Walker, "The Language of Amos," *Southwestern Journal of Theology*, IX (1966/67), 37-48; M. Weiss, "Methodologisches über die Behandlung der Metapher, dargelegt an Am 1,2," *ThZ*, XXIII (1967), 1-25; *idem*, "On the Traces of a Biblical Metaphor," *Tarbiz*, XXXIV (1964/65), 303-18; *idem*, "The Origin of the 'Day of the Lord' Reconsidered," *HUCA*, XXXVII (1966), 29-60.

§64. G. Fohrer, "Die Sprüche Obadjas," in *Studia biblica et semitica Vriezen*, 1966, pp. 81-93; C. A. Keller, "Jonas; le portrait d'un prophète," *ThZ*, XXI (1965), 329-40.

§65 E.-J. Bickerman, "Les deux erreurs du Prophète Jonas," *RHPhR*, XLV (1965), 232-64; R. Pesch, "Zur konzentrischen Struktur von Jona 1," *Bibl*, XLVII (1966), 577-81; P. L. Trible, *Studies in the Book of Jonah*, Dissertation, Columbia, 1964; H. W. Wolff, *Studien zum Jonabuch*, 1965.

§66 J. Dus, "Weiteres zum nordisraelitischen Psalm Micha 7,7-20," *ZDMG*, CXV (1965), 14-22; O. García de la Fuente, "Notas al texto de Miqueas," *Augustinianum*, VII (1967), 145-54; T. Lescow, "Das Geburtsmotiv in den messianischen Weissagungen bei Jesaja und Micha," *ZAW*, LXXIX (1967), 172-207; *idem*, *Micha 6,6-8; Studie zur Sprache, Form, und Auslegung*, 1966; J. T. Willis, *The Structure, Setting, and Interrelationships of the Pericopes in the Book of Micah*, Dissertation, Vanderbilt, 1966.

§67 S. J. de Vries, "The Acrostic of Nahum in the Jerusalem Liturgy," *VT*, XVI (1966), 476-81.

§68 A. S. van der Woude, "Der Gerechte wird durch seine Treue leben; Erwägungen zu Habakuk 2,4 f.," in *Studia biblica et semitica Vriezen*, 1966, pp. 367-75.

§69 A. S. van der Woude, "Predikte Zefanja een wereldgericht?" *NedThT*, XX (1965/66), 1-16.

§70 K. Koch, "Haggais unreines Volk," *ZAW*, LXXIX (1967), 52-66.

§73 H. J. Boecker, "Bemerkungen zur formgeschichtlichen Terminologie des Buches Maleachi," *ZAW*, LXXVIII (1966), 78-80; L. Kruse-Blinkenberg, "Jødedommen i den persiske tidsalder i lys af Maleakis bog," *DTT*, XXVIII (1965), 80-99.

§74 C. H. W. Brekelmans, "The Saints of the Most High and Their Kingdom," *OTS*, XIV (1965), 305-29; K. Koch, "Die Apokalyptik und ihre Zukunftserwartungen," *Kontexte*, III (1966), 51-58; A. Szörényi, "Das Buch Daniel, ein kanonisierter *pescher*?" *VTSuppl*, XV (1966), 278-94; D. J. Wiseman *et al.*, *Notes on Some Problems in the Book of Daniel*, 1965; F. Zimmermann, "The Writing on the Wall: Dan 5,25 f.," *JQR*, LV (1965), 201-7.

§76 J.-L. Koole, "Die Bibel des Ben-Sira," *OTS*, XIV (1965), 374-96; J. van der Ploeg, "Le Psaume XCI dans une recension de Qumran," *RB*, LXXII (1965), 210-17; P. W. Skehan, "The Biblical Scrolls from Qumran and the Text of the Old Testament," *BA*, XXVIII (1965), 87-100.

§77 R. E. Murphy, "The Old Testament Canon in the Catholic Church," *CBQ*, XXVIII (1966), 189-93; A. C. Sundberg, Jr., "The Protestant Old Testament Canon: Should it be Re-examined?" *CBQ*, XXVIII (1966), 194-203.

§78 S. Ben-Meir, "Variant Readings in Medieval Hebrew Commentaries," *Textus*, V (1966), 84-92; F. Díaz Esteban, "Los supuestos errores de la Masora," *Sefarad*, XXVI (1966), 3-11; G. Fohrer, "Hin zu den Quellen," *ZAW* LXXVIII (1966), 225-29; D. N. Freedman, "The Biblical Languages," in *The Bible and Modern Scholarship*, 1965, pp. 294-312; M. H. Goshen-Gottstein, "A Recovered Part of the Aleppo Codex,"

Textus, V (1966), 53-59; B. Keller, "Fragment d'un traité d'exegèse massorétique," *Textus*, V (1966), 60-83; A. Murtonen, "A Historico-philological Survey of the Main Dead Sea Scrolls and Related Documents," *Abr-Nahrain*, IV (1963/64), 56-95; Y. Ratzabi, "Massoretic Variants to the Five Scrolls from a Babylonian-Yemenite Ms.," *Textus*, V (1966), 93-113; H. P. Rüger, "Ein Fragment der bisher ältesten datierten hebräischen Bibelhandschrift mit babylonischer Punktation," *VT*, XVI (1966), 65-73; P. Sacchi, "Il rotolo *A* di Isaia; problemei di storia del testo," *Atti dell 'Accademia toscana di scienze e lettere "La Colombaria,"* XXX (1965), 31-111; P. W. Skehan, "The Biblical Scrolls from Qumran and the Text of the Old Testament," *BA*, XXVIII (1965), 87-100; S. Szyszman, "La famille des massorètes caraïtes Ben Asher et le Codex Alepensis," *RB*, LXXIII (1966), 531-51; I. N. Vinnikov, "O vnov' otkrytoj nadpisi k jugu ot Jaffy," *ArOr*, XXXV (1965), 546-52.

§79 J. Barr, "St. Jerome and the Sounds of Hebrew," *JSS*, XII (1967), 1-36; *idem*, "St. Jerome's Appreciation of Hebrew," *BJRL*, XLIX (1966/67), 281-302; A. Benoit and P. Prigent, "Les citations de l'Écriture chez les Pères," *RHPhR*, XLVI (1966), 161-68; J. W. Bowker, "Haggadah in the Targum Onqelos," *JSS*, XII (1967), 159-69; J. Cantera, "Puntos de contacto de la Vetus Latina con el Targum Arameo y con la Pesitta," *Sefarad*, XXV (1965), 223-40; S. Daniel, *Recherches sur le vocabulaire du culte dans la Septante*, 1966; F. Dunand, *Papyrus grecs bibliques (Papyrus F. Inv. 266), volumina de la Genèse et du Deutéronome*, 1965; G. Fohrer, "Hin zu den Quellen," *ZAW*, LXXVIII (1966), 225-29; H. S. Gehman, "Adventures in Septuagint Lexicography," *Textus*, V (1966), 125-32; D. W. Gooding, "An Impossible Shrine," *VT*, XV (1965), 405-20; *idem*, "The Septuagint's Rival Versions of Jeroboam's Rise to Power," *VT*, XVII (1967), 173-89; P. Grelot, "Les versions grecques de Daniel," *Bibl*, XLVII (1966), 381-402; J. G. Janzen, *Studies in the Text of Jeremiah*, Dissertation, Harvard, 1966; S. Jellicoe, "The Septuagint To-day," *ET*, LXXVII (1965/66), 68-74; R. Kasser, "Les dialectes coptes et les versions coptes bibliques," *Bibl*, XLVI (1965), 287-310; L. Kruse-Blinkenberg, "The Pesitta of the Book of Malachi," *StTh*, XX (1966), 95-119; M. McNamara, "Some Early Rabbinic Citations and the Palestine Targum to the Pentateuch," *RSO*, XLI (1966), 1-15; *idem*, "Targumic Studies," *CBQ*, XXVIII (1966), 1-19; C. A. Moore, "A Greek Witness to a Different Hebrew Text of Esther," *ZAW*, LXXIX (1967), 351-58; J. Reider and N. Turner, *An Index to Aquila*, 1966; L. G. Running, "An Investigation of the Syriac Version of Isaiah," *Andrews University Seminary Studies*, III (1965), 138-57; J. Shunary, "Avoidance of Anthropomorphisms in the Targum of Psalms," *Textus*, V (1966), 133-44; P. W. Skehan, "The Biblical Scrolls from Qumran and the Text of the Old Testament," *BA*, XXVIII (1965), 87-100; I. Soisalon-Soininen, *Die Infinitive in der Septuaginta*, 1965; O. Wahl, *Die Prophetenzitate der Sacra Parallela in ihrem Verhältnis zur Septuaginta-Textüberlieferung*, 2 vols., 1965; B. K. Waltke, *Prolegomena to the Samaritan Pentateuch*, Dissertation, Harvard, 1965; G. E. Weil, "Fragment d'une Massorah alphabétique du Targum Babylonien du Pentateuque," *Annual of Leeds University Oriental Society*, V (1963/64), 114-34; J. W. Wevers, "Proto-Septuagint Studies," in *The Seed of Wisdom* (Festschrift T. J. Meek), 1964, pp. 59-77.

§80 A. Benoit and P. Prigent, "Les citations de l'Écriture chez les Pères," *RHPhR*, XLVI (1966), 161-68; D. W. Goodwin, *Text-restoration Methods of the Baltimore School*, Dissertation, Brown, 1965; P. W. Skehan, "The Biblical Scrolls from Qumran and the Text of the Old Testament," *BA*, XXVIII (1965), 87-100.

INDEX

1. Index of Passages

(Only those passages are cited that are discussed outside the paragraphs devoted to the book in question.)

Genesis

Genesis 104
1–11 132
1:1–2:4*a* 87, 115
2:4*b*–3:24 88
2:4*b*-25 115
4:1 65
4:1 ff. 89
4:17 87
4:23-24 163
5 88
6:1-4 88
6:5–9:17 88, 113
9:6 69
9:20-27 115
9:25-27 162
10 115
10:8 ff. 152
11:1-9 90
12:10 ff. 115
15:1 155
15:9 ff. 72
16 115
16:11-12 66
18:22*b*-33 151
19 90
19:20 ff. 163
19:26 89
20 115
21 115
21:22-31 90
21:22 ff. 72, 92
23 72, 182
24:4, 10 121
25:1-6 163
25:27 ff. 89
26:26 ff. 72
27 89
31:44 ff. 72
32:10-13 84
32:25 ff. 163
34 93
35:17 65
37; 39–50 131
39:7 ff. 89
49 66

Exodus

Exodus 104
1–15 117
3 115
3:8 125, 150
4:1 ff. 89
4:24-26 163
12:21-23 117
12:24-27*a* 166
12:27 70
13:3-16 166
13:14-15 70
14:13 66
15:1-19 271
15:20-21 125, 163, 275
17:10 126
17:16 163, 274
20:1-17 68, 133, 166
20:18-21 144
20:24–23:9 134
21:2 ff. 70
21:12-17 70
23:10-19 69
24:1-2, 9-11 163
24:3 ff. 69
24:8 71
24:11 72
32:34 158
34:14-26 69

Leviticus

Leviticus 104
1–7 142
11–15 143
17–26 137
18 67, 101
18:7-17 47
19:3-12 69
19:13-18 69
23 101

Numbers

Numbers 104
1:46 184
2:32 184
4–6 143
6:24-26 182
9 70
10:35-36 66
13–14 126
15 143
15:32 ff. 71
16–17 92
18:8-32 143
19 143
21:14 279
21:14-15 156, 273
21:17-18 156, 273
21:21-31 126
21:27 38
21:27-30 156, 273
22–24 131, 274
22:28 ff. 89
23:9*b* 157
23:21-22 157
24 149-50
25:1-5 163

27 71
28–30 143
32:1-38 202
32:1 ff. 126
32:39-42 126, 198
36 71

Deuteronomy

Deuteronomy 25, 27, 104, 109, 116, 158, 185, 194
20:5-8 82
21:7-8 69
25:9 69
26:5 127
26:5 ff. 118
27:4-7 144
27:5-7 91
27:15-26 47, 70, 143
32 271
33 66

Joshua

Joshua 26
6:2 66
6:16 66
8:30-35 144
9:15 72
10:12 274
10:13 279
11:10 ff. 209
24:2 ff. 155
24:26 71

Judges

2:6-10 203
5 66, 275
5:12 275
5:15-17, 28-30 273
6:23 67
8:14 39
9:8-15 314
10:10 84
10:15 84
11:34 275
14:14 312
16:23 ff. 275
16:28 83
17–18 91

I Samuel

1–3 91
2:1-10 271
9 89
10:11 72
10:21*b*-27*a* 72
12 212
12:10 84
16:7 311
17 89
18:3-4 71
18:6-7 275
22:23 67
24:14 311
28:12 67

II Samuel

1:18 279
1:19-27 276
3:33-34 276
5:3 72
5:8 311
7:18-29 84
12 314
15:10 67
18:17 67

I Kings

3:4 ff. 98
3:16 ff. 89
5:12-13 309
5:16 ff. 72
5:17 67
8 272
10:1 312
10:1 ff. 333
12 72
12:24 m (LXX) 275
14:5 ff. 352
17:16 89
20:11 311
20:13, 28 409
21:13 69
21:17-19 354
22:17 355

II Kings

1:3-4 354
2:8 89
4:1 ff. 89
11:17 72
13:17 274
14:9 314
18:13, 17–20:19 370
19:9-14 84
20:1 352
22–23 167
22:8, 10 169
23:1-3 72, 175
23:8-9, 19 167
24:18–25:30 399

Isaiah

1:10 79
5:1-7 274, 314
5:8-10 444
5:11-13 273
5:20-21 309
6 265
7–8 361
8:16 40, 359
8:16-18 349
9:2 272
10:15 314
10:27*b*-32 444
14:4 ff. 276
21:12 273
22:13 273
23:15-16 273
24–27 271
28:4*b* 314
29:14 309

29:16 314
30:8 359
31:1-3 309
33 271
33:14-16 69
36–39 234
37:22 ff. 354
38:10-20 271
44:12-20 273
45:9 314
47 273
51:9-10 275
52:13–53:12 276
56:12 273
57:1-2 446
61:1 378
62 47

Jeremiah

3:21-25 266
9:16 38
9:19-21 275
14:2–15:2 271
14:7-9, 19-22 266
16:5 275
18:1-11 314
22:18-19 275
23:9 360
23:28 311
25:11 475
29:10 475
30:1-4 360
32 72
34:18 72
36 359
37:17 352
46:1 360
49 440
49:7 ff. 440
50:1 360

Ezekiel

Ezekiel 142
1:2 25
3:22-27 349
4–5 361
6 360
12:1-11 356
12:1 ff. 361
12:21–13:23 360
12:21 ff. 349
16 274
16:1-43 277
17:1-10 277, 314
17:18 71
18:5-9 69
19:1-9 277, 314
19:1-9, 10-14 277
19:10-14 277
21 360
23 274
24 361
24:15-24 356
24:15 ff. 275
24:25-27 349
26:15-18 276
27 276
28:11-19 276
31 276, 314
32:1-8, 17-32 276
33:21-22 349
34 361
44 185
48 204-205

Hosea

Hosea 158
2:4 65
5:15–6:6 271
6:1-3 266
6:7-11*a* 72
9:7*b* 349
10:3-4 72
14:2-9 271
14:3*b*-4 266

Joel

Joel 271

Amos

1:3 ff. 312
5:1-3 276
5:16 38
6:4-6 273
7:10 ff. 349

Jonah

2:1, 11 314
2:3-10 271
4:5 ff. 314

Micah

7:8-20 271

Nahum

Nahum 34
1:2 ff. 513
3:18-19 276

Habakkuk

Habakkuk 271

Zephaniah

1:12 311

Haggai

2:10-14 79

Zechariah

Zechariah 26
1:7 25

Psalms

2 269
2:7 65
6 267-68
8 264
13 267

15 69, 79, 266
18 25
18 B 270
20 270
20:7 ff. 352
21 270
22 267
24 266
24:3-6 69, 79
25 266
25:2 267
27 B 68
29 259
32 269
33 271
37 313
37:16 313
39 266
44 270
45 269, 274
46 265
47 264
48 265
49 313
49:5 313
51 25, 266
52 25
54 25
56 25
57 25
59 25
60 25
60:8-10 266, 352
62:12 312
72 270
73 269, 313
76 265
78 264, 313
78:2 313
78:44-51 191
82 265
84 265
85:9 ff. 352
87 265
89 B 270
91 313
93 264
95:7 ff. 352
96–99 264
101 269
103 271
104 259, 264, 315
105–106 264
107 269
110 269
111 47
112 47
116:13 268
122 265
130 266
132 270
133 314
134:3 270
136 269, 271
137 262
144 270
148 315

Job

Job 315, 322
1:21*b* 65
5:19-22 312
18 313
18:5-21 313
20:4-29 313
28 309, 313
31 69
33:14-15 312

Proverbs

1–9 309, 317
1:6 311-12
6:1-5 316
6:6-11 316
6:12-15 316
6:16-19 312
8 272, 313
9:1-18 313
10:6, 11 311
11:2*a* 308
11:9-12 316
11:24 308
15:13-14, 16-17 316
16:10 312
16:18 308
18:12 308
20:17 308
22:29 312
25:1 312
25:2-3 312
25:15 308
25:23 308
26:4-5 316
26:20 308
27:7 308
27:20 308
30 312
31:10 ff. 217

Ruth

4 72

Song of Songs

3:3 273
5:7 273

Ecclesiastes

Ecclesiastes 317
9:4 311
11:9–12:8 314

Lamentations

1 271
2 271
4 271
5 271

Esther

Esther 25
9:20 ff. 85

Daniel

Daniel 26
3:31–4:34 85

5:12 312
9 272

Ezra

9 272

Nehemiah

4:4 272
9 272

Other Writings

III Ezra 102, 481

I–III Maccabees 102, 481

I Maccabees
2:59-60 473
8:22 ff. 72

II Maccabees
2:13-14 485
15:36-37 255

Tobit 89, 102, 481
7:13 65

Judith 102, 481

Prayer of Manasseh 279, 481

Additions to Daniel 102, 279, 481

Additions to Esther 481

Baruch 279, 481

Epistle of Jeremiah 102, 481

Ecclesiasticus 481
24 272, 310
38:25 272
48:22 ff. 485
49:12 363

Wisdom of Solomon 481

Letter of Aristeas 102, 482, 493, 507

Jubilees 102, 482

Martyrdom and Ascension of Isaiah 482

Psalms of Solomon 279, 482

IV Maccabees 481-82

Sibylline Oracles 362, 482
iii.338 ff. 473

Enoch 362, 482

Ascension of Moses 362, 482

IV Ezra 362, 481
14:18-48 482

Apocalypse of Baruch 362, 482

Testaments of the Twelve Patriarchs 102, 482

Life of Adam and Eve 482

Odes of Solomon 482

Mark
13 478

II Corinthians
10:13 ff. 480

Galatians
6:16 480

II Thessalonians
2:4 478

Mishna Yadayim
iii.5 481

2. Selective Subject Index

(To supplement the Table of Contents)

Addition method, 114
Alphabetical songs, 270-71, 297, 314
Alphabetizing songs, 270-71
Amarna Letters, 122
Amen-em-opet, 173
Amphictyony, 207, 209
Ancient Near East, 100, 112, 116, 136-37, 141, 173, 175, 183, 190, 265, 276-77
Anecdote, 199, 209-10, 224, 232
Animal metaphor, 66
Annals, 227, 239
'Apiru, 122
Apocalyptic, 487
Apodictic law, 67, 174
Aramaic, 242, 472, 478
Archaeology, 28, 30
Archives, 39, 56
Art, 62
Audition (prophetical), 356

Balaam, 131
Baruch, 315
Biography, 61, 378
Blessing, 257
Blessing formula, 220
Book of the Upright, 102, 279
Book of the Wars of Yahweh, 102, 156, 279

Canaan(ite), 34, 136, 165, 200, 223, 259, 277, 284, 308, 331, 343, 368, 416, 472, 477
Cantata, 450
Casuistic law, 70, 174
Catechism, 116, 139
Christianity, 480
Chronicler's History, 195
Chronology, 60, 183, 213, 228, 230
Circumcision, 91
Composition method, 114
Confession, 269
Confidence, 269
Confidence, song of, 268, 277-78
Conversion, 425, 457, 463
Court style, 270
Court wisdom, 308-9
Covenant, 23, 167, 175, 178, 184, 221, 373, 383, 386, 396, 402, 424
Covenant Code, 144, 172
Covenant document, 72
Crystallization hypothesis, 110
Cult, 30, 117-18, 149-50, 258-59, 261 ff., 266, 269, 275, 285, 295, 380-81, 386-87, 392, 423, 437
Cult legend, 91, 210
Cult prophet, 270-71, 274, 396, 409, 429-30, 432, 445, 455, 458
Cultic centralization, 167-68, 170
Cultic pattern, 34

Day of Yahweh, 427-28, 430, 438, 456-57
Death, 65
Decalogue, 68-69, 72, 133, 139, 144, 149, 174
Deuteronomic theology, 417
Deuteronomistic History, 193-94
Diaspora, Babylonian, 185
Didactic narrative, 442
Didactic poetry, 269
Dirge, 257, 275, 296
Disciples (of prophets), 40
Discussion, 377, 469
Documentary hypothesis, 108-9, 114
Dream, 472, 474-75

Ecstasy, 343, 345, 349, 408-9, 412, 414-15
Educational wisdom, 309-10, 315, 421
Election, 150, 157, 178, 438
Elohist, 112, 144, 194
Enemy (in the Psalms), 268
Enneateuch, 104, 195
Enthronement songs, 264-65

Entrance liturgy, 270
Epithalamium, 302
Eschatology, 430
Etiology, 92, 200
Execration texts, 354, 367, 434
Exhortation, 354, 386
Exile, 190
Exodus tradition, 117, 125
Experience, secret, 349

Fable, 210, 306
Fairy tale, 442, 462
Festival legend, 253
Festival scroll, 249, 253
Form and function, 28, 112
Form criticism, 27-28, 112
Fragment hypothesis, 108, 110, 114

Gematria, 184, 187
Genealogy, 96, 127, 181, 250
Genizah, 491, 499, 512
Geographical saga, 90
God, dominion of, 239
God, names of, 108, 110, 115, 146, 152, 184, 294
Guide of self-examination, 69
Guilds of singers, 282-83, 294, 346

Ḫapiru, 122
Hellenization, 478
Heptateuch, 104, 195
Hero narrative, 208
Hero saga, 91, 201, 209, 219
Hexapla, 509
Hexateuch, 104, 193, 195
Historical and geographical lists, 96
Historical narrative, 98, 219-20, 234
History, 156, 184
History, analysis of, 190, 235-36, 247, 476
History, cyclic concept of, 213
Hittites, 259
Holiness Code, 145
Hymn, 188-89, 257, 258-59, 277, 319, 333, 371, 377, 436, 449
Hymn, monotheistic, 265, 294

"I" in the Psalms, 262-63
Innocence, psalms of, 268
Invective, 319, 354-55
Iranian influence, 477

Joseph novella, 131
Josephus (*Contra Apionem* i. 8), 482
Joshua tradition, 126-27
Josiah's reformation, 167-68, 391
Judah, 152, 165, 190
Judgment discourse, 377

King(ship), 54, 56, 63, 70, 210, 214, 217, 221, 225-26, 232, 235-36, 245, 248, 257 ff., 263, 269-70, 274, 301, 320, 365, 381, 396, 423

Lament, 257, 258-59, 270, 277, 297, 333, 387, 395, 452
Lament, communal, 296
Law, 183, 213
Law codes, 53-54
Law, Hurrian, 121-22
Legal form, 421
Legal reform, 136
Legend, 210, 219, 325, 472, 474
Legend, personal, 91-92
Levites, 214, 248
Library, 38
Lists, 96-97, 198-99, 204, 243-44, 306, 333
Litany, 258, 271
Literary forms, 27-28
Literary prophets, 349
Liturgy, prophetical, 270, 369-70, 386, 453
Love song, 257, 259, 302

Magic, 209, 356
Mari, 121, 186
Marriage, 65
Memoirs, 243
Midrash, 187, 442
Moses, 106-7, 156, 167-68, 173-74, 189
Moses tradition, 127
Motifs, 29, 112
Môt-yûmāt series, 69
Mourners, 275
Music, 283
Musical instruments, 263
Myth, 56, 88, 258, 306, 319, 416, 442, 462, 476

Nabi, 345
Naḥal Ḥever, 494
Names, non-Akkadian, 121
Nature saga, 90
Nature wisdom, 309
Nomad(ic), 124, 160, 163-64
North Israelite, 175
Northern Kingdom, 130, 137, 158, 169
Novel, 253
Novella, 249
Nuzi, 121

Occupation narrative, 124 ff.
Occupation tradition, 118
Octateuch, 104, 195
Officials, 309
Onomasticon, 307
Oracle, 265-70, 277, 352-53, 452

Parallelism, 45-46, 320, 322
Pārāšôt, 501
Parenesis, 174 ff.
Patriarchal traditions, 127
Penitential psalms, 257, 268
Pentateuch, 27
Pilgrimage song, 266, 295
Poetry, 257-58, 277
Poetry (literary), 259, 274
Poetry (religious), 266
Prayer, 243, 257, 259, 477
Prayer of the accused, 268
Preaching, 246
Priest, 70, 140, 185, 219, 268
Priestly Code, 27, 112, 137-38, 143-44, 191
Priestly theology, 417
Primal history, 87, 132, 149, 159, 163
Promise, 354, 371, 386
Prophecy, 150, 156, 173, 177, 189, 223, 235, 246, 273, 276, 278
Prophecy (prediction), 352
Prophetical legends, 232, 441
Prophetical saying, 225
Proverb, 305, 308
Pun, 66
Purim, 252-53

Qumran, 44, 45, 102, 187, 218, 225, 255, 272, 279, 362, 400, 453, 455, 473, 482, 487, 491, 493, 501, 506, 510

Redaction, 190-91
Redaction-history, 30
Redemption, 425
Resurrection, 475, 479
Ritual, 56-57, 258-59
Royal inscriptions, 199
Royal novella, 61, 98, 221

Saga, 250
Sanctuary, 156, 214
Sanctuary legend, 90-91
School, 35, 191
School, priestly, 445
Seder, 501
Seer, 345
Seer-saying, 355
Seminomads, 123
Sickness (in the Psalms), 268
Sinai tradition, 117, 125
Singers, 263
Sitz im Leben, 27
Soldier song, 259
Song, 209, 220, 225, 263-64, 266
Song of Moses, 189-90
Song of the Well, 156
Source strata, 114, 197
Southern Kingdom, 130
Speech, 246
Stylistics, 30
Supplement hypothesis, 108, 110, 114
Supplement method, 114
Symbolic action, 234, 349, 356, 409, 412, 420-21, 463

Taunt song, 156
Temple, 219, 221, 231, 235-36, 239, 248, 266, 283-84, 295, 384-85, 387, 392, 408, 452, 458-59, 478
Territorial claim, 124-25
Territorial history, 30
Tetrateuch, 104, 193, 195
Thank offering, 268
Thanksgiving, 188, 269, 371, 442
Themes, history of, 29
Theodicy, 334
Threat, 224, 319, 353
Topography, 30
Torah, 69-70, 103, 270, 385
Tradition, oral, 29
Traditio-historical criticism, 29, 113

Tradition-history, 113
Tradition and interpretation, 29-30
Travesty, literary, 302
Treaty, 175-76
Tribal god, 123
Tribal saga, 91
Tribal saying, 66

Ugarit, 38-39, 44, 57, 222, 282, 312, 322, 472

Victory song, 188
Vision, 356, 434, 453, 461-62, 472, 475-76

Wadi Murabba'at, 494
War, 66-67
Wisdom, 189, 269, 270-71, 371, 382, 387
Wisdom, practical, 309
Wisdom saying, 225
Wisdom school, 316
Wisdom song, 295
Wisdom teacher, 309-10
Work song, 259
Writing, 35

Yahweh as king, 264
Yahwism, 34 ff., 63, 94, 136, 164, 259, 270, 273, 276-77, 310
Yahwist, 111

Zion song, 262, 265

Also by Georg Fohrer

HISTORY OF ISRAELITE RELIGION

'A veritable quarry of information, familiar and novel, in parts closely argued, at times encyclopaedic in presentation, always arousing admiration at its fullness within brevity. A reliable and stimulating text-book for students, it will also be read with pleasure and profit by every preacher and scholar of the Old Testament.'

Expository Times

'The success of the book can be attributed to the fact that the author has used his erudition and skill to choose exactly the right (chapter) titles and, having chosen them, has written succinctly and authoritatively under them. Fohrer's views are clearly discernible throughout the book but, as he always presents the evidence in a balanced way, they are not obtrusive.'

Theology

2